ALSO BY EDWARD G. LENGEL

General George Washington:
A Military Life

World War 1 Memories:
An Annotated Bibliography

TO
CONQUER
HELL

TO
CONQUER
HELL

THE MEUSE-ARGONNE, 1918

THE EPIC BATTLE THAT ENDED
THE FIRST WORLD WAR

EDWARD G. LENGEL

A Holt Paperback
HENRY HOLT AND COMPANY
New York

A Holt Paperback
Henry Holt and Company, LLC
Publishers since 1866
175 Fifth Avenue
New York, New York 10010
www.henryholt.com

A Holt Paperback® and ® are registered trademarks of Henry Holt and Company, LLC.

Distributed in Canada by H. B. Fenn and Company Ltd.

Library of Congress Cataloging-in-Publication Data

Lengel, Edward G.
    To conquer hell : the Meuse-Argonne, 1918, the epic battle that ended the first world war / Edward G.
Lengel.—1st ed.
        p.   cm.
    Includes bibliographical references and index.
    ISBN-13: 978-0-8050-8915-8
    ISBN-10: 0-8050-8915-2
    1. Argonne, Battle of the, France, 1918.   2. World War, 1914–1918—Campaigns—Meuse River
Valley.   3. United States. Army—History—World War, 1914–1918.   I. Title.
    D545.A63L46 2008
    940.4'36—dc22   2007024461

Henry Holt books are available for special promotions and premiums.
For details contact: Director, Special Markets.

Originally published in hardcover in 2008 by Henry Holt and Company

First Holt Paperbacks Edition 2009

Designed by Meryl Sussman Levavi

Maps © 2007 by Rick Britton

Printed in the United States of America

1   3   5   7   9   10   8   6   4   2

To Sergeant George F. Shade,

150th Machine Gun Battalion (Reading Militia), 42d Division:

born 1892; gassed in the Meuse-Argonne, 1918; died 1942

And to my cousin, Sergeant Alvin C. York

God would never be cruel enough to create a cyclone as terrible as that Argonne battle. Only man would ever think of doing an awful thing like that.

—*Alvin C. York*

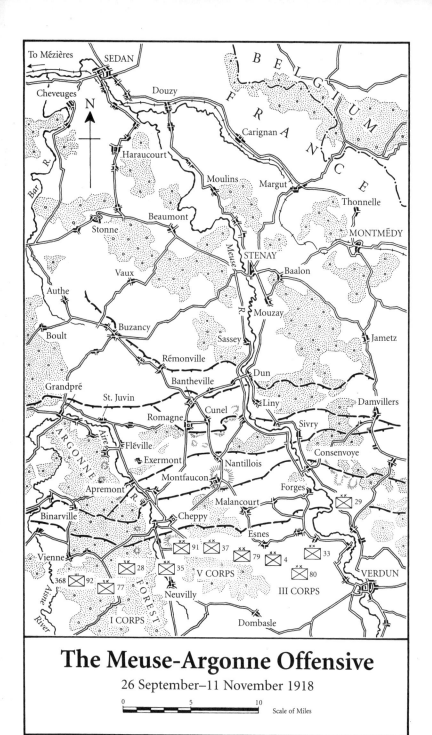

The Meuse-Argonne Offensive

26 September–11 November 1918

CONTENTS

———•◦•———

LIST OF MAPS   XV

PREFACE   1

PART I

CHAPTER 1
"All the Promotion in the World Would Make No Difference Now":
JOHN J. PERSHING   11

CHAPTER 2
The Cult of the Attack   21

CHAPTER 3
"Right or Wrong, My Country"   30

CHAPTER 4
"Retreat, Hell. We Just Got Here"   40

CHAPTER 5
"An Independent American Army"   47

PART II

CHAPTER 6
"Here Is the Golden Dream": The Meuse-Argonne   57

CHAPTER 7
"The Only Way to Begin Is to Commence"   66

PART III

PHASE ONE • SEPTEMBER 26–30

CHAPTER 8

"*You Boys Are My Kind. Now Let's Go In!*" SEPTEMBER 26   85

CHAPTER 9

"*We Began to Realize What Artillery Really Meant.*" SEPTEMBER 27   125

CHAPTER 10

"*Words Can Never Describe It, Nor Is the Mind Imaginative Enough to Conceive It.*" SEPTEMBER 28   147

CHAPTER 11

"*There Were Very Few Heroes That Morning.*" SEPTEMBER 29   161

CHAPTER 12

Relief. SEPTEMBER 30   186

PHASE TWO • OCTOBER 4–6

CHAPTER 13

"*God Damn It, Don't You Know We're Going Over the Top.*" OCTOBER 4   194

CHAPTER 14

The Lost Battalion: "*Our Mission Is to Hold This Position at All Costs*"   221

CHAPTER 15

"*Just Plain Murder.*" OCTOBER 5   235

CHAPTER 16

"*It Is Not a Dishonorable Deed to Give Up.*" OCTOBER 6   247

PHASE THREE • OCTOBER 7–11

CHAPTER 17

"*Their Faces Told the Whole Story of Their Fight.*" OCTOBER 7   255

CHAPTER 18

"York, I Hear You Have Captured the Whole Damned
  German Army." OCTOBER 8   275

CHAPTER 19

"We Are Going to Have a Very Hard Day." OCTOBER 9   283

CHAPTER 20

Beyond the Argonne. OCTOBER 10   298

CHAPTER 21

Last Gasp. OCTOBER 11   305

PHASE FOUR • OCTOBER 12–15

CHAPTER 22

"Like the Heat from a Blast-Furnace Door."
  OCTOBER 12–13   317

CHAPTER 23

"The Best Day's Work." OCTOBER 14   331

CHAPTER 24

"There Are Times When Even General Officers Have
  to Be Expendable." OCTOBER 15   346

PHASE FIVE • OCTOBER 16–31

CHAPTER 25

"Large Bodies Move Slowly, Though with Great
  Momentum When They Start"   359

VICTORY • NOVEMBER 1–11

CONCLUSION

"When I Get Back, You Can Wager I Will Be a
  Home Loving Man"   413

NOTES   437

SELECTED BIBLIOGRAPHY   459

ACKNOWLEDGMENTS   473

INDEX   475

MAPS

The Meuse-Argonne Offensive — *x*

The Western Front, 1918 — *42*

Central Meuse-Argonne — *87*

Western Meuse-Argonne — *196*

The Lost Battalion — *225*

Eastern Meuse-Argonne — *257*

Heights of Cunel and Romagne — *319*

Breakthrough — *383*

Meuse-Argonne Key

Woods *(Bois)*

Major Road

Minor Road

Towns & Villages

Hills *(Cotes)*

Ridges *(Cotes)*

German Defensive Positions

Rivers & Creeks

Canal

Marsh

Railroad

Farm

American Division — 78

American Regiment — 368 92

French Division — Fr 18

Fortified City

TO
CONQUER
HELL

———•◦•———

Reese Russell, a tall, slender, fun-loving, and handsome young man with jet-black hair and dark brown eyes, was thirty-four years old when the United States entered World War I in April 1917. He came from the little Appalachian mill town of Cedar Bluff in Tazewell County, Virginia, a place of quiet mountain charm where community picnics, summer bandstand concerts, and church revival meetings were the order of the day. He and most of his friends had never been more than twenty miles from home. Why travel, people joked, when they already lived in the most beautiful place on earth?

Russell registered for the draft in the summer of 1917, and the U.S. Army called his number soon afterward. Putting down his banjo and straw hat, he kissed his girl good-bye and joined the 317th Infantry Regiment of the 80th "Blue Ridge" Infantry Division, a unit made up of draftees from rural Virginia, West Virginia, and western Pennsylvania. He went to France and fought in the Battle of the Meuse-Argonne, at obscure places like Béthincourt and the Dannevoux. After less than a week in combat in the fall of 1918, he was evacuated to the rear, with poison in his lungs and demons in his mind. Neither ever left him.

In 1919 he came home to Cedar Bluff to spend "the rest of his life," as his daughter remembered, "traveling a lonely road, out of step with his family, his friends, and his surroundings." His lungs ruined, he could no longer breathe properly and collapsed periodically into uncontrollable spasms of coughing. He never spoke of what he had seen in France, and forbade his family to mention the war in his presence. His uniform, helmet, gas mask, rifle, and bayonet stayed packed away in a trunk, strictly off-limits to his family. When he wasn't looking, his children secretly opened the trunk and fingered the mementos. To them, he had become a remote presence. As they handled the items, the children tried to guess what their father had experienced in the foggy, shell-torn fields and forests of the bloodiest battle in American history, the Meuse-Argonne.

Russell began drinking as soon as he returned home. He drank through the economic recession of 1919, when an ex-Doughboy could not find a job, and the boom years that followed. He drank through the Great Depression, and during Franklin Roosevelt's presidential administrations, when the New Deal's Promised Land always seemed just a step away. In 1941 America entered the Second World War, and Russell drank even more, as if in sympathy for the GIs about to die, or in realization that his war—the so-called War to End All Wars—had been fought in vain. And he never slept. He went through the motions—lying down in bed between midnight and 5:00 A.M.—but he never closed his eyes in sleep, "unless," his daughter recalled, "one could call the stupor he fell into when he drank in his later years, sleep." Perhaps he feared that his dreams would take him back to the war. He died a broken man at age sixty-one. As his daughter heard taps played over his lonely country grave, a sense of relief enveloped her. At last, her father's torments had ended, and he could sleep.[1]

★

THE Meuse-Argonne American Cemetery and Memorial at Romagne, containing the graves of 14,246 soldiers who died in World War I, is the largest U.S. cemetery in Europe. Carefully tended by the American Battle Monuments Commission, the cemetery presents a splendid vista, with a beautiful Romanesque chapel overlooking rows of crosses and Stars of David on the green and gentle slopes of the hillside below. A beautiful spring or summer day that brings tour buses packed with tourists trundling out of Paris for the four-hour drive to the U.S. World War II cemetery at Omaha Beach, where crowds of teenagers giggle and banter while aged veterans and tourists walk among the graves, leaves the Meuse-Argonne cemetery quiet and largely deserted. Here and there couples or families stroll about, occasionally stooping to read a tombstone. Except for those making pilgrimages to the graves of great-grandfathers they never knew, or groups of soldiers on leave from nearby bases, the majority of these visitors are European, not American; and the civilian and military delegations that lay wreaths in the chapel, or children who lay roses or little bunches of wildflowers at graves, are most often French, Belgian, English, or German.

The Argonne Forest has become a resort for nature lovers and hikers. Farmers till the surrounding fields, where over a hundred thousand American soldiers spilled their blood in the autumn of 1918. American veterans' organizations have recently erected a few markers commemorating their regiments or divisions, but most monuments date from the 1920s or 1930s. They receive few visitors. The memorials at Montfaucon and Blanc Mont—the former a two-hundred-foot-high granite Doric column capped by a statue symbolizing liberty, and the latter an elaborately engraved yellow limestone tower sited atop a battle-scarred hill—are two of the most stunning American battlefield monuments anywhere. Though well tended by the American Battle Monuments Commission, they typically stand deserted. Two monuments erected by the states of Pennsylvania and Missouri near the towns of Varennes and Cheppy in the 1920s—the former a Greek-style structure beautifully situated overlooking the Aire River valley where thousands of Pennsylvanians died in 1918, and the latter a fine bronze sculpture of a triumphant female figure holding aloft a wreath—are neglected and in disrepair. Elsewhere in the Meuse-Argonne, markers and monuments to American units like the all-black 371st Infantry Regiment were mutilated by the Germans in World War II and have never been repaired; French farmers destroyed others, finding them a nuisance to their plows, and many have disappeared under brambles and weeds.

Many sites of heroism and agony in the Meuse-Argonne remain unmarked: places like Molleville Farm, where the 29th Division endured an inferno of fire and blood; the Bois de Fays, where the 4th Division suffered weeks of unremitting torment; the Bois des Ogons, where the 80th Division tore itself to pieces to defend a general's reputation; and the Bois de Rappes, where regiments of the 5th Division dissolved as they repeatedly took and retook the woods during a few grim days in October. Farms, forests, and fields all remain essentially as they were in 1918, and the visitor may easily envision the events of ninety years past. Sites where Americans won Medals of Honor remain unmarked—except for that of Corporal Alvin C. York, which researchers rediscovered nearly ninety years after the war ended. And while curio collectors have picked clean American Civil War battlefields and many World War II sites, visitors to the Meuse-Argonne can still trace individual trenches, rifle pits, bunkers, and craters and pick spent cartridges, rusted equipment, and (dangerously) unexploded ordnance out of the ground almost at will.

Back in the United States the neglect is just as marked. In Europe, Australia, and Canada the dwindling few veterans of the First World War are counted one by one and publicly memorialized on television and in newspapers when they die; most Americans pay scant attention to the departure of the last Doughboys. The burning curiosity that drove Reese Russell's children to ponder their father's old rifle and uniform and read his diary is all but gone today. German World War II and American Civil War militaria fetch high prices at public sales; similar items from World War I go cheap. Print and manuscript letters, diaries, and memoirs of American veterans of World War I gather dust in attics or are sold cheap on Internet auction sites. Veterans' papers and memorabilia, donated to national and local libraries and archives in hopes of enlightening future generations, typically go for decades without being examined by researchers. Johnny Reb, Billy Yank, and the GI live forever in the American psyche. The Doughboy has been forgotten.

*

Less than twenty years after the war ended, complained Brigadier General Dennis Nolan, who had served on General John J. Pershing's staff, hardly anyone could name, much less describe, America's greatest battle in the late war. "Veterans said to me in their speeches and in private that the American people did not know anything about the Meuse-Argonne battle," he said. "I have never understood why."[2] Fought over a period of forty-seven days, from September 26 to November 11, 1918, the Meuse-Argonne sucked in 1.2 million American soldiers, leaving 26,277 of them dead and 95,786 wounded. Almost all of these casualties came in a period of about three weeks of heavy fighting, and they amounted to about half of the total American casualties for the war. Twenty-two American infantry divisions participated in the battle, along with 840 airplanes and 324 tanks. About twenty-four hundred artillery pieces fired over four million shells, more than the Union army fired during the entire four years of the American Civil War. No single battle in American military history, before or since, even approaches the Meuse-Argonne in size and cost, and it was without question the country's most critical military contribution to the Allied cause in the First World War.[3] And yet, within a few years of its end, nobody seemed to realize that it had taken place.

The U.S. Army, distracted by downsizing and funding cuts, made no comprehensive attempt to digest all of the lessons it had learned from the largest and bloodiest battle in its history. It neither compiled a complete official history of America's military role in the conflict nor sponsored full-scale studies of the Meuse-Argonne or any other battle. Instead, departments and individual officers independently examined various aspects of the conflict, such as the roles of artillery and tanks, and buried their findings in specialist publications. Young officers who entered the army in the 1920s and 1930s knew more about the Battle of Gettysburg than the Meuse-Argonne. By the time the United States entered World War II in December 1941, the army had hardly learned the lessons of the first war, let alone begun to comprehend the conditions of the second.

In 1919, Frederick Palmer, a former war correspondent, wrote a chatty patriotic book titled *Our Greatest Battle (The Meuse-Argonne)*. Since then, only two books about the battle have appeared in print, both of them brief academic studies focusing on its operational and strategic aspects.[4] So far as the American public is concerned, the Meuse-Argonne might as well never have occurred. Although the battle receives passing mention in popular studies of the United States during the First World War, it gets nothing like the attention it deserves as one of the largest and most critical military engagements in the nation's history.

The Doughboy, meanwhile, remains a mystery. Millions of Americans have relatives—fathers, grandfathers, great-grandfathers—who served in the war. Who were these soldiers? What did they believe in? What did they experience? And how did they change? The nature of the war they fought remains a mystery too. Some books and movies portray it as a grand parade, with intrepid Doughboys flying planes, firing a lot of guns, sending the Germans packing home, and saving Europe. Others present the war as an endless charnel nightmare, with innocent men reduced to mud-soaked automatons, slaughtered en masse on a static battlefield of trenches and barbed wire.

The story of that generation, and its greatest fight in the Meuse-Argonne, is a tale of heroism—of untested draftees and recruits who went up against the best-trained army in the world, and drove it from some of the strongest defensive terrain in France. It is also a chronicle of tragedy—of thickheaded nationalism and military ineptitude that sent thousands of men uselessly to their deaths. More than anything, it is a story of transformation. In the Meuse-Argonne, over a million American soldiers learned that modern war had nothing to with the waving banners and glorious cavalry charges that stocked the pages of the books they had read in childhood. They saw thousands of comrades killed or disabled. They learned how artillery could blow a man to pieces, how machine guns could slash down dozens of soldiers at a time, and how poison gas could dissolve lungs. They witnessed all the stupidity, bravery, cruelty, kindness, and pathos of which humanity was capable. They discovered the meaning of comradeship on a deeper level than they had ever thought possible. They were physically and mentally stunted—and yet they grew.

Many men took their first steps toward greatness on the battlefields of the Meuse-Argonne. Flamboyant young Brigadier General Douglas

MacArthur led his brigade of the 42d "Rainbow" Division from the front. He promised to take a critically important hill even if it cost every drop of his men's blood, and survived an artillery bombardment that killed everyone around him. Brigadier General Billy Mitchell, commanding the U.S. Army Air Service, claimed to have proven airpower's potential, although the Doughboys claimed his fliers never showed up when it mattered. Colonel George C. Marshall single-handedly managed the biggest exercise in military logistics that the country had ever seen. Lieutenant Colonel George S. Patton led tanks in battle for the first time, saw a vision of his past-life "ancestors" in the clouds above the enemy lines, and split the skull of a terrified American soldier with his shovel. Captain Harry Truman distinguished himself under fire, even as the infantry division that his artillery battery supported collapsed. Private James M. Cain's harrowing experiences as a runner provided the material for one of his first stories. War correspondent Damon Runyon watched the exhausted, haunted men of the Lost Battalion stagger out of the Argonne Woods, and reported one of his first newspaper articles.

Other men became heroes in an instant, and then drifted into obscurity. Corporal Alvin C. York killed 32 German soldiers and helped to capture 132 more, along with thirty-five machine guns. The next morning he wandered over the empty battlefield, tormented with guilt and desperately seeking someone, American or German, to save. Private John Lewis Barkley occupied an abandoned French tank behind the German lines and single-handedly crushed an enemy counterattack. Lieutenant Samuel Woodfill put the marksmanship that he had honed on moose and grizzly bears in Alaska to use on the Germans, although he had to finish off his last two victims with a pickax. Major Charles Whittlesey led a composite battalion of Doughboys from Brooklyn and the western plains states through five days of hell, and emerged tormented by demons that made the remainder of his short life a misery.

For each man who found fame during or after the battle, there are thousands whose tales of valor, cowardice, death, and survival have been largely forgotten. Private Joe Rizzi, an Italian American fiercely loyal to his adopted country, left his parents and girlfriend with tears and simple ideals and learned to become a killer. Private Ernest Wrentmore, at age thirteen the youngest soldier in the American Expeditionary Force (AEF), killed Germans in hand-to-hand combat and nearly died from shrapnel wounds and gas inhalation. Lieutenant Farley Granger watched the Wild West Division dissolve in a frenzy of reckless gallantry and blood. Captain William J. Reddan led his company into a ravine reminiscent of the Valley of Death, losing all except thirteen of his original two hundred men. Lieutenant Colonel Channing Delaplane formed a rear guard of one against an overwhelming German counterattack. Lieutenant Colonel Theodore Roosevelt Jr. played a leading role in perhaps the most boneheaded battlefield maneuver in American military history. And Lieutenant General Hunter Liggett, who spent the first hours of every attack playing solitaire, led the American army to final victory in the biggest battle in its history. Unlike Pershing, MacArthur, Patton, and others, he—like the thousands of officers and common soldiers who followed him—is practically unknown today.

After the battle ended, American soldiers—and the legions of men and women who tended their needs in sickness and in health—acquired new understandings of their relationships with country, government, society, family, and friends. No two men came out of the Meuse-Argonne exactly the same. Some changed their political outlook. Some grew more idealistic or embittered. Some found God; others lost their faith. All, however, had changed. The country would never be the same.

PART I

CHAPTER 1

"All the Promotion in the World Would
Make No Difference Now"

—JOHN J. PERSHING

The sun rose on August 27, 1915, to a typical morning at Fort Bliss, Texas, from where Brigadier General John Joseph Pershing's 8th Infantry Brigade kept the peace along the troubled U.S.-Mexican border. Clouds of dust swelled and drifted as infantry drilled and cavalry patrols came and went, and shouted orders echoed among the adobe walls. Through one dust cloud rode Lieutenant James L. Collins, the general's aide, who had set out from headquarters for a routine two-hour horseback tour around the base. Pershing would normally have accompanied him, but this morning he had decided to stay behind and get some paperwork done, so Collins took the tour alone. The lieutenant had got only halfway through his tour when Pershing's orderly galloped up and called him back to headquarters on urgent business.

Pershing had accompanied the 8th Brigade to Fort Bliss back in April, leaving behind his wife, Frankie, and their four children at the Presidio military base in San Francisco. The separation had been difficult, for John and Frankie loved each other dearly and also doted on their children—three girls and a boy. Now, after four long months, his wife and children were finally about to follow him to Texas. Their departure from California was scheduled for August 28, and for the past several days the general had prepared eagerly for their arrival. "I'm tired of living alone," he confided to a friend. "I'm having my quarters fixed so that my wife and children can join me."[1]

When Collins arrived at headquarters, he found the usually confident, relaxed, and firmly in control general looking wide-eyed and desperate. "My God, Collins," he gasped. "Something terrible has happened at the Presidio! There's been a fire at the house!"[2]

It took time for Collins to get the general to explain: less than an hour before, Pershing had been working at his desk when the telephone rang. He picked it up without identifying himself. The caller, an Associated Press correspondent named Norman Walker, said, "Lieutenant Collins, I have some more news on the Presidio fire."

"What fire?" the general snapped. "What has happened?" Only then did the reporter realize that he had Pershing rather than his aide on the line. Horrified, Walker falteringly repeated a dispatch reporting that early that morning a fire had gutted Pershing's home at the Presidio. His wife and three of his children—Helen, aged eight; Anne, aged seven; and Mary Margaret, aged three—had perished of smoke inhalation. "My God! My God! Can it be true?" the general screamed. After a few moments in which the correspondent tried to offer his sympathy, Pershing's voice came back on the line, once more under control. "Thank you, Walker," he said. "It was very considerate of you to phone." Then he hung up.[3]

Two days later, the general's train pulled into the station at San Francisco. He had spent the last three hundred miles of the journey sobbing on a friend's shoulder, while Collins took charge of all his personal and official affairs. Pershing went immediately to the funeral parlor where the four caskets lay. Collins retired behind some drapes, but he could see the general kneeling in turn before each member of his family. About an hour later, Pershing asked to be taken to the ruins of his house. From there he went to the hospital where his five-year-old son, Warren, had stayed since his rescue. Pershing held the boy on his knee as they drove away from the hospital. Soon they passed the Fair Grounds, where in happier times the family had spent many a sunny afternoon. "Have you been to the fair?" the father managed to ask. "Oh yes," the son innocently replied. "Mama takes us a lot."

For the next weeks and months Pershing struggled to recover his self-control. At the funeral he stood with dignified poise, but his grief remained visible. He read each of the hundreds of letters of condolence, including one from his future enemy, the Mexican bandit Pancho Villa. He talked about the fire with friends, and tried to find some understanding and resignation. He sought solace in religion, and delved into staff paperwork with an intensity sometimes bordering on insanity. Occasionally, something made him break down, like an ill-timed comment, or the arrival of a trunk bearing his family's personal effects. In response to these moments he progressively walled himself in, retreating from the world, including acquaintances, friends, and what remained of his family. With Warren he shared a distant, embarrassed kind of affection.[4] For the Pershing family, a long and happy fairy tale had come to a tragic end.

★

Born in 1860 in Laclede, Missouri, one of nine children of a foreman on the Hannibal and St. Joseph Railroad, John J. Pershing had passed a happy but uneventful childhood. As a teenager he worked on his family's modest farm while teaching children at local country schools, including one for African Americans. Meanwhile he took classes at the Kirksville Normal School in preparation for a career as a teacher. After graduating in 1880, more on a whim than from any desire for a military career, Pershing took the entrance examination for the U.S. Military Academy at West Point, New York. He passed by a single point, and enrolled. He achieved middling grades at the academy, but his natural aptitude as a soldier—hitherto unguessed, for he did not come from a military family—earned him the rank of senior cadet captain before his graduation in 1886.

Commissioned a second lieutenant in the 6th Cavalry and sent to the frontier, Pershing participated in the army's final campaign against Geronimo's Apaches in Arizona, and witnessed the Sioux Ghost Dance rebellion in South Dakota in 1891. Taking time out to earn a law degree from the University of Nebraska in 1893, he returned to field service in 1895 as an officer with the 10th Cavalry, a unit of black "buffalo soldiers" stationed in Montana. He returned to West Point as a tactical instructor in 1897, earning the sobriquet "Black Jack" because of his command of black troops. When the Spanish-American War began in 1898, he rejoined the 10th Cavalry as a captain and fought at San Juan Hill in Cuba alongside Theodore Roosevelt. Pershing next went to the Philippines, where he helped to put down an insurrection by the Moro Indians in 1903 before returning to the United States. An experienced and highly respected field and staff officer, he had also earned a reputation as a rake. Rivals accused him—probably unjustly— of fathering several illegitimate children with Filipino women.

Pershing's star continued to rise. Appointed to the army general staff in Washington, D.C., he befriended powerful men, including Senator Francis Emroy Warren of Wyoming, a snowy-haired Civil War veteran who had won the Medal of Honor in 1863. As chairman of the Senate's Military Affairs Committee, Warren wielded much influence in Congress. He was also the father of Helen Warren, an athletic and intelligent if not pretty twenty-four-year-old girl known to family and friends as Frankie. John and Frankie met, and promptly fell in love despite the twenty-year difference in their ages. Senator Warren approved the match, and after a joyous one-year courtship the couple married on January 26, 1905, in a ceremony attended by President Theodore Roosevelt. Over the next six years Frankie bore four children, three daughters and a son.

Shortly after their wedding the Pershings went to Japan, where he served as a military attaché and observed the Russo-Japanese War. They were celebrating the birth of their daughter Helen in Tokyo in September 1906 when word arrived that President Roosevelt had promoted John from captain to brigadier general over the heads of 862 more senior officers. Critics spoke of nepotism and derided him as the president's pet. The newly minted general silenced them quickly, justifying his promotion through first-rate administration and staff work.

In January 1914 Pershing took command of the 8th Infantry Brigade at the Presidio in San Francisco. There he and his family enjoyed an idyllic life, with Frankie active in the women's suffrage movement while her husband managed the brigade. The couple spent all of their free time together, and with their active and happy young children. Far away to the southeast, however, Mexico had descended into a state of anarchy, with political and social unrest spreading across the countryside and even over the border into Texas. To quell that unrest, Pershing and the 8th Brigade were ordered to Fort Bliss, near El Paso. Then the Presidio fire of August 1915 wrecked his family and tore the joy from his life.

Pershing continued to advance his career after the fire, but without enthusiasm. "All the promotion in the world would make no difference now," he remarked after his promotion to major general in September 1916.[5] Yet duty continued to call. Six months before his promotion, Pershing took command of a punitive expedition against Pancho Villa. The campaign, which lasted until January 1917, failed to achieve its objective. Villa escaped, and Pershing's force of twelve thousand troops returned to Texas empty-handed. But the expedition had seized the imagination of Americans, and for the first time in his life, "Black Jack" became a household name. Press correspondents trotted after him almost everywhere he went, shouting questions about politics and world affairs.

The reporters especially liked to quiz Pershing about the war in Europe. For the first two years after the war began in August 1914, it had been second- or third-page news. Firebrands like former president Theodore Roosevelt had exhorted the United States to intervene, and a few adventuresome volunteers—like Ernest Hemingway and John Dos Passos—had gone to Europe as volunteer ambulance drivers, fliers, or soldiers. The vast majority of Americans, however, had no desire to become involved in another man's war. This remained true even after a German submarine sunk the British liner *Lusitania* in May 1915, killing 1,119 people, including 114 Americans. The sinking created deep popular resentment against Germany, but it did not spur any move for intervention, and in 1916 President Woodrow Wilson won reelection on a platform promising mothers that their children—in the parlance of a popular song—would not have to grow up to be soldiers.

In 1914–15, Pershing had closely followed the fighting in Europe. He even hinted to his superiors that he would like to observe some of the battles.[6] In the wake of the Presidio fire, however, he lost interest in European affairs, and the Mexican assignment took him mentally even further away from the trenches of France. He sympathized generally with the British and French in their struggle against Germany, and thought that American intervention might afford him a prospect of relief from the dusty wastes of southern Texas, but that was all. He felt no passion for heroism or the fight for justice against Teutonic baby killers. Nothing—even the deaths of hundreds of thousands of men in battles like Verdun or the Somme—moved him much anymore.

Kaiser Wilhelm II of Germany shocked Americans out of their indifference on February 1, 1917, announcing that unrestricted submarine warfare, which had ceased after the *Lusitania* affair, would resume. All merchant vessels entering European waters, he declared, might be torpedoed without warning, whether or not they belonged to one of the belligerent nations. Wilson's government broke off diplomatic relations with Germany, but the submarines attacked anyway. Public outrage grew as ships sank and Americans died. The interception and publication of a telegram from Arthur Zimmermann, the German foreign minister, suggesting that Mexico might declare war on the United States in return for New Mexico, Arizona, and even Kansas, marked the last straw. With his entire cabinet and the American people outraged, the peace-loving Wilson reluctantly asked Congress for a declaration of war. The United States entered World War I on April 6.

★

PERSHING's call to duty came on May 3, in a telegram from Senator Warren in Washington, D.C. It read:

> WIRE ME TODAY WHETHER AND HOW MUCH YOU
> SPEAK, READ AND WRITE FRENCH.

Pershing spoke French poorly, but he understood "the possibilities to be implied from Senator Warren's telegram"—namely, military command. He replied:

> SPENT SEVERAL MONTHS IN FRANCE 1908 STUDYING
> LANGUAGE. SPOKE QUITE FLUENTLY; COULD READ
> AND WRITE VERY WELL AT THAT TIME. CAN EASILY
> REACQUIRE SATISFACTORY WORKING KNOWLEDGE.

Soon another message arrived at Pershing's Texas headquarters, this time from Major General Hugh Lenox Scott, the army chief of staff. In code and marked "for your eye alone," it announced that the War Department intended to send a small force to France in advance of the still-forming national army. "If plans are carried out," Scott informed Pershing, "you will be in command of the entire force." Interpreting this to mean that he would command a division, Pershing prepared for a summons to Washington. It came in short order.[7]

Pershing's train arrived in Washington on the bright and chilly morning of May 10. Newspaper reporters mobbed the general as he stepped onto the platform, asking whether his summons to the capital had anything to do "with the election of a commander for a military expedition to France." Offering no comment, he stepped into a car that sped him to the War Department.[8] Pershing first entered the army chief of staff's office. General Scott, a sixty-three-year-old former Indian fighter, had entered the famous 7th Cavalry just after the 1876 Battle of Little Big Horn. "He was deaf," critics sneered, spoke in "grunts and the sign language," and went to sleep in his chair while conducting official business.[9] Pershing had little use for fossils and chafed at the chief of staff's unwillingness to get to specifics. Scott said that the government was considering sending a division of about twelve thousand men to France under Pershing's command. Later, a larger army would form. Just how large, nobody knew; nor did Scott explain where the soldiers would come from. Congress had just begun considering a military draft.

Leaving Scott's office little wiser than before, Pershing walked to the office of the secretary of war, Newton D. Baker. He found a thin, bespectacled man sitting behind a massive desk in an overstuffed office chair, reclining with one leg bent under his body and the other just barely reaching the floor. Baker neither looked nor acted the part of a secretary of war. As a boy, he had preferred books to tin soldiers and toy guns. As an adult, after becoming a solicitor and then mayor of Cleveland, he had rejected the honorary post as leader of Ohio's Boy Scouts because he considered the organization too militaristic. Woodrow Wilson named Baker secretary of war in 1916 because of his past political support for the Democratic Party, not because he had any qualifications for or particular interest in the office.[10]

Although they had little in common, Pershing liked the man. The secretary of war's mild exterior, he decided, masked a cultured, well-educated, and exceptionally gifted mind. Perhaps most important from Pershing's point of view, Baker believed in efficiency. "He was courteous and pleasant," the general observed, "and impressed me as being frank, fair, and businesslike. His conception of the problems seemed broad and comprehensive. From the start he did not hesitate to make definite decisions on the momentous questions involved."[11] As the war progressed the two would become unlikely, but firm, friends.

Baker confirmed that Pershing would command a division. A day later, however, he called the general back to his office and dropped the proverbial bombshell. Not one, but several divisions would go to France, and Pershing would command all of them as commander in chief. "My feelings may well be imagined," Pershing later wrote. "Here in the face of a great war I had been placed in command of a theoretical army which had yet to be constituted, equipped, trained, and sent abroad. Still, there was no doubt in my mind then, or at any other time, of my ability to do my part, provided the Government would furnish men, equipment and supplies."[12] He buried his fears, just as he had done with the memories of that night in August 1915. Now, as then, he lived on willpower.

✳

Pershing and Baker both believed in efficiency and organization. Unfortunately, others in the U.S. government did not. For years German satirists had mocked Americans as soft, corrupt, and lazy—good at making money but alien to war—and the accusation had some merit. As they attempted to prepare the army, the government, and the general population for war, Pershing and Baker found everywhere the same insularity and blithe carelessness. It would all work out right, people told them. Millions of American soldiers would go to Europe, swat the Germans aside, smite the kaiser, and return home in time for Christmas. Guns, uniforms, equipment—not to worry, they would come from somewhere.

The habits of years could not be broken in a day, but Baker had one important success early on: the institution of a military draft. In February 1917, six weeks before the declaration of war, the War College Division of the army general staff had submitted to General Scott a plan for creating a national army of four million men based on nationwide conscription. Scott endorsed the plan and passed it on to Baker, who in turn presented it to the president, urging his assent. Wilson complied, and Baker then assembled his War Department staff, telling them to draft a bill that the president could present immediately to Congress in case of war. They did so—though some of them reluctantly—and when the United States declared war on Germany in April the president secured speedy if not unopposed passage through Congress of the draft legislation, which became law on May 18.[13]

Organizing the draftees and volunteers into a national army presented a more daunting task. In April 1917 the U.S. regular army consisted of only about 137,000 men, with 181,000 more in the National Guard—the seventeenth largest army in the world, just behind Portugal's. Only a tiny fraction of its men had seen combat, and they had done so in places like Mexico, Cuba, or the Philippines. Few had any understanding of modern war. The army's officers were elderly, inexperienced, or both. Its soldiers, equipped with guns and accoutrements that dated back to the nineteenth century, knew next to nothing about modern tactics or weaponry. At least they could follow orders and fire rifles, however; the same could not be said for the hundreds of thousands of draftees and recruits who now poured into the army from every corner of America.

The Europeans had been able to call up millions of trained reservists in 1914. By contrast, the U.S. Army Reserve existed only after 1912, and the Officers' Reserve Corps, Enlisted Reserve Corps, and Reserve Officers' Training Corps had only appeared with the passage of the National Defense Act of June 1916. That same act belatedly established the National Guard—which in some states had not progressed in training or organization far beyond the Revolutionary War–era militia—as the army's primary reserve force, regularizing its training and organization. The National Defense Act was less than a year old in May 1917, and its implementation had been rudimentary at best. The recruits now joining the army were the rawest, greenest imaginable.

As Pershing and the War Department pondered how to transform this paper army into reality, orders came for the general's departure for France. Shortly afterward, on May 24, he and Baker met with President Wilson at the White House. Pershing looked forward to the meeting with the president as an opportunity to gain some specifics about the nature of his mission. Conversation between these two stiff and serious men failed, however, to transcend the standard formalities. Wilson at first avoided speaking with his general, preferring to discuss shipping with the amiable Baker. Finally the president turned to Pershing and abruptly blurted, "General, we are giving you some very difficult tasks these days." "Perhaps so, Mr. President," Pershing blandly replied, "but that is what we are trained to expect." He and Wilson exchanged a few words on the Mexican expedition and the general's 1908 visit to France before Pershing tried to steer the conversation back to the war.

"Mr. President," the general declared, "I appreciate the honor you have conferred upon me by the assignment you have given me and realize the responsibilities it entails, but you can count upon the best that is in me." Wilson evaded Pershing's attempt to open a substantive military discussion. "General," he replied quickly, "you were chosen entirely upon your record and I have every confidence that you will succeed; you shall have my full support." He then declared the conference concluded. No further meetings between the president and his top general would take place until after the end of the war.

Pershing admired the president's simplicity and "air of determination," but regretted Wilson's failure to discuss important matters, such as military cooperation with the Allies, supplies, munitions, recruiting, strategy, or— most important of all—war aims. Was he supposed to be fighting for a compromise peace, or unconditional surrender? While Pershing had no desire for civilian interference in military matters, at least a display of interest in them would have been nice. Wilson's aloofness had its positive side, as the general realized. "In the actual conduct of operations," he would recall, "I was given entire freedom and in this respect was to enjoy an experience unique in our history."[14] Yet it also left the army entirely bereft of guidance from its civilian commander in chief: the president of the United States.[15] The country had never fought a war that way before, and never would again.

★

FOUR days after meeting the president, Pershing assembled an ad hoc staff of 191 men and traveled to Governors Island, New York, where the liner SS *Baltic* waited to carry the first American military contingent to Europe. Elizabeth Marshall, wife of Captain George C. Marshall of the 1st Division, watched the general and his officers as they shuffled past her in the rain, "dressed in antiquated civilian clothes, coat collars turned up in the absence of umbrellas or raincoats." They didn't look like much. "Such a dreadful-looking lot of men," she told her husband, could not possibly "do any good in France."[16]

The staff's departure was supposed to be a secret, but every journalist in the country knew when and where it would take place. Ordered to appear at the dock in civilian clothes, many officers nevertheless wore military uniforms, and several sported army shoes or swords in scabbards dangling conspicuously from their civvies. The expedition's supplies had sat at the pier for two days, labeled "S.S. Baltic, General Pershing's Headquarters"; and the commander's orderly had prominently marked his handbags "General Pershing, Paris, France." And when the *Baltic* sailed just after 5:00 P.M., the signal guns on Governors Island fired a farewell salute reserved only for personages of note. The guns' boom could be heard all the way across the harbor.[17]

As the ship left shore, some of Pershing's aides had second thoughts. Perhaps they had not been careful enough, despite all their scrupulous attention to secrecy? What if a German U-boat somehow received word of the departure and surfaced to capture the general and his staff? What a coup that would be for the kaiser! After several minutes of terror and confusion, one aide had an idea: someone must act as Pershing's double in order to confound any inquisitive German submarine captains. Somehow the aides convinced the general to lend them a full-dress uniform, in which a hapless major spent the rest of the ten-day voyage strutting around the deck. The real Pershing stayed belowdecks, pondering the army's organization, command, transport, training, ordnance, equipment, and ultimate employment at the front. His officers helped him by preparing reports, and in their free time took French lessons and attended lectures on venereal disease. A standard of discipline and efficiency, Pershing knew, had to be set early on; but the real work would not begin until they reached Paris.

The Cult of the Attack

On June 28, 1914, a teenaged Serbian terrorist named Gavrilo Princip opened fire on a car carrying Archduke Franz Ferdinand, heir to the throne of the sprawling Austro-Hungarian Empire, and his wife, Sophie, through the Bosnian city of Sarajevo. One of Princip's bullets pierced the archduke's neck; the other entered his wife's abdomen. "Sophie dear, Sophie dear, don't die," Franz Ferdinand moaned as his wife slumped over in his lap. "Stay alive for our children." A few minutes later they were both dead. Princip tried to commit suicide at the scene, first with cyanide and then with his pistol, but Austrian police wrestled him to the ground and carted him off to prison. Already terminally ill with tuberculosis, he would die in captivity in April 1918, six months before the end of the war that his bullets had started.

Suspecting that the Serbian government had instigated the murder, Austria-Hungary issued an ultimatum. Serbia rejected it, and five days later Austria-Hungary declared war. That act triggered a network of alliances that bound Russia to Serbia, France to Russia, and Germany to Austria-Hungary. Britain, loosely committed to support France in the event of war, had been a guarantor of Belgian neutrality since 1839. When Germany invaded Belgium on the road to France, therefore, Britain intervened. By August 1914 the war had spread across the Continent, with Germany and Austria-Hungary fighting Britain, France, Russia, Serbia, and Belgium.

The guns of August 1914 sounded on multiple fronts, from the outskirts of Belgrade in Serbia to the Carpathian Mountains of northwestern

Austria-Hungary and the lakes and plains of East Prussia on the border of Germany and Russia. The most important fighting, however, took place in the west. In Belgium and northeastern France, Germany's main invasion force drove toward Paris; and along the Franco-German border in Alsace-Lorraine, a huge French army attempted to advance on the Rhine. In the north, the tiny British Expeditionary Force fought alongside the French and attempted to hold up the German advance; but thanks to better weaponry and an effective system of mass mobilization the Germans overpowered their enemies everywhere on the western front. Within a few weeks the kaiser's armies had successfully conquered most of Belgium and plunged deep into northeastern France. They nearly rolled into Paris before miscalculations by some German generals opened a gap in their lines. The French and British exploited the gap in early September, during the First Battle of the Marne. Pulling back from the outskirts of Paris, the Germans then tried to outflank the Anglo-French armies to the north; and as the Allies countered these moves in a series of engagements over the following two months, the battle lines extended all the way to the North Sea.

In the south, meanwhile, the French had opened the war by launching an all-out offensive across the frontier into Alsace-Lorraine. Contemptuous of defensive warfare, which they blamed for their defeat at the hands of the Prussians in 1870, the French generals employed the *offensive à outrance*, or offensive to the limit. This concept had emerged from the teachings of Lieutenant Colonel Louzeau de Grandmaison, prewar director of the Bureau of Military Operations and founder of what came to be known as the "cult of the attack." Success in battle, Grandmaison taught, depended not on numbers, firepower, or even good tactics, but on spirit, willpower, and simple élan—a word that Americans later translated as "guts." Following his advice, the French generals of 1914 told their troops to rely on their rifles, bayonets, and fighting spirit to carry them to victory against the German artillery, machine guns, and fortifications. Marching forward impetuously in tight ranks, splendidly attired in bright blue and red uniforms, the French fell in swathes, suffering three hundred thousand casualties in only a few weeks of fighting.

With no clear victor at the end of 1914, the war continued to spread, with each side gaining new allies and extending the fighting to new fronts. Over the following two years Great Britain, France, Russia, Belgium, and Serbia—the so-called Allies or Entente powers—were joined by Japan, Italy, Portugal, and Romania; while Germany and Austria-Hungary—the Central powers—allied themselves with Bulgaria and the Ottoman Empire, which consisted of Turkey and much of the Middle East. In eastern Europe, the Germans destroyed two Russian armies at the titanic and momentous Battle of Tannenberg in 1914, and over the next two years they conquered most of the region, including Serbia, Romania, and previously Russian-controlled Poland, Ukraine, and the Baltic states. This string of defeats helped reduce Russia to a state of civil unrest, and in February 1917 a revolution deposed the czar and installed a weak pseudodemocratic regime under the liberal socialist Aleksandr Kerensky.

By that time, Austria-Hungary was also near collapse. Her armies had performed dismally, and as nationalist sentiments in the Balkans grew stronger only German military and political intervention kept the government in place. The Ottoman Empire beat off an Anglo-French invasion force at Gallipoli and destroyed an Anglo-Indian division in Iraq, all in 1915; but in 1917 they had lost most of Palestine to the British while the Arabian Peninsula flared in revolt. Jerusalem fell to the British on Christmas 1917. The Italians, meanwhile, found a way to outdo even the Russians and the Austrians in the field of military incompetence, dashing themselves against Austrian Alpine positions in no fewer than twelve "Battles of the Isonzo" at tremendous cost in human life.

During the same period, a series of horrifically bloody battles took place on the western front, each of them on a scale eclipsing anything seen before. From February to December 1916 around the fortress city of Verdun, the French and Germans suffered a combined total of one million casualties; farther north along the Somme River, the British lost nineteen thousand dead in one day, July 1, and both sides took another million casualties as the battle dragged on into November. By 1917, the trench lines in France and Belgium had moved only a short distance to the east, remaining essentially the same as they had been in 1914.

*

THE Europeans learned, adapted, and improved new tactics and technology during the course of these great battles. The British and French experimented with tanks, and the Germans developed new infantry tactics employing *Stosstruppen*, or storm troops. Both sides became more adept in the use of artillery, aircraft, and poison gas, and improved techniques of attack and defense. Yet the learning process cost lives. The French launched their last major offensive of the war in April 1917. It failed disastrously. Many French regiments mutinied and refused to return to the front until the steady General Henri-Philippe Pétain took command and restored them to order. They had served notice of their discontent, however, and henceforward the

French army attacked with extreme caution, almost invariably withdrawing in the face of determined resistance. The British, bolstered by Dominion troops from Australia, New Zealand, Canada, and South Africa, had also suffered severely from three years of war; and a grinding offensive launched in Flanders in the late summer and autumn of 1917 wrecked several divisions. They could still fight, but their ranks were desperately thin.

The Germans were tired too. The kaiser's army had taken millions of casualties, and an Allied naval blockade caused severe shortages of food and consumer goods in Germany. But there were bright spots. By the spring of 1917 Russia neared collapse, with a restive population sick of war and a government increasingly incapable of carrying on the fight. When the Russians withdrew from the war, as they inevitably would, most of the more than one million German troops fighting on the eastern front could be transferred to the west. With that in mind, Germany's leaders prepared one final drive to end the war. By resuming unrestricted submarine warfare in February 1917, the kaiser and his ministers hoped to cripple Britain's sea supply lines and force her to sue for peace. America, they knew, would declare war against Germany in response; but it might take months or even years for the U.S. Army to assemble in strength. Before it did, the Germans intended to carry out the second phase of their plan: a massive land attack on France aimed at the capture of Paris. Bolstered by over a million veteran troops from the eastern front, the German army's chances of capturing Paris and ending the war looked very good indeed.

The Allies anticipated and dreaded the German offensive. Their only hope for beating the odds seemed to lie in bringing American soldiers to the front as quickly as possible. They saw two options. First, they could sit and wait while the untried Yanks built an army from scratch, trained it at home, shipped it overseas with all its supplies and matériel, and took over part of the front. Green American officers could then lead their equally inexperienced soldiers into battle against veteran and well-trained German troops. Alternately, the wizened French and British could take charge of their new comrades, shipping them quickly across the Atlantic, supplying them with weapons and other equipment, and training them under seasoned European officers. They could then incorporate the Americans into veteran European formations and send them to the front under European command. The second option seemed both wiser and more humane. Instead of paying in blood for their inexperience, the Americans could make immediate use of lessons that their veteran allies had learned over the past three years. And the British and French would have the troops they needed to stem the coming German offensive.

The British and French dispatched special missions to the United States in the summer of 1917 and presented their ideas for the role of the American forces in Europe. The British representatives were both paternalistic and blunt. American recruits, they said, should be arranged immediately into provisional battalions, and shipped to Europe with little more than the uniforms on their backs. On arrival they would be trained and then used as replacements for depleted British divisions fighting at the front. The French, who had taken time to study American psychology, phrased their suggestions more diplomatically. The Americans had "a highly developed national pride and a strong spirit of independence," the chief of the French military mission explained in a secret memo to his superiors.

> They are all convinced that their country is now predominant. They look upon it, under present circumstances, as holding the balance of power, by virtue of its enormous resources in men, money and supplies of all kinds, as compared with the other Entente nations, which have been more or less exhausted by the prolongation of the war. [Thus] they have decided not to submit to any subordination whatsoever, and have made up their minds to be placed on a footing of complete equality. . . . We must resign ourselves, and take counsel of patience. We gain nothing by being short with them. It is better to let their lessons sink in little by little, and to have their minds become convinced by degrees, as a result of practical experience. . . . [But] we must keep trying; it is incumbent upon us to hang on, since we have the force of logic and practical experience on our side. Besides, our American Allies, while the possessors of qualities which at times disconcert us, are gifted, in general, with a sound common sense, and, a spirit of fairness, which, together, finally put them on the right track. . . . Our real and only danger lies in failure to make allowances for the spirit of the American people, and for the idiosyncrasies of American mentality. In such case, we should proceed straight to defeat.[1]

Of course the Americans wanted to fight under their own flag, the French emissaries said; that was right and proper. But first, let them train and fight alongside French veterans at the front. After this brief but necessary tutelage, the Yank lion cubs would reach maturity and could be released to fight on their own. Then they would field the best army in the world.

Neither British forthrightness nor French delicacy impressed Wilson or anyone else in the American government. The European proposals, they believed, concealed a plot to diminish American influence in the postwar world and reduce them to junior status in the Allied coalition. To thwart these plans, Wilson and Baker insisted on a significant and *independent* military role for the U.S. Army on the western front. "In military operations against the Imperial German Government," Baker instructed Pershing, "you are directed to cooperate with the forces of the other countries employed against that enemy; but in so doing the underlying idea must be kept in view that the forces of the United States are a separate and distinct component of the combined forces, the identity of which must be preserved."[2] Pershing, who feared that excessive contact with the battle-weary British and French would demoralize his young soldiers, had reasons of his own for supporting the president's position. And he had just the right combination of patience and stubbornness to back it up.

★

PERSHING and his entourage arrived in Paris on June 14, 1917, and paid the obligatory ceremonial visit to Lafayette's tomb. A few months later, "raving mad" at the French capital's political and social distractions, he moved his staff 150 miles east to Chaumont, in the upper Marne region. There he took up residence in a house decorated with bizarre hunting trophies in what Captain George S. Patton called "the damdest taste you ever saw." His staff lived and worked nearby in a four-story, eighteenth-century barracks building.[3] Pershing would get to know those trophies well; for the rest of the war Chaumont functioned as the nerve center of the American Expeditionary Force.

Pershing selected his staff with extraordinary care and eventually assigned it to work in five main sections: Administration (G-1), from August 1918 under Colonel Avery D. Andrews; Intelligence (G-2), under the professorial, brilliant, and extremely brave Major (later Brigadier General) Dennis E. Nolan; Operations (G-3), under Colonel Fox Conner; Coordination (G-4), under Lieutenant Colonel George Van Horn Moseley, dealing with supply; and Training (G-5), under dour, hardworking Lieutenant Colonel Harold B. Fiske. Teams of young, intelligent, dedicated, and inexperienced junior officers served within each of the staff's five sections, working to build an army administration and keep it running efficiently. The most notable of these officers included Colonel Charles G. Dawes, a financier who became chief procurement officer; thirty-eight-year-old Captain Hugh Aloysius Drum, an assistant who later became chief of staff of the First Army; Major John L. Hines, an assistant who in 1918 rose to command the 4th Division and V Corps; and the erratic Patton, who served for a time as Pershing's aide before going on to command the U.S. Tank Corps.

Working from scratch, Pershing's staff officers—and the organizations that they created—established assembly and training areas, transport networks, supply and replacement depots, workshops, airfields, and hospitals, and many other elements essential to the formation and battle-readiness of the American Expeditionary Force, or AEF. They also established rudimentary systems of intelligence, liaison, and espionage, and grappled with questions of weaponry, unit organization, and chains of command. Though eager and hardworking, these officers were amateurs, and they made amateurs' mistakes. To help them along, Pershing created an Army General Staff College at Langres, France, where officers could find instruction and reference materials on all facets of staff work.[4]

The most critical issue facing the general and his staff revolved around the question of what kinds of tactics the army would employ at the front. Pershing's answer to this problem originated in his conviction that the British and French armies employed bankrupt methods of attack under inept, unimaginative generals. Three years of war, he believed, had demoralized their soldiers and exposed the sanguinary futility of their tactics. The AEF must not follow their example. Instead, Pershing wished to train his soldiers in methods reflecting a uniquely American—and thus superior—way of war.

Trench warfare, Pershing argued, had left European soldiers overreliant on machine guns, grenades, and light and heavy artillery, sapping them of the spirit necessary to carry any offensive through to victory. The only way to get around this was to employ time-honored American methods, centering on three main principles: the soldier, his rifle, and his bayonet. Most important was the soldier's spirit: his willingness to attack and win, regardless of cost. The right kinds of weapons could reinforce that attitude. "The rifle and bayonet remain the supreme weapons of the infantry soldier," Pershing declared on October 19, 1917; "the ultimate success of the army depends upon their proper use in open warfare."[5] An effective advance, he believed, consisted of successive infantry rushes followed by the establishment of fire superiority through accurate rifle fire and, finally, effective use of the bayonet.

Pershing based his tactical concepts on the U.S. Army's prewar *Infantry Drill Regulations* and *Field Service Regulations,* which emphasized lightly armed, fast-moving infantry. According to these regulations, artillery, tanks, and machine guns existed for the sole purpose of supporting the infantry's attempts to defeat the enemy with rifles and bayonets. Machine guns—the sine qua non of infantry combat on the western front—were "weapons of emergency . . . of great value at critical, though infrequent, periods of an engagement." They should not be employed "until the attack is well advanced, [and] should not be assigned to the firing line of an attack." Pershing thought that machine guns had their uses, especially in defense, but he feared that in the attack soldiers might become so dependent on their support that they would not advance without them. He felt much the same about artillery, tanks, trench mortars, grenades, and other weapons whose use had become widespread in Europe. He did not deny their usefulness on the battlefield, but worried about their psychological effect on the soldiers.[6]

Pershing sought to recapture the offensive mind-set of 1914. Trench warfare, he argued, could not continue forever. The day would come—*must* come if victory were to be achieved—of a return to maneuver and open warfare. American officers must anticipate that day by training aggressive soldiers. A breakthrough served no purpose if the men lacked the spirit to advance confidently, even recklessly, accepting heavy losses to take an objective by bypassing strongpoints and disregarding open flanks. This required willpower, or guts—the French *élan*. Since British and French military thinking had apparently become atrophied into dependence on attrition and trench warfare, Pershing doubted their readiness to seize the opportunity for victory when it came. The AEF must not be caught asleep.

Not everyone agreed with Pershing's ideas. His staff learned and experimented on their own initiative, and sometimes defied him. One staff officer annoyed Pershing by boldly opining that "the day of the rifleman is done. He was a good horse while he lasted, but his day is over. . . . The rifleman is passing out and the bayonet is fast becoming as obsolete as the crossbow."[7] The War Department, which sent its own independent missions to the AEF, also questioned the fixation on open warfare and suggested that American officers listen closely to British and French advice. In the field, officers would interpret Pershing's tactical doctrine—which he never promulgated officially—however they pleased. Some followed it blindly, discouraging artillery, machine guns, and grenades even as enemy fire cut their rifle-toting men to pieces. Others—in the time-honored American tradition of individual initiative—tested and then discarded official doctrine in favor of lessons learned from their European allies.

Ultimately, though, it was the infantryman on the ground—not Pershing, his staff, or the War Department—who lived or died by good or bad battlefield tactics. True, the American soldier had to follow orders, whether they originated in the studied decisions or careless whims of his officers; but the time always came when he made up his own mind. Fortunately the average American soldier of World War I—the legendary "Doughboy"—felt comfortable thinking and acting on his own.

CHAPTER 3

"Right or Wrong, My Country"

Twenty-year-old bricklayer Joe Rizzi watched a recruiting parade march through the streets of his hometown of Tarrytown, New York, on a spring afternoon in 1917. Led by firemen, the Masons, the Knights of Columbus, and the Salvation Army, and trotting briskly to the tune of "Over There," the marchers filed into an old ball lot. There they stood at attention as speaker after speaker mounted a platform to deliver fiery speeches denouncing Germany and urging Americans to enlist in defense of their country. Rizzi, who had been baptized Giuseppe Nicola Rizzi in Calitri, Italy, and immigrated to the United States when he was five, listened to the speeches with mounting excitement and pride in his adopted country.

> As I stood listening, it forcibly came to me that I was no longer a boy, but a man who must find a way to do the right thing. . . . My mind was in a turmoil trying to grasp this situation. "My adopted Country! Right or wrong, my Country." A patriotic feeling seized me, and talking it over with my brother we decided to enter the army to fight for our country.

After enlisting—he joined the 110th Engineers of the 35th Division—Rizzi walked home to eat with his family and break the news, a ritual being repeated in thousands of other homes across the country. "Pop," he said quietly after a long silence, "I am going away next week." "Yes," his father replied innocently. "Are you going to be gone long?" Rizzi froze and felt like he was choking. In his mind, the whole scenario had already been scripted. He had not expected this. "Well," his father repeated, becoming annoyed, "where are you going and how long will you be gone?" With an effort, Rizzi blurted out, "I've joined the army." His stepmother started to cry. "Just as I expected," his father muttered bitterly, returning to his meal.

Rizzi's girlfriend had been teasing and nagging him about joining the army. Otherwise, she said, people would call him a "coward" and a "slacker." When he told her that he had joined up and would leave within the week, however, she begged him to stay. "Gosh," Rizzi chided her, "you women would drive a man crazy. Well, I am going and cheer me up." Her parents allowed them to dispense with the usual chaperone and spend their final evening before his departure together. "It was worth the going," Rizzi believed, "just to find out that my girl loved me and she stated she would pray for me every night and day."[1]

Thousands and eventually millions of young men like Rizzi enlisted, or were drafted, into the U.S. Army in 1917. People called them Doughboys, but nobody knew why. In the Napoleonic era, British soldiers had eaten flour dumplings known as doughboys, and some said the British applied the term to their American cousins after witnessing their fondness for doughnuts. Others claimed that Americans had used the term since the nineteenth century because of the resemblance of the brass buttons on soldiers' uniforms to lumps of dough; that it was a play on the secretary of war's last name, thus "Baker's doughboys"; or that it referred to the American troops' relatively high pay compared to the British and French. It has also been claimed that cavalrymen during Pershing's Mexican campaign applied it as a derogatory term to the infantry, who became covered with the white dust that is a primary ingredient of adobe.[2]

Volunteers typically joined not because they understood the political issues involved in the war, but through a desire for new experiences and adventure, and a sense of duty.

Massachusetts schoolteacher William L. Langer thought that

after almost four years of war, after the most detailed and realistic accounts of the murderous fighting on the Somme and around Verdun, to say nothing of the day-to-day agony of trench warfare, it would have been all but impossible to get anyone to serve without duress. But it was not so. We and many thousands of others volunteered. Perhaps we were offended by the arrogance of the German U-boat campaign and convinced that Kaiserism must be smashed, once and for all. Possibly we already felt that, in the American interest, Western democracy must not be allowed to go under. But I doubt it. I can hardly remember a single instance of serious discussion of American policy or of larger war issues. We men, most of us young, were simply fascinated by the prospect of adventure and heroism. Most of us, I think, had the feeling that life, if we survived, would run in the familiar, routine channels. Here was our one great chance for excitement and risk. We could not afford to pass it up.[3]

Propaganda encouraged this attitude by whipping up patriotism and painting romantic and unrealistic portraits of the battlefield. "To young enthusiasts, such as we," remembered a soldier from West Virginia, "war consisted of following the flag over a shell-torn field, with fixed bayonet. Hadn't we stood for hours gazing at the recruiting posters? We could picture ourselves in the near future as pushing the Hun back from trench to trench, stopping only now and then to cut notches in the stocks of our rifles." Most recruits had a deep sense of obligation to the country that had nurtured them—even if it had done so for only a few months. "War had been declared and I thought my country needed me and I wanted to do my part," Walter E. Miller of Westbrook, Maine, explained simply. An Italian water boy declared more succinctly to his local recruiter: "Ma name Tony Monaco. In dees countra seex months. Gimme da gun."[4]

Not everyone wanted to go. In Buffalo, New York, a grocery boy drove to city hall in his work wagon to fill out a draft registration card. "Is there any reason why you shouldn't go to war in case you are called by Uncle Sam?" the clerk asked him. "Who the hell would drive the horse?" the boy nervously replied.[5] More often, men claimed exemption from service because they needed to support children, wives, or aged parents; and many were permitted to stay at home. Once selected, however, even draftees usually went to war uncomplaining, feeling that they owed it to their country. Conscientious objectors or simple "shirkers" were rare, although they received disproportionate notice in the media.

Inductees assembled in their local towns and cities before shipping out to divisional training camps across the United States—places like Camp Lee, Virginia; Camp Sill, Oklahoma; Camp Mills, New York; Camp Funston, Kansas; and Camp Lewis in Washington State. Many of these camps existed in name only, and soldiers who debarked from troop trains expecting lodgings often found dusty fields, virgin woods, and piles of lumber instead. The men immediately set to work building barracks—for officers first, of course—and other military facilities. Hard work and hot weather quickly divested them of any extra pounds.

Training, the recruits discovered, rested on two basic principles: drilling and marching. Day after day, week after week, they assembled, drilled back and forth, spun wooden rifles, and then departed for hot and dusty route marches. "Rumors of swift action in getting on with the war soon began to fade in the dust of the oval racetrack in front of the grandstand or in the endless inspections and inoculations," wrote a disgusted trainee at Camp Allen, Pennsylvania. Line of battle infantry and members of specialized services like the artillery and engineers all went through the same thing. "We followed the usual training," wrote Samuel E. Moore of the 37th Engineers: "5:15 A.M. first call, roll call, detail assignments [such as ditch-digging or latrine duty], setting up exercises, a run around the drill ground, then breakfast. After breakfast, drill till noon, more drill and/or a hike." Staige Davis Blackford, a medical student theoretically training to be a driver for the U.S. Army Ambulance Service, did not see an automobile or so much as learn how to change a tire before leaving for France. Up to that time, he recalled, training had "no effects particularly except that my mental condition went down and my physical condition improved."[6]

Equipment shortages often prevented specialized training. Major Charles DuPuy, assigned to train machine gunners in the 79th Division, found them armed with only "ten or fifteen Krag Jorgensen rifles [dating from 1896, before the Spanish-American War], and a few old Krag carbines, which were not much longer than a boy's Flobert rifle, the rest carrying wooden guns, which they had sawed from boards." Disgusted, the major ordered the men to throw their wooden guns into a bonfire and return the Krags to the depot. He trained them without weapons instead.[7] Many soldiers trained for months without guns before receiving shipments of the hated Krags, passed down from other camps.

The U.S. Army's official service rifle, the 1903 Springfield, equipped some infantry divisions, but the factories could not produce it fast enough to supply the entire AEF. Instead, the army turned to the Enfield rifle, which Remington and Winchester had produced in America for export to the British army. Slightly redesigned for issue to the U.S. Army, the Enfield had an extremely high rate of fire for a bolt-action rifle. The British had proven what this fine weapon could do in 1914, when their well-trained infantry had fired it so efficiently that the Germans thought they faced machine guns. The Americans never received the training necessary to reach British standards of fire discipline—many Doughboys would not receive their rifles until they arrived in France—but at least they were well armed.

Bayonets were distributed to the recruits promptly, and in good quantity. Attached to old rifles or even strapped to the end of wooden sticks, they suited the spirit of attack that officers tried to instill in their men. "We drilled and fought dummies with bayonets until we couldn't see straight," complained one recruit.[8] So much the better, drill sergeants told the dazed rookies, to make them into the ruthless warriors the army required. Once real rifles became available, marksmanship received particular emphasis in training. This, like bayonet practice, reflected Pershing's belief in the primacy of traditional weaponry on the battlefield. Infantry soldiers learned to rely on their rifles and bayonets, and were told to establish moral superiority over the enemy through confidence, energy, and drive.

Heavy weapons and equipment, such as machine guns, artillery, aircraft, trucks, and tanks, played no role in training in the United States. Machine gunners used sticks or old rifles; artillerymen made do with sawhorses and wooden guns; engineers learned how to do a million different things with rope; tank, ambulance, and truck drivers spent weeks pushing wooden boxes across fields; and airmen risked their lives flying antiques or just gazed longingly at the sky. Communications and signaling equipment was also scarce and often defective.

Such were the dividends of American industrial and military unpreparedness. U.S. factories had been shipping artillery shells to Europe for three years—the French and British accepted them out of desperation but derided their poor quality—but they could not produce equipment and ordnance on anything like the scale needed in 1917. Even textiles, one of the most advanced sectors in American industry, struggled to produce an adequate supply of uniforms for the troops, who often spent months training in their civvies. Conditions improved toward the spring of 1918, as modern rifles, trucks, and other equipment began reaching the training camps, but by that time many units had already gone overseas. Most of the men landed in Europe without having touched a machine gun or grenade, fired a cannon, operated signals or engineering equipment, or learned how to apply basic infantry tactics in either attack or defense. The Doughboys were as unprepared as the country that sent them.

★

WITH the exception of the 1st through 5th Divisions—regular army formations recruited from all over the country—most of the AEF divisions that saw action in France were regionally organized. Formed from individual states or groups of adjacent states, American divisions contained regiments of volunteers and draftees from specific cities or counties, and companies from individual towns or townships. This sensible arrangement eased recruiting and organization, fostered cooperation among officers and men, and helped to create a sense of esprit de corps. Thus, for example, the troops of the 28th Division (Pennsylvania National Guard) and 32d Division (Wisconsin National Guard) took pride in their origins by devising unique insignia, building traditions, and tracing their regimental and even company histories back to the Civil War and earlier.

All of this changed late in 1917, when the army gutted the National Guard divisions still training in the United States and reassigned many of their officers and men to other divisions ready for shipment to France. Untrained recruits and draftees, selected seemingly at random from all over the United States, filled the resulting gaps. This decision spawned some ridiculous mixtures—the 77th Division, for example, initially composed of recent European immigrants and urban toughs from downtown New York City, received a sudden influx of callow farm boys from the western plains—and seriously undermined unit cohesion and identity. Other troops underwent months of training only to be reassigned to labor battalions, while unnaturalized natives of Germany and Austria-Hungary were thoroughly trained and then kicked out of the army because of their origins.[9] Bonds cemented during training thus had to be established all over again, often between groups of men who had nothing in common.

The Doughboys became used to variety. "An infantry company could boast of most any sort of character," recalled an officer of the 79th Division. "One outfit alone included in its roster a murderer, several moonshiners and boot-leggers, a newspaper reporter, a professional baseball player, several lumber-jacks, a couple of 'ham' actors, a couple of high school professors and at least one lunatic." Many gangsters from Chicago and New York served with the 33d and 77th Divisions, including Jack "Legs" Diamond—who deserted rather than face the German machine guns—and "Wild Bill" Lovett, who would earn a Distinguished Service Cross in the Meuse-Argonne. Another notorious gangster, "Monk" Eastman, showed up at a recruiting station so scarred by bullet and knife wounds that the army doctors nearly rejected him, and went on to become a war hero with the 27th Division. Rural recruits, often deeply religious, were made of different stuff. Sergeant William Triplet's platoon of the 35th "Missouri-Kansas" Division "had one professed conscientious objector and one self-appointed minister of the gospel who abhorred the use of carnal weapons but their squadmates could be relied on to keep them in line."[10]

Perhaps the most striking thing about the AEF was its ethnic diversity. About 18 percent of army recruits were foreign-born, and 70 percent of them had lived in the United States for fewer than ten years. Major Charles DuPuy of the 316th Infantry Regiment, which originated from central Pennsylvania, needed interpreters standing at his elbow as he trained "Russians, Poles, Austrians, Germans, Italians, Turks, Sicilians, Greeks, Lithuanians, French Canadians, and Slavs of all the Slavic races." The 77th Division from New York stood out especially in this regard. Its officers, typically coming from wealthy Anglo-Saxon families, struggled to understand and relate to their men. "Krag-a-co-poul-o-wicz, G.," one officer of the 77th stuttered at roll call in Camp Upton, New York. He had to repeat himself twice before someone drawled, "Do yuh mean me? That ain't the way tuh say my name. Me own mother wouldn't recernize it." "Quiet. Say 'here,'" the officer snapped. "Then I ain't here," the feisty recruit growled sullenly. "That's all. I ain't here." The 77th Division's biggest ethnic contingent came from Manhattan's Little Italy. In France, German scouts would hear the New Yorkers chattering in their trenches and misidentify them as Italian army soldiers.[11]

Immigrant soldiers usually did not suffer severely discriminatory treatment. The same could not be said for soldiers of African American descent. Blacks had a long history in the U.S. Army dating back to the Revolutionary War, and in the decades preceding World War I they had served with distinction in places like Cuba and the Philippines. Not since the days of the Civil War, however, had they encountered such an overwhelmingly hostile and racist military culture. In April 1917, twenty thousand blacks served in the regular army and the National Guard. In the following months four hundred thousand more, mostly conscripts, entered the armed forces. Seventy-five percent of the blacks were assigned to labor units, where they did menial work in segregated and often appalling conditions. Only a small proportion entered combat. After toying with the idea of organizing black combat soldiers into separate units within white infantry divisions, the War Department decided to segregate them into two largely black divisions, the 92d and 93d. At Pershing's insistence, they trained under black junior officers and white general officers.

Such careful segregation failed to stem the resentment of whites who believed that blacks did not belong in the army. At best, white Doughboys treated their black comrades with patronizing contempt; at worst, they subjected them to excoriation and abuse. Tensions extended to the home front. In July 1917, white anger at the employment of blacks in war industries led to riots in East St. Louis, during which forty blacks and nine whites died, and six thousand African American families fled their homes. A month later, riots between white civilians and black soldiers in Houston ended with the execution of thirteen black soldiers who were disallowed the customary right of appeal to the War Department.[12]

Bringing order to this melting pot—or seething cauldron—of an army would have tried the most seasoned officers in the world. Eager and well educated but generally naive, most American junior officers had received little or no military training before the war began. Former teachers, accountants, and lawyers, they struggled to exert authority over their rougher and often more gun-savvy enlisted men, especially in units drawn from rural states like Tennessee and Wyoming. And unlike their British counterparts, American officers could not draw on any traditions of social deference. Instead they learned how to command on the job, often enforcing obedience simply through superior dedication or strength of character. Training camp eliminated some of the unfit, with officers obviously unsuited to field command being reassigned to staff or clerical duties, and more effective leaders taking their place. The real culling out of good from bad, however, would not occur until the trial by fire on the battlefields of France.

A similar process took place in the higher echelons of AEF command. Many of the U.S. Army's senior officers in 1917 were elderly, with minds rooted in the conflicts of the nineteenth century. They often lacked the energy and flexibility necessary to adapt successfully to modern warfare. Pershing removed ten of the thirty-two generals who arrived in Europe during the winter of 1917–18, calling them too old or mentally unfit.[13] Similar problems characterized command in the National Guard. Many Guard officers were political appointees with little or no military experience. This fact fostered bad blood between regular and Guard officers, and led to many needless and harmful controversies. Pershing, for one, made no secret of his disregard for National Guard officers. Yet the basic problem was the same throughout the AEF, and it could have only one solution: weeding out via intensive training and, eventually, combat.

In the autumn and winter of 1917–18, training camps across the United States disgorged thousands of tired, bored, and poorly trained men. No longer civilians and not quite soldiers, they marched to assembly areas and rode cross-country trains to cities on the East Coast. The busiest port of embarkation was New York. "I cannot adequately express or, describe, or convey our feelings, and when we passed that immortal gift, the 'Statue of Liberty' from our French brethren across the sea, not knowing when, if ever we would return," remembered Private Alexander Clay of the 33d Division, Illinois National Guard. "I thought to myself, and could only say, 'Laffayett we are coming to repay the debt of our gratitude to your country.'"

As the troopships crossed the Atlantic, the Doughboys whiled away their time by reading, writing letters home, or playing cards and crap games. But they never completely relaxed. For the first time, the Germans had become a tangible threat. Private Clay was chatting with two friends on the top deck when suddenly, "as a flash of lightening from a clear sky," the ship's whistle shrieked loudly enough, it seemed, to shatter their eardrums. Looking up, the soldiers saw two red flags fluttering. Turning to scan the ocean beyond the rail, Clay spotted something slashing toward them through the water.

> I said to my friends, "Look! Look! What is that?" My friends looked but didn't
> see anything. It had gone under the bow of the ship. In a few seconds believe
> me, we certainly heard the loudest noise in our lives. It was a torpedo from a
> German submarine. The ship tilted or listed over from bow to stern. I would
> say from 12 to 15 degrees.

Bugles blew, and soldiers scrambled out of every corner of the ship, hurrying into company formation before frantic officers. Water flooded compartments belowdecks, and Clay, peering through the hatches, saw packs, overcoats, and other equipment sloshing about. Men talked of what would happen if they had to jump overboard: "We were realizing that we now faced our Almighty maker. That only a very few moments, may be seconds to live, and [we are] on our way to Davy Jones's locker." The ship didn't sink, and eventually limped into a French port.[14]

Actual torpedoings were rare, and very few troopships sank, thanks to an effective convoy system and heavy destroyer escorts. But there were exceptions. On February 5, 1918, the transport *Tuscania,* loaded with engineers, was hit by a torpedo as it rounded the coast of northern Ireland in high seas. The torpedo struck amidships, sending a plume of flame and debris into the sky and destroying or damaging many of the lifeboats. The ship immediately listed heavily to starboard, and some of the remaining lifeboats flipped upside down as they were lowered, hurling soldiers into the freezing water. Soon all the lifeboats were gone, with most of the soldiers still waiting on deck. "The situation looked none too encouraging," remembered Private Henry Askew of the 20th Engineers, but "the boys showed few signs of nervousness."

Standing there, lining the rail, waiting for the next development, some six hundred of them smoked or talked quietly, discussing their plight. The remarkable part of it all was that they took everything in a matter-of-fact way with a sort of "well, what's next?" attitude. Occasionally a few would sing some little song, indicative of their feelings, such as "Where Do We Go From Here, Boys?" or "To Hell With the Kaiser." The absence of panic or effort and time in prayer was remarkable.

Eventually a destroyer came alongside and rescued most of the soldiers before the *Tuscania* sank. Over two hundred men went down with the ship.[15]

.　　★

In Europe, meanwhile, the French economy had degenerated into a shambles, and labor unrest threatened to spin out of control. British civilian morale plummeted under Germany's continuing submarine campaign, and some politicians questioned whether the war remained worth fighting. In northeastern Italy, Austrian and German forces launched a stunning offensive at Caporetto on October 24, shattering Allied resistance and nearly bringing Italy to her knees. Two weeks later, Russia collapsed into civil discord as the Bolsheviks took power in Moscow and St. Petersburg and drove Aleksandr Kerensky from power. Their leader, Vladimir Lenin, promptly made good on earlier promises to take his country out of the war, although the official peace treaty was not signed until March of the following year.

By the end of 1917 the Germans had followed through on their plan to withdraw a million battle-tested troops from the eastern front and send them west. They spent weeks practicing new "storm-troop" tactics and preparing for a final offensive aimed at destroying the exhausted Anglo-French armies and ending the war. Confident of victory, German politicians envisioned a brutal peace settlement that would leave Belgium and much of France under German occupation and turn eastern Europe into a colony for Teutonic settlers. Facing the long-dreaded enemy offensive, the British and French scrambled to organize their withered armies for defense. They begged the Americans to reconsider amalgamation, if only as a temporary solution to the mounting crisis. But Pershing and his superiors in Washington refused to budge. When the German offensive began on March 21, 1918, with not a single American soldier in place to help, the British and French armies quickly fell to pieces.

CHAPTER 4

"Retreat, Hell. We Just Got Here"

The German 1918 offensive slashed through the British and French armies with seeming inevitability. In an operation code-named Michael, seventy-one German divisions attacked twenty-six British divisions along a fifty-six-mile front in northeastern France. Spearheaded by elite groups of storm troopers, who infiltrated the British defenses under cover of heavy fog and disrupted communications and supply lines in advance of the main infantry assaults, the Germans drove the British Fifth Army back twenty-five miles before their commander, General Erich von Ludendorff, called a halt to the offensive's first phase. On April 9 he renewed the attack in Flanders, shattering the Portuguese Army Corps and surging through the Allied lines. As the Germans expanded and increased their pressure, the British ran desperately low on reserves. French reinforcements arrived slowly.

"There is no other course open to us but to fight it out," a desperate Field Marshal Sir Douglas Haig, the British commander, declared to his troops on April 11. "Every position must be held to the last man: there must be no retirement. With our backs to the wall, and believing in the justice of our cause, each one of us must fight on to the end. The safety of our homes and the freedom of mankind alike depend on the conduct of each one of us at this critical moment."[1] His troops heeded the call and slowed the German offensive, preventing it from wiping out the British positions in Flanders. By the end of April the Germans had nevertheless taken numerous vital positions and advanced to within twenty miles of the Channel port of Dunkirk. Ludendorff then deftly switched to yet another front, taking the French by surprise in an attack along the Aisne River on May 27. Obliterating the front lines with a massive artillery bombardment of high explosives and gas, the Germans poured through the resulting twenty-five-mile gap and advanced nine miles in the first day alone, taking some fifty thousand prisoners and eight hundred guns. Hardly anything remained between them and Paris, about fifty-five miles away.

On April 14, with the need for Allied unity more apparent than ever, French marshal Ferdinand Foch became Allied supreme commander for the western front. A wizened, sixty-seven-year-old career soldier who had fought in the Franco-Prussian War of 1870–71, Foch was urbane, religious, and incurably optimistic. In late August 1914, less than a week after learning of the deaths in battle of his son and son-in-law, he had supposedly reacted to a heavy German attack by reporting: "I am hard pressed on my right; my center is giving way; situation excellent; I attack." Like Pershing, he believed that willpower and élan won battles, not just big guns. "Action is the first law of war," he declared. "Of all mistakes only one is disgraceful—inaction. We must seek to create the course of events, not merely be passively subject to them; and above all we must organize the attack."[2]

Foch lacked the authority to order the Allied generals to do his bidding. Instead he worked to convince them through sheer force of personality. This was no easy feat, especially considering the kind of men with whom he had to deal. Douglas Haig, a cranky, fifty-six-year-old Scotsman with the grim pertinacity of a bulldog, had taken command of the British Expeditionary Force in December 1915. He had masterminded the horrendously bloody battles of the Somme in 1916 and Passchendaele in 1917, impressing some with his persistence and others with his apparently callous disregard for his soldiers' lives. Henri-Philippe Pétain, the grave, imperturbable "savior of Verdun" who had restored order to the French army after the mutinies following the disastrous Nivelle offensive of April–May 1917, was, like Haig, an extremely stubborn man who moved only when *he* felt inclined to do so. And then there was Pershing, perhaps the stubbornest man in France.

Up to the spring of 1918 the American Expeditionary Force had impressed only by its absence. Again and again the British and French had attempted to shame Pershing into handing over at least some of his men to their command. "If Great Britain and France had to go under," British prime minister David Lloyd George once scolded the general, "it would be an honourable defeat, because each had put the very last man into the army, whereas

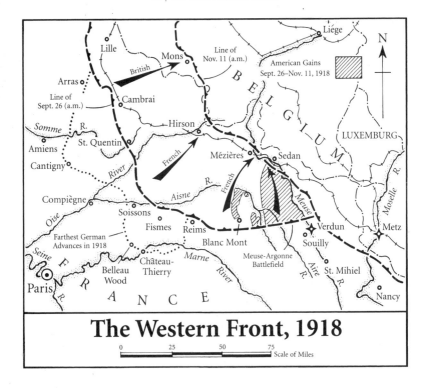

The Western Front, 1918

0   25   50   75
Scale of Miles

the United States would go under after putting in only as many men as had the Belgians. [Surely] the American nation would feel it a matter of prestige and national pride not to accept defeat after . . . hardly putting their little finger in the struggle." But Pershing remained unmoved. There would be no division of the AEF; it would enter the lines only as a single, distinct unit. Annoyed, Foch demanded whether he would let the Germans push the French back to Paris rather than compromise his views. Pershing flatly replied that he would. Foch then threatened to refer the matter to Wilson. "Refer it to the President," Pershing growled, "and be damned."[3]

By the spring of 1918, the Allied situation looked so desperate that even Pershing had to make concessions. By mid-April he had five fighting divisions at his disposal—the 1st, 2d, 26th, 32d, and 42d—and he agreed to place four of them on quiet sectors of the front in order to free British and French divisions for service elsewhere. He also agreed to accelerate the transportation of American troops to Europe by concentrating on shipping infantry only, without artillery, ordnance, and other heavy equipment. In March 1918, 60,000 American soldiers sailed to France; 93,000 departed in April, 240,000 in May, and 280,000 in June. Yet all of these troops remained undertrained and underequipped. An independent American army remained an apparently distant prospect.

★

THE 1st Division landed in France in June 1917, proudly waving the Stars and Stripes. French officials welcomed it enthusiastically, but civilians paid the Yanks little attention. As Captain George C. Marshall's ship pulled in, "a small crowd of the French inhabitants collected along the edge of the basin and at the end of the street to watch our arrival. Most of the women were in mourning. Very few men were in evidence. There was not a cheer, and the general aspect was that of a funeral." The Americans thought of themselves as saviors; but the civilians had seen it all before. Over three years, thousands of fresh-faced young soldiers—French, British, Australian, and many others—had marched gallantly off to battle. They always returned worn out, often demoralized, if they came back at all. American troops nevertheless interpreted the civilians' "studied indifference" as ingratitude.[4]

Marching through quiet, grubby streets of ports like Brest, the Doughboys assembled at railheads and boarded cramped boxcars in sooty old trains. These took them to assembly areas where they spent days or even weeks organizing before marching to training camps far inland. By the time they reached camp the men had fallen out of fighting trim:

> Toward the end of such a march husky men would blindly stagger to the roadside and drop in a ditch or shady place to come along later as best they could. Blistered feet, weak spines, fainting spells, dizzy spells, and well-nigh, broken shoulder blades were but a few of the tortures which urged the body to give up the fight. One was unconscious of all else except dirt and sweat, heat, blind staggers and bodily ills, and won the fight only by an almost superhuman muster of grit and will power.[5]

The Americans did not think much of the French countryside. Iowa farmer Joe Romedahl wrote to a friend: "Well I suppose you want to know how I like France and to tell the truth I don't. I don't like France. It may be allright but they are away behind the times. Most of the people here cut there oats by hand. If they seen us farm they sure would open their eyes." The filthiness of the French villages, typified by the tendency of many peasants to measure status by the size of the dung heaps that stood steaming in their yards, especially shocked the Yanks. Thinking they were doing the peasants a favor, the soldiers removed dung heaps from villages where they billeted. Villagers carefully replaced their precious piles after the Americans departed, only for new groups of well-intentioned Doughboys to raze them the next day. Eventually the peasants accepted such Sisyphean labors as a fact of life. As Major Charles DuPuy of the 79th Division marched his troops into one village, an old woman hobbled up to him and muttered, "Well, now that you Americans have come, I suppose you will start cleaning up the town with your brooms." She was right. Finding that the peasants had "lapsed into their old conditions" since the departure of the last American unit, DuPuy and his men decided "to do the work all over again and start in fresh."[6]

In camp, the Doughboys encountered the same training regimen they thought they had left behind in the United States: marching and drill, drill and marching. Morale reached rock bottom before crates of brand-new Enfield rifles and grenades arrived, and European instructors appeared offering courses on how to fight. Eager at last to learn something useful, the Doughboys flocked to the courses, but quickly grew disappointed. Refusing to believe "that these 'Yanks' had any previous training or ideas worth considering," British instructors talked down to them—insisting, for example, that the Americans throw grenades with a motion similar to bowling in cricket. Bluntly dubbing the posture "ridiculous," the Yanks threw them like baseballs instead.[7] French instructors carefully avoided any suggestion of superiority, lest their new allies become offended. One French general suggested discarding the word *instructor* in favor of *consulting expert* or *technical adviser,* to avoid wounding American pride.

✶

DURING the winter of 1917–18, four American divisions entered quiet sectors of the front, relieving French and British units for fighting elsewhere. Remembered Private Walter Corning:

> The fact that it was a quiet sector meant nothing to us. We were new in the game and everybody had visions of a continuous raging battle. Shrapnel flew around and bullets "phitted" as we bumped and splashed along the muddy "boulevard." Now and then a zing-g-g made us duck as a stray bullet ricocheted. We reached the front line in a light fog with only three minor casualties and felt relieved when we discovered that it was really quiet. Only the intermittent rat-a-tat-tat of one Jerry machine gun broke the silence out in front. Our hearts behaved and our knees stopped knocking. All signs of nervousness disappeared.[8]

Such light "seasoning" at least gave soldiers an idea of what flying bullets sounded like. To all practical purposes, however, the Americans remained untested. The initial division to see serious action was the 1st Division under Major General Robert Lee Bullard. On May 28, it attacked the German-held village of Cantigny, about fifty miles southeast of the center of the German offensive along the Aisne River, which had begun the previous day. Supported by French artillery and tanks, the Americans seized Cantigny with only minor losses and beat off several enemy counterattacks.

Despite its propaganda value for the Americans, the Battle of Cantigny did nothing to slow the German steamroller on the Aisne. On May 30, with the French government prepared to flee from Paris to Bordeaux, Pershing responded to Pétain's appeals for help by rushing two divisions, the 2d and 3d, to hold the front at the tip of the German advance. The 3d Division, which had been in France for only a few weeks, took up defensive positions along the Marne River near Château-Thierry. The 2d Division, including the Marine brigade under Brigadier General James G. Harbord, arrived shortly after. Together they held on to a six-mile front, stopping a heavy German assault on June 4 that brought the enemy to within fifty miles of Paris. Legend has it that when a French officer told a Marine captain to retreat, the American snarled: "Retreat, hell. We just got here."[9]

On June 6 the commander of the French XXI Corps, under which the two American divisions fought, ordered the Marines to make a surprise counterattack against German positions in and around Belleau Wood. Harbord and his men complied, almost too willingly. Attacking in waves across poppy-studded wheat fields against well-placed German machine guns, the Marines fell in dense swathes. They took 1,087 casualties in one day.[10] Three more weeks of heavy fighting followed as they contested Belleau Wood, often hand to hand. When the battle finally ended on June 26, Harbord's brigade had taken the woods at the cost of 5,200 casualties. This was war in earnest.

Belleau Wood marked the beginning of a long, painful learning process. The Marines had fought hard but employed clumsy tactics. "It became apparent," one Marine officer wrote, "that the reckless courage of the foot soldier with his rifle and bayonet could not overcome machine guns well-protected in rocky nests." Other problems included inadequate artillery preparation and poor use of grenades and machine guns—weapons that Pershing had considered supplementary to the almighty rifle and bayonet. The Germans noted the American infantryman's bravery and tenacity, along with the incompetence of his officers. "The American soldier is courageous, strong, and clever," one German staff officer reported in mid-June. "He is at his best in guerrilla warfare. [But] the manner in which large units attack is not up-to-date and leadership is poor."[11] For all their bravado, the Yanks could be beaten.

"An Independent American Army"

Quiet returned to the western front after the bloody encounters at Château-Thierry and Belleau Wood. The most dangerous phase of Ludendorff's massive offensive had stalled, thanks in part to the Americans. But the respite didn't last long. On July 15, guns once more thundered along the front as Germany resumed the offensive, in Champagne, southeast of the previous attack. This time, Foch was ready. The night before the Germans attacked, the French bombarded their areas of assembly. The next morning, German infantry overran the lightly held French front lines, only to slam into ferociously defended second and third lines. Nowhere could they make significant headway, and on July 16 Ludendorff called off the attack. For almost four months he had thrown every soldier he had into the western offensive. His troops were exhausted and reserves had grown dangerously thin.

On July 18 Foch launched his own counteroffensive against the western tip of the German salient near Soissons. The American 1st and 2d Divisions, rested and replenished since the previous month's heavy fighting, spearheaded the attack. "There was mists hanging low down close to the ground but it was a right pretty day. Too nice a day to die," remembered Corporal Joseph E. Rendinell of the 6th Marines.[1] As the troops advanced slowly through wheat fields and woods, German machine guns and artillery hit them from three sides. Casualties were heavy—some units lost up to 50 percent of their men and all of their officers—but the Doughboys continued stolidly on, absorbing their losses and pushing the Germans back. By July 22 the 1st and 2d Divisions had taken respectively sixty-nine hundred and four thousand casualties in an advance of seven miles.

Elsewhere along the German salient the U.S. 3d, 4th, and 26th Divisions, followed by the 28th, 32d, and 42d Divisions, drove the Germans steadily back. The fighting went on day after day, week after week, and for the first time the Doughboys gained a protracted look at the reality of modern war. "Men plunged to earth to the right and left of me," a corporal of the 42d Division said of one attack.

> Almost at every stride some comrade fell, stumbling forward lifeless, or falling to [catch his] wind and rock for a while through the first disordering sting of a fatal wound. Others just slipped down and lay low and still. . . . I saw these incidents, little nightmare incidents, flashed upon the screen of my vision in jumbled, jerky fashion, and I ran on feeling that the whole thing was just a dream, stopping to aim and fire as some chance gray uniform showed, and then blindly running on.

Men grew acquainted to sights of fields "strewn with our doughboys, gray faces in the mud, blue hands frozen to their guns."[2] For thousands of Americans, war's first innocence had passed.

Eliminating the Aisne-Marne salient by the end of July, American troops reached the Vesle River near a little village called Fismes. Across the river lay an even tinier village called Fismette. At the insistence of the French high command, elements of the 28th Division occupied it in mid-August as a bridgehead for later advances. The Germans responded by bringing up substantial reinforcements and deploying them around the bridgehead. The Pennsylvanians asked for permission to evacuate, but the French generals refused; on August 27 the Germans attacked, led by *Stosstruppen* with flamethrowers. Only 30 of the 230 Doughboys in the village escaped capture or scorching death. Anger at the disaster spread through the entire AEF, and many men swore they would never again fight under French command.

Elsewhere, the French and British erased practically all the gains the Germans had made earlier that year. British, Australian, and Canadian troops backed by over six hundred tanks attacked on August 8 around Amiens, shattering the German lines. They caused such panic that Ludendorff, calling it the "black day of the German army," offered his resignation; but the kaiser refused. As these battles took place, the Americans, who had lost almost fifty thousand men during the summer, began entering the lines in large numbers.[3] The war's supreme crisis had passed; for the first time, the Allies seriously outnumbered and outgunned the Germans on the western front.

✳

THE summer's successes enheartened the French civilians, who now swarmed to the docks as American troopships entered port, waving caps and calling the Doughboys saviors. *"Vive l'Amerique! Vive les Americaines!"* shouted one elderly Frenchman to a shipful of 79th Division troops. "Vive yourself, you damned frog!" a cynical Philadelphia Doughboy called back. Swarms of French urchins trailing oversized black cloaks greeted another group of Americans. Singing "Hail, hail ze gang all heeare, what ze ail do we ceeare," and demanding chocolate, chewing gum, and cigarettes "for papa," the children followed the soldiers through town. When the troops paused or fell out, young women and girls dashed among them, selling fruit or "detestable postcards" and slyly uncovering bottles of wine and cognac. Charmed by the children and the ladies, many of the soldiers traded equipment and rations in exchange for fruit or souvenirs.[4]

The summer had gone well, with the Yanks fighting successfully under European command, and Foch and Haig hinted that the arrangement should remain in place. Pershing remained determined to create an independent American army, however; by midsummer, with 1.25 million Americans in France, he finally had the forces available to accomplish that goal. An opportunity to push it through arose at a meeting of the Allied army commanders on July 24, when Foch presented a new strategic plan dubbed the "continuous offensive." In earlier years, the Allies had launched set-piece offensives at different times and places. From now on, Foch announced, Allied troops would attack on convergent lines against the broad German salient in France, driving the enemy back and denying him the chance to pause and reorganize. Haig and Pétain at first declared the idea too risky, but Pershing thought it would work—so long as an independent, well-prepared American army took part on its own section of the front. Pershing helped to bring the other two commanders around to Foch's plan; in return, Foch gave him what he wanted.[5] The American First Army, consisting of fourteen U.S. infantry divisions and French artillery, tanks, and transportation, was born in Lorraine on August 10.

Foch at first envisioned two powerful attacks in the north and south by the British and Americans, respectively, with a more limited advance by French forces in the center, and after meeting with Pershing during early August he assigned First Army to take the St. Mihiel salient, south of Verdun. The salient measured about two hundred square miles. The Germans had occupied it since 1914, and had used it in 1916 as a base of operations for their attacks against the fortress of Verdun. Its strategic value had since diminished, and most of the Germans had left it for more critical fronts farther north. The Americans, Foch decided, could easily clear the salient and free the important Paris-Avricourt railway line running through it.

Pershing liked the idea. The offensive seemed to offer an opportunity not just to clear the St. Mihiel salient, but to drive farther east toward the German fortress of Metz. Capturing that place would sever an important railway line, threaten the vital industrial regions of Briey and the Saar, and bring the war to the borders of German Pershing went to Foch's headquarters at Bombon on August 24 and excitedly presented his expanded plan, which involved seventeen divisions and 476,000 men against an estimated 2,000 German defenders.[6] Foch approved, and the stage seemed set for the first major American offensive of the war.

On August 30, however, Foch unexpectedly turned up at First Army headquarters and told Pershing that he had changed his mind. The salient, he argued, had no significant strategic value; let the Germans keep it. Instead, the Americans should leave nine divisions to contain the salient, and move the remainder of First Army about sixty miles northwest to support a much larger French force slated to advance through the Champagne and Meuse-Argonne regions. That advance would form the southernmost prong of a trident-shaped offensive, with the British delivering the northern thrust from Cambrai to St. Quentin and the French attacking in the middle along the Aisne. Horrified at Foch's plan, which assigned only a junior role to the Americans, Pershing exclaimed that it would ruin all of First Army's elaborate preparations for the St. Mihiel offensive. Recalling troops and supplies from their staging positions would waste time and reduce First Army to organizational chaos, possibly incapacitating it for weeks. Besides, the St. Mihiel salient threatened the right flank of Foch's intended drive in the Meuse-Argonne; it had to be eliminated.

Pershing and Foch shot angry glances at each other during pauses for interpreters' translations. Each had had enough—Foch of Pershing's obstructionism, and Pershing of Foch's apparent determination to thwart the formation of an independent American army.

"I do not want to appear difficult," Pershing said finally, but "the American people and the American government expect that the American army shall act [independently] and shall not be dispersed here and there along the Western Front."

"Do you wish to take part in the battle?" Foch demanded, his eyes flashing.

"Most assuredly," Pershing replied firmly, "but as an American Army and in no other way."

The argument continued and tempers worsened. "Your French and English comrades are going into battle; are you coming with them?" Foch asked patronizingly.

"Marshal Foch," Pershing raged, "you have no authority as Allied Commander-in-Chief to call upon me to yield up my command of the American Army and have it scattered among the Allied forces where it will not be an American Army at all."

"I must insist upon the arrangement," Foch rapped.

"You may insist all you please," the American shot back, "but I decline absolutely to agree to your plan. While our army will fight wherever you decide, it will not fight except as an independent American army."

The two men leapt up from the table simultaneously, and in his fury Pershing briefly envisioned punching the much smaller Frenchman. Thankfully for Franco-American comity, the moment passed. But Foch left without an agreement, and after two and a half hours all hopes of a "continuous offensive" seemed dashed. Bitterly, Pershing confided to his diary that the British and French "did not wish America to find out her strength."[7]

Another meeting took place at Bombon on September 2. This time Pétain, grave and taciturn but trusted by both Foch and Pershing, mediated a compromise. Pershing suggested abandoning St. Mihiel altogether and moving the entire First Army to the Meuse-Argonne, where it would take part as a separate element of Foch's concentric offensive. That, Foch replied, would delay his offensive for several weeks and give the Germans time to recuperate. Instead he suggested that First Army take on not one but *two* attacks—first St. Mihiel, and then the Meuse-Argonne—all in a period of two or at most three weeks. At St. Mihiel, First Army would attack and eliminate the salient, but without attempting to continue on to Metz. It would then shift to the Meuse-Argonne and lead the primary thrust of this portion of Foch's offensive, with French armies on either side attacking in support. The rub was that First Army would now have to fight two major battles on separate fronts sixty miles apart, within a period of two weeks. Yet Foch's new plan, as he no doubt expected, appealed to American vanity. Pershing was satisfied and optimistic. "In my opinion," he said, "no other Allied troops had the morale or the offensive spirit to overcome successfully the difficulties to be met in the Meuse-Argonne sector." He agreed to Foch's proposal, and the allies separated, best of friends once again.[8]

✳

ON September 12, 1918, over half a million American and 110,000 French soldiers attacked the St. Mihiel salient. The Germans offered little resistance; deeming their ground untenable, they had already begun to withdraw. Even so, the Americans caught them off guard. First Army eliminated the salient in four days, capturing fifteen thousand German prisoners and hundreds of artillery pieces and machine guns at the cost of fewer than nine thousand casualties. Yet the easy victory did not satisfy everybody. Brigadier General Douglas MacArthur, commanding the 42d Division's 84th Brigade, went to a forward observation post one evening during the attack and brooded over the fortress city of Metz, which he could just see in the distance behind the enemy lines. He could not understand why Pershing would not let him go and take it.[9]

The St. Mihiel offensive exposed serious problems in the AEF infrastructure. The huge American divisions—at twenty-eight thousand men, they could hold two European divisions[10]—had caused severe supply logjams behind the lines. Even basic necessities like food and water had taken days to reach troops at the front. Communications had also been poor. Units lost touch with one another, officers became disoriented and detached from their commands, and infantry failed to coordinate with artillery. Had the Germans resisted in force, the battle might have ended very differently.

Pershing expressed few concerns. His thoughts were more for the historic importance of First Army's victory. "We gave 'em a damn good licking, didn't we?" he gloated. America had convincingly demonstrated her dominance over the tired old nations of Europe. "Wave after wave of Europeans, dissatisfied with conditions in Europe, came to this country to seek liberty," Pershing lectured his intelligence chief, Brigadier General Dennis Nolan.

> Those who came had the will-power and the spirit to seek opportunity in a new world rather than put up with unbearable conditions in the old . . . those who came for that reason were superior in initiative to those, their relatives, who had remained and submitted to the conditions . . . in addition to this initial superiority in initiative they had developed, and their children had developed, under a form of government and in a land of great opportunity

where individual initiative was protected and rewarded. [In consequence] we had developed a type of manhood superior in initiative to that existing abroad, which given approximately equal training and discipline, developed a superior soldier to that existing abroad.[11]

The battle just ended, Pershing and his officers believed, had justified their efforts to maintain the AEF as an independent entity. With hundreds of thousands of troops marching north toward a new, bigger encounter with the Boche, Pershing's theories of American superiority would be tested as never before.

PART II

————•◦•————

"Here Is the Golden Dream":
The Meuse-Argonne

The Meuse-Argonne, a hilly region of forests and farms rimmed by stretches of battle-scarred wilderness, provided its German occupiers with some of the best defensive terrain on the western front. Topographically, it resembled a funnel. The American front, facing north up the spout, ran roughly twenty miles across from east to west. To the east, the broad and unfordable Meuse River flowed north-northwest from the fortress of Verdun, about seven miles behind the American lines, past Sedan, about thirty-five miles behind the German lines. A canal ran for several miles along the river's east bank; beyond that the German-held Heights of the Meuse, packed hub to hub with artillery, commanded the entire battlefield. To the west, the Argonne Forest ran north-northwest between the Aire and Aisne Rivers on the right and left respectively. Beyond the immediate vicinity of the front line, the forest remained largely unspoiled by war, with dense foliage and underbrush covering dozens of small ravines, hillocks, and streams.

Advancing north up the funnel's spout, with their right flank on the Meuse and their left flank in the Argonne, the Americans would first have to cross a wasteland of shell holes and barbed wire. This nightmarish swath ran west from the Meuse across swampy open lowlands and a series of low hills and shallow valleys before cutting a jagged scar through the Argonne Forest. Immediately north of this shell-torn region were more hills and valleys, dominated in the center by Montfaucon, a 1,122-foot-high butte crowned by the broken white walls of a shell-blasted village and the steeple of a long-abandoned church. The French had tried and failed to take Montfaucon on several occasions in 1914 and 1915, and the German crown prince had used it as an observation post for his own attacks on Verdun in 1916. It was the highest point in the whole sector and offered sweeping views of the surrounding terrain. The Americans had to take it before they could advance any farther north.

North of Montfaucon, the hills and valleys faded into even more difficult terrain. On the right the Meuse River took a sharp turn to the west, considerably shortening the front the Germans had to defend. In the middle rose steep wooded ridges, the Heights of Cunel and Romagne, between and around which narrow ravines shot off in all directions. The general effect of these ridges and ravines was to force the attackers into two defiles, each of them subject to German observation and crossfire. On the left, the Argonne Forest continued north until the Aire River, bounding its right flank, turned abruptly west past the village of Grandpré. Only after the Argonne had been cleared and the Aire River crossed on the west, and after the Heights of Romagne and Cunel had been cracked in the center, could the attackers break into the open country to the north—the wide top of the funnel. This region—a broad plateau—was fairly flat and open, and consequently more difficult to defend than the broken terrain to the south. The Germans would try to make sure the Americans never reached it.

The German defenses in the Meuse-Argonne dated back to 1914—with numerous improvements—and had long been considered impregnable. They ran in several minor and three major east-west belts, each named after a witch from the operas of Richard Wagner. The first major belt, the *Etzel-Giselher Stellungen,* lay three miles behind the initial front lines and included the strongpoint of Montfaucon. About four miles north of that was the second and strongest belt, the *Kriemhilde Stellung,* which included the Heights of Cunel and Romagne and the village of Grandpré. The third belt, the *Freya Stellung,* lay five miles farther north and constituted a weak, last-ditch position. Each of these belts consisted of multiple lines of interlocking trench systems, all well established and maintained and surrounded by forests of barbed wire. Multiple strongpoints—concrete pillboxes, wooden emplacements, and earthen redoubts carefully placed to maximize the advantages of terrain—anchored the trench systems. Between the strongpoints the Germans cleared lightly defended lanes, luring attackers into dead-end defiles stopped up with barbed wire. Attackers caught on the wire in these killing zones would come under fire from dozens of pillboxes, machine-gun nests, and mortars and artillery.[1] The Germans placed most of their heavy guns on the Heights of the Meuse to the east, but field batteries impregnated all the woods and ridges to the north and west, especially along the eastern edge of the Argonne Forest. Manned by superbly trained crews, these guns would subject the Doughboys of First Army to heavy and constant fire as they advanced north past Montfaucon toward the Heights of Cunel and Romagne.

Machine-gun nests anchored the German defensive system. A typical nest consisted of teams of two to six men manning one or several light or heavy Maxim machine guns—magnificent and reliable weapons with an astonishingly high rate of fire. The Germans planted them everywhere imaginable—in ravines, on hillsides, in or under trees, in bushes, in ruins, and even out in the open. Like the heavier strongpoints, machine-gun nests were deployed with a view to taking attackers in the flank or rear, or in killing zones in front of barbed wire or woods. They were mutually supportive, making it difficult to take them out one at a time. Snipers and riflemen with grenade throwers also frequently supported them against attack. Attackers could get at the nests only by pinning them down with mortars, machine guns, or rifles while small groups of infantry worked around their flanks and rooted them out with grenades.

The German dependence on machine guns constituted a virtue born of necessity. For four years, the kaiser's army had held up against everything that the British, French, Italians, and Russians could throw at it. The constant struggle had progressively weakened it, however, and by the autumn of 1918 much of the muscle had worn away, leaving a sickly frame of skin and bones with a fighting sparkle in its eyes. German divisions typically contained 50 percent or less of their normal complement of infantry, with many elderly, underage, or infirm soldiers. Morale varied from unit to unit, but a hardened group of veterans accustomed to victory and willing to fight to the death lay at the center of every division. The German commanders placed their weaker infantry, old men and boys, in the front lines and temporary positions, and put their best troops in the well-fortified second and third lines. Allied attackers often easily shredded the soft outer skin of the German defenses, only to break their fingers on the hard inner core.

German Army Group Von Gallwitz controlled the entire area from Metz to the Meuse-Argonne. Fifth Army held the Meuse-Argonne proper, with five divisions totaling seventy thousand men in the front lines, and another eight divisions in reserve. These divisions operated at about one-third strength, and American planners rated their fighting quality as poor. Farther back, over thirty divisions waited in reserve between the Meuse and Moselle Rivers. Pershing's intelligence officers estimated that the Germans could reinforce the front with four divisions on the first day of the American attack, two divisions on the second day, and nine on the third day. After that, the Germans could bring in ten more divisions from the west and seven from the east if they so desired.[2]

The weakness of the Germans' front line and the depth of their reserves forced two priorities on the Americans. First, they must break through and advance rapidly; second, they must divert or delay the German reserves by any means possible. The first priority depended on the aggressiveness and drive of the American infantry, and the second on ingenuity. In an era predating effective tactical air support, the fledgling American air service could not hope to prevent the German reserves from reaching the front. Instead, Pershing planned to distract them by creating a fictional American Tenth Army in the St. Mihiel sector. Agents spread gossip that the Americans planned a big drive toward Metz—something that MacArthur and many other generals genuinely desired. Five U.S. divisions remained in this sector, and in the days before the jump-off of the Meuse-Argonne operation they made noisy preparations to attack.

Scowling, bullet-headed, sixty-six-year-old General Max von Gallwitz, a crafty veteran who had fought in Russia, at Verdun, and on the Somme, commanded the German forces in this region of France. He knew the Allies were preparing an offensive, but did not expect them to attack the Meuse-Argonne. Instead, he believed that the French would advance along the Aisne while the Americans assaulted Metz. Incredibly, his agents did not inform him of the massive, clumsy movement of almost a million American and French troops toward the Meuse-Argonne, but hints were not lacking. During the night of September 18, German scouts reported "a continual noise of motors" in the area, but they later decided that some "Italians"—possibly men of the 77th Division—had entered the front lines. German raiders captured several American prisoners over the next few days, but although the Doughboys conveyed "a distinctly naive impression when interrogated," they offered no information on an impending attack. The Germans concluded that they were there for training only. On September 25, French deserters and a captured Doughboy gave hints of an attack through the Meuse-Argonne, but Gallwitz refused to believe them and stubbornly maintained his reserves around Metz.[3] This failure of German intelligence presented the Americans with a precious opportunity to score a striking victory in the Meuse-Argonne. They would have to move fast to take advantage of it.

For all their previous disagreements, Foch and Pershing agreed on one thing: the upcoming offensive must go forward with spirit and determination, and without regard to losses. It must be "as powerful and violent as possible," Foch proclaimed.

> If we do not give him time enough to pull himself together we shall be confronted everywhere with nothing but disorganized units, mixed up together, or, in any event, improvisations hastily made. The use of numerous machine guns can undoubtedly slow up or cover the enemy's retreat; but they do not suffice to create a solid defensive system, and at all events, small organizations properly manoevering can get the better of any such methods.

The American commanders, he continued, must show a "spirit of decision" and break through at all costs.[4] For Pershing, such words were superfluous. Confident that American soldiers were capable of deeds well beyond the reach of Europeans, he devised an attack timetable fit for an army of supermen.

Pershing planned an advance in three stages. The first stage would cover seven to ten miles, across the German frontline positions to the main enemy defensive system, the *Kriemhilde Stellung*. In the center, his forces would drive past and outflank Montfaucon, while a simultaneous push up the Aire River valley to the west forced the Germans to evacuate the Argonne Forest. With Montfaucon captured, the central attack would resume toward the Heights of Romagne and Cunel, the key positions of the *Kriemhilde Stellung*. Once the Doughboys had seized the heights—a project scheduled to take no more than several hours—they would advance to a line from Dun-sur-Meuse on the east to Grandpré on the west. The clearance of the Argonne Forest would meanwhile compel the German forces west of the Meuse-Argonne to evacuate the Champagne region and withdraw to the Aisne River. Counting on surprise and the weakness of the German frontline divisions, Pershing expected this first stage to take no longer than thirty-six hours to complete. If not, he predicted that German reinforcements would arrive in strength and drag the Americans into a slugfest lasting up to two months. That made a speedy advance imperative.

The second and third stages looked simple compared to the first. The second stage prescribed another advance of ten miles, across the weakly defended plateau north of Romagne to a line from Stenay to Le Chesne. This advance would outflank the German defenses along the Aisne to the west, opening the way to Mézières—about forty miles behind the German front lines—and Sedan. In the third stage, First Army would attack across the Meuse River to the east and clear the artillery-infested Heights of the Meuse.

After completing these three operations, First Army could take Mézières and, in combination with French and British advances from Cambrai to St. Quentin, cut the primary German railway line serving the central western front. That would leave the enemy with no choice but to conduct a full-scale withdrawal into Germany.[5]

Sixteen American infantry divisions arranged in three corps, with ten American and French artillery brigades, were detailed to accomplish this little project. Nine divisions would make the initial attack. On the right, III Corps, commanded by Major General Robert Bullard, would attack along the west bank of the Meuse with, from right to left, the 33d, 80th, and 4th Divisions. In the center, V Corps, under Major General George Hamilton Cameron, would lead the main strike against Montfaucon and the *Kriemhilde Stellung.* It consisted of, from right to left, the 79th, 37th, and 91st Divisions. On the left, I Corps, under Major General Hunter Liggett, would push through the Argonne Forest and the Aire River valley with, from right to left, the 35th, 28th, and 77th Divisions. Six American divisions, the 1st, 3d, 29th, 32d, 82d, and 92d, waited in reserve, along with the French 5th Cavalry Division. First Army also assumed operational command of the French XVII Corps on the right bank of the Meuse, although it would not participate in the initial attack. In the front lines, the American infantry would outnumber the Germans by over three to one.

Only three of the nine attacking divisions—the 4th, 28th, and 77th—had experienced serious fighting, and the worn-out 28th and 77th Divisions needed rest and replacements. The other six divisions were new to the front. Pershing understood the dangers of asking inexperienced forces to lead the attack, but he had no choice. Kept in reserve at St. Mihiel, they could move to the Meuse-Argonne more quickly than the veteran formations that had led the earlier offensive. A total of 2,775 artillery pieces, half of them manned by French crews, supported the offensive. Packed densely, with one gun per twenty-six feet of front, or 156 guns per mile, the artillery would bombard the German front lines and reserve positions for three hours before the beginning of the attack.[6] The guns would fire ahead of the Doughboys as they attacked at dawn, and move forward to new positions as they advanced. Such, at least, was the plan.

The air service, with 821 aircraft—French pilots flew one of every four planes—offered further support. During prebattle preparations, the planes would intercept and prevent enemy reconnaissance flights, and also spot for their own artillery. These duties would continue during the artillery bombardment and the initial ground assault, along with attacks on German troop concentrations, airfields, and observation balloons. After the infantry had broken through the main German lines, the aircraft could turn to "destroying the enemy's air service, attacking his troops on the ground, and protecting our own air and ground troops."[7] No infantryman could have faulted this plan; but the chief of the air service, Billy Mitchell, had innovative and ultimately controversial ideas about how to put it into practice.

The Doughboys did not entirely trust the artillery and planes to come through when it counted, but they had high hopes for the tanks. Allied propaganda claimed that the Germans did not know how to stop them. Almost two hundred tanks, mostly French-built Renaults with French or American crews, would participate in the opening assault. The American-manned tanks were commanded by the wealthy, athletic, and brilliantly insane Lieutenant Colonel George S. Patton. He had come to France in June 1917 as a thirty-one-year-old captain on Pershing's staff, eager to fight and consumed with a desire to "kill Germans."[8] Headquarters service did not offer ample opportunities for hand-to-hand combat, however, and Patton desperately sought a way onto the battlefield.

Tanks intrigued Patton. "There is a lot of talk about 'Tanks' here now," he wrote to his wife, Beatrice, in late September 1917, "and I am interested as I can see no future in my present job. The casualties in the Tanks is high that is lots of them get smashed but the people in them are pretty safe as we can be in this war. . . . I love you too much to try to get killed but also too much to be willing to sit on my tail and do nothing." Tanks fascinated Pershing too, and on the advice of a board of officers he created the Tank Department—later the Tank Corps—to oversee the new weapon's deployment in combat. Pershing appointed Lieutenant Colonel LeRoy Eltinge to oversee the department, and Eltinge offered to make Patton a tank officer. An enraptured Patton called the appointment "a thing of destiny. Of course there is about a fifty percent chance they [tanks] wont work at all but if they do they will work like hell. Here is the golden dream."[9] Impressed by the mercurial young captain's intelligence and devotion to duty, Pershing confirmed Patton's appointment and ordered him to establish the First Army Tank School at Langres, France.

Patton studied Renaults until he could have disassembled one and put it back together again, but his recruits at Langres had to train with old trucks until a shipment of twenty-five tanks arrived in March 1918. They had two-man crews, the driver and commander, with the latter doubling as a gunner for the turret-mounted machine gun or 37mm cannon. There were no lights inside, so when the hatches were closed the crews operated in the dark. The commander signaled the driver with a series of kicks: one in the back told him to go forward, a kick on the right or left shoulder meant he should turn, and a kick in the head signaled him to stop. Repeated kicks in the head meant he should turn back. Mechanically unreliable, they boasted a top speed of four to five miles per hour. Patton found the Renaults easy to drive compared to automobiles, however, and thought they were "quite comfortable though you can see nothing at all." "It is funny," he told Beatrice, "to hit small trees and see them go down. They are noisy . . . [and] rear up like a horse or stand on their head with perfect immunity. . . . The thing will do the damdest things imaginable."[10]

Patton's drive and nearly obsessive organizational skills impressed his superiors. Promoted to major in January 1918 and to lieutenant colonel a few months later, he took command of the 1st Light Tank Battalion in April. He organized the battalion into three companies of tanks, with two leading the assault echelon and the third following in reserve. In August, he took over the 1st Tank Brigade, consisting of the 344th and 345th Tank Battalions. These promotions failed to satisfy Patton, however, and he worried that the war would end before he saw combat. The prospect of a bloodless conflict literally gave him nightmares. It would, he groaned, "destroy my military career or at least give it a great set back."[11]

The opening of the St. Mihiel offensive on September 12 offered an opportunity for action. The 1st Tank Brigade had only begun receiving its Renaults two weeks earlier, however, and the last of them detrained only two hours before jump-off. Nearly hysterical, Patton screamed and waved the tanks off to the front, but most of them toppled into ravines and shell holes, broke down, or got lost without ever seeing combat. Patton did not do much better. Riding forward on top of a tank, he lost touch with headquarters and earned a dressing-down from his superior, Brigadier General Samuel D. Rockenback. It all went for naught, as the battle didn't amount to much. The Germans ran too fast, and the lumbering tanks couldn't catch up.[12] Patton hoped that the Meuse-Argonne would offer better opportunities for the glory he craved.

Tanks, planes, artillery large and small, a frontline infantry advantage of over three to one, high morale, the American spirit—Pershing could be forgiven for feeling optimistic about the coming battle. The Germans occupied strong positions, but their morale reportedly was poor. Nor did they appear to expect the coming attack. If the advantage of surprise could be maintained—American scouts wore French uniforms as they worked the front lines, and troops were told to accept death rather than capture in order to prevent the Germans from learning of the preparations—everything should work as planned. Speed, Pershing told his generals, was the thing. Each unit must attack, attack, attack, without wasting time worrying about casualties or its flanks. The only direction was forward. Wherever possible, infantry should bypass enemy emplacements. Small clusters of machine guns or the occasional bunker or pillbox could not be allowed to hold up the attack. To Pershing and most of his officers and men, the possibility of stalemate or defeat was unthinkable.

CHAPTER 7

————•••————

"The Only Way to Begin Is to Commence"

"W hen you hear somebody talk about doughboys singing when they're going to fight, you can tell him he's a damn liar and say I said so," growled a soldier in one of James M. Cain's stories. "Doughboys when they're going up in the lines they look straight in front of them and they swaller every third step and they don't say nothing."[1] Yet while soldiers did not sing as they entered the trenches, on route marches and in rest camps their lungs worked almost constantly. Cheery ditties like "Over There" and "Goodbye Broadway, Hello France" were popular, along with maudlin tunes like "Till We Meet Again." Many of the Doughboys' songs, however, were not fit for family consumption. "God damn / Thank you ma'am / Who the hell are we, / God damn / Christ Almighty / We're the infantry / We'll circumcise the kaiser with a piece of broken glass / And stick a rusty bayonet right up the bastard's ass," ran one soldier's adaptation of a popular song.[2]

"Our regiment loved to sing on the march," remembered a 42d Division private. "To say our songs were risqué would be putting it mildly. They were as bawdy as the collective imaginations of 3,000 horny men could conceive."[3] The standard lyrics to "Mademoiselle from Armentieres," a British popular song that civilians, including children, knew well, ran:

> *Oh, Mademoiselle from Armentieres,*
> *Parlez-vous*

> *Oh, Mademoiselle from Armentieres,*
>   *Parlez-vous*
> *Mademoiselle from Armentieres,*
> *She hasn't been kissed for forty years!*
> *Hinky-dinky, parlez-vous?*

The Doughboys—like the British Tommies—sang it differently. One of the least vulgar of the thousands of versions they improvised on the march ran:

> *Oh, Mademoiselle from Armentieres,*
>   *Parlez-vous*
> *Oh, Mademoiselle from Armentieres,*
>   *Parlez-vous*
> *You didn't have to know her long,*
> *To know the reason men go wrong!*
> *Hinky-dinky, parlez-vous?*

> *Oh, Mademoiselle from Armentieres,*
>   *Parlez-vous*
> *Oh, Mademoiselle from Armentieres,*
>   *Parlez-vous*
> *She's the hardest-working girl in town,*
> *But she makes her living upside down!*
> *Hinky-dinky, parlez-vous?*

> *Oh, Mademoiselle from Armentieres,*
>   *Parlez-vous*
> *Oh, Mademoiselle from Armentieres,*
>   *Parlez-vous*
> *The cooties rambled through her hair;*
> *She whispered sweetly "C'est la guerre."*
> *Hinky-dinky, parlez-vous?*

> *Oh, Mademoiselle from Armentieres,*
>   *Parlez-vous*
> *Oh, Mademoiselle from Armentieres,*
>   *Parlez-vous*
> *She'll do it for wine, she'll do it for rum,*

And sometimes for chocolate or chewing gum!
Hinky-dinky, parlez-vous?

Such improvisation amounted to a game; but, like child's play, it had serious underlying purpose. Most popular tunes were written by civilians and reflected their outlook on the war. By changing the lyrics, the soldiers made songs reflect their own experiences and concerns. Parents imagined their sons talking about home, family, God, country, and—perhaps with a little shudder at the thought—girlfriends. Actually, explained one Doughboy, "almost nine-tenths of the soldier's conversation concerns stories about women, the location of wine shops, the likelihood of being able to purchase cigarettes, the next trip to a bath house, what the censor did to the last batch of letters, what is the popular song back in the United States, what's the idea of fighting for France when they charge us high prices, and above all other subjects—'when do we eat?' "[4]

The Doughboys were changing. Clean-living farm boys from the Bible Belt learned to smoke, drink, gamble, and cuss well before they learned how to kill. Thousands of young men lost their virginity, many contracting diseases that forever separated them from the conservative, insular communities they had left at home. In France, the government managed prostitution as a concession that brought in revenue. The U.S. Army accepted this reality, and discouraged but did not try to prevent its soldiers from visiting brothels. Instead, officers lectured their men on safety and publicly humiliated those who had contracted venereal disease. The prophylaxis stations established in every camp nevertheless grew so busy that medical officers remained in attendance twenty-four hours a day, tending to a constant stream of patients.

At heart, though, the Doughboys remained creatures of their upbringing. Religion, for example, remained extremely important to most of them. Chaplains were treated with deference and respect. Though they remained Christians, however, the Doughboys had acquired a hard edge. That edge grew sharper as the troops entered combat in the summer and autumn of 1918. "We ceased to be human," explained the Reverend James R. Laughton, a pastor from rural Virginia serving with the 80th Division:

> We became beasts lusting for blood and flesh. We were no longer normal, but abnormal. Indeed the abnormal was the normal. It was a hard life. We lived hard. We fought hard. We dealt in hard terms. Men called one another names that, in civilian life, would have been insults. Soldiers swore going over the top, though they had New Testaments in their pockets and read them. Many

died with curses on their lips. . . . Men swore who never swore before, men who taught Sunday School classes back home. There was much to make them swear. The atmosphere was surcharged with profanity.

The troops nevertheless remained zealous in attending services.[5]

One thing that had not changed for most of the troops by September 1918 was their self-confidence. The Marines and a few army divisions had seen combat in the summer, although almost all veterans of the early fighting would consider it nothing compared to the Meuse-Argonne. Most American soldiers, however, had not yet developed the veterans' realism and instincts for staying alive. Like all young men who have not been in combat, the untested Doughboys believed they would live forever. Their officers reminded them that they were Americans—strong, fresh, and ready—bringing a new confidence and new way of fighting to a tired old continent exhausted by war. Their very appearance exuded strength, as combat artist Captain Ernest Peixotto observed: "Dressed in their khaki uniforms they looked strangely alike, emanating a powerful impression of ruddy, clean-shaven youth, of lithe, athletic bodies with strong, clean limbs—the only really youthful army in the field in 1918."[6]

✲

It was the biggest logistical undertaking in the history of the U.S. Army, before or since. In two weeks, six hundred thousand men, four thousand guns, ninety thousand horses, and almost a million tons of supplies would move sixty miles from St. Mihiel to the Meuse-Argonne, and relieve 220,000 troops of the French Second Army. Colonel George C. Marshall, a thirty-seven-year-old staff officer, ran the whole operation. Marshall, a serious, aloof, and methodical man with fiery red hair, had started the war as a lieutenant on the staff of the 1st Division. He soon became divisional operations officer, and his efficient staff work at Cantigny in May 1918 drew Pershing's attention. Two months later he joined First Army headquarters as an assistant in the Operations Section, and in August he was given the acting rank of colonel. He performed well during the St. Mihiel offensive, but had never demonstrated any aptitude for managing large logistical operations—especially nothing on the scale of the Meuse-Argonne offensive. He never could figure out why Pershing chose him for the job.

Marshall learned of his new assignment sometime on September 8 or 9 (he couldn't remember which), when Brigadier General Hugh A. Drum, Pershing's chief of staff, called him to his office. Drum—"Drummie" to his friends—was a prodigy. Thirty-nine years old, he was the son of Captain John Drum, who had been killed at San Juan Hill in July 1898. President McKinley appointed Hugh a first lieutenant shortly afterward, at the tender age of eighteen, and sent him to the Philippines, where he spent eleven years. While there he rose to the rank of captain, and on his return to the United States he joined the staff of the 2d Division. Querulous but extremely intelligent, Drum served as an instructor in military art at Leavenworth Staff College from 1914 to 1916 and organized the National Guard on the Mexican border as a member of Pershing's staff during the expedition of 1916–17. By September 1918, Drum had in effect become Pershing's right-hand man. Marshall listened respectfully while he spoke.

After tersely outlining the Meuse-Argonne offensive scheduled to begin in two and a half weeks, Drum told Marshall that he would be responsible for moving the troops to the new battlefront after the St. Mihiel offensive ended. Preparations must begin immediately; there was little time to spare. Marshall had to plan the withdrawal of American forces from St. Mihiel and provide for their relief by other Allied and American units; designate the roads to be used on the way north; schedule traffic timetables; arrange for motorized and horse-drawn transport for troops, guns, equipment, and supplies; lay out camps and billets on the road and at the front; and work with the French to replace their units on the Meuse-Argonne front with the nine huge American divisions that would lead the attack. All of this would have to be done as secretly as possible, preferably at night, lest the Germans observe the movement and bombard the packed roads with their formidable artillery.

After glancing at the map and the forces involved, Marshall saluted and left Drum's office. A growing feeling of horror possessed him. Unable to work or even to think, he left headquarters and walked along a nearby canal. The more he tried to grasp the task before him the more confused he became, until his mind seemed frozen in a block of ice. Spotting an elderly French fisherman, one of those who "forever line the banks of the canals and apparently never get a bite," the befuddled colonel sat down next to him. They did not exchange a word, but after watching the fisherman for half an hour Marshall felt a little calmer. He returned to his office, "still without any solution of the problem, but in a more philosophical mood." Starting with the principle that "the only way to begin is to commence," Marshall called a stenographer, spread out a map on the table, and set to work. In less than an hour he had come up with the outlines of a plan. Still unsure of himself, he sent it to Drum through a subordinate and then made himself scarce. The next morning Drum summoned Marshall to a meeting with the commander in chief. "That order for the Meuse-Argonne concentration you sent over last night is a dandy," Drum remarked jovially as they walked to Pershing's office. "The General thought it was a fine piece of work." Marshall proudly remembered the plan as "my best contribution to the war."[7]

On September 13, with the St. Mihiel offensive just under way, Marshall started moving troops toward the Meuse-Argonne. He had a system—the artillery would move first, then the reserve troops, and finally the frontline divisions—but he never figured out exactly how it worked in practice. "I often wonder," he later wrote, "how in the world the concentration was ever put through in the face of so many complications."[8] Three dirt roads and three light railways bore the traffic of fifteen divisions and three corps headquarters. Each division consisted of one thousand trucks carrying foot soldiers, ten-mile-long columns of horses and wagons hauling artillery and supplies, and masses of foot-slogging infantry and support troops dragging gun carts and carrying heavy packs. Vehicles, horses, and men moved at differing rates of speed, causing long halts and sudden surges in traffic. Accidents and breakdowns were common, and the logjams horrendous.

American, French, and Indochinese truck drivers—the latter, according to bigoted Doughboys, "sun-burned, almond-eyed, square-cheeked Chinks" who drove like "madmen"—teamsters, troops, and officers disagreed over who deserved priority at every intersection.[9] Marshall carefully distributed military police to manage traffic and settle disputes, but the young and inexperienced MPs struggled to keep vehicles and troops moving. They screamed and gestured ineffectively while vehicles collided and drivers cursed or started free-for-all fights that spread along columns like cinematic barroom brawls.[10] Driving along a road one night to observe the operation, Marshall witnessed a chaotic scene:

> a solid mass of transportation, mostly motor-drawn. There was no light of any kind, except occasionally from the exhaust flames of the large tractors hauling heavy guns. . . . The roadside was fairly well littered with broken trucks, automobiles—particularly Dodge cars—and motorcycles. I saw one aviation truck, from which a long hangar beam projected, sideswipe two machine-gun mules, incapacitating both and injuring the driver. Near Void there was a jam resulting from one busload of soldiers being driven into the river and the following truck wedged on the bridge. At this same point the following night another busload of soldiers crashed through the railroad gate and was struck by an engine, several of the men being killed and a number injured.[11]

Yet for all the accidents, traffic jams, rerouting, intermingled units, and fights, the troops did get there, on time and generally in one piece. And, miracle of miracles, the Germans didn't notice.

★

COLONEL William "Billy" Mitchell, a thirty-eight-year-old Wisconsin native who had served in the U.S. Army for twenty years, had responsibilities almost as onerous as Marshall's, but his personality was very different. Outgoing, independent, arrogant, intelligent, and hardworking, he never shied from a fight. Aviation fascinated him, and as a staff officer in 1916 he had taken flying lessons in hopes of becoming an army pilot. The army rejected Mitchell because of his "erratic" flying, but in March 1917 he became an observer with the Allied air forces in France.[12] He logged hundreds of hours of flying time as he studied British and French methods of aerial combat.

In the summer of 1917, Mitchell rose to the rank of colonel and became Pershing's chief air officer. Increasing power and influence made him insufferably cocky, alienating Pershing's staff officers—particularly Drum and Nolan—and, over time, even the commander in chief. Sporting a walking cane because he thought it made him look dapper, Mitchell emblazoned his aircraft with his personal symbol, an eagle in a circle, in a bid to pose as an "intrepid airman."[13] More substantively, Mitchell feuded with Pershing and his staff over the role of the air service. He demanded its independence, while Pershing insisted on its subservience to the army. This dispute fed Mitchell's deepening contempt for the army in general and the infantry in particular, whose officers he treated like a bunch of narrow-minded lunkheads. Pershing appointed Mitchell to a series of commands, finally making him chief of air service for First Army just before the St. Mihiel offensive, but never really trusted him.

Pershing and Mitchell held similar views of their British and French allies. Mitchell's observations of Allied aerial tactics had convinced him that they were too defensive in nature. He wanted his own fliers to be more aggressive, attacking in large concentrations and taking the fight to the enemy. Mitchell especially prized the principle of mass attack. The German fliers, he knew, tried to disperse Allied airmen by testing the whole front, and especially the flanks of any Allied ground advance. Mitchell told his fliers not to attempt to challenge the Germans everywhere. Instead, they must concentrate for maximum punch. By bombing and strafing only at critical points, he believed, they would have a decisive effect on the ground.[14]

When the United States entered the war, the army had 131 air officers, including only 56 pilots.[15] Mitchell and his fellow believers did a great deal to reverse that weakness, drawing on veteran pilots of the Lafayette Escadrille and sifting eager young recruits from the army and artillery. They flew French planes, which proved so excellent that the pilots quickly forgot the American-built Jennies that they had flown during training in the United States. By the fall of 1918, the American air arm, though not yet formidable by European standards, at least had some bite to it. At St. Mihiel, Mitchell successfully commanded over a thousand planes and quickly established American aerial supremacy. Yet although German aerial resistance at St. Mihiel was weak, the American planes suffered significant wear and tear. By battle's end, Mitchell had 845 airplanes left, but only 670 of them were fit for combat. Fewer aircraft would take part in the Meuse-Argonne offensive than in the much smaller St. Mihiel offensive that preceded it.

As preparations for the Meuse-Argonne began, Mitchell had to supervise the construction of new airfields, hangars, and billets in the terribly scarred terrain of the old Verdun battlefields, and the laying of hundreds of miles of wire for a new telephone system. He also had to arrange for the flow of needed fuel, spare parts, and other equipment and supplies to the area; all at night, on clogged roads, and under a tight schedule.[16] Most of Pershing's officers hated Mitchell too much to commiserate with him. At times it seemed that his only ally in France was Eddie Rickenbacker, a daredevil race-car-driver-turned-pilot who in 1917 had served as Pershing's and Mitchell's chauffeur. Rickenbacker and Mitchell were kindred souls, both enamored with speed and the thrill of flight. Gone were the days, however, when they could drive like maniacs around the Paris streets, scattering pedestrians before them.[17] The Meuse-Argonne demanded patience, foresight, understanding, and a willingness to cooperate with the forces on the ground. The Doughboys counted on their planes to protect them from above. It remained to be seen whether Mitchell would be able, or willing, to do everything they hoped.

The Doughboys' concerns were less complex than those of Marshall or Mitchell, but no less trying. Constant rain soaked their uniforms and plastered them with mud as they marched toward the Meuse-Argonne. Field kitchens disappeared in traffic jams, forcing famished soldiers to scrounge the countryside for food. Above all, they craved sleep. Will Schellberg, a machine gunner with the 79th Division, carried a pack weighing almost a hundred pounds, sometimes along with a fifty-seven-pound machine-gun tripod and a forty-seven-pound gun, and rode in a railway car so packed with soldiers that he "could hardly move." He slept in a leaky tent at night, woke up underwater, and drank stolen beer until he and his comrades could hardly stand. On reaching the reserve trenches he fell asleep immediately, only to wake up in the middle of the night almost swallowed in mud. Although the Germans were "shelling the hell out of us," he felt "so tired and played out that I wish one of those shells would hit me." He slept again, only half aware of the cat-sized rats running back and forth over his body. In the morning he discovered that they had eaten an entire bag of rations he had used as a pillow. On other nights the voracious creatures would eat through a can of corned beef and then eat the can too.[18]

After sleeping off their fatigue, the soldiers took stock of their surroundings. Veterans smirked at the trenches full of skulls and bones left over from the Battle of Verdun, the smells of gas, cordite, and rotting flesh, and the constant flash and rumble of gunfire. Green troops found the same sights grotesque and terrifying. Lieutenant Colonel Ashby Williams's battalion of the untested 80th Division arrived in the evening and camped in a harmless-looking field. After pitching their tents they discerned the crosses of an adjacent graveyard. Trucks soon roared in, bearing corpses from the front. "The foul odor of the trucks as they passed and their destination and evident mission sent a thrill of horror through me that I never felt before or since that time, although I have seen many horrible sights," he remembered.[19] Private James M. Cain slept in a folded tarpaulin next to a pile of supplies he had unloaded in the rain. Sometime during the night the rain stopped, and he woke to see the entire sky lit with "orange flashes like heat lightning—the guns of the western front." A trooper who had fallen asleep next to him also awoke and watched the lights. Cain heard him sobbing.[20] A few Doughboys drifted away toward the rear in the darkness, but most just shuddered and pulled their overcoats and blankets a little tighter around their shoulders.

Not all the fireworks exploded in the distance. One enemy salvo hit Lieutenant Colonel Williams's battalion as it waited in the woods for orders to move.

We could hear the explosion as the shell left the muzzle of the Boche gun, then the noise of the shell as it came toward us, faint at first, then louder and louder until the shell struck and shook the earth with its explosion. One can only feel, one cannot describe the horror that fills the heart and mind during this short interval of time. You know he is aiming the gun at you and wants to kill you. In your mind you see him swab out the hot barrel, you see him thrust in the deadly shell and place the bundle of explosives in the breach; you see the gunner throw all his weight against the trigger; you hear the explosion like the single bark of a great dog in the distance, and you hear the deadly missile singing as it comes towards you, faintly at first, then distinctly, then louder and louder until it seems so loud that everything else has died, and then the earth shakes and the eardrums ring, and dirt and iron reverberate through the woods and fall about you.

This is what you hear, but no man can tell what surges through the heart and mind as you lie with your face upon the ground listening to the growing sound of the hellish thing as it comes towards you. You do not think, sorrow only fills the heart, and you only hope and pray. And when the doubly-damned thing hits the ground, you take a breath, and feel relieved, and think how good God has been to you again. And God was good to us that night— to those of us who escaped unhurt. And for the ones who were killed, poor fellows, some blown to fragments that could not be recognized, and the men who were hurt, we said a prayer in our hearts.[21]

In time, the troops distinguished the different types of enemy shells. The worst were the "whiz-bangs"—88mm shells, precursors to the feared 88s of World War II. "You couldn't hear the shells until they lit," explained artillery lieutenant Bob Casey, "but you knew well enough when they arrived. Afterwards you could hear them coming at you for a good thirty seconds. It was the most uncanny crab-walk of sound any of us had ever heard, all of it due to the fact that the whiz-bang—the Austrian 88—is faster than sound." A group of soldiers might be sitting peacefully one second and blown to pieces the next, without a sound. Casey watched one group of men setting up a telephone exchange. "I looked over just in time to see a plume of smoke rising at Templeton's feet. Two men were staggering around with their hands in front of them. Two lay on the ground. Temp's horse was butting itself against a tree. My first thought was that somebody had been fiddling with a hand grenade. But as I ran over I saw a fresh crater that looked like the effect of shell." It was a whiz-bang.[22]

The German heavies—210mm naval (or railway) guns—had a different effect: "Whenever a 210 struck it burrowed into the soft mud, lifted the landscape and dropped it again, knocking everybody flat within a radius of 200 meters and leaving an echo, terrible, persistent, that numbed the ears. For minutes after tumbling branches testified to the ruin it had wrought."[23] The Doughboys also learned to fear the minenwerfer, or "minnie." A German heavy trench mortar, it fired high-explosive shells at an extremely high trajectory. A "plop!" from the enemy lines, signaling the firing of one of these monsters, would be followed by the appearance of a fat, black, fifty-pound shell spiraling slowly through the sky with a spectral screech—slow enough for the infantry to freeze in terror as they tried to figure out where it would land, before running for cover. Some ran the right way; others didn't. The terrible screams that followed as men were "cut in two or three pieces by the shells, legs, arms and heads being blown off," drove some soldiers out of their minds.[24]

The Doughboys never forgot the poison gas. Decades later, nightmares would wake them, choking and sweating, in the night. The colonel of one regiment arriving at the Meuse-Argonne told his troops to sleep with gas masks at the ready. They prepared their masks, but could not sleep. Gazing warily at the shifting shadows of no-man's-land, Doughboys dozed off only to jerk awake as barbed wire rustled, distant shells burst, or rats scuttled underfoot. Their nerves stretched taut. Midnight had just drifted eerily by when the men leapt to their feet at a sudden shriek of claxons and the rattle of rifle fire up and down the lines. Above the din came a frightened bellowing that seized them with a sharp twist of nausea: "Gas! Gas!" With trembling hands, the troops tore the masks from their pouches and shoved them on their faces.

One Doughboy who had misplaced his mask used his presumably final moments on earth to bid his pals good-bye and divvy out his possessions. An infantryman interrupted these funereal ceremonies by hissing, "Climb a tree, Jack, the gas stays close to the ground" between draws on his mouthpiece. The stricken Doughboy abandoned his farewells and shimmied up the nearest shell-blasted trunk, perching atop it like a shivering raven in the early morning mist. Nothing else happened for a time, and finally an officer drawled, "Masks off! No gas!" The words were no sooner said than "Jack" plopped earthward amid the cackling laughter of some French artillerymen who had watched the farce from a nearby road.[25]

The real thing was no laughing matter. The Germans had been using poison gas since April 1915. The British and French had followed suit with their own chemical weapons, but the Germans led the way in diabolical inventiveness. They started with chlorine gas, which caused violent retching and coughing, and then shifted to phosgene, which had a more insidious effect. A soldier might inhale it deeply without noticing, only to die within forty-eight hours as his lungs dissolved. Mustard gas, first used by the Germans in September 1917, was worst of all. This horrible compound caused no immediate effect, but a few hours after exposure a soldier would develop extremely painful blisters, especially on uncovered parts of his body, under his arms, and in his crotch. Then the eyes would burn and swell shut, causing temporary and sometimes permanent blindness. Finally, a soldier who had inhaled mustard gas would develop bleeding and blistering in his lungs as his mucous membranes dissolved, usually leading to a lingering, agonizing death. British nurse Vera Brittain saw many such cases, "the poor things burnt and blistered all over with great mustard-coloured suppurating blisters, with blind eyes . . . all sticky and stuck together, and always fighting for breath, with voices a mere whisper, saying that their throats are closing and they know they will choke. The only good thing one can say is that such severe cases don't last long."[26]

The Doughboys possessed a reasonably effective gas mask based on a British design. The masks were uncomfortable, however, and after long periods of use the eyepieces had a tendency to mist up—a serious problem in the Meuse-Argonne, where the troops often had to fight in foggy conditions. Many soldiers took their masks off to see where they were going, and ended up on hospital beds, retching their lungs out; others kept their masks on and blundered into German machine-gun nests. Training in use of the masks had been rudimentary, and many soldiers considered themselves lucky if they could get them on right side up. And they didn't protect the skin against blistering from mustard gas.

American chemical weapons were rudimentary by comparison. Among the first recruits to the U.S. Chemical Warfare Service was schoolteacher William L. Langer, who read in the newspaper that the army sought men who could speak French and German. Eager to put his knowledge of languages to use, Langer rushed to Boston in November 1917 and enlisted. He assumed that he would be put to work as an interpreter, but was instead caught up in the impersonal flood of the growing AEF and sent to join the 30th Engineers ("Gas and Flame") at Fort Myer, Virginia. Stunned at where he had washed up, Langer protested to his company commander that he had expected to be put to use as an interpreter, not in chemical warfare. "All you need in the Army," the commander replied, "is a strong back and a weak mind."[27]

Langer's comrades in the 30th Engineers, soon renamed the 1st Gas Regiment (Chemical Warfare Service), knew as much about chemical warfare as he did: nothing. Graduates of college technical schools and illiterate mechanics, salesmen, and shopkeepers, they spent all their time stateside marching on scorching-hot parade grounds, with endless drill, guard duty, inspections, and fatigues. On arriving in France in mid-July 1918, they still had seen no specialized equipment and knew nothing of their supposed trade. They spent several weeks digging field trenches before officers gave them basic instruction in firing smoke and gas and wearing gas masks. A few companies participated in the St. Mihiel offensive, but they fired only smoke. By the time the Meuse-Argonne offensive began, the U.S. Army's only chemical warfare unit still had not fired gas in combat.

Poor equipment and training extended to just about every branch of the AEF. Their Enfields and Springfields were good, with sharp bayonets and plentiful ammunition, but it all went downhill from there. Their heavy machine guns, usually French-made Hotchkisses, were extremely heavy and hard to bring forward. Their crews had received only rudimentary training. Most knew nothing about indirect fire—firing at a target you couldn't see—a critical battlefield art that the Germans had honed to perfection. The Germans also made extremely effective use of light and heavy machine guns, particularly the excellent Maxims, but the Americans had neither the training nor the weaponry. Some units received Browning Automatic Rifles—fine weapons cherished by the Doughboys—or the handy, reliable British Lewis gun. Most, however, had to make do with the clumsy, hiccupy French Chauchat, a gun that many soldiers "junked as absolutely useless."²⁸ The Doughboys had plenty of one-pounder (37mm) guns—portable weapons of British manufacture that proved useful against machine-gun nests and wood or earthen bunkers—but few rifle grenades and no light mortars. Most American officers and men had no notion of the tactical use of machine guns, grenades, and other support weapons.

In the less glamorous but even more critical arena of signals and communications the Americans were also dangerously unprepared. Two days before the attack began, a squadron of U.S. airplanes dropped leaflets over the American lines:

> Your signals enable us to take the news of your location to the rear, to report if the attack is successful, to call for help if needed, to enable the artillery to put their shells over your heads into the enemy. If you are out of ammunition and tell us, we will report and have it sent up. If you are surrounded, we will deliver the ammunition by airplane. We do not hike through the mud with you, but there are discomforts in our work as bad as mud, but we won't let rainstorms, Archies or Boche planes prevent our getting there with the goods. Use us to the limit. After reading this, hand it to your buddy and remember to show your signals.²⁹

All well and good, the Doughboys asked one another, but what were they supposed to signal *with*? Most of their communications and signal equipment was missing or broken, and no one knew how to use the rest. Heliographs, telephones, wireless equipment, rockets, and flares had been shipped overseas in pieces, not all of which had arrived, or had been ruined by seawater and careless stevedores. Telephone wires were of poor quality, insulated in cotton rather than in rubber and prone to breakage and short circuits. And training was so weak that even the so-called experts in the signaling units could not tell how to make their equipment work. Pioneers—like engineers—found that they had only tiny combat shovels to level ground, build bridges, and clear barbed wire. Good maps were scarce, and only platoon leaders had compasses.

✶

LATE in the afternoon of September 25, the troops turned in their blanket rolls and extra equipment, keeping only overcoats, helmets, gas masks, rifles with two hundred rounds of ammunition (a few carried bags of grenades), canteens, and light packs containing reserve rations and slickers. Falling into columns of squads with mules and carts, they bumped and jostled toward assembly points. Machine-gun squads, each man carrying a gun, tripod, or two ammunition boxes, wound single file through woods and underbrush, and along slippery, crater-strewn trails toward the front. Private Ray Johnson's machine-gun company of the 37th Division encountered a gauntlet of obstacles: "Old roots tripped us, vines that ran along the ground entangled our feet, trees felled by shellfire blocked the way, old barbed wire caught at our clothing and imbedded its barbs in our flesh, thorny bushes scratched our faces and hands, innumerable shell-holes, old and new, caught us unawares in the darkness, causing us to slip on their treacherous rims and slide into their watery bottoms."[30] Engineers marked unit boundaries and attack lanes with white tape that quickly disappeared in the mud, and established dumps for ammunition and other equipment. Signalers lay wires and set up telephone exchanges.

Gunners dragged their artillery into position and waited for the word to begin the bombardment. Batteries filled clearings, often hub to hub, and gunners worried what would happen if the Germans discovered them. Lieutenant Bob Casey, a portly young artilleryman with a relentlessly offbeat sense of humor and thirst for adventure—he would spend much of the rest of his life as a war correspondent in some of the most dangerous regions of the world—saw no cause for cheer in his battery's situation. "Just off-hand I shouldn't give a dime for our position," he wrote in his diary. "We are in an open space with a wooded country hemming us in on three sides. The clearing is so narrow that batteries could not be placed side by side across it. As things stand four of us are in here now, one behind the other, and will soon be shooting over each other's heads. One muzzle-burst and break the news to mother." Anticipating German counterfire—which usually included floods of mustard gas—artillerymen prepared a secret antidote: gas paste. A greasy, foul-smelling alkaline substance with "the consistency of tooth paste," it protected the skin against blistering. "As soon as their other duties permitted, the soldats peeled off their clothes down to the hide and shaved off such hair as had been overlooked [in previous actions]. . . . Every man in the firing battery is now denuded of hair on top of his poll, under his arm pits and between his legs. His underwear is soldered to him with 'Sag' paste and he is wondering if, after all, mustard gas might not be an improvement."[31]

Tanks—"funny, clumsy boxes built of steel and mounted on caterpillar tractors, or long, jointed steel belts that clawed at the road as they crept forward"—appeared by the dozen, clattering toward the front. The 1st Tank Brigade arrived from St. Mihiel on flatcars, and unloaded in the rainy dead of night while Patton bellowed and cursed. He wrote a letter to Beatrice that evening: "Just a word to you before I leave to play a little part in what promises to be the biggest battle of the war or world so far. . . . If the Bosch fights he will give us hell but I don't think he intends to fight very hard. . . . I am always nervous about this time just as at Polo or at Foot ball before the game starts but so far I have been all right after that I hope I keep on that way. . . . I love you you you always."[32]

The drizzly, dark night; the flashes of gunfire and occasional detonations among the assembling troops; the exhaustion; and the dread of anticipation— all took their toll on the infantry. Some men broke. One 77th Division soldier "refused to carry his pack. He was relieved of it and an officer ordered that his belt and pistol be taken from him. We soon came upon small detachments of French hurrying out of the lines we were to take over. As they came across the gullies our man mistook their uniforms for the gray of the enemy and started calling for his pistol and raving for us to do something. It was realized that he had broken under the strain and was sent back." Once in position, the troops waited dejectedly in knee-deep mud: "slimy rats played tag with us while we waited for our artillery to commence firing. . . . Waiting was the hardest job . . . the minutes seemed endless." The troops wore summer uniforms, and had not washed in at least a month. With the constant activity, from the march from St. Mihiel to the preparations for the attack, they had slept little for several days. The battle had not yet begun, and they were already exhausted.[33]

✳

MAJOR Charles Whittlesey, a tall, thin, thirty-four-year-old lawyer with a Harvard graduate's intellect and a New Yorker's sarcasm and wit, had been driven frantic in recent days by the need to keep his men under cover. His First Battalion of the 308th Regiment, 77th Division, was stationed in the village of Florent, six miles behind the lines. Forbidden from walking the streets by day, "the men were packed in barns like sardines, and had to pay Frenchmen to bring them water and soup and cigarettes. . . . We battalion commanders had to go to the jug at night and account for each of our victims." Ordered to reconnoiter his battalion's jumping-off positions, then still occupied by the French, Whittlesey and his fellow officers donned French helmets and overcoats in case Germans spotted them. "You should have seen the Frenchmen laugh when we passed," he told a friend, "for all the overcoats were the same size"; but he took it in good humor. He was more worried about the front lines, where villages appeared as if they had been "destroyed in the middle ages," and "systems of mossy caved-in trenches" had been assigned to hold thousands of troops before the attack. Whittlesey worked around the clock to bring his battalion safely into line and prepare it to jump off on September 26.[34]

Born in Florence, Wisconsin, Whittlesey had spent most of his childhood in Pittsfield, Massachusetts. He graduated from Harvard Law School in 1908 and established a partnership in New York City. He joined the army in 1917, and was commissioned a captain in the 308th after three months' training at Plattsburgh, New York. His promotion to major and commander of the regiment's First Battalion came just before the opening of the Meuse-Argonne offensive, and despite the entreaties of his adjutant he had not yet gotten around to replacing his captain's bars with a major's oak leaves. Whittlesey was brave—"absolutely indifferent" under fire, said his adjutant—smart, aggressive, and strict. His steel-rimmed spectacles and usually quiet demeanor reinforced his air of intellectualism. People found him difficult to approach, but his shyness didn't run deep, and he quickly warmed to any conversation. His sense of humor often left his friends laughing hysterically. Whittlesey's aggressiveness was instinctive—his quick march earned him the nickname "galloping Charlie." His strictness served to hide his inexperience as an officer and discomfort with the military life. He was not a hard man, but a sensitive, peace-loving individual who cared deeply for his soldiers despite their widely different social class and cultural background.[35]

★

MAJOR General Adelbert Cronkhite, commanding the 80th Division, announced at 5:30 P.M. on September 25 that H hour would come in twelve hours. "I think every man's heart beat a little faster at that announcement," remembered Lieutenant Colonel Ashby Williams; "at least mine did. It was especially annoying to have to listen to it beat in the silence that followed the announcement. . . . It was now a real, living, throbbing thought that in less than twelve hours we would go under an actual barrage and bare our breasts to the fire of the enemy's guns and maybe the steel of his bayonet." The general described the attack plan and told the officers to synchronize their watches. A tense silence followed. Then Cronkhite looked up and said: "Gentlemen, we have reached the time we have all been looking for, we are about to engage in the most serious business ever undertaken by man, and no one can tell who will come out of it. Gentlemen, may God be with you." The officers silently dispersed to organize their commands for the attack.[36]

Junior officers received the news a little less somberly than their superiors. A colonel of the 79th Division described the plan of attack to his lieutenants, captains, and majors, and predicted heavy losses. Every man, he said, must do his duty, whatever the sacrifice. The tension broke as soon as he left. "I'll appropriate your cigarettes and dog biscuit tomorrow, when you're yelling for Peter at the gates," one officer ribbed another, who replied, "Say, whop, you're mistaken. I'll be taking that five bucks you owe me from the last poker game, when you're with your monkey ancestors." The rest teased and joked in the same way—"happy-go-lucky, dare-devil young fellows," one of them remembered wistfully after the war.[37]

Each enlisted man dealt with the tension and fear in his own way. The chaplain of the 313th Infantry Regiment heard eight hundred confessions on September 25 alone. Elsewhere in the same regiment, two privates spent the evening "discussing the strangely persistent presence of the number '13' in and around their immediate neighborhood. It had been Friday, the 13th, when the regiment had arrived in the Bois de Pommes, preparatory to taking the Avocourt sector. That day, as soon as midnight had gone, would be just 13 days ago. The date of the attack was just twice 13. And there were 13 active men in the regimental intelligence section, and the regiment itself was the Three Thirteenth! Lucky or unlucky?" Soldiers wrote letters home, cleaned weapons or clothes, or kept to themselves. Some cried. Others just stayed with pals and talked—anything to avoid thinking of the morrow.[38]

PART III

CHAPTER 8

"You Boys Are My Kind. Now Let's Go In!"

SEPTEMBER 26

The rain stopped a few hours before dawn on September 26. As the black screen of clouds parted overhead, moonlight illuminated long rows of artillery waiting silently behind the American lines. As if the moon had given the signal, officers leapt from dugouts, raced to their crowded batteries, and shouted orders. "From basic deflection Left 20," Lieutenant Bob Casey's gunners cried. "On Number One open Five . . . With H.E. Normal, CR fuse, Load! Three thousand . . . Readee." Breeches clanged and fists jerked into the air as the minute hand touched the half hour. "Number One . . . Fire!" and "a dozen guns turned loose at once with a detonation that took one in the pit of the stomach. In thirty seconds Hell was loose once more and tons of shells were screaming over the hill toward No man's Land." The Meuse-Argonne offensive had begun.[1]

Reasoning that a short artillery preparation would maintain surprise, Pershing had scheduled the opening bombardment to begin three hours before the infantry attacked. French-built 75s, excellent weapons with high rates of fire, fired most of the shells. They had been brought as far forward as possible. Behind them, the heavies—105mm and 155mm howitzers, and immense twelve-inch battleship guns—belched ferociously. Sweeping east and west, north and south, they pounded the German first and second lines, supply dumps, and assembly areas. Hills, forests, and fields glowed with a halo of flame as the air crackled with the whistle of shells and the thunder of guns, including the "sharp, staccato bark" of the 75s, the "throaty roar" of the howitzers, and the "deep boom" of the naval guns. Eddie Rickenbacker, leading a predawn flight of five planes, watched the exploding shells create "a solid belt of flashes, lighting up the world."[2]

Captain Harry Truman's Battery D of the U.S. 129th Field Artillery had moved almost a hundred miles during the past week. Rain had turned roads into quagmires, spattering guns, horses, and men with a slick layer of mud. None of this bothered Truman as much as the two hundred men under his command. Feisty, sarcastic, and rebellious Kansas City Irishmen, they had worn out four commanders and earned their battery the nickname "Dizzy D" before he took over. On Truman's first day in charge, they had deliberately stampeded their horses and staged a free-for-all fistfight that sent four men to the hospital. Since then he had earned their respect as a no-nonsense commander, and they had impressed him with their steadiness under fire.

A few minutes before the bombardment began on September 26, Truman gave his men a pep talk. "It wasn't what you could call a speech," remembered Private Ed Condon, "just a quiet talk like an older brother sometimes has with a younger boy." But a few things that Truman said stuck in Condon's mind: "I want to tell you this, too, fellows. Right tonight I'm where I want to be—in command of this battery. I'd rather be right here than be President of the United States. You boys are my kind. Now let's go in!" Working silently like grim drones, Truman's gunners kept their 75s barking until they boiled the wet gunnysacks that had been draped over their barrels to keep them cool. He estimated that his battery fired three thousand rounds in four hours. The noise left him "deaf as a post."[3]

No one envied the Germans on the receiving end of the bombardment, but the American gunners didn't have it easy, either. An officer told Lieutenant Casey before the bombardment that there was "no such thing as a muzzle burst," in which the shell exploded prematurely in or just outside the barrel. But there was. Shortly after the guns opened fire, a muzzle burst shattered one of Casey's 75s and wiped out the crew. Another one of his gunners retracted his hand too slowly after pulling the lanyard. "The tube caught him on the counterrecoil and mashed his fingers under the rollers," Casey recalled. "Had a devil of a job getting him out. The gun was elevated almost straight up on end and so hot that nobody could stand near it, let alone handle it. Finally we got a duckboard and laid it over the muzzle. Eight or ten men took hold of it and pushed the tube down out of battery. Joe calmly stood up and pulled out what was left of his hand." Quickly reassembled, the gun resumed firing.[4]

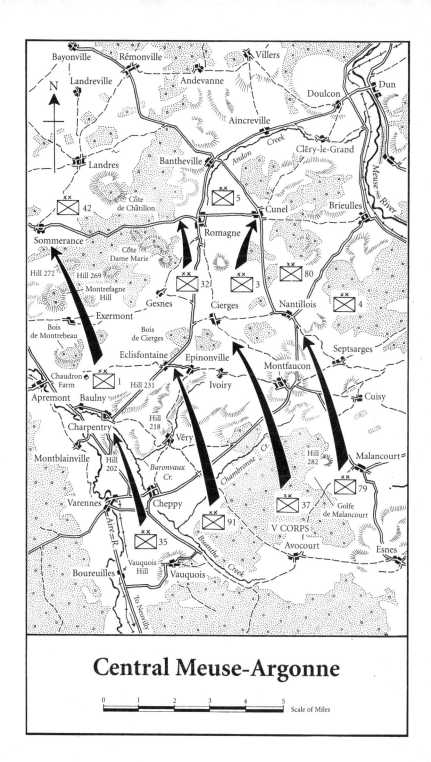

Central Meuse-Argonne

0 1 2 3 4 5   Scale of Miles

German return fire hit some of the American batteries, and shells landed among the infantry gathered for the attack. Lieutenant Edward Lukens came across the aftermath of a German salvo that had caught a company of the 80th Division: "Heads and limbs and torsos were seen scattered all over the ground where L Company had been, one fellow's body being smeared on a kitchen wheel as if the spokes had been a part of his own skeleton." Such episodes ratcheted up the tension among the waiting troops. "There was nothing to do," said a soldier of the 91st Division, "but sit and listen to those shells and wish and wish and wish, with the strongest wishing in you, that every one of the shells, big and little, meant the less Germans on the advance." Some soldiers shouted and cheered the American barrage, especially when they heard the thundering reverberations from one of the heavies. Others sat quietly, their minds spinning off in a million different directions. "It was my first time," recalled Private R. L. Dwight of the 37th Division, "and I hardly knew which would be most appropriate to cry or laugh."[5]

The barrage intensified as H hour approached, and "the metallic whiz of shells overhead merged into a continuous scream." The rippling light of gun flashes spread along the line, creating a false daylight. Luminous dials of synchronized watches glowed eerily as the minutes counted down to 5:30. In the last twenty minutes the barrage grew heavier, until the ground trembled to the sound of a million colliding express trains. The Doughboys shuddered and gritted their teeth.[6]

Ten minutes before H-Hour, officers told their men to get ready. The doughboys gripped their rifles tightly. . . . Machine-gunners looked carefully over the guns, testing their mechanism, and making sure that the tripods were clamped and strapped tightly. The ammunition and water boxes were inspected to make sure that the belts of cartridges were not jammed and that there was plenty of water. The steam hoses and spare parts kits were given the "once-over." Helmet straps were adjusted, waist-belts given a reassuring little hitch, pack straps fixed comfortably, and leggings fastened securely.[7]

Men prayed, held charms, or performed superstitious rituals. Some chatted. Some even napped. Officers carried out a thousand duties and worried if they would show fear or let down their men. "Among the men there was no elation, no joy of battle," recalled Sergeant Maximilian Boll of the 79th Division. "We spoke to one another with subdued spirits and arranged with one another to have our best buddy carry home a message to our folks just in case we didn't make it." At 5:30, all their divergent thoughts merged into one:

"This is it; this is what I've been preparing for; this is the moment to which all the other moments of my life have been pointing." Shouted orders erupted all along the line: "F Company, Over!" "E Company, Ahead!" "Third Platoon, advance! Combat groups about thirty paces. Scouts Out!"[8]

Fog and smoke draped the battlefield as the soldiers heaved forward, their nostrils stinging with the odor of high explosive. Dim figures moved across the battlefield, dropping into shell holes and popping up again, covered with slime and mud, on the opposite sides. At Souilly, where Pershing had set up First Army headquarters on September 21, journalists scribbled tales of Doughboys going over with a throaty cheer, shouting, "Remember the *Lusitania*!" In reality, the men "went forward eating, smoking cigarettes, chewing tobacco, and when they did holler at the Boche it was invariably a less romantic and more vulgar word that they yelled."[9]

"At zero hour we started on our greatest of all adventures," remembered Private Joe Rizzi. "I cannot truthfully say that I was not somewhat afraid, yet I remember I did not in the least hesitate to scramble up the trench on the word, 'Let's go.'" Climbing out, Rizzi reached for a root. It gave way, toppling him "ass over head" backward. "Hey, Woppy, we are going this way," called a sneering corporal as Rizzi pulled himself out of the mud. "Oh nuts," he yelled back, and ran to catch up with the first wave. As dawn broke, he saw Americans advancing on every side:

> The sight was ferociously beautiful. The officers were ready to lead with the attitude of "come follow me but don't go unless I can go." This was shown in their stride and set faces. The sergeants with their rifles raised high for a guide to the infantry, cussed the luck that they were behind their leaders. Then came the man who bears the brunt of everything, the doughboy. This first line seemed to radiate with energy and fighting spirit. Impatience was evident in their faces and each step advanced they could not seem to understand (neither could I) why in hell we couldn't run instead of walk and thus have it over with. It was not very long before we all found out the reason why.[10]

Private Ray Johnson of the 37th Division, a Cleveland native and company runner with a reputation as a humorist, wasn't joking now. He "felt a welling up of strange sensations" as he hauled his machine gun across no-man's-land.

> When a man felt it, his teeth clenched involuntarily, his chest rose and fell rapidly, his fists automatically closed tightly, and with a very perceptible tremor his muscles pulled together rigidly. We were undergoing that "keying

up" without which a man could not possibly endure the terrific strain required of him. It must be much the same sensation which causes the tautening ripple of muscles and bristling of hair on a dog's back when he scents danger or a fight. After a short time the keyed-up feeling seemed natural and we took no further notice of it.

The adrenaline surge helped the soldiers to keep moving as the German shells started to fall:

Now and then one of the dusky forms [Americans] would stagger, reel, and crumple in a heap; struck by a flying bit of shrapnel or a shell fragment. Again, there would come a blinding flash and a terrific explosion—four or five comrades disappeared. It was ugly, sickening, unnerving, but our training and our "keying up" overcame the nausea we could not help but feel. The only effect was a further tightening of the jaws.[11]

Pride, the sense of being part of a great nation on a historic mission, urged many of them on. Looking around, the Doughboys saw—or sensed, depending on the thickness of the fog—"an armed host, every man going in one direction, with one purpose, and all advancing in relentless systematic order. We were a part of it! Call it egotism if you will, but we felt that great pride of our nationality coursing through our veins. We were Power, and nothing could stop us. We were Americans!"[12]

★

MAJOR General Robert Bullard, a tall, athletic, fifty-seven-year-old Alabaman who had commanded the 1st Division at Cantigny, led III Corps—containing, from east to west, the 33d, 80th, and 4th Divisions. A West Point graduate and Pershing favorite, Bullard had drive—and a ruthless disregard for losses. The day before the attack began, he sternly commanded his officers not to worry about their flanks. In every fight, Bullard told them, "I had heard division, brigade, and regimental commanders excuse their failures to continue the advance by blaming the units on their right or left for failing to come forward with them." In this battle, he would "take no such excuse . . . each of your divisions maintains its reserve for the very purpose of protecting its flanks."[13] There would be no complaints. They would attack, whatever the cost.

The 33d "Prairie" Division, Illinois National Guard, reflected the diversity of the state from which it hailed. Two of the division's four regiments, the 129th and 130th, consisted almost entirely of midwestern farm boys. The

131st and 132d Regiments, by contrast, came from Chicago's toughest working-class neighborhoods. Before the war, many of the men had marched and rioted with the Industrial Workers of the World, or "Wobblies," a socialist labor organization that had once dominated Chicago's working-class politics. Now they had joined the Illinois National Guard—once their hated enemy—to fight for their country. Major General George Bell Jr.—a corpulent, jovial-looking man, but reputedly the "most exacting inspector general" in the army's history—commanded the division, which had seen fighting that summer under British command elsewhere in northeastern France.[14]

None of the Prairie Division's soldiers had ever seen anything like the pitted, corpse-infested swamp that awaited them on September 26. The division's front faced north with its right flank resting on the Meuse, which flowed northwest; beyond that, to the northeast, loomed the dreaded Heights of the Meuse, thick with German and Austrian artillery. From those heights, the enemy could observe and pulverize any movement on the river's west bank. Ahead, to the north, a marsh oozed around the banks of Forges Creek, which flowed roughly west to east. Shell holes, filled with dense stews of water, mud, rotten equipment, and human and animal remains topped with dense coatings of scum and vegetation, pitted the landscape, amid tenuous islands of stringy grass. Rusty barbed wire, broken guns, unexploded grenades, tattered clothing, and human bones—remnants of an unsuccessful French attack two years before—lay about everywhere. Grim-faced Germans, carefully concealed behind tufts of swamp grass, manned Maxim machine guns.

The French avoided this charnel domain, declaring it impassable; but in the early morning darkness of September 26, American engineers ventured into the swamp, scurrying from hole to hole as they laid paths for the infantry to follow at daylight. Forging nine passages across the marsh marked with lines of broad white tape, the engineers laid duckboards and unrolled fascines—coils of brushwood—across the creek and its associated rivulets and bogs. They also defused mines and cleared strands of wire. At daybreak, instead of returning to their lines, the engineers stayed in the swamp with their tottery makeshift bridges, in some cases standing up to their armpits in slimy shell holes to shore up the planks as the infantry passed overhead.[15]

Led by the Chicagoans, with the 132d Regiment on the left and the 131st on the right, the Prairie Division advanced into the fog- and smoke-covered swamp, separating into nine columns along the rows of tape laid by the engineers. Progress was slow, and the rolling barrage, intended to move just ahead of the soldiers as they advanced, soon outdistanced the infantry. German artillery shelled the swamp, blindly at first but with increasing accuracy as the fog lifted later that morning. Fortunately the shells plunged deep into the mud before exploding, showering the Doughboys with sticky slime but leaving most of them unhurt. Seeking to avoid German machine gunners and snipers, many troops abandoned the duckboards and jumped into water-filled shell holes, wading across with rifles held overhead, hauling one another out onto the small grassy islands, and plunging onward for more of the same. Others slithered toward the German machine-gun nests, which they destroyed with grenades.[16]

The Germans had not expected the Americans to attempt to cross Forges Creek, and did not adequately garrison the Bois de Forges on the swamp's northern edge. Moreover, many of the enemy troops were not even German. They had been recruited from the French-claimed border region of Alsace-Lorraine, and their morale was poor. Most of them threw up their hands and surrendered as the angry, mud-covered Chicagoans emerged from the swamp; the rest fled until "the entire skyline in front was dotted with fleeing Boche." The only enemy troops to put up a serious fight were the artillery crews, who manned their guns, firing over open sights, until killed or disabled. By noon the Americans had entered the village of Forges and captured about fourteen hundred prisoners, including the staff of a divisional headquarters. They also seized entire batteries of artillery, ammunition, and crates packed with brand-new machine guns.[17]

The Prairie Division had met its objective for the day, which was to capture Forges and advance to the westward bend of the Meuse. With a German counterattack unlikely, the Illinoians scraped the mud from their uniforms, sampled seized provisions that they dubbed "Kanned Wilhelm," and wandered through captured German dugouts fitted with electric lights, telephones, bunkbeds, and stoves.[18] Their biggest concern at this point was the German artillery on the Heights of the Meuse. But the enemy guns fired over their heads, pounding the 80th Division, which had been supposed to keep pace to the left.

★

GENERAL Bullard thought that the 80th "Blue Ridge" Division "contained many North Carolinians, who, with me at least, always have the reputation of being very steadfast, reliable soldiers." In reality, it consisted of draftees from Appalachian Virginia, West Virginia, and western Pennsylvania. The division's commander, Major General Adelbert Cronkhite, a short, swarthy regular army officer with a gremlinlike face, was known for bullying recruits and sympathizing with blacks in the military. Both made him unpopular among his soldiers. They had arrived in France in June 1918 and trained under the British in Picardy, without seeing any fighting, but they still considered themselves elite troops, frontiersmen in the old-fashioned American mold.[19]

The division's 319th and 320th Regiments, both from western Pennsylvania, led the assault on September 26. Preceded by a rolling artillery barrage that churned up clots of mud and unmentionable debris in no-man's-land, the troops crossed marshy ground similar to that facing the 33d Division. Halfway across the swamp, they waded through Forges Creek and slogged past the remains of Béthincourt. "There wasn't enough of that town standing to shelter a pair of field mice," a Doughboy wryly observed; "it was flat."[20] The Germans did not show much fight, and the Blue Ridge boys emerged from the swamp onto a rising open slope.

The advance continued over open ground for another two miles. Here and there, Germans scampered away like scared deer. The Pennsylvanians reacted as if they were on a hunting trip in the Alleghenies. One group of Doughboys spied some Germans frantically trying to hitch up their horse-drawn artillery piece. Sensing an opportunity for some sport, the Americans watched the Germans harness a horse and then shot it down. The Germans cut the dead animal loose and harnessed another. The Doughboys gleefully killed that one too. After repeating this process three or four times they grew bored and fired at the whole team, which fled in all directions. "Among the three 'Bosche' there was a large fat one, who seemed as round as a butter ball," one American recalled. "We all centered our fire on him, but as he ran in a zig-zag course and was quickly getting out of our range, one of the officers in the party secured a rifle and commenced firing on him. He at once increased his speed and ran so fast that his overcoat tail stood straight out behind him that one could have played marbles on them. The officer, who was an excellent shot succeeded however, in getting him just as he was entering the woods."[21]

As the troops scattered in the fog to take potshots at fleeing Germans or plunder souvenirs from prisoners and corpses, the regiments lost formation.[22] The Pennsylvanians were crossing a road running across their line of advance when the fog suddenly lifted and enemy machine guns opened fire from a line of woods. Caught in the open, the Doughboys dropped their souvenirs and darted for shell holes, bushes, or dips in the ground. Many toppled over dead or wounded, and the rest were paralyzed with terror. German planes arrived at the same moment, strafing the helpless infantry. Mortar and rifle-grenade teams eventually blasted the enemy machine-gun nests out of the woods, but as soon as they had finished, German infantry charged the scattered American lines. Fortunately a machine-gun battalion arrived just in time, mowed down the enemy soldiers, and sent the survivors scurrying back into the woods. German artillery shells cracked among the treetops as the Americans pursued, showering them with branches, wood splinters, and shrapnel.

Lieutenant Edward Lukens entered the woods at the head of a support battalion assigned to seek out and destroy enemy snipers, machine-gun nests, and dugouts. His men had stuffed their pockets with grenades and looked like "some mob of anarchists or blackhanders." Joking and chafing with carefree abandon, they acted "like a lot of boys on a 'pirates' game" as they went about their work. As his squad prowled among the trees, Lukens discovered the entrance to a German dugout. Peering down, he saw movement in the darkness and pulled out a grenade, striking the cap against his helmet:

> At the sound of the hissing fuse, there came from the dugout the most unholy conglomeration of yells that I ever heard from human throats—screams of terror and abject pleading. But six seconds is too short a time to negotiate a surrender; they had kept hidden too long and could not possibly claim to be regarded as prisoners. The fuse was already going and down the hole went the bomb.

Lukens jumped back as the grenade exploded, followed by a cloud of dust and smoke. As the smoke cleared, shouts of "no more" became distinguishable, and eight terrified but uninjured Germans piled out of the dugout. Finding "something ludicrous and at the same time contemptible in the way they screamed for mercy," Lukens and his men disgustedly refused the Germans' offer to shake hands for sparing their lives.[23]

By dusk the 80th Division had advanced almost four miles to just south of the village of Dannevoux, where a supply depot that the Germans had set on fire burned brightly in the twilight. The heavy resistance of earlier in the day had left the Blue Ridge Division well behind the 33d and 4th Divisions to the right and left, and as the troops settled down to rest, orders came to continue the attack past Dannevoux toward a ridge overlooking the Meuse River, a little over a mile ahead. By this time, many of the troops had not slept for over sixty hours, and officers had to kick or shake their men awake. Many soldiers revived briefly and then fell back asleep. The remainder stayed conscious long enough to resume the advance, which the Germans fortunately did not resist. At midnight, with its right resting on a hillcrest above the Meuse and its left slanting back about a mile behind to the west, the Blue Ridge Doughboys collapsed into a line of vague heaps snoring in the darkness.[24]

★

For the 4th "Ivy" Division—a "fighting machine" whose bucolic nickname, a play on the Roman numeral IV, belied its record as a tough combat unit—September 26 was a day of missed opportunities. Major General John Leonard Hines, a "driving, hard-fighting, unrelaxing soldier," commanded the division. A forty-nine-year-old West Virginian and West Point graduate, he had seen combat at San Juan Hill and in the Philippines. "It was said of him," remarked the war correspondent Frederick Palmer, "that he was the best linguist in the A.E.F., as he could be equally silent in all languages, including English." The taciturn Hines reminded him of the legendary "Western sheriffs who do not talk before they shoot." In the spring and summer of 1918 he had led a brigade of the 1st Division at Cantigny and beyond, earning a Distinguished Service Cross, promotion to major general, and command of the 4th Division. A regular army formation organized at Camp Greene, North Carolina, the division—consisting of the 39th, 47th, 58th, and 59th Regiments—had arrived in France in May 1918. During the Aisne-Marne offensive in July and August, it had taken a whopping 5,627 casualties.[25]

Like III Corps' other two divisions, the Ivy Division had to cross a dense, mist-covered swamp after dawn on September 26. Following the engineers, with the 39th and 47th Regiments leading from left to right, Hines's troops moved downhill into the shallow valley formed by the brook. As elsewhere, the engineers cut lanes through coils of barbed wire, marked paths around the numerous shell holes, and laid fascines and footbridges for the infantry to follow across the swamp. After a few hours the infantry emerged from the bottom of the valley and ascended the open slope on the other side. As expected, the troops found the German frontline trenches shattered and mostly deserted.[26] The novice 80th Division had scattered at this point to hunt for loot and souvenirs, but the veteran Doughboys of the Ivy Division anticipated harder work ahead. Advancing cautiously, they waited for the enemy machine guns to open fire.

The bullets began flying just as the division reached the German intermediate positions south of Cuisy. The enemy had dispersed his nests widely, but the regulars knew how to handle them—one by one. After working forward methodically for three hours, the Americans swarmed over the ridge, took Cuisy and Septsarges, and pushed forward all the way to the Bois de Septsarges—an advance of five miles. In the process they captured forty German 77mm and 150mm guns, along with dozens of machine guns and seventeen hundred prisoners. Enemy resistance disintegrated.

Lacking orders to advance farther, the Ivy Division stopped to rest and consolidate as the afternoon slipped away. Major J. A. Stevens of the 47th Regiment halted his troops shortly after noon along the northern edge of the Bois de Septsarges. Scouts reported no enemy troops to his front, while to his left around Nantillois—a mile north of Montfaucon—only a few Germans could be seen. The 79th Division on the left remained held up at Montfaucon, and Stevens yearned to wheel west and cut off the German strongpoint. Crossing of divisional boundaries had been strictly forbidden, however, and the major spent the next few hours waiting and watching as enemy reinforcements poured in to his left and front. By 4:00 P.M. the opportunity to take advantage of the German collapse by advancing farther or assisting in the capture of Montfaucon had disappeared. "We had an uneasy feeling," Stevens later reported, "that, despite the local success in our own sector, something had gone wrong somewhere."[27] Ninety minutes later, orders came to resume the attack. A deluge of rifle, machine-gun, and artillery fire flattened the first wave of Doughboys as they jumped off, and the advance went nowhere. Stevens had a sinking feeling that there would be trouble tomorrow.

✶

"Boys, it's here," Captain "Big Ben" Hewit told his company of the 316th Regiment, 79th Division, just before they jumped off. "It's every man for himself. Save your rations. Remember, you're on your own now, but don't forget that I'll be with you." Hewit's men always remembered his unusually calm and quiet demeanor that morning. Later, they guessed that he knew he would not live to see home again.[28]

Hewit's division belonged to V Corps, which Pershing tasked with breaking the center of the German defenses from Montfaucon to Cierges and the Heights of Cunel and Romagne. This, First Army's primary assault, demanded experienced troops and daring commanders, but V Corps, commanded by the mild and unimposing Major General George Cameron, consisted of three green divisions. The 79th, which Pershing expected to seize the all-important strongpoint of Montfaucon, was the weakest of the three. Organized at Camp Meade, Maryland, in August 1917, it originally consisted of draftees, including many immigrant coal miners, from Maryland, the District of Columbia, and Pennsylvania. The army gutted it during the winter of 1917–18 to provide troops for other formations, however, transferring 65 percent of the division's original personnel to other units. Their untrained replacements came from states like Ohio, West Virginia, and Rhode Island.

Major General Joseph Kuhn, a fifty-four-year-old West Point graduate who had spent most of his military career as an engineer before becoming president of the new Army War College, took command of the 79th in 1917 and set about molding it to his disciplinarian tastes. He demanded flawless drill, neat dress, and lusty singing on the march. Newspapermen dubbed it "Kuhn's Singing Army." They approved of the general, as did most of his soldiers—before the battle began. "Most of the time, the General was a pretty snappy-looking soldier," wrote novelist James M. Cain, who served in the 79th. "He was about medium size, and he had a cut to his jaw and a swing to his back what look like them pictures you see in books." Like his officers and men, Kuhn had never participated in combat.[29]

By the early morning of September 26, 1918, the Doughboys of the 79th had lost some of their pep. Haggard, sodden, and muddy after several rainy, sleepless nights, they faced a landscape unlike anything they had ever seen. To the north, beyond Avocourt, blobs of fog scudded over jagged hills and ravines speckled with dense clots of shattered trees and underbrush draped with barbed wire. Water-filled shell holes covered practically the entire area.[30] The French had lost three hundred thousand men here during the Battle of Verdun in 1916. Almost four miles beyond, on the horizon—at first invisible behind the fog, but palpably present nonetheless—stood the Heights of Montfaucon, capped by the bleached skeletal ruins of what had once been a village. From here, the Americans knew, the Germans could observe the whole surrounding country; and they had dug in with machine guns and artillery. To the right of Montfaucon lay another strong German position along a ridge fronted by woods, the Bois de la Tuilerie.

Kuhn ordered the 313th "Baltimore's Own" and 314th Regiments to lead the attack, supported by artillery, engineers, and two French tank battalions equipped with Renaults and gigantic, clunky St. Chamonds. He expected his men to advance boldly, telling them that they faced only one exhausted German infantry regiment.[31] The infantry jumped off at 5:30 A.M., their rifles bristling with bayonets. The artillery fired a rolling barrage, and the 1st Gas and Flame fired superfluous smoke shells into the fog. As these plopped and hissed on the ground, some troops screamed "Gas!" and donned their masks.

A few panic-stricken Doughboys dashed back to their trenches; furious officers drove them forward again. The Germans answered with a barrage of high explosives. To Private Will Schellberg, a young machine gunner from Baltimore serving in the 313th, it seemed that "all hell broke loose" as he dodged shells that showered him with dirt. He and the other Doughboys recovered their nerve quickly, however, and they shouted and cheered as they advanced.[32]

They found the first German line mostly vacant, with trenches shattered and the yellow gas-stained earth torn into innumerable craters. Stunned and shaken Germans appeared, begging to surrender. Most of them were grizzled, middle-aged, and happy to be alive. Others looked dangerous—like two husky, glowering prisoners that a lieutenant of the 314th ordered an Italian American private to escort to the rear. The private walked off with his charges and reported back to the lieutenant after a suspiciously short interval. "What did you do with the prisoners?" the lieutenant demanded. "I tended to them, sir," he answered with a sheepish look. Eager to stay at the front rather than waste time escorting prisoners, he had killed them.[33]

At one place, seventeen German soldiers surrendered to an American machine-gun company. The Doughboys brought their captives before the company captain and asked what to do with them. "I'll take care of that," he snapped and, taking a machine gun, he massacred the lot—one of them "just a kid."[34] Private Maximilian Boll of the 315th Regiment, a son of German immigrants, witnessed another incident of brutality late in the afternoon of the same day as he entered a captured enemy trench with a companion named Bergmaier:

> Suddenly we see a German boy about sixteen years of age run across the field to our left. He is carrying no weapons and is obviously a messenger who has lost his way. He seems bewildered and frightened. One of our men, a heavy-set Italian-American, a Corporal Corrado, goes after him with his bayonet. It is poised to be plunged into the boy. We are some distance away but Bergmaier and I as well as other men in the line yell "Let him alone." But Corrado is about to plunge his bayonet into the lad when a shot from the nearby German line knocks Corrado off his feet, wounding him. The German boy is on his knees and quickly gets out his first-aid kit but is pushed away. We had been led to believe that the Germans were known to carry poisonous first-aid kits with them.

Boll's comrades captured the boy and escorted him behind the lines, where a captain, enraged by the loss of several of his men during the battle, summarily executed him. Another captured German soldier approached a group of Americans and begged for water. "In reply," said a witness, "one of the men put a revolver to the German's head and shot him through the temple."[35]

Enemy shellfire remained persistent but inaccurate, allowing the Americans to continue their steady advance. On the right, the 314th bypassed the ruins of Malancourt at 7:30 A.M., without bothering to search the rubble. On the left, the 313th advanced through the shattered Bois de Malancourt and encountered only sporadic resistance. The fog and smoke lifted suddenly around 9:00 A.M., however, exposing a chaotic panorama. Ordered to advance in thin lines at regular intervals, the inexperienced Doughboys had instead dispersed in clumps, some surging ahead and others dawdling behind. The rolling barrage had outpaced all of them, and no longer provided any cover. The 315th and 316th Regiments, ordered to follow in reserve, had intermingled with the leading units, disorganizing supply parties and communications. The Renaults and St. Chamonds rumbled aimlessly, sometimes sliding into shell holes.

Dozens of enemy snipers and machine-gun nests emerged from hiding places in trees, earthworks, and pillboxes in and around Malancourt, firing into the flanks and rear of the advancing troops. Simultaneously, the Americans slammed into heavy resistance to their front. On the right, German fire pinned down the 314th half a mile north of Malancourt. A lieutenant, a sergeant, and four privates from this regiment cleared a network of barbed-wire defenses and moved over the crest of a knoll when the fog lifted. An automatic rifle opened fire on them from a clump of bushes ahead, and "as if by prearranged signal, enemy machine guns, automatics and snipers located in trees, gullies, and bushes ahead and on the flanks, opened with a hot fusillade which filled the air with snaps, cracks and whines of flying lead. Cut weeds, flying gravel and the harsh cracks of the bullets were proof enough that the patrol had located the resistance—and were in a bad trap." The sergeant fell, shot through the head; two privates were hit in the legs and another in the stomach. The lieutenant, carrying his revolver and two grenades, slithered through the mud and rolled into a shell hole, wondering how he had survived. "When the helmet rings with the cracks of 'close ones' and bits of flying gravel play a tattoo," he later explained, "one just naturally feels weak in the stomach and expects everything to suddenly turn black." The 314th remained stuck for another five hours. It attacked again at 2:00 P.M., but covered only a short distance before the troops had to take cover in a slimy hollow.[36]

On the left, the 313th emerged from the Bois de Malancourt into the open, sloped Golfe de Malancourt. Looking up as the fog lifted, the

Doughboys experienced a horrible, gut-sinking moment. To their right ran a jagged north-south ridge, capped to the right front by an eminence called Hill 282; to their left and front lay dense woods, the Bois de Cuisy. Carefully placed pillboxes and machine-gun nests impregnated the entire area, in crevices and shell holes, among the trees and behind clumps of bushes. All of them opened fire at once, slaughtering the Americans at point-blank range.

Caught in the crossfire, officers hearkened back to the instructions they had received before the battle: "Commanders when confronted by a situation must not vacillate between conflicting situations, but act! In case of doubt, choose the bolder solution. It is seldom wrong to go forward. It is seldom wrong to attack. In the attack it is much better to lose men than to fail to gain ground." Time after time the Doughboys attacked machine-gun nests and pillboxes head-on. After the Germans mowed them down or immolated them with flamethrowers, others took their place and attacked anew. The Americans took an average of twenty casualties for each German emplacement. They received no artillery or machine-gun support.[37]

Snipers' bullets flew everywhere as Will Schellberg and another soldier tried to mount a machine gun in the Golfe de Malancourt. Hearing a sudden noise, Schellberg turned to find his buddy shot by a sniper through the heart. One of Private Casper Swartz's comrades got up on his knees, muttering, "I'll get them with this Brownie Automatic." As he raised the gun to his shoulder he suddenly fell backward, motionless, with a bullet through his brain. Another sniper hit one of Swartz's lieutenants behind the left ear and the bullet came out his cheek, but the officer refused to leave until forced to do so by his men. Of the 313th's three battalion commanders, one, Major Benjamin Pepper, took a rifle bullet through the head as he charged into the Golfe de Montfaucon, crying, "Come on, boys, follow me and give 'em hell"; another, Major Israel Putnam—a direct descendant of his Revolutionary War namesake—died in the same way during an attack that evening. The third, Major Jesse R. Langley, had both of his legs shattered by bullets from a German machine gun.[38]

The fighting in the Golfe de Malancourt raged for five hours until the enemy, threatened by the advances of the 37th and 4th Divisions on either flank, abandoned Hill 282. The Doughboys then advanced into the Bois de Cuisy, uprooting the Germans after four more hours of combat. It was now 6:00 P.M. Sodden, exhausted, and devastated by the day's losses, the men of the 313th halted and dug in.[39] On the right, the 314th remained pinned down north of Malancourt. Behind, officers directed attacks on pockets of German resistance and attempted to extricate reserves that had become entangled in the front lines.

French reconnaissance aircraft had flown over division and corps headquarters all day, dropping "ragged little messages and scraps of maps with lines roughly streaked across them, trying to show where they thought they had seen the leading units." Unable to make sense of the movements taking place below them, or to differentiate between Germans and American troops, the pilots claimed that the 4th, 37th, and 79th Divisions had taken Montfaucon and advanced well to the north. Kuhn, believing that the German strongpoint had fallen, ignored his troops' calls for artillery and tank support. Not until sometime between 6:00 and 7:00 P.M. did he discover his division's true position. Pershing, scolding that the delay threatened the advance of the entire army, ordered Kuhn to attack immediately and take Montfaucon that very night.[40]

Colonel Claude B. Sweezey, a hard-bitten West Point graduate and thirty-year army veteran who chomped an unlit cigar and spoke in a deceptively soft stutter, commanded the 313th Regiment. Soldiers marveled at the colonel's bravery and apparent immunity to enemy bullets: "Constantly under severe shell-fire with machine-guns pouring streams of lead around him, jumping from shell-hole to shell-hole with a field telephone in his hand . . . he seemed to have a charmed life, for again and again men were knocked out near him, while he remained untouched throughout the action." Promised artillery and tank support, Sweezey prodded his miserable men out of their holes and prepared them to attack. The evening drew on, but still the tanks didn't come. Finally, at around 8:00 P.M., several gaudily painted Renaults chugged up, manned by French crews. After surveying the German positions, the French commander asked Sweezey for an infantry screen to accompany the tanks. The colonel curtly replied that he could not spare the men, whereupon the Frenchman declined to proceed. "All right, we'll do it without you," Sweezey barked, and ordered the attack to begin.[41]

Two tanks eventually followed the "Baltimore's Own" Regiment out of the Bois de Cuisy at 9:00 P.M., but they might as well not have bothered. Not a single artillery piece fired in support as the infantry advanced about two hundred yards—Montfaucon lay over a mile ahead—to the crest of a ridge. As they reached the crest the night lit up with an explosion of machine-gun fire, high-explosive shells, and grenades, and the Renaults turned around and rumbled back into the woods. The infantry stayed and fought for a time, only to flee after taking heavy casualties at the hands of an invisible enemy.

Sweezey, the regiment's only unwounded officer, composed a message to division headquarters describing the attack's failure. With the telephone lines cut and no runners available, he seized a pigeon, tied the message to its leg, and let it go. The bird flew up into a tree and stayed there all night.[42]

✷

THE 79th Division's failure to take Montfaucon did not necessarily doom Pershing's timetable for the offensive. The 4th and 37th Divisions had driven respectively northeast and due west of the German strongpoint, and by concurrent thrusts to the west and northeast they stood a chance of cutting it off. Major General Hines, commanding the 4th Division, suggested the idea to his corps commander, Major General Bullard, that afternoon. Hines said he had the reserves to do it, and if the 37th Division agreed he could start that night. Bullard at first approved, but called the operation off a short time later. The countermand may have come all the way from Pershing, who didn't like his divisions to operate outside their prescribed boundaries.[43]

At the front, officers of the 313th and 314th Regiments picked up the pieces of their shattered commands. Wounded men huddled in the Bois de Cuisy or stretched out on the slopes north and west of Malancourt, tended by overworked medics and stretcher-bearers. Behind the lines, men and vehicles jammed the only road to this part of the front. Ambulances could get neither back nor forward through the huge traffic jam, and forward aid stations overflowed. Gerald Gilbert Jr., working at one such aid station, jotted in his diary: "Worked hard all day treating the wounded . . . some of them were awful sights for the shrapnel had just about torn them to pieces . . . they were coming in so fast we had to continue all through the night. Did not get any sleep."[44]

Wounded men lay in the mud for up to eighty hours as priests and ministers moved among them. Reverend Hal Kearns, an Episcopalian, carried a crucifix for the consolation of dying Catholics and learned to recite the prayers they liked to hear. He took charge of a burial detail that afternoon. "Our men were falling in such numbers," he later wrote, "that it was no longer possible to send those who had made the great sacrifice back to the burial grounds in the rear; they must be buried on the battlefield."

> Bodies were borne on stretchers and accumulated in convenient, easily designated spots where burial grounds were created, each burial ground being carefully marked on field maps so it could be located later. All valuables were taken from the body and marked to be sent home. One identification tag was

left on the body, the other fastened to the marker, which was often made either from canned goods boxes or split sticks and placed at the head of each grave. Where possible, religious services were held at each interment but often we worked under such heavy shell fire that there was opportunity to utter only a word of prayer as we lowered the bodies into their temporary resting places.[45]

Orders came down from General Pershing that night, via V Corps: "There should be no delay or hesitation in going forward. . . . All officers will push their units forward with all possible energy. . . . Commanders will not hesitate to relieve on the spot any officer of whatever rank who fails to show in this emergency those qualities of leadership required to accomplish the task that confronts us."[46] The attack on Montfaucon would resume the next morning.

☆

First Lieutenant Robert Weise of the 37th Division witnessed an unforgettable sight as he advanced with his troops on the morning of September 26. Looking to his right and left, he saw a seemingly endless line of soldiers moving forward, bayonets glistening, comrades with a common purpose. The panorama thrilled him and made him proud. Three days later he would describe very different scenes in his diary, with soldiers clinging miserably to patches of gas-soaked mud, or in panicked retreat.[47]

The 37th "Buckeye" Division, Ohio National Guard, was as green as the 79th Division, but with a somewhat easier assignment. Led by the 147th and 145th Regiments on the left and right and sheltered by the same rolling barrage and dense fog that prevailed elsewhere along the lines, the Buckeyes jumped off on schedule and advanced quickly through the Bois de Montfaucon, reaching the woods' northern edge by midmorning. Private Ray Johnson found the old German front line "literally pulverized. Everywhere, on every side—nothing but yawning shell craters, cluttered with broken timbers, twisted bars of steel from dugout roofs, broken rifles, torn German packs, and all sorts of debris. It gave the impression that a gigantic series of dynamite charges had been exploded simultaneously and had turned the whole terrain upside down." The troops clambered over this mess and marched up the open ridge to the north. Then the fog lifted, and German snipers and machine-gun nests sprang up in front, on the flanks, and behind. They took a grisly toll. As Johnson watched his buddies die, feelings of horror and vengefulness churned within him; but all he could do was keep moving forward.[48] The Buckeyes cleared the ridge after severe fighting and approached Ivoiry, west of Montfaucon.

As the Buckeyes advanced, the 145th Regiment on the right sent patrols eastward to make contact with the 79th Division. They moved up the western slopes of Montfaucon and actually penetrated the outskirts of the ruined village on its peak before discovering that the German positions there remained intact. Another patrol set out at dusk and poked about briefly on Montfaucon's forward slopes, returning unmolested. Despite these signs of vulnerability, no attempt was made to pressure the German defenders or otherwise assist the 79th. Instead, the Ohioans stopped half a mile south of Ivoiry and hardly more than a stone's throw west of Montfaucon. With both sides on this small but critical part of the battlefield content to leave each other alone, the Doughboys dug foxholes and settled down for the night.

★

PRIVATE Morris Martin, a diminuitive, red-haired, blue-eyed soldier known as "Speedy," attacked at dawn with the troops of the 361st Regiment, 91st "Wild West" Division. The pitted, black earth might have reminded him of the Craters of the Moon in his native Idaho:

> The ground was torn up and heaved into mounds; trees were shattered, and only stumps remained; great shell holes yawned here and there, and occasionally a long concrete pill box would be seen still standing. And entwined through all this debris were great quantities of tangled barbed wire which had been battered down by artillery fire. Our putties were soon torn to rags. Being in the last wave of the advance, we presently began to see results of our barrage. Fresh shell holes, still smoking; newly splintered trees, and occasionally a dead German.

Farther ahead, he found dead Doughboys from his own outfit. These, the first he had seen, gave him a "decided shock. . . . We were beginning to be impressed by the grimness of our task, although we could not as yet appreciate what lay in store for us in the days to come."[49]

"Powder River, Let 'er Buck!"—the 91st Division's war cry—echoed strangely in the machine-gun-infested morasses of the Meuse-Argonne. This left-hand division of V Corps, consisting of draftees from the Rocky Mountains and the Pacific coast, was completely untested, but the men were unashamed of their inexperience. Organized into the 361st (Oregon and Washington), 362d (Montana), 363d (California), and 364th (California)

Regiments—all intermixed with natives of Nevada, Utah, Idaho, Wyoming, and Alaska—the troops of the 91st Division prided themselves on their self-reliance. Pershing visited the division's commander, Major General William Johnston, on the day before the battle, and decided the troops were ready to go. They didn't need him to tell them that—they knew it already.

The division jumped off at dawn on September 26, with the 363d, 361st, and 362d Regiments in line from left to right, covered by a rolling barrage. Fog shielded the Americans from enemy observers, and there were no casualties. They found the enemy's frontline trenches abandoned except for a fox terrier that burst yapping from a trench and joined the Doughboys' advance.[50] Passing across a narrow valley, they entered the Bois de Cheppy, a fog-shrouded wasteland of shattered logs, stumps, barbed wire, and bracken. Sniper bullets pinged through the fog, and Private Martin watched his comrades warily circle the few trees still standing, like dogs treeing a raccoon. Unable to see the treetops through the fog, the Doughboys fired blindly. Sometimes a sniper's body hit the ground with a thud. But they didn't get them all.

After advancing two to three miles, the Americans emerged from the northern edge of the Bois de Cheppy into an open ravine. The fog lifted at that moment, revealing to Private Martin a glorious sight:

> Glancing to our right and left as far as we could see, were long lines of American soldiers pressing eagerly toward their objectives. In this bright sunshine, with the green woods as a background, these long lines of khaki clad figures advancing brilliantly across the grassy plain gave me a thrill which I shall never forget.[51]

But the thrill soon dissipated. As the troops entered the ravine, German machine guns became visible on the opposite side. At the same moment, enemy snipers and machine guns popped up from among the blasted woods to the rear. The Doughboys took heavy fire from all sides. Reserves and attacking waves had intermingled in the fog, clumping together and blundering into crossfires. As befitted the Wild West Division's motto of self-reliance, however, they sorted themselves out quickly. Through the remainder of the morning and into the afternoon the Doughboys imposed their will on the Germans, taking out snipers and machine-gun nests and working around the flank of the main enemy defensive line. By midafternoon the German defenses had collapsed.

For Private Martin, the war became for a brief moment almost enjoyable again as German soldiers surrendered by the dozen. Some episodes offered comic relief:

> At the opposite end of the trench from where our soldiers were a lone German suddenly appeared and started trotting toward our men with the evident purpose of surrendering along with the rest of his comrades. A one-pounder on our ridge started firing point blank at him. A one-pounder shell explodes upon contact, and as each shell would strike near this fellow it would explode, enveloping him in a cloud of dust and smoke. He never was hit, and as each shell exploded in his very face he ran faster until the men firing the one-pounder got to laughing so hard that they had to stop shooting, and the runner escaped. I was glad, for he deserved a break after that heroic race with death.[52]

The next stage of the advance took the Wild West Division across open hills and valleys toward the village of Epinonville. The American rolling barrage had passed forward long ago, and there was no longer any effective artillery support. The Germans, on the other hand, had found their range, and they plastered the Americans with well-aimed shellfire. On the left, the 363d Regiment inadvertently strayed westward into the zone of the 35th Division—which lagged well behind—and took the town of Very; on the right, the 362d Regiment assaulted the next German line of defense in front of Epinonville.

Colonel John H. Parker, who had already won three Distinguished Service Crosses as an officer of the 26th Division and now commanded the 362d Regiment, had "never seen a stronger line nor one more stubbornly held" than the one before Epinonville. His men—Montana ranchers and cowboys—nevertheless "swept forward with hardly a delay through these formidable trenches, driving the Prussian Guards in front of them like a flock of sheep, and paid no attention whatever to the tremendous cross fire of high explosives and shrapnel that was rained upon them." Their momentum carried them over a steep ridge, across a valley, through an orchard, and into the outskirts of Epinonville, which they entered at 6:30 P.M. Here they spent half an hour consolidating their lines and rooting through hurriedly deserted German dugouts, where they found several pairs of binoculars (eagerly seized as souvenirs), half-finished glasses of beer (quickly consumed), and "a magnificent fur coat," which, passed from man to man, had everybody laughing.[53]

They were not to enjoy the bonanza for long. On the right, the 37th Division had not taken Ivoiry; on the left, the 361st and 363d Regiments had also not kept up. As a result the 362d had both flanks exposed, with strong enemy forces, backed by artillery, hidden in woods to its front. As darkness fell these forces infiltrated toward and around Epinonville to the east and west. Lieutenant Farley Granger of California, his men exhausted and unable to repel the enemy infantry, decided to pull his men back to the woods south of the village.[54] The Doughboys pulled back out without casualties, but thoroughly discouraged. The 362d would have to retake Epinonville the next day.

The 91st had done well despite this last disappointment, advancing five miles against determined German resistance. In the course of its advance the division had left behind a wake of destruction, as described by Lieutenant Bob Casey, who dragged his battery forward that evening: "Smashed caissons, dead horses and dead men filled the ditches all the way forward," he wrote, and everywhere he saw smashed machine-gun nests with dead Germans splayed about. Casey also found "dressing stations on both sides of the road in the open and under sheds," and "men lying face up in the mud outside the stations with tickets on their breasts waiting for the ambulances that will arrive, God knows when." The 91st Division's route was "plastered with the finest collection of busted wagons and human guts in this end of France," an officer cautioned Casey. "Watch your step."[55]

✯

Major General Hunter Liggett, commanding I Corps' three divisions to the 91st Division's left, quietly played solitaire while his soldiers attacked on the morning of September 26. A staff officer, he believed, "has done everything he could before H day, or if he has not it is too late now. He can do nothing more until the first reports come in. To try to follow the infantry is folly; he can see much less than he can on a map at headquarters." Besides, playing cards helped to relieve the pressure and clear his mind. "That is as good an anodyne as I know. It saves you from nail biting and pacing the floor until your nerves are shot."[56]

Born in Reading, Pennsylvania, in 1857, Liggett had graduated from West Point in 1879 and served in the Spanish-American War and in the Philippines, eventually commanding a brigade. A keen student of military history, he had also served as president of the Army War College. People knew him as an excellent officer and leader of men: opinionated but tactful, independent but loyal, and confident without being self-centered. He was both smart and levelheaded. As Bullard assessed, Liggett "had the valuable faculty of seeing what was important and what not; and he did not waste his time or attention on what was not going to count."[57]

Liggett's age—he was sixty-one in 1918—did not at first endear him to Pershing, who preferred youth and physical fitness. He and other officers also balked at Liggett's bulk, for at over three hundred pounds, he was the fattest general in the AEF. But weight did not preclude energy: "His great bulk might impress you as a physical weakness," said Bullard. "It was not. He was active enough; he went when it meant anything to go. He was strong and hard; I have seen a big horse fall with him, pitching him a great distance on a hard, rough road, from which he rose without strain or injury." More important, as Liggett remarked, although "there is such a thing not only as being too old to fight but too fat . . . that disqualification is the more serious if the fat is above the collar."[58]

Of Liggett's three divisions, the 35th, 28th, and 77th, the first-named was by far the weakest. Composed of Kansas and Missouri National Guardsmen and draftees from Minnesota and the Dakotas, it was nicknamed the Santa Fe Division. Consisting of the 137th, 138th, 139th, and 140th Regiments, it had arrived in France in May 1918 and trained with the British and French before spending a brief period on the quiet Vosges front. The division remained in reserve during the St. Mihiel offensive, transferring to the Meuse-Argonne front as the right-hand division of I Corps. Pershing called the 35th Division's Doughboys the "best looking lot of men I have got in France."[59] Tall, burly, blond farmers of Scandinavian stock, they possessed an air of calm and determination. But they were reluctant warriors. Strongly religious, many of them had expressed ambivalence about the war. Their training, moreover, had been poor even by the sorry standards of the AEF, and they still felt more comfortable with pitchforks than Enfields. Hands accustomed to plows cradled rifles awkwardly, and minds used to slow, steady work froze in situations requiring instant decision.

· The Santa Fe Division's most dangerous weaknesses were its administrative disorganization and poor-quality officers. Major General Peter Traub, a stubborn, cocky regular army officer, commanded the division. Not trusting his National Guard subordinates, whom he derided as political appointees, Traub abruptly relieved both of his brigade commanders and all four of his regimental commanders on September 21, just five days before the Meuse-Argonne offensive began. Their replacements lacked combat experience and did not know their troops. The Doughboys resented these changes, and administration from company to brigade descended into chaos as the new officers shuffled and reorganized their commands.

The division deployed with its right flank resting on the blasted remains of Vauquois Hill, which the French and Germans had contested for four years, and its left flank straggling along the hill's western slopes toward the town of Boureuilles on the east bank of the Aire River. Liggett ordered Traub to bypass Vauquois Hill and sweep north through the Aire Valley to Cheppy, Exermont, and the main German defenses on the Romagne Heights, eight miles beyond. The 138th and 137th Regiments would advance on the right and left respectively, while the 139th Regiment mopped up Vauquois Hill, which the Germans had mostly evacuated. Patton's 344th Tank Battalion would advance in support.

Private Milton B. Sweningson of the 138th waited in a trench atop a small bluff during the predawn hours. Above, a clear sky full of stars preached serenity and peace. Ahead, to the north beyond the dark trenches and craters of Vauquois Hill, the fog-choked valley glowed with light of a different kind. "The whole expanse seemed to be sparkling," Sweningson remembered. "I knew that it had to be the shells exploding out there, but it seemed very unreal. . . . The scene was so wonderful, so inspiring, so unbelievable—and so threatening." The image would return to him every December in Minnesota after the war, robbing each Christmas tree or store window display of its message of joy.[60]

The assault began on schedule at 5:30 A.M. On the right, the 138th jumped off from the eastern slopes of Vauquois Hill and scrambled downhill past craters and scraggly bushes into the fog. Visibility dropped to zero, blinding the soldiers and causing them to topple over bracken, drop rifles and bags of grenades, and stumble into razor-sharp banks of barbed wire. The German guns remained silent, however, and the troops disentangled themselves and tumbled to the bluff's base. From here they advanced north across open country, dimly aware of the presence of dozens of German pillboxes and machine-gun nests around them.

The leading American wave followed a road and approached a little bridge over Buanthe Creek at 8:30 A.M. Beyond the creek the road climbed a bluff, atop which stood the village of Cheppy. The banks of the creek seemed peaceful until the mist parted temporarily, revealing dense coils of barbed wire, pillboxes, and earthworks in woods behind the creek and along the bluff. At that moment the German guns woke up, sending sharp stabs of light through the fog and creating a deafening rattle that echoed amid screams and hoarse commands. The mist surged and swirled, concealing the main German line and other machine guns and snipers that fired from the flanks and rear. The Americans groped out the German positions one at a time. Private Nels Wold, a tall Swede from Winger, Minnesota, slipped into the fog and methodically silenced four enemy machine-gun nests. He returned to his platoon and gravely turned over eleven German prisoners to his lieutenant before disappearing again in search of a fifth nest. He never returned, receiving a posthumous Medal of Honor.[61]

For every German machine gun or sniper destroyed, another took its place. The First Battalion's commander, Major Sauerwein, died from a bullet through the head as the fog lifted at 10:00 A.M. Trapped in the open, the Doughboys fell in heaps, panic spreading as officers became casualties. Captain Alexander Skinker of St. Louis took two volunteers, one with a Chauchat and the other carrying ammunition, and plunged through the fog against the steel and concrete pillboxes of the main German line. After the carrier was shot, Skinker took his place and fed the Chauchat until he fell dead, earning another posthumous Medal of Honor.[62]

Colonel Henry Howland, the 138th Regiment's commander, spent the morning in a shell hole three hundred yards behind the lines. Appointed only the day before the attack, he struggled to extricate his men from the death trap into which they had fallen. As he considered his options, two French tanks rolled across a field near his position. Assuming that their crews were French, Howland sent his interpreter—a merry, cultivated young Frenchman named Sergeant Morel—to make contact. Morel leapt out of the shell hole and ran across the shrapnel-swept field. Miraculously unhurt, he jumped in front of one of the tanks, shouting and waving his arms. The tank stopped and a little trapdoor on the front popped open. The driver stuck out his head and stared for a moment at the excited Frenchman. "Well, what the hell do YOU want?" the tanker drawled.[63]

Delighted that the tanks were American, Howland ordered them forward alone, without infantry—as if they could single-handedly ford the creek, smash the barbed wire, churn through the woods, scale the seventy-five-foot bluff, flatten the German pillboxes, and take Cheppy. Firing their machine guns valiantly, the tin cans rumbled across the valley toward the creek—hesitated—and turned back. All they had accomplished was to stir up the German hornet's nest a little more, and as soon as they left the infantry fell under renewed and intensified bombardment. The Doughboys dug deeper and hoped for salvation. Howland, his hand shattered by an enemy shell, prayed for more tanks.[64]

★

LIEUTENANT Colonel George S. Patton began the morning at Neuvilly, half a mile east of Captain Harry Truman's battery position. His orders were to remain at headquarters while two companies of the 344th Tank Battalion under Major Serano Brett advanced to support the infantry. Patton tried to stick it out, but at 6:30 A.M. he gathered his staff and bolted off to the front, hoping to find Brett's tanks and take command. The fog still lay thick, and although Patton heard firing and tantalizing creakings and rumblings everywhere he could see nothing. By 10:00 A.M. he had arrived at a crossroads five hundred yards south of Cheppy. The fog began to lift at this point, but no tanks appeared, only groups of confused-looking Doughboys.

As the fog thinned, German fire swept across the battlefield until, said Patton, "we were shot at to beat hell with shells and machine guns." He and his entourage scuttled behind a narrow-gauge railway cut while the infantry scattered. "We hollored at them and called them all sorts of names so they staied," Patton wrote to his wife two days later, "but they were scared and some acted badly, some put on gas masks, some covered their face with their hands but none did a damed thing to kill Bosch. There were no officers there but me."[65] Disgusted at such apparent cowardice, Patton rounded up soldiers and herded them forward, only to watch them fall back again as the enemy fire intensified. It was all he could do to keep the infantrymen from breaking to the rear.

Patton's retrograde movement at least put him in touch with his tanks, which had become bogged down in a heavily cratered trench system a football field's length behind his original position at the crossroads. Before dawn, the engineers had filled in trenches and craters so that the tanks could jump off quickly. During the advance, they had jogged behind the tanks, directing them past obstacles, laying fascines, building causeways, filling in trenches, and when all else failed digging them out of the mud. They did all this under almost constant enemy fire.[66] By the time Patton found the tanks, however, they had become intermingled—and collectively stuck—with two battalions of French Schneider tanks and several reserve infantry companies. The Germans opened fire on this logjam, knocking out some of the tanks and forcing the infantry and engineers to take cover.

"To Hell, with them—they can't hit me," snapped Patton as he jumped up and stormed across the open to the tanks stuck in the muddy trenchworks. Bellowing and raging, he ordered the infantry to get up and dig them out. Those who did not obey immediately discovered that with Patton around it was more dangerous to stay under cover than to brave the enemy shells. "I think I killed one man here he would not work so I hit him over the head with a shovel," he later wrote. "It was exciting for they shot at us all the time but I got mad and walked on the parapet. . . . At last we got five tanks across and I started them forward and yelled and cussed and waved my stick and said come on. About 150 doughboys started but when we got to the crest of the hill the fire got fierce right along the ground. We all lay down."[67]

For possibly the only time in his life, Patton was afraid. His hands were clammy with sweat, his mouth felt like it was full of flint, his body trembled, and he wanted to run. A believer in reincarnation, he thought of his previous lives as soldiers from ancient times to the nineteenth century. Looking up, he envisioned his progenitors staring at him from a cloud bank over the German lines. Under their reproachful gaze, his fear disappeared. Saying "it is time for another Patton to die," he started forward, shouting, "Who comes with me?" and waving his pistol, expecting certain death. Only six soldiers accompanied him, and four were hit right away. Then a machine-gun bullet smashed through Patton's upper left thigh and ripped out through his bottom. He hobbled on for another forty feet before collapsing and lapsing into shock. Patton's aide, a Private Angelo, dragged him into a small shell hole, where he lay for another two hours as German fire slashed overhead, thinking of his grandfather who had been wounded at Cedar Creek during the Civil War. Evacuated later that day, he spent the rest of the autumn recovering in a hospital. It would be another twenty-four years before he returned to battle.[68]

Patton had made his first important contribution to American military history. Thanks to his bravery, the 344th Tank Battalion had started forward again; and at about noon eight tanks emerged on Colonel Howland's left. He sent them forward in another attack. This time the Doughboys—learning from previous mistakes—advanced behind the tanks. They fired their rifles at every stop, while heavy machine guns and one-pounders raked the German positions. The tanks and support weapons suppressed the enemy fire long enough for the infantry to reach the creek, ford it, and attack the enemy nests and pillboxes. Tossing grenades through gun slits and bayoneting crews, the Americans dismantled the German line and scaled the bluff toward Cheppy. An hour later, they swarmed into the town and rounded up hundreds of German prisoners, along with tons of booty. Their discoveries included a stockpile of guns stamped with the insignia of the Bethlehem Steel Works. The guns had been made in Pennsylvania, sent to Russia, captured by the Germans, brought to France, and recaptured by the Americans.[69]

Colonel Howland, in a state of physical and psychological collapse, was evacuated. His replacement, Colonel H. W. Parker, ordered the 138th Regiment to reorganize in Cheppy before resuming the advance in mid-afternoon. German resistance had by this point practically disappeared, and by sundown the regiment reached positions along the southern slopes of Hill

218, half a mile north of Very. Sergeant William S. Triplet of the 140th Regiment, a tall, husky, seventeen-year-old Missourian, came across the remains of the 138th's attack later that afternoon. The fields in front of Cheppy were covered with dead and dying Americans lying amid putrid shell holes and smoldering pillboxes.

> They'd pushed in with the same esprit as Picket's brigade at Gettysburg and with about the same results. The stretcher bearers were gathering them in and lining them up in the cover of a clump of trees where a trio of medics were applying bandages. I walked by one man that the stretcher men had passed up. He had one eye, looked the size of a peach, hanging out on his cheek by a thick white string and just as I glanced at him the other eye winked, at least it looked like he was winking at me. Gave me a hell of a start. Then I saw why he hadn't been picked up. He'd been shot in the head and the pressure had forced one eye out when the bullet had exploded his brain. The poor devil was still alive but the medics were too busy to waste time on a man who had no chance of living.[70]

On the left, the 137th Regiment advanced west of Vauquois Hill against little resistance until 9:30 A.M., when it reached a line between Cheppy on the right and Varennes on the left. Varennes, a historic village where revolutionaries had captured King Louis XVI during his attempted flight from France in 1791, sat in a bowl-shaped valley straddling the Aire River. The 28th Division was supposed to take the west end of the village and the 35th Division the east, but both divisions had trouble making headway against the well-entrenched German garrison. Half-ruined stone houses and a roofless church held machine guns, mortars, and rifle pits, as well as several 88mm guns that fired at the Americans over open sights. The whiz-bangs savaged the infantry and broke up the advance. No American artillery support was available, for the guns could not move forward through the cratered terrain and traffic jams. That left the infantry to suffer and endure as best it could. The regiment's commander, Colonel Clad Hamilton, collapsed in exhaustion. An officer found him lying on his back in a shell hole, arms and legs splayed, eyes closed, mumbling out orders but unable to move. The 137th, like the 138th, sat helpless for the rest of the morning.[71]

The 139th Regiment at first had an easier time than either of the leading formations. The regiment's commander, Lieutenant Colonel Carl L. Ristine, was mentally and physically tougher than Howland and Hamilton combined. As a student, he had founded the University of Missouri's basketball team and served as captain of the undefeated football team, while at the same time becoming the Missouri Valley college tennis champion. Ristine's soldiers knew him as a hard-boiled "man-driver." He allowed his soldiers no time to worry about Vauquois Hill's reputation for swallowing attackers, but sent them ahead against the enemy entrenchments. Fortunately the Germans had all but abandoned it before the American attack. Within half an hour, "two American soldiers were seen advancing over Vauquois with a remarkable flag—the Stars and Stripes on one side and the French tricolor on the other. They ambled joyfully along, apparently under their own orders, and were soon lost to view."[72]

Ristine and his officers congratulated themselves. The French had tried for four years to take the hill; the Americans captured it in less than an hour. Fired up as if his team were ahead 35–0 at halftime, Ristine drove his regiment northward. Within an hour his men stepped on the heels of the 137th Regiment, which had ground to a halt. Ristine could not understand the delay and went to look for the 137th's commander. He found Colonel Hamilton in his shell hole. Why, Ristine demanded, had the advance stopped? Staring glassily at the sky, Hamilton groaned that it would be suicidal to push farther without artillery support; they must wait for the guns to come forward. Ristine disgustedly turned away. The 137th had not only stopped; it was disintegrating. General Traub was out of communication, and Ristine lacked the authority to take command of the regiment on his own. The 139th was supposed to remain in reserve, but Pershing had also repeatedly insisted on the need to press the attack. Ristine made up his mind. If the 137th could not do the job, the 139th—conquerer of Vauquois Hill—would. He ordered his regiment to advance through the 137th and continue the attack.[73]

The 137th, already shaky, fell apart as the 139th pushed forward. Some soldiers sidestepped to the east or west; some slunk rearward; and others joined the advance. Though ill-conceived and poorly executed, Ristine's advance at least came at the right time. As it began, six companies of tanks and 28th Division infantry launched a coordinated attack on Varennes, to the northwest, seizing the village by early afternoon.[74] Had that attack not taken place, the German guns might have massacred the men of the 137th and 139th as they struggled past each other. Ristine marched his troops east of Varennes to Hill 202, south of Charpentry. Liggett ordered the advance to resume from Exermont to Apremont, but communications had completely broken down, and neither Ristine nor Howland received the message. Ristine—some officers already derided him as an "inexcusable bonehead"—was anyway too busy trying to disentangle his command, which now consisted of the mixed elements of two regiments.[75]

The 35th Division had advanced a respectable total of three miles for the day. Organizationally, however, it was in bad shape. On the right, the 138th Regiment had taken heavy casualties and undergone a change in command. On the left, the wretchedly led 137th no longer existed as a coherent fighting force. Its unscheduled replacement, the 139th, remained reasonably fresh but had become disorganized. Only the 140th, still in reserve, remained in full fighting trim. General Traub, meanwhile, wandered about from place to place, out of touch with the front. His inexperienced staff officers, unsure what to do in his absence, procrastinated or issued contradictory orders. Poor signal equipment, inadequate training, and chaotic troop movements interrupted communications with headquarters and among frontline units. The 35th Division had become a dangerously weak link in the American front.

✳

"THEY struck me as the best soldiers I had ever seen," Brigadier General Dennis Nolan said of the men of the 28th "Keystone" Division. "They were veterans, survivors who didn't seem to be oppressed by the death of other men, their comrades; they were accepting it as part of the thing, with a very fine psychology, and if they had a chance to sleep they went to sleep and slept until we woke them to get ready for another attack. They were good." Organized in August 1917 from the Pennsylvania National Guard, the division was arranged into the 109th, 110th, 111th, and 112th Infantry Regiments. Fifty-eight-year-old Major General Charles H. Muir, nicknamed "Uncle Charley" despite his decidedly uncuddly appearance, commanded the division. Stocky and clean-shaven, with a perpetual scowl and inflexible personality, Muir was one of First Army's few generals to have experienced combat firsthand. During the Spanish-American War he had served as a sharpshooter and earned the Distinguished Service Cross by picking off the crew of a Spanish artillery piece. He also served in the Philippine Insurrection and the 1901 expedition to China during the Boxer Rebellion. In the summer of 1918, Muir led the 28th Division through the terrible Aisne-Marne battles, when it took 8,772 casualties. His men trusted him, not least because he "had the strength of character . . . to stand up to an Army staff when he knew that its orders were impracticable."[76]

As the center division of I Corps, the 28th Division began the morning of September 26 half in and half out of the Argonne Forest. Its main thrust would take place in open terrain on the right, where the 110th Regiment started next to the 35th Division just south of Boureuilles, and the 109th

Regiment straddled the Aire River. American tanks and mobile artillery would back up those regiments as they attempted to push rapidly north, out-flank the Germans in the Argonne, and force them to withdraw. On the left, the 112th Regiment would keep pressure on the enemy by advancing slowly through the Argonne. "Up until this time I thought I had seen a lot of combat in France," recalled Private Duncan Kemerer. "But nothing compared to what lay ahead."[77]

The division's three machine-gun battalions opened fire simultaneously to support the attack, which began at 5:30 A.M. behind a rolling artillery barrage. Fog and terrain caused the usual problems, especially for the tanks; but the veteran infantry maintained cohesion and kept going in the proper direction. On the right, the 110th advanced easily through tall grass and rusty old barbed-wire emplacements, taking Boureuilles—a "few walls standing mournfully above yawning craters and masses of crumbled masonry"—by 10:00 A.M., while the 109th kept pace to the west. The fog lifted at midmorning, and ahead the troops saw thick clouds of smoke rising from the gray stone and whitewashed stucco of Varennes. Sunshine reflecting off the buildings and trees—some shattered, others still leafy and apparently untouched—added a strange ambience to the scene.[78] Within moments, German machine guns in and around Varennes erupted in a furious barrage.

The Keystone Division's officers and men didn't panic, but worked around and behind the enemy emplacements. The first wave infiltrated Varennes within an hour, and tanks systematically wiped out the German positions around the village. In Varennes, the Pennsylvanians picked off snipers and grenaded cellars with cool efficiency until German resistance collapsed. By noon the village was in American hands. Pausing to reorganize, the troops extricated all sorts of loot, including vegetables from carefully tended gardens and crates full of live rabbits that ended the evening as stew in the officers' mess. In the streets, the corpses of disemboweled Germans lay "oozing upon the pavement."[79]

German resistance increased during the afternoon. General Muir, watching one of his regiments preparing to assault some German machine-gun nests, turned to the regimental commander. "I think I'll command one of those companies myself," he snapped, and sprinted away before the stunned colonel could reply. Rushing and dodging from hole to hole, to "the amazement and great glee of officers and men," Muir reenacted his previous role as a sharpshooter. Enemy shells landed all around him, but he "manifested as much agility and energy as the youngest private" and helped to destroy one machine-gun nest before rejoining the colonel. "That was fine!"

Muir sighed, as if he had just returned from a summer picnic.[80] Even exploits such as these could not break the German defenses, however. The 110th reached a plateau about a mile north of the village, but bogged down under flanking enemy fire because of the inability of the 109th Regiment and 35th Division to advance on the left and right respectively. The advance got no farther.

In the Argonne to the west, the 112th Regiment ran into trouble immediately after attacking. The German defenses, bolstered by a "maze" of barbed wire laced from tree to tree, held firm. Terrain that the Doughboys could have covered in a few minutes under normal circumstances now took hours, as the men "had literally to cut and hack their way through yard after yard." By 4:00 P.M. the 112th had advanced to the southern slope of Côte des Perrières, south of Champ Mahaut, a distance of about a mile. The 109th and 110th had advanced farther—three miles—but it would take much more than that to uproot the Germans from the Argonne. By evening, "the Pennsylvania men looked back almost longingly to what they had regarded at the time as hard, rough days along the Marne, the Ourcq and the Vesle. In perspective, and from the midst of the Argonne fighting, it looked almost like child's play."[81]

★

PRIVATE Aldred Hoyles of the 307th Regiment, 77th Division, recalled his comrades as "a bunch of New York prison men," the type who would just as well "shoot you as to go to the right place in School."[82] He was not far off the mark. The 77th "Statue of Liberty" Division included many Jewish, Polish, and Italian laborers from New York City's Lower East Side, along with draftees from the city and adjoining counties. Tough men, they gave their division a tough reputation. But in 1917 and 1918, many of them were transferred to other divisions. Their replacements, from the 40th "Sunshine" Division, California National Guard, and other western and midwestern units, were quiet, respectful, and deeply religious farm boys. Abysmally trained, many did not know how to fire their rifles. Yet even the remaining New Yorkers, though tough, were no veterans. Although the division had arrived in France in the spring of 1918 and played a modest role in the Aisne-Marne battles, it had not been seriously tested in combat.

The 77th Division had gone through five different commanders since its formation in August 1917. The most recent, fifty-four-year-old Major General Robert Alexander, had been appointed in August 1918. Born in Baltimore, Alexander studied law before enlisting as a private in the U.S. Army. He served for three years in the ranks before rising to the rank of lieutenant in 1889. Over the following ten years he served on the frontier and in the Spanish-American War, commanding a company and earning citations for gallantry. He subsequently fought during the Philippine Insurrection—where he was wounded by a bolo—and in Pershing's Mexican expedition. Alexander became a colonel in August 1917 and served in a variety of staff assignments before becoming a major general and commander of the 77th Division a month before the opening of the Meuse-Argonne offensive.

Alexander's appointment to command the Statue of Liberty Division sparked gossip and speculation in First Army. True, he had risen through the ranks, had seen some action as a young man, and had energy and drive. But he was no leader. Brash and sarcastic, Alexander heaped responsibilities on subordinates and infuriated them with constant prodding. As an administrator and a strategist he was mediocre. A firm believer in Pershing's doctrine of rifle and bayonet over massed firepower, he regularly disregarded the importance of artillery. Major General James G. Harbord speculated that Alexander, whom he called a "stuffed shirt," had been appointed by accident because of a clerical error.[83]

Liggett did not ask much from Alexander or his division on the first day. The 77th Division's positions stretched along a frontage of five miles, all within the Argonne. Ahead lay "a bleak, cruel country of white clay and rock and blasted skeletons of trees, gashed into innumerable trenches, and seared with rusted acres of wire, rising steeply into claw-like ridges and descending into haunted ravines, white as leprosy in the midst of that green forest, a country that had died long ago, and in pain."[84] Hoping only to pressure the Germans until the 28th Division outflanked them to the east, Liggett ordered Alexander to advance slowly and methodically.

The infantry knew nothing about woodland combat. Many soldiers had never seen a forest before coming to France, and neither they nor their officers had received any useful training on the navigational tools, tactics, and weaponry necessary for success in the Argonne. Instead, four days before the attack, Major Whittlesey and the other battalion commanders received a memorandum titled "Questions for a Battalion Commander to Ask Himself Prior to Taking Over and While Occupying a Portion of the Front Line." The questions, an officer observed, "were of a soul-searching nature, suggestive of an almost morbidly meticulous introspection. Somehow they sounded a little like Thomas À Kempis—though perhaps without all the common sense which is the mark of the genuine mystic." Junior officers received a similar "devotional manual" titled "Questions a Platoon Leader Should Ask Himself on Taking Over a Trench and at Frequent Intervals Thereafter." Soldiers received weapons that they had never seen before and did not know how to use. "They issued us bombs," reported Whittlesey, "and at the last second, after dark of the night when we were to pull out—with no candles available and every one set to go—they tried to issue some new-fangled rifle grenade affair—very complicated with a tail." Division headquarters ordered the men to discard other, supposedly expendable items, such as tents, blankets, overcoats, and raincoats; reserve rations were not issued.[85]

The Statue of Liberty Division jumped off at dawn, with the 308th, 307th, 306th, and 305th Regiments in line from left to right. The Doughboys quickly became lost in a bank of incredibly dense fog that nullified, "in one chilly breath, all the carefully planned instructions in regard to liaison, the vital necessity of keeping in touch."[86] Advancing with bayonets fixed, they walked in a half crouch, squinting into the fog and peering at luminous compasses. Men followed anyone they could see, assuming that the other guy was going the right way, and coalesced into clumps of soldiers stumbling in every direction. One officer of the 307th found himself, "with my striker and two runners, adrift in a blind world of whiteness and noise, groping over something like the surface of the moon."

> One literally could not see two yards, and everywhere the ground rose into bare pinnacles and ridges, or descended into bottomless chasms, half filled with rusted tangles of wire. Deep, half-ruined trenches appeared without system or sequence, usually impossible of crossing, bare splintered trees, occasional derelict skeletons of men, thickets of gorse, and everywhere the piles of rusted wire.[87]

Sight failed the soldiers, and hearing was unreliable too—in the fog it could not be determined whether the thump of the rolling barrage, the crack of a rifle, the jangle of equipment, or a shouted command came from left, right, ahead, or behind. With sight and hearing confused, the soldiers found their sense of smell strangely intensified:

> Even more depressing than the lack of vision . . . was that dank breath of the Argonne, saturated, until by dawn the atmosphere had passed mellowness, with the odor of stagnant, muddy pools, hiding beneath treacherous carpets of tangled wire grass and bringing to the nostrils of the new crusaders a reminder of the awful slaughter which had left another carpet on this mutilated soil in those historic days [in 1916] when a barrier of horizon-blue poilus had hurled back the Crown Prince's army.[88]

The Argonne's distinctive odors would remain for many soldiers the most powerful and haunting memory of those terrible weeks in the autumn of 1918.

Major Whittlesey had developed a cold and could not raise his voice above a whisper, making it impossible for him to gather his men in the fog. With his headquarters company of the First Battalion, 308th Regiment, following behind, he grabbed a pair of wire cutters and jogged ahead, clipping through the German barbed wire. He quickly outpaced the infantry, which lingered far behind.

The fog's dispersal at midmorning revealed the 77th Division's disorganization, as shouts wafted through the rising mist:

> "Hello—who are you?" some sergeant hailed from the bottom of the ravine.
>
> "Company B," answered one platoon working about in circles on the slope.
>
> "Where in hell is C Company?" inquired another detachment, floundering through the scrub brush to the left. No one answered—no one knew where he himself was, to say nothing of volunteering information to others.[89]

Whittlesey and some others had pushed ahead as far as a mile, but the mass of the infantry remained behind, wandering among the shattered trees and shell holes. All four regiments had become jumbled, with battalions and companies intermixed or lost in the woods. Officers collected any men they could find and sent them forward, but by early afternoon their attacks had degenerated into local, uncoordinated actions with no fixed objective. German machine guns broke up the attacks and kept the Doughboys dodging for cover. The troops' dispersal helped to keep casualties light, but by dusk all forward movement had stopped. "Everything was confusion," said a soldier, "and everybody seemed to be lost." Lacking food, overcoats, and blankets, the soldiers made themselves as comfortable as possible on sodden leaves and mud, under dripping trees. Whittlesey thought "it might have been worse." It would get worse soon enough.[90]

✶

THE westernmost formation in the Meuse-Argonne was not a division, and not even officially part of First Army. It was the 368th Regiment of the 92d Division, an African American unit consisting of draftees, mostly poor blacks from the Deep South. Sarah Sand, a nurse from North Dakota, had seen them during a posting near Columbia, South Carolina:

They were coming in droves, unkempt, and some hobbling their way towards a large barracks. . . . A white officer was in front of this barracks lining them up. Inside the barracks they were made over before they reappeared—no longer barefoot and unkempt negroes, but well-groomed soldiers of Uncle Sam. There seemed to be an instant change; their step became alert and quick, and their manner changed as if by magic. Were they not soldiers fighting for our principles, born in our country, raised under our flag, wearing proudly our uniform?[91]

What they experienced afterward severely tested their pride in their country. Even by AEF standards, the 92d and 93d Divisions—the latter another all-black division—received the worst clothing, equipment, and training. The 92d Division's staff and field officers down to the rank of major were white, but some six hundred lieutenants and captains were black. Like their white counterparts in the other divisions, the black officers were poorly trained amateurs eager to serve but unfamiliar with modern warfare. "The Commanding Officer is doubtful whether some of these colored officers can ever be made efficient," an inspector reported in January 1918. "They do not possess the necessary education or intelligence." The same inspector called the black enlisted men, "as a general rule, illiterate and uneducated and of a low order of intelligence."[92] The white officers expected little from their charges, and little is what they got.

The 92d Division arrived in France in July 1918 and trained with the French, but saw no serious fighting before transferring to the Meuse-Argonne. The only barrages the troops experienced were fired by German propagandists, who sought to exploit racial tensions in the AEF and back in the States. "Do you enjoy the same rights as the white people do in America, the land of Freedom and Democracy, or are you rather not treated over there as second-class citizens?" asked one leaflet that the Germans had dropped from airplanes.

Can you go into a restaurant where white people dine? Can you get a seat in the theater where white people sit? Can you get a seat or a berth in the railroad car, or can you even ride, in the South, in the same street car with white people? And how about the law? Is lynching and the most horrible crimes connected therewith a lawful proceeding in a democratic country? Now, this is all different in Germany, where they do like colored people, where they treat them as gentlemen and as white people, and quite a number of colored people have fine positions in business in Berlin and other German cities.

"We know what they say is true," black soldiers said to their officers, "but don't worry; we're not going over."[93]

Considering the 92d not battle-ready, Pershing kept it in reserve during the Meuse-Argonne offensive, except for the 368th Regiment. He assigned that regiment to an ad hoc formation called Groupement Durand, a liaison formation between First Army and the French Fourth Army. Officially, the 368th formed part of the French 1st Dismounted Cavalry Division. While the French division advanced northward along the west bank of the Aisne River, Groupement Durand would keep astride on the east bank, simultaneously protecting the French and American flanks from German infiltration in this wooded area and maintaining communications between the allies. Its combat role was expected to be minimal.

Colonel Fred Brown, the 368th Regiment's white commander, had "never seen anything equal" to the barbed wire that faced his troops on September 26. "There were two or three kilometers of solid mass of French and German wire . . . the whole country . . . was covered with this mass of barb wire and covered with second growth brush. The new growth had grown up through this barb wire and was absolutely impenetrable."[94] When the regiment, led by its Second Battalion, jumped off in the morning, the troops discovered that the artillery had done nothing to cut the enemy wire. No heavy wire cutters had been supplied to the regiment, so the infantry had no choice but to follow any available lane or gap. This—along with the fact that none of the officers had maps—exacerbated the confusion caused by the fog, and elements of the Second Battalion became badly separated during the advance. The confusion continued all day, and as darkness fell, the troops wandered in a jungle terrain of wire and bracken under enemy machine-gun and mortar fire. Also subjected to strafing runs by enemy airplanes, the Americans dispersed in disorder, and the Second Battalion's major ordered a withdrawal.[95] The infantry had managed an advance of half a mile, but it lagged well behind its neighbors on the left and right. A half-mile gap had opened between it and the 77th Division, with no liaison; on the left, the regiment maintained only tenuous contact with the French.

✱

THE first day's results had been mixed. On the right, III Corps had done well, with the 33d, 80th, and 4th Divisions advancing roughly according to schedule. V Corps' 37th and 91st Divisions had also kept a strong pace, and the 35th Division of I Corps had advanced a healthy three miles despite serious disorganization. The biggest problems were in the center, where the 79th

Division had stalled on the German defenses at Montfaucon; and on the left, where the 28th Division had slowed down before tough German opposition. The failure to take Montfaucon especially troubled Pershing. The 79th Division's problems threatened to slow his main attack, allowing Gallwitz time to rush in reinforcements.

Pershing had other worries too. One was logistical. As soon as the attack began that morning, traffic had piled up behind the lines as artillery, ambulances, supply wagons, and infantry clogged the few available roads to the front. These traffic jams had lengthened throughout the day, making movement practically impossible:

> All about, cursing, lashing mule-skinners, straining mules and eager horses. M.P.'s keeping the lines from tangling. Excited staff-officers tangling things up and cursing everyone else. All this thru seas of mud. Wagons miring, breaking; horses struggling. Trucks and wagons, stuck in the mud, unceremoniously turned over in the ditch. . . . Occasionally a German shell landed within a half or quarter-mile on either side. If they had found that road, choked with horse and humanity—God![96]

By midnight it became disturbingly apparent that First Army would have to attack on the twenty-seventh without artillery support or additional supplies of ammunition, food, or water, all of which remained stuck on the roads; and that the wounded would have to spend the day in the open, without access to medical care except for field dressings.

A second problem involved the growing evidence of disorganization and command confusion. Several divisions had, or shortly would, show signs of confusion at all levels of command, from major general all the way down to lieutenant. Generals were out of touch, colonels were incompetent or otherwise incapacitated, and captains and lieutenants could not keep their men in hand. This failure in command contributed to serious problems in tactics, especially with green divisions like the 80th, 79th, 37th, 35th, and 77th. Intermixture of units because of fog and poor direction-finding disrupted the advance. The Americans also blundered into German kill zones, froze under cover, or milled about under fire. Officers had not been taught how to eliminate strongpoints, and ordered suicidal frontal attacks. Such attacks were also usually unsupported. Instructed during training that success on the battlefield depended on rifle and bayonet, the Doughboys had received only cursory training in the use of hand grenades. Some soldiers discarded them before the battle began. Officers often neglected to call for mortar or machine-gun support, or found it unavailable. American heavy machine gunners had not learned to fire indirectly, and their barrages caused only modest damage to the enemy.

★

BILLY Mitchell, flying over the lines according to his custom, observed First Army's difficulties from above. The traffic jams behind Cameron's V Corps particularly worried him. What if the Germans caught wind of the congestion? A large air assault on Cameron's supply lines, followed by a counterattack against the 79th and 37th Divisions, might collapse First Army's center. Hoping to prevent such a disaster, Mitchell emphasized two basic principles. First, he kept his planes concentrated, rejecting German attempts to disperse them along First Army's flanks. Second, he sent them ahead of the main axis of First Army's advance, bombing and strafing roads, railroads, supply depots, infantry assembly areas, and airfields. Mitchell hoped that these tactics would keep the enemy planes continually on the defensive, too busy repelling attacks against their rear areas to bother with bombing First Army's supply lines, strafing the infantry, or observing for the German artillery. Yet although Mitchell's plan may have distracted the German fliers from First Army's supply lines, it did nothing to keep them away from the infantry. German planes strafed and bombed the Doughboys at will, and observed for their artillery, with no interference from American planes.[97]

Every failing of First Army, Pershing believed, could be attributed to one thing: lack of drive. That night he sent a message to the corps commanders, who passed it on to the divisions: "The Commander-in-Chief commands that division commanders take forward positions and push troops energetically, and the corps and division commanders be relieved of whatever rank who fail to show energy."[98] The attack would continue as planned, without regard to losses.

CHAPTER 9

"We Began to Realize What Artillery
Really Meant"

The rain resumed with a vengeance at the end of the battle's first day, sending rivulets across fields and woods scattered with corpses. By dawn on the twenty-seventh it increased to a downpour, reducing the Doughboys to a lower state of wretchedness than they had ever imagined possible. Not a speck of their clothing remained dry, not even the spare socks and underwear that they kept in their packs. No one had eaten a hot meal for days, and with ration parties unable to reach the front they received no food, hot or cold. Against orders, many dined on emergency rations, sopping wet German bread and sausages, or captured tinned rations—"Kanned Wilhelm"—some of it dating from 1914. Some members of the 80th Division found barrels of beer, complete with spigots, pump, and glasses, and emptied them greedily.[1] The only fresh water came from rain that the soldiers collected in raincoats or ration tins. Under such conditions, the attack's resumption came almost as a relief. In any event, the Doughboys assured themselves, it couldn't be any worse ahead than where they were.

Bullard's III Corps had met most of its objectives on the twenty-sixth, so the 33d and 80th Divisions—except for the 320th "Pittsburgh" Regiment, which attacked and occupied the Bois de Dannevoux—got to rest on the twenty-seventh. The Ivy Division, meanwhile, attacked at daybreak from the northern edge of the Bois de Septsarges. Major General Hines, hoping to outflank Montfaucon to the west and not expecting serious resistance, ordered his men to press northward through Nantillois to the Bois des Ogons and the Bois de Fays; but a storm of German artillery and machine-gun fire slowed their advance to a crawl and then stopped it entirely. Sheets of shrapnel and high explosive enveloped them. Lacking artillery support, the Doughboys turned around some captured 77mm field guns and fired random salvos, but to no effect. Gas drifted amid the mist and rain, forcing the men to don their masks, but in the moisture-laden atmosphere the eyepieces clouded up. Unable to see, with bullets and shells shrieking past and exploding on every side, wet, hungry, and jaded from lack of sleep, the Doughboys slid back toward the cover of the woods they had just left.

For a brief moment, the veteran, rock-solid, reliable men of the 4th Division broke and ran—the enemy fire was too heavy, and they were just too tired. By 9:45 A.M., they had withdrawn behind Hill 295 on the left and into the Bois de Septsarges on the right, leaving behind hundreds of dead, plus wounded who made their way back to cover as best they could. The shock was so great that for the rest of the day Hines could only hold on to the lines his troops had started from in the morning. The Germans fortunately launched no counterattacks, but their artillery fired constantly. Meanwhile the rain intensified, filling trenches and foxholes with water and further tormenting the men, many of whom shuddered and coughed with pneumonia.[2]

★

JAMES M. Cain, a 79th Division runner, spent the wet and dreary night of September 26–27 trying to maintain communications between division and brigade headquarters. As the light faded on the evening of the twenty-sixth, Cain had trotted behind Brigadier General "Slicker Bill" Nicholson, the forty-two-year cavalry veteran commanding the 157th Brigade, who sought a new command post close to no-man's-land:

> And what we was walking over was all shell holes and barbed wire, and you was always slipping down and busting your shin, and then all them dead horses and things was laying around, and you didn't never see one till you had your foot in it, and then it made you sick. And dead men. The first one we seen was in a trench, kind of laying up against the side, what was on a slant. And he was sighting down his gun just like he was getting ready to pull the trigger, and when you come to him you opened your mouth to beg his pardon for bothering him. And then you didn't. Well, we went along that way for a hell of a while. And pretty soon it seemed like we wasn't nowheres at all, but was slugging along through some kind of black dream what didn't have no end.

Finally Nicholson stopped and pointed to a piece of corrugated iron lying in the mud. The new brigade command post would be there, he told Cain and his buddy; they could go back to division headquarters and tell Major General Kuhn.

The two runners returned by a different road, walking silently, sunk in morose thoughts, until "a bunch of rats come outen a trench and began going up the road in front of us, hopping along in a pretty good line, and Shep said they was trench camels, and that give us a laugh, and we felt better." At divisional headquarters, they found Major General Kuhn blustery, cranky, and unshaven with "his eyes all sunk in." Cursing Nicholson for not maintaining contact, Kuhn savagely scribbled a message. Cain, almost asleep on his feet, jerked awake as Kuhn barked out his orders for Nicholson to attack at dawn, by then just a few hours away. As an afterthought, Kuhn told Cain that he planned to move divisional headquarters to Malancourt. Mounted on a weary old nag, Cain departed for the front. He thought he knew the way, but this time the landscape looked different—ironically, by filling in shell holes and resurfacing roads overnight, the engineers had obliterated the only familiar points of reference. After a couple of miles the rain clouds glowed in anticipation of the dawn, and Cain began to panic.

"That order in my pocket, it weren't getting no cooler, I'm here to tell you. It was damn near burning a hole in my leg, and a funny hicuppy noise would come up out of my neck every time I thought of it." Nobody would tell Cain where to find the brigade command post. Suspecting that he might be a spy, they wouldn't even tell him the identity of their own units. "AEF," some soldiers yelled; others drawled "YMCA" and moved on. Cain felt like he had become lost in a lunatic asylum. Finally he discovered that he had strayed several miles to the west, among the troops of the 37th Division. Sobbing uncontrollably and beating his horse, he raced back the way he came, leaping shell holes and startling groups of soldiers near the front lines. Dawn had broken, and he could hear the sound of heavy firing up around Montfaucon.[3]

★

WILL Schellberg and his machine-gun crew spent the night trying to sleep in the mud next to their gun. Lacking blankets, they covered themselves with overcoats and slickers that kept out only some of the rain and none of the cold. They chattered and shivered all night, unable to sleep amid the frequent shell explosions and gas alarms. Every half hour, it seemed that the shrill rattle of the gas claxons forced them to sit up and fumble for gas masks with ice-cold fingers. Ten minutes later would come the "all clear," and shortly after that another gas alarm.[4]

A heavy fog settled on the valley overnight, concealing Montfaucon's crest. During the morning the fog slowly departed, leaving ghostly blobs of mist clinging to the church tower on top.[5] Shivering uncontrollably, soaked through, living on emergency rations, and low on ammunition, the Dough-boys moved forward through sheets of rain, supported only by a battalion of 75s and a company of heavy machine guns. As elsewhere, traffic jams and bad terrain had prevented most of the supporting artillery from getting forward.

On the right, the 314th Regiment moved forward at 4:00 A.M. Advancing a thousand yards ahead of the rest of their company, a captain and six soldiers sought to find and eliminate German machine guns before they could hinder the main advance. They had covered only a short distance before a voice in the dark shouted a challenge in German. Whispering, "Let's capture this German," the inexperienced captain yelled, "Comrade," crept a little way forward, and then fired his .45 as the rest of the party rushed forward. Sergeant Andrew Kachik, a devoutly religious Pennsylvania coal miner, described what happened next:

> Well all hell broke loose. It was a machine gun nest. My captain disappeared [he had been captured]. . . . When the machine gun started shooting at us, it made a glaring red light and the star shells the Germans shot in the air made a lot of light. I dropped to the ground and made myself as flat as I could. I didn't dare to move, not even a muscle. I waited until the star shell went out. I crawled back to the road and found a big shell hole on it. So I stayed there all by myself. I sure was scared. I didn't know what to do. I knew that I had to get out of there while it was still dark. The machine gun was about fifty steps away from me. I am not ashamed to say that I prayed fast.

Three more Americans tumbled into Kachik's shell hole. He urged them to get out while it was still dark, but they decided to wait until the company rescued them. It was a poor choice. When daylight came, the Germans lobbed rifle grenades into their shell hole. In a panic, all four of the Americans tried to get out at once. The first two fell instantly. Kachik and the other soldier found a roadside ditch and slithered down it on their stomachs. Every time they tried to get up on their hands and knees, the bullets forced them down again. After crawling three hundred yards they reached their company, and found that in the dark they had bypassed not one, but *five* German machine-gun nests before their captain recklessly charged the sixth; the rest of the company had taken five hours to deal with the first five.[6]

This fiasco aside, the 314th did get forward, albeit slowly. Individual machine-gun nests caused the Americans trouble, but the Germans recognized the danger to their left flank and did not try to hold for long. Advancing toward the Bois de la Tuilerie east of Montfaucon, the Americans crossed corpse-strewn fields and woods and reached their objective about noon. At one place, they entered an abandoned trench system packed with "scores of bodies shrouded in the German dull, gray-green uniforms," one of which revealed "the upturned face of a young German, about sixteen years of age [with] an expression with something of the puzzle of DeVinci's Mona Lisa. The innocent, child-like, questioning wonderment seemed to indicate that he had left this life puzzled as to what it was all about."[7] Private Boll found four bodies next to an enemy gun emplacement, apparently dead.

> As I look, one of them lifts an arm as if in a gesture for help; then a series of pistol shots scream out behind me. There some ten feet in back of me is our bugler, Isaac Kevitch. He is emptying his revolver at the wounded German who throws up his arm then rolls to the side on his face. I am dumb-struck. I just could not have seen what I did see![8]

On the left, the 313th advanced toward Montfaucon. French tanks, mostly light Renaults but with a few heavies sporting hull-mounted 75mm guns, moved in support. Enemy artillery fired on the Doughboys, but the German infantry offered no serious resistance until the 313th reached the south slopes of Montfaucon at about 9:00 A.M. As the infantry scaled the hill the clouds parted briefly, and the sun reflected weirdly over the misty hills and valleys. At the same moment ten German heavy machine guns shredded the American lines, and showers of hand grenades tumbled down the hillside.[9] But the resistance didn't last long. By noon the last of the Germans had withdrawn, leaving Montfaucon in American hands.

"Awful carnage—torn bodies of 313th Infantrymen, Germans, and horses, lying in piles amid rubble and wrecked caissons and carts; in the cemetery, coffins and skeletons of German soldiers blown from their graves by the bombardment" greeted the conquerors. They also found hundreds of frightened Germans hiding in dugouts. Private Joshua Cockey confronted three of them as they huddled in their bunks. " 'Get out of here!' he roared—a gaunt, filthy, ragged American, with a trembling pistol, gone clean mad with battle. 'Get out of here before I count three! One-two-three!' And then he blew out the brains of the German in the middle bunk. The others tumbled out in terror." Surrendering enemy machine gunners were shot on sight.[10]

Any illusions that the Americans had about advancing north of Montfaucon with the same ease they had that morning were quickly shattered. "From that point on," Major Charles DuPuy remarked, "we began to realize what artillery really meant."[11] The German infantry had withdrawn, but their artillery and machine guns had ranged carefully on Montfaucon and its northward slopes. As the 313th and 314th moved toward Nantillois that afternoon, enemy fire blasted them savagely. Exhausted and out of food and water, the Americans withdrew. The German artillery fire continued unabated all night, turning Montfaucon into a churning Hell. "My God, it was awful," Sergeant Edward Davies of the 315th wrote in his diary.

> We lost men right and left. . . . The cries of the wounded and dying was awful and I can never forget them. Everywhere you could hear them crying for "First Aid." The hospital men did their best, but everytime a shell landed we lost men. What a weird night it was. The shells bursting in the darkness and star shells coming up from behind the hills and flashes of the machine guns as they blazed away ahead of us. I am wondering if any of us will be alive by morning. . . . I think all of us realize what war means by this time.[12]

James M. Cain had stumbled into divisional headquarters at 11:00 that morning to find Major General Kuhn "all smeared up with mud and looking like hell." Kuhn demanded to know whether Cain had delivered the message to Brigadier General Nicholson. "No, sir," Cain replied, trembling. "What!" Kuhn howled. "Then what are you doing coming in here at this hour?" "I got lost," Cain whimpered. The general "never said nothing," he recalled. "He just looked at me, starting in from my eyes and going clear down to my feet, and that there was the saddest look I ever seen one man turn on another. And it weren't nothing to do but stand there and hold on to the reins of the goddam horse, and wish to hell the sniper had got me."

Moments later, Nicholson strode in. Kuhn switched his glare from Cain to the tall, stern-faced brigadier. " 'Where have you been?' he bellowed. 'And what do you mean, breaking liaison that way?' 'Been?' answered General Nicholson, bellowing even louder. 'I've been taking that hill, that's where I've been—I moved on Montfaucon and took it! And what do you mean, 'breaking liaison'? Two of your own couriers knew where I was—and I posted guides for them, every foot of the way.' . . . So they began to cuss at each other, and the generals can outcuss the privates, I'll say that for them." Cain saluted and slinked away.[13] The generals were still yelling when a carrier pigeon, its left wing shattered and bleeding, flapped into headquarters. A piece of paper attached to its leg bore news of Montfaucon's capture.[14] Kuhn, apparently, was too busy screaming to notice.

✳

WHEN the Ohioans of the 37th Division swept forward to the western outskirts of Montfaucon on September 26, they had passed two abandoned German 155mm howitzers squatting impassively in the mud like steel toads. The guns remained untended until dawn on the next day, when two squads of Doughboys in dripping slickers heaved the monsters around in the slurping mud and lobbed shells toward the German lines. They would provide the division's sole artillery support that day.

The Buckeye Division's orders for September 27 were to capture the few stacks of brick and mortar that constituted the village of Ivoire and advance another seven miles north to Bantheville. German resistance seemed negligible at first, and as Private Ray Johnson moved his machine gun forward, stopping to fire at the retreating enemy before shifting to another position, he recovered some of the sensations of invincibility that he had felt during the early stages of the previous day's advance. For a few brief minutes the Doughboys felt unstoppable, their strides lengthened and their backs straightened.

Johnson's machine-gun section had just entered a shallow, open valley northwest of Montfaucon when "suddenly hell broke loose from three sides; machine guns opened up on us from both flanks and front, whizzbangs exploded amongst us, trench mortars, Minnie Wurfers, 'flying pigs,' and big H.E.'s descended upon us with terrifying crashes, and rifle fire augmented the extreme danger of our predicament." Men ran for cover, but found none except for a few shell holes, logs, and bushes. "Dozens were almost literally riddled with bullets. . . . Men running for cover toppled down in their tracks; others were stricken where they lay, by flying shrapnel and shell fragments; many more were blown to bits by direct hits from big shells or killed by concussion." In an instant, the peaceful little valley had become a slaughterhouse.

Johnson and the other survivors crawled back up the valley's southern ridge, while several French tanks chugged down the open slope toward them. A smack; a roar of flame; a rush of smoke; and the German artillery knocked out the tanks one at a time. Soldiers clustered around the wrecks, found that the smoke only drew more enemy fire, and resumed their painful crawls to safety. The wounded relied on comrades to drag them out. Many would-be rescuers—like Lieutenant Albert Baesel of the 148th Regiment, who won a posthumous Medal of Honor for trying to carry away one of his corporals—paid the ultimate price. Finally some American heavy machine guns set up along the ridge and covered the withdrawal. Ivoire had fallen, but the 37th Division had nothing left to give. The Buckeyes remained under cover for the rest of the day, drenched by rain squalls and wondering how they were ever going to cross that valley.[15]

✫

SPEEDY Martin of the 91st "Wild West" Division had endured a miserable night. Pelted by wind and rain, he had huddled in a small shell crater with a friend and the company bugler.

> A cold wind sprang up and we twisted and squirmed trying to keep warm. Finally we took out our bayonets and dug out dirt and piled it in ridges in the direction from which the wind was coming to act as a windbreak. We curled up together like a couple of pups, after taking our blouses off and using them as blankets. However, it was no use, and we continued to shiver until morning.

Many soldiers awoke with pneumonia or severe rheumatism that forced them to sit out the day's attack. Martin later regretted that he had not been among them.[16]

The 91st Division's first objective for September 27 was the village of Epinonville, located picturesquely on a ridge one mile due west of Ivoire. The 362d Regiment had taken it on September 26, but had withdrawn that evening under fire. The reoccupying Germans worked around the clock to fortify the village with trenches, redoubts, and machine-gun nests. They also reinforced their positions in woods and orchards north, east, and west of the village, so that if the Americans succeeded in capturing Epinonville they would be forced out again just as quickly and decisively as they had been on the previous day. As the Germans worked, the Americans waited miserably in holes and puddles in a little hollow. The westerners disregarded the hollow's formal name, Baronvaux Creek, preferring to call it Death Valley, Death Hollow, or Deadman's Gulch.[17]

The 362d Regiment from Montana led the attack on Epinonville on the twenty-seventh, as it had on the previous day, with Private Martin's 361st Regiment from the Pacific Northwest in support on its left and the 363d and 364th Regiments attacking farther west against the tiny hamlet of

Eclisfontaine. The Montanans attacked just before 6:00 A.M., and made easy progress until they approached the top of the ridge, when their own artillery began shelling them. For those who experienced it, the bombardment was "the worst, the most sickening experience of the whole war." Fortunately a savior was at hand: Colonel John Henry "Gatling Gun" Parker, the regiment's commander, a hero of San Juan Hill who had already been wounded and decorated several times in the present war. "A towering figure, easily six feet three, with his enormous pipe smoking and brandishing a cane like a young sapling," Parker waved his cane and swore until his voice echoed across the entire field. The men followed him safely out of the barrage and into the outskirts of Epinonville.

Energized by the presence of their charismatic commander, the Americans destroyed the German emplacements in Epinonville. Then they attempted to push beyond, only to run into a hail of enemy artillery and machine-gun fire. Parker directed his men to dig in, and deployed machine guns and riflemen around the village's northern perimeter. The Americans concealed themselves well; a company of German infantry, apparently thinking that the 362d had withdrawn, sauntered toward the village across an open clearing. Captain Elijah Worsham of the regiment's machine-gun company watched them advance until they reached point-blank range, when he ordered his three concealed guns to open fire. Surprised, the Germans first "stood huddled in temporary paralysis" and then fled as the machine guns "played back and forth over them like a hose with a wide-spraying sprinkler."[18]

This defeat served only to enrage the Germans further. Minutes after the last German soldier had scuttled out of sight, the enemy laid a furious bombardment along the American line. The inability of the 37th Division to advance past Ivoiry on the right meant that a great deal of the enemy fire came from that direction, into the 362d's open flank. German aircraft, braving the same weather that had grounded the American planes, strafed up and down the lines. Miserably, the Doughboys withdrew. They attacked twice more that day and took Epinonville each time, only to withdraw again, leaving behind scores of dead and wounded. "To have to fight an elusive enemy that spit lead at us and then crept sullenly away without clashing, and then to be pulled back from the hard earned conquest as an angry bull-dog is jerked back by his chain, seemed to be the fate of our Regiment," complained Lieutenant Farley Granger.[19]

Private Martin participated in a similar debacle with the 361st, attacking alongside the 362d to the west. Advancing toward Epinonville, his battalion took shelter from an enemy barrage in a sunken road just below the village.

Each time the Doughboys tried to advance, the Germans drove them back with heavy losses. A one-pounder section took potshots at the enemy positions, without results. Meanwhile the enemy barrage intensified, zeroing in on the sunken road. Groups of German infantry became visible, evidently planning a counterattack. American machine gunners held them back for the moment, but their stocks of ammunition dwindled. When they ran out of bullets, the Germans would attack. Martin's officers worried that the enemy infantry would work around the battalion's flanks and wipe it out.

Private Martin now came into his element. The battalion needed a runner to contact regimental headquarters and request support, and "Speedy" was the natural choice. Crawling through long grass and weeds and then bolting full throttle for the rear, he braved fire both from the ground and from above. German planes flew everywhere, strafing and calling down artillery on everything that moved. He found the regiment's colonel, the levelheaded William D. Davis, pacing back and forth on a hill, "apparently oblivious of all the screaming and exploding shells, and the hail of machine gun bullets," and delivered his message. On the way back, a German shell landed next to Martin and shattered his left arm. But his battalion made it back.[20]

Farther west, the 363d and 364th had smashed through thick belts of barbed wire covered by machine guns and advanced toward Eclisfontaine. Lieutenant Frank L. Thompson of the 363d wrote in his diary that "we had gone about 200 yards when 'tst-tst-tst-tst!' and we did an Annette Kellerman for Mother Earth. . . . I heard a moan from behind and saw a man trying to get up,—then he bent over as though to vomit and the blood gushed out in a stream from his mouth." The regiment got nowhere, and rage and frustration again vented itself on prisoners, as Thompson witnessed: "Saw a tank driver kill a wounded German in cold blood. Shot him three times with his pistol before he finally got him."[21]

Lieutenant Deming Bronson, a Seattle native serving with the 364th, had twice been severely wounded on September 26 and ordered to report to a first-aid station. He nevertheless participated in the initial attacks on the village and single-handedly killed an enemy machine gunner. During the withdrawal, Bronson insisted on being the last man to leave, and suffered a near-direct hit from an enemy shell that shredded both of his arms. Dragged out of the line, he spent the night with his command before seeking medical treatment, earning the Medal of Honor.[22] Even a hundred Lieutenant Bronsons could not have held Eclisfontaine, however. As at Epinonville, the Americans took the village only to withdraw. The division's net gain for the day was zero.

Each attack left a nightmarish aftermath. Casualties grew so heavy that musicians from the divisional marching band were pressed into service as stretcher-bearers. They worked under constant artillery fire alongside bedraggled squads of enemy prisoners. Model T ambulances shocked everyone with their ability to bounce and rattle over trenches and shell holes, but even they could not traverse the shattered ground south of Eclisfontaine and Epinonville. Most of the wounded either had to wait for the stretchers, or crawl or stumble out on their own. Dressing stations were established back in Death Valley, where wounded soldiers lay for hours, unattended by overworked doctors and orderlies as German artillery blindly but effectively searched the valley. As elsewhere along the line, no fresh food or water could make it through the clogged rear areas to the front lines, and the Wild West Division's soldiers had to survive on emergency rations and water drawn from the filthy stream at the bottom of Death Valley.

★

September 27 brought the already-confused 35th Division closer to dissolution. The previous evening had ended with the 138th Regiment, bloody and exhausted, on the right; on the left, Lieutenant Colonel Carl Ristine had pushed his 139th Regiment to the front, passing through the shattered 137th Regiment. Ristine had acted against orders, but division commander Major General Traub ordered the 139th to continue ahead while the as-yet-untested 140th Regiment leapfrogged the prostrate 138th on the right. The 139th and 140th would then advance toward the division's original objective, three miles north of Fléville.

Poor staff work caused two different attack orders to enter circulation, preventing a coordinated advance. On the right, Lieutenant Colonel Channing Delaplane's 140th passed through the 138th at dawn and advanced northwest, with weak artillery support, up the broad, open slopes of Hill 218. The Germans had festooned the hill, an important observation point, with massive coils of barbed wire, which held up the Americans at the crest. Wire clippers went to work with maddening slowness as German 77mm field guns and Maxim machine guns, which had preregistered on Hill 218, delivered horribly accurate volleys on the infantry from long range. There was no escaping the bullets and shells, as Sergeant William Triplet discovered to his horror:

> [The Germans] were artists with machine guns, used them at two thousand
> yards or more, placing them well back where the trajectory of the bullets
> would follow well down the curve of our reverse slopes. Then the gunner

would range in with bursts of ten and when he saw just one bullet kick up dirt on the crest he'd clamp his gun at that elevation knowing that the other nine bullets were making life miserable for anybody on the reverse slope behind the crest.[23]

The 140th stopped, pinned down, below the crest.

On the left, Ristine's 139th waited for artillery support until 9:00 A.M., and then advanced without it. The regiment moved north-northwest, following Buanthe Creek up a valley past the base of the western slopes of Hill 218. As the Doughboys advanced, the village of Charpentry became visible below the crest of a ridge above the creek. To Private Joe Rizzi, the unspoiled little town, with its church steeple rising erect on the skyline, seemed to say, "Hell shall never prevail against me."[24] The defiance was more than picturesque.

Three roads left Charpentry. One passed south into the valley and across Buanthe Creek. Another ran north and west toward the shattered remains of Baulny. The third ran east for a short distance and then split. One fork went southeast across a narrow valley and up over the crest of Hill 218 toward Very; the other, an old Roman thoroughfare, cut directly northeast along a ridge toward Romagne. The Roman road, which overlooked the 139th advancing up the valley below Charpentry, and the 140th pinned down on Hill 218 to the east, was lined by tall, stately, but shell-shattered old trees. German machine-gun nests sprouted funguslike from the base of each tree, and barbed wire covered the slope below the road all the way down to the valley.

The 139th attacked up the ridge toward Charpentry while Sergeant Triplet watched from his uncomfortable post on Hill 218. Puffs of smoke rose from the Roman road as Maxims raked the American infantry struggling upward, and black fountains of dirt and smoke exploded along the ridge's base. As the explosions cleared, ant-sized figures of soldiers tumbled down the valley. "Five minutes later another section of the hill would jump a hundred feet into the air and the little figures would scurry away again, some of them back toward the first strike. The Jerries had saved one hellish big howitzer."[25] The inexperienced Lieutenant Colonel Ristine packed two battalions into the first wave of his attack, and thereby doubled his losses to no purpose. Charpentry and the ridge remained firmly in German hands.

As the attack bogged down, German planes swooped from the low-lying rain clouds and either strafed the American infantry or observed for the enemy artillery. One plane seemed to have singled out Private Rizzi for destruction.

I want to say that the plane scared me more than I ever was scared in my life. I really thought he was firing directly at me and I could almost see his features when he was coming at us. I was trying to force myself into my fox hole and cover myself with my equipment, all the while shaking my fist at him and shouting, "You, you son-of-a-bitch. Come down and just let me get one poke at you." I was scared—and believe me, there must have been hundreds like me.[26]

At noon the attack resumed, this time with tanks; but the "wonder weapons" did no good. On the right, where Triplet's 140th languished on Hill 218, five Renaults—two mounting 37mm guns and the other three with machine guns—lumbered down the hill's forward slope, popping their guns randomly at the unseen enemy. They returned ten minutes later, unable to cross the creek at the bottom of the valley. Ashamed to return in futility, the tankers drove back and forth on the crest of the hill, firing at the German machine guns along the Roman road while Triplet and other Doughboys tried to avoid being crushed under the tracks. German fire followed the tanks as they rattled back and forth, spraying the unlucky infantry with bullets and shrapnel. Finally the Renaults ran out of ammunition and withdrew down the hill's rearward slope; the infantry assault was canceled, and Triplet and his comrades "settled down to a comparatively peaceful life of sniping again."[27]

On the left, the 139th attacked Charpentry again, alongside several tanks that followed the southern road across Buanthe Creek, and waddled painfully up the slope toward the village. The Germans, with clear observation down into the valley, knocked out the tanks with antitank rifles.[28] The infantry got about a thousand feet up the slope before heavy casualties forced them to turn back again. American mortars plastered some machine guns on the ridge, but failed to get the attack going again. The day looked like a complete washout, an impression reinforced all afternoon by the lashes of cold rain that swept across the ridge and down the valley.

✶

PERSHING, "not satisfied with the Division being stopped by machine gun nests here and there," angrily demanded that Traub launch another attack that afternoon. Officers were equally harsh on their men. "The 140th held up by a lot of Germans!" howled Lieutenant Colonel Channing Delaplane, the regiment's fiery commander. "It simply must not be!" Called "Dogface" for his bulldog's scowl, Delaplane's confidence and decisiveness energized his men even though he had taken command less than a week earlier. The Doughboys needed the boost, for their long, uncovered route of advance—across the broad open crest of Hill 218, down its equally open northwestern slopes, across a creek, and up the ridge on the other side toward the Roman road—did not inspire confidence.[29]

Several batteries of artillery miraculously penetrated the traffic jams and arrived in time to support the attack. Captain Harry Truman's Battery D had entered Cheppy at about 11:00 that morning. His usually voluble Irish gunners became "quiet as a church" on passing a pile of dead infantrymen that the German machine guns had ripped to pieces. The 75s unlimbered in a nearby orchard, and the men cut down trees to clear fields of fire while Truman, ordered to act as forward observer for the battery's fire on Charpentry, went forward to a shell hole on the front lines. He had been there only a few minutes when the American infantry stationed nearby withdrew out of sight, leaving him high and dry. Truman quickly scuttled back to another hole.

The barrage began a few minutes later. Truman phoned directions, and the 75s barked. German planes strafed Battery D and dropped grenades while the Irishmen fired back with rifles. One man grabbed a machine gun and swung it about like an out-of-control fire hose, causing his comrades to dive for cover. Fortunately he caused no casualties, and the Germans only killed two horses. Truman kept feeding targets to his guns, which pounded Charpentry with eighty-two shells before he spied another target to the west across the Aire: a German artillery battery. The enemy guns were in the 28th Division sector, and the orders on divisional boundaries were so rigid that he could expect a court-martial if he fired across them without permission. Reasoning that the guns might leave before his superiors gave him clearance for action, he ordered his 75s to open fire. Forty-nine shells slammed the enemy battery within two minutes, wiping it out. Sure enough, ten minutes later Truman's phone rang. His colonel screamed into the earpiece, threatening a court-martial. "Go ahead!" the captain shouted back. "I'll never pass up a chance like that. We plastered 'em." That was the last he ever heard of the affair.[30]

Sergeant Triplet of the 140th walked among his men on Hill 218 at 5:20 P.M., whispering that they would attack in ten minutes. It was growing dark, and the rain had settled to a steady drizzle.

> We all settled our packs, put one in the chamber and five in the magazine, and lit our smokes. I filled my pipe, feeling very nervous and shaky, just like before the kickoff in a football game. Then a whistle blew from the fourth platoon

area, another from the first platoon ahead, and I blew mine. They climbed out, slinging bayonet⁴ ⁷ ˡes, and started walking.

The troops advanced in a broad, loose phalanx, with five yards between each man, fifty yards between sections, one hundred yards between platoons, and two hundred yards between companies. The German machine guns along the Roman road, which had quieted down since the mortars hit them a few hours earlier, resumed firing with unabated fury. Men dropped everywhere, but with Delaplane at their head the infantry continued.

Triplet reacted instinctively to the slashing bursts of the enemy machine guns:

> It's odd how a man under fire will tilt his head forward and lean into his helmet like it was an umbrella in a hard rainstorm. It would take four helmet thicknesses to bounce a bullet. I noticed that they were all leaning into the storm—foolish. And then I caught myself doing it too. It felt safer, peering from under the brim—stupid.

As they got farther down the slope into the valley the Doughboys discovered that they had reached a blind spot below the trajectory of the German machine guns. Except from some long-range artillery fire, they were "safe as in church." Delaplane would not allow them to pause, however, and he drove them chest-deep across the freezing creek and up the slope on the other side. Once more in the Germans' view, the infantry struggled through the barbed wire while enemy potato-masher grenades tumbled among them. Clipping and climbing, unthinkingly as if in a dream, the Doughboys took their casualties and kept going. Then, suddenly, they reached the Roman road.[31]

Surging over yet another line of barbed wire, where some men remained strung up, "chopped to bloody rags," the infantry charged northeast along the road from one nest and shattered tree to another. Triplet now discovered that "the trees along the road had been strung with wire interwoven with brush and poles ten feet high as camouflage or screen to keep the French balloon observers from spotting traffic on the road." Behind two gaps in this artificial hedge, clusters of Germans fired through the camouflage and lobbed grenades over the top.

> On this side we were piling up, mixing platoons and companies, shooting at glimpses of movement, and heaving F-1 grenades over the hedge. A man couldn't feel safe anywhere. Our men were tearing at the brush and poles with brute strength and awkwardness and jamming themselves into impossible holes.[32]

Finally the Americans penetrated the screen, and the Germans fled, abandoning their machine guns along the ridge. "Wild-eyed" with frenzy, the Doughboys charged pell-mell after the fleeing enemy. Their officers could not make them stop. The frustration and rage that had been building since the previous morning boiled over unchecked, and they bayoneted every German they caught. Private Rizzi joined the mayhem:

> The sight of the mangled bodies [of his buddies] brought curses and prayers that we might get at the cause of that butchery. We vowed no more prisoners if those bastards wanted war in that fashion. We swore that they would get it. Gritting our teeth, we pushed on. . . . Our minds were becoming warped, not stopping to figure that our artillery was doing the same to those poor unfortunate wretches. . . . I had become as vicious as the rest.[33]

The Doughboys' rage did not abate until the 140th had captured the entire ridge, Charpentry included, and Delaplane got them settled down and dug in for the night. Alongside came the 139th—still intermingled with elements of the 137th—which had attacked up the ridge below Charpentry in "a line just as straight & regular as though we were in our drills at Camp Doniphan" and braved German machine guns and flamethrowers to take the ridge's western edge and the village of Baulny.[34] The 140th had really broken the German positions and taken Charpentry, however, and as Delaplane's men recuperated they thought of themselves as elite troops:

> We had taken the enemy's guns. We had wiped out his flock of machine gunners. We had shown how we could die. We had learned that we could count on each other to the limit. We had entered the battle-line a green regiment, and received our baptism of fire. Tonight we were veterans.[35]

As Rizzi observed:

> Our nerves were mighty strained. We were crabbing about everything in general—hunger, cold and fatigue. Still, the last puff of a cigarette would be split up; the last bit of chewing tobacco was passed around; the last can of corned willie shared. You see, we were all buddies. The canteen of water was passed around. The one who had the water would be the last to drink and he sure would cuss at the fellows if they would insist on his drinking first. It was the same with the smokes or eats or what have you. God never could create human beings so unselfish, so devoted and so tender as my buddies. The beautiful memories of loyalty and comradeship still linger, memories deeply implanted in our souls.[36]

Midwestern farm boys had become men. Men had become soldiers. And soldiers had become comrades.

★

THE 28th Division fought two very different battles on September 27. On the right, the Pennsylvanians advanced over the rolling, open hills on the west bank of the Aire River; on the left, they struggled through the cragged and misty woodlands of the Argonne. Neither flank had it easy. On the right, the 109th and 110th Regiments attacked in fog and rain, crossing a cratered grain field, sliding down the bank of a shallow ravine, and hauling themselves up the other bank. Above, they reached a cratered plain, with the gray walls and red roofs of Montblainville visible less than a mile ahead. They were in the open now, and machine-gun and sniper fire from the village and woods to the west stabbed at them through the fog. The Doughboys took severe casualties, but stormed the village efficiently. By 8:00 A.M., they had reached positions three hundred yards north of the village, where they ran into such heavy enemy fire that they had to stop and dig in. Later that morning they broke up a German counterattack, but as the rain increased to a downpour the Doughboys could not follow it up with an attack of their own.

Farther west, in the Argonne, the 111th and 112th Regiments marched uphill through foggy, sodden woods toward the German trenches on Champ Mahaut. Maxims opened fire as the Doughboys reached the crest, forcing them to pause before hurling themselves over the ridge toward level ground. At every step men fell, victims of an unseen enemy somewhere in the fog. "We walk forward always on the lookout for holes and depressions to drop into," Corporal Harold Pierce wrote in his diary.

> At every stop we lie down. The air is filled with rushing, snapping, cracking sounds, sometimes close and sometimes far away as the Boche fire blindly into the fog hoping by luck to get someone. Ricochet bullets scream horribly when deflected by a twig. . . . Dimly through the fog we can see the files and combat groups moving slowly. When they move we move and when they halt we halt. . . . We come to a woods road, the men ahead stop and take refuge behind trees, and I remain on one knee. I can barely see the figure of a man behind a tree fifty yards in front of me. Suddenly a crackle of bullets and in front a man screams, then flops into the bushes, his throat gurgling, moaning, kicking and thrashing around. His kicks gradually cease a long sigh and it is all over. It was the bugler from "F" Company and he got it through the neck. I lie down on my face and shiver and cover my head with a blanket

I found this morning to keep out the sound. Bing Johnson also crawls under with me and though we realize the blanket is no protection yet it will keep out the sights.[37]

The advance continued for about half a mile before the men could take it no longer. By nightfall the regiments—less dozens of men killed, wounded, or mentally incapacitated—had withdrawn to their original positions of the morning. The Argonne had begun to reveal the evils held hidden in its mists.

☆

THE city dwellers and western plainsmen of the Statue of Liberty Division had by this time grown intimately, horribly acquainted with the Argonne. Many swore that after the war ended they would never look at another tree in their lives.

All four regiments of the division attacked on the morning of September 27, most with artillery support. The division had not advanced far on the twenty-sixth, so the guns did not have to move up. But the Germans were ready. After hours of fighting from tree to tree, the line crept forward a few hundred yards, and many soldiers died. The Doughboys attacked again in the afternoon and knocked out some machine-gun nests, but made no significant gains. Dozens more soldiers fell dead or wounded. A third attack at dusk got a little farther—four or five hundred yards—mainly because the Germans had withdrawn. But the Americans felt no sense of progress. They had captured some woods, but ahead the trees grew closer, the vines and thickets denser, and the earth fouler with the mingled essence of rotting leaves and flesh. By now, nature herself seemed an enemy:

Huge trees tower protectingly above their brood of close-grown sapling, branches interlacing overhead until no patch of sky is visible and the light is the sickly half-light of early dawn. The ground hides under a maze of trailing vines, prickly bushes, rheumatic tree branches, imbedded in soggy leaves, with here and there a clump of rank fern. The undergrowth is so tangled as to give the impression that nature had gone on a debauch and later, viewing the havoc, in a moment of self-spite had added to her riotous handiwork. No birds sing. No living thing moves. Like the seared leaves, like the rotting tree trunks, it is a place of death.[38]

The sights and sounds of fighting in these woods presented unique horrors. Private Henry Smith discovered "hell on earth" when his battalion advanced up the slope of one fog-choked ravine "in the face of machine gun fire, German hand grenades, known as potato mashers, trench mortars and snipers. The screeching of the men who were hit was blood curdling." Some, such as Colonel A. F. Prescott of the 308th Regiment, collapsed after such episodes and had to be relieved. Most reacted like Private Ralph John of Marmath, North Dakota, who had begun the fight with a naive "feeling of wonderment at what we might see or learn." After two days in the Argonne he "didn't think anything of stepping over dead bodies of men with whom I had started out or wading through a pool of blood." Many soldiers kept themselves and others going with crazy jokes or songs; without them, John confessed, "many fellows would have gone raving mad."[39] Such individual methods of coping became especially important in the absence of officers, who grew fewer with each passing hour. Soon, sergeants would lead many companies in place of dead, wounded, or mentally incapacitated captains and lieutenants, while privates and corporals took command of squads and platoons.

✳

Colonel Fred Brown assembled the officers of his African American 368th Regiment, 92d Division, on the morning of September 27. He ordered them to attack at daybreak, with the Second and Third Battalions in front from right to left, and the First Battalion in reserve under French control. Major Mox Elser, commanding the Second Battalion, could not understand how the regiment's mission had changed from liaison to assault. In any event, he told Brown, his men were in a "muddled fix" and he wanted them held back for reorganization. The colonel overruled him. The troops would go forward.[40]

The Third Battalion jumped off on schedule and maintained a reasonably good pace, covering a mile against sporadic resistance from enemy snipers and machine guns. Elser's Second Battalion started late and got nowhere. His company and platoon commanders lost their way and wandered aimlessly, stumbling occasionally into enemy emplacements that pinned them down. For his part, Elser was incapable of keeping his battalion together. By nightfall it had become dangerously disorganized, but worse was to come.

✳

By the evening of September 27, Pershing had become seriously annoyed with First Army's lack of progress. His troops had captured Montfaucon and Charpentry, and dented the enemy lines in a few places, but the Germans had repulsed them everywhere else. Unable to conceive of an effective defensive system built around machine guns—and entirely discounting the enemy artillery—Pershing could not understand why his intrepid American soldiers had not advanced farther. In his mind, victory depended on willpower; if the advance had stalled, the will to win must have been lacking. "Our advance is somewhat checked by rather persistent action of Germans with machine guns," he wrote in his diary. "This is due to a certain extent to the lack of experience and the lack of push on the part of the division and brigade commanders."[41] First Army must simply push harder.

War correspondent Frederick Palmer found an atmosphere of "forced optimism" among Pershing and the other officers at First Army headquarters: "Our ambition was soaring for a decisive success on the 28th. We had been delayed a day, but we should yet carry through our daring programme. . . . Drive, and again drive; keep moving; the enemy would eventually yield. He must yield. Once we broke his resistance, then the going would be swift and easy against his shattered units." Even so, Pershing and his generals realized that "the 28th was a critical day: the day when it was to be decided whether or not we were to fight a siege operation, or to carry the whale-back [the Heights of Cunel and Romagne] in a series of rapidly succeeding rushes."[42]

A tour of the lines—traffic jams permitting—would have given Pershing a more complete impression of what his Doughboys had to deal with. On the right, in III Corps, the 33d and 80th Divisions had captured their objectives; but the 4th Division had shuddered to a complete halt, leaving the Blue Ridge Division's left flank in the air. In V Corps, the 79th Division had captured Montfaucon, but could not advance farther. Worrying rumors claimed that the division's soldiers had "scattered like sheep" under enemy fire, and that officers with drawn pistols had herded them forward.[43] The 37th Division had scratched a few hundred yards toward Ivoiry and collapsed in exhaustion, while the 91st Division thrashed and bled in front of Epinonville and Eclisfontaine. On the left, I Corps' 35th Division had captured Charpentry at the cost of heavy losses and increasing disorganization. The 28th Division's right half had captured Montblainville while its left foundered in the Argonne, where the 77th Division endured torments worthy of horror author H. P. Lovecraft. Signs of shakiness had also appeared on the far left flank, where the 92d Division's 368th Regiment advanced hesitantly toward Binarville.

At the front, thousands of wounded Doughboys remained untended under the merciless rain. The ambulances still couldn't reach them. Even more critically, fresh water, food, and ammunition could not get to the front. The troops' canteens had gone empty, but at least they could collect rain from shell holes. As a rule, soldiers considered it safe to drink from a shell hole inhabited by frogs or toads—that meant gas had not poisoned the water.[44] Without food supplies, however, the Doughboys went hungry. Emergency rations had already been eaten and captured German stores quickly disappeared. They had run low on ammunition too, and scavenged cartridges and grenades from the dead and wounded.

The Doughboys looked in vain for support from above or behind. Bad weather had grounded most of the American planes—although the rain didn't seem to bother the German fliers—and except on the far left, where the 77th Division had hardly advanced past its starting positions of September 26, artillery support was nonexistent. The guns just couldn't make it up through the traffic. Lieutenant Bob Casey struggled to get the guns of his field battery forward, only to find that

> all the wheeled materiel of the A.E.F. is on the road out of Avocourt and all of it bound toward the Front. Ambulances are stalled in the ditches. They can't get back and men who might have had a chance for their lives are dying because nothing can be done with them. . . . What to do? Not much of anything. The road through Avocourt was paved with vehicles—a double column of them stretching for indefinite miles forward and back—locked hopelessly, end to end and hub to hub. . . . An M.P. colonel making a futile effort to straighten the tangle raged back and forth in front of us. He was swearing like an insane man and tears were rolling down his cheeks unheeded.[45]

In desperation, the colonel ordered all the ration carts into the roadside ditch. He had been ordered to give priority to artillery and ammunition.

Flying over the front, Billy Mitchell found congestion

> worse . . . than I had ever seen on a battlefield. In addition, the troops immediately behind the front, being new at the game, built any number of fires in the woods which at once disclosed their positions. When I first saw it, it looked like the best target that I had ever seen for aviation on any field. The Germans, I knew, would not be slow to take advantage of it.[46]

Hoping to keep the German fliers busy defending the *Kriemhilde Stellung,* Mitchell concentrated his planes against the Heights of Romagne and Cunel ahead of V Corps. At the same time, he ordered his First Pursuit Group to maintain a constant patrol of only three hundred feet, "in fact, almost down among the infantry," over the American supply lines. "Had we not done this instantly," Mitchell later claimed, "I believe that this whole mass of transportation would have been destroyed and burned."[47]

The Germans never attacked First Army's supply lines on a large scale, but the power to do so remained within their reach. As Private Rush Young moved up with reserve elements of the 80th Division near Béthincourt, two enemy planes descended over the crowded roads.

> We all made for the trenches along the roadside, thinking we would be wiped out. Back they came and we began to rain showers of machine gun bullets at them. They were not flying up the column, but across from one side to the other. . . . The only time during the war I had ever seen the Colonel engaged in combat was now. He . . . began to fire at them with his pistol for all he was worth. I often wondered what he thought he could hit with a pistol, shooting at an airplane in flight.

After the Germans departed, a few Allied planes arrived and flew around. When they left, the enemy planes returned and repeated their strafing act. Amazingly, they inflicted only light casualties on the soldiers packing the narrow road, "just as helpless as the proverbial snowball in Hell."[48]

General Max von Gallwitz, Pershing's German adversary, felt more confident with each hour that passed. The beginning of the American offensive had found his frontline units unprepared and left many of them shattered. They had lost some ground on the twenty-sixth. Today, however, his soldiers had held fast, allowing time for reserves to come into the lines. If his front held for another day, Gallwitz felt certain he could hold the Americans for weeks, even months. "On the 27th & 28th," he later wrote, "we had no more worries."[49]

CHAPTER 10

"Words Can Never Describe It,

Nor Is the Mind Imaginative Enough to

Conceive It"

SEPTEMBER 28

"There is evidence that the enemy is retiring from our own front," Pershing announced to his troops on September 28. "Our success must be followed up with the utmost energy, and pursuit continued to bring about confusion and demoralization, and to prevent the enemy from forming his shattered forces. I am counting on the splendid spirit, dash and courage of our army to overcome all opposition. Our country expects nothing less."[1]

At the front, far away from Pershing's desk at Souilly, American morale plummeted after another rainy night. The Germans kept up a scattered but steady barrage of gas and artillery all along the line, causing relatively few casualties but preventing the bone-weary Doughboys from getting any rest. Enemy infantry infiltrated the American positions in several places, rattling sentries who thought they were under full-scale attack; in the morning, German snipers and machine gunners opened fire from positions that had been "captured" the previous day. From the packed roads below Avocourt, artillery lieutenant Casey could see that all was not well at the front: "We had been told by French instructors that panicky infantry betrays its condition with rockets. Whether or not that is true the northern sky was a vast set piece of fireworks until we quit watching it at 2 o'clock."[2]

★

III Corps again remained stationary along the Meuse on the right. On the left, the 80th Division's 320th Regiment and the 4th Division attacked together. They advanced about a mile before the Germans stopped them. The 320th advanced through the Bois de la Côte Lémont without any trouble, but as the troops reached the woods' northern edge the Germans socked them with an artillery barrage and an infantry counterattack. The Americans pushed the Germans back, but they could not advance any farther across the open ground north of the woods. The Ivy Division meanwhile captured the Bois de Brieulles and a German storehouse full of munitions on the right, and helped the 79th Division to take Nantillois on the left; but when the troops tried to continue farther toward the Bois des Ogons and the Bois de Fays—later scenes of some of the worst fighting of the war—German counterattacks pushed them all the way back through the Bois de Brieulles. Hines tried to push his men farther but eventually gave in and let them rest.[3]

German artillery fire from the Heights of the Meuse reached an awful intensity by evening. There was no escaping it; the enemy held the entire corps under observation, and could hit practically wherever they wished. The mental pressure of the constant bombardment grew more terrible with each passing moment. Private Rush Young found his top sergeant "trembling like a leaf. I couldn't understand what was wrong with him, and asked him if he was cold. He could not answer. . . . The wounded and dying were groaning and calling for help. 'I'm hit, for God's sakes help me,' was the cry. It was almost unbearable. Some were shell shocked and were screaming maniacs. From the way they were screaming you would think they were shot to pieces."[4] The shells, combined with sleeplessness, hunger, fatigue, and the constant chilling rain, propelled the men into a hazy dreamworld of pure instinct, where only the will to live remained.

*

PRIVATE Maximilian Boll of the 79th Division spent the night of September 27–28 lying under a poncho in the mud on Montfaucon, feeling "the quivering of the ground from the crashing shells and the sensation of feeling dirt fly and fall over me from near-by hits." He rose to find his 315th Regiment in the front lines and preparing to attack the village of Nantillois, one mile ahead across an open valley. Officers gave Boll and the rest of the men no time to think of their hunger and misery, but drove them into the attack at first light. The day before, German fire had swept across the valley and blasted the Americans back to Montfaucon; this time, the enemy guns remained silent until the Americans reached a ridge just south of the village. Then they opened up with "the most hellish machine-gun and artillery fire of the entire Argonne fight." Assisted by the Ivy Division on the right, the 315th butted through at the cost of 40 percent casualties, and took Nantillois, along with a battery of German 77s, by 11:00 A.M.[5]

The 315th advanced half a mile farther north to Hill 274, which sloped gradually eastward toward the Bois de Brieulles, where the 4th Division was fighting. Ahead, across a narrow valley traversed on the left by a road that led past a small cluster of buildings known as Madeleine Farm, lay the dense Bois des Ogons. This marked the first outpost of the main German defensive line, the *Kriemhilde Stellung*. The Heights of Cunel and Romagne were two miles north, beyond a series of fortified woods and ridges. Allied artillery had so far left the *Kriemhilde Stellung* untouched, and the troops manning it were fresh and ready.

Billy Mitchell's aircraft had only barely reconnoitered the German defenses. Boll and his comrades could see many of the pillboxes, rifle pits, trenches, and machine-gun nests that infested the Bois des Ogons, but there was no artillery available with which to hit them. Major General Kuhn nevertheless did not hesitate. Gathering together a few light and heavy French tanks, he flung his jaded infantry headfirst into the German hornet's nest.

The attack went over at 4:30 P.M. The troops at first felt reassured by the tanks' presence, but the sense of security quickly evaporated. German machine gunners directed a steady stream of fire against the Renaults, and although most of the bullets bounced off, "many a leaden messenger, thus deflected, found its way into a gallant soldier lad advancing behind. It was like a carom shot on a pool table." German artillery blew up the tanks one by one. "It seemed as if each single boche sought out one of the tanks," an American remembered. "It bowled them over one at a time with a regularity that was heart-breaking." Turning back was impossible, so the surviving French tankers bailed out and fled pell-mell for the rear. An American lieutenant grabbed one of the tankers, demanding, "What's the matter with the tanks?" "Too much boche artillery," the Frenchman screamed, tearing free and cursing the "fool" Americans.[6]

The Doughboys continued without the tanks. How any of them made it to the woods, Sergeant Edward Davies wrote in his diary, "is more than I can tell. Bullets just pelted around us like hail. The bottom of my rain slicker was cut to ribbons." The German fire intensified as the Americans reached the woods, forcing them to "fight for every inch of ground," but they eliminated several enemy machine guns. The order to retreat left them stunned:

We were making good progress when we were ordered out of the woods. Word had been received that the Germans were going to set the woods on fire, so we had to give it up. Lieut. Bagans actually cried when we had to evacuate, he said it had cost so much to take the woods, it seemed a crime to give them up now. We got out just in time for the Germans started a terrific bombardment and almost leveled the woods.

A few survivors made it back across the shell-swept field to Hill 274, which Davies found covered with the bodies of his comrades. Over four hundred others, dead or wounded, stayed all night on the field or at the edge of the woods, slashed by shrapnel and bullets or choked on gas.[7]

General Kuhn sent the 315th's reserve battalions in another head-on attack at 6:00 P.M. Half dead from lack of sleep, the Doughboys "dragged themselves to their feet and staggered forward. They were so exhausted that they did not seem to have strength even to cry out, but went forward with jaws drooping and eyes listless." The attack ended in failure, like the others. As night fell, the Doughboys huddled under steady rain and German bombardment on Hill 182, drinking water from gasoline cans that still had blobs of gas floating on the surface and listening to the screams of their wounded buddies trapped on the field in front of the enemy lines. "The night of September 28, 1918, can never be erased from the minds of the men who were there," one soldier later recalled. "Words can never describe it, nor is the mind imaginative enough to conceive it." By morning, they had rechristened Hill 274 "Suicide Hill."[8]

"I'm all in," Davies wrote that evening in his diary, sitting in a shell hole with mud up to his waist.

Hungry and thirsty, I haven't eaten since yesterday morning. About 10 P.M. the Germans started to shell our position, God it was awful. Saw a man blown to pieces just below where Monty and I were lying. . . . I am sick and disgusted with this life. It seems to me that the men who are killed are better off. This is simply a living death, Hell can hold no terrors for me after this. We are not men any more, just savage beasts. There is no fear in me now I would go forward willingly and play the game. If I come thru I am thankful, if not—well its simply part of the game.[9]

To the left, the 316th Regiment entered the front lines in place of the 313th Regiment, which had been devastated the previous day. Captain "Big Ben" Hewit's company jumped off at 7:00 A.M. and encountered the usual assembly of German machine guns, mortars, whiz-bangs, high explosives, shrapnel, and gas. An observation balloon directed German heavy artillery from east of the Meuse, and "the big shells arrived with monstrous roars and crashes that tore holes in the earth as big as a house." Men fell in sheaves, but "on we pressed, running, flopping, firing. Dull explosions, scarcely heard amid the uproar, were followed by sinister puffs of yellow—Gas!" Badly wounded soldiers, too weak to put on their masks, died. Another soldier evaded the gas and crawled to the captain, clutching something in his hand. "I've lost a lamp," he said with a grin and opened his palm to reveal his right eye, which had been torn out by a machine-gun bullet.[10]

Major John Baird Atwood, commanding the regiment's Third Battalion leading the attack, called a halt near the edge of the Bois de Beuge and ordered his men to take cover. Ahead lay a railroad embankment. The German machine guns were too well dug in behind it to take head-on without needless slaughter. Atwood sent word back to regimental headquarters asking for artillery and machine-gun support to suppress the enemy positions so that he could resume the advance. In reply, the regiment's commander, Colonel Oscar Charles, curtly ordered him to attack. Atwood obeyed. His troops, five hundred men in two companies, went forward with him at their head. Within moments he was dead, shot in the face.[11] His two companies, hit by overwhelmingly strong enemy fire, almost fell to pieces.

Ben Hewit's men needed him now, more than ever. A six-foot-two-inch mining engineer from the Rocky Mountains, he looked and acted like God had created him with this situation in mind. "We've got to reach that railroad cut or be shot to pieces," he cried, and led his men in a dash for the embankment. Most of them made it, but a bullet had pierced the captain's wrist. "Damn! One stung me!" he mumbled, fingering the hole. A soldier asked him to go back and have the wound dressed. "No," Hewit replied, "tie it up. I can use my right arm. What would my men think of me if I let a little thing like this send me back?"

Company F continued, driving through the Bois de Beuge and then across an open valley to a smaller wood called Bois 268. Here the Americans came under heavy fire, especially from one well-entrenched German machine-gun nest. Fortunately, the company had been equipped with a number of Browning Automatic Rifles. A lieutenant called out for volunteers to outflank the enemy nest. Several riflemen responded, but only one was necessary. John Thomas, an Albanian restaurateur from Philadelphia, took a Browning and advanced under fire for hundreds of yards, outflanking and destroying the nest. "I tried to shoot fast enough to make them think a whole Platoon was on top of them," he explained. "But I was more scared than they were."

As the Americans captured Bois 268, waves of German soldiers, looking "like clouds of gray insects against the hazy horizon," attacked from the northwest. Captain Hewit watched them through his field glasses and ordered his machine gunners to open fire. The Germans melted away. The German artillery next attempted to blow the Americans out of the woods, which became "an inferno of detonations, flying tree-trunks, howling shrapnel, and the moans of wounded men"; but Hewit wouldn't budge. Retreating, he reasoned, would cost more casualties than holding on. The Americans stayed, firing back at the Germans from time to time with their one-pounder "toy cannon." After dark, the soldiers dug into reserve rations, plundered dead soldiers' packs for food, and filled their canteens with water from shell holes. Looking like wild men, with scraggly beards, sunken eyes, and filthy uniforms, they retained little of the optimism they had felt on September 26. Captain Hewit kept his men going, talking and joking with each of them as he visited their posts through the night.[12]

Private Ray Johnson and the other soldiers of the 37th Division needed rest. They had seen enough Hell in two days, especially in the valley northwest of Montfaucon where the Germans had slaughtered so many of them on September 27. But the generals were not done. The attack must proceed, they insisted, without regard to casualties or open flanks. Officers who hesitated would be relieved on the spot. So the Buckeyes—wet, haggard, and sleepless, with hunger pangs gnawing at their bowels—attacked again at 6:30 A.M., without artillery support. Onward they stumbled across the valley; this time with no casualties, for the Germans had withdrawn the previous night. This caused no cheer—they were too tired, and had been disappointed too many times before. Mechanically the Doughboys pressed on, across a road, down a slope, through the village of Cierges, and over a ridge beyond. "No sooner had they disappeared," reported an officer of the 91st Division watching the Buckeyes advance from the west, "than back they came—pell-mell—with H.E. and shrapnel helping them along. They were in full retreat—a mob."[13]

An enemy counterattack smashed the leading battalions of the 37th, which fled back through Cierges and scattered across the hills and valleys to the south. Fortunately the Germans did not press hard. Johnson's machine-gun squad had managed to stay together during the rout, but a leaden sense of fatalism consumed them. "The constant harassing we were undergoing began to tell on our nerves, which had been in a state of tension for so long that they began to frazzle. The steady rain increased the irritation we felt. We could not fight shell-fire; just had to take our medicine and hang on." Johnson settled his men that evening in a shell hole, but the sound of screams from a nearby dressing station soon had them verging on hysteria. Slinking away, they found a shell hole half filled with stinking, icy water—but at least it was quiet. They stayed there all night, racked by cramps, rheumatism, and nightmares.[14]

Major Oscar F. Miller, an Arkansas native who had moved to California and joined the 91st Division in Los Angeles, was as exhausted as his men of the First Battalion, 361st Regiment. He had accompanied them forward on September 26, and had participated in their disastrous attacks on the German positions outside Epinonville on the twenty-seventh. He advanced with them again on the morning of the twenty-eighth, when the 361st and 362d Regiments swept through Epinonville, which the Germans had abandoned, and into the enemy-held Bois de Cierges beyond. The Germans had used the woods for years as a rest camp, and had fortified them well. Snipers and machine guns covered every path, and wire hung from tree to tree. Determined infantry manned camouflaged pillboxes, dugouts, and foxholes. It was like the Argonne, although much smaller, and it took the men of the Wild West Division several hours of hand-to-hand fighting to clear the woods to their northern edge. During the fighting, Major Miller passed out from exhaustion. His men dragged him to the woods' edge, where he regained consciousness and resumed command.[15]

From the northern edge of the Bois de Cierges, Miller and his men overlooked an open east-west valley, at the bottom of which lay the buildings and trees of La Grange aux Bois Farm. Beyond the farm, the far slope climbed steeply for almost four hundred yards to the village of Gesnes, atop a ridge about a mile away. From their positions along that ridge—part of the *Kriemhilde Stellung*—the Germans observed the whole valley, which they swept with artillery and machine-gun fire. Ordered to continue attacking at all costs, Miller walked back and forth through the woods, organizing his battalion and preparing it to cross the valley. The Doughboys went forward with him at their head.

The German guns pummeled the Americans as soon as they entered the valley. As they passed La Grange aux Bois Farm and mounted the slope on the other side the Doughboys showed signs of breaking, just like the 37th Division beyond Cierges to the right. Miller was the engine that kept them going. Leading as always from the front, he kept walking even after taking a bullet in his right leg and another through his right arm. Though staggering, he ignored his wounds and cheered the troops onward through the enemy barrage. The Doughboys were well up the slope and nearing the ridge when Miller took a final bullet in the abdomen. He would not let them pause, but kept yelling until he fainted from loss of blood. The battalion thereupon halted, leaderless and exhausted. Miller died a few days later.[16]

Epinonville and Eclisfontaine—the latter taken on this date by the 363d and 364th Regiments—were advanced positions, not part of the main system of enemy defenses. The Germans had not intended to hold them for long. Gesnes, a strongpoint in the *Kriemhilde Stellung,* was different. There, the enemy played for keeps. And although the Wild West Division had shown more grit than its neighbors to the east and west—whose inability to keep pace exposed its flanks to enfilading enemy fire—it had not made any significant progress. Stuck in the open, the Doughboys suffered for the rest of the day and the following night from machine guns, high explosives, and gas. Heavy rain fell continuously as the Americans, who had fought for three straight days without fresh food or water, searched for some kind of shelter. Wounded and exhausted soldiers hid in craters, foxholes, and old German dugouts, or sat in the rain propped against shattered tree stumps.

★

THE Missouri-Kansas Division had done well so far, advancing five miles over two days and taking Charpentry Ridge in a stirring assault on the evening of September 27. September 28 began with Lieutenant Colonel Delaplane's 140th Regiment, on the right, still occupying the ridge road north and east of Charpentry, and Lieutenant Colonel Ristine's 139th holding the ridge above Baulny to the west. Ahead, the regiments faced a series of open slopes and ravines, the most prominent feature being Montrebeau Wood, about a mile ahead on the left. Dense with trees, thickets, and emplacements occupied by the fresh German 52d Division, the wood covered a broad, craggy hill that overlooked much of the surrounding country. Its capture was essential to I Corps' advance east of the Argonne. The 35th Division's commander, Major General Traub, had no particular plan for taking it; but Pershing lashed him forward, demanding attack without regard to artillery support, terrain, or the state of the German defenses.

Traub took little interest in coordination and planning, preferring to wander along the lines, brandishing his swagger stick and shouting fiery, irrelevant commands. He lived on coffee and cigarettes. Traub's staff scattered in the process of trying to follow him around the battlefield. Brigade and regimental commanders, most of whom he had appointed only a few days earlier, gave up trying to consult division headquarters and acted independently.[17] The 137th and 139th had become so intermingled that they no longer functioned as separate units; the 138th no longer existed as a fighting force, instead lending companies and provisional battalions to the 140th. Traub reorganized the four regiments into two provisional brigades, but defined the new organizations so vaguely that nobody knew what they meant.

A stiff, cold wind drove rain into the Doughboys' faces as they advanced at dawn. On the right, Delaplane's 140th was quickly driven back under German fire. To the left, the 137th and 139th repulsed a German counterattack and then launched a succession of random, uncoordinated attacks. Their overall commander, Lieutenant Colonel Ristine, had become lost in German-occupied territory west of Montrebeau Wood on the evening of the twenty-seventh. He would not turn up until the early morning of the twenty-ninth, disguised in a German helmet and overcoat. In the meantime, his officers and men acted on their own, without artillery or air support and under severe artillery and machine-gun fire. Bands of infantry and tanks nevertheless inched across the shell-strewn valley past Chaudron Farm, up a short open slope, and through Montrebeau Wood.[18]

In the woods, junior and noncommissioned officers led improvised units, using rifles, grenades, and the ubiquitous one-pounders, and knocked out the German emplacements one at a time. Fighting according to a loose, improvisational code worked in the short term. By late afternoon, under a steady rain, the troops had established a badly confused and intermixed front line along the northern edge of Montrebeau Wood. Only Delaplane's 140th maintained any cohesion, although it too had suffered badly; the division's other three regiments now existed in name only. Small groups of walking wounded, unable to get medical attention at the front, streamed toward the rear; others lay on the cold and muddy ground under German bombardment. With no food or water, little ammunition, and few officers, the Missouri-Kansas men were going to need all the pluck they could muster.

★

BUGLER Wayne DeSilvey of the 112th Regiment, 28th Division, described the events of September 28 very simply in his diary: "Still more Hell on the earth."[19]

The Keystone Division's objectives for the day remained unchanged: to advance as far as possible on the right in order to outflank the German defenses in the Argonne. On the far right, the 110th Regiment assaulted Apremont, which stood bastionlike atop bluffs facing the Aire River to the north and east. The Americans first attempted to approach the village via the riverbed, only to find that the bluffs bristled with German machine guns. Returning to their original positions, they then attacked from the south across an open plateau. German machine guns and artillery lashed the Doughboys as they crossed the plateau beside a few tanks, but they continued to advance. Entering the village, they battled the Germans in close-quarters combat that left the gutters "bright red with blood." Apremont fell in the late afternoon. The Germans immediately counterattacked from the north, but were slaughtered below the village.[20]

Just east of the Argonne, the 112th attacked at 6:00 A.M. from a ravine south of Montblainville toward Le Chêne Tondu Ridge. Corporal Harold Pierce advanced with the first wave. Leaving the ravine, he and his comrades moved cautiously in open order across a road, through an orchard, and into a gently sloping field. The dark woods of the Argonne loomed to the left; ahead, across a farm road, stood a small copse. Shelling was light, and Pierce and his fellow veterans grew careless. Minds strayed to thoughts of dry clothes, food, and sleep. Suddenly a terrible, concentrated burst of machine-gun fire opened up from the copse ahead and the woods on the left. Men yelled, tumbled, and dove for cover in the tall grass. Pierce's entire battalion had fallen into a trap.

Some Doughboys rose to their knees and fired back with their rifles, but the well-hidden enemy guns shot them down. Pierce measured his predicament. Flight was impossible; the Germans had the whole field covered and could detect any movement in the grass. Rushing the guns would be equally suicidal. Although the grass concealed the Doughboys, it offered no real protection. There were no shell craters, ditches, or knolls. Pierce and his comrades could only hug the ground, squirm into real or imagined hollows, and pray.

Panic spread as the minutes dragged by. Wounded men screamed and thrashed in the grass, but no one dared bring them aid. Some soldiers sprinted for shelter and were hit immediately. The Germans machine guns raked the field methodically, back and forth. Finally somebody started digging. The ground was soft, and soon everybody clawed the dirt with spades, rifles, and hands. Pierce—steadied by the presence of his lieutenant beside him, calmly lying propped on his elbow and chewing tobacco—dug too.

> I lie on my side and start the hole. Bullets crackle a few feet overhead. . . . I can hear the crackling coming closer and I push myself as low in the ground as possible, the crackling misses my head by a few inches and passes on. I dig furiously, a few shovels full in front of me, the crackling returns toward me, dust flies in a line coming at me, the bullets are over my head again, snapping viciously, they are over and I am digging again. . . . I shovel frantically, a few

more and I will have six inches of dirt, the bullets are swinging back at me, my helmet is not right, if I lay my head to the side and flat on the ground my head is not so safe, if I point it to the ground my shoulders are not covered. Inches count now. . . . A few more inches of dirt and I am safe. I hope there are no rocks in this ground. Lieut. Ogrum chews and spits. The wounded cry "first aid." . . . It seems like hours till my hole is a foot deeper but it is only a few minutes. At last I am safe from the guns, more than a yard of dirt in the front and if I lie still they cannot hit me.[21]

Four hours later, a group of men rushed forward through the grass to Pierce's left, threw themselves to the ground, and calmly began setting up a machine gun. He wondered how long they would last. Craning his head around, Pierce saw other machine-gun crews running up and mounting machine guns and one-pounders in the orchard. The German guns opened fire, but this time they were answered by the "strong, hard persuasive note" of the American machine guns and the chugs of the one-pounders. Bark flew from the trees as the Germans came under fire. Then, "another sweet sound, the soothing screaming shriek of seventy fives from a battery just set up behind us." The artillery ranged too close to the infantry, causing some soldiers to leap out of the grass and sprint toward the orchard. The Germans efficiently mowed them down. The artillery quickly adjusted its range, however, and the forest and copse exploded with shellfire. Then Pierce heard "another note in the orchestra, the clank of tanks, the sweetest, softest music of all." Thanking God fervently, he watched the Renaults plod stolidly into the woods, oblivious to the German artillery. As they disappeared the shellfire moved on, and the Doughboys could stand up in safety. Half of the battalion had been killed or wounded in that nameless field.[22]

Crossing the copse through lanes that the tanks had flattened in the underbrush, the remnants of the 112th reached the wooded base of Le Chêne Tondu Ridge by midafternoon. They took cover behind trees and rocks or in old trenches, and waited. A short machine-gun and smoke barrage on the ridge followed, after which officers ordered the attack. At 4:00 P.M. the soldiers started up the ridge through clotted underbrush. With every step they expected an avalanche of German grenades. Nothing happened, however, until the Doughboys crested the ridge two hours later, when "a perfect Babel of jabbering and yelling" began as large numbers of Germans, mostly old men, approached with their hands up.[23] As darkness fell, the regiment established a line atop the ridge along an old sunken road. There was no support on the right, where the 109th had spent the afternoon repelling German counterattacks west of Apremont, or on the left, where the 111th had made no progress against the German defenses in the Argonne. Fortunately the Germans did not take advantage of the resulting gaps. Pierce and his buddies—those who remained—tried to sleep in the sunken road, which became a muddy stream overnight under increasingly heavy rain. Hundreds of others, dead or wounded, lay strewn in the wake of the day's advance. The ambulances still could not get forward to evacuate them.

★

WHILE the 77th Division prepared to attack in the early morning of September 28, a ration detail—the first in two days—appeared, bearing such delicacies as cold cabbage, beef, bacon, and bread. After German artillery hit some chow lines, officers ordered their men to eat alone or in pairs.[24] The Doughboys' initial advance at 5:30 A.M. met only spotty resistance—the Germans had again withdrawn during the night—and they continued past ravines, knolls, and patches of woods with colorful names like Abri St. Louis, Abri du Crochet, Boyau des Chemins, and Bagatelle Pavilion. After gaining about a mile, however, the Americans hit the new German line of defense and the same story began again, worse than before. The Germans had cleared small lanes through the wire and underbrush, luring the Americans into death traps registered by machine guns and the deadly, high-trajectory minenwerfer mortars. The underbrush prevented the Doughboys from using their mortars, one-pounders, and even grenades, which tended to bounce off obstacles and explode prematurely.

As the 77th Division's attack broke down into small-unit and individual combat, trickery and even savage cruelty became common on both sides. The rules of warfare meant nothing in the Argonne. First Lieutenant Dwite H. Schaffner of Company K, 306th Regiment, led his men that afternoon in an attack on a ridge called St. Hubert's Pavilion. They drove the enemy off after extended hand-to-hand combat. Three counterattacks followed, during which the Germans slipped machine guns through the woods around Company K's flanks and subjected the Americans to enfilading fire that caused heavy casualties. Schaffner found one machine-gun nest and personally wiped it out. Just before the third counterattack, several Germans appeared, walking toward the Americans with their hands up and crying "Kamerad," the usual cry of surrender. The Doughboys had let them approach to within five or ten yards when another group of Germans, well armed with pistols, rifles, and hand grenades, leapt up behind the sham deserters and opened fire. Several Americans died in the ensuing firefight. Schaffner furiously leapt out of his trench and charged among the Germans, firing his pistol and tossing grenades. Finally he spotted the enemy commander, a captain, shot him point-blank, and dragged him by the collar back into the trench. After a probably none-too-delicate interrogation, the mortally wounded officer revealed his company's strength and position. The information thus obtained helped Schaffner to deploy his men effectively and hold his position for another five hours against repeated attacks from three sides.[25]

Major Whittlesey, who had spent the afternoon leading four companies of his battalion of the 308th from tree to tree in "machine gun Indian warfare," consulted his map at dusk and discovered that his command had become isolated from the rest of the regiment in a ravine one hundred yards southwest of the aptly named Moulin de l'Homme Mort. The growing dark and heavy rain made withdrawal impossible, but Whittlesey characteristically did not panic. Instead he formed his men into a hollow square for defense against all directions. He sent a runner back to headquarters—wherever that was—with a message asking for rations and ammunition, stating that "we have suffered considerably from lack of drinking water; the men are very tired but in good spirits." For the men, trying to sleep in wet funkholes where everyone felt "his whole body was wrapped in iced towels," it was "a ghastly night of uncertainty and sudden alarms, of bursts of fire coming from none could say where, of hunger, and of long, long hours of drenching darkness."[26]

✯

FARTHER west, the African American 368th Regiment, 92d Division, attacked toward the village of Binarville, which years of shellfire had reduced to "simply a name painted on a board nailed to a tree." Advancing through the dense woods along the Argonne's western edge, the regiment met only slight resistance until the early afternoon. German artillery and machine guns then opened fire in earnest. The Second Battalion fell to pieces immediately. Major Elser, the battalion's white commander, became hysterical and had to be relieved on the spot. The Third Battalion took a little longer, but it broke too. Untrained and unmotivated captains and lieutenants withdrew their companies in disorder, without waiting for orders, and allowed their men to scatter. Colonel Brown tried to rally the troops, without success. He later derided white and black officers and men as indistinguishable in their cowardice. Binarville remained in enemy hands, and the Second and Third Battalions of the 368th ceased to exist.[27]

*

By the evening of September 28, even Pershing could not deny that the Meuse-Argonne offensive looked close to failure. I and V Corps on the left and center particularly worried him. Driving to the front in his staff car that morning, Pershing took ninety minutes to cover two and a half miles of road behind the 35th Division—that with the priority right-of-way due to the commander in chief. Stuck in traffic, Pershing stood up and harangued some bewildered Missouri-Kansas men on why they should break through the enemy lines. Eventually making a breakthrough of his own through the miles of guns, horses, vehicles, and swearing MPs, Pershing arrived at I Corps headquarters to find Liggett full of reasons why his troops had not advanced farther. The terrain was horrendous. The German troops were stubborn, and their defenses diabolically efficient. The Americans were by contrast exhausted, untrained, and poorly equipped.

Pershing's own assessment of the reasons for the delay remained unchanged. It all came down, he thought, to disorganized, inexperienced, and timid officers. Some needed replacement; others just a kick. Sensing confusion at 28th Division headquarters, Pershing assigned two members of his staff, Colonel Arthur Conger and Brigadier General Dennis Nolan, to supplant "inefficient officers" of that division and bring things back to order. He also decided to replace the 35th, 37th, and 79th Divisions with the veteran 1st, 3d, and 32d Divisions. The relief could not take place for another few days; in the meantime, Pershing told Liggett's chief of staff to phone each division commander and "tell him that he must push on regardless of men or guns, night or day." Back at his own headquarters that evening, Pershing wrote in his diary that he had done everything in his power "to instill an aggressive spirit" in the generals.[28] He apparently had no sense of the plunging morale of the rank-and-file infantry. He might have inferred it from the wretched weather, the lack of food, fresh water, and sleep, and the long casualty lists; but neither he nor any of his generals had ever experienced this kind of war.

———•••———

"There Were Very Few Heroes That Morning"

SEPTEMBER 29

September 29 dawned darkly, with heavy rain clouds belching intermittent rain squalls and drizzle—ensuring another day of misery for the infantry. The Germans had by now moved another six divisions into the line and had an additional five in reserve. Their primary line of defense, the *Kriemhilde Stellung,* remained completely intact. According to the original plan, it should have been breached on September 26; three days later, in most places the Americans had not even tested it.

For the troops of the 80th "Blue Ridge" Division, the last twenty-four hours had seemed like a waking nightmare. German artillery from across the Meuse subjected them to a hideous, unending bombardment. Rumors of German infiltration and counterattacks swept the lines all night, until Lieutenant Edward Lukens found he could no longer control his men. Firing at shadows and even throwing hand grenades, they seemed about to panic. Fortunately, orders came for the 80th to withdraw into corps reserve, while the still relatively fresh 33d Division expanded its front westward. "Our joy at finding we were relieved is beyond description," Lukens wrote in his diary. On the way out, his company carried wounded soldiers who had lain in no-man's-land for two days without food or water, and passed a long succession of burial details moving in the opposite direction.[1]

★

THE Ivy Division still had some fight left in it. At 7:00 A.M., the 58th and 59th Regiments left the reserve and moved to the front, attacking with light artillery and machine-gun support. The 59th advanced on the right through the Bois de Brieulles to open ground beyond. On the left, the 58th assaulted the eastern portion of the heavily defended Bois des Ogons. Colonel Frederic Wise, commanding the 59th, had led a battalion of the 5th Marines in Belleau Wood. His men called him Old Fritz Wise. Tough and ornery, he had driven his officers and men mercilessly during training camp. "Whenever he'd address you," said Lieutenant Lemuel Shepherd, "it'd be 'goddamn you, Mr. Shepherd' or whatever your name would be." At Belleau Wood, Wise led well, fought hard, and finally "cracked up," suffering a nervous breakdown that briefly put him out of action. Since then he had been a little easier to get along with.[2]

Old Fritz Wise knew how the Germans fought in the woods—how they cleared lanes in the underbrush to create kill zones, and how their snipers and light machine gunners, hidden in tree platforms, waited until the attackers had passed and then opened fire from behind. The night before the attack, Wise sent a memorandum to his company commanders. They were to comb their companies for "country boys," especially those used to hunting squirrels, and organize them into squads. These "squirrel squads" would advance about a hundred yards behind the first infantry wave, keeping their eyes on the trees. Their targets were German snipers. Drawing on another hard lesson that he had learned in Belleau Wood, Wise predicted that the advancing Doughboys would pass large numbers of German corpses. They were to bayonet each of these before moving on. The colonel had seen too many Marines killed by Germans shamming death. It wouldn't happen again.

The new tactics worked well at first. Wise's "squirrel squads" picked off more than fifty snipers from the treetops. And the infantry advanced carefully, bayoneting every German they found, avoiding kill zones, and disabling captured enemy machine guns lest the Germans infiltrate behind the lines and set them working again. None of his Doughboys, Wise noted proudly at day's end, had been shot in the back. But lots of them still died, their bodies scattered through the woods and piled up in stacks before the enemy machine guns.[3] Private Rush Young and his comrades, feeling like "drowned rats . . . covered with mud from head to foot," advanced through the woods over a gray-green carpet of dead and wounded, the latter exclusively American. Enemy machine guns seemed to fire at them from every direction:

They were watching every road and pig path and had machine guns trained on them. The minute you stuck your head out to cross, bullets would go S-p-i-n-g s-p-i-n-g all around you. It was almost impossible to cross a road or path in this forest. We would go to the edge and take a long pole and stick our helmet on the end of it and slip it out onto the path to see if there was any fire before we started across.[4]

By early afternoon the 59th had taken the Bois de Brieulles, but the open ground beyond was a different matter. As soon as the infantry left the woods, an "anihilating barrage" hit them from the front and right flank. German heavy artillery from across the Meuse, including massive 210mm railway guns that had been used to shell Paris, shook the ground with titanic explosions that obliterated entire squads and sent geysers of dirt, equipment, and flesh far into the sky. The Ivy Doughboys hugged the ground for a while, and then withdrew to the woods.[5] The German shells followed them.

The 58th on the left had similar experiences as it tried repeatedly to enter the Bois des Ogons. Advancing in the open through a light morning mist, the Doughboys encountered a storm of machine-gun and artillery fire. Further torment came from above in the form of enemy airplanes that descended through the mist, strafing and dropping clusters of hand grenades upon the advancing infantry. Other planes hovered above, spotting for the German artillery, which fired with pinpoint accuracy. Shattered and demoralized, the regiment withdrew toward Nantillois, which had itself become a "cauldron of fire" under constant bombardment from German artillery. American artillery replied only weakly, and the air service was absent.[6]

Back at Souilly, Billy Mitchell received reports of German planes strafing the Doughboys and spotting for the artillery. The infantry thought the enemy pilots flew with leisurely insolence, as if knowing that American aircraft would never appear. Mitchell refused to believe it. His pilots had assured him that the Germans were too busy defending their own rear areas to bother with the front. Suspecting that the infantry were simply jittery or trying to excuse their own incompetence, he dispatched his information officer to the front. The officer rode his motorcycle around for a while, occasionally getting off to walk along the lines, and reported back that he had not seen a single enemy plane. Satisfied, Mitchell told the infantry that there were no enemy planes overhead. They had simply mistaken American planes for German. They could thank their own poor training for their inability to tell the difference.[7]

★

THE 79th Division "attacks in thick columns, in numerous waves echeloned in depth, and preceded by tanks," a German staff officer reported to General Gallwitz on September 29. "This kind of attack offers excellent targets for the fire of our artillery, infantry and machine guns. Provided the infantry does not allow itself to be intimidated by the advancing masses but remains calm, it can make excellent use of its weapons, and the American attacks fail with the heaviest losses." General Kuhn, the division's commander, did not care what tactics his officers employed so long as they attacked. Invigorated by gallons of coffee and cartons of cigarettes, he also spared little thought for the sufferings of his men. When the 315th Regiment's colonel reported that his Doughboys were "too weak for further advance without food," Kuhn replied simply that no food was available, and ordered the regiment to attack. The 315th's objective: the Bois des Ogons and Madeleine Farm, with help from the 4th Division.[8]

"Daylight is indeed welcome after this night of torture," Sergeant Edward Davies of the 315th wrote in his diary on the morning of September 29. "We are soaked thru and chilled to the bone. . . . I am so weak that I can hardly stand. None of us have [had] any food or water for days now. My throat and tongue feel like sandpaper. I have discarded my pack, I haven't the strength to carry it any further." Nevertheless, at 7:00 A.M., "strained almost to the breaking point by three days of continuous fighting, the troops gathered themselves together and with a cheer rushed upon the woods ahead." The four functional tanks remaining in the sector accompanied the infantry. They were promptly destroyed. Again the Germans let loose an "annihilating" fire from ahead and on both flanks, smashing the first wave of infantry and forcing the survivors to withdraw to their starting lines on Hill 274. The enemy shells followed them, and once again they withdrew, leaving behind fresh piles of dead.[9]

Demoralized and wasted, the 315th practically imploded. Sergeant Maximilian Boll, escorting wounded men to first-aid stations, encountered many shell-shock victims, particularly "a big six-foot farmer boy who had completely lost his nerve during the night. Whenever a shell passed overhead, which was often, he would cringe in terror, bury his head in his arms and wince as if in great pain." Behind the front he found crowds of stragglers looking for food and water, while an officer and a chaplain on horseback implored them to return to the front. Private Irwin Rentz of the 314th met a group of 315th soldiers retreating in disorder down the road. They told him that his regiment, hitherto in reserve, had become the division's last line of defense.[10]

Captain "Big Ben" Hewit, who had led his men through conditions that would have routed veteran formations, now paid his final debt. Attacking without artillery support, the 316th rammed itself against the German lines without gaining an inch. Officers and men fell in scenes of slaughter, and Hewit took de facto command of two companies, his own and another that had lost all its officers. Leading from the front, his soldiers last saw him waving his bandaged hand to urge them onward. They found his body the next day. "Thus died our gallant Captain," eulogized Company F's historian, "in a veil of dingy, wind-blown smoke upon that rain-swept field."[11]

Shattered and leaderless, the 316th fell apart, just as the 315th had done. Private Harry Frieman, a Russian Jew who had fled pogroms in his country only to be drafted and sent back to Europe, watched Brigadier General "Slicker Bill" Nicholson ride among a crowd of stragglers who had drifted away, screaming for them to return to the lines. Turning to Frieman and his comrades of the 313th, Nicholson told them to shoot stragglers on sight.[12]

The 79th Division had disemboweled itself, leaving its remains scattered across the battlefield. Artillerymen found "so many corpses of the 79th Division on the hillsides that some had to be dragged away to make a path through which ammunition could be brought to the guns without driving over the bodies." Private L. V. Jacks had a "perfect windrow" of bodies near his battery, and counted thirty-nine dead in one heap.[13] Master engineer LeRoy Haile wandered through a field of dead men still under German bombardment:

> For those who do not know what a field strewn with dead resembles, here it is, what had been men now looked like lots of discarded clothes scattered about, most of us had overcoats and these were all then in view, they did not seem to have men inside them. Packs, gas masks, and all sorts of equipment was all around. Then, too, the dead looked so small, they seem to shrink up. . . . The shelling was intense and they started using high explosive and gas. The gas and fumes and croton oil made me deathly sick and I vomited and was scared almost to death, this matter of being brave is a lot of talk, and I am sure there were very few heroes that morning.[14]

Pictures such as these did not make the newsreels back home.

★

LIEUTENANT Bob Casey's 75s fired relentlessly in support of the 37th Division on September 29, but as he watched the infantry attack he wondered if the guns served any purpose:

Line after line of doughboys moved slowly up the hill in extended order, their rifles at the port.

They would come to the crest. The Maxims would stutter. They would tumble down like dominoes in a row. Litter bearers would come forward on a run.

Another scattering line of infantry. . . . Another five or six silhouettes on the crest. . . . Another comment from the machine guns. . . . Another rush of litter bearers. . . .

And so on endlessly.[15]

Consuming the last of their water and provisions, sometimes chomping on raw coffee and sugar, the Buckeyes attacked at dawn.[16] The German artillery opened fire immediately, knocking out ten French tanks and enclosing the American infantry in an ever-tightening "box" barrage. Caught in a trap straight out of Edgar Allan Poe's "The Pit and the Pendulum," the Doughboys panicked and fled back through the barrage, which shredded them mercilessly. "Our nerves," confessed Private Ray Johnson, "were now in a state of collapse."

Most of the 37th's officers concluded that the time had come to call off the attack, but a few remained determined to carry on. The colonel and major of Johnson's regiment paced through the mud, arguing, as their men huddled miserably nearby. The colonel spoke of the heavy German gas and shellfire and predicted an enemy counterattack, but the major begged him not to hold back. One more attack, he insisted, would break the German lines. "There would be no half-way measure," he cried, "they'd go through!" The colonel interrupted the major and ordered him to prepare for defense, saying he would take full responsibility for canceling the attack. The expected German counterattack never materialized, although many prayed for it as a distraction from the ceaseless, enervating rain.[17]

✶

LIEUTENANT Farley Granger's Montana Doughboys had gone three days without hot food or coffee. Cold and wet, they scraped remnants from ration tins, sipped tainted water, and shivered under blankets pilfered from German corpses. Bombarded constantly for three nights, they snatched fragments of sleep amid intermittent gas alarms. Many were sick. Yet even as the soldiers' strength ebbed, morale remained high. On September 29 they attacked without hesitation, not stopping to consider whether their officers' orders made sense or, as Granger later realized was the case, if they amounted to "madness."[18]

"Attack with utmost vigor and regardless of cost," V Corps' generals had been told.[19] The 91st Division's commander, Major General William Johnston, liked those kinds of orders. A gritty career soldier from Cincinnati, Ohio, he paid no heed to enemy bullets and shells. Gesnes, he insisted, must be taken. As preliminaries, Johnston directed the capture of Tronsol Farm on the division's left, and the consolidation of La Grange aux Bois Farm—which Major Miller had taken at the cost of his life on September 28—on the right. With these strongpoints anchoring its flanks against possible counterattacks—a necessary precaution since the neighboring divisions still lagged far behind—the Wild West Division could advance to Gesnes and beyond. Johnston ordered the battle-weary 362d Regiment to take that village while the 363d and 364th attacked farther west, across a ravine and into the woods on the opposite ridge. He scheduled the attack for 3:30 P.M.

Colonel John "Gatling Gun" Parker, the 362d's fierce but thoughtful commander, did not like Johnston's orders. Gesnes, he observed, lay one mile ahead across open ground, all of it "double enfiladed by machine guns and subject to the highest concentration of artillery fire that I have ever seen." German heavy artillery was already pummeling his men sheltering in the Bois de Cierges; it would tear them to pieces once they stepped into the open. Moreover, two enemy-occupied hills overlooked Gesnes from the north, and the right flank remained open. If the Doughboys took the village, the German guns would turn it into an inferno. "The position can be taken," Parker warned, but only "if it is desired to pay the price, which will be very severe loss." Johnston responded unsympathetically. "The whole army is being held up because this brigade has not taken all the objectives assigned to it," he declared. "The brigade will attack [with the] 362nd Infantry leading, and will carry the town of Gesnes without halt, regardless of cost."

Lieutenant Granger watched Johnston's orders being read to his regiment's officers. One major didn't care; he had gone batty. The others listened somberly and turned to one another in disbelief. The thing was impossible, a captain gasped; "our losses would be terrible." "To hell with the losses," another captain replied; *"read the order."* As the officers prepared their men, Granger slipped to the edge of the Bois de Cierges and looked through his binoculars toward Gesnes.

Every square yard was visible from the higher hills beyond, occupied by the enemy, and the concrete pill-box on hill 255, and every foot swept by machine-gun and artillery-fire. Protection there was none—not even concealment for one man. The gullies between the hills were swept by enfilading fire from the wooded hills above Gesnes, and the hillsides were commanded by nests hidden in the flanks.

There was no time to think about it. At 3:30, Granger's captain turned to him and quietly said, "Well, Farley, let's go." Granger gave the signal and the men leapt forward into a storm of steel.

The isolated notes of the French 75mm field guns supporting the attack instantly disappeared in a concert of German machine guns, mortars, whizbangs, and medium and heavy artillery firing high explosives, shrapnel, and gas. Some of the Montanans cried "Powder River," but no one could hear them. "Perhaps the charge of the Light Brigade was more spectacular, more melodramatic and picturesque," said Granger, "but not more gallant."

> It is one thing to ride knee to knee in the wild delirium of a cavalry charge under the eyes of Armies; it is something else to plod doggedly on, so widely scattered as to seem alone over a barren hillside against an unseen enemy's invisible death, singing its weird croon as it lurked in the air and stinging swiftly on every side. Man after man fell but the others continued on through a "hell" of shrapnel and machine gun fire as would be impossible to exceed.

Colonel Parker led from the center of the first wave, tall, stout as an oak, waving his walking stick, and shouting for the men to follow him. They did. Parker was hit once, twice, and kept going. His men followed over one hill after another, heads and shoulders bent into the storm. With every minute the attacking ranks thinned, and the olive-drab carpet of dead and wounded grew thicker. Hit a third time, Parker crawled into a shell hole full of wounded soldiers. Peering over the rim, he could see only dead and wounded men, with a few soldiers dodging for cover. Of the attacking battalion there remained no sign. Fearing that it had disintegrated and expecting a counterattack, Parker tossed all of his maps, orders, and other papers to the bottom of the shell hole. Burn them all, he told his wounded companions, and get ready; the Germans might appear at any moment.

Unseen by Parker, small groups of Doughboys still stalked toward Gesnes. Lieutenant William Hutchinson, a bespectacled, balding young intelligence officer from California, decided that "speed was the essential thing." Sprinting ahead with a few other soldiers, he reached a clump of bushes in a little gully, just east of the village and next to a road. A hundred yards ahead he could see a crossroads, with an abandoned tank—a Renault captured and used by the Germans—surrounded by dead soldiers. Keeping close to the road bank, Hutchinson led his men in rushes toward the tank; but others had gotten there first. A few minutes earlier, some Doughboys had pounced on and disabled the Renault, shot its crew, and turned the machine gun on a nearby German emplacement before heading for Gesnes. The tank was splattered with blood, inside and out.

Lieutenant Granger, who had attacked with the group that disabled the tank, joined the charge into Gesnes. After "the satisfaction of some bayonet work," the Americans cleared the town of Germans although its streets remained full of gas. Gathering together what remained of the regiment, Granger and some other officers decided to occupy the hills north of Gesnes rather than waiting in town at the mercy of the enemy artillery. After a brief preparation, the Montanans dashed uphill at full speed. Lieutenant Hutchinson once more found himself in the midst of the first wave among begrimed Doughboys wildly shouting, "Powder River—let 'er buck." The surprised Germans fled at first, and many were shot down or bayoneted before the rest took cover and turned on the Americans with rifles and grenades. Hutchinson dove into a shallow ditch packed with Doughboys returning fire, but several enemy machine guns enfiladed the ditch from a distant ridge. "What really took place here," said Hutchinson, "can never be adequately described." The ditch was so crowded with men that machine-gun bursts passed through several men at a time. One short spray of bullets shattered Hutchinson's eyeglass case and gas mask satchel, hit a private through the brain, and severed a sergeant's spine.

To Hutchinson, "it looked as though we would be wiped out entirely":

> I told the men to keep up their fire and make it just as hot as possible. My plan was to hold out until dark, then in the event that no reinforcements arrived to wave back to the town or to some point just south of it. I figured that the Germans would soon get their artillery into action and knew that they could blow us off the map if it was working right.

The German artillerymen fortunately concentrated on Gesnes, perhaps fearing to hit their own men; but the French gunners had no such compunction. Shelling the hill with a ferocity that had been absent in the initial attack, they blasted the ditch and surrounding areas until a fireworks display of flares convinced them to lift their fire. As dusk approached, the ratio of dead to living men in the ditch grew higher and Hutchinson prepared to call the retreat. Finally, just at sundown about two hundred reinforcements charged up the hill, "very much like the most realistic melodrama or harrowing movie."

Cheering, Hutchinson's men joined the charge, cracking the German lines and throwing their artillery, which had been firing downhill over open sights, into panic. Enemy gunners struggled to hitch their guns, drivers lashing their bucking horses, but many didn't make it out in time. By 5:30 P.M., the 362d had captured both hills overlooking Gesnes, along with dozens of prisoners and several artillery pieces.

Hutchinson, "tired—more tired than I had ever been before," plopped down to rest in the ditch while his men dug ditches and foxholes along the hill's crest, and sentries occupied shell holes in the forward slope. As it grew dark, he got up and walked back toward Gesnes, passing dozens of wounded men shaking uncontrollably from chill and loss of blood. Hutchinson ordered them carried to a shed, and after wandering around the blasted village without finding any other officers he started back up the hill. On the way he pilfered some cabbages from a field and ate them with relish, dirt, worms, and all. Back on the ridge, he collapsed into the ditch he had occupied during the afternoon's attack and fell asleep next to stacks of unburied corpses. Before midnight an officer, spotting Hutchinson's bald head—he had lost his helmet during the day—jostled him "awake." The officer gave an order and walked away. Hutchinson mumbled something in reply, and fell back asleep. Only later did he learn that the officer had told him to withdraw from the hill and evacuate Gesnes.

The 362d had advanced well ahead of any other regiment in the division, and with the 37th Division still two and a half miles behind, the right flank was dangerously vulnerable. German artillery fire intensified every moment, and when daylight came it might obliterate the regiment entirely. As Colonel Parker had predicted would happen, all the day's sacrifices had gone for naught. "We were all so tired that we did not have much feeling one way or the other at the time," Hutchinson recalled, "but later the full truth dawned on us. We were withdrawing to the point from which we had started the attack. The whole terrible afternoon and hideous night to follow were all for nothing. We were simply ahead of the organizations on our flank. The attack had been made at a terrible cost thru an ill-advised order."[20]

The withdrawal was if anything more nightmarish than the attack. "The night," a soldier remembered, "was black and cold and rain that was half sleet fell at fitful intervals. The moaning cries of the wounded seemed to come from everywhere out of the darkness. Here and there a man was found wandering about among the dead and wounded like a lost child; rendered so by the terrible shock and horror of the carnage."[21] Wounded soldiers assembled for evacuation, while Doughboys piled corpses to be left behind.

Hutchinson, awake in earnest after several prods and kicks from his men, led a "sad little procession" of soldiers, each of them carrying a stretcher or with a wounded comrade around his shoulders:

> It was quite cold with a strong wind blowing the rain in our faces. We stumbled along floundering thru shell holes and every now and then picking up wounded men who had not been brought in off the field. . . . Many times the stretchers gave way or the stretcher bearers stumbled and fell. The wounded would groan and curse and the column would halt until they were ready to move forward again. No one was sure of our direction and not one compass in the company would work. I had two of them both full of water or broken. We must have been going in a circle for two hours, as we did not seem to make any headway. The landmarks all looked strange but, of course, country always looks differently at night.

Dazed in exhaustion or sobbing in despair, Hutchinson's men wandered hopelessly until one soldier who claimed to have a "highly developed sense of direction" from living on the frontier volunteered to lead them back to safety. He did, escorting them back to the Bois de Cierges just before daylight.

Lieutenant Granger had joined the list of casualties. The previous evening, "with a machine gun bullet through my canteen, four holes through my loose trench coat and one more noticeable through my ankle," he had hobbled back through Gesnes, across a field covered with dead and dying, to a first-aid station in the Bois de Cierges. The station was "a crowded mass of shell torn bodies," and Granger decided to continue toward the rear. Miraculously, he found a Ford ambulance and hitched a ride next to the driver. He was still counting his luck when a shell struck near the ambulance and tossed it off the road. The men inside were unhurt but the Ford was totaled. Granger resumed his pilgrimage on foot. Finally he reached a dressing station, and orderlies put him on a truck for transport to a hospital in the rear. The ride, over shell-torn and congested roads, lasted many hours. Granger spent it in a small compartment with two other soldiers, one of them screaming and sobbing, and the other moaning for his mother. With time to meditate, he pondered "who was responsible for this costly order of attack, why this needless sacrifice of precious lives."

Colonel Parker, who Granger met at the evacuation hospital, proudly boasted that "I did not see in the whole regiment a single case of cold feet nor a single yellow streak." There had certainly been a lot of red. Lieutenant Hutchinson, calling roll on the morning of September 30, found that only 39 of the 146 men who had started out with him the previous afternoon remained standing. The 362d had, as a whole, taken 50 percent casualties in one afternoon. And for what? It had ended up where it had started. The 363d and 364th Regiments to the west had hardly begun their own attacks against the ridge west of Gesnes when a massive German counterattack against the 35th Division forced them to turn left and defend their flank at Tronsol Farm. The flank held, thanks to a hasty spoiling attack by the divisional engineers and some well-directed fire by the 348th Machine Gun Battalion, but that was all.

In one day's fighting the 91st Division—one of the best under Pershing's command despite its lack of previous battle experience—had been torn to pieces, without taking and holding a single inch of ground. It had done better than its neighbors, but that was a dubious honor. By nightfall the 37th and 35th Divisions lagged, respectively, three and four miles behind on the right and left, leaving the 91st badly exposed and holding a much wider front than originally intended for it. Worse, the 35th neared collapse, placing the Wild West Division in serious peril.[22]

★

PERSHING visited the headquarters of the 35th Division on the afternoon of September 28. He knew that it was disorganized and had taken heavy casualties and that the men were tired. But he did not tour the front lines, and neither he nor Major General Traub—who had wandered all over the battlefield for four days—had any idea of conditions there. After looking over maps and speaking with some staff officers, Pershing ordered Traub to keep attacking "regardless of cost."[23] In doing so, he opened the door to catastrophe.

No words could do justice to Montrebeau Wood on the morning of September 29. The Missouri-Kansas Division had captured the wood the previous afternoon, at terrible cost. Bodies and pieces of bodies littered it now, alongside shattered and discarded equipment, shrapnel, unexploded shells, and cracked canisters seeping gas. Boglike shell holes, blasted pillboxes, and splintered logs and branches concealed prone forms of men huddled against icy rain falling from a black sky. German shells exploded everywhere, illuminating the nightmare scene with brief flashes of light, but the soldiers didn't notice and didn't move.

As dawn approached, officers tried to organize their soldiers for the attack that Pershing demanded. It was not an easy business. Many of the men they tried to rouse were dead; others had to be shaken and kicked repeatedly before they rose, sodden and dazed like zombies from the grave.[24] There was no coffee, only a little cold food. This revived the Doughboys a bit, but with awareness came a sinking realization that the officers were telling them to attack—again. Sergeant Triplet reviewed his platoon of the 140th Regiment:

> The outfit looked terrible and I knew just how they felt, exhausted, sleepy, hungry, worn down, and sick. Worse, they didn't feel lucky any more. They'd lost the soldier's bullet-proof ego, that feeling that "others may get hit, but I never." I knew how they felt because I felt the same way. I knew that the next time I stuck my head out in the open I'd catch a bullet in the teeth. Not even the clowns were wisecracking any more.[25]

Traub ordered the division to attack at 5:30 A.M. behind a rolling artillery barrage, without fixed objective but in the direction of Exermont and the Bois de Boyon. No provision could be made for coordination, or for reserves. The division's four regiments were so intermingled as to be practically indistinguishable, and their battalions no longer existed as such. Provisional brigades had been organized, but only on paper. In practice, the men just followed whatever officer happened to be closest.

A smattering of artillery fire announced the moment of attack. Whistles blew. Officers shouted. And nothing happened. After four minutes, about 125 Doughboys appeared from the woods on the left and cautiously followed a major across muddy fields toward Exermont. They flopped down in a ravine southwest of the village and sat there for several minutes, until artillery and machine-gun fire hit them from three sides. Individuals, small groups, and then the entire formation got up, "and quietly, without orders and without panic, slowly retired to the protection of the woods from which they had just come."[26] The major begged them to stay. They ignored him.

That ended the attack on the left. The 137th and 139th, theoretically holding that part of the line, were leaderless. Lieutenant Colonel Carl Ristine of the 139th had just returned from his sojourn behind enemy lines and hardly knew where he was. The 137th's commander, fifty-two-year-old Colonel Clad Hamilton, had spent most of his life at a desk in a Topeka, Kansas, law office. Montrebeau Wood broke him. That morning, while watching the 125 men advance toward Exermont, Hamilton suddenly felt dizzy. "I'm gassed," he croaked to an aide, and collapsed. He had to be carried out on a stretcher.[27]

On the right, Lieutenant Colonel Channing Delaplane led about one thousand men from the 139th and 140th—the remnants of the 138th could not get organized—north out of Montrebeau Wood. A few tanks joined them, but the American artillery lent no support. The German guns were alert. "A horrendous howl-rumble-scream of incoming shells and our world exploded with a hundred thunderclaps," said Sergeant Triplet. "The battalion to our right disappeared in a cloud of haze, smoke, and flying mud. Fifty yards in front of us the mud was jumping in fountains." German 77s behind Exermont fired at them over open sights; their shells, coming in on a flat trajectory, skipped off the ground in front of the Americans and ricocheted, slicing men to pieces. Triplet saw the mud boil underfoot and inferred that machine guns were firing at them too, but in the cyclone of noise he couldn't distinguish the sound of the bullets. He knew there was gas, too, for he could see men breathing through the mouthpieces of their gas masks, leaving the face masks dangling free under their chins to maintain visibility. "Good idea," he thought, "but just at the moment I was too worried to bother about a mask."[28]

After five hundred yards the tanks quit and turned back. The infantry, as usual, kept going. Lieutenant Colonel Delaplane, limping from shrapnel in his leg, led them on.

> In the stunning, dumbing gust of war the men sensed with their physical bodies rather than their minds, that death was pouring past them in a flood. As if they were walking forward through a driving hailstorm they turned their faces to leeward and, leaning forward against the blast, pushed ahead with the point of shoulder offered to the gale.[29]

Halfway to Exermont, the Doughboys passed a cluster of dead bodies, remnants of an American attack that had wandered horribly off course the previous day. In a tiny hut they found two wounded men who had lain untended for twenty-four hours.[30] Machine-gun nests held them up, but the Americans stormed and destroyed them with savage, almost mindless fury. The German artillery barrage intensified as the troops approached Exermont, and Sergeant Triplet ran ahead as fast as he could, covering two hundred yards before he dove into an old sunken farm lane. Only a dozen men remained in his company.

As Lieutenant Colonel Delaplane reached the outskirts of Exermont, only four hundred of his original thousand men remained standing. Ahead, a bridge spanned a small creek. A platoon of the 139th under Lieutenant John McManigal reached it first, but a German machine gun on the other side of the creek mowed most of the men down before they could cross. McManigal, followed by Private Ernest Simpich, charged ahead regardless.

Brigadier General John J. Pershing and Marshal Ferdinand Foch at the latter's country home, 1918. Their cheerful poses belied the strained nature of their relationship.

Lieutenant Colonel George S. Patton and a Renault light tank at the First Army Tank School, Langres, France, in July 1918.

Supply wagons at a foggy crossroads in the Argonne Forest, September 1918. During the battle's first days, traffic jams caused frantic scenes behind the front lines, and left the Doughboys without food or water.

American field artillery firing from the ruins of Varennes by the Aire River, September 1918. German artillery was much more effective and caused terrible casualties.

77th Division Doughboys and French liaison officers prepare to advance into the Argonne Forest, September 26, 1918.

German barbed wire blanketed much of the Meuse-Argonne battlefield, severely slowing the American advance.

American tanks (French-made Renaults) advancing into battle, September 1918.

Tanks moving up near Boureuilles with the 28th Division infantry on September 26, 1918, the first day of the Meuse-Argonne battle. The Doughboys had high hopes for the tanks, but most of them either broke down or were blown to scrap by the German artillery.

Wounded soldier pauses to rest on the way to an aid station in Septsarges (visible in background), near Montfaucon, in September 1918. To reach the aid station, he would have to cross ground swept by German machine-gun fire.

77th Division Doughboys rest in a captured German trench in the Argonne Forest, September 26, 1918. Opportunities to rest would become rare in the days that followed.

Captain Harry S. Truman in France, July 1918. His battery of field artillery saw heavy fighting in the Meuse-Argonne, and on one occasion it was thrown into battle in a last ditch effort to halt an overwhelming German counterattack.

General Hunter Liggett, commanding I Corps and, after October 16, 1918, First Army. Quietly brilliant, he orchestrated the First Army's final breakthrough on November 1, 1918.

Major Charles Whittlesey (*front row, left*), commander of the famous Lost Battalion, and the headquarters company of the 308th Regiment, 77th Division.

African American infantry of the 92d Division advancing under camouflage netting toward the front in the Argonne Forest, September 1918. Brave but poorly led by their white officers, they were labeled cowards and ignominiously pulled out of battle after a few days in combat.

Street scene in Exermont shortly after its capture by troops of the 1st Division on October 4, 1918. Note the dead German soldier in the foreground.

The same scene moments later, with 1st Division Doughboys running for cover as Exermont comes under German artillery fire.

"Prisoners and Wounded" by the American war artist Harvey Thomas Dunn.

Corporal Erland Johnson, 58th Regiment, 4th Division, in the Bois de la Côte Lémont, October 2, 1918. The stresses of combat fatigue are etched on his face.

Shattered French church near the Argonne Forest serving as a first-aid station, October 1918.

"In the Front Line at Early Morning" by Harvey Thomas Dunn.

Looking west toward Châtel-Chéhéry and Hills 244 (*left*) and 223 (*right*), showing the open ground over which the 112th Regiment, 28th Division, advanced on October 7, 1918.

Photo taken from the crest of Hill 244, looking north toward Hill 223. The capture of this critical ground on October 7 led to the capure of the Argonne Forest and the relief of the Lost Battalion.

Private John Lewis Barkley, winner of the Medal of Honor near Cunel, October 7, 1918. From a post in an abandoned French tank, he single-handedly broke up a German counterattack on the 3d Division.

Father Francis Duffy, Chaplain of the 165th "New York" Regiment, 42d "Rainbow" Division. Stolid and brave, he ministered to the troops on the front lines, and criticized American generals for pointlessly wasting their soldiers' lives.

Alvin C. York at the site of his Medal-of-Honor–winning exploit on October 8, 1918. Photo taken in February 1919.

Brigadier General Douglas MacArthur (*left*), commanding the 84th Brigade, 42d "Rainbow" Division, with his chief of staff, in March 1919. MacArthur claimed to have survived a German artillery bombardment that killed every man around him.

General Charles P. Summerall, commanding 1st Division and, after October 16, 1918, V Corps. "General Summerall may be a son-of-a-bitch," his men said, "but thank God he's *our* son-of-a-bitch." Photo taken in 1926.

"Sunday Morning at Cunel," painting by Harvey Thomas Dunn. The Heights of Cunel and Romagne held the key to the German defenses.

American soldier inspects a German Maxim machine gun on the citadel overlooking Grandpré and the Aire River, one of many that inflicted terrible slaughter on the 78th Division in October 1918.

German machine-gun bunker near Etrayes. Nearby lay the body of a 79th Division Doughboy who was killed shortly before the end of the war in November 1918.

Dead Americans of the 79th Division awaiting burial near Etrayes on November 11, 1918, the last day of the war. They were among the 26,000 American soldiers who died in the Meuse-Argonne.

Victims of the Meuse-Argonne: amputees at Walter Reed Hospital, Washington, D.C., January 1919. Almost 100,000 soldiers, according to official figures, were wounded in the Meuse-Argonne, but thousands more casualties, especially victims of poison gas, never appeared on the official lists.

Sergeant Alvin C. York on troopship returning home in May 1919. The ghosts of the Meuse-Argonne would haunt him for the rest of his life.

A puff of dirt broke from the back of McManigal's mud-encrusted tunic, and he crumpled down on the bridge, a bullet hole in his chest. Another machine-gun burst hit Simpich in three places, breaking his thigh, shattering his kneecap, and puncturing his calf.[31]

The remainder of Delaplane's men bypassed the bridge and forded the stream in several places. Destroying the German machine guns, they entered the village and fought house to house with grenades and bayonets. The German garrison was not large, and its few survivors fled. Delaplane followed them a few hundred yards north of Exermont and dug in. He had six men with him and a few hundred more straggling behind.[32] Over the next few hours he collected the stragglers in a hastily dug ditch, unsupported on either flank and in full view of the enemy. Lieutenant McManigal and Private Simpich, unnoticed by their comrades, meanwhile crawled off the bridge and slithered down the muddy bank to get water from the stream. The lieutenant, weak and unable to talk for the blood that kept bubbling out of his mouth, slid up to the waist in the slimy water.

By noon, Delaplane's exposed force was the only organized American unit in the area. The 138th, which had been unable to move that morning, tried to push forward with 850 men but broke under German artillery fire and withdrew. Its commander, Lieutenant Colonel James S. Parker, died in the attack, leaving a captain in charge of the regiment. The 137th and 139th remained prone. The Germans had meanwhile withdrawn the shattered 1st Guards Division, which had been fighting the Missouri-Kansas Division since the offensive began. In its place they inserted the 5th Guards Division, commanded by one of the kaiser's sons, and the relatively fresh 52d Division. These now commenced a counterattack, carefully infiltrating around Delaplane's flanks and through the cracked and dispersed 35th Division lines all the way back to Montrebeau Wood. At the same time the German artillery, directed by airplanes, methodically eliminated American trenches and emplacements, down to individual foxholes.

By the time Delaplane's men realized what the Germans were up to it was almost too late. At 1:00 P.M., enemy soldiers entered Exermont and the colonel ordered an immediate retreat. With Delaplane at their rear, firing a Chauchat, the Americans fled across the rolling fields above Exermont, leaping hedges, shell holes, and innumerable corpses. Germans popped up along the way, firing rifles and hurling grenades, and the Doughboys tackled them head-on. The village once again erupted in close-quarters combat as the Americans forced their way through the streets, across the bridge, and back toward Montrebeau Wood. Delaplane inspired the men through it all, firing his Chauchat until it grew red-hot in his hands. "That new colonel is a fightin' son of a bitch," said a Doughboy. "Dogface they call him, Dogface Delaplane. He can shoot too. Got him a Chauchat and was right there with the rear guard all the way back from town."[33]

Lieutenant McManigal and Private Simpich, still in the stream below Exermont, heard Delaplane and a few Doughboys pound across the bridge overhead and watched them run off toward Montrebeau Wood, firing wildly. Soon they heard the more measured tread of the German pursuers. The two wounded Americans kept quiet, and the Germans moved on. Next came two Doughboys bearing a stretcher. Simpich shouted for help, but the soldiers told him that they had been taken prisoner and could only pick up German wounded. They left and never returned. Around midafternoon a German soldier walked across the bridge and saw the two wounded men, the lieutenant half in the stream and Simpich lying nearby. He gazed at them quietly for a moment and then raised his rifle, aiming it carefully between McManigal's eyes. The lieutenant, "in that neutral state between consciousness and delirium," watched the German apathetically, wondering irrelevantly whether he would need to take up as much slack in his rifle's trigger as Americans did with the Enfield.

Simpich spoke sharply in German. Amazed, the enemy soldier replied, and the two men commenced a heated argument. Finally the German shouldered his rifle and stalked angrily away, evidently deeply offended at being prevented from making what seemed to him like a mercy killing. Simpich had told him that other Americans could see the bridge, and that if he killed McManigal they would find him and "take him apart, one joint at a time." The wounded men would stay there by the stream for another two days and nights, McManigal delirious with the sensation that he had left his body and was hovering above it, until the Germans finally took them prisoner.[34]

Delaplane arrived in Montrebeau Wood at around 2:00 P.M. and discovered that the entire line had collapsed. Germans had infiltrated the woods from every direction, scattering the Americans and taking dozens of prisoners. Panicked officers shouted contradictory orders, trying to rally their units, or just ran. Someone clutched an order from Traub sanctioning a withdrawal from Exermont. Bayonets flashed and grenades exploded, engulfing the woods in a maelstrom of violence. By 3:00 P.M., the Germans had begun forming an infantry line on the woods' south edge, while many Americans, lacking orders, continued to hold positions on the north edge.[35] As they grew aware of the situation, the remaining troops in the woods fled madly. Frightened Doughboys streamed across the open ground south of the woods and were shelled savagely. The 35th Division was in a state of rout.

The only units in the division still capable of fighting were the 110th Engineers, under Lieutenant Colonel Edward Stayton of Missouri, and the 128th Machine Gun Battalion. They occupied old trenches below Montrebeau Wood, the engineers on Hill 231, and the machine gunners on a ridge just north of Baulny. Knowing they were the last line of defense—the only hope, in fact, of preventing a complete German breakthrough—the engineers worked furiously to improve their positions, oblivious to the routed infantry that streamed continuously past. They arranged their trenches around one central strongpoint, an old German pillbox facing the wrong way. Above, columns of smoke rose and drifted from burning dumps set alight by German artillery, nearby and in the zones of the 28th Division on the left and the 91st Division on the right. Massive German counterattacks were under way in those sectors too. Major General Traub, who had spent the morning in Baulny, meanwhile discreetly departed for points south. One of his staff officers fired a message to corps: "Germans are coming right on us."[36]

German aircraft spotted the engineers and machine gunners, and heavy artillery fire soon "traveled back and forth on the lines in a wicked arpeggio of thunderous chords, rising from upheavals of earth and rolling clouds of acrid, yellow smoke, blurring the view from our sweating engineers. For further distraction there flew overhead from moment to moment rounds of high-breaking shrapnel from the left rear out of the Argonne Forest."[37] Many officers went down, but noncoms took over and the men remained steady. Soldiers wrapped casualties in blankets and tenderly placed them in old German dugouts.

Just before dusk, German infantry filtered out of Montrebeau Wood in small groups and darted closer to the American lines. Their attack seemed to come from all directions, first here, then there, giving the Americans no time to concentrate and keeping them guessing where the enemy would come from next. The engineers and machine gunners held, sometimes beating the Germans off with picks and shovels. As the Americans repulsed the first German attacks, officers coaxed some of the stragglers hovering behind Hill 231 into rejoining the lines. Captain Ralph E. Truman, the 140th's intelligence officer and a cousin of Harry's, waved his pistol and threatened to shoot anyone who tried to retreat.

The batteries of Captain Harry Truman's artillery regiment were now practically in the firing line. A number of French batteries cooperating with them hitched up and fled. A French officer shouted to D Battery that they should pull out too, and one of Truman's Irishmen socked him in the jaw. Truman and his fellow battery commanders instead lowered their guns to a flat trajectory, preparing to fire over open sights.[38] Farther back, I Corps ordered the 82d Division to prepare to leave the reserve and move into the lines in case the 35th Division fell apart.

But the Germans didn't come. The day's fighting had disorganized them too, and they had suffered heavy losses. Instead, they settled down in Montrebeau Wood as darkness fell. The Americans on Hill 231 could hear them all night as they methodically eliminated the small groups of Doughboys that had been left behind. There was nothing anyone could do to help the isolated soldiers. Yet although the division was a wreck, the line—thanks to the heroics and quick thinking of the engineers and machine gunners— remained intact.

Somehow, Joe Rizzi found a moment during the fight for Hill 231 to look to the west toward Apremont, in the 28th Division zone: "Shells were falling, dust flying and fire breaking out in several sections of the town. Its grimness seemed to impart, 'Now that you fools have left me a mere skeleton, what in hell more do you want of me? I am not worth having.' "[39] The Germans evidently thought Apremont very much worth having. They were dying for it by the score.

The 110th Regiment, holding Apremont, and the 109th, just to the west, attacked early on September 29 but made little progress. Then the Germans swarmed in from the northwest, down the valley of the Aire. They attacked, were beaten back, and attacked again. The Pennsylvanians followed up each German repulse with a thrust of their own, and were defeated in turn. It settled into a contest of wills—a match between two sluggers, each trying to inflict maximum damage and outlast the other.

The Americans had several tanks from Patton's Tank Corps, but German field artillery—77s brought up for this purpose—blasted many of the flimsy Renaults to pieces. Enemy infantry finished off several others before the Americans got wise. Propagandists claimed that foot soldiers always ran from tanks, but the Germans were no longer afraid. They had fought the steel monsters for two and a half years. Unsupported by infantry, tanks fell easy prey to antitank rifles and determined soldiers toting satchels of grenades and other explosives. Adapting from experience, the Americans detailed infantrymen to escort the big machines into battle. Private Maurice De Frehn, who had drifted away from the 112th, was rounded up as a straggler near Apremont and pressed into service as a tank escort. "Keep your eyes opened for those dutch men," an officer warned him, "that they dont climb up on the front of the tank as they are very clever at it."[40] Tanks had been billed as saviors of the infantry. Now the infantry protected *them*.

By late afternoon the Germans had gained the upper hand in the contest for Apremont. Each thrust and counterthrust ended a little closer to the village. Just before 6:00 P.M., divisional headquarters ordered the Americans to organize Apremont as a strongpoint and defend it to the last. A few minutes later, a German wave—at least three battalions of infantry, with heavy machine guns—surged down the valley of the Aire, up the bluffs, and into the village. Dusk had fallen, and as darkness swathed the rain-swept streets it grew difficult to tell friend from foe. Dim shapes ran from house to house, lit by bursts of rifle and machine-gun fire or the flashes of grenade explosions.

Many grim encounters took place. A machine-gun company from Reading, Pennsylvania, turned a corner by the church and ran into a group of Germans coming the other way. Both sides opened fire at point-blank range before scattering. A wild, running melee ensued. One American lieutenant, shot through the lungs, lay dying in the middle of the street. Another lieutenant ran, firing his pistol at fleeting shapes of coal-scuttle-helmeted soldiers, and became lost. Eventually he found himself back near the church. Circling it slowly, he almost tripped over a German machine-gun nest. He waved his pistol and took three prisoners.[41] There were just too many Germans, however, and by evening the village had fallen under their control.

On the left, attacks and counterattacks surged back and forth over Le Chêne Tondu Ridge. The 112th, which had spent the previous night in a sunken road on the ridge's crest, withdrew early that morning to permit an artillery barrage on the German-occupied opposite slope. The barrage, fired by naval guns, six-inch howitzers, and 75s, sent trees and dirt flying everywhere and created a massive cloud of smoke. Instead of hitting the Germans, however, it fell mostly along the sunken road. When it ended, the 112th Regiment climbed the ridge, crossed the shell-blasted crest, and ran straight into a furious blast of enemy fire. A counterattack then forced it off the ridge entirely.[42]

By 8:00 P.M. the 28th Division had lost both Apremont and Le Chêne Tondu Ridge. But changes were under way. That morning Pershing had relieved Brigadier General Thomas Darragh, who commanded the 55th Brigade, which was holding Apremont, and replaced him with his own intelligence chief, Brigadier General Dennis Nolan. A forty-six-year-old West Point graduate, Nolan looked austere and professorial, which he was. But he was also a former football player—he had been an All-American at West Point—and a decorated soldier who had won two silver stars in Cuba. A brilliant intelligence officer and military administrator, Nolan also had that quality that Pershing valued most, drive. He helped to bring focus back to 28th Division headquarters and turn the tide in the fight for Apremont.

Night attacks frequently end in disorganization and defeat, but Nolan decided to take the risk. Reasoning that the Germans must not be allowed to dig in, at about 9:00 P.M. Nolan sent his troops back into Apremont one more time. Fighting in near-complete darkness but stirred by their new brigadier general, who came up to direct the fighting personally, the Doughboys pried the Germans out of the village and sent them fleeing back down the bluffs to the valley of the Aire. The line had been reestablished, but Nolan knew the Germans would come again. In preparation, he ordered his troops to establish four strongpoints around Apremont. He also got the 109th Field Artillery to send four 75s up for defense of the town.[43]

On the Keystone Division's left, meanwhile, another attack recovered at least part of Le Chêne Tondu Ridge. The bloodied and wasted 112th Regiment had halted while a battalion of the 111th sidestepped into its place. "Never before did we see such a steep hill to climb," said one Doughboy; "it was almost straight up and down." The 111th climbed it anyhow, and had nearly reached the sunken road when the American artillery fired another heavy barrage. It landed on neither the Germans nor the 111th, but on the unlucky 112th. "Everybody," a company war diary reported simply, "ran for their lives." The friendly fire fell for five minutes before somebody found a flare gun and signaled the gunners to raise their fire. They complied, and finally started hitting the German lines. With heavy casualties, the 111th took the ridge crest and pushed a little beyond into the woods on the far slope, while the 112th spent another night in the sunken road.[44]

"I want to get out of all this mess, it's too terrible," Private Charles Minder wrote to his mother on the night of September 29. A member of the 77th Division's 306th Machine Gun Battalion and a German American, Minder had sworn to himself and his family that he would not kill anyone during the war. He had just broken that pledge. Earlier that day, watching from a shell hole as Doughboys advanced up a hill in front of him, Minder had seen a German officer directing his machine-gun crew "to shoot down the Infantry, which he was doing very nicely. From the angle where I was, I could see everything very plainly, as I was almost on his right flank. The Infantry boys couldn't see the machine gun nest very well. I opened up our gun and let him have it, I was so sore at the moment. He was hitting our Infantry; they were falling one after another. It was terrible! I had to shoot."

After the action, Minder went over to the machine-gun nest. He found one German unconscious and the other barely opening his eyes. Looking at his face, a terrible thought came into Minder's mind: Had he just killed his uncle Franz, who lived in Germany?

> I didn't know what to say or do. I stood there dumb. The others had gone on. I lifted his head, and blood spurted from the wound on the side of his neck. I asked him, *Sint sie nicht Franz Barg, von Bremen aus?* He opened his eyes very slowly again and looked at me. He tried to talk but couldn't. I didn't know what to do and started to cry. The man opened his eyes once more and smiled as I grasped his hand; then his eyes closed, and he was still. He gave one slight gasp and passed on. I knelt there for a little while just dumb. I couldn't think or do anything. Of course, he was not Uncle Franz, but I kept thinking of him in the German lines and my cousins there too. An officer came along and started hollering at me: "What the hell are you doing there? This is no time for souvenir hunting! Don't you know we are advancing? Leave those dead Germans alone! Come on!" I gathered up the ammunition boxes and followed on. I was so heartsick I couldn't talk.[45]

The 77th Division took what the Germans gave them, and not much more. The 305th Regiment, on the right flank, advanced a mile thanks to a German withdrawal. The 306th, to its left, advanced half a mile. The 307th received no gifts, but butted in grim futility against a machine gun–infested ridge concealing the Depôt de Machines, a huge and vitally important German supply dump.[46] Teams of Doughboys with jam-prone Chauchats loped through the woods, tackled enemy nests, and returned on stretchers and sporting bandages and slings. German artillery fired with deadly accuracy.

The 308th, on the left flank, had a more complicated problem. Four of its companies had become isolated during the previous evening in a wooded ravine about half a mile southeast of Binarville. The two officers in command of the force, Majors Charles Whittlesey and Kenneth Budd, had decided to stay put and wait for relief. They spent a difficult night under rain so heavy that it filled foxholes to the brim with mud and water. Now, on September 29, the troops had run out of food and were getting low on ammunition. Scouts found Germans everywhere, making standard communications with regimental headquarters impossible. Whittlesey and Budd had four messenger pigeons and used all of them during the day, reporting their positions and calling for food and ammunition. "We understand," they explained in one message, "our mission is to advance, and to maintain our strength here."[47] And so they stayed. By evening, however, relief remained far off.

Lieutenant Colonel Frederick Smith, a quiet, competent officer, had briefly taken over the regiment after the removal of Colonel A. F. Prescott the previous day. Prescott's replacement, the nervous and irritable Colonel Cromwell Stacey, assumed command on the morning of September 29. He sent Smith with two officers and ten soldiers bearing ammunition to find and relieve the isolated companies. Smith's guide led him deep into the woods and then strayed off course, leading the party beyond the regiment's left flank and into view of a German strongpoint. As the Germans opened fire, Smith yelled for his men to take cover, drew his pistol, and emptied it into the enemy positions fifty yards away. Shot in the side, he popped up again and kept firing until his men were under cover. He then hobbled over to where his men had dropped some ammunition, and dragged back two boxes of grenades—all "in plain view" of the enemy, which kept up a steady fire. He attempted to spot the machine guns in hopes of rushing them, but the Germans saw him first and shot him down. His death earned him a posthumous Medal of Honor, but left Colonel Stacey still without any idea of how to reach the isolated companies.[48]

Whittlesey did not depend only on carrier pigeons to communicate with headquarters. Late that afternoon, he ordered Lieutenant Arthur McKeogh, who had been leading Chauchat teams against German machine-gun nests, to take two enlisted men and find a way back to the regiment. McKeogh picked Privates John J. Monson and Jack Herschowitz—the latter a German Jew whom the lieutenant teasingly called a "buttonhole maker"—to go with him. Bearing pistols, the trio slipped through the woods and moved cautiously for forty-five minutes until they found a trail leading south. Jogging along, they turned a corner and ran headlong into two German officers. Both sides fired. McKeogh took a bullet in the arm, and one of the Germans died with a shot to the head. The other ran away. Fearing that he would bring back help, the Americans ran and hid in the underbrush.

McKeogh and his companions stayed concealed until sunset, when they set off again, crawling on their elbows. After what seemed like miles of mud and bracken, the lieutenant spotted low shapes in the darkness and decided they were either stumps or German helmets. Slight movements revealed that they had blundered into a warren of enemy foxholes, and the click of a rifle's safety told McKeogh that their presence had not gone unnoticed. He jumped up and screamed, "Spread out and beat it!" The Germans opened fire, and the Americans ran "hell bent through the brush." McKeogh saw what looked like an open ditch, jumped in, and landed feetfirst on a German soldier. The lieutenant straddled him like a horse. Another soldier stood facing him, gaping in surprise. McKeogh recovered first. Pulling out his automatic pistol, he fired two shots into the standing German's face, and fired again between his legs into the other soldier's back. He then leapt out of the trench and fled, pursued by "an uproar of shots and flashes." A root snagged his foot, and he tumbled down a slope into a pile of leaves. He hid there while the Germans searched, heard the report of distant pistol fire—Monson had killed another German—and then took off again under cover of a heavy rain squall. All three Americans—including Private Herschowitz, who was sick with influenza and running a fever of 105 degrees—made it to Colonel Stacey's command post later that night, completing a journey that earned them several decorations. More important, they brought information that would lead to the rescue of Whittlesey and his men.[49]

✳

GEORGES Clemenceau, the fiery old French premier known as the Tiger, visited First Army headquarters at Souilly on September 29. His persistent advocacy of amalgamation had made him unpopular there, but the Frenchman beamed happiness and goodwill. The Americans had captured Montfaucon, and by way of thanksgiving he had come to inspire them with his personal presence. He would go to the front, cheer the Doughboys, and visit Montfaucon. Pershing tried to talk him out of it. Montfaucon, he said, remained under enemy fire. Moreover, although Pershing did and would continue to deny that road congestion existed as "a general condition" behind First Army, he admitted that at this moment there might be just a bit more traffic than usual because of the impending relief of the 35th Division by the 1st Division.[50] Clemenceau, who rarely changed his mind on any subject, would have none of it. Over four years of war he had seen the entire western front, and during the Battle of Verdun—a much bigger affair, he might have reminded Pershing, than the Meuse-Argonne—he had driven every inch of these same roads. He thought he had seen everything. He hadn't.

Clemenceau set off in his limousine, revving up his powerful voice to clear slow-moving trucks and wagons out of the way. Five miles from Montfaucon his car came to a dead stop. A long line of trucks, cars, wagons, carts, artillery, and horses, surrounded by a milling mass of soldiers, snaked over the hills ahead. None of the soldiers and drivers cursed like they had during the battle's first days. Instead, they stood about, smoking cigarettes and looking bored. They had evidently been there a long time. The Tiger refused to accept the halt as anything more than temporary. Yet although he yelled, and his driver honked his horn, the other drivers only smiled and waved cheerfully. They could not move their vehicles aside more than a few inches. Enraged at their stubbornness, the seventy-seven-year-old premier jumped out of his car and marched across the shell-pocked fields to a hill about a mile ahead. His escort, a French captain, found him there an hour later, hopping mad. From the hill, Clemenceau could see the incredible congestion extending northward all the way to Montfaucon, still a mere pimple on the horizon. Cursing, the premier turned and walked back to the car, which the driver turned around with difficulty and drove away.[51] The premier nurtured his anger all the way back to Paris. First Army, he decided, needed new leadership.

Pershing had fought bitterly for an independent American army and got what he wanted. Now his pigeons had come home to roost. Clemenceau's chief of staff saw the American commander in chief at Souilly and pitied him:

> I could read clearly in his eyes that, at that moment, he realized his mistake. His soldiers were dying bravely, but they were not advancing, or very little, and their losses were heavy. All that great body of men which the American Army represented was literally stuck with paralysis because "the brain" didn't exist, because the generals and their staffs lacked experience. With enemies like the Germans, this kind of war couldn't be improvised.[52]

How far Pershing sensed the shakiness of First Army is a mystery. Several divisions, he knew, needed immediate relief, and he had already arranged for their replacement. To that end a brief pause had become necessary. While some local attacks continued on September 30, First Army as a whole shifted to the defensive. For the most part, though, Pershing remained optimistic in the soundness of his overall plan. Bring some veteran divisions into line, replace inefficient commanders, clear up the occasional supply bottleneck, and resume the attack, and the German defenses would buckle. Of that he felt sure.

Pershing made frequent visits near the front and encouraged his generals to do the same. His rank and importance, however, precluded him from actually entering the lines, and there is no indication that he understood or even thought much about his soldiers' situation.[53] He passed columns of battle-weary Doughboys on his regular trips to and from corps and division headquarters, and sometimes stopped to give impromptu speeches, but his assessments of First Army's situation made no reference to battle fatigue. Instead, Pershing attributed episodes of weakness to disorganization and ineffective command. He understood that soldiers might straggle or even break under fire, but instead of exploring the conditions that led to demoralization he insisted that the officers enforce both strict, West Point–style discipline and a "high standard of sportsmanlike cooperation that appeals to our fine young American soldiers." When that didn't work, officers should handle shirkers on the spot by shooting them down. If they felt squeamish, the officers could arrest cowardly soldiers for later trial and execution.[54]

Yet if Pershing made no allowances for fatigue in his soldiers, he also made none for himself. Constant work and strain eroded his physique and even his posture. He lost weight, his Mexican tan faded to a "ghostly gray," his eyes were sunken, and he slumped at his desk.[55] But he never complained. It was a commander's duty to lead under all circumstances and bear up under even the heaviest strain without asking for sympathy. No one could tell Pershing what suffering meant. The Doughboys must bear trials in the same way he did. Willpower sufficed for him. It should be good enough for them.

—•◆•—

Relief

SEPTEMBER 30

The last day of September dawned windy, rainy, and cold. Soldiers, many of them ill with pneumonia and dysentery,[1] shivered in water-filled trenches and foxholes, German artillery fire crashing around them. In such circumstances they were happy for small blessings. Here and there, food and water had finally made it to the front. The occasional ambulance bumped around shell holes to dressing stations and evacuated wounded Doughboys, many of them nursing wounds inflicted days earlier. The finest blessing of all was reserved for those who heard the divine word: relief.

On the right, III Corps' 33d and 4th Divisions remained static while the 80th Division temporarily withdrew. In the center, V Corps' three divisions were all being relieved. The 79th Division, "Kuhn's Singing Army," wasn't singing now. According to the official tally—almost certainly an understatement—the division had taken 3,591 casualties since September 26. The survivors didn't feel much better off than the comrades they had lost. Major Charles DuPuy described them as

> a handful of men, their faces drawn, their eyes sunken with a dead look, and almost all affected more or less from shell shock, and so weak were some that they died of exhaustion on the trip to the rear. Others were so used up that they could not carry their ammunition belts and rifles, being just able to stagger along at a pace of not more than a mile and half an hour. When they

finally came out of the fight, with more than one-third of their horses and mules killed, dragging their mule-carts by hand, they looked more like a defeated force than a victorious one.[2]

✳

OFFICERS were as exhausted, physically and emotionally, as their men. Colonel Oscar J. Charles of the 316th Regiment, whose senseless attack orders had nearly destroyed his regiment, reported to his medical officer that he felt "run down due to lack of rest and nourishment" and "had lost his usual energy and pep." The doctor evacuated Charles to Neurological Hospital No. 1, diagnosing him with "anxiety neurosis in line of duty."[3] After treatment the colonel returned to duty, probably to his men's dismay. The story was the same with the troops of the 37th "Buckeye" Division, which had suffered 3,060 casualties since September 26, and the 91st Division, which had taken almost 4,700 casualties in the same period. The troops of the Wild West Division, a few days earlier among the most eager and aggressive men in First Army, had descended to a state of "loggish stupor." The division's units had shrunk to mere husks of their former selves. One company had only 18 men out of its original 179; lieutenants or sergeants commanded many of the others.[4]

For I Corps, the fighting had not quite ended. At Apremont, Brigadier General Dennis Nolan's Doughboys easily repulsed a German counterattack; the 35th Division, broken and routed on the previous day, faced a more serious assault against its rearguard positions on Hill 231. Harry Truman's battery was in the thick of the fight, as always. Runner Paul Shaffer carried an order to the battery as it fired in support of the 110th Engineers. Running frantically from shells that seemed to scream "Where are you, Corporal Sergeant Shaffer?" he "reached the battery in nothing flat, as muddy as an alligator, all the skin off my nose."

> Captain Harry S. Truman was standing there, his tin hat pushed on the back of his head, directing salvos into some spot toward the northeast. He was a banty officer in spectacles, and when he read my message he started runnin' and cussin' all at the same time, shouting for the guns to turn northwest. He ran about a hundred yards to a little knoll, and what he saw didn't need binoculars. I never heard a man cuss so well or so intelligently, and I'd shoed a million mules. He was shouting back ranges and giving bearings.
>
> The battery didn't say a word. They must have figured the cap'n could do the cussin' for the whole outfit. It was a great sight, like the center ring in Barnum and Bailey at the close of the show, everything clockwork, setting fuses, cutting fuses, slapping shells into breeches and jerking lanyards before the

man hardly had time to bolt the door. Shell cases were flipping back like a juggler's act, clanging on tin hats of the ammunition passers, the guns just spitting fire—spit-spit-spit-spit.

Then Captain Truman ran down the knoll and cussed 'em to fire even faster. When he ran back up the hill still cussin', I forgot how I didn't want to get killed and I ran with him, even though my bit tongue was hanging out and a tooth sticking through my lip. I couldn't see our infantry. It must have been driven back to the little knoll, trying to crawl around and change front. Beyond it was some mighty fine grazing land, and at the far end a clump of woods, pretty leaves still on the autumn trees. The leaves were falling fast, shells breaking into them. This time Captain Truman had his binoculars on them. I finally made out what he saw. There were groups of Germans at the edge of the woods, stooping low and coming on slowly with machine guns on their hips, held by shoulder straps. He shouted some cusswords filled with figures down to the battery, and shells started breaking into the enemy clumps. Whole legs were soon flying through the air. He really broke up that counterattack. He was still there being shot at when I came to my senses and got off the knoll.[5]

The Germans didn't come again, and the remnants of the 35th Division withdrew that night. It had taken, according to initial reports, more than 8,000 casualties, a figure later officially revised to 6,006.[6] In either case, the toll of Missouri-Kansas men was far higher than any other division in the line. The survivors were wretched, exhausted—and transformed. During the first two days of the offensive, they had confidently expected victory, and then sought vengeance for the deaths of their comrades. Those feelings had now disappeared, replaced by feelings of bitterness and, for some, disillusionment. "There was no sign of revenge in this sorry looking bunch of men," observed Joe Rizzi.

> Our lesson was severely taught us. Our enemy fought on because he thought just as we all thought, "Right or wrong—my country." Company A finally realized this like every other man who had fought. England never did anything for us. France had done less. . . . But, here we were fighting. Fighting for what? To justify five words with deep meaning—"Right or wrong, my country."[7]

Ultimately, though, only one thing mattered to the Doughboys: "the fact of being alive *and back in the world*."[8]

✱

THE 77th Division, alone of all the units in First Army, continued attacking on September 30. The Argonne was cold—in the morning the ground and trees glistened with frost, and the mud was half frozen—and denser than ever. Private Minder's depression grew deeper with every moment he spent there. "I feel like a man of fifty, my bones ache so," he wrote. "What if I do get hit; it might get me out of this mess! I don't want to kill anymore."[9] But the Doughboys soldiered on.

Captain Walter Rainsford's company of the 307th Regiment waited in the woods that afternoon while the artillery fired a desultory barrage against the Germans. The barrage ceased, and "at once the whole forest began to echo with a sound like a hundred pneumatic riveters at work. We moved forward into a close wall of foliage, combed and re-combed by the traversing bullets, and we fired blindly into the leaves as we went. The noise was deafening." Rainsford led his company to the top of the ridge before the Depôt de Machines and paused. As happened all too often in these woods, two of his platoons had disappeared from sight. After a few minutes, a redheaded Irish runner named Patrick Gilligan emerged from the foliage and saluted Rainsford with a grin. The missing platoons followed behind him. "Never fear, Captain, and praise God it's here that we are and in time for it all, and yourself so safe," the private said. An instant later he fell with a bullet through the brain.

Rainsford's company pressed on to a point four hundred yards east of the later site of the "Lost Battalion," when the Americans heard voices shouting, "*Kamerad, kommen Sie hier*" and saw German helmets poking out above the bushes. Rainsford's favorite sergeant, a mild-mannered Englishman, started toward them. The captain called for him to stop. "It's all right, sir," the sergeant replied. "They're most anxious to surrender." The next moment he pitched over, mortally wounded, and Rainsford fired his pistol into the trees. Three other Germans came out of the woods on the left, hands raised in surrender, and again crying "*Kommen Sie hier*." Before the Americans could react, the Germans dropped to the ground as a machine gun opened fire above their heads.[10] More of this bitter, lawless kind of fighting took place during the afternoon into the evening, before the regiment finally broke through and captured the Depôt de Machines with tons of usable heavy equipment.[11]

The 308th had meanwhile rescued its four isolated companies, thanks to information provided by Lieutenant McKeogh and his two companions. Major Whittlesey and his men returned to the lines tired and thirsty, but still confident and unbeaten. They thought they had survived the worst.

The 77th Division's officers blamed Whittlesey's predicament in part on the withdrawal of the African American 368th Regiment from his left flank. That unit had fallen into disorder over the previous two days, and by the morning of September 30 the French had already pulled most of it out of the line. The First Battalion remained temporarily in line on the right, but the French Fourth Army issued orders for it to sit quietly while French dismounted cavalry assaulted Binarville to its left. It was then supposed to withdraw into reserve. The orders went awry, however, and did not reach the battalion until evening. In the meantime, the Americans joined the attack. They entered Binarville two hours later, ahead of the French. A day later they withdrew.

This achievement did not of course prevent the battalion's white commander from denigrating his men. "Every time the many halts under none too severe fire were made," he later testified, "I personally and often at the point of the pistol literally drove forward the battalion."

> Without my presence or that of any other white officer right on the firing line I am absolutely positive that not a single colored officer would have advanced with his men. The cowardice shown by the men was abject. The officers when I was personally present did not run but carried out orders but immediately the advance began it almost as soon stopped as soon as the officers and men were beyond the sound of my voice. . . . The fighting spirit does not exist among the men, they are rank cowards, there is no other word for it.[12]

No official attempt was ever made to gather testimony from the 368th Regiment's black officers and troops. Their perspective on the battle remains unknown.[13]

✳

THUS ended the Meuse-Argonne offensive's first—but by no means bloodiest—phase. Casualty estimates vary, and in fact nobody, not even Pershing or his staff, knew how many soldiers had been killed or wounded. Official postwar estimates were usually whittled down from after-action reports and did not include many "temporarily" incapacitated soldiers who left their units and returned after periods ranging from a few days to several weeks—for example, the lightly wounded and gassed, the fatigued or shell-shocked, and stragglers. Thus, the official tabulation of verified killed and wounded for the nine divisions in combat from September 26 until early October is about twenty-six thousand. However, if one includes the incapacitated—soldiers who returned to duty eventually but nevertheless had to be deducted from their division's combat strength for part, or all, of the remainder of the war—the figure must be at least twice that number. Some recent, unofficial estimates of First Army's actual losses for the last five days of September approach seventy-five thousand.[14]

Simple statistics, of course, cannot tell the whole story, especially the human impact. For tens of thousands of men, casualties of war, the battle had just begun. Private Morris Martin, the little red-haired runner from the 91st Division who had been badly wounded in the arm on September 27, learned this when he reached an evacuation hospital the following day:

> My first impression was that I had been carried into a slaughterhouse by mistake. There must have been fifteen or twenty operating tables, and they were all occupied. They slapped me onto a table and I had a few moments to glance around before they started to pouring the ether to me. It was a horrible sight. Blood, mangled arms, legs, heads and bodies. Some limbs had been shot off; some were being taken off, and the nauseating smell of blood, mixed with ether was all over the place. I was thankful when I lost consciousness, and drifted off to blissful forgetfulness.

He woke up in a large recovery ward, with the sun shining through the windows and white-clad nurses moving from bed to bed. But the sense of relaxation didn't last. His previous experiences had brought home the physical toll of battle. Now he witnessed the emotional toll. The ward, he wrote, echoed like Bedlam with the cries of shell-shocked men. "Some were laughing; some were crying, while some were swearing like the proverbial sailor." He and they could still hear the distant rumble of guns at the front.

> I knew that the rest of the boys were still pushing on. Lying there in the nice clean bed, I gave myself over to some reflections. I recalled what Turner had said the day before when he was helping to dress my arm. Something about getting out of this Hell and having a chance to rest and get enough to eat anyway. Those boys up there were still in that Hell, and the end wasn't in sight yet. Closing my eyes I could still see those mangled and bloody bodies of my buddies, and I began to wonder what it was all about.[15]

✱

ARTILLERY, not machine guns, caused the largest number of casualties— about 75 percent, according to some estimates. Shrapnel caused terrible wounds that were much harder to treat than bullet wounds. They were more difficult to close, recovery took longer, and infection was more common. Gas was even more insidious. Many thousands of soldiers took what seemed like only light whiffs of gas and remained in service, never reporting as casualties, only to find days, months, or even years later that their lungs had been damaged. Some, weakened by gas, fell victim to illnesses like influenza and pneumonia.

Combat fatigue, trauma, and stress were only dimly understood. Men called them shell shock or war neurosis without knowing what the terms meant. Many mentally debilitated soldiers who would have been evacuated today remained in the line and were never reported as casualties. Understanding officers gave them light duties until they seemed to have recovered. Less understanding officers called them cowards and drove them back to the front, or—like Patton, who claimed to have killed a frightened Doughboy with his shovel—physically abused or even killed them. Badly shell-shocked soldiers who reported to hospitals were treated with all the tools that doctors and nurses had at their disposal—which is to say, sympathy, rest, food, and clean beds—but without psychological expertise.

The casualties overwhelmed First Army's medical system. All the heroic work of doctors, nurses, and orderlies could not keep up with the immense flow of sick and wounded. Harvey Cushing, a Harvard surgeon who had served for years with the British in Flanders, had never seen the likes before, and neither had his fellow doctors. One doctor from a nearby unit staggered into Cushing's hospital on October 2, reporting:

> Late cases—awful wounds—hospital on a hillside—promised an evacuation with 20 ambulances last night—100 severely wounded brought down to the roadside ready to be loaded—no ambulances came till noon the next day, and then only three—dreadful condition of cases brought in, many of them three days old—often from 24 to 30 hours in the ambulance on the way down without food—frequently the ambulances bring in dead.

On October 3, the AEF reported that sick and wounded soldiers occupied 84.7 percent of its hospital beds, along with 60 percent of its emergency beds. A week later, it reported the base hospitals 107.9 percent full, with 73.3 percent of its emergency beds occupied.[16] Thousands of the men in these beds had fallen sick, with sixteen thousand new influenza cases reporting to army hospitals in the week ending October 5.[17]

Women, particularly those of the Army Nurse Corps, played a central role in caring for the wounded. By the end of the war, 21,480 women served in the Army Nurse Corps, with hundreds more in the Red Cross.[18] Among the latter was Sarah Sand, who had been born in Norway in 1884 and immigrated to Grand Forks County, North Dakota, when she was eight. She began nursing studies at age sixteen, received her diploma in 1905, and became director of nurses at Bismarck Hospital in 1916. In 1918 she volunteered as a Red Cross nurse, and reported to Base Hospital No. 60 at Bazoilles-sur-Meuse in early October. She took charge of its surgical ward just as trainloads of terribly wounded men began pouring into camp. Sand and her fellow nurses barely had time to treat the men before other trains carried them away to hospitals in Paris or England, making room for the next wave of casualties from the front.

> Many a time when these poor wounded lads would be barely cleaned up, their wounds dressed, and they seemed to have a chance to live, the officer would come in and order the ward to be vacated. . . . Then it became necessary to transfer their poor maimed bodies from the cot to the stretcher and then on to the train. Some would plead to be allowed to stay just a little longer but there were no favors shown. Others were coming from the hospital train from the Argonne . . . and room had to be made for them.

And all the while, doctors, nurses, and orderlies fell ill from influenza, making adequate staffing and treatment almost impossible.[19]

The YMCA provided women with another important opportunity to serve, sometimes very close to the front. Two sisters from Kentucky, Mary and Sunshine Sweeny, would earn gallantry citations for donning helmets and moving all the way up to the front lines in order to provide the troops of the 82d Division with food, hot chocolate, and coffee.[20] Thousands of others provided refreshments in rest camps. Some women volunteers drove ambulances—usually surreptitiously—or served as switchboard operators for the Army Signal Corps. Perhaps the best-known woman to all the Doughboys, however, was the Broadway singer Elsie Janis, who toured the western front for six months, doing shows for large crowds and sometimes inviting soldiers onstage for sing-alongs. Her shows later became models for the USO.

The importance of the work performed by the women and men of First Army's various support services is impossible to overestimate. The first five days of the Meuse-Argonne had been difficult, but they would seem easy compared to the horrendous fighting that would take place during the first three weeks of October. The Doughboys had a long road ahead. They were going to need all the help they could get.

CHAPTER 13

———•·•———

"God Damn It, Don't You Know
We're Going Over the Top"

OCTOBER 4

Corporal Freddie Stowers was a farmhand from Sandy Springs, South Carolina, and the grandson of a slave. He was also a Doughboy in the 371st Regiment of the African American 93d Division, which attacked German positions on Hill 188, near Ardeuil in the Champagne, on September 28. As the Americans crept closer to their objectives under fierce machine-gun and artillery fire, the Germans resorted to a ruse they had used elsewhere with considerable success. Ceasing fire, they left their trenches and signaled that they wanted to surrender. Stowers and his comrades responded as the Germans hoped, leaving cover and drawing cautiously closer. When they were one hundred yards away, the Germans leapt back into their trenches and opened fire, with devastating effect. The Americans did not flee, but pressed their attack. Stowers urged his men on, helping them to destroy an enemy machine gun and penetrating the second trench line before falling, mortally wounded.[1]

On September 29, First Lieutenant George S. Robb, a white officer from Salina, Kansas, led his platoon of the black 369th "Harlem Hellfighters" Regiment against German positions near Séchault in the Champagne. Severely wounded by machine-gun fire, he remained with his unit until another officer peremptorily ordered him to report to a dressing station. Robb obeyed, and returned forty-five minutes later. He stayed with his troops all night, and the next morning was wounded again. Still refusing to leave, he led his men in further attacks until a whiz-bang killed his commanding officer and two other officers, and hit Robb in the shoulder and hand. He remained with his company for the rest of the day, leading them through and beyond Séchault as their advance continued in the Champagne.

An African American National Guard unit attached to the French Fourth Army, the 93d had been attacking since September 26 into the Champagne, a flat and fertile region of wheat fields and small villages across the Aisne River to First Army's left. It advanced over Bellevue Signal Ridge to the villages of Ardeuil and Séchault and beyond, taking more than two thousand casualties and severely denting the German defenses in that region.[2] Elsewhere, British and French troops enjoyed even greater successes. In Picardy, British attacks on September 27 and 29, supported by the U.S. 27th and 30th Divisions, had shattered the Hindenburg Line and driven several miles through the German defenses. Another attack in Flanders had sent the Germans in full-scale retreat, forcing them to abandon the Channel ports. And on September 29, a combined Anglo-French offensive had crashed into the German positions between Lo Fère and Péronne. The only unsuccessful Allied army at the end of September was the American First Army, in the Meuse-Argonne.

✶

ON October 1, while First Army rested and reorganized after five days of brutal combat, an unwelcome visitor appeared at Pershing's Souilly headquarters: Foch's chief of staff, General Maxime Weygand. He had come to present a new battle plan. On First Army's right, the German artillery on the Heights of the Meuse had inflicted serious casualties on III and V Corps and disrupted their advance. Foch proposed to deal with this problem by expanding the offensive east of the Meuse, adding two or three fresh American divisions to the French XVII Corps, which would be placed under Pershing's command and hurled against the German positions there. The catch to Foch's plan came on First Army's left. Not enough progress, he intimated, had been made in the Argonne Forest. He therefore proposed to insert the French Second Army between the American First Army and the French Fourth Army. This new army would absorb the American 77th Division and possibly also the 28th Division, which would no longer operate under Pershing's command.

Pershing assumed that the plan had originated with Clemenceau, and was not far wrong.[3] The French prime minister had not forgotten what he had witnessed at Montfaucon, and had been lobbying for Pershing's removal. But

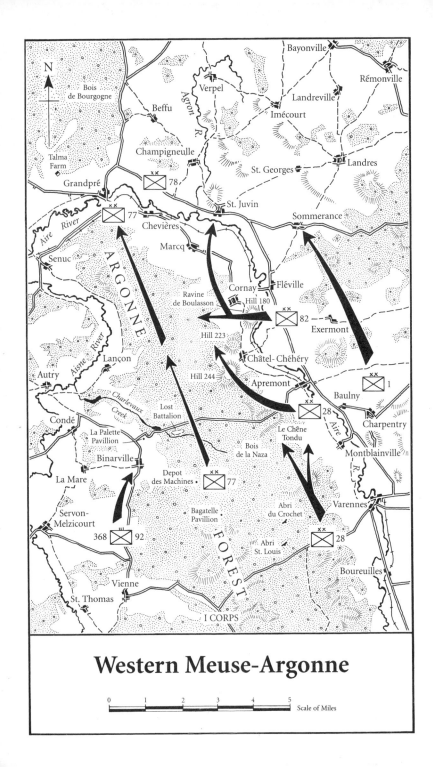

Western Meuse-Argonne

Scale of Miles

there were other detractors too. General Pétain, who had served so well as a mediator during the amalgamation controversy, had written to Foch on September 30 that the reasons for the breakdown of First Army's attacks could be found "less in the resistance of the enemy than in the difficulties experienced by the American General Staff in moving its troops and in supplying them under the conditions created by the advance of the American First Army on September 26."[4] Pétain had in fact originally suggested placing the French Second Army in the Argonne, although he had left open the question of whether it would serve under American or French overall command; Foch had decided on the latter.

Pershing accepted the need to extend the offensive east of the Meuse—albeit not right away—but refused to relinquish control over the Argonne Forest sector. Most of the reasons he gave Foch were tactical and logistical, but he also insisted that the plan entailed "dismemberment of the American First Army at a moment when its elements are striving for success under the direction of American command." Foch accepted Pershing's critique and did not press the plan further, but he insisted "that your attacks start without delay and that, once begun, they be continued without any interruptions such as those which have just arisen." This patronizing insinuation that Pershing had unnecessarily suspended the offensive on September 30 touched a sore spot. "The Marshal quite overstepped his bounds of authority in writing such a letter to me," Pershing raged in his diary. "Any observations from him as to my way of carrying out my attack are all out of place. I will not stand for this letter which disparages myself and the American Army and the American effort. He will have to retract it, or I shall go further in the matter." Foch relented, but the bad feeling remained. Sensing the French breathing down his neck, with his honor and the honor of the AEF at stake, Pershing would drive his troops harder than ever before.[5]

For all that Foch, Pershing, and the other generals bullied and pushed, however, it all came down to how much the soldiers could take. For the past five days, they had endured far greater hardships than most of the generals could comprehend. Pershing had seen nothing comparable in Cuba, the Philippines, or Mexico. Rain and cold, hunger and thirst, sleeplessness and fatigue were the least of it. The Doughboys had faced high explosives, shrapnel, mustard and phosgene gas, and most of all machine-gun bullets. They had been strafed and bombed. They had charged across rain-, shell-, and gas-soaked fields to capture woods and villages that had to be given up hours later. They had seen friends die for nothing in such fruitless attacks, or lie wounded for days with no aid except field dressings.

Pershing's unwillingness to consider the human cost did not prevent him from seeing and attempting to correct other problems before the offensive resumed. Infantry officers had a disturbing tendency to attack machine guns frontally, in human wave attacks. Pershing ordered this to stop. Officers were to seek flanks wherever possible, and although they should cooperate with other units they must take care to avoid the kind of mixing that had doomed the 35th Division.[6] He also saw, and ordered officers to deal with, supply blockages and instances of poor liaison between the infantry and the artillery and air service. Two fundamental defects remained uncorrected: poor training and wretched equipment. These would haunt First Army for the rest of the war.

Not just the infantry had underperformed; so had planes, artillery, and tanks. Billy Mitchell—no self-deprecating man—deflected criticism of the air service by accusing the infantry of misusing their signaling equipment and firing on their own planes. Army investigators were less forgiving with the artillery, accusing it of spotting targets poorly and wasting ammunition, along with a whole host of other blunders. Artillery officers had ordered a battery of eight-inch howitzers to send out a "roving gun," told a field artillery regiment to fire an immediate barrage while on the march, and instructed a battery of howitzers to open fire on a German observation balloon. The Germans, used to their own very high standards of gunmanship, regarded the American artillery with frank contempt.[7] American and French tanks had also been ineffective, utilizing amateurish tactics based on the assumption that they had only to drive straight at the enemy soldiers to make them run. Instead of running, the Germans destroyed them.

Then there were the German defenses. The Americans had not breached the *Kriemhilde Stellung,* nor even dented it. Three intact strongpoints west of the Meuse still faced First Army. These were, from right to left, the Heights of Cunel, north of Montfaucon beyond the Bois des Ogons, Madeleine Farm, and the Bois de Fays; the Heights of Romagne, north of Ivoiry and Epinonville beyond Cierges and Hill 250; and the northern half of the Argonne, especially on its northeastern flank around Châtel Chéhéry and Cornay, from where heavy concentrations of German artillery overlooked the routes of advance toward the Heights of Romagne. Each of the three German strongpoints supported the others. Gallwitz had also heavily reinforced them, First Army intelligence estimated, with at least twenty-six German and one Austrian division, with seventeen in reserve. His forces now amounted to about 125,000 men. The Germans had likewise bolstered their artillery and air forces, bringing in among other units the infamous former flying circus of Baron Manfred von Richthofen, now commanded by Hermann Göring.[8]

Pershing planned to resume the attack along the entire twelve-mile front. On the right, III Corps, with the 33d, 4th, and 80th Divisions in line from east to west, would capture the Heights of Cunel. In the center, V Corps, with the veteran 3d and 32d Divisions from east to west, would take the central Heights of Romagne. On the left, I Corps, with the 1st, 28th, and 77th Divisions from east to west, would clear the Argonne, particularly its eastern edge, and also push through Exermont and Fléville to the western edge of the Heights of Romagne. Pershing considered the attacks of III and I Corps subsidiary to the main effort of V Corps in the center. He specified that both the right- and left-hand corps should act in support of V Corps as soon as they had taken their own objectives.[9]

The plan's simplicity, Pershing believed, would increase its chances of success. "The thing to do," he insisted, "was to drive forward with all possible force." Unfortunately, the Germans knew exactly when and where the Americans were coming. On the evening of October 3, Gallwitz's troops brought in five talkative prisoners from the 32d Division, who announced that the attack would begin the following morning and outlined its objectives. Gallwitz, who had already heard details of the American plan from other intelligence sources, took immediate measures to shatter it as soon as it began.[10]

✦

BULLARD's III Corps had already endured days of constant shelling from the enemy artillery sited atop the whaleback east of the Meuse. Shrapnel and gas had caused hundreds of casualties and disrupted supply lines, forcing soldiers, ammunition, and provisions to move only at night. Artillery batteries, finding it almost impossible to position themselves out of sight, lived day and night in clouds of poison gas. By the time the corps attacked toward the Heights of Cunel on October 4, it was already seriously damaged and disorganized.

The 4th Division attempted to drive ahead through three patches of woodland, the Bois de Fays, the Bois de Malaumont, and the Bois de Forêt. If successful, the advance would drive a wedge into the eastern end of the *Kriemhilde Stellung,* allowing the division to seize Brieulles and push west along the Heights of Cunel. The 80th Division, having presumably breached the German positions in the Bois des Ogons, would simultaneously attack the heights from the south.

General Hines ordered the Ivy Division's 58th Regiment to lead the attack across an open ravine and into the Bois de Fays. The Doughboys jumped off at dawn behind a rolling barrage of shellfire from French 75s that raced quickly ahead through the Bois de Fays, while French tanks rolled and coughed alongside. Mist wreathed the ravine, limiting visibility to about two hundred yards. A promised smoke screen failed to appear on the right, however, and the fog lifted quickly. Halfway across the ravine, German observers spotted the Americans. The enemy artillery, which had been pounding the 4th Division's lines of supply, redirected its fire against the infantry and inflicted severe casualties while knocking out most of the tanks.[11]

The infantry found the fighting in the Bois de Fays more to their taste. Instead of just serving as targets for German shells, they could hit back. German snipers and machine gunners received no quarter as the Doughboys slashed forward through the Bois de Fays and the Bois de Malaumont, crossed the Cunel-Brieulles road, and pushed toward the southern edge of the Bois de Forêt. The surge didn't last long, however, before the German artillery regained the upper hand. The 58th's right flank dangled in the open. It had also badly outpaced the 80th Division to the left, leaving it in a dangerous salient. German field artillery plastered the Americans with high explosive and shrapnel, while heavy howitzers from east of the Meuse shook the ground with explosions that sent columns of dirt and debris hundreds of feet into the air. Gas shells fell in profusion, splashing the woods and fields with mustard gas and creating billowing clouds of phosgene. The Doughboys had to fight in their masks, making it more difficult to spot enemy snipers and machine gunners.

German shellfire fell with particular fury on the ravine south of the Bois de Fays, isolating the 58th's first waves from their support. No reinforcements or ammunition could be brought forward into the woods. Enemy airplanes swarmed like hornets, strafing, bombing, and directing the German artillery. Mitchell's fliers were invisible—as usual—and the German planes just kept coming despite the efforts of antiaircraft machine guns.[12] Attacked from above and on almost every side, the Doughboys withdrew to the northern edge of the Bois de Fays, leaving only a few outposts in the Bois de Malaumont.

Sensing weakness, the German infantry counterattacked immediately; but the Ivy Division's officers did a superb job of preparing their positions. As a reinforced company of Germans approached the eastern edge of the Bois de Fays, entering a small valley just outside the woods, American machine guns laid a swath of fire just behind them. American riflemen simultaneously worked toward the valley's edge, raking the Germans' flank and routing them completely. Unheeding their officers' orders to halt, many Doughboys pursued, capturing or bayoneting several Germans, but their impetuousity carried them too far. Caught in open ground toward Brieulles, the Americans took heavy casualties from German machine guns before their officers shepherded them back into the Bois de Fays.[13]

The next two weeks were the worst the Doughboys ever experienced. "It is said," wrote Sergeant Major James Block, "that the Bois de Fays means 'Woods of the Fairies.' Were I to name it, I would call it 'The center of Hell.' Any man who ever spent any time in those woods from the 4th to the 17th of October, knows that even that term does not adequately express the true situation."

> The shell torn woods were wet and muddy; everything was wet and damp, raw, cold and clammy. Not a breeze blew to clear the gas laden air. The sun never shown, it was always dark and murky. Down the sides of our fox holes, water trickled or seeped through the walls. From all sides came the odor of death or decay, mangled bodies of men everywhere. Our bodies ached from the cold and wet. The foul surroundings made one sick at heart. We were hungry, yet unable to eat but little of the food which came up. For hours at a time we were forced to be without water, for to go after it was to gamble with death. The mental strain was maddening, the physical strain exhausted us, yet we had to be alert. Sleep was impossible. The enemy counter-attacked time and again, but was repulsed each time. . . . When the Boche were not counter-attacking, they were shelling our positions. We had to lay there and hold. We had to take all the punishment with our hands tied.[14]

Such horrible realms of experience forever seperated the Doughboys from the desk-bound generals under whom they served. Men like Pershing and Bullard, who never set foot in a place like the Woods of the Fairies, could not understand how it sapped drive and morale.

✻

PRIVATE Rush Young, a Blue Ridge Doughboy waiting to attack on the morning of October 4, had changed profoundly in the past nine days. Though a draftee, he had not at first been an unwilling soldier. When his number came up in March 1918, he had left his farm in Loudoun County, Virginia, without complaints, joining the 80th Division's 318th Regiment. Outgoing and cheerful, he had seen the humor in training and enjoyed the comradeship of his fellow soldiers. One and a half weeks of combat and shellfire in the Meuse-Argonne transformed him into a living contradiction. On the outside, he maintained a quiet optimism and good humor that encouraged his nerve-wracked comrades to seek his moral support. Inside, he witnessed the miseries of war with awestruck horror, and mused bitterly on the callousness and stupidity of generals who sent men to certain death. Not until he wrote his memoirs fifteen years after the war did Young admit that he, too, had been near to breaking.

Young had joined a burial detail on October 2. He dragged and piled bodies and body parts all day, until two hundred dead soldiers lay stacked for burial. Several were friends of his, foxhole comrades with whom he had shared letters, jokes, and life stories. Young stared as the bodies were laid side by side in a ditch, their faces covered by raincoats and helmets. "There were no tears," he remembered, for "such would not be fitting at a time like this. The pain was too great for that." But his blood ran cold. "One minute," he mused, "you may be joking and the next you are in Eternity." Rejoining his company, Young found his surviving comrades sitting in their foxholes, trading irrelevant jokes to keep their minds off the explosions, the groans of the wounded, and the screams of the shell-shocked all around them. "If this had lasted much longer," he later confessed, "we would all have been crazy."[15]

The German artillery had severely pummeled the 80th Division since September 26, causing widespread demoralization before it withdrew from the lines at the end of the month. Instead of moving the 80th into reserve, however, III Corps' commander, Major General Bullard, had marched it right back to the front. There, in the first four days of October, the German artillery east of the Meuse had subjected it to a perpetual, appalling bombardment. Rocked and blasted for four days, the division again began to crack, but Bullard and the division's commander, General Cronkhite, refused to change their plans. The Blue Ridge boys, they insisted, must do their part in dismantling the eastern ramparts of the *Kriemhilde Stellung*.

The approaches to the first objective, the Bois des Ogons, were thick with corpses of men from the 4th and 79th Divisions, but their mute testament to the futility of frontal attacks failed to impress Cronkhite. "The reputation of the Blue Ridge Division is at stake," he warned his men. At dawn, the Virginian 317th and 318th Regiments, bolstered by extra machine-gun companies, mobile field artillery, and three companies of French tanks, would assault the Bois des Ogons head-on. The regiments would then drive northward quickly and join the 4th Division's attack on the Heights of Cunel. That strongpoint should fall in a day or two, he believed. Cronkhite's officers and men, he later discovered, felt a "decided lack of confidence" in the plan.[16] But by then it was too late.

The attack did not begin well. On the right, the foremost battalion of the 317th got lost on its way to the front. A reserve battalion replaced it, but the change delayed the attack for half an hour, losing the support of the rolling artillery barrage and the tanks. The German counterbarrage hit the Dough-boys as they jumped off and followed them across open hills and valleys. They had advanced halfway to the Bois des Ogons when massed machine guns hit them from the east, west, and north. A few soldiers stumbled on to the woods' southern edge, encountered a concentrated blast of high explo-sives, shrapnel, and gas, and withdrew to their original front lines. Another attack that afternoon ended in the same way.

On the left, the 318th's Second Battalion—which the Virginians called the "Gray Squirrels," with the "Red Squirrels" of First Battalion and the "Fly-ing Squirrels" of Third Battalion—jumped off at 5:30 A.M. A savage German counterbarrage, including mustard gas, hit it immediately, making the ef-forts of the Allied artillery seemed like the windmillings of "a small boy." Dozens of men fell dead before they left their positions. The Gray Squirrels pressed on regardless, helmets tilted against the storm, through plumes of dirt and smoke. They advanced over a low ridge, into a broad valley, up the slope of Hill 274, and across a deep swale toward the Bois des Ogons. Light and heavy French tanks preceded them as far as the swale, where a direct hit blew one of them to pieces. The rest turned about and fled, pursued by buzzing clouds of shellfire.[17]

When the tanks disappeared the German artillery released its full fury upon the infantry, raking it from the front and both flanks. Half blind be-cause of the masks they had to wear and no longer in formation, the Dough-boys blundered onward. Small groups of infantry reached the woods' edge and dug in, but most of the battalion remained stuck in the shelterless swale as small parties of Germans with light machine guns closed in on both flanks. Ahead, the rolling barrage had passed out of sight. Behind, companies of supporting infantry and heavy machine guns disappeared in sickly clouds of mustard gas and never emerged. Unsupported, raked by shellfire, and pressed on three sides, the troops in the swale broke and fled. The survivors huddled on the rear slope of Hill 274, pounded by regular, cruelly accurate blasts of shrapnel that cut whole squads to pieces at a time.[18]

Major Jennings Wise, the Gray Squirrels' commander, had lost more than half of his officers. His remaining men clustered in shell holes, refusing to advance into the swale. "It's murder to try to cross that place," they cried. He did not try to force them. Although the gas had dispersed, a line of shattered telegraph poles across the hill's crest helped the German artillery to target accurately. German planes droned back and forth, apparently competing to see who could most accurately plop bundles of grenades into shell holes packed with Doughboys. One private leapt out of a shell hole, shrieking insanely. Wise ordered some soldiers to gag the private and sit on him. His wailing unnerved the others; it reminded the major of a gorilla's cry.[19]

Private Young's Red Squirrels—First Battalion—meanwhile formed up along a hedge fence below Nantillois and prepared to advance in support.

> As we moved along the fence it was a mortal sight to see the lifeless bodies of soldiers, mostly German, in green uniforms lying all under this hedge fence in every conceivable way. Expressions on their faces showed that they had been gassed and died in agony. Many still had their masks on and had been mowed down with machine-gun fire. Their coat collars were torn open in their struggle for breath, and they had turned a dark purple from the effects of the gas. Some were burnt from the mustard gas, lying in shell holes as though scalded by boiling water.

Young and his comrades crossed the hedge and marched past Nantillois—a "smouldering mass of ruins" under perpetual shellfire—toward Hill 274. In the bright sunshine the men made easy targets for the German artillery. Gas shells kept falling too, but as there was little wind the Doughboys did not don their masks unless a cloud got too close. Instead, they walked with hands clasped on their noses. That was a mistake, as they soon found out. Some inadvertently plopped down into yellow-brown craters full of mustard gas and were severely burned, blinded, or died in agony. Other soldiers began sneezing uncontrollably in a misty ravine. There was no humor in the situation. A victim of sneezing gas could not put his mask on and keep it in place. A subsequent dose of poison gas meant death. Many men died in that ravine. The Red Squirrels stopped behind Hill 274, unable to advance farther. The soldiers crouched in shell holes, "calling on their Lord to help them as never before."[20]

Cronkhite had another go just after dark, ordering a battalion of the 319th to leapfrog the 318th and attack the Bois des Ogons. The Germans were ready and inflicted heavy casualties on the Americans in the swale below the woods. One company nevertheless penetrated a gap in the German lines and advanced about a mile into the woods. The company blasted several enemy dugouts and even entered a barracks complex before it realized that it was alone and fought its way back to the swale.[21]

Cries of wounded soldiers echoed all night, while American and German patrols crept about the swale in search of injured comrades. Occasionally the patrols crossed paths and exchanged fire, while stretcher-bearers attempted to evacuate the wounded. When they could not find any wounded, they carried corpses. As the night dragged on, Major Wise struggled to keep his Gray Squirrels on Hill 274 alert, in case of enemy counterattack. Though still, they didn't really sleep. They just lay about, torpid and unresponsive. When shaken, they responded groggily. Then they reverted to a trancelike state that Wise attributed to the effects of constant shell concussion and gas. Farther back, stragglers wandered rearward through Nantillois, which erupted and burned under repeated shellfire in an all-night fireworks display.[22]

★

MAJOR General George Cameron's V Corps had only two divisions—the 3d and the 32d, from right to left—with which to capture the Romagne Heights, the central strongpoint of the *Kriemhilde Stellung*. Both of them were veteran formations, however, and relatively fresh. The 3d Division was a regular army unit reinforced by a leaven of draftees. Made up of the 4th, 7th, 30th, and 38th Infantry Regiments, it had left the United States in the spring of 1918 and fought along the Marne River in June and July before following the German withdrawal to the Ourcq River and the Vesle at the end of the summer. It took more than seven thousand casualties during that period. The division's commander, Major General Beaumont Bonaparte Buck, was a snappy, mustachioed Texan with a penchant for leading from the front. A veteran of the western frontier, the Spanish-American War, and the Philippine Insurrection, Buck had commanded a regiment and then a brigade of the 1st Division in the spring and summer of 1918. On July 21 he had won the Distinguished Service Cross for leading the first wave of his forces in the capture of the town of Brezy-le-Sec. He took command of the 3d Division in August.

The confident, veteran 3d Division regulars relieved the bedraggled 37th and 79th Divisions on October 1, and quickly discovered that there was more to this war than they had thought. The Germans conducted no fighting withdrawals, but clearly meant to stay. Their artillery seemed to have endless supplies of ammunition. Gas clouds floated everywhere. Perhaps most disconcerting, the Germans had control of the air. With von Richthofen dead, the Allied air services claimed to have won the skies of France. If so, where did all of those enemy planes come from? Two hours after the 38th Regiment took its positions at the front, flight after flight of German fighters descended upon them. The pilots did not just pursue large targets, but seemed to seek out individual foxholes. Billy Mitchell might deny that these planes existed, but they caused genuine casualties. In desperation, the 38th's colonel ordered all of his troops to fire on the planes with their rifles, with predictably negligible effect.[23]

Among the 3d Division veterans marching to the front was Private John Lewis "Jack" Barkley. He came from a family of soldiers, and his father and grandfather boasted that "from Revolutionary days on, whenever America got into trouble there'd always been a Barkley in the fight." When America declared war on Germany in April 1917, eighteen-year-old Jack—fit, patriotic, and handy with a gun—had tried to enlist, but the army wouldn't accept him because he stuttered. Jack despondently returned home from the recruiting office, and his father shook his head and "guessed the Barkleys were petering out." Determined to keep trying, Jack left his small town of Holden, Missouri, and traveled to the state draft board. His physical exam went well, but when the doctors asked him questions they discovered his stutter, and their smiles turned to frowns.

"Hell no!" said one. "They'll never let you get anywhere."

"God damn it," yelled the other. "We're not picking orators. We're picking fighting men!" And so they let Barkley in.

The good-byes didn't last long. There were his parents, an ill brother, his dogs, and his old horse. And there was his girlfriend, to whom he got engaged just before leaving for training camp. On the whole, though, Barkley had led a solitary life:

> I hadn't any close friends. It's so much easier to go out to the woods with a gun and a couple of dogs than to try to make friends with people, at the risk of making a fool of yourself instead, every time you open your mouth. I'd spent more days alone in the woods than I ever had at school—and a good many nights. Out there it was easy to forget that everybody laughed at me when I tried to talk.

Barkley's fellow recruits laughed at him too, but only at first. Though small, he knew how to fight. After a few brawls they respected and accepted him. At scout and sniper school, he fit right in. Daniel Boone "was some sort of ancestor," and as a child he had modeled himself on the frontier legend. The specialized training continued in France, where he was taken from his unit—the 4th Regiment of the 3d Division—and sent to intelligence school under French officers. After graduation he was assigned to his battalion's intelligence section. He and his select group of comrades—including Jesse James, a tall, heavily muscled, three-quarters Cherokee Indian; "Nigger" Floyd, a huge, dark-skinned, Choctaw/Cherokee who had served in the army since the Boxer Rebellion; Mike De Angelo, a wiry little Italian and feather-weight boxer from Philadelphia; Norosoff, a Brooklyn Jew; and Sergeant Nayhone, a Syrian from New York City who spoke with a Middle Eastern accent—were given rifles with telescopic sights, pistols, close-quarters weapons, and maps. Officially scouts and snipers, they operated more like a semi-independent Special Forces unit.

By the time the 3d Division joined the battle in the Meuse-Argonne, Barkley and his comrades had seen a good deal of action and had become used to bucking authority. But on the morning of October 3, his confidence received a shock. Just after chow came mail call, the highlight of every sol-dier's day. Barkley received several letters from his family and one from his fiancée. He put the others in his pocket and opened the letter from his girl. "Dear Jack," she wrote, "I'm going to make this very brief and to the point."

> And she did. She thought a lot of me, but I'd never get out alive anyway, so it wouldn't make any difference to me. She was going to marry the boy she'd been going places with, to try to keep him from having to go into the army.

Barkley paced around alone for a while, cleaned his rifle, and cursed. His bud-dies started a game of blackjack, and pestered him until he joined. He played for a few minutes and then threw his cards down and plodded back to his tent. Norosoff was there. "You can't kid me," he said in his Brooklyn accent. "Somethin's eatin' you. What is? Bad news from home?" Barkley told him.

"Gee, that's tough," Norosoff replied, and the two lapsed into silence. After a while he spoke again: "Maybe you ain't got this thing straight, Barkley. Maybe it ain't so bad when you know about it."

"I got it straight all right," Barkley growled, and went to sleep.[24]

✻

THE 3d Division's objective on October 4 was to advance to the eastern base of the Heights of Romagne, a little over two miles ahead. Getting there would not be easy. On the right, the 4th Regiment, starting from the northern edge of the Bois de Beuge, would have to climb a slope to the forested Hill 268, de-scend into an open ravine, seize the wooded crest of Hill 250, cross another ravine, and storm the Bois de Cunel—all in plain view of the German strongpoints in the Bois des Ogons and Madeleine Farm to the east. On the left, the 7th Regiment, starting just north of Cierges, would have to cross several rolling hills into a ravine, climb the grassy slopes of Hill 253 to the rabbit's warren of enemy emplacements at its top, and then advance across a mile of open ground to Mamelle Trench, a German position at the base of the Heights of Romagne. French tanks would provide support.

The 4th Regiment attacked at dawn and promptly ran into the same deluge of German artillery fire that plagued the rest of First Army, mostly from the guns east of the Meuse. The infantry climbed up the slope to the undefended woods on Hill 268, but when they tried to push farther across the open ground toward Hill 250 the Germans hit them with such a terrible concentration of artillery and machine-gun fire that they had to withdraw. The French tanks, meanwhile, trundled merrily ahead, sweeping around Hill 250 and out of sight. The Germans held their fire until the tanks had left the infantry well behind and then destroyed all of them.

The 7th Regiment jumped off late. The 1st Gas and Flame fired a protective smoke screen, but the smoke clouds only served as markers for the German artillery. Hit hard by enemy shellfire, the advancing infantry lost formation and suffered terrible losses.[25] By late afternoon the 7th had advanced under a mile, into the ravine below Hill 253. There the Doughboys waited, taking casualties from artillery and aircraft, until a larger, more effective smoke screen at 4:00 P.M. covered a further advance over Hill 253. They might as well not have bothered; within minutes, heavy enemy fire forced the regiment to withdraw back to the ravine.

Private Barkley watched the infantry's futile attacks and appealed unsuccessfully for permission to lead raiding parties against German snipers. Frustrated, he and his comrades eventually killed the snipers without permission, but even this was unsatisfying—they wanted to do more. After dusk, Barkley was ordered to take a detail of five men and eliminate a German howitzer. This looked more worthwhile than killing snipers. The German gun sat under camouflage netting in a large pit near no-man's-land, and as Barkley and his men snuck up to it they could hear the gunners quietly talking. The Americans were about to attack when one of them tripped over an old helmet. The Germans yelled and bullets flew, but Barkley's men had their grenades ready and hurled them through the netting while he fired his pistol.

After confirming that the gun crew was dead, Barkley withdrew. Not until he reached headquarters did he realize that he had neglected to spike the gun. Reasoning that it was his fault, he went back alone. He found the gun as he had left it, except that one of the crew he had thought dead—one he had shot with his .45—made a hideous snoring noise as his life ebbed away. Barkley tried to ignore the noise as he packed the gun's barrel with rocks, but the snoring unnerved him and he yearned for the German to hurry up and die. Barkley finished his work, and left in a cold sweat and shaking with chills. The memory of the dying soldier's "damned snoring" would fade quickly in the frantic terror of the events that followed.[26]

✳

OCTOBER 4 was Major General William Haan's birthday, but he had no time for celebration. A West Point graduate from Indiana who had served in the Spanish-American War and the Philippine Insurrection, Haan commanded the 32d Division—the "Red Arrow" or "Les Terribles," as the French called it. Organized from National Guard troops and draftees from Michigan and Wisconsin, the Red Arrow was one of the most regionally homogenous divisions in the AEF. Unlike most others, it had not been gutted with transfers and replacements before going to France. Containing the 125th, 126th, 127th, and 128th Infantry Regiments, the division had participated in fighting along the Aisne River from July to early September, performing well under fire and taking about sixty-five hundred casualties. Haan, the son of German immigrants, stood apart from many other AEF generals in that he felt a genuine affection for his men, many of whom shared his Teutonic ancestry.

The commander of V Corps, Major General Cameron, had trouble deciding what to do with the Red Arrow, first ordering it to occupy the 37th Division's former sector and then moving it west into the 91st Division's old positions. Such indecision, Haan complained to his diary, was enough to make the angels cry, but what came next "made the angels have galloping consumption." On October 3 Cameron ordered the division, fresh into the lines, to attack the next morning against Gesnes, one of the strongest parts of the *Kriemhilde Stellung*. The 91st Division had bled itself white trying to take the place in late September; Cameron ordered the 32d to seize it within a few hours. The Red Arrow was then to advance another mile over broken terrain and strong German emplacements to the western reaches of the Heights of Romagne—all in one day.

With no time to plan, Haan could only arbitrarily assign jump-off times and places, pass the orders on to his brigadiers and colonels, and "hope to God our infantry will get there in time."[27] He put the 126th and 127th up front from right to left, with the other two regiments in reserve, and ordered them to attack at dawn. Tanks, he said, would accompany the infantry. He made no promises of artillery support, for the very good reason that neither he nor anyone else knew who commanded the guns or where they were. In the past few days the divisional artillery had shifted around even more than the infantry, and its officers were being relieved and replaced at a breakneck pace. The artillery might fire in support, or it might not. Either way, the objectives remained the same.

Captain Paul Schmidt's company of the 127th moved into position in the early morning. Worn out from marching back and forth, with no idea where they were or what they were supposed to do, Schmidt and his men thought only of rest. They dozed for a few hours until 6:00 A.M., when an order came from First Battalion headquarters. Written three and a half hours earlier, the order indicated that a rolling barrage toward the enemy lines—wherever those were—would begin at dawn. Schmidt's company was to follow the barrage and attack immediately. Already the captain could hear explosions in the distance, and they got closer as he frantically roused his troops. Only when the explosions began did the Doughboys realize that the incoming shells were German rather than American.

Two men approached Schmidt as he tried to hold his company together amid the crashing enemy shellfire. One wore a French officer's uniform, and the other sported overalls and a helmet. Pointing to a few tanks idling nearby—Schmidt had not noticed them in all the excitement—they said they had been ordered to support the infantry. Schmidt told them to get ready; the attack would begin at once. Instead of running to their tanks, however, the Frenchmen hesitated. One turned pale; the other trembled. When they didn't move after a few minutes, Schmidt ordered his company to attack without them. He never saw the tanks again.

Fog hindered German observation, but not enough to prevent the counterbarrage from killing and wounding many Doughboys in the fields below Gesnes. It also caused Schmidt and other officers to lose their bearings, breaking up whatever formation they had managed to attain during the morning's panic. When the sun broke through in midmorning, the wandering clumps of American infantry made easy targets for the German machine gunners. Schmidt hurried what he could find of his company to the shelter of a small ravine. A quarter mile to his left, Gesnes dissolved under rising clouds of smoke and dust. To his right, more infantry took shelter in the ravine and along a road embankment leading east from the town. Officers from both attacking regiments darted about, yelling orders, but to little effect. The 128th's colonel was just as confused as his troops in the line. His maps had been drawn on a much larger scale than those of his company commanders, whose own maps omitted many important landmarks.

Schmidt's ravine provided little shelter. German machine gunners—masters of indirect fire—could hit it at several points, as could the artillery, guided by their omnipresent planes. Casualties piled up, and by midafternoon Schmidt was one of the last officers of his battalion still standing. Hoping to find better cover, he ordered his men to move up the west end of the ravine toward Gesnes. Shells and bullets followed them as they emerged from the ravine just outside of the village. There they made a gruesome discovery. Bodies, almost all of them Doughboys of the 91st Division, lay in thick windrows where the German machine guns had cut them down a week before.

A small ridge rose northeast of Gesnes. Schmidt led his troops up its rear slope, but German shellfire killed and wounded men at every moment. Shallow foxholes, craters, and corpses offered the only shelter. Schmidt sent a runner to regimental headquarters reporting his position and requesting orders. The runner returned to tell him that his company was out of position; it should be on the opposite side of Gesnes, attacking north into some German-occupied woods. The colonel ordered Schmidt to take his company there immediately without waiting for support. "Use tanks when possible," he said. Schmidt looked at his men sprawled in their shell holes, thought of the tanks and their nervous drivers, and decided to stay put. Darkness came within the hour, and the Doughboys dug their holes a little deeper and fell asleep. Schmidt spent the night in a hole, his only companion a dead soldier.[28]

The only soldiers in Gesnes were dead. The Germans had withdrawn a few days before, preferring to turn it into a slaughterhouse for the Americans rather than hold on to it directly; their infantry and machine-gun positions in the woods north of the village remained untouched. At day's end, the Red Arrow occupied a line running roughly along the Cierges-Gesnes-Exermont road. German snipers, machine gunners, and artillery maintained a lethal barrage along the line for most of the night. For all of the sympathy Haan felt for his troops, he was miserably uninformed. Unaware that his division had taken Gesnes only in theory, he accepted it as a fitting birthday present and wrote complacently in his diary that enemy artillery fire had been insignificant throughout the day. At the front, meanwhile, men wrote in their diaries of a "hellish bombardment" that had inflicted "terrible losses" and left the attacking regiments "shot to pieces."[29]

✸

MAJOR General Charles P. Summerall, the 1st Division's commander, was one of the war's most colorful and controversial figures. Robert Bullard first met him on New Year's Day, 1899, at an insurgent-besieged post in the Philippines. Bullard commanded an infantry regiment that had become pinned down in an attempt to break out of the post, and Summerall, an artillery lieutenant, appeared at a critical moment with a light artillery piece and a Gatling gun. He deployed the pieces in the open and directed their fire on the insurgents while the infantrymen looked on in amazement.

> Summerall was strutting up and down in the open, his chest was stuck out, and he was behaving as if he were on parade. It was an inspiring sight, and under its effect it was easy to lead the line of infantry forward, run the enemy out of his position, and chase him for six or seven miles.[30]

This fiery individual with a deceptively mild face had been born in 1867 in Blount's Ferry, Florida. He graduated from West Point in 1892 and became an artillery officer, serving in the Spanish-American War, the Philippines, and the Boxer Rebellion. He then served for several years as senior instructor of artillery tactics at West Point. In the summer of 1917, as head of the artillery section of an independent mission that the War Department sent to France to evaluate the formation of the AEF, Summerall had confronted Pershing over the weakness of the American artillery. Almost alone among American general officers, he insisted on the primacy of firepower—as opposed to rifles, bayonets, and willpower—on the modern battlefield. According to Pershing's then chief of staff, James G. Harbord, Summerall "carried his argument as nearly to the limit of courtesy as I have ever seen an officer go and escape unrebuked."[31]

Pershing admired Summerall's tough-mindedness and promoted him from one position to another, eventually making him commander of the 1st Division's artillery brigade. In July 1918, Pershing promoted Summerall to major general and appointed him to command the entire division. On July 19, Summerall earned the Distinguished Service Cross "for extraordinary heroism" by exposing himself to enemy fire near Soissons while rallying his troops. Ruthlessly efficient, Summerall showed no pity for shoddy and timid soldiers. He also developed a reputation for callousness, a victory-at-all-costs attitude that sent Doughboys to their deaths without qualms. But he got results. "General Summerall may be a son-of-a-bitch," one of them said, "but thank God he's *our* son-of-a-bitch."[32]

Summerall's division, the Big Red One, was organized in May 1917 from regular army units serving on the Mexican border and elsewhere. It consisted of the 16th, 18th, 26th, and 28th Infantry Regiments, along with support units. In June 1917 it became the first division to leave for Europe, and it took the first American casualties of the war four months later. The 1st Division fought in the first important American engagement of the war, at Cantigny in May 1918, and then participated heavily in the summer's fighting, taking 12,271 casualties from April 19 to July 23. It took another 500 casualties at St. Mihiel in mid-September.

The 1st Division possessed a pride and swagger absent elsewhere in the AEF. Its officers and men thrived on the conviction that they were the best trained and equipped, and most irresistible fighters in the entire army. They had been the first in everything and—so they thought—had seen it all. Such confidence all too easily led to arrogance and a belief that they could fight the entire German army on their own. This in turn bred resentment among soldiers who did not belong to the 1st Division's exclusive club. By the end of the war, while the Big Red One was the most beloved division at army headquarters and the most popular in the United States, most Doughboys from other units hated it.

Donald D. Kyler represented the ideal 1st Division soldier. A handsome farm boy from Whitley County, Indiana, he was only seventeen years old in 1918 but determined to fight. With the connivance of his family he deceived his local recruiter and entered the 1st Division's 16th Regiment. The army was all he hoped it would be, and more. He loved his uniform and wore it with pride. He enjoyed training, from route marches, drills, and rifle ranges to spit-and-polish parades. So enthusiastic was he, and such a good marksman, that in France his officers promoted him to corporal and put him in charge of any detail, such as escorting prisoners or punishing malingerers, that required a "degree of fanaticism." A veteran sergeant counseled Kyler not to go to extremes, but he rejected the advice.

> I tried very hard to be all soldier, and foolishly expected others to be also. With evil doers and malingerers I felt a personal animosity. By that time a strong instinctive attachment bound me to my company, the regiment, the army. It was quite apart from patriotism or the love of one's country. In fact, it might be called antipatriotism in our society.[33]

On one occasion, Kyler bayoneted a German prisoner who hesitated to obey his command.

Such ruthlessness had its uses at the front, especially in the sector assigned to the 1st Division on October 4. It had entered the lines in place of the shattered 35th Division, and faced a victorious enemy—the elite German 5th Guards Division reinforced by the 37th and 52d Divisions—occupying the blasted, corpse-strewn remnants of Montrebeau Wood. Summerall chose to attack with all four of his regiments, with the 16th, 18th, 28th, and 26th Regiments in line from left to right. Their overall direction of attack was northwest along the east bank of the Aire River. Kyler's 16th Regiment on the far left flank would, with the 18th Regiment, be responsible for driving the Germans out of Montrebeau Wood and taking Fléville, Exermont, and Hill 240—also known as Montrefagne—beyond. The other two regiments would advance over a series of ravines and ridges toward the imposing Hill 272, which guarded the western approaches to the Heights of Romagne. It was difficult and well-defended terrain, which was why Liggett had chosen the 1st Division to take it.[34]

The attack began at dawn with a barrage that stood two hundred yards ahead of the jump-off line for five minutes and then rolled slowly toward the enemy. The Doughboys hardly noticed the support. Just after they left their trenches a curtain of German artillery fire swept down, dicing and pulverizing the 35th Division corpses that carpeted the fields and adding fresh bodies to their midst. Fortunately Summerall had instructed the infantry to spread out, and the casualties were not as severe as they could have been. As the morning fog lifted, a vast plume of smoke appeared over a supply dump hit by the German artillery. Airplanes dodged in and around the plume like hornets defending their nest. For once, American fliers were challenging the German planes.[35]

Forty-seven Renaults of the 344th and 345th Tank Battalions supported the attack, but only three remained operational at the end of the day. Their crews took 84 percent casualties. Some helped destroy machine-gun nests or provided suppressing fire; others spluttered aimlessly, unable to get their bearings because of all the shell holes that forced them to take long detours. One mistake could be deadly for the tankers. Corporal Harold Roberts, a tank driver from San Francisco, came too close to the edge of one water-filled crater. His Renault tumbled in and immediately sank. There was one escape hatch; whichever of the two-man crew opened it might make it out, but the water would certainly rush in and drown the other. "Well, only one of us can make it out," Roberts told his gunner, "and out you go." He pushed the gunner through the hatch, and drowned.[36]

Kyler's 16th Infantry Regiment, advancing with the Aire River on its left and Montrebeau Wood on its right, took fire from both flanks as it approached

Exermont Ravine. To the right, on the other side of the ravine behind Montrebeau Wood, Kyler could see Exermont. It had been assigned to the 18th Regiment. Ahead lay the 16th Regiment's objective, the town of Fléville. To get there, Kyler's Company G would have to pass a small wooded gully that extended south from the ravine, almost on the boundary between the 16th and 18th Regiments. As the company approached the ravine, German machine guns and infantry concealed in the gully opened fire into the Americans' flank and halted their advance.

Company G's commander, Captain Allen Wildish, studied his map. He was addicted to chewing tobacco, and when under stress he chewed until the juice trickled down the front of his tunic. His jaws worked furiously now. No one had told him about the gully, and it was not marked on his map. A frontal assault on it might cost many casualties and waste valuable time. Wildish's lieutenants stood by in indecision for several minutes until one remembered that Kyler took all the dirty jobs. The captain called the eager young corporal over and ordered him to take one man and circle around the gully to the right. Kyler might be able to do something from there; if not, Company G would only lose another two men.

Kyler attached his bayonet and put two grenades in his pockets. Followed hesitantly by the other man—who probably regretted being assigned to accompany the bloodthirsty corporal—Kyler moved around the gully and approached it from the southeast, crawling and leaping from hole to hole. As he approached the underbrush on the gully's edge he heard two machine guns, a mortar, and several rifles working below. Abandoned by his companion, Kyler crawled between the bushes to a point within grenade-throwing range of the unseen enemy. He took the grenades from his pockets, pulled the pins, and hurled them into the gully. As the second grenade left his hand he snatched his rifle and rushed forward. Firing from the hip, he killed one startled German soldier, just as the grenades exploded, and leapt over a bluff into the gully. He landed directly on one German and felt his bones crunch beneath his feet as he skewered another on the end of his bayonet. A third ran off, bleeding from a grenade wound. Kyler had eliminated one machine-gun nest.[37] The rest fell to the other men of Company G, who had heard the firing and moved forward to help.

After clearing the gully, the 16th Regiment moved through the ravine, stormed several German trenches and emplacements, and entered Fléville. The German artillery had registered the town in advance, and heavy shellfire brought the buildings tumbling down around the Doughboys as they moved through the streets. They had advanced farther than anyone else in the division and were exposed on both sides, however, so the regiment's commander pulled his troops back to the northern edge of Exermont Ravine.

To the right, the 18th Regiment had stormed the German trenches below and in Montrebeau Wood with bayonets and grenades. They emerged on the woods' northern edge to find the German artillery waiting for them. Machine guns also opened fire as the Americans advanced down the ravine's open southern slope. Exhausted and with their ranks badly thinned, they continued through Exermont, which the Germans had left unoccupied, and climbed the far slope of the ravine to the foot of Montrefagne. A few stolid survivors continued all the way to the top. They stayed there, dazedly watching the Germans prepare a counterattack while the shelling intensified, until they came to their senses and withdrew. The remnants of the regiment formed a line on Exermont Ravine's northern edge at the foot of Montrefagne, and waited for the night.

"God damn it, don't you know we're going over the top at 5:35," Lieutenant Maury Maverick yelled to his company of the 28th Regiment as it formed up and prepared to attack past the eastern edge of Montrebeau Wood. A fiercely independent Texan, he would serve in the 1930s as a Democratic congressman from San Antonio and coin the term *gobbledygook* to describe the language used by President Roosevelt's government bureaucrats. No gobbledygook passed Maverick's lips as he paced up and down the lines in the predawn darkness of October 4. The enemy lines were silent—some said they had already retreated, but Maverick had the unsettling feeling that they were just waiting. Sure enough, "the Germans simply waited, and then laid a barrage of steel and fire."

> At this moment of 5:35 everything happened that never happens in the storybooks of war. . . . There were no bugles, no flags, no drums, and as far as we knew, no heroes. The great noise was like great stillness, everything seemed blotted out. We hardly knew where the Germans were. We were simply in a big black spot with streaks of screaming red and yellow, with roaring giants in the sky tearing and whirling and roaring. I have never read in any military history a description of the high explosives that break overhead. There is a great swishing scream, a smash-bang, and it seems to tear everything loose from you. The intensity of it simply enters your heart and brain and tears every nerve to pieces.[38]

At the beginning of the advance, Maverick's company numbered two hundred men. A few minutes after the attack started, half of them were dead or wounded. As the last remaining officer, he took command of the company. The next highest-ranking soldier was a corporal.

With "nothing to do but keep on going," Maverick tilted his head into the storm. Giving the Doughboy's tin helmet more credit for stopping power than it deserved, he held his head down in hopes that it would deflect enemy bullets. Then he had second thoughts. What if a bullet hit him in the chin and tore off his jaw, leaving him horribly disfigured for life? He held his head up, and reconsidered. What if a bullet hit him in the mouth and knocked out all his teeth, or cut through his eyes and left him blind? Glancing up, he realized in a moment that his helmet was gone. In the excitement that morning he had worn it on top of his cap. It had slipped off without his feeling it.

"This was no time to be worrying about hats," he told himself. "We had to advance." Ahead, he saw trees interlaced with immense coils of barbed wire. In the middle, a single lane passed through the wire. In that lane lay dozens of American corpses—a death trap. Certainly a German machine gun waited on the other side. "I did not want to go through that lane. But the men began to waver a little and I figured it would not be right for me to lay down or stop, so I moved ahead. I said to myself, 'This is one of the finest dilemmas I have ever been in. I must go through that lane, call for my men if I don't get killed, and get a hat. I need a hat. I need a hat.'" Maverick picked through the lane, stopping briefly to try on helmets from dead soldiers, and emerged safe on the other side. A German machine gun was there, sure enough, but its occupants were dead, one of them slumped over his gun. Maverick formed his men to resume the advance through the woods when a shell burst over his head, ripping out a large piece of his shoulder blade and collar bone and knocking him to the ground. A medical man joined him, and applied bandages.

> As he lifted me from the ground, I looked at my four runners, and I saw that the two in the middle had been cut down to a pile of horrid red guts and blood and meat, while the two men on the outside had been cut up somewhat less badly, but no less fatally. It reminded me of nothing I had ever seen before, except a Christmas hog butchering back on the Texas farm.[39]

Maverick's 28th Regiment, and the 26th Regiment to its right, continued the advance over broken, machine-gun- and sniper-infested country. They traversed the eastern end of Exermont Ravine and fought bitterly to capture two heavily fortified farms. Machine-gun emplacements made of logs overgrown with moss and shrubbery took a heavy toll. The veteran 1st Division troops expertly infiltrated between the German strongpoints and destroyed them before moving on. There was much bayonet work too, with no prisoners taken on either side.[40] Eventually, they seized their objectives. But as the regiments had advanced well ahead of the 32d Division, German artillery methodically flailed their right flank. Being first was not always best.

Overall, the Big Red One had advanced about one and a half miles, farther than any other division on October 4. Its losses had been severe—2,057 casualties in one day—but the 1st Division had upheld its reputation as the most hard-driving unit in the AEF.[41]

✮

BRIGADIER General Dennis Nolan, the former football star and intelligence officer who Pershing had put in charge of the 28th Division's 55th Brigade on September 28, had successfully held on to Apremont against repeated German attacks, but the enemy showed no signs of giving up. On the morning of October 1, while all of the other divisions in First Army—except for the luckless 77th, fighting in the Argonne—rested and refitted, Nolan suspected that his troops had more fighting ahead. The 28th's commander, hard-driving Major General Charles H. Muir, wanted to spend the day straightening out the lines with limited attacks. Nolan instead prepared his brigade to resist an all-out German attack against Apremont.

A cyclone of German shells crashed into the American lines just before Muir ordered his infantry to move forward. Twenty minutes later a huge swarm of German infantry—an entire division in mass formation—poured southward over the fields toward Apremont. Making no pretense of flanking or infiltration, the Germans had launched one of their biggest counterattacks of the entire battle. Nolan had deployed the 109th and 110th Regiments in rifle and machine-gun pits on the bluffs along Apremont's northern perimeter. Two strongpoints, a gravel pit and a graveyard, anchored the line, along with a few 75mm field guns. In addition, several battered Renault tanks—the remnants of Patton's old 344th Tank Brigade—waited in a ravine south of town. The tankers had not received training in defensive tactics—no one had thought of using them except to attack—but Nolan gave them specific instructions on what to do.

The German artillery barrage lifted as the field-gray tide of enemy infantry approached Apremont. Racing from position to position, Nolan ordered his men to keep quiet as the Germans advanced. The first enemy wave had approached to within twenty-five yards when he ordered the Doughboys to open fire. With rifles and machine guns, they caught the Germans in converging streams of fire. The enemy soldiers hesitated, attempted to fire back, and fell in heaps. Some scaled the bluff as far as the cemetery wall and traded pistol shots, grenades, and bayonet thrusts with the Americans at point-blank range for several minutes, but they were unsupported and eventually tumbled back down the bluff, most of them dead.[42]

As the enemy attack lost momentum, Nolan called in his own artillery and the tanks, which rumbled in pairs around Apremont's eastern and western bluffs and plowed into both ends of the German lines, crushing and machine-gunning the bewildered infantry. The German artillery attempted to respond and shelled its own men. Shattered, the enemy infantry turned and fled. The Doughboys pursued, cheering, along with six tanks, but quickly reeled back before heavy machine-gun and artillery fire that disabled five of the tanks. They withdrew to Apremont.

Nolan's officers counted one thousand dead enemy soldiers around Apremont, most of them middle-aged and elderly men. Their teenaged officers had flung them into the attack with pitiless disregard for losses. Machine guns had killed most of the Germans; others had been crushed by tanks or blown to pieces by American and German artillery. The many prisoners that Nolan's troops brought in included a pale young officer whose hands shook uncontrollably. Nolan gave him a cigarette and lit it. After a few minutes the officer calmed down enough to speak through an interpreter:

> He asked me if I knew of the atrocity I had committed there that morning. . . . I asked him what he meant by that word as I didn't understand what he was talking about. He said "Your sending those tanks against our halted lines. You forced every soldier in those lines to choose the manner of his death this morning, whether he would be killed by machine gun fire, because everyone felt if they moved from their position they would be killed by machine gun fire,—or whether he would be run over by the tanks." He said "I had to make that decision myself."

Nolan pitied the German, yet also felt vindicated. He had long considered First Army's use of tanks uncreative. The day's action proved that tanks could not only attack, but also form a "vital element" in any defensive action. Nolan had also demonstrated the quality of his own leadership. "While we were up there fighting we saw him going from shell hole to shell hole, never bending his head," one of his lieutenants later wrote. "This is what gives men grit. I never saw the general we had before outside of the dugout, the new one was always leading us."[43]

To the west, along the borders of the Argonne, the Keystone Division's 111th and 112th Regiments had a more difficult time. On October 1 and 2 they tried repeatedly to take the crest of Le Chêne Tondu, an important ridge that dominated all the open ground to the east in the Aire River valley. The Americans could not flank the ridge; they had to assault it directly. Again and again they surged over the crest to assault the German trenches on the rear slope, but came to grief every time and withdrew back to the sunken road they had occupied since September 28. After nightfall, Corporal Harold Pierce and his fellow Doughboys huddled together for comfort, amid a realm of all-too-realistic nightmares. "Above our heads bullets snap and crackle," he wrote in his diary. "We talk of home and God. The terror of the night is upon us. We realize the hopelessness and uselessness of it."[44]

A constant attrition of casualties sent morale plunging among the troops of this once-proud, veteran division. "During the day," testified private Paul Compton of the 111th, "we were forced to keep close to the ground, not even so much as moving the foliage about us, for fear of drawing fire . . . when 'Jerry' did open up, we could see the bark flying from trunks of trees two or three feet above our heads. . . . Lines of wounded men were constantly going back to the rear." His company, which had 240 men on October 1, had by the fourth been reduced to less than 100. The division as a whole had taken 2,916 casualties by that time, a severe loss to its frontline strength.[45] Even so, and despite the fact that the Pennsylvanians had received almost no rest since September 26, Pershing still expected them to attack on October 4. The Argonne had to be cleared.

All four regiments of the 28th Division participated in the attack, encountering the same type of German counterbarrage that disrupted First Army's advance all along the line. On the right, Nolan's 109th and 110th Regiments weathered the enemy shellfire and advanced through a dense fog bank for a mile down the Aire River valley. They met only weak opposition before German machine guns held them up in front of the village of La Forge and the adjoining wooded Hill 180. On the left, the troops of the 111th were too jaded to advance, and the 112th flung itself against Le Chêne Tondu only to suffer another bloody repulse. Major Generals Muir and Liggett suspected that they were going to have to come up with some more creative method of prying the Germans out of the Argonne.

—•·•—

"Our Mission Is to Hold
This Position at All Costs"

THE LOST BATTALION

On September 26, First Army had ordered the 77th Division to advance slowly through the Argonne Forest, maintaining pressure on the German forces there, while the 28th Division, driving aggressively north through the Aire River valley, and the French, attacking into the Champagne, outflanked the enemy respectively to the east and west. Nobody had expected the Statue of Liberty Division to conquer the Argonne by itself. The German defenses were too strong, the terrain too difficult.

Since then, the division's mission had changed to one of all-out attack. One factor in the change was the unexpected strength of the German artillery on the forest's northeastern fringe. From those positions the enemy batteries raked not just the 28th Division, advancing up the Aire River valley, but also 1st Division and all of V Corps, attacking the Heights of Romagne. This forced Pershing on September 29 to revise I Corps' objective. Previously, he had assumed that the Argonne would fall once V Corps had seized the Heights of Romagne. Now, the commander in chief ordered that "if the heights cannot be taken, the necessary part of the Foret d'Argonne [to a point west of Apremont] must be taken to maintain our positions already gained."[1]

The 77th Division's altered plan of attack also owed much to the generals' strong egos. Foch pushed Pershing; Pershing pushed I Corps' commander, General Liggett; Liggett pushed the 77th's commander, Major General Alexander; Alexander pushed his brigadiers; they pushed their colonels; the colonels pushed their officers and men; and instead of advancing slowly but steadily against positions that the Germans would anyway have abandoned, the Statue of Liberty Division assaulted them headlong. Generals and officers had become intoxicated with the spirit of the attack and passed it on to their men. "The Division was not so well trained for its task as we would have liked to have it," Alexander admitted, "but the spirit of officers and men was beyond all praise. Whatever could be accomplished by devotion to our cause and by determined courage would, I knew, be achieved."[2]

Spirit and courage could not compensate for lack of training, however. By late September the 77th had sustained severe losses in the Argonne, with regiments dwindling to the size of battalions, and battalions to companies. Raw replacements from a "depot division"—an emasculated former fighting unit—filled the gaps. Many of the replacements were recent draftees who had received only cursory training before being shipped to France—cannon fodder, essentially. Among the 77th's replacements, most of whom came from the western plains states, "many had not fired a rifle, and had never seen a grenade. They had no idea of target designation, and had to be told how, where, and when to shoot."[3] Flung into the attack almost as soon as they arrived, alongside officers and men who did not know their names and clutching rifles they could not load, many died without firing a shot.

Major Whittlesey's First Battalion, 308th Regiment, had received its share of replacements a few days before. Although they had experienced some fighting, the replacements remained newcomers, shunned by the other men—there was a vast cultural difference, after all, between Brooklyn and Wyoming—and still poorly trained. Unused to the stress and exertions of combat, they were past exhaustion. "I was near all in," a replacement from Montana complained. "I took the bayonet off my rifle because I had to catch myself from falling two or three times, and I was afraid I would fall down on my bayonet."[4] The veterans felt little better. None of them had rested since September 26, and many had not received fresh food and water.

First Battalion nevertheless attacked at 6:00 A.M. on October 1, moving forward from L'Homme Mort with Second Battalion—now under the command of Captain George McMurtry, a granite-faced but good-humored former Rough Rider—in support. Advancing through thick underbrush and wire past a wrecked German headquarters building surrounded by corpses, Whittlesey's battalion suffered so many casualties during fighting for a strongly defended apple orchard that the medical detachment could not handle the constant flow of wounded.[5] By 10:00 A.M. the Americans had reached a crossroads half a mile east of Binarville, which the 368th Regiment had taken the previous day before the French occupied it. To the right was a densely wooded north-south ravine, about six to eight hundred yards wide. Ahead, on the west side of the ravine, German-held trenches and machine-gun emplacements stretched across a steep wooded hill. Whittlesey tried to take the hill from the front and to the right, but failed to make any progress before nightfall.

Captain McMurtry's Second Battalion took positions in the ravine, where Private John Nell discovered abandoned German barracks consisting of dugouts and log buildings clustered along a light railway. Decaying corpses littered the area, including one carcass that Nell found particularly bothersome:

> There was a little car sitting on the track with board sides and both ends open. A dead German with his head and feet sticking out over both ends of the car was stinking terribly. I recall he had a sandy red mustache. I gave the car a shove with my foot, and the car ran about a hundred feet then left the rail. This got the terrible odor away from us.[6]

McMurtry established Second Battalion headquarters in one of the buildings. Regimental headquarters occupied a dugout another two hundred yards back down the ravine. Colonel Stacey, the regiment's high-strung commander, worried that the Germans would shell the dugout if they detected any activity there, and discouraged visitors.[7]

To the east, the 307th, 306th, and 305th, from left to right, had also attacked early in the morning, without result. The 305th, following paths that engineers hacked through the woods and improbably towing two 75mm guns, made it as far as the crest of a ridge in the Bois de la Naza. The 306th, facing "diagonally crossing gaps through the forest, to cross which, we learned earlier in the game, it was necessary either to dash or to crawl on our stomachs" under fire of enemy machine guns, advanced to the southern edge of Charlevaux Valley, which continued west to the northern end of the ravine occupied by McMurtry's battalion.[8] The 307th advanced all the way across the valley to the Charlevaux Mill road on its northern side, but had to withdraw under fire. By nightfall it occupied positions on the east side of the ravine, to the 308th's right.

✳

The saga of the so-called Lost Battalion began on October 2. Brigadier General Evan Johnson, commanding the 154th Brigade (307th and 308th Regiments), was visiting the lines early that morning when Major General Alexander called his headquarters and left a message:

> You tell General Johnson that the 154th Brigade is holding back the French on the left and is holding back everything on the right and that the 154th Brigade must push forward to their objective today. By "Must" I mean must, and by "today" I mean today and not next week. You report heavy machine gun fire, but the casualty lists do not substantiate this. Remember that when you are making these reports.

Johnson was incredulous. How could he hold up the French on his left or the 153d Brigade on his right when *they* lagged behind *his* brigade? He called Alexander back and tried to explain the actual state of the front lines. Was it wise to press the attack when it might leave his brigade further exposed? Alexander, who had spent much of the previous day exploring his new headquarters in an elaborate German complex equipped with kitchens, mess halls, "bath houses, with both hot and cold water, moving picture theaters, bowling alleys of concrete and almost everything else calculated to make life pleasant," brushed him off. On October 2, he told Johnson, the French planned to launch a major attack north of Binarville while the 28th Division assaulted Le Chêne Tondu. They both counted on the 77th Division to help break the German line. If Johnson did not attack immediately and without regard to losses, Alexander told him over the phone, "he would get some one else who could." Johnson obeyed.[9]

The objective of 154th Brigade was the ridge north of the Charlevaux Mill road, which the 307th Regiment had briefly reached the previous day. This time, the 307th didn't get anywhere. Attacking at 7:00 A.M., the regiment's Second Battalion reached a dense screen of barbed wire. The American "barrage" that preceded the advance had not even slightly damaged the wire, and German rifles, machine guns, and rifle grenades hacked the Doughboys to pieces before they could start using their wire cutters. The Americans withdrew. By chance, one company penetrated a gap in the German wire and advanced as far as the road, but the commander feared becoming isolated and pulled back.[10]

Whittlesey's battalion also attacked that morning, only to find the German positions on the hill still impervious to frontal assault. Scouts reconnoitering the eastern slopes of the ravine told him that they had found another way forward. Between nine and ten o'clock they had advanced up that side of the ravine to within six hundred yards of the Charlevaux Mill

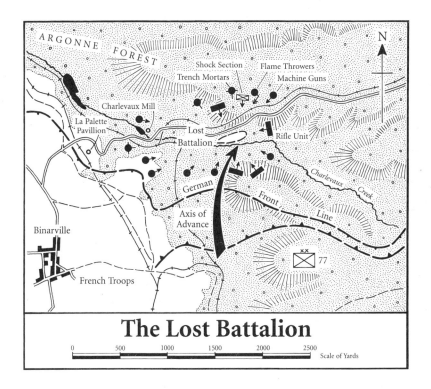

The Lost Battalion

road before meeting any enemy resistance. When Whittlesey received an order from Colonel Stacey to resume the attack at 12:50 P.M., therefore, he decided to drive a wedge into this apparent gap in the German lines. First and Second Battalions would move out together. Companies D and F would advance on the west of the ravine, applying enough pressure on the Germans on the hill to keep their attention away from their flank. Below the ravine's eastern edge, meanwhile, Companies B and C would advance behind a light screen of scouts, followed by Companies A, E, G, and H, and Companies C and D of the 306th Machine Gun Battalion. Whittlesey didn't worry about his own flanks. The 307th Regiment was attacking again on his right. On his left, reports said that the French had already advanced two miles.

★

RATION details appeared just before the attack began, and issued a day's worth of food to all except two companies, which were forced to advance without it. Ammunition also did not arrive in quantity. The Doughboys had about two hundred rounds per rifle, five boxes of ammunition per machine gun, and a small number of grenades. At least they had entrenching tools and some signal flares. In case those ran out, Whittlesey's aide carried a few messenger pigeons.

"Leaders, get your men up!" Whittlesey ordered as several batteries of 75s opened fire at 12:30 P.M. "Let's go! Forward!" he cried twenty minutes later, and the attack began. The broken, wooded terrain forced the Americans to advance in single file by platoons, and although officers issued orders to prevent all unnecessary delays, telling the men to urinate or defecate where they stood rather than leave their column, progress was slow. Snipers, "all over the damn place," caused the biggest delays. Whittlesey eventually grew exasperated at the stop-and-go advance, and yelled, "Advance until the last man drops!"[11]

The Germans did not offer any organized resistance, except for a few dozen middle-aged reservists who quickly surrendered, and the persistent snipers. By midafternoon the companies on the east side of the ravine—less ninety casualties from snipers—had moved up a branch of the ravine to the western edge of Ridge 198. Below lay the shallow, wooded Charlevaux Valley, at the bottom of which ran tiny Charlevaux Brook. The far slope rose thirty feet, at a 60-to-70-degree angle, to the regiment's objective, the Charlevaux Mill road. Above the road rose a sheer embankment, about ten to fifteen feet high; above that, in places, was a ledge, or another steep slope.[12]

Whittlesey had left two-man runner posts every two hundred yards along his route of advance to maintain contact with the rear, and although his troops detected some enemy activity to their left—where most of the snipers were—the major felt secure enough to enter the valley and advance to his objective. The Americans clambered down the slope and crossed a swampy area to the brook, where they discovered a little plank bridge. The vegetation was thin here—the Germans had cleared some of the valley for use as a drill field, and a dirt road ran alongside the stream—and the Americans could see a long way to left and right. The Germans saw them too, and inflicted several casualties as Whittlesey's men double-timed across the bridge. He ordered them to climb the far slope and dig in, below the road. The steep slope offered good protection against enemy artillery, and the trees and underbrush grew thickly, concealing the troops from snipers. By dusk the Americans had gouged dozens of rifle and machine-gun pits and foxholes in the rocky soil. The holes would get a little deeper each day.[13]

With standing orders to hold here until support arrived, Whittlesey deployed his troops in a roughly oval-shaped perimeter about three hundred yards long and sixty deep. Companies E, G, A, C, B, and H were arranged from right to left, with machine guns—nine in all—on each flank. Men with unreliable Chauchats took positions around the perimeter. Whittlesey and McMurtry occupied a foxhole near the center. The major sent a message reporting his positions to Colonel Stacey via the runner posts and ordered his men to eat supper—uncooked, of course.[14] Four medical men tended the wounded.

As the westernmost formation in First Army, the 308th Regiment relied on the French to cover its left flank. The liaison unit, the 368th Regiment, had departed, but the French were supposed to have filled the gap. So far, however, Whittlesey had seen nothing of his allies. They were supposed to have advanced far beyond Binarville to a German stronghold to the northwest, La Palette Pavilion. Why, then, did the enemy still seem so active in that direction? Were they preparing to withdraw? He sent two privates, George Newcom and John Hott, to find out.

Crawling from bush to bush below the road, Newcom and Hott worked westward until they detected the outlines of Charlevaux Mill. They heard some soldiers on the road above them, chatting indistinctively. Unsure if they were friend or foe, Newcom took cover. Hott, less wisely, blurted, "What outfit is that up there?" In reply, an entire squad of Germans emerged from the trees and pointed their rifles at the hapless private. Newcom, still concealed, aimed his rifle at the German squad leader, thought the better of it, and lay still as the enemy soldiers took Hott's rifle, searched him, and led him off down the road. When they left Newcom returned to Whittlesey. There were no French to the west, only Germans. And they looked as if they meant to stay.[15]

Unbeknownst to Whittlesey, the attack against La Palette Pavilion had failed, and the French had withdrawn in disorder all the way back to Binarville. They were now well *behind* Whittlesey's position. On the right, meanwhile, the Statue of Liberty Division's other three regiments had all bogged down. The 305th and 306th had made no progress at all. The 307th had advanced as far as the Charlevaux Valley's southern rim, and then withdrawn. Just before nightfall, Johnson received Whittlesey's report of his advance to the Charlevaux Mill road, and decided to see if he could take advantage of it. He shifted a battalion of the 307th west into the ravine through which Whittlesey had advanced that morning, and ordered it to follow the same route. The battalion did not get into position until after nightfall, however, and only its leading company, Captain Nelson Holderman's Company K, made it as far as the valley. The other companies got lost in the dark and returned to their original positions. Holderman, who had served in the California National Guard since 1904 and "took to soldiering like a kitten to catnip," joined Whittlesey during the early morning of October 3. His seventy-nine men would be the major's only reinforcements.

The German forces around Whittlesey were tired, disorganized, and surprised by the advance through the ravine. At first they did not know what to do about it; but their confusion did not last long. Realizing that the Americans were unsupported, on the evening of October 2 they began working around Whittlesey's flanks, especially the left. The men of Company H could hear the enemy soldiers moving but could not see them. Once or twice the Germans threw grenades or fired machine guns to test their defenses, and the Americans fired back, illuminating the woods with brief flashes, but there were few casualties. Those would come later.

General Johnson phoned divisional headquarters late that evening. General Alexander's chief of staff, Colonel J. R. R. Hannay, picked up the phone. Johnson told him of Whittlesey's advance, but also reported the dangerous exposure of both his flanks. Hannay listened, hung up, and phoned back shortly after. "General Alexander says, 'Congratulations,'" he stated blandly. "I do not consider it a matter for congratulations," replied Johnson, probably struggling to contain an apoplectic fit, "but I wish to put him absolutely in possession of the facts."[16]

Johnson phoned Alexander again at about 2:00 A.M. on October 3 to report that Whittlesey's command was in danger of being cut off. "The information did not, at the time, make a very deep impression," Alexander later confessed. Johnson had reserves, including the 308th's Third Battalion. These should suffice to protect Whittlesey's left flank. Alexander had anyway just received a pleasant message from the corps commander. Liggett had extended to Alexander and "the entire 77th Division a most cordial expression of his gratification at the steady, solid progress made since the beginning of the operation now under way. . . . The difficulties of the terrain are fully understood and the amount of ground gained is notable, while your supplies and communications are thoroughly satisfactory." With praise such as this, Alexander had no time to bother with the niggling complaints of his brigade commander, whom he had begun to dislike.[17]

✫

THE Germans sealed the pocket by daybreak on October 3. Infiltrating through the woods to Whittlesey's left and right, they met on Ridge 198 south of Charlevaux Valley, plugging the northern end of the ravine. It did not take long for Whittlesey to learn he was surrounded. At daybreak, he ordered Company E, fifty men under Lieutenant Karl Wilhelm, to attack down the west side of the ravine and establish contact with Companies D and F, which had remained there the previous day. Wilhelm's force moved cautiously toward the ravine when a voice in the woods called out, "Americans?" The veterans took cover; but one soldier, evidently a newcomer, obligingly called back that they were, indeed, Americans. "What company is that?" the voice inquired. "E!" several Doughboys replied. Then silence. A scout that Wilhelm sent to find E Company's interrogator disappeared. Finally, the lieutenant ordered his men to resume their advance. As they stood up, several grenades thumped down the hill and rolled through the leaves. As they exploded, the Germans opened fire from all sides. Eighteen men made it back to Whittlesey and reported what had happened. Wilhelm and a sergeant crawled on, and made it all the way back to regimental headquarters around midnight. The rest of the men of Company E were killed, wounded, or captured.[18]

Forty minutes after the remnants of Company E returned to their foxholes on the slope, Whittlesey ordered Captain Holderman's Company K to move south across Charlevaux Valley and reopen communications with the rest of the brigade. Holderman, who had been so ill the previous day that he could barely walk, led his men into the valley and across the brook. Holderman's men raced across the dirt road and up the ravine's southern slope to Ridge 198. The Germans, who had patiently allowed Company K to advance into their midst the better to destroy it, then opened fire from all sides. Holderman doggedly pushed his men on through two networks of barbed wire before giving it up as a bad job and leading them back with many wounded—the dead had to be left behind. He reported back to Whittlesey late that afternoon. The runner posts had been wiped out. They were surrounded.

The troops in the perimeter—554 in all, counting Companies E and K—had spent a busy day. At 3:00 P.M., the Germans hurled showers of potato-masher grenades down from the ridge above the road. The Americans fired back but no enemy came—evidently they were just probing their positions. At sunset, German infantry assaulted both flanks while more grenades rolled down the slope. Whittlesey had placed his machine guns well, and they beat back the enemy infantry without much trouble. More galling were the enemy trench mortars, or minenwerfers, which, because of their high trajectory, could hit them easily from emplacements in the valley or higher up the slope.

The Americans could only dig deeper. "There were long periods of time," one soldier remembered, "when all one did was lie there and hope nothing made a direct hit in your own particular funkhole."[19]

Whittlesey released three carrier pigeons during the day, all of which made it safely to lofts at Alexander's ornate headquarters complex near Champ Mahaut. "Germans are on cliff North of us in small numbers and have had to evacuate both flanks," the first message read. "Situation on left flank very serious." The others reported shortages of food and supplies and requested artillery support. All were too terse to represent the situation as it really was. The Americans had no more grenades, and machine-gun ammunition was running out. Soldiers experimented with different types of leaves in place of tobacco, for all the cigarettes had been smoked. They had finished their food the previous day; in desperation, men licked salt and pepper from condiment cans. This only increased their raging thirst. Water could be found only in the slimy brook or a nearby spring, both of which the Germans had covered. Several men who tried to draw water were wounded. Whittlesey posted a guard to prevent further attempts during the day, but the Germans continued firing at the watering places even at night.[20]

By nightfall on October 3, 25 percent of Whittlesey's force had become casualties. There were no fresh bandages, and only three enlisted, semiqualified men from the medical corps to provide aid. And of course there was no disinfectant or anesthetic. Whittlesey never forgot the "moans and half-suppressed cries" of men who "strove to grit the little devils of pain and anguish between their teeth." But neither Whittlesey nor McMurtry was ready to quit. "Our mission is to hold this position at all costs," they instructed their company commanders. "No falling back. Have this understood by every man in your command."[21]

Such was the 77th Division's situation on the morning of October 4, when First Army attacked all along the lines in an attempt to crack the *Kriemhilde Stellung*. Alexander had met the previous evening at Liggett's headquarters with Generals Summerall, Muir, and George B. Duncan of the 1st, 28th, and 82d Divisions, the latter unit still in reserve. Liggett hoped for great things from the 1st Division, as did the rest of First Army. If successful, the German positions in the Argonne would be unhinged. In the meantime, 77th Division must attack in full force, in coordination with the French on their left— although how that could be accomplished without any kind of liaison remained open to speculation. Reports of Whittlesey's situation had reached I Corps, and thoughts of the disastrous consequences to American morale if the isolated troops surrendered lurked at the back of everyone's minds.

The 77th's attack ended where it began. On the right, the 153d Brigade assaulted a ridge in the Bois de la Naza and accomplished nothing. The 307th Regiment, striving to force its way through strands of barbed wire sixty to eighty feet deep, also failed. At noon Johnson ordered his brigade to resume the attack at 4:30, with the 307th pushing abreast of the surrounded troops on the right while the Third Battalion of the 308th attacked up the west side of the ravine to relieve them from behind. The 307th took heavy casualties but briefly penetrated about five hundred yards down the east side of the ravine. The 308th's Third Battalion, however, made only a pathetic attempt to get forward. Colonel Stacey, the regiment's commander, had suffered a nervous breakdown.

Stacey had gone to pieces that evening when Johnson informed him over the phone that the remnants of his regiment would attack again the next day, October 5. "I do not believe that at any time during the fighting in the Argonne Forest, the Brigade and Division Commander had a correct appreciation of the enormous difficulties encountered," Stacey later asserted. "I could tell from the impatient and unreasonable messages and orders I received that they had no idea of the actual conditions." He was correct—like many other generals in First Army, Alexander and Johnson were completely out of touch with the front—but the 308th nevertheless needed a leader, and Stacey was not the man. He begged Johnson to transfer him to a command in the services of supply. Johnson refused, but passed Stacey's request on to Alexander, adding that the colonel's conduct had been "weak in the extreme." Alexander responded by ordering Johnson to relieve Stacey. Johnson protested; the only man available to take the colonel's place was a captain, Lucien Breckenridge. Alexander replied "that the command of the regiment was immaterial so long as the officer at its head could and would fight." Stacey went.[22]

The surrounded troops grew more miserable with each passing hour. Hunger pangs had grown severe, and the sufferings of the wounded were indescribable. Whittlesey released two of his last three pigeons by early afternoon. "Many wounded here when we can't evacuate. Need rations badly," read his first message. "Situation is cutting into our strength rapidly," the second message reported. "Men are suffering from hunger and exposure, and the wounded are in very bad condition. Cannot support be sent at once?" The Germans attacked repeatedly, and Whittlesey's well-entrenched men beat them back without too much trouble. Yet there was no way to defend against the grenades that fell out of nowhere, the snipers who fired and moved to new positions, and the trench mortar shells that exploded without warning, leaving men torn and screaming.

At about 2:45 P.M., a salvo of high-explosive shells landed on the valley's southern slope. The trapped Doughboys cheered, thinking that their artillery was aiming for the German positions behind them. Then, as Whittlesey described it, "increasing in intensity, the barrage crept down the slope, crossed the marshy bottom of the ravine where it hurled mud and brush into the air, and settled directly on our position." The Germans gladly augmented the 75mm shells with a minenwerfer barrage of their own. The Doughboys took about thirty casualties, including several shell-shocked men who got up from their holes and wandered away to be killed or captured. Whittlesey decided to release his last pigeon, named Cher Ami, in an attempt to stop the barrage. "Our artillery is dropping a barrage directly on us. For Heaven's Sake stop it," he scrawled on a piece of paper, and attached it to the pigeon's leg. But the bird seemed to feel honor-bound to remain with the surrounded troops. Upon release, it flew into a nearby tree and perched there, preening itself. Whittlesey and his men hurled debris at the stubborn pigeon as it stared at them, unperturbed. Finally a private climbed the tree, shaking branches and shouting at the pigeon to leave. Sensing that it was not wanted, the bird finally departed its ungrateful friends, circled two or three times, and headed south. The barrage ended at 4:20, either because of a previously set firing schedule, or the bravery of Cher Ami.[23]

Whittlesey struggled to maintain morale among his soldiers. Wounded men moaned and screamed; the dead lay unburied. Some soldiers engaged in fisticuffs. Now and then the sound of machine-gun fire crept closer from the south, convincing the men that they were about to be relieved, only to fade away again. Planes flew overhead. Sometimes they were Germans sighting for the artillery, and sometimes they were French and Americans. Whittlesey signaled the Allied planes with flares and cloth panels, and they dropped supplies, but all of the parcels landed within the enemy lines. He tried to cheer the men, but his choice of words was not always fortunate. Sometimes he gave them patriotic tripe—telling them, for example, that "there are two million Americans pushing up to relieve us." At other times he gave historical lectures, remarking that "the English forces held out at Lucknow for forty days without any trouble at all."[24] The Brooklyn toughs and western farmers had no idea where Lucknow was, or what it had to do with them, but the major's coolness impressed them. Once, pinned down by enemy machine guns, Whittlesey turned to McMurtry and sarcastically said, "*Most* unpleasant," like he was "criticizing the flavor of a cup of tea." Few realized that he cried in his sleep.[25]

McMurtry and Holderman showed that they too were fine leaders. McMurtry, who had already severely bruised his knee, was fighting off a

German counterattack when a grenade exploded nearby. The grenade's wooden handle flew into his back, but he kept walking around, oblivious of the protruding wood, until Whittlesey noticed and abruptly pulled it out. McMurtry roared in pain and turned on the major. "If you ever do that again," he swore, "I'll wring your neck."[26] Holderman had several painful wounds that festered on the verge of gangrene. Yet he and all the other officers remained calm, even cheerful, visiting the wounded and scrambling from one foxhole to another to encourage the men.

✦

REPORTS of the surrounded troops' predicament spread quickly through the AEF. By the evening of October 4 the Doughboys were all talking about it. Would the trapped men be rescued? Could they break out? Did anyone at First Army headquarters know or care? A lot rode on the answer to the last question, and Pershing knew it. In purely military terms, a weak battalion didn't mean that much. The British, French, and Germans had thrown away much larger formations without a second thought. But American soldiers and the civilian public would be unlikely to forgive such wastage. Battle casualties, however pointless, could be explained away as necessary sacrifices of war, but the destruction or surrender of an isolated battalion could not be justified so easily. And the press had already got hold of the story. On October 3, a reporter with the United Press transmitted a report of the Charlevaux fighting to his cable editor, who responded, "Send more on Lost Battalion"—by lost, he meant doomed.[27]

Pershing and his generals thus could not afford to ignore Whittlesey's command as they drew up plans for the continuation of the second phase of the Meuse-Argonne offensive. With the exception of the advance of the 1st Division—achieved at heavy cost in casualties—October 4 had been a day of bloody disappointment for First Army. Every attack had failed, with no serious progress toward the capture of the vitally important Heights of Cunel and Romagne. The drive against these must of course continue, and Pershing issued orders for V and III Corps to attack again on October 5 with no change in objective.[28] German artillery, from the Heights of the Meuse to the east and the fringes of the Argonne to the west, continued to pour devastating flanking fire into First Army's infantry. Yet with Whittlesey's predicament an additional and equally vital objective had to be inserted into the American plan of attack. The Lost Battalion must be relieved.

The German commander, Gallwitz, had fewer concerns. On the afternoon of October 4 he toured the front, visiting aid stations and talking to his wounded soldiers. They were surprisingly cheerful. The Americans had suffered "terrific losses," the German soldiers said, and their vaunted artillery, tanks, and planes had proven completely ineffective.

> The men related with pride how tank attacks had been resisted, reporting that many tanks were destroyed by artillery and machine guns. One lieutenant blew up with his guns not less than three of those monstrous tanks, if current rumors meant anything. Our flyers, too, gave a very good account of themselves. They not only brought in important information in regard to the development of the fighting, but also succeeded in preventing the enemy from observing movements in our rear. . . . The whole Fifth Army felt in the best of humour, on account of having completely repulsed a superior opponent.[29]

Almost two million American soldiers, Gallwitz knew, were now in Europe. And this was the best they could do?

CHAPTER 15

"Just Plain Murder"

OCTOBER 5

M ajor General Robert Bullard, III Corps' commander, thought the beleaguered 4th Division troops in the Bois de Fays could use a little
pick-me-up—not coffee, but encouraging words. "You are there. Stay there,"
he told them. Easy for *him* to say, soldiers like Sergeant Major James Block responded. "The enemy had been 'sapping' hell out of us for days. We had to like
it and call it good. How much better it would have been if those last words
had been changed to this—'Attack the enemy and tear him to shreds.' "[1] But
no attack orders came. Instead the troops hunkered down and endured torments that never seemed to end.

The Bois de Fays formed a salient in the German lines, fully exposed to
enemy fire on all sides. Artillery on the Heights of the Meuse registered every
spring, road, and footpath, making it a terrifying and often deadly journey to
get water or carry a message. Enemy observers beyond the river or in planes
hovering above detected the slightest movements and picked out crowded
trenches and foxholes with insidious accuracy. Enemy planes bombed the
woods all day, spreading a sense of helplessness and terror. Gas—mustard,
phosgene, and even tear—drifted through the woods at unpredictable intervals, causing terrible casualties among troops who did not wear their masks
all the time. At night, Colonel Frederic Wise watched the remnants of his
59th Regiment hobbling out of the woods, their gas-infected eyes oozing
fluid, "one man who could see a little, in front, leading the others, totally

blinded, who held on to little sticks, extending from hand to hand, to guide them."[2]

Every night, German snipers and machine-gun teams entered the woods in small parties, penetrating gaps in the American lines on either flank. In the morning they opened fire from every direction. Nowhere was safe. A Doughboy could be hiding in his foxhole one moment and find a grenade in his lap the next. The stench of death, from dozens of unburied bodies in the thick underbrush, floated everywhere. At night, soldiers dragged as many bodies as they could find to the southern edge of the woods and buried them in mass graves, but plentiful supplies of fresh corpses appeared the next day. Survivors recalled the broken, the hysterical, and the shell-shocked; more than anything, they remembered how men's eyes grew dull, their movements mechanical.[3] Total strangers sharing the same shell holes forged comradeships that lasted only for a few days, until one or both were killed or until they withdrew from the woods and returned to their units. Often they did not even know each other's names—they just knew that they were in it together.

☆

Major Jennings Wise, commanding the Gray Squirrel Battalion of the Blue Ridge Division's 318th Regiment, woke before daylight on October 5. General Cronkhite had sent his officers a message, the same as the one he had given them yesterday: "The reputation of the Division is at stake. The Bois des Ogons *must* be taken!" He did not mention the danger to his *own* reputation should the Blue Ridge Division fail. Give up the attack, the ferocious Bullard had told him in a confrontation at divisional headquarters, "and you are a goner; you'll lose your command in twenty-four hours." As Wise trolled about in the dark, trying to lash his scattered and demoralized troops into formation, he confronted a trembling lieutenant who had spent the previous day hiding in a cellar. "Where have you been?" Wise demanded. Before the lieutenant could answer a shell hit nearby, killing him instantly. A little later he came across another young lieutenant. This one was not scared; he had just finished officer school and rushed to the front lest he miss the fighting. As he reported for duty a shell had burst in his face. "I'm afraid I'm blind," he said, as Wise rolled back the lids of his burnt-out eyes.[4]

Private Rush Young of the Red Squirrel Battalion took advantage of the misty morning to brew coffee in his foxhole, since the Germans couldn't see the smoke. As the fog lifted he looked out of his hole toward Nantillois, through which the Gray Squirrels and other units advanced to the attack. Vaguely human figures stumbled aimlessly, unable to see through their gas masks and stunned by the shells that fell around them. German planes strafed them and darted about, directing artillery. Machine gunners lugged their guns forward to support the attack, but as soon as they set up, lines of German shells crumped across the fields, knocking them out in bloody punctuations. Officers stood about, studying their maps in idle futility. Meanwhile, "all along the ridge I could see boys being mowed down by machine-gun fire, and the runners were being picked off by snipers. Another runner would try his luck, by running to the wounded or dead one, getting the message and trying to get it through. Down he would go and another would try."[5]

The Gray Squirrels tottered back after about two hours of fighting, along with the defeated troops of two other regiments. Major Wise led the remnants of his battalion along a sunken road below Nantillois and found it "filled level with stiffened bodies." Many of them were from his battalion, which had entered the Meuse-Argonne with one thousand men and now numbered about three hundred. The survivors were half dead themselves. Among the battalion's supply wagons, Wise discovered a shell-shocked private who had escaped from a field hospital to which he had been sent the previous day, "half-starved, crawling on hands and knees among the horses." The private seized Wise by the knees and begged not to be sent away. "I'll tend yo' horses if only yo'll lemme stay," he whined. The major ordered him back to the hospital.[6]

The Red Squirrels' turn came at 10:00 A.M., and Private Young and his battalion advanced past Nantillois over heavily cratered fields. German artillery harassed them until they reached the relative safety of a ravine. Above was a shelterless ridge; 150 yards beyond that lay the Bois des Ogons. There was a pause while the company commanders, many of them sergeants taking the place of dead or wounded captains and lieutenants, tried to settle the men for the final advance. The soldiers, "shivering and shaking in their shell holes, praying to God Almighty to help them," knew that crossing the hill would be "just plain murder." Young took cover in an old German machine-gun nest back in the ravine while he waited for the attack order. The German artillery had spotted the ravine, and shellfire intensified as Young huddled in the muddy hole. Another American flopped down next to him. It was his friend Private Willie P. Mitchell, crying and trembling uncontrollably.

Young, his company's unofficial father-confessor, tried to console his friend. "Don't let it get on your nerves, we will make it all right," he said. "No, Young," Mitchell replied, "I'll never get across that ridge alive." Young tried to smile. "Oh, cheer up," he said, and talked about other things. But Mitchell wasn't listening. At noon, the order came to advance, and the two soldiers sat together while Young prayed for them both. "We must go now, Mitchell," he said. "I will go first and you follow . . . see you in the woods." "Good Bye," Mitchell called as Young climbed out of the hole. Young shouted, "Don't say good bye," and ran as fast as he could toward the hill. A German shell killed Mitchell moments later.

Young left the ravine and climbed the hill, past the wreckage of a German plane flanked by the bodies of its young pilot and a Doughboy. The slopes trembled with German shellfire, and puffs of gray smoke drifted by. He found the men of his company crouched in shell holes just below the crest. Between each shell burst he could hear the cries of the wounded and the screams of the shell-shocked, who "had become crazy, wild, raving maniacs. It is a terrible feeling, because you are not conscious of what you are doing. They had to be held down or knocked out, because they fear nothing then." Everyone wondered what the Bois des Ogons held in store for them. Young was glad he didn't know.

> An officer's whistle blew and the Red Squirrels jumped off for the attack. As we reached the crest of the hill, it was one solid sea of shell craters, not one foot of land remained that had not been torn up by the big shells. Machine guns were popping in every direction. Off we went for the woods as fast as we could go. Whiz-Bang, Whiz-Bang, Crash! Crash! And a big shell burst in front of me just at the edge of the woods, scattering chunks of human flesh all over the ground. On a limb of a tree about ten feet high, hung a man's leg with the shoe and wrap leggins still on it. Poor soldier! Who could he be?

Three heavy tanks that had somehow made it up the ridge accompanied the advance. They were all knocked out within the first few minutes. Their French crews, clad in grimy uniforms, bailed out and headed for the rear. Lieutenant Robert Higgins, later a football star at Penn State, did not see the French getting out of their tanks—or so he later claimed—and assumed that they were Germans. The lieutenant had a strong arm, and he hurled grenades at the tankers with unusual gusto. He kept them running from hole to hole for five minutes until he "recognized" them as allies and allowed them to pass. The French stalked back over the ridge, cursing and saying "most everything uncomplimentary about the American soldier."

Private Young and about 175 men of his company—another 75 had fallen since crossing the ridge—made it into the woods. Officers studied their maps and decided to advance. Surprisingly, they met little opposition, advancing for about two hundred yards and finding a hurriedly abandoned German barracks that seemed as large as a town. Nearby, they discovered a teenage German soldier who had been chained to a tree with his machine gun. His hands were in the air and he had "a smile on his face a mile long." An escort took him and a few other prisoners to the rear while Young and his comrades explored the barracks, awestruck at the boardwalks running through the woods from one building to another and the carefully tended gardens.

The surreal peace didn't last long. As the Americans explored the houses, concealed German machine guns and snipers opened fire, hitting several officers and men. Trench-mortar shells and whiz-bangs followed the machine-gun bullets. "What in the Hell was coming off, anyway?" Young wondered. Where was their support? Why hadn't any other Americans come in on the flanks? An officer ordered the company to take cover in a ditch, but the Germans kept slamming them "with everything from G.I. cans down." A whiz-bang burst near Young, blowing a sergeant's head to pieces and decapitating a lieutenant.

The Americans fixed bayonets, but no German counterattack came. As it grew dark, Young opened a can of bully beef and pulled some pieces of hardtack out of his pack. His canteen was empty so he walked down the ditch in search of water. He found none, and finally sat down on what looked like a log: "It felt soft and a terrible odor came up from it. It was a dead German, and I had sat on his stomach. As the last breath was squeezed out of him, he groaned. My hair stood straight up, I never had such a funny feeling in my life. I completely lost my appetite and threw the corn wooly away." His battalion was relieved that night.[7]

The 80th Division spent the entire day attacking the Bois des Ogons. Almost everywhere the troops made short advances with heavy casualties before the German artillery drove them back to their original positions. Some units broke, leaving behind dozens of prisoners. Other companies entered the woods and either lost their way or fell victim to German grenade, mortar, and artillery attacks. Some disintegrated; others, like Young's, held on to tiny toeholds in the woods. Finally, at 6:00 P.M. Cronkhite sent his entire division forward, only to find that the Germans had withdrawn entirely from the Bois des Ogons. So far as they were concerned, the woods had served their purpose.

★

MAJOR General Beaumont Buck's 3d Division had been dubbed the Rock of the Marne for its stubborn defense of that river back in July. It encountered a bigger rock on October 5. The day before, the division had tried unsuccessfully to break the German positions on Hills 250 and 253, en route to the eastern reaches of the Heights of Romagne. It pulled back that evening to recuperate, while enemy reinforcements, including infantry, machine guns, and light artillery, dug in and waited for the Americans to attack again. At dawn on October 5, the men of the 7th Regiment stepped over the bodies of their fallen comrades, through the same ravine they had crossed the previous day, and charged up Hill 253. Beaten back, they attacked again and again, ending the day on the hill's southern slopes. To their right, the 4th Regiment moved out silently under cover of heavy fog, approaching the woods on Hill 250. The fog lifted while the trees were yet 150 yards away. Immediately, dozens of German machine guns opened fire, along with rifles, mortars, and 88s. The slaughter was unbelievable. Buck nevertheless poured in his reserves and launched further attacks at eleven and two o'clock, each of which ended the same way.[8]

Jack Barkley—"Punk" to his Indian comrades—had not seen any fighting since knocking out a German artillery piece the previous night. His Third Battalion, 4th Regiment, remained in reserve all day. The inactivity ended near dusk, when he learned that one last attempt would be made against Hill 250 in the dark. Two companies of Third Battalion would lead the advance, accompanied by Barkley's scouts. Expecting close fighting in the woods, he exchanged his rifle for a sawed-off shotgun and readied his pistol, trench knife, and grenades.

Admonished to silence, the Doughboys crept forward, dropping to the ground when enemy flares lit up the sky and trying not to trip over the wounded men and corpses that littered the fields. Suddenly rifles and Chauchats opened up. A soldier yelled, "Let's go!" and Barkley's squad jumped and ran toward the woods as the German machine guns came to life. The left-hand company had moved quickly and entered the woods before the Germans could hit it in the open. The right-hand company was not as fortunate. Barkley found it still outside the woods and beset by a swarm of German infantry. Groups of soldiers battled back and forth, firing from the hip and swinging rifle butts. One American accidentally whacked Barkley on the head, causing him to drop his shotgun. He didn't bother looking for it, but ran toward the woods.

Barkley had not yet made the tree line when he tripped over a machine gun mounted at the side of a hole and fell into it headlong. Someone else leapt in after him a moment later. A boot landed on Barkley's left hand. It was German. Fortunately Barkley had his pistol ready in his other hand and shot the enemy soldier, who fell dead on top of him. He was still struggling to get free when another soldier jumped in the hole. This one yelled, "Where in hell's the rear?" in a New York accent and ran off into the darkness without waiting for an answer, leaving Barkley alone with his dead companion. He wedged the body into a sitting position in the corner—it was too heavy to lift—and stayed as far away from it as he could.

The sounds of fighting eventually petered out. Neither side had won; the soldiers just huddled in any shelter they could find. In his hole, Barkley could hear that

> the night all around was filled with cries, groans, curses. In English. In German. In languages I didn't know. Cries for water, for help, for death. Once I heard one boy ask another if he had any chewing-gum. I wouldn't have minded having a little myself. Another boy babbled over and over for hours it seemed to me, "What is this war? What's this war for? What is this damned war?"[9]

☆

Lieutenant Harold Woehl's battalion of the 126th Regiment, 32d Division, attacked just after dawn on October 5. His men moved down a long slope through artillery and machine-gun fire and clouds of gas until they reached a crossroads on the Gesnes-Cierges road. Woehl found everything there in "indescribable confusion," with officers trying unsuccessfully to reorganize their men amid ever-growing piles of dead and wounded.[10] His battalion remained pinned down near the crossroads for the rest of the afternoon, and two more attacks by the regiment's other battalions likewise ended in failure. The Red Arrow's right had bogged down.

Captain Paul Schmidt's company of the 127th Regiment, occupying a ridge just outside Gesnes on the division's left front, stayed put until headquarters found him early that afternoon. Off to the west, Schmidt learned, elements of the regiment had occupied two woods in the morning fog, the Bois de la Morine and the Bois de Chêne Sec, after hand-to-hand fighting. The goal now was to secure Gesnes by capturing Hill 255 and the Bois de Valoup, to its northwest and northeast respectively. A two-hour barrage, the colonel told Schmidt, would hit these positions beginning at 1:45; it was essential that his company should "keep up right behind it." The barrage amounted to ten shells fired over a span of ninety minutes, each of which landed on Hill 255 to no apparent effect. Schmidt's battalion moved out anyway, with orders to pass through Gesnes to jumping-off positions on its northern outskirts. As they approached the village a converging fire of enemy machine guns hit them from three directions, forcing the Doughboys to run pell-mell toward the buildings while German artillery dealt "hammering blows that shook the ground while the thunder of cannon reverberated among the hills that surrounded the town."

In Gesnes, Schmidt's men stumbled upon a scene straight out of the Apocalypse. At least fifty unburied, stinking bodies of 91st Division soldiers and innumerable dead horses littered the town, many of them chopped into bloody chunks by artillery shells that had fallen since they met their deaths a week earlier. Clouds of red dust rose from crumbling walls and terra-cotta roofs as the German guns registered hit after hit. The Americans darted through as fast as they could, as if fearing the dying village would suck them in. Several never made it. The rest reached the shelter of an embankment rimming the village's northern edge. Ahead they could see the German gun emplacements on Hill 255 and in the Bois de Valoup, and the enemy gunners running in and out of their holes. By then it was dark and too late to attack. Headquarters compensated for the abortive assault by reporting that the regiment held Gesnes. The Doughboys may have felt more like the shell-blasted village held them.[11]

★

Lieutenant Charles Butler's 28th Regiment occupied the center of 1st Division's lines, north of Exermont at the foot of Montrefagne. Butler's company had spent the night in funkholes, eating cold rations—wryly called "canned heat"—and watching German artillery systematically dismantle Exermont below them. Halfway through his meal, Butler turned to one of his men. "I don't mind eating surrounded by these dead Germans," he said, "but that Yankee leg lying by that shellhole gives me the chills. Would you mind picking your way down there and tossing it into that shell hole?" With a cheery remark the private crawled over and casually tossed the puttee-wrapped leg into the crater. At dawn the officers blew their whistles, and the Doughboys climbed out of their holes. The private grabbed Butler's arm and pointed to a ditch. "There it is, Lieutenant," he said excitedly. "The mate to the leg I tossed into the shellhole last night!"[12]

The 28th Regiment attacked the eastern end of the Montrefagne while the 18th Regiment attacked the west. The regiments crossed an open, shell-swept draw and then scaled the hill's lower slopes, on which the Germans had dug several deep trenches and dugouts replete with machine guns. Soldiers fell in clumps, a group of fifty being killed in front of one small trench system alone. Fighting swept along the slope as the Doughboys charged, withdrew before counterattacks, and charged again. Sergeant Michael Lewis of St. Louis showed an aptitude for taking out machine-gun nests, capturing at least ten machine guns and forty-four prisoners in actions later rewarded by a Medal of Honor. Lieutenant Butler—more of a regular guy when it came to fighting machine guns—shot a German gunner with his .45, but missed another who ran to take his place. The second German swung the gun around to face Butler, but before he could fire, one of the lieutenant's men killed him with a lucky shot fired from the hip.[13]

Finally, the two regiments won the hill by merit of "extermination"— quarter was neither asked nor given—and paused to reorganize. German shellfire intensified, and when the Americans tried to resume the attack that afternoon they got no farther then the edge of some woods at the base of Montrefagne's northern slope. Ahead of them loomed the rugged heights of Hill 272, a "hive" of German machine guns and artillery.

On the right, the 26th Regiment fought over the wooded, machine-gun-infested crest of Hill 212, engaging in the same kind of close-quarters combat that typified the battle for Montrefagne. The regiment next advanced across a succession of woods, clearings, and small valleys, infiltrating in small groups around German strongpoints rather than moving in formation, toward the Bois de Moncy on the right and Ariétal Farm on the left. The Americans captured both of these points after severe fighting, but shellfire became so strong—the Germans on Hill 272 overlooked the entire sector—that further movement was impossible, except through the woods to the northeast.

First Army tactics had changed since September 26 in at least one significant respect. Then, divisional boundaries had been sacrosanct. Now, Liggett instructed his generals in I Corps to assist their neighbors whenever possible, even when that meant crossing boundaries. When the 26th Regiment's attack ended on the afternoon of October 5, therefore, Summerall authorized its colonel to send a strong patrol northeast through the Bois de Moncy to Hill 269—a wooded height in the 32nd Division's zone. His intention was to aid Haan's division, which remained half a mile behind the 1st Division, by disrupting the communications and supplies of the German forces facing it. By capturing the hill, the patrol would also save the 32d Division the trouble of assaulting it frontally.

The patrol set off. The Germans, not expecting Americans to apply such unorthodox tactics—experience had taught them that Pershing's generals only attacked head-on—made no attempt to stop the patrol, which dutifully occupied Hill 269's western slope and captured numerous prisoners in the process. Summerall reported the move to Haan and Liggett, naturally assuming that he had done something positive. Subsequent events would show that his good intentions had unhappy results.[14]

✯

WITH the exhausted 28th Division inactive on October 5—except on the right, where the 109th Regiment occupied the village of La Forge—the 77th Division faced its worsening predicament in the Argonne alone, unsupported to the west or east.

Whittlesey's command in Charlevaux Valley was in bad shape. "It was the worst mess I ever saw," remembered a private. "Comrades all shot up and lying around under trees and every place you looked. It was worse when you crawled down to the foot of the hill after water. Dead bodies all around the water hole, and the water had lots of blood in it, but it tasted good anyway." The torments of the wounded intensified, with infections spreading through the reuse of soiled bandages. Enemy snipers, machine guns, and trench mortars were active as usual. Morale was poor. "We were literally waiting," said Private Nell, "for our time to die."[15]

At around 10:00 A.M. the trapped soldiers heard a sound that simultaneously encouraged and terrified them. Back on Ridge 198, shells whipped into the German positions, filling the air with sounds of falling timber and screams—along with "flying Dutchmen and parts of the same." So far so good, but the explosions drew closer, crossed the valley, and worked slowly toward the slope as the Doughboys cringed deeper into their holes. Then the shellfire skipped the American positions and landed on the Germans beyond the road above. The artillery knew their positions! Yet the American and French guns did not necessarily work in concert. At 3:00, a French plane buzzed overhead for a few minutes and disappeared. A little later a torrent of 75mm shells tore in from the southwest onto the Americans' right flank, causing relatively few casualties but sending morale back into a tailspin.[16]

Sounds of firing continued to echo from the south. After German machine-gun barrages and grenade attacks, which filled the forest with sounds "like a thousand riveting machines," the Doughboys cocked their ears to hear if the firing had come any closer. By late afternoon, it seemed farther away than ever. That evening the temperature dropped, and a light but cold drizzle sifted down through the shattered trees, adding to the suffering of the wounded. "Their suppressed moans and the impending danger of attack at any moment united to keep many heavy-lidded eyes wide open. And in the solemn watches of the night, these eyes could only see a vision of despair.

Where was the help that every one had expected long before things had come to such a terrible state?"[17]

At 5:30 P.M., General Alexander dispatched a message to Whittlesey by plane. "Our troops now attacking German Trenches in ravine Southeast of Moulin de Charlevaux," it read. "The Division Commander directs that you retire and fight your way through, attacking the Germans from the rear while our troops engage their front." The message fell far off to the west, within French lines. It was well that it did, for the 77th Division's other regiments were nowhere near being able to coordinate a breakout with Whittlesey's exhausted command. To the east, the 305th and 307th Regiments made no progress in their morning attacks, while the French 1st Cavalry Division, pushing toward La Palette Pavilion to the west, fell back before a strong German counterattack.[18]

Alexander ordered the 154th Brigade's commander, Brigadier General Johnson, to leave his headquarters and coordinate the afternoon's attacks from the front, but it did no good. The attack, led by a battalion of the 307th and the Third Battalion of the 308th, began at 2:45 and reached a point two hundred yards south of La Palette Pavilion, but the troops could neither hold there nor penetrate the enemy wire. They withdrew at 5:30, just as Alexander dispatched his message to Whittlesey ordering a breakout in conjunction with nonexistent "troops now attacking German Trenches in ravine Southeast of Moulin de Charlevaux."

To the Germans, the Lost Battalion looked increasingly vulnerable. The French attacks against La Palette Pavilion were pathetic; the 77th Division was ineffective; and the 28th Division had made no headway. The surrounded force in Charlevaux Valley, which some German estimates placed at two thousand men, appeared weak, possibly near capitulation. True, the 1st Division's advance east of the Aire River was worrisome, and must eventually force the Argonne's abandonment. But when had the Americans ever attacked in any direction but straight ahead? Another attempt to crush the Charlevaux pocket seemed worth the risk. Lieutenant General Richard Wellmann, commanding the German I Reserve Corps fighting in the Argonne, asked for a battalion of elite *Stosstruppen* equipped with flamethrowers to augment his force surrounding the American pocket. He was given thirty-six hours to destroy the Americans before his corps pulled out.[19]

★

AT I Corps headquarters that evening, General Liggett put aside his playing cards and peered at his map. The 77th Division had gone nowhere in the

Argonne. German artillery on the northeastern fringes of that forest continued to ravage his infantry, and Whittlesey remained cut off. The 28th Division still had not taken Le Chêne Tondu, and its drive down the Aire Valley had stalled. The 1st Division, however, had covered three miles in two days, all the way to Fléville and Montrefagne. In doing so, it had fulfilled the function originally assigned to the 28th Division—namely, to outflank the Argonne from the east. Pershing had assumed that the Germans would react to such an advance by abandoning the forest. But they had not done so. Perhaps they thought they were calling the Americans' bluff. Perhaps they were so fixated on finishing off the Lost Battalion that they did not notice the danger to their flank. Whatever the reason, Liggett resolved to make them suffer for their mistake.

———•◦•———

CHAPTER 16

"It Is Not a Dishonorable Deed to Give Up"

OCTOBER 6

Jack Barkley woke to a foggy dawn in the woods on Hill 250. The evening before, his group of irregulars had assaulted the woods with two companies of the 4th Regiment, 3d Division. The attack had ended in confusion, leaving soldiers of both sides scattered in foxholes and craters among the trees. Overnight he heard Doughboys and Germans knifing one another in the dark, and in the morning he found the corpse of a German officer near his hole. In another hole nearby sat his Native American buddy Floyd, sporting a Luger and a silver pocket flask—once full of schnapps but now empty— that he had taken from the officer after bayoneting him. Barkley crawled over to Floyd's hole as shapes of soldiers appeared in the mist around them. Soon the fog dispersed, and the sounds of fighting resumed.

The two American companies controlled only the southern rim of the woods. German artillery pummeled and churned the open ground to the south, preventing reinforcements from coming up. The German infantry, meanwhile, seemed stronger and showed indications of preparing a counterattack. If the enemy attacked in force, the outnumbered Doughboys could either fight where they stood or retreat through that murderous barrage. Barkley and his two Indian comrades, Jesse James and Floyd, decided to move deeper into the woods and find out what the Germans were up to. Barkley, who looked like a midget next to the two towering Indians, didn't reveal his doubts about their chances of survival. They already called him "Punk." If he backed out, they might think of worse names.

Shoving pistols in their waistbands and shouldering rifles with belts of ammunition, the three men set out. Dodging among trees and crawling through small meadows and patches of undergrowth, they moved deeper into the woods. After Floyd knifed a sentry in the back, they entered a small hollow. In it they found the bodies of seven Americans, a sergeant and six privates, laid in a row. Their pockets had been ripped open and their bodies plundered of anything of value. Each of them had been killed, execution-style, by a single shot. Floyd and Jesse glanced at each other, wordlessly, but Barkley knew them well enough to expect "trouble for the next Germans they ran into."

Farther on, the trio pushed through a patch of bushes and entered a small clearing. Ten feet in front of them was the center of a column of German infantry—four squads of riflemen and two squads of machine gunners carrying two Maxims. An officer stood nearby, about to send them into action. The Germans and Americans looked at one another in stunned surprise. Floyd reacted first and shot the officer, Jesse fired his pistols, and Barkley killed three Germans with his rifle. The Germans, apparently thinking they were under attack by a large force, scattered for cover as Barkley dropped his rifle and pulled out his pistols. The three Americans fired again and dove back into the thicket—just in time, as the Germans had begun to recover and return fire with rifles and grenades.[1]

This little firefight seemed to wake up the woods, and sounds of firing echoed from all directions as Barkley and his comrades—Floyd shot in the arm and Barkley without his helmet—worked back toward the American lines. After joining Mike, the Italian prizefighter, they returned to combat. Some reinforcements had finally made it up, and the Doughboys had returned to the offensive. German infantry, machine gunners, and snipers contested every patch of trees. The newer American replacements, Barkley noticed, died first—"they tried to hurry things too much." The veterans took their time. Barkley's group did as they pleased:

> We were free lances in that fight—Jesse, Floyd, Mike, and I. We ranged up and down the line wherever the hunting was best. We were under no one's orders. When one of us had lined up on some German crew he'd pass the word. If the nest was within long range of Mike's shotgun all four of us would bombard it. On the singles, we worked as individuals. It was a damned busy morning. They were certainly killers—those two Indians and that little Italian. I didn't realize until afterward that I was a killer too.[2]

By midafternoon the Americans had cleared the woods of Hill 250, capturing thirty German soldiers, thirty-five machine guns with ammunition, and three disabled French tanks.[3] The 4th Regiment's commander tried to push his men farther, out of the woods' northern edge and across an open valley into the Bois de Cunel, but the Germans had the valley covered with artillery and machine guns. The Americans backed off and consolidated their lines, with the Germans not far away.

During the fighting, Barkley had picked up a helmet and put it on in place of the one he had lost that morning. Only after the firing receded did he notice a tingling on his scalp and discover that the inside of the helmet had been splashed with mustard gas. Washing with water did no good, and as the day went on the pain got worse. Jesse's eyes had been irritated by gas that seeped through the splintered eyepiece of his mask, and Floyd's wounded arm was badly swollen. Barkley stitched the arm wound with twigs at Floyd's direction and got an excruciatingly painful iodine bath on his head in exchange.

That evening, battalion headquarters ordered Barkley to scout the German lines and report by midnight. Tired, hungry, and with the top of his head agonizingly sore, he borrowed Mike's shotgun and a belt of shells. He found the front lines—evidently along Hill 250's eastern edge near Madeleine Farm, where Germans still held a toehold in the woods—"about as hot a place as I wanted to be in." The Germans were alert, firing intermittent bursts from their machine guns, shooting flares, and sending out frequent patrols. Barkley crawled back and forth until midnight, but as hard as he tried he could not penetrate their lines. The opposing lines were extremely close, and soldiers yelled to one another in the dark. "Hey, Fourth Infantry!" the Germans shouted, cursing the 4th Infantry, the AEF, and Woodrow Wilson. After each curse they tossed a grenade or fired their machine guns. The Americans answered with equally fruity remarks about the kaiser. Barkley couldn't believe how personal some of the shouts became.

> They got hold of some of our names. One German kept yelling at a Polack in our outfit who had a name that sounded like Kolchak to me.
>
> "Hey, you Cupjack!" the German would yell. "Pring dose krenades over here!"
>
> Then he'd laugh and turn loose a burst of machine-gun fire.
>
> His talking and shooting gave away his position. As soon as he was sure where the German was, Kolchak crawled over there and shot him with his Springfield.

At midnight Barkley returned to headquarters and confessed that he had not been able to gather any information. The officers seemed too preoccupied to care. Both sides, it seemed, had big plans for October 7.[4]

General Liggett, I Corps' commander, also had plans for the following day. If successful, his forces would liberate the Lost Battalion and cut off the Germans in the lower Argonne. If they failed, the Germans would capture Whittlesey's command and maul or even destroy I Corps. The outcome depended on the tired, battered 28th Division, and the novice 82d Division, commanded by a general whom Liggett's aide considered "as thick as mud and not worth a damn."[5] Liggett presented his plan to his chief of staff, Brigadier General Malin Craig; Pershing's chief of staff, Major General James McAndrew; Brigadier General Hugh Drum; and Major General George B. Duncan, commander of the 82d "All-American" Division and his chief of staff, Colonel Raymond Sheldon. The 1st Division's advance on October 4–5, Liggett explained to the assembled officers, had created a gap between Fléville, on that division's left, and the villages of Châtel Chéhéry and La Forge, in the Aire River valley about a mile and a half to the southwest. If the 82d Division, I Corps' only reserve, advanced through that gap, across the Aire and into the Argonne Forest in conjunction with a westward swing of the 28th Division, it could take the German forces facing the 77th Division in the flank and rear and force their quick withdrawal. The only danger—a serious one—was that the 82d Division would expose its right flank to attack from the north.

Liggett proposed that the attack begin the next morning, October 7. In less than a day, therefore, the 82d Division would have to move eight miles over traffic-clogged roads, deploy along the east bank of the Aire River, ford that river—all its bridges had been destroyed—and attack into an unreconnoitered area against strong enemy opposition. Duncan, who had taken command of the division only a few days before, knew little about his troops, except that they were raw and poorly trained draftees. Liggett's plan, he protested, would try a veteran formation; for untried novices it was a prescription for disaster.[6]

The French officers attached to I Corps rejected the plan, as did everyone on Liggett's own staff, except for Craig. The timetable was too tight, they said, the advance too dangerous. Liggett nevertheless insisted, and Pershing's representatives, McAndrew and Drum, approved. Unlike the others, they saw the bigger picture. The plan was risky, true, and might well fail. But the cause justified it. Something had to be done to rescue the men of the Lost Battalion. Their capitulation or destruction might be just a matter of hours. The ramifications of such a disaster for American morale were too frightening to contemplate.

Among the soldiers charged with carrying out Liggett's plan was a tall, heavily freckled soldier with a thick red mustache, Corporal Alvin C. York. A deeply religious, semiliterate farmer from Fentress County, Tennessee—one of the poorest counties in the United States—York was a draftee and deeply uncomfortable with shedding human blood, whatever the cause. The War Department refused to grant him conscientious objector status, however, and his battalion commander and others succeeded in convincing him that military service was not inconsistent with God's word. York served, but he never grew comfortable with war. Bayonet training with straw dummies left him feeling "queer to think I might have to cut up human beings. I still didn't want to kill. I still did feel somehow that it was wrong—terrible wrong for human beings to take each other's life."

All of which is not to say that York felt at all uncomfortable with guns. He grew up in an era when guns and hunting were inescapable staples of American rural life, and like Jack Barkley, another country boy, he was an excellent marksman. Yet York was a different kind of man. Where Barkley, like many Doughboys, thrived on gambling, drinking, cussing, and combat, York preferred the simple life.

> I had put all of the drinkin' and fist-fightin' away behind me. I left it back home on the Kentucky line. I didn't have a drink all the time I was in France. I didn't have a fist fight or an argument. I didn't swear or smoke either. I wasn't any better'n any of the other boys. It was jes my way of livin', that was all.

York said nothing about the Lost Battalion in his diary in early October. Other thoughts occupied his mind. "We went out on the main road," he wrote on October 5, "and lined up and started for the front and the Germans was shelling the road and airoplanes was humming over our heads and we were stumbling over dead horses and dead men and shells were Bursting all around me." Faced with such sights, he could only look up to Heaven and spread his hands. "Then it was," he wrote, "that I could see the Power of God helped man if he would only trust him."[7] That—and a steady rifle.

★

Major Lyman S. Frasier, commanding the 1st Division's Third Battalion, 26th Regiment, roused his troops from their positions around Ariétal Farm in the early morning and hustled them toward the eastern slopes of Hill 272.

That towering eminence, an important outer stronghold of the *Kriemhilde Stellung,* would be difficult to take head-on, but Summerall thought his troops might snip it off by infiltrating around its flanks. As Frasier's battalion advanced steadily around the hill, with other troops approaching it from the south and west, he heard sounds of heavy firing from the front. A German barrage smashed into his command post, knocking out his phones and killing several operators. Moments later, dozens of panicked soldiers ran past—1st Division men could run too, as it turned out—shouting that the Germans had launched a surprise counterattack into their right flank. The battalion was in retreat.

With his telephones out of commission, Frasier sent runners to his company commanders telling them to hold on, and he requested supporting fire from the divisional artillery and machine guns. He then rounded up about forty of his retreating troops and drove them back to the front. The enemy, he discovered, had indeed broken the perimeter of his battalion. The Doughboys quickly regrouped under Frasier's direction, however, and with support from the artillery and machine guns, they launched a counterattack of their own. They routed the Germans and inflicted heavy losses.[8] Further advances against Hill 272 were called off, however. To take it, 1st Division would have to pay a heavy toll in blood.

✳

SECOND Lieutenant Maurice S. Revnes, a theatrical producer from Philadelphia and New York, knew nothing about machine guns. On September 27, after serving as a staff officer and camp theatrical director, he was nevertheless appointed to lead a platoon in Company D of the 77th Division's 306th Machine Gun Battalion. Less than a week later he became trapped in Charlevaux Valley with the rest of Major Whittlesey's command. Revnes did his duty, carrying a message under fire and leading patrols, until an enemy grenade blew off half of his foot on October 3. He spent the next few days in his foxhole, tired, hungry, and in excruciating pain. He endured the repeated enemy counterattacks. He suffered through the artillery barrages. He heard taunting cries of "Cheese!" "Cigarettes!" "Canned beef!" "Jam!" "Chewing tobacco!" and "Chocolate!" as the Germans plundered supply parcels intended for the Lost Battalion that had been dropped within their lines. And he worried as the sounds of firing from the "relieving" troops come closer and then faded away. By the sixth, Revnes had reached the limits of his endurance.[9]

That afternoon, a private crawled over to Whittlesey's foxhole and gave him a letter endorsed by Revnes:

If our people do not get here by noon [on October 7], it is useless for us to keep up against these great odds. It's a horrible thing to think of, but I can see nothing else for us to do but give up—The men are starving—the wounded, like myself, have not only had no nourishment but a great loss of blood. If the same thought may be in your mind perhaps the enemy may permit the wounded to return to their own lines. I only say this because I for one, cannot hold out longer, when cornered as we are it strikes me that it is not a dishonorable deed to give up.

Whittlesey read the message silently and made his way over to Revnes's foxhole. He spoke with the lieutenant quietly for a while, attempting gentle encouragement and even bringing out the old Lucknow chestnut. In the end, he was curt and direct. "There is going to be no surrender," he barked. "Are you game to go on?" Revnes meekly responded, "I am." Turning to a noncom as he left, Whittlesey said, "If you see any signs of anybody surrendering or see a white flag or anything, you shoot him!"—not realizing that the noncom had coauthored the note.[10]

Revnes's letter was not the only sign of crumbling morale among the surrounded troops. Soldiers approached Whittlesey throughout the day, asking for permission to break out individually. Knowing that such attempts would likely fail, encourage the enemy to attack, and lead to the disintegration of his command, he refused. But he clearly could not hold the men together for much longer. By the end of the day, both of the machine guns on his left flank were out of commission. One remained on the right, with ammunition sufficient for only twelve minutes' firing. The soldiers had to scavenge rifle cartridges from corpses, which had begun to fester badly but could not be buried. Grenades, and food, were but a memory.[11]

Back at General Alexander's headquarters, reports arrived that the German government had applied for an armistice on the basis of Woodrow Wilson's Fourteen Points. The president had presented the points to Congress in January 1918 as a statement of American war aims. Since then they had become popular in both the United States and Europe as moderate proposals that would punish Germany's wrongs without alienating her people, and ensure future peace. But Alexander saw no reason to end the war too soon. Anyone "with a sufficiently wide mental horizon to appreciate the facts," he declared, knew that effective peace terms could only be "dictated by the Allies *on German soil.*" Even so, he gloated, "America's might had been displayed, and the enemy saw the handwriting on the wall."[12]

Returning to the problem of his starving and suffering troops in Char-levaux Valley, Alexander refused to consider the possibility that Whittlesey "might have yielded to circumstances and surrendered." Air service reports assured him that they had successfully resupplied the surrounded troops. One message relayed a pilot's report that he had "dropped pigeons and says that he dropped the cage overboard in good shape and that the parachute opened so he thinks the pigeons were delivered all right." "They feel pretty good about that, do they," a headquarters officer replied. "Good work, that's fine business."[13] Eleven days' constant fighting had exhausted the 77th Division's other regiments, however, as well as the French to the west. Their chances of breaking through to the surrounded troops were next to nothing. The Germans, meanwhile, remained full of fight. They did not intend to hold on to the Argonne for much longer, but they planned to bag the Lost Battalion before they left.

CHAPTER 17

"Their Faces Told the Whole Story
of Their Fight"

OCTOBER 7

While the Lost Battalion languished, the French Fourth Army had enjoyed astonishing success in the Champagne off to the west, thanks in large part to the U.S. 2d Division. Composed of two Marine and two regular army regiments under the command of Major General John A. Lejeune, the 2d was a battle-tested, hard-bitten outfit. Rivalry—sometimes friendly, often not—between the Marine and army troops, which constantly tried to outdo each other, made it particularly ferocious in battle. Entering the lines near Sommepy on October 2, it was told to take Blanc Mont Ridge, the most important enemy defensive position in the Champagne, which the French had repeatedly tried and failed to take. Deeming a frontal attack on the ridge suicidal, Lejeune had instead deployed his regulars on the right with orders to drive northwest against Blanc Mont's eastern end, while the Marines on the left attacked the ridge's western end.

Lieutenant Lemuel Shepherd advanced with the 5th Marines at dawn on October 3. He had been at Belleau Wood and St. Mihiel, but both battles seemed like skirmishes compared to Blanc Mont. "As far as I'm concerned," he told an interviewer many years later, "October 3 at Blanc Mont was the toughest day of the war. And I think most of the men with me agreed." Supported by artillery and tanks, the 2d took the crest of Blanc Mont after three hours of some of the most terrible fighting of the war. Three men, Private Frank J. Bart of the U.S. Army, and Private John J. Kelly and Corporal John

H. Pruitt of the Marines, earned Medals of Honor. The division captured the remainder of the ridge on October 4, and then pushed north to the village of St. Etienne. It was withdrawn from the lines on October 10 after suffering 4,754 casualties.[1] In taking Blanc Mont, Lejeune's men had broken the center of the enemy's defensive system in the Champagne.

*

First Army had less to show for its fighting during the first week of October. Phase two of the Meuse-Argonne offensive, amounting to a head butt by V Corps against the center of the *Kriemhilde Stellung,* had hit a brick wall. Pershing hoped for better results from phase three, beginning on October 7. The new assault would consist of a one-two-three combination punch at the German defenses: a left by I Corps into the Argonne on October 7; a right by the French XVII Corps—built around two American divisions, the 29th and 33d—against the Heights of the Meuse on October 8; and an all-out attack by V Corps on the Heights of Cunel and Romagne on October 9. Pershing intended the combination to extend the battle to a wider front, forcing the Germans to fight all along the line and allowing the Americans to take advantage of their greater numbers.

The operation east of the Meuse had been under consideration since the beginning of October. German heavy artillery, firing from the ridge running along the river's east bank, had flogged the 4th, 80th, and 3d Divisions practically into the ground, paralyzing III Corps and much of V Corps and preventing any further movement toward the Heights of Cunel. Clearing the ridge would be a tough job—the Germans had constructed extremely strong defenses along its southern approaches—but it had to be done. Pershing accordingly withdrew the 33d Division from III Corps, and assigned it and the 29th Division to the French XVII Corps alongside two French infantry divisions. The American divisions made up two-thirds of the corps' numerical strength and would do the bulk of the fighting after the attack jumped off on October 8. III Corps, reduced to the 4th and 80th Divisions, would hold its positions until XVII Corps had made at least moderate progress toward clearing the ridge.

*

Just after midnight on October 7, a provisional battalion of the 3d Division's 4th Regiment tried to infiltrate across the open valley between Hill 250 and the Bois de Cunel. The Americans hoped to launch a surprise attack at daylight. But the enemy was alert. Three times the Doughboys crawled into the

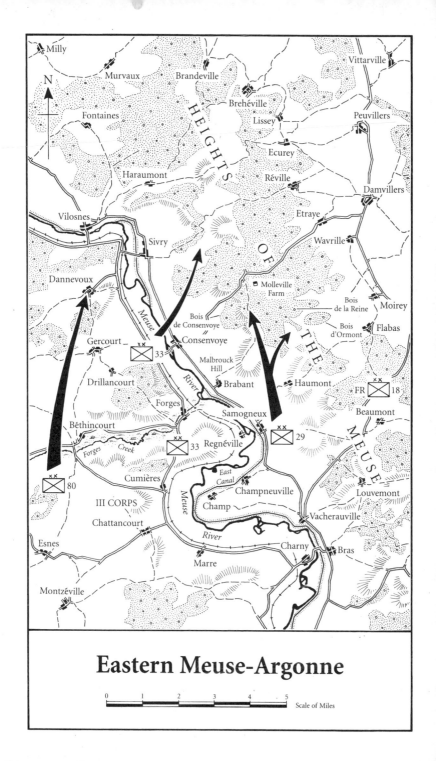

Eastern Meuse-Argonne

0 1 2 3 4 5
Scale of Miles

open, and three times the Germans fired flares, raked them with machine guns and mortars, and forced them back. German reinforcements meanwhile poured into the Bois de Cunel and formed up among the trees in preparation for a powerful daytime counterattack. They did not reckon on Jack Barkley, who went out to face them alone.

Hill 250, occupied by the 4th Regiment, formed part of the southern ridge of an open valley. Across the valley lay another wooded ridge, the German-occupied Bois de Cunel. From between these two points, the valley ran northwest behind Hill 253, to the 4th's left. An open, unoccupied ridge running northwest along the lower rim of the valley connected Hill 250 to Hill 253. The Germans still held the crest of Hill 253, although the 7th Regiment occupied its southern slopes. The trouble was that nobody—including airplane pilots, for it was a rainy day—could see into the valley behind Hill 253. What were the Germans up to? Were they reinforcing Hill 253? Were they preparing a counterattack? Jack Barkley's superior, Sergeant Nayhone, ordered him to follow the unoccupied ridge, take a position overlooking the valley beyond Hill 253's northern slope, and find out. His position would be in no-man's-land, close to the enemy lines, dangerously exposed, and well beyond help should the Germans find out he was there. To Barkley, it looked like a suicide mission.

"If you want to bump me off, for God's sake do it here!" he yelled during a face-off with the sergeant in a candlelit command post just after midnight on October 7.

"We've got to have information," Nayhone replied. "You can see for yourself there's no way out. Somebody's got to go." He reached out his hand, and Barkley, after a brief hesitation, shook it.

"I know you'll do the best you can. . . . And no hard feelings!" the sergeant said.

"All right," Barkley replied. "No hard feelings! . . . But write a nice letter home to my folks."

Accompanied by two signal corps men carrying a phone and laying wire, Barkley followed the ridge for two hours and settled into a deep crater. The signalers gave him the phone—set not to ring, but to make a slight buzz—and trotted off in the dark. Hopefully any German patrols that came across the wire they had laid would not think to trace it—and hopefully it would not be cut. Barkley tested the phone, and Nayhone spoke on the other end. "Don't phone anything not of major importance," the sergeant said in his Middle Eastern accent. "You're too close to them. They might hear you." Nayhone instructed him to call at short intervals all night to test the connection, but not to say anything unless the sergeant asked him a question. Instead, Barkley should scratch the mouthpiece with his fingernail. When he made an actual report, he must do it in code.

Thirty minutes later, Barkley heard shouted commands and clattering equipment in the woods on the other side of the valley. The Germans seemed to be shifting to Barkley's left, directly opposite Hill 253. He picked up the phone, reported the movement to Nayhone, and sat back to wait and listen. He was up to his knees in mud, and smelled a powerful stench from the dead bodies that covered the ground around his crater. Woozy from hunger and lack of sleep, Barkley rubbed his gas-burned scalp in hopes that the pain would keep him awake, with limited success. Sometimes he didn't realize he had fallen asleep until the phone buzzed and Nayhone's voice yelled at him over the line.

At daylight, Barkley found that he had chosen his post well. He had an unobstructed view over the entire valley, from Hill 250 behind and to his right, to Hill 253 ahead and to his left. He also discovered what had made all that noise during the night. In the woods on the opposite side of the valley from Hill 253, German troops moved busily about, evidently with the intention of crossing the valley in front of Barkley and launching a counterattack against the 7th Regiment on the southern slopes of Hill 253. Barkley reported to Nayhone and awaited the Germans' next move while contemplating the dead Doughboys whose bodies lay in dense windrows over the hillside. In the early afternoon an enemy barrage began, landing on Hill 250 and sweeping west toward the southern edge of Hill 253. Nayhone reassured Barkley over the phone. "Stay with it as long as you can," he said. "Take care of yourself. If anything . . ." And the line went dead.

With his phone line cut, there seemed nothing left for Barkley to do except return to headquarters. Seventy-five yards away along the ridge, however, he saw an abandoned French light tank—evidently one of those that had swept heedlessly around Hill 250 during the fighting on October 4. Dozens of dead Germans scattered the ground around it, and Barkley imagined what he could do with a machine gun in that tank when the Germans moved into the valley. Nearby, he spotted a Maxim light machine gun and some boxes of ammunition among a cluster of dead Germans. Their comrades likely would have disabled the Maxim by removing its breechblock. But then Barkley remembered what an officer had told him at intelligence school. The first chance he got, the officer had suggested, he should take the breechblock out of a captured German machine gun and carry it with him— you never knew when it might come in handy. Barkley checked his hip pocket. The breech, which he had picked up many weeks before, was still there.

Dodging from hole to hole, Barkley reached the machine gun without being spotted. Across the valley, he saw Germans at the edge of the woods with grenades, machine guns, and other equipment. They looked ready to move. Suddenly a smoke barrage fell between him and the Germans, and the soldiers disappeared from view. In an instant, Barkley realized what he could accomplish under cover of the screen. Grabbing the gun and ammunition, he sprinted for the tank and hopped inside. The little Renault was empty, except for a bloody leather helmet on the floor. Its turret machine gun had been removed.

Barkley examined his Maxim. Its breechblock, as he expected, was missing, so he snapped his spare into place and it fit perfectly. Except for a nearly empty water jacket—the Maxim was water-cooled, to prevent overheating—the gun seemed in excellent working order. The next priority was ammunition. Barkley had picked up a few boxes, but not enough for extended firing. Fortunately, a number of dead enemy machine gunners lay nearby, surrounded by boxes of ammunition that the Germans had never got around to recovering. Barkley gathered up the boxes, stuffing as many inside the tank as he could and stacking the rest just outside the hatch. He climbed in, emptied several boxes of ammunition, and slung up the belts for easy access with one across his shoulder. Then he rotated the turret to face the woods where he had seen the Germans. He avoided poking his gun out the gun port, lest they see it and discover something was amiss.

The gun port was too big for the Maxim—it had been built for a larger weapon—and Barkley would have only partial protection from enemy bullets. But with the smoke screen fading, it was too late to back out now. Barkley tried not to think. "My legs felt wobbly. I hoped if there was any God, he'd give me the breaks. Then I forgot everything, for through my port I'd caught a glimpse of movement at the edge of the woods." Moving in squad columns and sending up flares, the Germans marched out of the woods and into the open, passing diagonally across Barkley's front toward Hill 253. He estimated five or six hundred men, an entire infantry battalion. The closest were two hundred yards from his tank.

Turning the turret slowly to follow their progress, Barkley waited until the end of the German formation had left the woods and the front had begun climbing Hill 253. He then took a deep breath, edged his gun out through the port, chose his direction of fire, exhaled, aimed the gun toward the waist of the nearest enemy soldier, and pulled the trigger. When the Maxim erupted, the Germans reeled in surprise. None of them, evidently, could tell where the fire was coming from. For a few moments they stood paralyzed. Then they saw the Renault and looked for cover. But they were caught in the open.

Barkley fired the Maxim in alternating short and long bursts. "The German who had carried that gun," he discovered, "had her beautifully adjusted. She fairly purred." He raked the infantry, and then massacred a group of officers. One of them, a "big fat fellow," fell as he waddled toward the woods; another tried to pull him in, and Barkley shot him too. The Germans had meanwhile begun to return fire with rifles and machine guns. As each bullet hit the turret Barkley thought his eardrums would explode. Several bullets got in through the gun port, some of them evidently fired by a smart enemy sniper. Miraculously, they didn't hit Barkley, and he kept firing. The gun overheated, and when it started to smoke he emptied his canteen into the jacket. The water boiled and evaporated immediately, almost scalding his hands. Barkley had to slow his rate of fire.

Eventually a patrol of about twenty Germans separated themselves from the rest and moved toward the tank. They carried two light machine guns and a lot of grenades. Barkley killed one of the machine gunners, but the other made it to a shell hole about seventy-five yards away.

> That fellow with the Maxim used his head. He started firing straight at the barrel of my gun. If he had hit it he'd have put the gun out of commission. I whirled the turret toward him. He was a brave man. He stood up in his shell hole and, with head and shoulders exposed, he tried to beat me to getting a burst home. The odds were all on me. I swung the sights just below his gun and fired. I was sorry. But it had to be one of us.

With the second machine gun out of action, the rest of the patrol ran up and threw their grenades. The grenades bounced off harmlessly, but as the infantry moved closer, one of them eventually would find a hatch or the port. They ran quickly from cover to cover, and Barkley couldn't get at them. Suddenly a shell burst among them—a German 77—and the infantry fled.

With one crisis gone, Barkley faced another. That artillery piece could blow his tank to scrap. He frantically searched for the gun as the shells crept closer. Two explosions straddled him in quick succession as he sighted the gun at the edge of the woods, six hundred yards away. Before he could pull the trigger, "there was a terrific crash—on the tank, in the air, inside the tank. A sharp blow against my chin—a ringing in my ears—and blackness." He came to consciousness with a strangling sensation and a weight on his chest.

The weight came from a heavy box of ammunition, which he threw off; the strangling came from smoke, intense heat, and lack of air. Blood poured from Barkley's nose, and his throat was scorched and dry. He craved air and water. Then he realized that no bullets were ricocheting off his tank. He threw open the turret's rear hatch and pushed his head out, gasping. When he had recovered sufficiently to look around he saw the Germans still climbing Hill 253, this time under fire from American machine guns. They showed no interest in Barkley, apparently thinking him dead.

Barkley got back in the tank, closed the door, and examined his Maxim. The stock was cracked but otherwise it looked all right. Getting his ammunition back in order, he rotated the turret back to where he had seen the 77 just before he was hit. He found it, the gunners walking unconcernedly about it. Six hundred yards was a long way, but Barkley measured the range carefully. He fired a whole belt at the artillery piece, saturating it thoroughly. The 77 gave him no more trouble after that, but the German infantry woke up—no doubt cursing heartily—and again peppered the Renault with bullets.

The Maxim started jamming repeatedly. Barkley cleared the jams, but the rate of fire slowed until it became single shot, like a rifle. Figuring the end had come, he slid down into the driver's compartment and waited for a chance to bail out and run for the woods. Then he saw a can of thin oil. Grabbing the can, Barkley climbed back into the gun compartment and poured the oil into the water jacket. It worked, just in time for him to fend off another grenade-toting German patrol. As the patrol fled, he resumed firing on the infantry struggling up Hill 253. The oil in the gun jacket boiled, filling the turret with acrid black smoke. Then the gun jammed again, and Barkley thought his part in the war had ended.

> I just sat there, with my head in my hands, waiting. I told myself I was waiting for the gun to cool off. But it was really the end I was waiting for. I couldn't hold out much longer with a gun that would fire only once in a while.

Suddenly, he heard the sound of artillery shells bursting nearby. This time they were not aimed at his tank. Instead, they exploded all along the northern slopes of Hill 253 among the German infantry. American infantry and machine gunners joined in, and soon the Germans could take no more. Breaking, they ran back down the hill, through the American barrage, across the valley, and into the woods on the other side. Barkley opened the tank door and tumbled to the ground outside, feeling half dead and sick to his stomach. An American officer and twenty-five men from the 7th Regiment walked toward him.

"What the devil are you doing here?" the officer asked, looking incredulously at Barkley's filthy uniform and blood-matted whiskers. Barkley replied that he had been in the tank. "You certainly look like hell," the officer replied, and after directing the bedraggled private back to his regiment he and his patrol moved off. As Barkley staggered back along the ridge and into the woods, he heard explosions behind him. Looking back, he saw a salvo of huge, six-inch shells exploding around the tank. The German heavy artillery had finally found his range.[2]

✯

GENERAL Summerall, commanding the 1st Division, called up the 32d Division's commander, General Haan, on October 7 and told him about the patrol that he had sent on the previous day to Hill 269, to the 32d's left front. Summerall had assumed that the Michigan-Wisconsin troops would assault the hill in short order, but they had not done so. Now the patrol had become isolated, and what was the 32d going to do about it? Haan had not been consulted on the patrol's venture, but he reluctantly agreed to send four companies of the 128th Regiment to rescue it. The results did little to improve the Big Red One's popularity.

First Lieutenant Edmund P. Arpin, a twenty-four-year-old woodsman from the town of Grand Rapids in northern Wisconsin, commanded Company F. He kept his men under cover until they reached an open area five hundred yards from the hill's base. Dividing them into three waves of forty men each, Arpin led the first wave in a rush across the clearing toward a tiny, brush-fringed gully. The Germans immediately spotted the movement and saturated the Americans with machine-gun and artillery fire as they hopped over the gully and scrambled onward. Soldiers fell on every side; some to crawl into shell holes and others "just to beat a little tattoo upon the ground with heels and hands and at last lie very still." Bullets sliced the air under Arpin's nose, sucking his breath away, but he did not pause or look back. Waving his men onward, he loped up the hill's wooded slope, through a misdirected American artillery barrage, and toward the crest.

Arpin found the crest abandoned. He also discovered that only four Doughboys had made it with him this far. Unperturbed, he ordered his dazed, mud-spattered men to spike the enemy machine guns while he looked around. No Germans or Americans were in sight. Where were the men he had been supposed to rescue? And what had happened to his support? Turning to the south, Arpin pulled out his handkerchief and frantically signaled the rest of his company to advance. Nothing happened. He whipped off his coat and flapped it in the wind. Still nothing happened. After several minutes with no success, Arpin explored further. Sticking a .45 in his belt and holding a captured German Luger in each hand, he led his little party along a path through the underbrush. After a hundred yards he sighted a group of Germans standing in a small clearing about thirty feet away, pointing and laughing at the dead and wounded Doughboys down in the valley.

Arpin fired his Lugers, but they quickly jammed, so he pulled out his .45. The Germans fled before he fired many shots. He then returned to his men and led them back along the crest. In a minute they saw a single German sneaking toward them along the trail. Arpin's sergeant aimed his rifle, but the lieutenant—perhaps feeling a little cocky after scattering the previous group of Germans—motioned that he would use his .45 instead. Before he could fire, however, the surprised German yelped wildly, performed an Olympic-quality back somersault, and "dove headlong over an extremely steep slope on the reverse side of the hill, tearing through the brush, yelling like a maniac." Forgetting for a moment the seriousness of their situation, Arpin and his sergeant collapsed in laughter.

Working back to the point where he had originally reached the crest, Arpin again signaled for support, to no avail. German troops milled about among the trees and bushes on the hill's north side, their movements gradually becoming more purposeful. Arpin and his men fired on the Germans, killing several, but obviously they could not think of holding out against an enemy attack. "Thoroughly nauseated," Arpin led his men back down the hill to find his company all but destroyed. The German barrage had caught and scattered the second and third waves; of the first wave, only Arpin and his four men remained. He reported that there were no Americans on Hill 269. There must be some mistake, headquarters replied. The patrol was there, 1st Division insisted. They were surrounded—desperate—and they had to be saved. What kind of men let their fellows down like this? General Haan gave the order, and the attack resumed. Three times, Arpin watched as other companies assaulted the hill; three times they came back, bloodied and reporting that the only men up there were German.

Only later did Haan's men discover that the hill had two peaks. The 128th Regiment had attacked the hill's actual crest, while the patrol occupied a lower spot some distance away. No one could tell why the 1st Division soldiers had not attempted to contact the Red Arrow troops as they stormed the crest. Nor had the patrol been in such immediate danger as 1st Division had suggested. That night a battalion of engineers contacted the patrol and pulled it out with ease, leaving Lieutenant Colonel Glen Garlock, commanding the 128th, wondering why so many of his men had died in search of phantoms. He blamed Summerall and his 1st Division. "Probably no other division in the American army could have forced us to send out three detachments on such a 'wild goose chase,'" he complained. "The First had so much prestige it was unbelievable it could be wrong."[3]

✳

THE most critical fighting of October 7 took place in the Argonne, where the untested 82d Division attempted to execute a major part of Liggett's plan to rescue the Lost Battalion and capture the entire forest. Composed of a mishmash of draftees from east of the Mississippi—half of them recent immigrants, and many not even citizens—the "All-American" 82d Division possessed an ironically appropriate nickname.[4] Its four infantry regiments, the 325th, 326th, 327th, and 328th, arrived in Europe in July 1918 and trained with the British before entering a quiet sector near Toul. The All-Americans took about one thousand casualties at St. Mihiel, but most of them remained as green as the day they had entered basic training.

The division's commander, Major General George B. Duncan, was a West Point graduate and an old Pershing comrade who had served in Cuba and the Philippines, and on the army's general staff. Perhaps his greatest asset in Pershing's eyes was his experience with the 1st Division, whose 26th Regiment and 1st Brigade he had commanded during the spring and summer of 1918. An army observer called Duncan "a good, rough soldier, a good general, fearless, aggressive and self-reliant"—just Pershing's kind of man.[5] On October 4 he took command of the 82d Division, its previous commander having left to become the U.S. military attaché in Greece. Some thought him a fathead, but no matter: Duncan liked to attack.

On October 6, Liggett ordered Duncan to insert the 82d into the gap between the 28th and 1st Divisions and attack west-northwest, across the Aire River and into the Argonne. Duncan directed his troops to hurry forward overnight, cross the river, and attack at dawn on the seventh, with the 327th Regiment on the right taking Hill 180 and pushing northwest across a ravine into Cornay, and the 328th on the left attacking due west toward Hill 223. The operation nearly collapsed before it began. Rain, congested roads, and enemy artillery hindered the night march, and the infantry reached their jumping-off positions late.[6] Fortunately, the officers kept their troops well organized, and the two regiments successfully crossed bridges that the engineers had built overnight, formed up along an old railroad track, and attacked.

The 327th cleared the lightly defended crest of Hill 180 within an hour. After pausing to rest, however, the troops found the Germans prepared to resist their further advance toward Cornay. Clobbered by heavy fire, the regiment's companies attacked halfheartedly and then withdrew to the slopes of Hill 180 and the Ravine de Boulasson that bordered it to the northwest. The 328th, arriving in position much later than its sister regiment, passed through La Forge at about 4:30 A.M. and crossed the Aire under fire from German artillery. Disorganized, the 328th failed to advance at first but finally got going toward Hill 223 at about noon. The 28th Division on the left had meanwhile already attacked—its right flank exposed by the 328th's delay and thus raked by German shellfire—and occupied the hill's southern slopes before the All-Americans lurched onto its northern end at about 12:30 P.M.

Corporal Harold Pierce of the 28th Division watched in horrified fascination from a nearby hill when the inexperienced 328th advanced again that afternoon against strong German resistance.

> I pity these men for ahead of them is a two mile stretch of open country under observation. Officers new to the front making another mistake. I say a prayer for them and then watch through field glasses, fascinated to see the slaughter. . . . The battalion starts in perfect alignment and reaches the middle of the first field. Over in the German horizon there is a "crunmph," the telltale whistles as a salvo speeds to them. Most of them take it standing up, another sign of green troops. The next salvo of seventy-sevens comes and before the shells burst the entire line disappears in the tall grass. They rise a little disorganized and press on. Another salvo and again they disappear, rise slowly after the bursts and again move forward. The shells come oftener, the battalion loses contact and bunches confused, but still moves on. Soon they are all running forward all formation gone as the shells search the ground and find many victims. About half make the stretch even with us. . . . Back in the field men are moving slowly back, limping, carrying others while many more must be sprawled out dead.[7]

The advance broke down, and the regiment organized a line along the crest of Hill 223.

Corporal Alvin C. York's battalion of the 328th spent the day in reserve, ensconced in impromptu foxholes along a roadside. But although he didn't participate in any fighting, what he saw was bad enough—aircraft buzzing "jes like a lot of hornets," and German heavy artillery blowing men to pieces. A machine-gun battalion across the road was literally disemboweled before his eyes.

> And oh, my! We had to pass the wounded. And some of them were on stretchers going back to the dressing stations and some of them were lying around moaning and twitching. And oh, my! The dead were all along the road and their mouths were open and their eyes, too, but they couldn't see nothing no more nohow. And it was wet and cold and damp. And it all made me think of the Bible and the story of the anti-Christ and Armageddon. And I'm a-telling you the little log cabin in Wolf Valley in old Tennessee seemed a long, long way off.[8]

The All-Americans had captured two undefended hills and advanced about half a mile, not nearly enough to fulfill Liggett's plan of driving the Germans from the Argonne. Unless the shattered, exhausted 28th Division could accomplish more, the Lost Battalion might be finished.

★

THE Keystone Division's attack swung like a steel door, with the hinge on the left, where the 56th Brigade's 111th Regiment struggled for the blood-drenched crest of Le Chêne Tondu. On the right, General Dennis Nolan's 55th Brigade—with the 112th and 110th Regiments from left to right—swung outward from the northwest to the west, crashing against Châtel Chéhéry. That village rambled along the foot of a long, uneven, north-south ridge. The 110th, in conjunction with the 82d Division's 328th Regiment, attacked Hill 223, which formed the ridge's northern end. The 112th simultaneously assaulted the ridge's southern end, Hill 244. That hill formed a crucially important part of the German defensive system. Its capture was imperative for the success of Liggett's plan.

The 110th, covered by a screening force from the 109th, crossed a pontoon bridge at La Forge and took up positions along the riverbank while the 112th, starting at Apremont on the Aire's west bank, moved into position on its left. The two regiments jumped off at 5:00 A.M. behind a rolling barrage. On the right, the 110th advanced through heavy machine-gun fire, found the northern end of Châtel Chéhéry undefended, and pushed on to Hill 223.[9] It paused there, waiting for the 328th to move into position on the right and the 112th to seize Hill 244 on the left. The 328th appeared in the early afternoon. The 112th, caught in a bitter struggle for Hill 244, took longer.

Colonel James Shannon of the 112th was a friend and West Point classmate of Brigadier General Douglas MacArthur, and an officer through and through. His men loved and trusted him. "He appears like a real man, not stuck up and seems to know his stuff," Corporal Pierce enthused. In the cold and foggy predawn hours of October 7, Shannon formed up his regiment and sent it west toward the southern end of Châtel Chéhéry. Preceded by a thin skirmish line, the Doughboys moved silently and carefully across an open field, halting frequently to lie down in the long, wet grass. At 5:00 A.M. the rolling barrage began, and the infantry picked up speed. Pierce described the advance:

> We break into a trot for a hundred yards, then about two hundred from the town we begin to charge, a regular old time infantry charge. The enemy machine guns and infantry, now awake to their danger, see us. Bullets whip by, hit the ground and stir up the dirt. The entire regiment is on the run forward, down a sunken road, climb the bank, running fast. . . . A wide patch of barbed wire is ahead but we make a running broad jump and clear it as bullets spatter into the wire. For the first time I see ahead and behind the town a large cliff where the German's guns are flashing. We run through an orchard as a shower of bullets hit the ground beside me and hand grenades from the cliff burst in front. A man to my front curls up and rolls over on his side, with a pained look on his face. We pass him on the run, cross the main street and into the houses under the cliff.[10]

There were no Germans in Châtel Chéhéry, but from the ridge above they peppered the houses and streets with grenades and machine-gun bursts. Shannon ordered one of his three battalions to attack directly west up the steep slopes of Hill 244 while another circled around and attempted to outflank it from the south. It was the last order he ever gave. Moments later, he and his second in command were almost simultaneously cut down by German machine guns, and a captain took command of the regiment.[11] Corporal Pierce watched his beloved colonel's life ebb away in a crowded wine cellar in the center of town:

> The room is filled with badly wounded men. Colonel Shannon is there, shot through the neck, mortally wounded, gasping for the breath that will soon leave his body. . . . Another man is on his back, unconscious, with a big piece

out of his head and his brain showing. I watch him, fascinated, as his hands rise slowly toward the terrible hole in his head, then a first aid man grabs his arm and pulls it down. But the unconscious man repeats the movement. Groans, moans and gasps and I decide to leave this place.[12]

The troops attacking west up Hill 244 made little progress, but the battalion that Colonel Shannon had sent around to the south captured a line of machine guns along the hill's rocky lower slopes. Three hundred yards above that, enemy infantry and machine guns had dug in behind dense coils of barbed wire that the American barrage had failed to cut. Enemy artillery began hitting the Doughboys, who took cover in shell holes that had been fortuitously left by the otherwise off-target U.S. artillery. But there was no way out. Either they retreated—most likely to be shot in the back by the German machine guns—or went forward. They chose the second option. Leaping from their holes, the Pennsylvanians took devastating losses as they slashed through the barbed wire. A fraction made it through—just enough to do the job. They leapt into the enemy trenches, bayoneting and hurling grenades with a fury that unnerved the defenders, who broke and withdrew. Another day would pass before its slopes were entirely cleared of defenders, but for all intents and purposes Hill 244 had fallen into American hands.[13]

Although the 28th Division had not driven far into the Argonne, the 112th Regiment's heroism and sacrifice at Châtel Chéhéry and Hill 244 paid immediate dividends. Had it failed to take these important points, the Germans would have gained an extra day or two of time—enough, perhaps, to finish off the Lost Battalion. By succeeding, the regiment drove a wedge into the Germans' left rear and made their positions in the lower Argonne untenable. In reaction, the Germans abandoned Le Chêne Tondu and withdrew into the woods. The 111th Regiment, which had tried for days to capture the ridge, gratefully occupied it and continued west toward the village of La Viergette through steadily increasing rain.[14] Liggett's plan had worked. The Germans were in retreat.

★

Private Lowell R. Hollingshead—Company H, 308th Regiment, 77th Division—was haunted by recurring dreams of juicy steaks and fat potatoes, and every time he woke up the hunger pangs became stronger. An Ohioan who had joined the 308th as a replacement in late September, he felt no particular loyalty to his officers, Whittlesey included. But he was no coward. He just wanted to get out, find some food, and fight another day. Whittlesey stubbornly insisted that there would be no attempts to break out. Hollingshead had other ideas.

That morning, he joined a group of eight soldiers near the creek in the valley. None of them knew one another, but all had the same purpose: find a food parcel, and "shoot it out with the Germans." Some of the men were veterans; some, like Hollingshead, were replacements getting their first terrible dose of war. One of them, Private Henry Chin, was a member of the Young China Association back in New York's Chinatown. The soldier who stood out most, however, was Private Robert Dodd, a full-blooded Paiute Indian from Nevada. Everyone assumed that Native Americans made excellent guides, and by unanimous consent the soldiers asked Dodd to lead them to food or safety.

Dodd led them with quiet confidence, moving short distances through the woods with frequent rest breaks—the men were weak and could not exert themselves much—and dropping to hands and knees where the underbrush offered sufficient cover. The soldiers had finished a break and were moving off again when Dodd paused, raised his hand, and motioned them to take cover—too late. In an instant, machine guns opened fire all around them, killing five of the soldiers, including Chin, and badly wounding all the rest. Dodd was shot in the leg and shoulder; Hollingshead took a bullet in his thigh. Soon some German soldiers came over, covered the dead soldiers with branches, and tended the wounded. Hollingshead played dead until a German aimed a Luger at his head and prepared to pull the trigger. When he yelled "*Kamerad!*" the German lowered his pistol and helped him to his feet.[15]

The Germans treated their four wounded prisoners kindly and escorted them back to headquarters. There they were given food—which they gobbled greedily—and cigarettes. Lieutenant Heinrich Prinz, a handsome, dapper young officer, interrogated them. Each American insisted that Whittlesey's command was huge, well supplied, and not even remotely interested in surrender. Prinz, who had worked before the war in Spokane, Washington, needed only a glance at the ragged, famished men to know better. He asked Hollingshead, the only prisoner able to walk, if he would carry a message back to his comrades. After asking and being permitted to read the message, the private agreed. Prinz gave him some bread and cigarettes, a cane, and a white flag on a stick, and had him led back to the American lines.[16]

Hollingshead hobbled back into Charlevaux Valley at about 4:00 P.M., and the American sentinels brought him to Whittlesey. The major had endured another difficult day. His command unquestionably verged on collapse. A German attack at noon had barely been repulsed. Men dribbled away in ones and twos, trying to escape. Ammunition was low, the men weak, the wounded dying, and it had begun to rain. Whittlesey took the German message and read it silently. Typos and misspellings notwithstanding, its meaning came through clearly enough:

> The Bearer of the present, Cowell [*sic*] R. Hollingshead, has been taken prisoner by us on October [blank]. He refused to the German Intelligence Officer every answer to his questions and is quite an honourable fellow, doing honour to his fatherland in the strictest sense of the word.
>
> He has been charged against his will, believing in doing wrong to his country, in carrying forward this present letter to the Officer in charge of the 2nd Batl. J.R. 308 of the 77th Div. with the purpose to recommend this Commander to surrender with his forces as it would be quite useless to resist any more in view of the present conditions.
>
> The suffering of your wounded men can be heard over here in the German lines and we are appealing to your human sentiments. A withe [*sic*] Flag shown by one of your men will tell us that you agree with these conditions.
>
> Please treat the Crowell R. Hollingshead as an honourable man. He is quite a soldier we envy you.[17]

Whittlesey passed the note to his officers without comment. When they had finished, McMurtry later testified, "there was a good smile all around among the crowd of us, because, first we knew that the Germans felt that they could not take us and secondly . . . the fact that they had tried to wipe us out every day and had been trying to wipe us out every day since we had been in the position and then had written us a note stating that they would like to have us surrender in the name of humanity, it didn't just exactly 'g' in our minds." Whittlesey carefully folded the note and put it in his pocket. "Go back to your post," he told Hollingshead, without word or sign of reproach. He then ordered his men to take in the white cloth panels that they had been using to signal the airplanes, lest the Germans mistake them for "withe Flags."[18]

Word of the surrender ultimatum spread rapidly through the valley, causing Whittlesey's men—according to postwar Lost Battalion mythology—to react with a burst of patriotism and pride. Injured soldiers with stinking, gangrenous wounds are said to have crawled out of the muddy shell holes in which they had lain for days, grabbing rifles and cartridges and preparing to repel the coming attack. Officers and soldiers, hitherto downcast, miserable, and thinking of escape, supposedly revived in a moment, sharpening their bayonets on stones and grimly imagining how they would plunge them into

German bellies. "Go to hell!" they cried. "Kiss our American asses! Come over and get us, you Dutch sons of bitches!" Allowing for patriotic hyperbole elicited after the action by newspaper reporters looking for good copy, there is no question that the men of the Lost Battalion had decided not to go down without a fight. They must have wondered, however, whether they could hold out for much longer.

The German commander, Lieutenant General Wellmann, had waited all day for the *sturmbataillon* that army headquarters had promised to lend him for the elimination of Whittlesey's command. His own troops, meanwhile, had become increasingly exposed. By midafternoon the Germans surrounding the Lost Battalion had been pushed back into a vulnerable salient. To the west, the capture of Blanc Mont had forced the Germans to evacuate La Palette Pavilion. To the east, the 28th Division's capture of Hill 244 had unhinged Wellmann's left flank, forcing a withdrawal in the eastern Argonne.[19] The *sturmbataillon* finally arrived just before Hollingshead set off to deliver the surrender ultimatum. It turned out to consist of only sixteen men and a few flamethrowers. When Whittlesey did not respond to the ultimatum after half an hour, Wellmann ordered his troops to attack. It was an act of desperation, a gambler's final throw.

The attack marked the fiery climax of the Lost Battalion's saga. Machine guns and trench mortars opened fire, grenades hurtled down the slope, and enemy infantry carefully infiltrated forward from tree to tree. The flamethrowers came last, spewing liquid fire that incinerated trees, underbrush, and a few unlucky Doughboys. They were slow-moving, however, and marksmen quickly put them out of action. The flamethrowers enraged the Americans—in World War I they were considered immoral weapons, worse even than gas—driving them into a bloodthirsty frenzy. Looking like haggard, wild-eyed barbarians, the Doughboys leapt out of their holes and bounded off through the trees, killing Germans left and right and whooping with glee.[20] The Germans would not come again.

✯

GENERAL Alexander, the 77th Division's commander, spent the morning of October 7 in front of a disability board, testifying on the mentality of Colonel Stacey. Returning to headquarters, he learned that his division's attacks into the Argonne had once again failed miserably. His artillery had fired all night, and a section of the 1st Gas and Flame had even lobbed phosgene gas shells against the enemy instead of their usual smoke, but without effect.[21] The enemy wire remained as thick as ever, and the Maxims extremely active.

By midday, however, the attacks of the 28th and 82d Divisions had caused the Germans to start withdrawing from Le Chêne Tondu and the ridge in Bois de la Naza. Alexander's 306th and 307th Regiments followed immediately, inflicting considerable casualties on the Germans and collecting many prisoners. With the German lines crumbling, General Johnson ordered the 307th's First Battalion to advance up the north-south ravine south of Charlevaux Valley, capture Ridge 198, and relieve the Lost Battalion.

Whittlesey and McMurtry were sitting in their foxhole a little after 7:00 P.M., talking in low voices, when a runner hurtled in between them. An American officer and a few men had just appeared on the right, the runner breathlessly reported. They wanted to see the commanding officer. Relief had arrived.

The men of the Lost Battalion were too exhausted to celebrate. There were no demonstrations of joy; there was no cheering. Instead, men turned to one another and silently shook hands, or quietly told wounded soldiers about the good news. The relieving troops distributed all the reserve rations they were carrying and stood guard while Whittlesey's soldiers ate and went to sleep. In the morning trucks and ambulances arrived and officers prepared the men for departure while the YMCA distributed chocolate. Only 194 of them could still walk; 144 more had to be taken out on stretchers. The rest of the Lost Battalion's original 554 men left in coffins.[22]

Newspaper correspondents arrived too, obligingly shuttled forward by an army command happy to publicize the story now that it had a happy ending. They found Whittlesey sitting on a stump, next to a group of filthy, bearded men. The reporters peppered the major with questions—who was he, where did he come from, did he think he would make it out alive, how had he outwitted the Hun, and so on. Whittlesey stopped them. "Don't write about me," he said, "just about these men." He gestured to the soldiers beside him, and spoke of how patient they had been. "New Yorkers and Westerners— all fine." He said nothing about the dead, but they were very much on his mind.

The newspapermen—one of them a "skinny fellow" in a "strange uniform" named Damon Runyon, a correspondent for the *New York American*— watched the soldiers file away to their trucks. Patriotic phrases leapt to the reporters' minds. "Out of the fog of fighting that hangs over the Forest of the Argonne came limping to-day Whittlesey's battered battalion which made the epic defense in the dark glades beyond," Runyon gushed. "Out of this scullery of war the American infantryman is emerging as the greatest fighter the world has ever seen." Another correspondent, Thomas Johnson, enthused that the men of the Lost Battalion "would not give in. The eyes told that. Those of us who were there and saw them, as the Pioneers turned the first spadeful of earth for the others, knew that here indeed was a holy place." Soldiers' reflections were deeper. Instead of cheering the rescued men as they shuffled to their trucks, the relieving Doughboys watched in silence. "I couldn't say anything to them," one of them said. "There was nothing to say anyway. It made your heart lump up in your throat just to look at them. Their faces told the whole story of their fight."[23]

CHAPTER 18

"York, 1 Hear You Have Captured the Whole
Damned German Army"

OCTOBER 8

The first blow of Pershing's one-two-three combination against the *Kriemhilde Stellung*—a strong left against the lower Argonne—had found a soft spot. The German defenses in the Argonne had crumbled as I Corps swept victoriously forward. The time had now come for the second blow, a right hook east of the Meuse. The Heights of the Meuse, which the Germans had held since 1914, consisted of one great north-south ridge surrounded by hills, woods, and ravines. Starting from their positions north of Samogneux, the Americans first would have to cross between three and five thousand yards of fields and open slopes. They would then enter dense woods—the Bois de Chaume, the Bois de Consenvoye, the Bois de la Grande Montagne, and the Bois d'Etraye, from left to right—covering steeply ascending hills and ridges. A road bisected the woods, running northeast from Consenvoye and uphill along ridges and through woods to the towns of Etraye and Damvillers. Halfway to Damvillers, the road passed Molleville Farm at the bottom of a steeply sloping clearing on the right.

The French XVII Corps attacked the heights on October 8 with four divisions from right to left, the French 26th and 18th Divisions, and the American 29th and 33d Divisions. The French divisions, reinforced by battalions of colonial Senegalese soldiers, were ordered to advance toward the town of Flabas. The most important attacks would be made by the 29th Division—attacking from the northern outskirts of Samogneux across open slopes into the Bois de Consenvoye, past Molleville Farm, and all the way to the Bois de la Grande Montagne—and the 33d Division, which would cross to the east bank of the Meuse near Brabant and advance north through the village of Consenvoye, into the Bois de Chaume, and along the top of the main ridge.[1] To ensure surprise, the French limited their artillery support to a rolling barrage beginning just before H hour at 5:00 A.M.

The 29th "Blue and Gray" Division, a National Guard formation, consisted of two "blue" regiments—the 113th and 114th from New Jersey—and two "gray" regiments—the 115th, from Maryland and Delaware, and the 116th, from Virginia. None of the division's soldiers, some of whom were replacements from New England and the Midwest, had seen any combat. Their commander, Major General Charles G. Morton, ruled them with "an iron hand" as if they were children, but his authority was not absolute. During this operation, his troops would be subject to French command. The 115th and 116th Regiments, attached to the French 18th Division, were deployed north of Samogneux and told to attack toward the Bois de Consenvoye. French troops flanked them to the right, and the 113th and 114th Regiments followed in reserve. The 33d Division, meanwhile, would cross the Meuse and join the 29th on the left as it pushed north.

Company and platoon leaders blew their whistles at 5:00 A.M., as the rolling barrage shrieked overhead. The men had not been permitted to smoke cigarettes for several hours, and lights winked in the early morning darkness as smokers lit up. As the dawn grew brighter, lines upon lines of American and French infantry stretched right and left, advancing with rifles held at port: Allies with a common purpose. To one American officer it "presented the initial effect of a vast maneuver . . . a glorious and never to be forgotten sight." Enemy shells arrived as the leading wave trampled the first belt of barbed wire underfoot, raking the infantry from left to right and front to rear. The American officers had deployed their men at wide intervals, however, so the casualties were not crippling. The assault waves moved steadily on.[2]

The Americans advanced two miles, along an old canal basin, across a long hill, through shell-torn trenches and barbed wire, and over three open ridges. Skittish Austrian infantry fled before them, "hell bent for Vienna." They made good target practice. "If they are going to keep up at this rate," the Doughboys joked, "we'll have to get motorcycles to keep up with them." At midmorning, the troops approached the main enemy line of resistance, which ran over the crest of Malbrouck Hill and along the wedge-shaped southern edge of the Bois de Consenvoye. On the left, the 115th faced Malbrouck Hill; on the right, the 116th approached the Bois de Consenvoye. Both regiments halted under strong enemy fire, but while the 115th stayed put, the 116th recovered and assaulted the woods. By noon the southern Bois de Consenvoye had fallen into American hands.[3]

German machine guns, particularly from Malbrouck Hill, ripped into the 116th's flanks. To make matters worse, artillery and airplane attacks on the open area south of the Bois de Consenvoye cut communications from headquarters and prevented reinforcements from coming up. Captain Ewart Johnston of Winchester, Virginia, ordered his company of the 116th to fix bayonets and assaulted Malbrouck Hill, catching the Germans by surprise. The booty included over two hundred prisoners, including a battalion commander and his staff, eighteen heavy machine guns, a food dump, an ammunition dump, and several artillery pieces. The attack into the woods then resumed, with such gusto that three members of the regiment earned Medals of Honor. Growling "I'll get them," Sergeant Earl Gregory of Chase City, Virginia, dashed into the woods with his rifle and a mortar shell that he used as a grenade. He captured a machine gun with three soldiers, a German mountain howitzer, and a dugout with nineteen prisoners.[4]

Similar episodes of bravery took place on the left, where the 115th faced even stronger enemy emplacements. Lieutenant Patrick Regan of Middleboro, Massachusetts, arranged a group of volunteers into three automatic rifle teams. He sent two teams against the flanks of one large, four-machine-gun enemy nest and led the third directly from the front. The Germans severely wounded Regan and another member of his team, and killed two others. Pulling out his pistol, Regan leapt into the middle of the enemy nest and screamed for the startled gunners to surrender. They did—all thirty of them. The lieutenant remained at the head of his platoon until his company commander ordered him to report to a first-aid station. Only then did he realize his pistol wasn't loaded. In another episode, Private Henry Costin of Baltimore joined an automatic rifle team and continued attacking an enemy machine gun after it had mortally wounded him and killed all of his comrades. He fired his rifle until he collapsed, suppressing the enemy position and allowing the rest of his company to capture a hundred prisoners and several machine guns.[5]

The American attacks eventually bogged down despite the outstanding heroism of individual soldiers, with the 115th substantially behind the 116th to its right. The Blue and Gray Division had advanced three miles, a respectable distance but well short of the objectives assigned to it at the beginning of the day. And the hard part of its assault on the Heights of the Meuse had yet to come.

✯

THE Illinoians of the 33d Division had not attacked since September 26, but for almost two weeks the German artillery east of the Meuse had pounded them with shrapnel, high explosives, and gas. The orders to cross the river and come to grips with their tormentors came as a welcome relief. They would have gladly stormed the gates of Hell if it meant getting rid of those guns. Overnight the engineers constructed two bridges over the river at Brabant-sur-Meuse and Consenvoye, and at 9:00 A.M. two battalions of the 132d Regiment crossed the Meuse at Brabant and turned north along the road to Consenvoye. They took heavy fire from the village and the Bois de Consenvoye until machine guns and automatic riflemen suppressed it. The Doughboys entered Consenvoye by noon, capturing dozens of bedraggled Austrian prisoners and a cache of British Lewis guns, which the Doughboys happily used to replace the despised Chauchats.[6]

A battalion of the 131st Regiment crossed the bridge at Consenvoye while the 132d continued north-northeast toward the Bois the Chaume and the Bois de Consenvoye. Caught in the open between these two machine-gun-infested woods, the regiment didn't get very far. The Germans had many antitank rifles and used them against the infantry, inflicting wounds "too horrible to describe." The Illinois Doughboys didn't lose their cool, but formed combat teams with Browning Automatic Rifles, one-pounders, trench mortars, and machine guns. Working singly or in tandem, they dismantled the enemy emplacements one at a time. Two soldiers, First Sergeant Johannes Anderson of Finland and Private Clayton Slack of Plover, Wisconsin, earned Medals of Honor by capturing enemy emplacements with dozens of prisoners. But it was not enough.[7] By nightfall the 132d had covered two and a half miles, but it remained exposed outside the woods, two hundred yards north of Consenvoye on the left and a hundred yards south of the Bois de Chaume on the right. A lot more fighting would be required to conquer the Heights of the Meuse.

✯

THE 82d Division had to make good progress, and fast. With the 28th and 77th Divisions exhausted and unable to push forward vigorously—the Statue of Liberty Division hardly moved at all despite encountering no more opposition than a hostile German police dog—the only chance of cutting off the Germans before they escaped the Argonne rested with the All-Americans.

With that in mind, Liggett boldly ordered General Duncan to drive his troops westward from Hills 180 and 223 to Cornay and La Besogne, all the way to the Argonne's western edge. He asked for too much. On the right, the 327th Regiment attacked at 6:00 A.M., with fifteen tanks in support. A few minutes after jump-off, with the troops and tanks advancing and already under fire, the 327th's commander, Colonel Frank Ely, received new orders from brigade headquarters changing the direction of the attack. He had to halt the troops, disengage them from the enemy, and then send them forward again in a new direction. It took the rest of the day for the regiment to cover the half mile from Hill 180 to Cornay. It entered the town just before dark and mopped it up, but as the position was exposed—under fire from both friendly and enemy artillery—the regiment withdrew to the southeast just before midnight.[8]

On the left, the 328th Regiment attacked from Hill 223 and advanced half a mile in three hours against strong enemy resistance. A further attack late that afternoon carried it another half mile to Champrocher Ridge, but, like Cornay, this conquest had to be abandoned. The only success came on the division's extreme left, or southern flank, where the 328th's Second Battalion—Corporal Alvin C. York's outfit—pushed a mile west of Hill 223 to a road and light railway.

York had spent the previous night lying out in the rain and mud until he was "wet through and dirty and kinder tired." The misery continued as his company crossed the Aire on a rickety wooden bridge and groped through a German gas barrage, "slipping and sliding, or falling into holes and tripping over all sorts of things and getting up again and stumbling on for a few yards and then going down again," to Hill 223. The Doughboys waited for a supporting barrage. None came, but they attacked anyway, bayonets fixed, at 6:10 A.M. York, in a supporting platoon, watched German machine guns cut down the men ahead of him "like the long grass before the mowing machine at home," until it seemed none of them were left. The survivors hit the ground and took cover. Further advance seemed impossible.

No sudden heroic impulse seized York. He didn't leap up and take on the guns single-handed. Instead he hugged the ground with the rest of the Doughboys while officers died trying to rally the men. York's platoon sergeant eventually gathered seventeen men and ordered them to work through the underbrush to the left so that they could take some enemy machine guns in the flank. Led by Sergeant Bernard Early, the detachment successfully moved across the brush-strewn valley and up a forested ridge on the other side. On the ridge they held a conference. Some of the soldiers suggested driving straight along the ridge into the German flank, but Early and York decided to penetrate farther, swing around, and take the enemy from behind.

As the little American detachment continued through the woods down the ridge's far slope, two Germans wearing Red Cross bands jumped out of the bushes and ran like "scared rabbits." The Americans called for them to surrender and fired some shots, to no avail, so they followed the fugitives down the ridge and across a little stream. On the other side, the Doughboys discovered another several dozen Germans standing around a little shack.[9] There were officers, orderlies, runners, and stretcher-bearers, all unarmed and some in their shirtsleeves. Their ranking officer, Lieutenant Paul Vollmer—the Americans misidentified him as a major—surrendered immediately. Sergeant Early ordered his men to line up the prisoners. Just as he gave the command, German machine gunners on a nearby hillside opened fire, yelling as they did so for the prisoners to hit the dirt. Early fell, riddled by six bullets; so did two corporals and six men. Corporal Murray Savage, York's best friend, was shot to pieces, with hundreds of bullets tearing the clothes from his body. The rest of the men took cover. The prisoners, several of whom had been killed, waved their arms and called for their comrades to stop firing, but machine guns continued firing in a building crescendo until the air was "plumb full of death."[10]

York had taken cover on a slope a little beyond the command shack. He did not choose the position—it was just where he happened to be standing when the enemy opened fire—but it could not have been better situated. The nearest Germans occupied ditches and gun pits on the hillside above him, about twenty-five yards away. Because of the slope, they had to raise their heads up above the rims of their earthworks in order to see York and the other Americans below. That made them excellent targets. York, being somewhat separated from the rest of the group and farther up the hillside, was the only man in a position to take advantage of it.

Lying down, then up on one knee, York worked his rifle like the expert marksman he was. He did not think of his victims as people. They were targets, like the ones he shot during competitions in Tennessee, or turkeys, like the ones he used to hunt. He could not give the Germans a chance to see him and take aim; he had to keep their heads down. So whenever an enemy soldier raised his head, York "jes teched him off." This went on for several minutes, until he had used several clips and his rifle had become red hot. The Germans shouted orders; he didn't know the language, but he could guess that they were trying to figure out what to do. Finally a lieutenant and five men jumped up and charged downhill with fixed bayonets.

The Germans were brave. They had twenty-five yards to cover, and must have figured that York would be able to kill some of them. They never imagined that he would be able to hit them all. A rifle didn't work that quickly, but York still had his pistol and pulled it out fast.

I teched off the sixth man first; then the fifth; then the fourth; then the third; and so on. That's the way we shoot wild turkeys at home. You see we don't want the front ones to know that we're getting the back ones, and then they keep on coming until we get them all. Of course, I hadn't time to think of that. I guess I jes naturally did it. I knowed, too, that if the front ones wavered, or if I stopped them the rear ones would drop down and pump a volley into me and get me.

He got them all, and then returned to his rifle.

York had been fighting by instinct. The suddenness of the engagement hadn't given him time for anything else. But his conscience was not dead, only suppressed; and it crept slowly back into his mind. These were *men* he was killing. And he didn't like it. He kept firing, but after every couple of shots he yelled, "Give up and come on down." They didn't hear him, didn't understand, or simply wouldn't think of surrendering to a single marksman. The fight would have continued, and York might have run out of ammunition, had not Lieutenant Vollmer intervened. Shortly after the defeat of the German bayonet charge, he crept up the hillside to York.

"English?" the lieutenant yelled.

"No, not English," York called back.

"What?"

"American."

"Good Lord!" Vollmer gasped. He knew that the English regulars could work miracles with rifles; they were some of the best-trained soldiers in the world. Perhaps he thought York was an English adviser shepherding the callow Yanks. That an American—particularly from a green division like the 82d—could behave so calmly and fire so accurately evidently came as a shock. After a moment he said, "If you won't shoot any more I will make them give up."

"Well, all right," York replied. "I will treat you like a man."[11] Blowing what sounded like "the whistle on a peanut stand," the lieutenant called for his men to come down and give up. They obeyed, leaving their trench and throwing down their weapons. York called them over. One of them had a concealed grenade and tossed it at the corporal, but it missed and York "teched him off."

The rest of the American detachment emerged cautiously from behind trees and underbrush and helped guard the prisoners. They were hesitant about escorting so many Germans back to the American lines. Vollmer, who had worked in Chicago before the war, suspiciously asked York how many men he had. The corporal curtly replied that he had "a-plenty," and ordered the Doughboys to gather the prisoners, make them carry Sergeant Early and the other wounded Americans, and move out. York put Vollmer at the head of the column and walked behind with his .45 trained on the German's back.

The lieutenant suggested they go back through a gully. York refused, electing instead to cut straight back across the ridge through the German front line. On the way they encountered an enemy machine-gun nest, but York forced Vollmer to order the crew to surrender. All of them did, except one whom York killed. His conscience was fully awake by now, and the necessity of killing that last German tore him up inside. He never forgot the incident, and frequently had to convince himself that he had no other choice. But the column made it back successfully.

"Well, York, I hear you have captured the whole damned German army," Brigadier General Julian Lindsey told him back at headquarters.

York replied that he had "only" brought in 132.[12]

✶

For all the acts of bravery that took place in the Argonne and on the Heights of the Meuse on October 8, First Army had made little progress in either sector. That did not worry Pershing unduly. The Argonne would fall soon, though the German rear guards continued to fight stubbornly. And though the conquest of the Heights of the Meuse promised to be a long and bloody business, his purpose there had been not just to clear out the German heavy artillery, but to "increase the fighting front of the army and thus engage and consume the maximum number of enemy divisions."[13] The critical point was not the left or right, but the center, where the attack would resume on October 9. Everything depended on it. If the Heights of Cunel and Romagne could not be taken, the *Kriemhilde Stellung* would never crack—and the Meuse-Argonne offensive would never succeed.

CHAPTER 19

"We Are Going to Have a Very Hard Day"

OCTOBER 9

Cold rain fell all night, drenching the ground and filling shell holes to the brim. It stopped before dawn, and a thick, dreary fog oozed over the ground. The fog would lift in the afternoon, and leaden skies would erupt with another downpour, harder than before. Private Charles D. Dermody of Lebanon, Illinois, a scout with the 33d Division's 132d Regiment, felt relaxed despite the miserable weather. He and his buddy Roy Dixon shared a shell hole just south of the Bois de Chaume. It had been a wet night, but Dermody had dry tobacco and Dixon had dry matches, and they rolled and lit cigarettes. "Between the two of us," Dermody remembered, "we had it made." Another buddy, Private Bertog, was antsy; he wanted action. "What are we stopping here for?" he yelled. "We can't win the war sitting here. Let's go up in those woods and see what's in there." A Doughboy in a nearby hole cried, "Hey you fellas, there's machine guns in there." But Dermody and Dixon were already convinced. "We know it—that's what we're going after," they called back. "There's no machine guns in there, that's just your imagination," Bertog chimed in cheerily as the three men hitched up and climbed out of their holes. He was wrong. "We found out," Dermody recalled, that "there were plenty of guns in there."

The 33d Division's morning barrage began at 6:00 A.M. and rolled north forty minutes later, followed by the 132d Regiment, its First and Second Battalions in line from left to right. Fog concealed First Battalion's advance over open ground along the riverbank, and it encountered only slight opposition. Second Battalion did not have it so easy. Following Dermody and other scouts into the Bois de Chaume, it ran into numerous German machine-gun nests, all of them dug in and ready. Gunfire and hand-to-hand fighting erupted as Private Dermody and his two companions entered the woods. After about a hundred feet the Germans detected them and opened fire. They took cover, but bullets flew at them from behind. Figures in wide-brimmed helmets crept through the fog. Snipers? No—Americans, firing wildly at everything that moved. The scouts leapt into a shell hole. "I don't mind the Germans shooting at us," Bertog grumbled, "but these Yanks are liable to kill a fellow."

The scouts joined the first line of infantry as it passed, alternately walking and crawling through the tangled undergrowth. The enemy fire intensified every minute, and grenades bounced off trees and hurtled through the air. Doughboys fell around Dermody, faster than he could count—including Dixon, who went down with a bullet in his knee and shrapnel rattling off his helmet. Another soldier walking next to Dermody took a bullet through the center of his forehead. He took another two steps and pitched forward on his face. Men sometimes kept walking, Dermody learned, even after wounds that caused instantaneous death. Men who took a little longer to die would often make the most matter-of-fact comments: "They got me," they would cry; or, "I got hit," "I'm hit," or "I got that one."

As casualties mounted, Dermody, Bertog, and the soldiers they had joined grew more cautious. They picked slowly through the underbrush, alert for snipers, rifles carried at the ready as if they were big-game hunters. Emerging from the underbrush, they saw a plank road that the Germans had used to move artillery and supplies. Knowing that concealed German machine guns often turned such open spaces into death traps, Dermody and the others stepped back into cover. They were thinking about how to get across the clearing when seven Doughboys walked up the plank road in single file. Dermody's group hissed at them to take cover, but the Yanks paid no heed and walked blithely on. Within thirty seconds, all of them were dead, "melted down one by one" before the German machine guns.

Second Battalion nevertheless reached the northern edge of the Bois de Chaume by noon, alongside First Battalion, which had advanced on the left to within a few hundred yards of Sivry-sur-Meuse.[1] Badly bloodied and short on ammunition, Dermody's battalion paused just beyond the tree line and dug in along the crest of a hill. The fog lifted as the Doughboys worked their spades, revealing a brush-filled valley directly ahead and another hill about nine hundred yards distant. It also exposed a large concentration of German infantry, only fifty yards away. The opponents gazed at each other for several minutes, stunned, until the Germans fled for the opposite hill. The Americans, weakened by the fighting in the Bois de Chaume, could not exploit this apparent weakness. Instead, they hunkered down while artillery and machine-gun fire poured in from the front and flank, directed by aerial observers and augmented by strafing Fokkers. Unable to hold in the open, the Doughboys pulled back to the Bois de Chaume, determined to "hold the lines to the last man."[2]

The real danger, it turned out, did not come from the front. To the right, the 29th Division had been supposed to keep pace with the 132d Regiment. Instead, it repulsed a weak German attack that morning and spent the rest of the day sitting on its hands. The Germans took advantage of the 29th's inaction by infiltrating the eastern Bois de Chaume. They found an undefended two-thousand-yard gap behind Second Battalion's right flank and advanced aggressively through it to attack the Americans in the flank and rear. Gun teams from the 124th Machine Gun Battalion tried to seal the gap, but the Germans methodically destroyed them.[3] The infantry at the woods' north edge turned and fought, but the outcome was inevitable. By evening, Second Battalion had abandoned the entire Bois de Chaume and withdrawn to its positions of that morning. To avoid being exposed, First Battalion had pulled back as well, to its original positions just north of Consenvoye. The Germans captured hundreds of American stragglers, including a wounded Private Dermody. Another group of Americans, more than one hundred men from Companies F and G, was surrounded in the woods.

This disastrous end to the day concealed one important reality: east of the Meuse, the Germans were near the breaking point. In authorizing the offensive's extension to this sector, Pershing had hoped to put severe pressure on his adversary's meager reserves—and he achieved just that. "Fighting east of the Meuse was particularly violent today," Gallwitz recorded in his army war diary for October 9. "It almost forced the Fifth Army to employ its last reserves on the battle front. The situation was serious. There were no reserves available worth mentioning."[4] On October 8, the 29th and 33d Divisions had essentially annihilated the 1st Austrian Division. Higher-quality German infantry entered the lines on the next day and played a central role in driving the 132d Regiment out of the Bois de Chaume. But they had played their last card. Behind the Germans already in the front line, nothing remained.

★

GENERAL Bullard's III Corps was little more than a wraith. Two weeks of combat and intense, unrelenting bombardment had mauled the 4th and 80th Divisions so badly that they could barely function. But Bullard refused to consider the Doughboys' sufferings. Confronted with reports of demoralization at the front, he declared that they had become infected with the European disease—sitting in trenches and begging for more artillery support instead of taking up their rifles, fixing bayonets, and attacking the enemy. He accused generals who mentioned the soldiers' exhaustion of losing their nerve. The 80th Division's commander, Major General Cronkhite, had hesitated to attack the Bois des Ogons; Bullard threatened to relieve him. The 4th Division's commander, Major General Hines, asked for his beleaguered troops to be pulled out of the hellish Bois de Fays. "No," Bullard sternly told him, "we've got to stay there; we give up nothing."[5]

Bullard knew of only one cure for the malaise. Pershing's orders for October 9 gave III Corps a supporting role. It was only supposed to watch out for the flanks of the French XVII Corps on the right and V Corps on the left, while preparing to advance on further orders. Bullard decided that the survival of his corps depended on a more aggressive policy. Only one thing, he believed, could revive his men and get them thinking about victory: attack, attack, and again attack. Somewhere Colonel Grandmaison, the architect of France's offensive philosophy in 1914, must have smiled.

Bullard ordered the Ivy Division to attack at dusk, peremptorily refusing Hines's request for a delay.[6] The 7th Brigade, with the 39th Regiment on the left and the 47th Regiment on the right, moved up that afternoon through the Bois de Fays.

> The march up to the front line was a march of horror. Several paths led through the Bois de Fays and all were strewn on both sides with dead bodies. In one spot lay more than sixty men and in another over two hundred. Gas, artillery shells and machine gun bullets rained on them.[7]

One hour before jump-off, the Germans laid down a devastatingly accurate barrage of high explosives and gas on the Bois de Fays. Some of the shellfire came from the southeast, making the troops think their own artillery was hitting them. The 47th Regiment, shattered and disorganized, abandoned the attack. The 39th Regiment, equally shattered and disorganized, continued. It was dark, and the Doughboys could not tell the way ahead:

> In the failing light and amid the thick underbrush little could be seen through the goggles of the masks. The shell-fire seemed to increase with

every passing minute. The roar of heavy shells could be heard coming from the rear. Soon the darkness in the thick woods became almost impenetrable. The men in the front lines fell. The men behind stumbled over their dead or wounded comrades as they advanced against their invisible enemy. They had nothing to guide them but the sound of their officers' voices. They could not see. They fell over the barbed wire which the Germans had wound low through the underbrush and between the trees. The advance stopped. The word was passed along the line to withdraw and the men filtered back by ones and twos.[8]

Dozens more men had died without gaining an inch of ground, and without seeing a single German soldier.

✫

THE 80th Division had taken 1,824 casualties since October 4, suffering from such heavy and incessant artillery and gas attacks that the troops had to wear their masks almost all of the time, even as they slept. Bullard, encouraged by the 3d Division's capture of the Bois de Cunel on the left, nevertheless ordered the 80th to attack at 3:30 P.M. The 319th and 320th Regiments led the assault from left to right. On the right, the 320th departed the nightmarish Bois des Ogons and advanced about half a mile, taking Hill 275 and the left edge of the Bois de Fays. As soon as the Americans paused to reorganize, however, a powerful German counterbarrage hit them. The terrible noise of "bursting shells, of the hideous crying of particles of flying steel," forced Lieutenant Colonel Ashby Williams to shout at the top of his voice as he attempted to form his men.[9] The American artillery responded with a sound akin to a mouse's squeak, scattering a few random shots over the German-held Bois de Malaumont, but the infantry could go no farther.

The 319th, on the left, also suffered from a heavy barrage of machine-gun, mortar, and artillery fire. Pummeled and slashed, the Doughboys advanced through the ruins of Madeleine Farm to a light railway and trench half a mile farther north. There they took fire from three directions, for they had outpaced the 318th on the right and the 3d Division on the left. The German infantry filtered through gaps between the advancing companies and severely disorganized their advance. Three companies nevertheless pushed ahead another mile, through an undefended gap in the enemy lines and all the way into Cunel, where they surprised the staffs of two German battalions and captured more than two hundred prisoners. The Doughboys herded the prisoners into a church, locked it, and looked around. In a couple of hours, they—members of a tattered, seemingly half-dead division full of draftees—had captured one of the central strongpoints of the *Kriemhilde Stellung.*

The situation was dangerous. The Americans in Cunel had advanced a mile ahead of their support on either flank. And the Germans, particularly those in the Bois de la Pultière on a ridge just north of town, could see everything they did. Yet the Doughboys had already accomplished the improbable. Might they next achieve the impossible, pushing into the Bois de la Pultière and seizing complete control of the Heights of Cunel? Their officers thought they could. Posting guards on the church, they ordered their men to shoulder rifles and continue advancing. Major General Cronkhite, meanwhile, got on the phone to the divisional artillery. His orders were to lay a barrage along Cunel's northern perimeter in case the Germans launched a counterattack. He never imagined that the troops in Cunel might try to push farther north.

The Americans advanced past a tree-lined crossroads north of town and were approaching the Bois de la Pultière when the friendly barrage fell among them. The timing could not have been better for the Germans. At that moment, they poured down from the wooded ridge in a massive counterattack. The outnumbered Americans held their ground for a while, but when the Germans infiltrated around their open flanks they had to pull back. Severe close-quarters combat took place in and around Cunel until midnight, when the surviving Doughboys took advantage of the darkness to retreat back to their main line of advance, about a mile behind. The glory had proved all too brief; the reality, that the Germans would not surrender Cunel without a bitter fight, was all too painful.

✫

GENERAL Cameron's V Corps, now containing the 3d, 32d, and 1st Divisions, along with the 91st Division's 181st Brigade, advanced on October 9 with the objective of conquering the Heights of Romagne. No one had any illusions that it was going to be easy—least of all Private Jack Barkley, whose exploits in the abandoned tank on the seventh had wrecked an entire German battalion. On the eighth, the 3d Division's 38th Regiment, moving up in place of the 7th Regiment, had tried to clear the crest and rear slopes of Hill 253, only to be stopped cold with heavy casualties. The morning of the ninth found the regiment's Doughboys "huddling in small scooped-out holes on the southern slope of Hill 253," with the enemy lines no more than seventy-five yards away. To the east, the 30th Regiment, replacing Barkley's 4th, looked across the valley toward the Bois de Cunel. Its objective was to cross the valley, take those woods, and push on to Cunel and the Bois de la Pultière. The 38th, meanwhile, would finish off Hill 253, cross the open valley beyond, and storm a strong German defensive system known as Mamelle Trench—part of the *Kriemhilde Stellung*—which ran below the crest of the opposite ridge.

A few days earlier, the 4th Regiment had tried to cross the valley between Hill 250 and the Bois de Cunel and been torn to shreds. The 30th had better luck. Advancing under cover of heavy fog, it crossed the valley without trouble and entered the woods at 10:00 A.M., receiving fire only from Madeleine Farm, on the right flank. The 80th Division had not yet attacked at this point, so the 3d Division Doughboys crossed the divisional boundary and stormed and captured the farm. The 30th Regiment reached the northern edge of the Bois de Cunel at noon. The German infantry had withdrawn across an open valley to Hill 272, but the Americans encountered such heavy shellfire when they ventured beyond the tree line that they had to stop and dig in. Nor, as it turned out, had the Germans given up on the Bois de Cunel. Many snipers had stayed behind—even this late in the war, there never seemed to be any shortage of volunteers for such suicide missions—and as the Americans stopped the snipers shot at them from behind. It would take all night to clear them out.

The 38th Regiment faced two problems. First, General Buck assigned it jumping-off positions a quarter mile behind the enemy lines. Second, and thornier, the Germans seemed extremely reluctant to give up Hill 253. When the Americans tried to take the hill that morning, enemy machine guns stopped them. The second time, they flanked the enemy positions. After an hour of fighting, in which so many officers fell that a corporal had to take command of one company, the Doughboys gained positions from where they could take the Germans in enfilade. Hill 253 finally fell by midmorning, and the advance continued.

With two battalions leading and one in reserve, the Americans moved north through the valley, past the twisted steel scraps of Barkley's tank and dozens of German corpses, and toward a small brook. Nearby stood a concrete pillbox reinforced with logs, looking much like an "old Indian blockhouse," except for the machine gun spitting death through the port. It was an isolated emplacement, and the infantry outflanked it and forced the Germans inside to surrender. The Americans crossed the brook and ascended a gently sloping hill without a speck of cover. Officers spaced their men at wide intervals as they advanced. It was a wise precaution. From Mamelle Trench ahead and emplacements on either flank, German machine guns swept the hillside with bullets. Dozens of Doughboys fell dead or wounded, but enough survived to cut through the barbed wire and assault the German trenches. Bayonets and pistols were the weapons of choice in the close-quarters fighting that followed. The enemy infantry defended stubbornly, with machine-gun and grenade posts at every corner. Other Germans appeared from the Bois de Cunel, jumping into the trenches or setting up machine guns on hummocks and in craters. The Americans fought stubbornly too, and after about an hour they cleared the trench system and drove the Germans back into the woods and over the hill.

With Mamelle Trench secured, the Doughboys continued another three hundred yards to the hill's open crest. A battery of 88s on another hill a mile away fired shrapnel at them as they advanced. The whiz-bangs exploded close to the ground—five to ten feet—and chopped soldiers to bloody rags, while the wounded crawled desperately for the few craters and depressions that dotted the slope. The Doughboys nevertheless passed over the hill's crest just after noon. A few patrols even entered Romagne, just a quarter mile ahead on the left, and returned with prisoners. The two battalions leading the assault had been reduced to the size of companies, but they had taken an important outpost of the *Kriemhilde Stellung* and advanced to the brink of the Heights of Romagne.[10]

*

GENERAL Haan did not look forward to October 9. "I am inclined to think we are going to have a very hard day," he told his diary. "The 32nd Division is going up against a very hard proposition—a thoroughly organized position which is reported well-armed and has good artillery behind it."[11] He had reason for concern. His division had advanced about a mile north of Gesnes. Ahead lay the strongest point of the *Kriemhilde Stellung,* an outcropping of the Heights of Romagne called Côte Dame Marie. This crescent-shaped ridge a mile west of the village of Romagne was about five-eighths of a mile long, with the horns pointing toward the American lines. The eastern horn projected directly south, with a rounded apex called Hill 258. From there the ridge rose steeply half a mile northwest to Hill 287. A short distance west of that was Hill 286, which formed the crescent's western horn.

Côte Dame Marie could not be taken frontally. At the crescent's center, the ridge rose fifty feet in a sheer wall of rock. The Germans had laid thick belts of barbed wire at the ridge's base, backed up by well-sited machine guns. Any attempt to scale the central ridge could only result in massacre. The alternative, to assault one or both of the crescent's horns and drive along the crest of the ridge, would also be difficult. The Germans had dug formidable infantry and machine-gun emplacements at the bases and on the approaches to Hills 258 and 286. They had also strung barbed wire and dug trenches east of Côte Dame Marie, into a valley and about half a mile south of Romagne, and established outposts and strongpoints in the various hills, ravines, and woods below and on either side of the ridge.[12]

Haan understood that his men faced an exceedingly complex task, requiring careful preparation and creative tactics. There must be no repeat of the fiasco of October 4, when officers and men had gone into battle with inadequate or conflicting maps. Haan therefore prepared a "special maneuver map" of the area around Côte Dame Marie and distributed copies of it to all of his officers, all the way down to company commanders. Each officer would thus be working on the same general plan, which was to attack south and southwest of Romagne and penetrate the outer German defenses. Once this had been accomplished, the 126th Regiment on the right would seize Romagne and drive northwest into the Bois de Romagne and the Bois de Bantheville. The 125th Regiment, to the left, meanwhile, would seize Hill 258 and attack simultaneously along the crest of the ridge and into the woods north of Côte Dame Marie.[13]

Lieutenant Harold Woehl of the 126th led his platoon forward just after 8:00 A.M. on October 9. His regiment encountered no opposition as it advanced for about half a mile through extremely dense fog. When the fog lifted, "like a clap of thunder, the fireworks started." The Americans found themselves on the north slope of a low ridge, with the Germans dug in along the crest of another ridge only a hundred yards away. The enemy machine gunners immediately opened fire, and the first wave of infantry melted away. Among those hit was a lieutenant who had been commissioned on October 1 and assigned to Woehl's company six days later. On arrival he had told Woehl that he looked forward to learning about conditions at the front. A German machine gun raked him across the stomach, and he died a few days later.

The forward movement nevertheless continued at other points of the regiment's front, and with the help of a few tanks the enemy's first line was broken. Some units even reached the southern outskirts of Romagne until the Germans counterattacked and drove them back. By late afternoon the regiment had dug in along a ridge east of Côte Dame Marie.[14]

A German counterbarrage slammed into the 125th just as it jumped off that morning, inflicting severe losses on the attacking companies. The fog caused more confusion and intermixture. The regiment nevertheless covered about a mile through the Bois de Valoup and approached the German defenses at the base of Hill 258. By that time the 125th was completely disorganized and in no condition to attack. Its officers ordered the men to dig in and get ready for the following day. Haan's plan had gone well so far. "Our troops fought fine," he wrote in his diary, "and although we had rather heavy casualties we nevertheless had small casualties for the work we accomplished." In reality, the Red Arrow Division had only stepped up to Côte Dame Marie's grim face and looked her in the eye. The real test had yet to come.[15]

★

Captain Allen Wildish, the tobacco-chewing commander of Corporal Donald Kyler's company of the 1st Division's 16th Regiment, knew something was wrong as soon as the fog lifted that morning. To the east, he could see the division's other regiments attacking the enemy around Hill 272; to the west, across the Aire, the 82d Division drove farther into the Argonne. Just to his front, meanwhile, German infantry massed around Fléville, obviously preparing a major counterattack against his battalion. Wildish knew he could not hold them back for long. Badly depleted by fighting and attrition since October 4, his company lacked adequate ammunition and had no machine guns, mortars, or rifle grenades. Instead of trying to hold the line, therefore, Wildish planned a fighting retreat. Selecting his best marksmen—including Kyler, who once again landed a dirty job—he deployed them in rifle pits ahead of his main positions. The rest of his men would fire into the flanks of the Germans as they overran the rifle pits—as they surely would—and advanced to the south.

Kyler selected a pit and moved in with his rifle and hundreds of cartridges. He cut a little slot in the bank, poked his rifle through it, and surveyed the ground in front of him. The field of fire was excellent—if only he had a machine gun! Kyler stayed low, waiting for an enemy barrage, but none came. Instead, the Germans gathered in small groups and advanced, with their right on the Aire and their left on the base of the broad open slope that climbed eastward to Montrefagne. He held his fire until the Germans were about four hundred yards away. Then he and the other riflemen aimed and fired carefully, picking off the enemy soldiers one at a time. Several Germans toppled over at the first volley. The rest dove to the ground, fired back, crawled a little way forward, and fired again. They didn't hit anything, but they kept getting closer.

Occupying a pit at about the center of the thin American line, Kyler fired steadily. He took deliberate aim, particularly at enemy officers, and tried not to panic. But Germans kept coming, until several hundred were just outside grenade range. They still weren't hitting anything—their rifles and light machine-gun bullets either hit the gun pits' earthen banks or flew harmlessly overhead—but pretty soon they would be able to hurl grenades and rush the Doughboys with bayonets. Kyler didn't use Corporal York's turkey-shooting technique of firing at the followers first; he simply shot those nearest to him. As they continued to approach he just pumped bullets without even trying to aim—the Germans were so close that it was impossible to miss anyway. Kyler's rifle became so hot that he could hardly hold on to it.

Suddenly, the Germans stopped. Kyler kept firing, and more and more enemy soldiers fell. Then they broke. Some ran; others dragged or carried wounded comrades. The Doughboys showed no mercy to any of them. They just fired and fired until nothing moved. When it was over, Kyler slumped in his hole. The whole right side of his body seemed like a mass of blood and bruises. His right hand was covered with blood from dragging across rocks while working the rifle bolt; his right shoulder was bruised from the recoil; and his right eye, cheek, and chin were all bruised from being bumped by the gun as he fired. His left hand, burned from touching the rifle barrel, provided a little balance.[16]

✻

For the rest of 1st Division, the day's fighting centered on Hill 272, a wedge-shaped, east-west ridge about half a mile north of Montrefagne. Craggy, wooded, and strongly defended, it had held up the Big Red One since October 4. The 26th Regiment had attempted to take it on the eighth, and had failed miserably. On the following day, Summerall brought the 16th Regiment's First Battalion over from the left flank and deployed it at the northern base of Montrefagne. The battalion was reasonably fresh, having been kept in reserve for the previous few days, and ably led. Its attack would be supported on the left by the 18th Regiment, which would push north through the hills and woods between Fléville and Hill 272, and on the right by the 26th and 28th Regiments, which would drive past Hill 269 through the Bois de Moncy to Hill 263, a little northeast of Hill 272. Summerall made certain that all of his available artillery and heavy machine guns worked together to support the attack.

A regiment of heavy 155mm howitzers announced the attack by pounding the crest and lower slopes of Hill 272. The 16th Regiment's First Battalion followed the barrage, jumping off at 8:30 A.M. into a pea-soup fog. The leading companies separated in the fog but crossed the valley and arrived at the hill's base at about the same time. Instead of attacking frontally, as many inexperienced formations had been wont to do, the Doughboys infiltrated through gaps and crevices between and behind the enemy machine-gun nests, which they outflanked and destroyed. Taking many casualties but aided by cover of fog, the Americans methodically eliminated fifty German machine-gun nests and captured the entire hill in less than two hours. This exploit forced the Germans to abandon the positions they had been holding in front of the 18th Regiment on the left, and undercut their defenses in the Bois de Moncy and Hill 263 on the right, which fell to the combined efforts of the 26th and 28th Regiments.[17]

✶

CORPORAL Kyler stayed in his rifle pit all night. He wanted to sleep, but the groans and whimpers of the wounded Germans in the field in front of him kept him and his comrades awake. The Doughboys endured it for hours until a young private from Montana, snarling that he would shut them up, took his bayonet and crawled silently off into the dark. After a while the cries ceased and the soldier returned. Nobody said a word in protest. "Our attitude was that they were better off than we were," Kyler recalled. "Their misery was over."[18]

✶

THE 82d Division had fought hard for two days, but—Corporal York's exploits aside—not accomplished much. Its two frontline regiments, the 327th and 328th, were in bad shape. "All of us," reported Colonel Frank Ely of the 327th, "are more or less gassed and ineffective."[19] But if two days in the line had ravaged the All-Americans, the state of the 28th Division—which had endured a bloody summer, followed by almost continuous combat since September 26—can scarcely be imagined. Sensing that the Pennsylvanians could take no more, Liggett moved them into reserve and ordered the 82d Division's fresh 325th and 326th Regiments into the front lines. These regiments would attack northwest and north toward La Besogne, while the 327th and 328th attacked northwest through Cornay.

The plan should have worked easily. That morning, all of the Germans in the Argonne had been ordered to evacuate the forest and cross to the other side of the Aire River to its north. And all went well at first, with the 325th and 326th driving rapidly into the fog-choked forest against practically no opposition and the 327th and 328th, which had been skirmishing with the Germans all night, seizing Cornay. Then disaster struck. The German 41st Division, which had been defending Cornay, did not receive the withdrawal orders until after its commander ordered a full-scale counterattack on the town around noon. The Doughboys in the town—elements of the 327th and 328th—barricaded themselves in houses as the German infantry closed in from three sides. The Americans fell back, crushed into an ever-shrinking perimeter, until the captain in charge, having more wounded than able men under his command, decided to surrender. "We have done all we can men, we shall all be killed if we stay," he explained to his terrified men. The Germans took 166 Americans prisoner, and recaptured Cornay.[20] The shattered 327th and 328th withdrew to the positions they had occupied two days earlier when the All-Americans first entered battle.

★

Corporal York did not participate in any of this fighting. His mind was elsewhere, with the dead and wounded men he had left behind in that little valley on the previous day. Unable to stop thinking about them, he asked his captain for permission to return there with two stretcher-bearers. Perhaps somebody could still be saved. The valley was in American hands, and it had already been searched. There were no wounded men there, only corpses; but the captain understood that York needed peace of mind, and let him go.

York found the valley littered with bullet-riddled equipment, helmets, and other things he couldn't mention. "Everything," it seemed, was "destroyed, torned up, killed—trees, grass, men." He combed the underbrush and wandered among the bullet-splintered trees. He called out to the wounded—and the dead. Whether they were Americans or Germans didn't matter—he just wanted to salvage something, to bring out somebody alive. But no one answered.

> I jes couldn't help thinking of the boys that only the day before was alive and like me. Dymowski—dead. Weiler—dead. Waring—dead. Wins—dead. Swanson—dead. Corporal Murray Savage, my best pal, dead. Oh my, it seemed so unbelievable. I would never see them again. I would never share the same blanket with Corporal Savage. We'd never read the Bible together again. We would never talk about our faith and pray to our God. I was mussed up inside worser than I had ever been. I'm a-telling you when you lose your best buddie and you know you ain't never going to see him again, you sorter know how terrible cruel war is.

Unable to save any lives, York prayed.

> I prayed for the Greeks and Italians and the Poles and the Jews and the others. I done prayed for the Germans too. They were all brother men of mine.

Maybe their religion was different, but I reckon we all believed in the same God and I wanted to pray for all of them.[21]

He, like Major Whittlesey, could never understand why they had died while he survived.

★

IN the Argonne Forest, the 77th Division's advance continued. Private Charles Minder of the 306th Machine Gun Battalion described it to his diary:

> We saw some pretty bad damage all along the hike today. I saw at least two hundred dead bodies lying all over the place, in every possible position. I saw one fellow, with his head bandaged, down on his knees. He passed on while kneeling. One fellow was completely blown to pieces, and half of his body was hanging on a branch of a tree, one arm on the ground, and his two legs about ten yards away. It was the most ghastly sight I've ever seen. The smell of the dead is terrible in the woods.[22]

By day's end the Statue of Liberty Division had advanced to just south of La Besogne and had established contact with the left flank of the 82d Division. The German commander, General Gallwitz, was not in the least bothered; the Argonne had outlived its usefulness. Instead, he felt "satisfied with the results of the day in so far as they yielded a great number of shining examples of bravery. It had been demonstrated that, even within numerically weak units, much reliable strength was left." Buoyed by his troops' continuing ability to hold back the far more numerous Americans, he denounced President Wilson's peace proposals as inconsistent with the honor of Germany.[23]

Gallwitz's only major concern was the exhaustion of his troops and the state of his reserves. Nothing, he knew, could be done—Germany had long ago called on her last manpower reserves—but he asked Ludendorff for help anyway, if only as a matter of form:

> Troops have fought superbly in most instances, but those in the front line are almost exhausted. Reserves have been committed and they are, likewise, weakened. . . . It is feared that the line of Fifth Army cannot be held much longer without further support. In view of the importance of the mission of this Group of Armies which is acting as the fulcrum for the operations of all of the armies fighting to the west and north, I request that additional forces be brought up.

Ludendorff replied with vague promises of eventual help. "However," he warned, "in view of the lack of troops, of which Your Excellency is well aware, Group of Armies Gallwitz must put into the fighting front every unit which is at all fit for employment in battle."[24] As Foch might have said, *tout le monde á la bataille*—everyone to the battle! Neither side would hold anything back from the coming struggle.

CHAPTER 20

————— ·•·•· —————

Beyond the Argonne

October 10

Lieutenant Joe Lawrence of the 113th Regiment, 29th Division, scanned the ground over which his men were about to attack. He didn't like what he saw. The enemy could see everything; there would be many casualties. The men around him realized it too. Lawrence's first sergeant stepped up and handed him his field glasses. "Here, Lieutenant," he said, "you will need these glasses. I won't." He then turned and fled, taking all of the company's signal flares with him. Other men disappeared too, turning up days later under arrest or in field hospitals with self-inflicted wounds. Lawrence eventually got used to such desertions as a routine preceding every attack. But he would miss those flares. Without them, it would be impossible to signal the artillery to stop shelling its own men.[1]

The 113th's New Jersey Doughboys had taken positions on the 29th Division's right front on the evening of October 9, replacing the 116th's battle-weary Virginians. Just after midnight, however, the commander of the French 18th Division—to which the 29th Division was attached—shifted the 113th eastward into a zone previously held by French infantry, and ordered it to attack at dawn. The Americans were told that their new objectives, the Bois de la Reine and the Bois de Chênes, lay beyond a steep, partially wooded slope; but that was all. The French provided them no maps or intelligence of any kind. "We had no guides," testified an American lieutenant, "and hardly knew where we were going. We only knew approximately where our positions lay, and no one could be found who did know." Officers desperately tried to gather information before H hour, without success.[2] They anticipated ugly business ahead.

After a laughably weak preparatory barrage, the attack began. The Doughboys moved light, without packs and carrying few grenades, but they were huffing and puffing by the time they reached the top of the steep slope. The first wave moved over the crest and advanced into a clearing. Then the storm began. From a camouflaged trench 150 yards ahead and woods on either side, dozens of German machine guns opened fire with a shattering barrage that wiped out the first wave. The soldiers in the second wave pressed on, crawling and rushing past dead and wounded comrades, but they were quickly pinned down. The French had encountered this death trap the previous day and withdrawn, but had not bothered to warn the Americans.

Lieutenant Lawrence looked to his right, where French infantry had started alongside the Americans, but the Poilus had turned and fled back down the slope. German machine guns promptly moved into the gap and fired into the 113th's right flank. A signal rocket went up from the enemy trench, and within moments artillery shells exploded in the clearing, "screaming and screeching, louder and louder, striking the ground in front or behind with a deafening, demoralizing crash, hurling dirt and debris all over us." The shellfire became more accurate every minute, as a German observation plane dropped markers for the artillery. The Doughboys clumped together under the shellfire, although Lawrence and the other officers ordered them to spread out. Another German airplane strafed back and forth over the clearing, methodically lashing the halted troops.

Though frightened and bloodied, the Americans did not flee. The few surviving officers signaled the attack, and their men picked up their rifles and rushed forward. Some reached the edge of the woods and dove into the enemy trench, yelling like maniacs and slashing with bayonets. The Germans fled into the woods, followed by battle-crazed Doughboys who cut them down without mercy. Chaos ensued. Rifle shots and screams echoed everywhere as Americans and Germans rushed among the trees. Gathering together a few men, Lawrence advanced into the woods. He had not gone far when some panic-stricken Doughboys hurtled past, pursued by whizzing bullets. Farther ahead, two soldiers crouched behind trees, firing at an unseen enemy. "Don't go down there, Lieutenant," one of them shouted, "the Boches are coming." Lawrence ignored them and kept going.

The lieutenant cautiously led his men down a winding forest road. Around a bend, the Americans encountered a halted column of three dozen

Germans, with officers poring over a map. "Boches!" yelled a Doughboy, who shoved Lawrence off the road into some bushes and then fled. American and German soldiers scattered in a wild melee, firing in every direction. Falling back into the woods, Lawrence gathered some men behind a light railway embankment. The Germans attacked a short time later, but the Americans sent them back into the underbrush with a point-blank rifle volley. The shrieking, agonized cries of wounded and dying Germans made Lawrence wonder whether some of them were women.

The Germans kept sniping all afternoon, and just before dusk they began preparing a counterattack. Lacking adequate ammunition, Lawrence decided to hit them with a bayonet charge. The ruse worked. Leaping over the embankment with a shout, the Americans scattered the Germans and drove them away, taking several prisoners. The pursuit continued to the edge of an open ravine, where the Doughboys stopped and picked off the Germans as they fled to the north. Lawrence took grim pleasure in watching their death pirouettes. "The Germans that were struck would leap into the air and fall to the ground writhing and twisting," he observed; others "would crawl a few yards and lie still." Lawrence led his men back into the woods and formed a ragged line as dark fell. The 113th had advanced to the northern edges of the Bois de Chênes and the Bois de la Reine, but at a terrible cost. It had been fresh at the beginning of the day; now it was a shattered wreck. Wounded Americans lay about in the woods all night, begging for water. German gas shells finished many of them off. Wounded Germans could not be cared for, and many were shot.[3]

The 29th Division's left-hand regiment, the 115th, attacked over more familiar ground: the steep western ridges of the Bois de Consenvoye toward Richêne Hill, and the edges of the Molleville Farm clearing. It also enjoyed close liaison with the artillery—and received no dubious "help" from the French. Jumping off just before 8:00 A.M., the regiment advanced slowly under heavy machine-gun fire, until the artillery laid an accurate barrage on the enemy positions along the lower slopes of Richêne Hill. Twenty minutes later, hundreds of shaken Germans emerged from their dugouts and surrendered. The regiment pushed forward another half mile to a railroad, where it formed a line. Along the way the Doughboys wiped out several machine-gun nests. The German machine guns "were in action until they saw it was no longer possible to avoid capture or death," an American lieutenant reported that evening. "Due to excitement and poor shooting on the part of some of our men some of them escaped. The large number of prisoners captured was an accident."[4]

★

THE 115th's advance past Richêne Hill relieved some pressure on the right flank of the Prairie Division, which had completed its crossing of the Meuse and attacked with its reserves in place. Jumping off at dawn, two battalions of the 131st Regiment advanced into the Bois de Chaume and the Bois Plat Chêne, rescuing a hundred men from the 132d Regiment who had been left behind the previous day. German machine guns and aircraft maintained a steady fire on the Americans, but the 131st successfully crossed the woods to the southern edge of an open ravine. Crossing the ravine, they drove back a weak line of German infantry and continued up a wooded ridge to an abandoned defensive system. Exhausted, the Doughboys plopped into old shell holes and trenches. They would get to know those holes very well.

The Illinoians had advanced to a line roughly even with Sivry-sur-Meuse. Ahead lay an extremely steep ridge rising northeast to the Borne de Cornouiller—otherwise known as "Corned Willy Hill." To their right and rear, where the 29th Division still lagged a mile behind, the woods swarmed with Germans. They fired on the Americans all day; the number of men holding the line grew fewer while the dead and wounded piled up. The Germans counterattacked twice, pounded the Americans with shrapnel, high explosives, and gas, and infiltrated like weevils behind the division's right flank. By late afternoon, casualties in the frontline battalions approached 50 percent, and signs of panic appeared among officers and men.[5] They had advanced four miles in three days. But without help on the right flank—and soon—they might have to give it all up.

★

GENERAL Bullard ordered an airplane to fly over the Bois de Fays and drop leaflets praising the troops of the Ivy Division for their bravery, and encouraging them to "stick." Then he issued another attack order, sending the 39th Regiment forward to another round of slaughter. Surging forward, then back, then forward again several times under brutal rifle, machine-gun, and artillery fire, the Americans ended about where they had started. By now they were no longer soldiers, but automatons. Their ranks had grown so thin that at least one company was commanded by a corporal. No matter; Bullard ordered them to attack again in the afternoon. They did, and once more were driven back. "I shall remember this as one of the finest if not the finest deed that I have known," Bullard wrote in his memoirs. He never forgot their "drive." They never forgot his either.[6]

The 80th Division had done well on October 9, nearly crashing the gates of Cunel. But Pershing and Bullard remained dissatisfied; the Doughboys and their commanders still seemed to lack the requisite spirit and drive. To stir them up, Bullard forwarded a message expressing Pershing's "great dissatisfaction with the progress of the attacking divisions, taking into consideration the fact that the enemy is not now holding his front with sufficient strength to counterattack and is, therefore, very evidently holding it merely with successive machine gun positions." Officers must "get in personal touch with front line conditions," the commander in chief demanded, "and see to it that energetic measures are adopted at once to reduce these machine gun nests."[7] Of barbed wire, mortars, grenades, and heavy artillery firing gas, high explosives, and shrapnel, Pershing said nothing. Nor did he address the fact that those "mere" machine-gun nests fired real bullets.

Lieutenant Colonel Ashby Williams, commanding the 320th Regiment, roused his men after midnight on October 10 and ordered them to attack the Bois de Malaumont. They had spent the past two weeks under fire with little sleep, and many soldiers had trouble breathing from the accumulated effects of gas. They nevertheless drove the Germans out of the woods and reached the Brieulles-Cunel road by 7:00 A.M. At daylight, with the 319th Regiment to its left advancing from the north edge of the Bois des Ogons, the 320th attacked again. German machine guns and 88s opened fire as they attempted to cross the road, forcing them back to their original positions. A savage drubbing at the hands of the American artillery followed, providing a fitting end to a miserable day.[8]

★

On October 9 the 3d Division had captured Mamelle Trench and the Bois de Cunel, advancing to the verge of the Heights of Cunel and Romagne. The Germans remained unbroken, but they seemed to be falling back; one more big push might kick in the door. And so on October 10 the 3d Division attacked, again and again. Each time it seemed that just a little more energy, a little more drive, a little more sacrifice might tip the balance; and each time the Doughboys tumbled back, exhausted, panic-stricken, and fewer than before. At 4:00 P.M. the troops were recalled, and the artillery laid a two-hour barrage on the German positions. At 6:00 P.M. the troops attacked again, and slammed into a stone wall. The battalion commanders ordered a retreat—and a few Doughboys crawled back down the hill. The Germans had no intention of retreating any farther.

A battalion of the 30th Regiment made one final attempt to crack the enemy lines in the dark at about 10:00 P.M. The troops crawled forward slowly, freezing when German flares lit the sky and moving again after they sputtered out, until the advance units were within a stone's throw of the enemy trenches. Then something—the rattle of a canteen, an indiscreet movement, a muffled cough—alerted the Germans and they opened fire. Bullets ripped into the Doughboys as they jumped up and charged the trenches. After close-quarters combat in the dark, the Americans captured a long stretch of the enemy trench. With the Germans still holding the flanks and no reserves to exploit and widen their toehold, however, they had no chance of holding on.[9] With dozens more Doughboys dead and wounded, the regiment withdrew. The 3d Division had nothing to show for the day.

★

ON October 9, the Red Arrow Division had advanced toward the flanks of Côte Dame Marie, the central stronghold of the Heights of Romagne. General Haan's plans for the tenth remained unchanged: attack toward Romagne and Hill 258, Côte Dame Marie's eastern peak, and drive northwest, capturing the remainder of the ridge. "The men are physically all in," Lieutenant Harold Woehl of the 126th Regiment wrote in his diary on October 10, "and a lot of their nerve is gone. Capt. Jankoska is on the verge of a breakdown but carries on with Company H. We need relief and we need it *BADLY*." But relief was a long way off. For now, headquarters had one thing to say: attack.

The 125th and 126th Regiments attacked in line from left to right, but neither got any farther than the southern slopes of Côte Dame Marie or the outskirts of Romagne. Woehl's battalion of the 126th was reduced to only sixty-six men out of an original strength of almost one thousand. German counterattacks kept the Americans at arm's length, and constant gas shelling forced the troops to wear masks all day. Haan expressed disappointment. "Today was entirely without result as to progress," he wrote in his diary, and his division was "considerably exhausted and disorganized"; but he still had hope that things would turn out all right. "There was not however much artillery fire today, and the men should have considerably recovered." Rested and ready, they should have all their drive back in time for the morning's attack.[10]

★

FOR Liggett's I Corps, October 10 was a day for celebration and the licking of wounds. After over two weeks of bitter, nightmarish fighting, the Argonne Forest finally fell to the Americans as the 77th and 82d Divisions advanced all the way to the south bank of the Aire River. The Germans, who had inflicted a humiliating defeat on the All-Americans at Cornay on the previous day, withdrew without putting up a fight. Summerall's 1st Division, meanwhile, followed the Germans as they pulled back to the *Kriemhilde Stellung*, from Sommerance to the north edge of the Bois de Romagne. For all their advances, the Doughboys did not feel victorious. "Physically we were wrecks," one of them attested. "Many of our men could not speak above a whisper owing to the action of gas on the vocal cords. We were weak but were not sick. We were just wornout. We had lost all track of the days of the weeks and of the months. All we knew about definitely was daylight and dark." Another Doughboy watched the Big Red One leaving the front a couple of days later and told one of the soldiers: "I thought you were the worst bedraggled, worn out, broken up and dishevelled bunch of men I ever saw at any place or at any time. Your clothes were in rags, you were mud from head to foot, and as you walked you staggered. I said to myself, 'These men have been through hell and have had a miraculous escape.'"[11]

CHAPTER 21

Last Gasp

OCTOBER 11

The Meuse-Argonne offensive's third phase, begun on October 7 with fresh troops, new ideas, and a wider front, neared its end. I Corps had cleared the Argonne, and V Corps had captured the approaches to the *Kriemhilde Stellung.* The 29th and 33d Divisions of the French XVII Corps had taken a few miles of territory east of the Meuse, and while they had not seized the heights, they had drawn in most of Gallwitz's remaining reserves. But the casualties had been enormous—1st Division alone had taken 6,314 casualties since October 4—and the fatigue incalculable. With the *Kriemhilde Stellung* nicked and dented but still intact, America's power was fading—and the Germans knew it.[1]

★

ON October 11, the 29th Division reached the worst death trap east of the Meuse: Molleville Farm. With the division's 113th and 115th Regiments too exhausted for further fighting and the 114th in reserve, Major General Morton decided to hurl the 116th against Molleville Farm, which had to be taken before the advance could continue toward the Heights of the Meuse. American troops held the woods south and west of the farm clearing, while the Germans occupied those to the north and east. Considering an attack on either flank impracticable, Morton ordered the 116th to advance across the clearing from the south. It was foggy, and there would be no artillery barrage, so it seemed possible that the Americans might take the farm, climb the slope, and enter the northern woods before the Germans could react.

The attack didn't go as Morton planned. Jumping off at 6:00 A.M., the Doughboys quickly captured the farm, but as they climbed the fog-covered slope the Germans awakened to their presence. The enemy machine gunners had already registered every part of the clearing and had only to pull their triggers. Converging from the north and east, bullets killed or wounded many of the Doughboys and forced the rest to the ground. Some soldiers in the leading wave had advanced almost to the road before the firing began, and managed to rush into the northern woods and capture some gun pits. The rest withdrew, or died where they stood. Two more attacks after the fog lifted ended in even greater slaughter, as German artillery pounded and Fokkers strafed the clearing. After nightfall, the troops who had reached the northern woods crawled back across the corpse-strewn clearing to their original lines. The heavy casualties that the 116th Regiment had suffered seemed to indicate that a change of tactics was in order, but Morton could think of only three solutions—more artillery, more men, and greater drive. With these ingredients in place, they were confident Molleville Farm could be taken.[2]

✱

PRIVATE Edward Loudenbeck of the 4th Division entered the front lines on October 11. "I never have seen so many dead," he told his diary. "Here is where it takes willpower to go on and face death."[3] The Ivy Division had been in combat and under fire since September 26. Its regiments and companies were skeletons of their former selves, and its men were tired and sick, many of them with influenza. Officers were few, and morale low. Fortunately— or unfortunately—General Bullard had more than enough willpower to go around. So long as he remained in charge of III Corps, there could be no question of rest and recuperation. The 4th Division would attack.

The attack plan was the straight-ahead affair that AEF commanders typically preferred. It called for the 39th and 47th Regiments to drive across a clearing and a road into the Bois de Forêt east of Cunel. Both regiments were in bad shape, especially the 39th, which had lost its colonel and his entire staff to a gas attack that morning. Yet at jump-off, while the 47th quivered, shifted a little, and lay still, the 39th crossed open ground under machine-gun and minenwerfer fire and entered the forest. Crossing a narrow-gauge railroad, the Doughboys pushed all the way to the woods' northern edge, capturing two hundred Germans and several machine guns. But the advance came at a cost. Early the next morning, American artillery accidentally shelled the 39th, inflicting two hundred casualties and causing the regiment to break up and flee to the south. A lieutenant colonel from the 47th barely managed to stop the panic-stricken Doughboys and herd them back into line.[4] Another week and a half would pass before the Ivy Division was relieved.

Bullard had enough willpower for the 80th Division too, and the Blue Ridge boys hated him for it. But First Army was no democracy, and when Bullard called the attack, Cronkhite and his men obeyed. The Germans, who seemed to understand what kind of general commanded III Corps, were waiting for them. At the exact moment of jump-off, 7:00 A.M., a counterbarrage "like a monster hail storm" butchered the Doughboys until the dead lay in heaps. The attack, led by the 319th and 320th Regiments, failed immediately. The troops were cut down, and their supporting teams of one-pounders and machine guns were blown to pieces. The lead battalion of the 319th broke and fled, forcing cooks, quartermasters, and clerks to enter the front lines until the reserves could come up. The American artillery capped the fiasco by repeating "the now-familiar process of shelling the wrong place." Some small detachments inched a little closer to Cunel, but that was the limit of the day's advance. It was also the end of the battle for the 80th Division, at least for a time. That afternoon, Bullard finally moved it into reserve.[5]

Just before dusk, Lieutenant Edward Lukens plopped into a shell hole where Lieutenant Colonel Ashby Williams had established a command post. Several officers were there, talking with men from the incoming 5th Division. All of the Blue Ridge officers were more or less nerve-shattered—one had suffered a nervous breakdown, and the others were "on the verge of it"—but happy in the knowledge that they were about to get out. Nobody could have anticipated what happened next. In an instant, Lukens was lying dazed on his back, his limbs shaking and his ears ringing. For a minute he couldn't speak or understand anything going on around him, until a voice calmly asked someone to put a tourniquet on his leg. A runner lay nearby, quietly inspecting his left foot, which had lost two toes, and his right leg, which had been ripped open by shrapnel. Two men had disintegrated, leaving the ground "strewn in a wide radius with quivering chunks of human flesh." A right hand, severed at the wrist, lay just outside the shell hole.

Lieutenant Colonel Williams had been buried alive. "I suddenly found myself under the ground as if by magic," he recalled, "with a ringing in my ears as of many bells. There was a sense of great bewilderment—for the act was quicker than thought, and I remember my first thought was: 'I am not dead, I am thinking.'" After a few moments he pushed his helmeted head through to the surface, but his arms remained pinned to his sides. His major lay half-buried next to him, and the two carried on a discussion that neither of them could understand until someone dug them out. Grabbing a stick to lean on, Williams staggered away, past a human liver, a leg, and part of a stomach, "still warm with the blood of life so recently departed."[6]

★

THAT evening, Bullard received marching orders of his own. Pershing wanted him to command Second Army, then being formed to the east near Toul. Much as he appreciated the promotion, Bullard hated to leave. "I make no pretense of loving a fight, but I hated to quit this one," he proclaimed in his memoirs. In his view, he had left behind a proud legacy. "My corps had fully attained its objectives and was ready for another push."[7] He just felt bad that he would not be there to do the pushing.

Major General George Cameron, commander of V Corps, was also reassigned. The official story was that he wanted to go back to his old division, the 4th; in fact, Pershing thought him ineffective and allowed him to stay with the Ivy Division for only a short time before sending him back to the United States.[8] Pershing assigned the 4th's current commander, Major General Hines, to take over III Corps in place of Bullard.

Before leaving, Cameron tried once more to break the *Kriemhilde Stellung*. "This morning we received Division orders to push forward in another attack," Lieutenant Harold Woehl of the 32d Division wrote in his diary. "Everyone was exhausted and sick, and muddy, and hungry. The Division order was 'one-of-those-things.'"[9] The story was much the same all along the line. The 3d Division's 30th and 38th Regiments launched several frontal attacks against the Heights of Romagne and Cunel, and were driven back with heavy losses. The 32d Division, still facing the southern slopes of Côte Dame Marie, also endured a frustrating day. In combination with the 91st Division's 181st Brigade, the Red Arrow attacked from dawn till dusk, but Côte Dame Marie and the *Kriemhilde Stellung* remained completely intact.

In the aftermath of these attacks, Captain Emil Gansser of the 126th Regiment passed a lone soldier sitting on the edge of a shell hole with a piece of stale bread on his lap. The soldier's face was a picture of "mental confusion and utter dismay," and he wiped away tears with a dirty handkerchief. Gansser asked him why he was not with his company. Between sobs, the boy replied that he had been drafted from a farm in late August 1918 and sent to the front only a week after landing in France, without having been taught to fire his rifle. Gansser silently sympathized with the soldier and gently told him to rejoin his company as soon as he could. He hoped the boy got away before some spit-and-polish martinet found him.[10]

Major General Liggett's I Corps, fresh from conquering the Argonne, faced a new tactical situation. For the past two weeks, the Aire had flowed along the corps' eastern boundary; now the river formed a barrier to its front. About two miles north of Fléville, the Aire turned sharply to the left and meandered past St. Juvin and Grandpré, two villages on its north bank. The Germans had organized both of these villages for defense, and destroyed all of the bridges across the river. The 82d and 77th Divisions, coming up from the south, would have to find a way to cross the river and seize the villages; but even then they wouldn't be facing the main enemy line of defense. That line, a branch of the *Kriemhilde Stellung* called the *Hindenburg Stellung,* lay another half mile farther north.

Liggett's right-hand division, the 82d, straddled the Aire, with the 325th and 327th Regiments below Sommerance, on the river's east bank, and the 326th and 328th on the other side near Marcq. Major General Duncan ordered the 325th and 327th to push north and northwest to Sommerance and St. Juvin, while the 326th, with the shattered 328th in reserve, crossed the Aire and attacked St. Juvin from the south. The plan went awry at the start. On the right, befuddled brigade officers imagined that the enemy had withdrawn and assigned jump-off positions for the 325th and 327th that were well behind the German lines. Promised tank and artillery support never arrived, and the infantry pushed straight ahead at the German positions.

The 325th marched north along the road from Fléville to St. Juvin, leaving a bloody trail of men and horses hit by German artillery. Colonel Walter Whitman, the regiment's commander, stood in full view at a crossroads about a mile southeast of St. Juvin, waving his men on despite fire from enemy machine guns. Dead bodies surrounded him. Captain John Taylor stood nearby, telling his men that the machine-gun fire was American and that the gunners would soon get their range right. The next moment, two soldiers next to Taylor fell dead, and another wounded. "Our Machine Guns are sure Hell," a Doughboy quipped.

As the Doughboys continued over a small creek and approached the foot of a ridge, enemy machine guns forced them into a small ditch running along the roadside. They continued in single file along the ditch until their officers ordered them to climb the open ridge. Artillery and machine guns fired at them all the way, but the most demoralizing attacks came from above. "German planes were flying very low throwing Grenades and ripping up our lines with Machine Guns," Captain Taylor later wrote. And where were the American fliers?

> Our own Planes were again careful not to come out, as usual. The moral effect of the presence of one of our own Planes is wonderful, until of course the men see him get away at a break-neck speed when an enemy Plane appears on the scene. The men feel that when *they* take almost impossible chances, walking into Machine Gun Nests Etc., that our Planes ought to at least take a little chance.

A German machine gun singled out Corporal Fred Takes, and he dove to the ground. After a few moments he tried to crawl on his elbows, but the machine gun opened up on him again. Deciding to play it safe, he remained still and pretended he was dead. After another few minutes the machine gun seemed to have forgotten him, and he sprinted toward an embankment next to a dirt road running along the ridge's crest. He found over a hundred other Doughboys huddled there, too terrified to move although German snipers were picking them off one by one. Finally a lieutenant took charge. Ordering the men to fix bayonets, he yelled, "Ready, let's go," and the men charged across the ridge, down a bank, and into a ravine. Bullets whistled past "like rain," and the lieutenant was shot, but he waved the soldiers on. They climbed another hill and then jumped into a thicket, where they collapsed or fainted in exhaustion. Ordered to hold their positions "at all costs," the soldiers dug in and stayed there all night, haunted by the sounds of the wounded crying and calling for aid.

On another part of the hill, Second Lieutenant Raiford Wood's machine-gun company dug in along an embankment surrounded by telephone wire from a nearby German relay station. That afternoon the Germans counterattacked his positions from the northeast. Directing his men to keep up their fire, the lieutenant calmly operated a captured Maxim. All seemed well until some infantry on both his right and left lost their nerve and fell back. The Germans pursued, threatening to surround the detachment. Wood, hit in the chest by an enemy bullet, refused to let his men withdraw, ordering them to open fire with their .45s once the Germans got within pistol range. The stubborn defense worked; reserves came up just in time, and the enemy fell back. The 325th consolidated its positions on the ridge, and advanced no farther.[11]

The 327th captured Sommerance at a cost in casualties that reduced it to a combat strength of 12 officers and 322 men, while to the west the 326th crossed the Aire under cover of fog, using bridges that the engineers had constructed overnight. As the attacking companies moved toward St. Juvin, however, the fog lifted and the German machine guns cut them to pieces. The Americans withdrew, digging in along a railroad embankment on the river's south bank. Farther west, the 77th Division had less success in fording the river than did the All-Americans. The engineers tried to build bridges but failed, either because the river was too wide or too deep, or the enemy fire was too strong. Scouts roved along the embankment, looking for possible fords, but discovered nothing. Getting across the river would prove a major problem at the beginning of the Meuse-Argonne offensive's fourth phase.

✯

"THE strain was too great," an officer said of Pershing as First Army's latest attacks against the *Kriemhilde Stellung* broke down; "this last battle had overloaded him." Normally the figure of health, he seemed to have aged a decade over the past few weeks. His hair had turned gray, and deep wrinkles lined his face. Most disturbing, his nerves seemed to be failing. "I feel like I am carrying the whole world on my shoulders," he confided. Riding past his soldiers in a staff car, Pershing sat erect, implacable, and impassive as always; but out of public view it was a different story. On one occasion in early October, Pershing collapsed sobbing in the backseat. "Frankie . . . Frankie," he cried, invoking his dead wife. "My God, sometimes I don't know how I can go on."[12]

The pressures were many. The traffic jams that had initially plagued First Army had eased, but the supply situation was becoming a nightmare. The Allied decision to give priority shipping to infantry during the spring and summer of 1918 had caused massive shortfalls in the supplies and equipment needed by several sectors of the AEF. According to official reports, the medical corps lacked 23 percent of its required supply tonnage; the chemical warfare service 51 percent; the signal corps 52 percent; and motor transport—upon which all the other services depended—81 percent. Bottlenecks in American and French ports and railways prevented supplies from reaching the front, as did shortages in motor and horsedrawn transportation.[13]

Six months earlier, people had spoken of a million Doughboys in France, and how America would tip the balance and lead the war-wasted Allies to victory. The American and French generals who had squandered thousands of Doughboys in senseless frontal attacks had done so with the supposedly limitless supply of replacements at least partly in mind. Now, however, the AEF approached a manpower crisis. When Pershing assessed First Army's frontline strength on the night of October 9–10, he discovered that he needed ninety thousand replacements to bring his divisions back to full strength, and that he could draw on only half that number of men before the end of the month. Many factors contributed to the wastage, including poor battlefield tactics, influenza, and straggling. Pershing's response to the crisis, which included reducing rifle companies from 250 to 175 men, and breaking up divisions not yet in combat and using their troops as replacements for divisions already at the front, smacked of desperation.[14] It was as if America had been fighting for four years instead of four months.

Pershing also had to deal with his rapidly deteriorating relationship with the War Department and its authoritarian chief of staff, Peyton C. March. The secretary of war, Newton Baker, encouraged and supported the overworked commander in chief during a visit to France in the autumn of 1918, but with March it was a different story. A stickler for military punctilio, March insisted that he, not Pershing, possessed supreme authority in the AEF. Pershing vehemently disagreed, and a mutual dislike developed that degenerated into sniping and obstructionism. The constant bickering proved a major distraction for Pershing and his staff, and helped to undermine the AEF administrative apparatus.[15]

Pershing's relationship with his allies, meanwhile, had reached a new low. Field Marshal Douglas Haig's contempt for his American counterpart, freely confided to his diary, was but thinly veiled in public. David Lloyd George, the British prime minister, didn't like him either. Pershing was "most difficult," Lloyd George told a colleague on October 12, and First Army was "quite ineffective."[16] And then there was Clemenceau. The French prime minister, a Pershing-hater ever since his unpropitious visit to the front in September, was now openly calling for the American's removal. On October 11 he drafted a letter to Foch complaining of "the inaction of the American troops, so prejudicial to the Allied armies, while the battle was actually raging." Clemenceau did not blame the American soldiers for their "inaction." They, he imagined, "quivered with impatience as they waited for the days that were to bring them to glory." Rather, he faulted Pershing, who would not act, and Foch, who would not command.[17]

Removing Pershing now, Foch replied, would only enrage the Americans. Nor could the Allies expect to gain anything by bullying the American commander in chief. Instead, they should gradually reduce the size of Pershing's command by finding excuses to divert American divisions to French and British armies. Foch spoke more bluntly in a meeting with Pershing at Bombon on October 13. "On all other parts of the front the advance was very marked," he pointed out, but "the Americans were not progressing as rapidly as the others." Pershing claimed that his efforts in the Meuse-Argonne had diverted German troops from other fronts. Foch replied that he was interested only in results. "No more promises!" he snarled. "Results!" The lecture continued: "I judge only by the results. . . . If an attack is well planned and executed, it succeeds with small losses. If not, the losses are heavy and there is no advance."[18]

✴

No shrinking violet, Pershing stood up to every attack on his command, and every criticism of his officers and his troops. Yet he too realized that only results mattered. With that in mind, he made a shocking decision: effective October 16, he would relinquish command of First Army in favor of Major General Liggett. Pershing would become an army group commander, technically still responsible for First Army and General Bullard's new Second Army near Toul, but without controlling the actual conduct of the battle. In effect, he was kicking himself upstairs—a remarkable and surprisingly humble decision for a man of his ego. Pershing also enacted sweeping changes among First Army's corps commanders, appointing Major General Joseph Dickman—a fiery, temperamental man who looked like a bespectacled bulldog with indigestion—to command I Corps in place of Liggett; Major General Summerall to command V Corps in place of Major General Cameron, who took over the 4th Division; and Major General Hines to command III Corps in place of Bullard. All of these changes boded well for the troops in the Meuse-Argonne.

Other changes were being enacted without Pershing's knowledge or consent, by the troops on the ground. During the offensive's first two weeks, American tactics had been stale, old-fashioned, and sanguinary, and many generals remained enamored with the kind of frontal attacks that the French had employed in 1914. On the battlefield, however, regiment, battalion, and company commanders learned quickly, along with their troops. They learned, for example, to disable German machine guns before bypassing them; to use light infantry weapons such as regular and rifle grenades, one-pounders, mortars, and automatic rifles effectively; to suppress the enemy with indirect machine-gun fire; and to practice fire-and-movement tactics against fortifications and emplacements. Artillery gunners also improved their techniques, learning which types of ammunition were most appropriate for certain situations, and cooperating more effectively with the infantry.[19] Tanks were being used more creatively too, although by mid-October not enough of them were left to have much of an impact at the front.

★

Of all the AEF's service commanders, Brigadier General Billy Mitchell was the most forward-thinking, creative, and—ironically—resistant to change. From the infantry's perspective, the U.S. Army Air Service had been less than ineffective; it had been invisible. German aircraft had roved over the battle-field at will since September 26, the Doughboys claimed. And while the en-emy bombed, strafed, and directed artillery, the American fliers never showed up. Mitchell and his supporters—including Major General Liggett—responded to these accusations by conjuring a magnificent illusion. All those bombing, strafing, and observing planes, they declared, could not possibly be German. The enemy had only a handful of planes remaining, all of them flown by desperate teenage pilots. Those planes swarming over the skies were not German, but American; the only shame was that the Doughboys could not tell the difference. "An impression seems to prevail in some quarters that our forces are at the mercy of German aeroplanes," Liggett declared, "when as a general rule the aeroplanes are our own."[20]

This fantasy did nothing to convince the infantry; they knew what they had seen and continued to see at the front. If all of those planes were American, they asked, then why were they machine-gunning and dropping grenades on their own troops, and dropping signal flares in the vicinity of U.S. infantry and artillery? True, the infantry had been poorly trained in aircraft identification and air-ground communications, as had many pilots. Yet the firsthand evi-dence remains far too strong to admit any doubt that, in practical terms, the Germans controlled the air above the Meuse-Argonne for almost the entire battle. The airmen worked hard, but Mitchell's obsession with strategic and tactical bombing prevented them from conducting the close air support so critical to the infantry. Instead, he preferred to engage them in more glam-orous operations behind the enemy lines.

On October 9, Mitchell's fliers reported a large concentration of German infantry east of the Meuse. Without consulting Pershing, his staff, or any in-fantry generals, Mitchell decided that the enemy intended to cross the Meuse and attack III Corps. Ordering all of his bombers into the air, along with three hundred French planes, he sent them to bomb the enemy troops, supply dumps, and a railroad. Mitchell then ran over to Pershing's headquarters, hus-tled him and his officers outside, and pointed out the beautiful formation of airplanes flying overhead. In reality, Gallwitz had neither the infantry reserves nor the boats or bridging equipment to launch any kind of attack across the Meuse; but Mitchell would always claim that he had single-handedly saved

First Army's bacon. The raid, he claimed, marked "the dawn of the day when great air forces will be capable of definitely effecting a ground decision on the field of battle." Hugh Drum noted more accurately that "while our big flight was in the air, as if on parade . . . German airplanes were over our front lines bombing and machingunning [*sic*] our infantry with serious effect on their morale."[21]

★

DIPLOMATIC developments gave Pershing and the Doughboys greater reason for hope. On September 29, the kaiser had met with the two most powerful men in Germany, Paul von Hindenburg and Erich Ludendorff, and agreed to pursue peace talks with President Wilson. It was a profoundly humiliating step for all three of them. Kaiser Wilhelm II—vain, boastful, but deeply insecure—had helped to instigate the war in 1914 by pushing Austria-Hungary to punish Serbia, and spent the rest of the war as a figurehead, without any significant political or military power in the country he supposedly ruled. Hindenburg, a seventy-one-year-old Prussian aristocrat, had taken titular control of the German army in August 1916 as its chief of staff. It was Ludendorff, however, who effectively ran the army despite his seemingly innocuous position as quartermaster general. Brilliant but cynically acerbic—he later would become a prime supporter of Adolf Hitler's Nazi Party—the fifty-three-year-old Ludendorff had devised the plan for the March 1918 offensive, which had come to grief during the summer. That these three men should have decided to treat for peace was an indication of the parlous state of the German military.

Forwarded through Switzerland, the peace proposal reached Wilson on October 6. Though unacceptable—the Germans sought an end to the war without preconditions—it was a start. On the eighth, the American president responded that the Allies would not even consider a suspension of hostilities until the Germans withdrew from all the occupied territories, and demanded that Germany accept the fairly moderate preconditions for peace that he had enunciated in his Fourteen Points. The German chancellor, Prince Max of Baden, agreed on October 12, and over the following days the belligerents exchanged notes discussing a possible armistice. Clearly, the end of the war was near—if not in 1918, then in 1919.

These events contributed to the atmosphere of optimism that pervaded Pershing's headquarters as he prepared the Meuse-Argonne offensive's fourth phase. As a prelude, Pershing withdrew two divisions, the 1st and the 80th, and replaced them with the 42d and 5th Divisions. He also shuffled several other divisions along First Army's front. From east to west, the French XVII Corps contained the 29th and 33d Divisions; III Corps contained the 4th, 3d, and 5th Divisions; V Corps contained the 32d and 42d Divisions; and I Corps contained the 82d and 77th Divisions. XVII Corps and I Corps would continue attacking on the east and west flanks. Pershing's main objective, however, was for the 5th and 42d Divisions to achieve a double envelopment of the German positions at Romagne and Côte Dame Marie. The 5th would attack north from Cunel to the Bois des Rappes. The 42d, meanwhile, would attack west of Côte Dame Marie, advancing north from the Bois de Romagne to the Bois de Bantheville. If successful, these two attacks would meet north of Romagne, cutting off the Germans around Côte Dame Marie or forcing their withdrawal, thus easing the 32d Division's task of taking that forbidding ridge. It was an ambitious plan, but Pershing gave his troops little time to prepare. The main attack would jump off on October 14.

CHAPTER 22

"Like the Heat from a Blast-Furnace Door"

OCTOBER 12–13

On October 12, two hundred soldiers of Captain William J. Reddan's company of the 114th Regiment, 29th Division, entered a ravine choked with barbed wire and skeletons. Just thirteen returned.

The French 18th Division had been trying for some days to take the Bois d'Ormont, just beyond the 29th Division's right flank, but without success. Deeming his troops too exhausted, the French commander brought in two battalions of the American 114th Regiment to do the job. French guides led the New Jersey Doughboys into position, gestured vaguely toward the woods ahead, said the enemy was there, and walked away.[1] As on previous days, the Americans received no information on the enemy positions or their objectives, and very little time to prepare. That the French regarded them as expendable was plain to all.

Captain Reddan reconnoitered the woods, and discovered that his battalion faced a thousand-yard-deep ravine. Using his field glasses, he could make out thick coils of barbed wire at the far end. White objects lay thick in front of the wire. They were skeletons. Unnerved, Reddan approached his battalion commander. Did they really have to attack into that ravine? Yes, the major replied, they did. But the French had told him not to worry. The Germans were broken and would retreat without resisting.

Gunfire announced the dawn, intensifying as the sun climbed through the sky. To the west, the Germans attacked the 113th Regiment behind a heavy artillery barrage and nearly broke through. Meanwhile, Allied artillery and heavy machine-gun fire raked the Bois d'Ormont. The shellfire intensified until 6:59, when burgeoning white clouds announced the beginning of the smoke barrage. A minute later, Reddan's B Company, one of two companies in Second Battalion's first wave, attacked directly up the ravine while First Battalion advanced over the western slopes to its left. Two French infantry regiments, ordered to move forward on either flank, advanced only a short distance before quitting and returning to their trenches. Reddan never noticed them. As his company entered the ravine it encountered German rifle and machine-gun fire "like the heat from a blast-furnace door." Five minutes later, the German artillery opened fire with what seemed like every gun in the kaiser's arsenal, devastating Second Battalion before it had advanced halfway up the ravine.

At training camp in New Jersey, the Doughboys had been taught rifle marksmanship and how to use their bayonets. But here the enemy was invisible, except for the occasional soldier in the distance running from one position to another. And the Germans had marksmen of their own. The machine-gun fire, most of which came from east of the ravine where the French had not advanced, was galling enough; but the enemy snipers, firing from high ground all around the ravine, were deadly. They seemed especially adept at picking off officers, noncoms, and runners, and killed every man that Reddan sent to report B Company's positions. The American and French artillery and machine guns had meanwhile stopped firing, forcing the infantry to resort to Chauchats, rifles, and pistols to suppress the well-camouflaged enemy positions. Heavy casualties quickly reduced the battalion to one thin line, with "each man getting forward from shell hole to shell hole, or from bush to tree stump, or any other cover available." Only "unadulterated grit" kept the Doughboys going.

The infantry took cover behind a slight bluff near the head of the ravine, among piles of skeletons wearing tattered French uniforms. Pushing bones and rusty, shrapnel-torn helmets and rifles aside, they tried to get a view of the enemy wire. The artillery had not even touched it. Reddan hardly had time to absorb this terrible information before German infantry charged down the east side of the ravine in an all-out counterattack. The Doughboys fired with an efficiency that did credit to their rifle training, but the Germans used cover and their grenades effectively. Reddan's men held on. The company to his right fell back, however, allowing the Germans to fire into B Company's flank. Seeking a way out of the crossfire, some Americans attacked the barbed wire with cutters while their comrades fired rifles and Chauchats overhead, but the Germans massacred them with artillery and grenades.

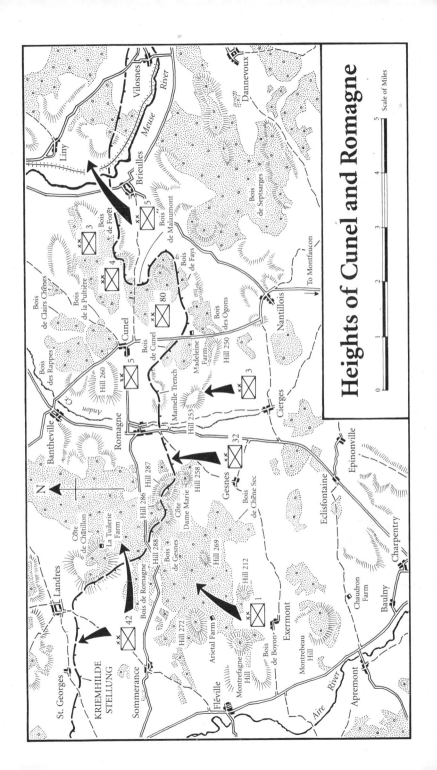

Heights of Cunel and Romagne

Scale of Miles

0   1   2   3   4   5

Reddan's men were the only Americans remaining in front of the wire. The troops to his right had fallen back before the German counterattack, and First Battalion on the left had withdrawn. Farther back, Second Battalion's second and third waves were pinned down, their ranks growing steadily thinner. Wounded men lay scattered all the way down the ravine, groaning for water and screaming in pain, but no one could reach them. After a few hours, a runner somehow made it through to B Company. Reddan read the message he carried. "The Brigade Commander insists that the position be held," it said. "A company is being sent up to your assistance." He waited a few more hours, but the promised company never arrived. Finally, with only about forty men left, Reddan decided on a desperate maneuver: move right under cover of darkness, and try to get through or around the enemy wire.

After dusk the enemy fire subsided, and Reddan quietly called his men together. A few shapes moved toward him in the dark. He gave them all time to arrive, and then took a head count. B Company, two hundred strong in the morning, had been reduced to thirteen men. It was every officer's worst nightmare: not to die, but to live—while losing his entire command.

> I have never felt more alone at any time in my life; what happened to me from then on was of no consequence, death or wounds could not have been worse. In fact death would have been a relief. Picture if you can that terrible ravine, full of our own "buddies," wounded, dying and dead. Your boys. . . . Many long, weary months had been spent in training these men so that when they went into battle they would at least have an even chance for their lives. Now all to be seen was death and desolation, and to hear the awful cries of the wounded, for whom we could do nothing.

Reddan's sanity snapped. Screaming for his men to follow, he turned and walked back down the ravine, making no effort to stay quiet or keep concealed. His mind was filled with visions of finding the officers responsible for the attack and showing them what their stupidity had wrought—perhaps even killing them. He remembered nothing of the journey back except the cries of the wounded, which were to haunt his dreams until the end of his life.

Reddan's thirteen men partly dragged and partly carried him out of the ravine. Afraid that he would injure himself or someone else, they took away his trench knife and revolver while he yelled and raved like a madman. He spent the night in a dugout under the care of a medical officer, who kept feeding him sedatives. Every few minutes he woke, screaming "slaughter," and on several occasions he had to be restrained physically from leaving the dugout and storming the battalion command post. Several days later, while convalescing, Reddan met a French officer who praised the Americans' bravery and then put his finger to his forehead, saying, "114th Regiment, American, *beaucoup de malade ici.*" The meaning of the gesture was clear to Reddan: "we were sick in the head." When he angrily asked why the French had failed to advance and protect the American left flank, the officer matter-of-factly replied that "there was too much artillery and machine-gun fire to advance through."

Reddan did not sock the French officer in the mouth. Instead, he reflected on whether the French actually knew something that the Americans did not.

> After four years of actual contact with the enemy and having made numerous attacks on trench positions, they were undoubtedly qualified to know what kind of fire it was possible to advance through with a minimum of losses. We, in our enthusiastic ignorance, had attempted to do what the French and the Germans, with their experience, knew to be impossible.[2]

Later that day, the commanding German officer issued a communiqué congratulating his troops on defeating the American attack, which had been carried out "with a reckless exposure of the infantry" attacking in dense masses. The 114th Regiment reported 939 casualties, most of them in Second Battalion. It had been annihilated.[3]

★

THE Germans, still holding the *Kriemhilde Stellung* but not content to leave well enough alone, launched repeated local counterattacks against the American lines. These small actions hardly registered in official records or communiqués, but cost the Doughboys a lot of stress. "Their infantry counterattacks, though not very heavy in numbers, were extraordinarily vicious," reported Colonel "Old Fritz" Wise of the 4th Division. "Parties of fifty to a hundred of them would worm their way through the underbrush and behind trees close to our line of fox holes, with a couple of machine guns. After a few bursts of machine-gun fire, they would attack with fixed bayonets. They never made any headway. But they kept us in a constant flurry of vicious small dog fights up and down the line day after day." One of the Germans' favorite targets was Jack Barkley's 3d Division, which became caught up in "red-hot fighting" in the Bois de Forêt. The fighting wore the division down so badly that the 30th Regiment, reduced to battalion strength, had to be organized into four provisional companies.[4]

German artillery applied additional pressure, especially on those unlucky enough to lie within range of the heavy guns east of the Meuse. Many men who went through the war without entering the front lines lost their minds because of the artillery alone. "It takes real men to stand this continual pounding by artillery," wrote Sergeant Major James Block of the 4th Division.

> Under such fire, and in those surroundings, all the sensationalism, all the heroism is removed. The long fatiguing days and nights of patient suffering; the continual exposure to miserable weather such as is found no where else on earth; the horribleness of the whole scene, all tended to deaden one's faculties. Men moved about like mere machines. No man could rest in that cold and mud with gun fire for a lullaby. As one by one (sometimes two or three at a time) we saw our pals "go west," we resigned ourselves to fate, and patiently waited our turn. If the end would only come quickly when it did come. But no, we linger on, passively enduring what seemed certain death. But it was not the fear of death, so much as the fact that we were suffering the tortures of a living death, unable from our support positions to strike back at the foe.[5]

"The men couldn't stand much more of this," attested Lieutenant Joe Lawrence of the 29th Division. "We had it for four days and were hungry, hollow-eyed, exhausted. Some of them were losing their minds." One of his runners, a likeable German-born kid named Pulveritis, went to the rear with a message and didn't return. Lawrence's captain, named Grassey, exploded in rage when he found Pulveritis and another runner sleeping behind the lines in an old dugout:

> Grassey drew his gun and threatened to shoot both of them. They protested hysterically that they were not yellow—they were worn out, dead tired. He sent them sobbing back to the hell from which they had sought to steal a little relief. Pulveritis had hardly gotten back to his foxhole when a shell exploded almost in his face, ripped his steel helmet open, and tore off part of his scalp and face. He lived.[6]

Rest and recuperation came only to those soldiers fortunate enough to be relieved from the front. On October 12, the 80th and 1st Divisions departed the lines in weary columns, while the fresh young soldiers of the 5th and 42d Divisions moved up to take their place. The usual chaffing passed among veterans and newcomers. As Private Rush Young and his comrades of the Blue Ridge Division marched away, looking "like tramps with bloody ragged uniforms and long whiskers just plodding along, too weak to keep any kind of formation," some snappy 5th Division regulars mocked the weary draftees whom they were about to replace. "Do you call yourselves American soldiers?" they cried. "Just wait until we get to the front we will show you rookies how to fight." "You're damn right we are American soldiers," an angry Blue Ridge Doughboy called back, "and good ones at that." Eventually the razzing ended, and the regulars quietly asked, "Buddy, how is it up there? Where are the Huns?" "Just go to the front," Young and his fellows replied, "and you will find out damn quick where they are and no one will have to show you."[7]

★

Lieutenant Samuel Woodfill could not wait to get to the front. Born in 1883 in Jefferson County, Indiana—frontier country near the Kentucky border—he had been raised on "stories about war and shootin'" told by his father, a Mexican War and Civil War veteran. Woodfill dreamed of being a soldier, and spent every day with a gun in his hands. At age eighteen, he joined the army and went to fight in the Philippine Insurrection. After four years he decided that the army offered "a glorious life," and signed up for a second term, this time in Alaska. He served there for eight years, developing his marksmanship by hunting big game such as caribou, moose, and grizzly bear. After being transferred to Kentucky in 1912 and the Mexican border in 1914, Woodfill rose to the rank of lieutenant in 1917 and was appointed to the 60th Regiment, 5th Division.[8]

Organized in December 1917 at Camp Logan, Texas, the 5th "Red Diamond" Division contained mostly "old army" regulars, with a few volunteers and draftees. Consisting of the 6th, 11th, 60th, and 61st Regiments, it arrived in France in the spring of 1918 and saw minor combat during the St. Mihiel offensive. Fifty-eight-year-old Major General John E. McMahon, who had served with the artillery for thirty-one years, took command of the division in December 1917. Thin, brittle, and dour, he had reputedly slept through the St. Mihiel offensive, and took forty-five seconds to sign his name.[9] He had never been tested in a serious battle, and neither had most of his men. But they all were eager to prove they could fight.

Woodfill reconnoitered the front lines during the night of October 11–12, as his division prepared to replace the 80th Division. Trolling through no-man's-land in the dark, he stepped on a tiny wooden bridge and detonated a German booby trap. The explosion knocked him on his back and he lost consciousness. He awoke with the rain beating in his face, feeling like "an iron rod had been driven right through my ears," and his nose bleeding profusely.

Stunned but not seriously wounded, Woodfill stumbled into a shell hole and fell asleep. It rained heavily all night, and in the morning he nearly floated out of the shell hole, which had filled with water.

Attack orders came a few minutes before 6:00 A.M. Woodfill's Third Battalion and a machine-gun company would advance north along an old railway, past Cunel and into the Bois de Pultière. There they would conduct a "combat reconnaissance" of the enemy positions. "In other words," Woodfill enthused, "over the top and fight!" The rain had stopped, and the Doughboys advanced in thin skirmish lines, bayonets fixed, through a heavy fog. The fog lifted as the soldiers entered a clearing south of the woods, and the German machine guns and artillery opened fire. A sergeant next to Woodfill grunted, took three steps, and toppled over dead on the railway track. An exploding shell knocked two others head over heels, but they got up, snatched their rifles, and continued to advance. Dozens more fell and never moved again. A boy who had lied about his age in order to enlist cracked under the fire and started shooting wildly; a soldier tackled the kid and hurled him under a bush.

Unwilling to ask his men to do anything he would not do himself, Woodfill waved them to take cover and rushed ahead alone. He dove into a shell hole and tried to figure out where the German machine guns were located while bullets flew so close that he felt their heat on his face. He eventually spotted the guns, one of them in an abandoned stable to his right, another in the woods ahead, and a third in the church tower in Cunel. Taking careful aim with his rifle, Woodfill emptied a clip into the tower window. The machine gun fell silent. Then he aimed at the stable and fired into a hole where a board had been removed in the gable. That machine gun stopped firing too. All those days spent hunting in Alaska had paid off.

With the machine gun to his front still firing, Woodfill dodged to one hole, then another. Suddenly he felt out of breath—the hole was filled with mustard gas! Better face bullets than this creeping death. Gasping, eyes streaming, throat burning, Woodfill leapt out of the hole and looked for another. He found none—only a little clump of bracken. He dove behind that, waited a moment, and then crawled away. He dragged himself around a knoll, over a road, and into a ditch, which he followed to a small gravel pile. He could still hear the machine gun rattling. Laying out his .45 and a clip of rifle ammunition, Woodfill slowly slid his rifle over the gravel and lifted his head. He saw the machine gun, forty feet away in some bushes. Eyes still streaming from the gas, Woodfill peered at the well-camouflaged gun until he could trace the outline of the gunner's head.

Woodfill aimed, fired, and the gunner went down. Almost immediately, another German took his place. Woodfill fired again, and another German pushed the corpse aside and took the machine gun. He killed four men this way, but there were six in the nest. The fifth German tried to crawl away, and died instantly. The sixth jumped and ran. Woodfill, who had emptied his rifle clip with no time to reload, grabbed his pistol and dropped the German.

Reloading his rifle and picking up his pistol, Woodfill ran across the road to the nest and found it full of corpses with their heads blasted apart. He continued into the woods past an apparently dead German officer. Leaping up suddenly, the German grabbed Woodfill's rifle and wrested it away. But he was not as quick with his Luger as the American was with his .45. The officer fell, shot in the gut; Woodfill ripped off his shoulder strap for a souvenir, took his Luger, and moved on. He found the woods filled with fighting Americans and Germans. Dashing from tree to tree, Woodfill discovered a group of enemy machine-gun nests behind some bushes. Falling to the ground, dodging bullets, and dueling with a sniper, he crept toward one of the German nests. He killed all the tenants, picking them off one at a time, and then captured three teenage ammunition carriers whom he sent to the rear.

Finding yet another active enemy machine gun, Woodfill slid on his belly to a good firing position and killed the crew as he had at the other nests. He was moving forward to spike the gun when another group of Germans opened fire. Woodfill sprinted for the only cover he could see, a trench. It was full of Germans, but he had his .45 ready. He shot one German before he ·could raise his Luger, but the .45 jammed as another enemy soldier rushed toward him from behind. Woodfill grabbed the closest weapon he could find, a long-handled pick, and swung it with both hands onto the head of the German, who "fell like an ox." Turning around, he barely evaded a bullet fired by the first German, who had only been wounded. He killed him with the pick, too.

By this time most of the German emplacements in the southern Bois de Pultière had been cleared, but the enemy artillery increased its fire until the Americans deemed it prudent to withdraw. They brought a good number of German prisoners with them. Back at the battalion command post, Woodfill reported to his major, who asked how he had treated the Germans. "I got a few," Woodfill said. "Yeah, I know you did," the major replied. Word got around. Eventually it got all the way up to Pershing, and Woodfill received a Medal of Honor. He never returned to active duty, though; that night, wounded by a German shell and weakened by gas, Woodfill rode an ambulance away from the front.[10]

"Looks like Woodfill's boys are rounding up some prisoners," Captain

Edward Allworth said to his runner, Private Henry Monroe. "Yes, that's right—they're on their way to the rear. Woodfill's having quite a day for himself."

"Yes sir!" the runner excitedly replied. "If we could clean out those bastards on the heights, we could mop up this area in a hurry!"

The captain didn't know it, but his runner's name wasn't really Monroe; it was Ernest L. Wrentmore. And he had lied about his age. A doctor's son from West Farmington, Ohio, he was husky and muscular, standing five feet, six inches tall and weighing 145 pounds. He would turn fourteen years old in November.

Allworth, a quietly confident former college fullback from Portland, Oregon, looked like a boy, too, although he was twenty-three. In less than a month, he would earn a Medal of Honor.

As Wrentmore and his captain watched Lieutenant Woodfill lead his prisoners away, the Germans woke up. First a machine gun sprayed the rim of the shell hole in which they were sitting. Then their artillery opened fire. "Captain," Wrentmore screamed over the noise of exploding shells, "we've got to get the hell out of here! We'll be blown to bits if we stay here any longer!" The next moment a shell landed with a powerful "wharmp!" throwing both of them into the bottom of the hole under a small avalanche of dirt and rocks. "Come on! It's now or never!" Allworth cried after a moment. He leapt out of the hole, waving the boy and some nearby soldiers to follow him in a mad rush to safety.

Men fell everywhere, "some crying like babies, some changed into driveling spectres of humanity from shell shock, some going down, never to rise again," as Allworth and his runner charged full-tilt for cover. Near their trench they scrambled past a soldier huddled in a listening post, no more than a shallow hole. A shell crashed in, and the two fugitives dove to the ground. As they crawled into the trench, Wrentmore heard "a wild scream, a scream that made the blood run cold." It was the soldier in the listening post, writhing in agony on the ground. German machine guns opened fire, ripping the post to pieces, but the soldier kept screaming. Wrentmore and some others who had made the trench begged Allworth to let them go out and rescue the soldier, but he refused. It was too dangerous. So they waited until dark, and crawled out to the now silent listening post. They found the soldier, an acquaintance of Wrentmore's, mercifully dead; but it had taken him a long time to expire: "In his mad frenzy, from shock and pain, he had torn every shred of clothing from his body. He had been hit more than one hundred times, and a large splinter of jagged steel had pierced the roof of his mouth."

"My God!" the shaken thirteen-year-old mused. "If this is the result of only one day, what will it be tomorrow . . . and the next day—and the next!"[11]

★

CORPORAL Donald Kyler's outfit of the 1st Division marched away from the lines on October 12. Every man in it had been transformed by his time in the Meuse-Argonne. Some of them had broken; others had grown and matured. Still only seventeen years old, Kyler had become ruthless, not just to the enemy but to his own men. He had frequently threatened to shoot them if they misbehaved. Inside, he had grown cold:

> I had seen many men, my friends, my acquaintances, and others, maimed and killed. At no time, either at the front or behind the lines, was I ever away from the sound of battle. Sometimes it was faint and far away, but always there. At first, I had been very much afraid. Then gradually, insensitiveness to danger, so far as fear was concerned, came. I realized danger with my mind, and could take measures to counteract it, but the emotions life or death were sort of blocked out. It seemed to me then as though the dead were luckier than I was. I could see no end to the war, and did not expect to survive it. It did not seem probable at the time. I was tired physically and mentally. I had seen mercy killings, both of our hopelessly wounded, as those of the enemy. I had seen the murder of prisoners of war, singly and as many as several at one time. I had seen men rob the dead of money and valuables, and had seen men cut off the fingers of corpses to get rings. Those things I had seen, but they did not effect me much. I was too numb. To me, corpses were nothing but carrion. I had the determination to go on performing as I had been trained to do—to be a good soldier.[12]

The 42d Division replaced the 1st Division at the front. A veteran formation, it was, after the Big Red One, the AEF's most celebrated unit. Composed of National Guard units from twenty-six states and the District of Columbia—thus its popular name, the Rainbow Division—the 42d had been organized at Camp Mills, New York, and arranged into two brigades, the 83d and 84th, containing the 165th (New York), 166th (Ohio), 167th (Alabama), and 168th (Iowa) Regiments. It arrived in France in November 1917, and entered combat in July 1918, suffering more than seven thousand casualties that summer, and another thousand at St. Mihiel. The division's commander, Major General Charles T. Menoher, was a West Point graduate and career artillery officer with a stiff, humorless manner.

The 42d had its share of celebrities, including Brigadier General Douglas

MacArthur, commander of the 84th Brigade. Born in Little Rock, Arkansas, in 1880, MacArthur grew up at Fort Selden in Texas, to which his father—Civil War Medal of Honor winner Arthur MacArthur—had been posted. While there he learned how to ride and shoot, "almost," he later claimed, "before I could walk and talk."[13] Graduating first in his class from the U.S. Military Academy at West Point in 1903, MacArthur served for the following ten years in engineering assignments all over the world. His only combatlike experience came during an intelligence mission to Vera Cruz in 1914, but he performed very well as a member of the War Department's general staff from 1914 to 1917. After the United States entered the war he became chief of staff of the 42d Division, and then a brigadier general commanding the 84th Brigade.

MacArthur's vanity and conceit rivaled that of the AEF's two other most prominent prima donnas, George Patton and Billy Mitchell. Refusing to don the army's humble regulation helmet during visits to the front, he wore a crushed military cap tilted at a jaunty angle, along with a turtleneck sweater and a long purple muffler. Tight, shiny boots encased his legs. He also had the dangerous habit of neither wearing nor even carrying a gas mask.[14] MacArthur's personal bravery and abilities as a leader of men only partially overshadowed his modest military intellect. As with many other American generals, he was not above sacrificing Doughboys' lives to satisfy his personal pride.

Other Rainbow Division celebrities fought with the 83d Brigade's 165th Regiment. Recruited from working-class Irish neighborhoods of the Bronx, the regiment proudly trumpeted its association with the Civil War–era "Fighting 69th" New York Regiment. Lieutenant Colonel William "Wild Bill" Donovan, a thirty-five-year-old former college football player from Buffalo, New York, commanded the regiment's First Battalion. A successful lawyer from a wealthy family who had married into an even wealthier family, Donovan was an adventure-seeker who reputedly put his own advancement above the safety of his men. During World War II, he would found the Office of Strategic Services, or OSS, the precursor of the CIA. Father Francis Duffy, pastor of the Church of the Savior in the Bronx and a well-known Catholic thinker, had been the 165th's senior chaplain since the Mexican expedition. Fiery, devout, and brave, Father Duffy would become America's most famous military chaplain.[15]

✳

RECONNOITERING the front just before his troops moved into position, MacArthur discovered a "desolate and forbidding terrain," with hills and "wooded valleys of death" amid an endlessly unfolding series of ridges. The biggest obstacle was the Côte de Châtillon, a large, wooded ridge just to the 84th Brigade's front. Deciding that "the previous advances had failed because it had not been recognized . . . [as] the keystone of the whole German position," MacArthur "proposed to capture the Côte de Châtillon by concentrating troops on it, instead of continuing to spread the troops along a demonstratedly unsuccessful line of attack."[16] Actually, no attempt had been made to capture the ridge earlier for the very good reason that the Americans had not come anywhere near it until that day—but no matter; MacArthur was correct in his assessment of the position's importance.

Sick and exhausted—a whiff of gas had caused him to spend the better part of the day vomiting uncontrollably—MacArthur had just finished drawing up his plans of attack on the evening of October 13 when Major General Summerall, the former 1st Division commander now in charge of V Corps, walked in. The usually sharp-as-a-tack general looked jaded, so MacArthur gave him a blistering-hot cup of black coffee. Caffeine performed its usual miracles. After a few sips Summerall bellowed, "Give me Châtillon, MacArthur. Give me Châtillon, or a list of five thousand casualties." "If this Brigade does not capture Châtillon," MacArthur replied, "you can publish a casualty list of the entire Brigade with the Brigade Commander's name at the top." Tears sprang into Summerall's eyes, and he stared speechlessly at the brigadier for a few moments before leaving. MacArthur's heroic pronouncement soon became a hot topic of discussion among the men. Hearing that the general had proclaimed his willingness to accept 100 percent casualties, one Doughboy quipped, "Generous son of a bitch, ain't he?"[17]

Father Duffy said Mass on a knoll as the men of the Rainbow Division marched into line and prepared to attack. Other chaplains would have used the occasion to lecture the troops on life, death, and getting their souls in order for the coming fight, but Father Duffy did not. "The frequently recurring rows of rude crosses which marked the last resting places of many brave lads of the 1st Division were an eloquent sermon on death," he decided, "so that no words of warning from me were needed." Instead, he carried on his business matter-of-factly, allowing the Doughboys to muse for themselves.[18] He would be hearing their confessions soon enough.

✳

CORPORAL Alvin York's battalion entered the front lines near Sommerance on October 12. The 82d Division was officially at rest, recuperating and preparing for another attack. But German artillery kept things hot, killing

Doughboys steadily until the dead could no longer be buried. "Oh my I cant tell you how I felt," he wrote in his diary, "when those big shells would come over and burst then I heard my comrades crying and mourning." As men died, he and the other God-fearing men in the battalion could only turn their eyes to Heaven and say:

> *Good by old pal, your body sleeps heer 'neath the sod,*
> *Your soul I pray has gone home to God.*

He made camp that night near the corpses, feeling "oh how lonely how sad no tongue can tell." Thoughts of the men he had killed, and of comrades he had been unable to save, drifted across his mind. "I cant know," he meditated, "the greenwood tree that leads into the vale beyond. Not yet. . . . But yet God was with me. Is God with you if not please don't do as many others have done—Put it off too long."[19]

Sergeant Frederick Hawke of North Andover, Massachusetts, a member of the division's 325th Regiment, was less inclined to be religious or sentimental. Entering combat for the first time on the eleventh, he had adopted a personal "motto": take no prisoners. Hawke attempted to kill the first surrendering German he saw, but as luck would have it another Doughboy stepped in and took the man prisoner. The sergeant worked off some of his feelings by picking off fleeing German soldiers with his rifle, but remained unsatisfied. On October 12, still eager for a face-to-face confrontation with the Boche, he attacked and destroyed an enemy machine-gun nest. He killed two of the Germans as they fled, and the rest knelt at his feet like "curs." He did not kill them. Instead, he kicked one with his hobnailed boots, prompting the terrified German to give him a box of cigars and beg him to stop. Hawke looted the rest, taking all their food.[20]

War, as York understood, sometimes brought out the worst in a man.

"The Best Day's Work"

Jack Barkley, his head nearly bald from mustard gas burns, was back in the front lines. His two Native American friends, Jesse and Floyd, still called him "punk." But they respected him a little more since that affair of the tank.

Barkley's division, the 3d, occupied a salient east of Cunel, which the 4th Division had created on October 11 by driving into the Bois de Forêt. The 4th Division had then sidestepped to the east while the 3d Division took its place. On the right, Barkley's 4th Regiment and the 30th Regiment were ordered to attack north and northwest toward Hill 299 and the Bois de la Pultière; on the left, the 38th and 7th Regiments would stay put while the 5th Division leapfrogged them and drove toward Cunel and beyond.

A cold drizzle settled in as the dog-tired Doughboys of Barkley's battalion shambled off that morning, climbing out of a ravine, up a slope, and toward a road running parallel to their front. German machine guns cut down many of the Americans in the open before they reached the woods on the other side. They nevertheless "waded on," entering the woods and killing dozens of Germans in a "sullen rage." Barkley, Jesse, and Floyd butchered a crowd of Germans in a ditch, and then came under fire from enemy infantry in an old quarry at the base of a steep hill. About three hundred feet square, with a mouth thirty feet wide, the quarry commanded the road. Sheltered by the hill and out of sight of the enemy artillery, it looked like it might make a good command post once the Germans had been cleared out. "Let's rush them out of that quarry," Jesse said.

Fifty Americans contested the quarry against the same number of Germans in a point-blank melee of Lugers, Mausers, Springfields, and Colts. Barkley found his small size an advantage in close-quarters combat, as the enemy preferred to rush big guys like Jesse and Floyd first. It was all over in a matter of minutes. Ten Americans had been killed, and many more wounded. All the Germans died—according to Barkley, because he and his comrades always aimed for the head. The aftermath looked like the floor of a butcher's workshop: "The floor was covered with the bodies of the dead and wounded. The walls and our clothes were spattered with blood and brains." The Americans converted the quarry into a strongpoint and drove back a German counterattack. They didn't expect to remain there for long, as the advance was supposed to continue the next day, but as it turned out, Barkley would spend the remainder of his time at the front huddled behind its bloodstained walls. By war's end, it looked less like a strongpoint and more like a prison.

In war, a soldier's knowledge horizon usually doesn't extend beyond his own squad, company, or at most battalion, so Barkley didn't know that the 4th Regiment had failed to take its objective, Hill 299. He also didn't know that Cunel had been taken, or that the 30th Regiment had advanced as far as the northeastern edge of the Bois de la Pultière. Still less did he or anyone else in his outfit know of the incredible slaughter that had been wrought among the Red Diamond Doughboys of the 5th Division.[1]

✴

ERNEST Wrentmore and his friends in the 60th Regiment gathered in the predawn hours of October 14 and gravely wished one another luck in the coming attack. As H hour approached, the thirteen-year-old felt so jittery that he could barely keep still. His comrades were nervous too, but they weren't shaking: "Their faces were set, their eyes gleaming, and they gripped their rifles until their knuckles were white. It was as though there was a final realization that some of us would not make it. Or perhaps all sense of feeling had left us, leaving only machines." Captain Allworth, who must have suspected Wrentmore was a little underage, ordered him to keep close by. Allworth wouldn't give him a rifle, either, but the boy didn't mind; he had gathered an arsenal of his own. It included two .45s, a dagger, a large trench knife, and enough ammunition for a platoon.[2]

As the easternmost formation on the divisional front, the 60th would pass through the 3d Division's left and advance to Cunel and the Bois de la

Pultière, followed by the 61st Regiment in reserve. Farther west, the 11th and 6th Regiments, from right to left, would make the main attack. Their objective was to attack northwest across the open ridge between Cunel and Romagne, continue over open slopes between two German-held woods, the Bois des Rappes and the Bois de Bantheville, and take the town of Bantheville. The regiments would then drive farther northwest up the open slopes of Le Grand Carré Farm, and hopefully link up with the 42d Division as it attacked northeast. They would come under flanking fire all the way—unless the 32d Division on the left took Romagne, and the 60th Regiment on the right captured Cunel, the Bois de la Pultière, and the Bois des Rappes. The plan was incredibly ambitious considering the proven strength of the German defenses. Pershing believed it should succeed in a day or two.

An unidentified soldier deserted from the 5th Division early that morning. He made his way over to the German lines, found an officer, and told him everything he knew about the American attack. In response, from 6:00 to 8:00 A.M. the Germans laid the strongest counterbarrage that the Red Diamond men had ever seen, causing heavy losses and disrupting the companies on the line of departure. The attack nevertheless began as scheduled at 8:30 A.M., and the Doughboys surged forward through woods and across fields "thick with the dead and wounded of the previous day's fighting."[3]

Wrentmore's 60th Regiment went forward shouting wildly, "like an avalanche, expecting to take everything in front of us," and slammed headlong into a "band of steel." Doughboys, including many of Wrentmore's best friends, fell all around him while he continued unscathed, thinking he was bound to catch it soon. The muddy fields south of Cunel became "one huge sea of death . . . like a scene from the infernal region" as the Doughboys advanced. Gas canisters plopped, and gray or yellow clouds drifted across the ground. Stretcher-bearers wearing gas masks darted from hole to hole, trying to reach the wounded before they choked. Some American heavy-machine-gun teams supported the attack, and with their assistance the Doughboys extinguished several nests. In Cunel, snipers occupied windows, doorways, and the church tower; beyond, the western Bois de la Pultière was studded with trenches, dugouts, and pillboxes. These had to be blasted out one at a time.[4]

Wrentmore became separated from Captain Allworth in the woods, and joined a pandemonium of hand-to-hand combat. The boy's .45s, once a joke, now came in handy. He was firing at one German when another charged him with a leveled bayonet. Fortunately Wrentmore's friend, a burly Pole nicknamed Polock, stood nearby. He crushed the German's skull with the butt of his rifle, splashing brains everywhere. Wrentmore did not notice his lucky escape, but kept firing both pistols at every German he could see. He fired them point-blank at one soldier about to attack Polock, and saw the man's face disappear as he fell like lead. "Jeez keed! Jeez keed!" the Pole yelled. "Me nevar know you fight dees damn Boche lak hell. You one damn good fighter!" With that he sprinted off to continue fighting, and Wrentmore went to find the captain.

He found Allworth recovering from a near-miss explosion that had driven a large piece of shrapnel into his pistol belt. The captain had a job for Wrentmore. The 3d Division had become separated on the right; Allworth wanted him to carry a message telling the nearest company of that division to close the gap. "Captain Allworth, I'll do my best!" the boy gasped. "If I don't make it, you'll know that I tried!" And off he ran.

Machine-gun bullets and artillery shells flew everywhere, forcing Wrentmore to take cover every few seconds in underbrush or behind trees. One burst of bullets slammed into him as he fell, and it took him a few moments to realize, first, that he was alive; and second, that his gas mask had been torn to shreds. Running on, through a clearing, into underbrush, and across another clearing, he stumbled upon a group of Germans who had been blown to pieces by one of their own artillery shells. He assumed they were all dead, until one of the blood-covered Germans raised his pistol.

> The lousy Hun, I thought to myself, here he is dying, but still rotten enough with the lust to kill to want to knock me off, as his last gesture on this earth. It had to be one of us—I shot him before he could get the bead on me. I moved closer to the dead Jerry, and saw that I had done him a good turn. Both of his legs had been blown off, and he was bleeding terribly.

Wrentmore found a 3d Division officer, delivered his message, and successfully made it back to his unit. He found it dug in about five hundred yards shy of the north edge of the woods, exhausted and under bombardment. Allworth and Wrentmore settled in a shell hole, opened a can of tomatoes, and tried to gather their nerves. Wrentmore knew he would never be the same:

> I was numb—no feeling left—petrified, and in a state of panic every moment. I had passed the point of being scared. I cringed and dodged each time a close one would shriek by, but that was a natural, almost involuntary reaction. I seemed to have lost all realization of the value of life. My comrades were dying all around me or receiving severe wounds, and they cried for help or cursed the damnable Boche as they were carried off the battlefield. This, too, had to become routine, or you would go mad. The nerves could take the

incessant pounding of gun fire, but to become emotional over the loss of a friend, buddy, or comrade would be to lose complete control. You had to become a piece of wood, or you'd never make it.[5]

Farther west, the 6th and 11th Regiments had endured an equally difficult day. Captain Emil Gansser of the neighboring 32d Division watched them attack over the brow of the ridge between Cunel and Romagne as if they were on maneuvers back in the United States:

> When they approach within gunshot range of the enemy in the trenches, fingers of flame spurt from the muzzle of mausers and automatics. Men are falling to the ground by the score. The deplorable carnage is appalling, yet the thinning waves come walking on without firing a shot in return. Not until the survivors of the leading waves reach a dry creek bed midway to the trenches, do these intrepid doughboys drop into shell-pits or hastily dug foxholes and end their costly advance which could have been attained after dark with scarcely any losses. They are learning the technique of advancing into battle the hard way, the same as we had to do.[6]

The regiments managed to cross the Romagne-Cunel road running parallel to the 5th Division's front on the ridge crest and move a short distance over the open ground beyond before intense German fire pinned them down. They took shelter on the reverse slope of Hill 260, well short of their objective; "further advance, until the woods on right and left were cleared, meant disaster, even extinction." German artillery bombarded the Doughboys and their lines of supply, blowing up the divisional signal dump at Septsarges and triggering a massive fireworks display as multicolored flares shot into the sky.

The 5th Division had advanced half a mile. And its frontline strength had been reduced to that of a brigade.[7]

★

It was a big day for the 32d Division. Although the 42d and 5th Divisions to the left and right were launching major assaults around both sides of the Heights of Romagne, that didn't mean the Red Arrow could take it easy. Major General Haan wanted Côte Dame Marie, and he meant to take it today. "Our troops are up against wire and will have a hard job," he wrote in his diary, "but I hope it goes O.K. I have impressed with all my force on Brigade and Regimental Commanders the fact that the position can be carried if they can impress their men in the same way, and get them into the full spirit of the matter."[8]

One of Haan's generals attempted to inspire his battle-weary troops with a stern message:

A few hundred yards to the north of you the remnants of the decimated crack divisions of the German army are clinging desperately to the pivotal point of their bruised and broken line, on which hangs the fate of their Emperor and the Empire.

The 32nd Division was sent to this sector to shatter that line. You are shock troops, "Les Terribles," the French call you. "Fighting sons o'guns," the Americans call you. You are the very flower of our army. You that remain up there on the front have been tried by fire. The skulkers have skulked—the quitters have quit. Only the man with guts remains.

Machine guns? You have captured thousands of them. And you took them standing up. The only way to take machine guns is to take them. No use lying down on the ground. They have plenty of ammunition and they aim low.

Shells? Shell casualties are only three per cent of the total.

Tired? You have been in the line two weeks. Your enemies have been in five weeks, prisoners say they have gone thru hell. . . .

The Americans must succeed. It is not enough to say, "I'll Try."

Your resolve must be "I Will!"[9]

What the Doughboys jokingly referred to as the "electric order" did little to rev them up. When Lieutenant Harold Woehl's men received their attack orders, they could hardly contain their dismay. "Oh Lord, Our God," Woehl scrawled in his diary, "is there no help for the little remnant that is left of Company H?"[10] But that didn't mean they wouldn't fight.

Haan ordered three regiments, the 127th, 126th, and 128th, from left to right, to attack at 5:30 a.m. The 128th would be responsible for taking the town of Romagne, while the 126th and 127th would drive up the eastern and western slopes of Côte Dame Marie. Each attack depended to some extent on the others. If the 128th, in particular, took Romagne, it would greatly ease the work of the 5th Division to the right and the 126th Regiment to the left.

Private Horace Baker, a devoutly religious country boy from Monroe County, Mississippi, felt out of place among the Wisconsin dairy farmers who made up his 128th Regiment. Every Sunday morning his mind went back to the little country towns and crowded churches of his native Mississippi. He took refuge in prayers and the New Testament that slipped naturally into his hands everywhere he went. It helped him to bear—though not to make sense of—the horrors around him. On October 14, he kept up his courage by singing church hymns as he moved toward the lines. Finding that the songs did not harmonize with the noise of exploding shells, and that in fact he could hardly hear his own voice, he gave it up.

As Baker's company advanced, a soldier overbalanced by his heavy pack fell down, and a sergeant named Flynn cursed him. "Isn't it terrible for him to be swearing this way and he to face his maker so soon?" Baker thought. Several days earlier, the sergeant had decided he wasn't going to make it. His men tried to talk him out of it, but secretly they believed him. Now he was cursing as if he would live forever. For his part, Baker had spent the last few minutes before H hour thinking of "home and loved ones, of my buddies on that battlefield, of my soul's condition, of the future, of food, of bullets, of victory, of death." Although it would be his first time in the attack, he wasn't scared; not because he was exceptionally brave, but because his nerves had been on edge for too long. He just felt a little chilly.

Baker had imagined a long line of men jumping off to attack as one. Instead, at 8:30 A.M. an officer climbed lazily up an embankment, pointed randomly at a squad of soldiers, and sent them forward. A few moments later he told another group to go. Then he pointed at Baker's squad. "Well, I guess, we'd better go," Baker mumbled to his comrades, and started forward. The first thing he saw was his burly corporal, his face covered with tears. He was wounded, he said, and couldn't go any farther. Then the man next to him stiffened and fell heavily to the ground. "Poor fellow, he is dead!" Baker thought as he passed on.

Ahead, hundreds of Doughboys advanced over a shell-pocked hillside toward what Baker later learned was the village of Romagne. Without thinking, he stepped into a shallow hole made by a 37mm shell. Some passing soldiers teased him, joking about his being completely concealed from the enemy now that his feet were covered, and he moved on. His thoughts turned to the weapon he was carrying, a French Chauchat:

> I had not yet been taught how to shoot it but evidently it would shoot, so, loading it, I set it down as it should have been and began trying to work the thing. I tried this thing and then that and finally I accidentally let loose a contraption and the thing went "Bam!" I looked to see if it was pointed toward the Germans and it was, so, I had not hit any of our own men.

Satisfied, Baker walked on, firing the Chauchat toward Romagne and gradually starting to enjoy it although he had to stop every few moments to clear a jam. "Quit shooting that chau-chay!" an angry officer shouted, and Baker had to stop. Bewildered—"here I was in the midst of a battle with orders not to shoot," he thought—and with "nothing to do," Baker jumped into a shell hole. He found Sergeant Flynn there, dead with a bullet hole between his eyes. A few minutes later, Baker saw Germans leaving Romagne with their hands up. For once, they had been caught unprepared. Aided by some companies of the 125th Regiment, the 128th had outflanked the German trenches, broken into the town, and continued for another half mile beyond, taking hundreds of prisoners.[11]

The 128th's coup at Romagne profoundly influenced the fighting to its left, where the 126th struggled toward Hill 258 on the eastern horn of Côte Dame Marie's crescent-shaped peak. That regiment had experienced a difficult morning because of disorganization caused by a command mix-up, and could not advance farther than the enemy's outer defenses. Romagne's fall forced the Germans to withdraw to their main positions on the lower slopes of Hill 258. The 126th followed to the main belt of enemy barbed wire and pushed through a gap, but German machine guns felled them in heaps before they could reach the other side. After several more attempts, the commander of the regiment's Third Battalion ordered Captain Edward B. Strom of Grand Rapids, Michigan, to take a combat patrol of seven men and penetrate the enemy wire at another point, silencing the machine guns covering the main gap. Equipped with rifle grenades and other weapons, the patrol cut through the wire and crawled up the slope, moving from shell holes to trees under heavy fire. When they had got far enough, Strom and his men made effective use of their rifle grenades, plopping them into German machine-gun nests as far as 150 yards away. Aided by "almost supernatural luck" and without a casualty, the patrol put ten machine guns out of action and opened the way for the 126th to advance through the gap and up the ridge to Hill 258.[12]

The capture of Hill 258 unhinged the German positions atop Côte Dame Marie, as Haan had hoped it would. That morning, Captain Paul Schmidt's company of the 127th's First Battalion had advanced toward the wire below the ridge's western horn. An overzealous officer blew his whistle early, and the Germans opened fire. "Men fell like pins struck by a ball on a bowling alley" as the Doughboys advanced to the edge of the enemy wire, upon which hung several 91st Division corpses. The Americans hacked desperately at the wire and were shot down, until only 150 men remained in Schmidt's battalion. Then the 126th broke through to the east, and everything changed. As the enemy defenses crumbled, the 127th surged up the ridge's western horn and drove along its crest. By evening, the Germans had abandoned Côte Dame Marie and fled into the woods to the north.[13]

For almost three weeks, First Army had crashed head-on into the *Kriemhilde Stellung,* the primary German defensive line in the Meuse-Argonne. Thousands of Americans had died in those attacks, without cracking the enemy positions. Now, thanks to the bravery of seven men, the most critical point in the *Kriemhilde Stellung* had fallen. "I consider this the best day's work that the 32d Division has yet done," Haan wrote in his diary that evening. "A German officer, who was captured today, stated that the attack of our Division was the best planned and best executed of any division's, British or French, that he had come in contact with except one Scottish Division, who wore kilts and they don't count."[14]

✦

The Rainbow Division's 84th Brigade faced rough, wooded terrain on October 14, while the 83d Brigade had to advance over mostly open ground devoid of cover. MacArthur's 84th, on the division's right, occupied positions in the Bois de Gesnes just west of Côte Dame Marie. The brigade's right-hand regiment, the Iowan 168th, attacked up a steep wooded ridge, Hill 288, while the Alabaman 167th advanced across its lower western slopes. The two regiments were then supposed to drive through the Bois de Romagne to the critical Côte de Châtillon, a mile to the north. The 83d Brigade on the division's right occupied a line that ran from just north of Sommerance and across an open ridge to the northwestern rim of the Bois de Romagne. The New York 165th Regiment on the right was ordered to advance over mostly open ground past the western edge of the Côte de Châtillon toward Landres–et–St. Georges, while the Ohioan 166th attacked over similar terrain from Sommerance toward a different town, St. Georges.

Major Lloyd Ross, commander of the Iowa regiment's First Battalion, led the assault on Hill 288. "Ross is the absolute key to the whole situation," MacArthur told his staff, and he was right.[15] The Germans defended fiercely, and inflicted heavy casualties. The inability of the 32d Division's 127th Regiment to advance that morning allowed the Germans on the western edge of Côte Dame Marie to maintain a steady fire on Ross's men. Gradually, the Iowans crept up Hill 288's lower slopes and took the crest in the early afternoon. MacArthur led the attack from the front. "If this is good, I'm in it. And if it's bad, I'm in it too," he supposedly told a Doughboy.[16] The hill was taken, but the Iowans could not go any farther. That afternoon, MacArthur telephoned Major General Menoher:

Have taken Hill 288. The fighting has been of the most desperate character. The battalion which took the hill is very badly shattered [it had taken about 65 percent casualties] and I am making replacements. The position was splendidly entrenched, heavily wired and strongly manned. It had to be taken inch by inch in the most sanguinary fighting. It was superbly defended and heroically won.[17]

★

THE Alabama regiment, meanwhile, pushed all the way to the lower slopes of the Côte de Châtillon, despite severe casualties from German machine guns firing into its flanks. Sensing that its advance had created an opportunity, MacArthur phoned Menoher that evening and suggested a two-pronged night attack against the Côte de Châtillon, with the Iowans advancing from the south and the Alabamans from the southwest. There would be no artillery or small-arms firing; instead, the infantry would take the German positions by bayonet alone. The plan sounded intriguing and heroic, and Menoher gave MacArthur the green light to carry it out. But when Major Ravee Norris of the Alabamans heard of the order, he phoned regimental headquarters. "It is nothing short of murder," he yelled into the mouthpiece. "I am sorry, Norris," came the reply, "but this is a direct order and must be obeyed." Downcast, Norris passed the order on to his company commanders. "What in hell does this order mean?" they shouted. "Such an attack will never succeed. You know that, Norris, as well as we do!" Menoher learned that the men considered the plan crazy or came to that realization himself, and ordered MacArthur to cancel it. Instead, he instructed the divisional artillery to bombard the Côte de Châtillon all night in preparation for a conventional attack at dawn.[18]

★

"DONOVAN is one of the few men I know who really enjoys a battle," said Father Duffy of Wild Bill Donovan. "He goes into it exactly in the frame of mind that he had as a college man when he marched out on the gridiron before a football game, and his one thought throughout is to push his way through."[19] On October 14, Donovan's impetuosity earned him a Medal of Honor, and also got many of his men killed.

The New York regiment attacked at 8:30 A.M. and moved quickly over the open terrain between the northwestern edge of the Bois de Romagne and the town of Landres–et–St. Georges. The 1st Division had fought unsuccessfully to take this ground a few days before, and the Irishmen paused occasionally to gape at hideously contorted corpses. After crossing a sunken road,

Donovan suddenly noticed men being hit all around him. "Where in hell is that coming from?" he yelled. "From the Côte de Châtillon, of course," his major replied. Deciding it was safer to keep going than stay put, Donovan ordered his men forward. Unfortunately, with the Alabama regiment falling farther and farther behind on the right, the flanking fire became steadily worse as they approached Landres–et–St. Georges. Eventually the New Yorkers had to take cover, about half a mile south of the village and immediately west of the Côte de Châtillon. Sergeant Michael A. Donaldson of Haverstraw, New York, earned a Medal of Honor here by rescuing several wounded men, and Donovan earned another by braving enemy fire to encourage his troops. "Come on, fellows, it's better ahead than it is here," he said, strutting back and forth conspicuously while German machine-gun bullets tore up the dirt around him; or, "Come on now, men, they can't hit me and they won't hit you." But even such bravery could not silence the German guns. Late that afternoon, Donovan called for an artillery barrage against the wire and then sent a fresh battalion ahead to attack. The men found the wire uncut, and the Germans slaughtered them.[20]

On the far left, the Ohio regiment attacked at 8:30 A.M. from lines about two hundred yards north of Sommerance, and covered about half a mile before the Germans stopped them well short of St. Georges. The enemy artillery doused the Ohioans with enough mustard gas to stop a division, and their planes—flying unopposed as usual—directed accurate artillery fire. "The enemy has continued his resistance with undimished fury," Lieutenant Colonel Noble Judah wrote that evening in his summary of intelligence, "and has at no time showed any tendency to withdraw or surrender."[21] The Côte de Châtillon still seemed miles away.

☆

THE 82d Division attacked on October 14 with the self-appointed objective of taking the battered town of St. Juvin. Officially, the 77th Division, on the left, was supposed to take the place, but the All-Americans—who had yet to take and hold a town by force—hoped to get there first. General Duncan placed his 326th, 325th, and 328th Regiments in line from left to right, with the 327th in reserve. Unusually, a company of the First Gas and Flame would fire in support, not just smoke but gas too.

Everything seemed to be going well for the 328th as it jumped off at 8:30 A.M., but then a large concentration of troops from the Rainbow Division's 166th Regiment blundered into its path. It took the 328th's colonel two hours to clear them out and get his regiment moving again. Around noon, elements of the regiment penetrated the German wire about half a mile southwest of St. Georges, but heavy artillery fire drove it back to the St. Georges–St. Juvin road, where it spent the remainder of the day.

In the center, the 325th covered about a mile and took a few dozen prisoners, including, as Lieutenant Herman Ulmer reported, one that the troops decided to save for dinner:

> As we passed over the first hill a jack rabbit came streaking out of the barrage in front of us. How even a rabbit could live in that hail of explosives is a mystery. It was running as no rabbit has ever run before, quite bewildered, and not knowing which way to turn. So calm were our men, and so normal, even though they were advancing to attack, that a number of them turned to shoot at the rabbit. It was killed, and a man in Company C carried it under his arm the rest of the day.[22]

Abreast of the 328th, however, the regiment encountered severe enemy fire that forced the Doughboys to take cover before they could cut the enemy wire. Corporal Fred Takes took cover in a shell hole just in front of the wire and spent fifteen minutes there "with my face in the dirt afraid to look up. There were so many shells and bullets flying. When I looked up no one was in sight. I soon beat it back thinking the Germans were coming over." He and some other men dashed back from hole to hole, not stopping until they had covered three miles all the way back to Fleury, where they joined First Army's growing mass of stragglers.[23]

On the left, the 326th attacked at 8:30 A.M. and made rapid progress past the eastern outskirts of St. Juvin. German machine guns fired from St. Juvin into the regiment's left flank as it advanced, providing a good pretext for a little diversion from the official line of attack. Veering left, some infantry and machine gunners entered the town in the early afternoon, ahead of the 77th Division, and fought house to house until they had captured St. Juvin's eastern half. The Statue of Liberty Doughboys came up later, and the two divisions shared the wrecked town like a crusty old loaf of bread.

★

THE 77th Division, as General Alexander put it, "stood on the threshold of the open country."[24] But two major barriers remained before the division could finally break free: first, the Aire River; second, the villages of Grandpré and St. Juvin, and the German trenches beyond. Though tired, the Statue of Liberty Doughboys longed to puncture those barriers and march north into the plains. Memories of the Argonne had everyone feeling more than a little claustrophobic.

The Aire River flows west from St. Juvin to Grandpré, traveling for about three miles through a broad open valley. South of the river, a road ran west from Marcq—a mile southwest of St. Juvin—for a mile to the tiny village of Chevières. From there, the road continued west for just over another mile before turning north and crossing the river on a bridge—demolished in 1918—to Grandpré on the German-held north bank. A railroad on a steep embankment, following the same course between the road and the river, offered cover to the Americans as they approached the Aire from the south. North of the river, another narrow road linked St. Juvin and Grandpré. A mile north of St. Juvin, a steep ridge ran roughly west from the village of Champigneulle through the densely wooded Bois des Loges, past two farms, and into the Bois de Bourgogne. The main enemy defenses, and the German artillery, were located along this ridge.[25]

Major General Alexander considered attacking Grandpré and St. Juvin at the same time, but decided he didn't have enough artillery to support both attacks. Instead, he ordered the 307th and 308th Regiments to push small patrols across the river below Grandpré, and between Marcq and Chevières. All their attempts failed until the 308th got a few dozen infantrymen across the river north of Chevières after dusk. The focus of the day's fighting, however, was to the east, where Alexander ordered the 306th to cross the Aire east of Marcq and advance north and west on St. Juvin, while the 305th followed in support.

The 306th's First Battalion left Marcq at 8:30 A.M., but instead of marching east as Alexander had specified, it moved north toward the riverbank immediately south of St. Juvin. The mistake had terrible consequences. There was no cover at that point on the riverbank. Worse, there was no way to cross. Instead of withdrawing, the battalion commander held his men in full view of the enemy while the scouts ran back and forth, desperately trying to find a place to bridge or ford. German artillery and machine guns on the high ground north of the river methodically ravaged the battalion until it practically disintegrated, at which time its commander pulled it back to a more sheltered position and dug in.[26]

Horrified at the blunder, which he attributed to "the malign influence of trench warfare doctrine," Alexander phoned General Edward Wittenmyer, commander of the 153d Brigade, which contained the 305th and 306th Regiments, and chewed him out. Meanwhile, Major Archibald Thacher, a New York City lawyer commanding the 306th's Second Battalion, found a crossing place about a thousand yards east, where the Aire split into two shallow streams under the protection of a wooded bend. Thacher reported his discovery to the regiment's commander, Colonel George Vidmer, who ordered him to lead his battalion and two companies of the Third Battalion across the river at that place. Thacher moved his troops out at 2:00 P.M. They crossed about five hundred yards of open ground before they reached the crossing place, which was sheltered by trees. German artillery heavily shelled the leading company, but the bulk of the troops made it to the river safely. More Doughboys fell as they waded across the first stream to a heavily wooded island, reducing the leading company to sixty men. After pausing briefly to reorganize and fix bayonets, they crossed the second stream to the opposite bank.[27]

As his troops took cover in a sunken road out of sight of the German artillery, Thacher saw 82d Division troops falling back before a German counterattack to the east. He ordered some of his men to help repulse that attack and then pivot west toward St. Juvin, while the remainder attacked the town directly from the southeast. Captain Julius Ochs Adler of New York City—who would command the 77th Division during World War II—advanced with Company H at the head of the troops attacking St. Juvin. Moving "in gang formation" along the Fléville–St. Juvin road, Company H had reached a point near the town when an 82d Division officer trotted over to Adler and struck up a conversation. "You don't intend entering St. Juvin with that handful of men?" he asked incredulously. Adler, who had about fifty riflemen and one machine gun remaining in his company, nodded his head. Not only that, he said, but after taking the town Company H would swing north and capture Hill 182 on the ridge to the north. There were "beaucoup Boches" in the town, the 82d Division officer warned, with plenty of machine guns, but Adler laughed, saying he would take the place in thirty minutes and then send back for him.

Adler was right, but also very lucky. His men entered St. Juvin at about 3:45 P.M., but some 82d Division infantry had already penetrated the town from the northeast a short time before. The Germans focused their efforts on repelling the first incursion, fighting the All-Americans house by house. When Adler's company came into St. Juvin from the other side, the Germans gave up. Taking about 350 prisoners, Adler's company pushed rapidly through the town to its northern outskirts. As the captain passed the last house with two other men, he saw a German soldier running away. Adler and his companions pursued the German all the way to the base of Hill 182, where another 150 or so enemy soldiers stood bewildered on the crest. Audaciously, Adler and the two other Americans climbed the hill, firing at the Germans above them. Joined by a Chauchat team and another group of ten soldiers, they closed to within point-blank range. Incredibly, the enemy soldiers—who outnumbered the attackers by about ten to one—waved white flags or fled.[28] A part of the last natural barrier between the 77th Division and open country had been definitely breached.

★

EAST of the Meuse, the 29th and 33d Divisions had stalled, and the German heavy artillery remained intact. The Blue and Grays still had more fighting in store, but the Prairie Division, after a few local attacks through October 17, had nothing left in the tank; it would be pulled out of the lines on the twentieth. III and V Corps continued to take heavy punishment from the German artillery and from stubbornly held enemy emplacements. Pershing's plan to capture the Heights of Romagne in a vast pincer movement had made little progress, and the 5th and 42d Divisions had been badly mauled, with heavy casualties. At Côte Dame Marie, however, the 32d Division had cracked the *Kriemhilde Stellung;* and at St. Juvin and Hill 182, the 77th and 82d Divisions had breached the Aire River defenses and taken the first steps toward the plains beyond. Much remained to be done; but at long last, after three weeks of fighting, victory had come firmly within First Army's grasp.

CHAPTER 24

"There Are Times When Even General Officers
Have to Be Expendable"

OCTOBER 15

Death reaped another bloody harvest from the grain fields of Molleville Farm on October 15. At 7:30 A.M., American artillery, trench mortars, and machine guns announced an impending attack by opening fire on the German-held woods to the north and east of the farm clearing. Twenty minutes later, the Third Battalion of the 29th Division's 116th Regiment advanced. Fog obscured the first wave of Doughboys as they moved into the clearing, but German rifles and machine guns opened up as soon as the second wave emerged from the southern woods. Brutal German fire from the eastern woods collapsed the entire first wave, and Doughboys fell like ninepins.

Colonel Reginald Kelley, commanding the 116th, could not see his troops in the fog, but believed that they had successfully crossed the clearing. Eager to follow up the apparent advantage, he ordered his headquarters company—including staff officers, clerks, runners, signalers, medics, and others—to form a skirmish line and enter the clearing. A major would command them; Kelley intended to follow a few minutes later. The headquarters men brandished their pistols nervously as they advanced in rushes through the fog. With bullets flying and men falling on all sides, they lost direction and veered to the right. The Americans could see nothing until the northern tree line emerged far away to their left. Turning to that direction, they ran for the trees at full speed, hoping for shelter and not knowing the woods were full of Germans. In one of those bizarre flukes of battle, the enemy apparently mistook the rush for a full-scale attack and withdrew as the Americans reached the trees.

The Germans soon realized their mistake, and the headquarters company scattered as bullets and minenwerfer shells landed among them. Before long the major and his adjutant were the only unwounded men remaining in the company. While the adjutant dashed off through the fog to seek help, the major pulled the rest of his men back into a shallow ditch running along the road at the top of the clearing. The ditch grew thick with bodies, and "several men escaped with their lives by being buried beneath the bodies of their less fortunate comrades." Unwittingly, however, the headquarters company had paved the way for the infantry—a nice change of pace, many of the enlisted Doughboys must have thought—and eventually some soldiers moved up to the corpse-clogged ditch and established a thin line in the woods. In the process they cleaned out several machine-gun nests, bayoneting their occupants. The Germans counterattacked this line repeatedly over the remainder of the day, until the Americans ran out of ammunition and had to fight off the attackers with rifle butts and bayonets. They held, however, and by evening Third Battalion had taken a tenuous hold on the north edge of the Molleville Farm clearing. The battalion had been reduced to 30 percent of its original strength.[1]

✴

"THE optimistic reports of yesterday have gradually given way to more pessimistic ones," General Hines, the new III Corps commander, wrote in his diary on October 15. With three regular divisions in the stable, his corps should have been First Army's strongest. Instead, it was the weakest. The 4th Division, which had been in the line since September 26, was so worn down that it could only hold the territory west of the Meuse that the 33rd Division had vacated several days before. The 3d Division had withered to skeletal proportions. On visiting the division's headquarters, Pershing was so alarmed that he relieved its commander, Major General Beaumont Buck, effective October 18. And the 5th Division—the vaunted Red Diamond, fresh and ready just three days earlier—was disorganized and demoralized. Hines inspected the division on this date and found it "jumpy," with stragglers numbering around twenty-five hundred. Matters were even worse at headquarters. "It appears," he wrote in his diary, "that the entire 5th Div. has been used by piling in all remaining reserves, elements are disorganized and crowded in Bois de la Poultiere beyond which they cannot advance." Pershing confronted the division's commander,

Major General McMahon, about the disorganization, and asked about his men. They were very tired, McMahon said. "Probably," Pershing fired back, "it was the division commander who was tired." Disgusted, he relieved McMahon, also effective October 18.

Though generals came and went, for the Doughboys little changed. The 3d Division's battalions had shrunk to the size of companies, and its companies to the size of platoons. Yet it still received orders to attack. The 4th and 7th Regiments, their battalions combined into provisional formations, jumped off in the early morning. Neither of them got anywhere. The Germans holding the Bois de Clairs Chênes, Hill 299, and the eastern part of the Bois de Forêt easily hurled the Americans back, inflicting heavy losses. Even nature seemed against the Americans; a tree fell on the 4th Regiment's commander, Colonel Halstead Dorey, during an artillery bombardment and severely wounded him.[2] By evening, engineers had to reinforce the shattered infantry regiments in the front line.

*

BACK in America, teenaged boys spent their weekend hours in the autumn of 1918 reading books like *The Army Boys on the Firing Line* and *Tom Swift and His War Tank*. Thirteen-year-old Ernest Wrentmore had no time for books. A private in the 5th Division, he had already experienced horrors that most adults had never dreamed of. Though exhausted, he could not sleep. Thoughts of home and visions of Hell wracked his mind:

> I'd seen enough of this hellish nightmare! Seen men torn to pieces, men I'd been talking to a few moments before. I tried to shut my ears to the groans and cries of my buddies who had been mutilated by shot and shell. Never had there been anything that could compare with the ugly viciousness of what my eyes were seeing! The horrors of this war were beyond human conception! The body and brain of my thirteen years were hard put to withstand much more.

"Christ, Harry," he told a comrade, "if this don't let up soon, it'll be curtains for me." But more—much more—lay in store for the boy and his fellow Red Diamond soldiers.

General McMahon deployed Wrentmore's 60th Regiment and the 61st Regiment in line from right to left, and ordered them to attack at 8:00 A.M. Their objective was to clear the rest of the Bois de la Pultière, and then take the Bois des Rappes. Heavy rain and fog provided some concealment, but it could not stop the German machine-gun bullets that slashed through the Doughboys as they advanced, "forging ahead, firing their rifles, yelling, and cursing—always cursing," through the Bois de la Pultière. Some of the most brutal fighting of the entire Meuse-Argonne battle followed, with no quarter asked or given. Germans and Americans contested the woods savagely, while the German artillery shells rained down on friend and foe alike. Stuck in the middle, Wrentmore thought he would lose his mind despite the steadying presence of Captain Allworth:

> Those of us who still lived, who were able to move, in body if not in spirit, wanted to drop to our knees and implore God to stop this horrible slaughter of mankind. Added to the thunderous roar of heavy gunfire was the constant whine of bullets and the angry shouts of war-maddened men as they met in mortal combat. It was enough to drive us out of our minds. Hadn't we passed the point of normal reasoning? There was nothing left but to move forward—and kill, move forward—and kill; or to be killed. The screams of weary fighters almost overcame me as they dropped from the sudden crash of machine guns or were pierced through with the dreaded shrapnel.

As the rain thinned to mist, and the wind abated to a light breeze, Wrentmore instinctively sensed that these were the ideal weather conditions for gas. And he was right. Through the leafless treetops descended clouds of phosgene, exuding an odor of newly mown hay as they settled to the ground. Splotches of yellow appeared on the ground too—mustard gas. The clouds drifted to and fro as the men continued fighting. Some soldiers were shot, some blown to pieces, some asphyxiated, and others burned inside and out by the horrible mustard. And all about lay bodies in every conceivable contortion, mangled as if by the mad rush of a runaway train.

Killing, Wrentmore learned, could be cathartic. At one point, he happened on a concealed German soldier and shot him with his .45. "You son-of-a-bitch," the boy screamed as he kicked the dead soldier and slashed his uniform, "you'll never murder any more of our men!" Shortly afterward the fight tipped in the Americans' favor. The Germans in the Bois de la Pultière fled and the Doughboys pursued, "yelling like a band of Comanches," to the woods' northern edge. But when they tried to dash across the open space beyond into the Bois des Rappes, a cyclone of enemy fire drove them back. Captain Allworth and other officers then requested a box barrage on the German positions, which the artillery fired into the early afternoon. The advance then resumed, with the soldiers infiltrating into the Bois des Rappes in small groups rather than advancing in line. More savage fighting followed until dusk, when the 60th and 61st established tenuous lines on the northern edge of the Bois des Rappes.

Both regiments had been devastated by casualties. Seventy-five men, for example, remained in the 61st's First Battalion. Captain Allworth called Wrentmore and asked him to carry a message back to regimental headquarters reporting the condition of the men. Feeling as if he were "burning up," with his insides "raw clear down to my belly," the boy could hardly speak; but he pulled himself together, took the message, and headed back toward the Bois de la Pultière. Shells exploded around him, but he no longer attempted to dodge them. "What the hell's the use?" he thought. He had just passed the clearing between the two woods when he heard a dull thud in the ground just in front of him. Gas! It was too close to avoid, and he wasn't wearing a mask. His lungs filled with the pungent odor.

> I became deathly sick. I dropped to my knees, retching and gagging. I tried to regain my feet. I couldn't make it! I became weaker and weaker, as I started to cough and choke up. What'll I do? Its got me for sure this time—went through my befogged brain. I tried to yell; no sound came forth. I sank to the ground, then, "lights out."

He came to on a stretcher, coughing and choking, and passed out again. He woke up again as a shell hit nearby and toppled one of the stretcher-bearers. He felt pins and needles in his legs, and then passed out again. Waking a third time, Wrentmore found himself in a first-aid station. But he still wasn't safe, for German shells fell furiously.

> I saw men lying on stretchers everywhere, and the Goddamned Boche were firing on the wounded and helpless! Every time a shell would scream its way into a part of the building, a voice would cry out, "I'm hit! I'm hit!" Or there would be the cries that would end in a blood-curdling gurgle. Maybe it was the quickest way out of this hellish tournament.

Wrentmore survived; an ambulance carried him away later that night. But his war was over.[3]

Wrentmore had not delivered his message, but later that evening a shell-shocked officer stumbled into 61st Regiment's command post. He told the colonel that his battalion and company commanders had all been killed or wounded along with most of their men and that the survivors were fleeing the Bois des Rappes. The colonel did not question the officer's account, which was accurate as to casualties but not about the supposed retreat.

Instead, he went to brigade headquarters and passed it on. The brigadier reacted to the report by ordering the troops to be rounded up and sent back, but word of the retreat continued to pass around until it reached General McMahon. He, like the colonel, did not seek verification of the rumor. Instead, he overruled the brigadier and ordered the survivors of both regiments to leave the Bois des Rappes and retreat to the northern edge of the Bois de la Pultière. Most of the troops did so, but many could not be found by messengers in the woods and remained until the following morning, when they withdrew. All the day's fighting and casualties had gone for practically nothing. The Bois des Rappes, won at such cost and then abandoned, would have to be taken again.[4]

✳

An "air of tranquility" reigned at the 126th's regimental headquarters on the morning of October 15. The 32d Division had captured Côte Dame Marie, the central strongpoint of the *Kriemhilde Stellung,* at the cost several thousand casualties. The Michigan and Wisconsin Doughboys were all in, and ready for relief. Surely they had done enough? Surely the time had come for the division to enter the reserve? 89th Division officers had been seen roving around the front lines—the Germans had captured one of them who went too far forward on a reconnaissance—and everyone expected that division to replace them soon. Then a message came from General Haan's headquarters: by General Pershing's orders, the attack would continue. "The brass hats are surely driving the division beyond the utmost limit of mental and physical endurance," Captain Emil Gansser complained.[5]

The attack moved forward with the 127th, 126th, and 128th Regiments again in front from left to right. The 128th made no progress, advancing as far as Hill 254 immediately to its front and then falling back before a counterattack. The 126th, conquerer of Côte Dame Marie, had received no rations since October 13 due to heavy German shelling of the rear areas, but it nevertheless pushed forward half a mile to the northern edge of the Bois de Chauvignon. Captain Paul Schmidt's 127th Regiment advanced abreast of the 126th until it reached the edge of a clearing below La Tuilerie Farm, on the eastern edge of the Côte de Châtillon, where the Germans let forth "an almost unbelievable storm of shot and shell. Machine guns, trench mortars, anti-tank, artillery and gas shells met us as we reached the clearing. Our lines staggered from the blow, wavered for an instant and then retreated into the woods leaving behind several killed and wounded." The regiment withdrew to the woods and remained there for the rest of the day, while the Germans sent over so much gas that several men were killed by direct hits from the canisters. Schmidt's men spent a disheartening night:

> The rain continued to come down in torrents and the shelter holes occupied by the men filled up with water, leaving us with only one alternative, viz: getting out of the water and exposing ourselves to the enemy shell fire and possible death, or to remain in the holes with our bodies submerged in the cold water. Between the two, we decided to remain in the shelter holes. . . . Dysentery aggravated the already bad condition and the men began to speculate on what would happen to them were they compelled to remain in this position all night. To add to the horror of the situation, our own artillery shot several shells into our lines about three o'clock in the afternoon.

Thoughts of relief provided hope, until a message arrived announcing that the division would stay put. "It proved," wrote Schmidt, "to be almost the last straw." General Haan wrote in his diary that "the spirit of our troops is still fine, but they are getting very tired and I hope they will not have to stay in much longer."[6]

✱

GENERAL Gallwitz took great pride in his East Prussian 41st Division, which faced the American Rainbow Division from Landres–et–St. Georges to the Côte de Châtillon. On October 14, the East Prussians had "repelled not less than four massed American attacks, partly in hand-to-hand fighting, while maintaining their position."[7] On the following day it would be more of the same. It seemed the Americans never learned. They just kept coming, head-on every time, taking terrible losses but never stopping; perhaps they planned to keep attacking until every one of them was dead.

Nature provided the Americans with a symbol of good fortune to start their day, in the form of a rainbow that appeared as the fog cleared away. "Our men regard this as an omen of good luck," artilleryman Elmer Sherwood wrote in his diary, "and shout to each other encouragements and orders to press on."[8] But the gunners were well behind the lines. At the front, no one had time to look overhead for anything but gas clouds.

On the right, MacArthur's 84th Brigade launched another round of attacks against the Côte de Châtillon, and La Tuilerie Farm flanking the ridge's eastern side. The Alabaman 167th Regiment sent out only patrols, but the Iowan 168th attacked north from the crest of Hill 288 and advanced half a mile through the Bois de Romagne to Hill 242, just beyond which lay La Tuilerie Farm. Working around both sides of the hill to the woods' edge, the

Iowans stormed the farm, extinguishing some machine-gun nests but without capturing all the buildings. The Germans on the Côte de Châtillon, looming above the farm to the west, inflicted heavy losses on the Iowans and forced them to withdraw. The Americans came back in the afternoon and took all the farm buildings except the barn, but again the German machine guns on the heights forced them back into the Bois de Romagne. Some companies had been reduced to fewer than fifty men. Iowa medic Lawrence Stewart stayed busy tending his regiment's casualties from this and the previous day's fighting; among them was an officer who struggled to pry the West Point graduation ring from his severed left arm.[9]

The 83d Brigade, with the New York and Ohio regiments in line from right to left, meanwhile struggled to pierce the wire between St. Georges and Landres–et–St. Georges. The Germans laid their wire thick and defended it well, but their positions ran along an open ridge—good tank country. Brigadier General Michael Lenihan, the brigade commander, promised that sixteen tanks would support the attack when it began at 7:30 A.M. behind a rolling barrage, but none appeared as H hour approached. Colonel Donovan consulted Lenihan and the division commander, Major General Menoher, and all three officers agreed: the infantry must not wait for the rattletraps, but go forward alone so as not to lose the rolling barrage. The Irishmen and Ohioans, supported by the 117th Engineers, jumped off and advanced toward the enemy wire. They made no attempts at infiltration or combined arms tactics—indeed, there were precious few arms to combine, since the tanks had not shown up and the division had run out of bangalore torpedoes. Instead, the Americans just tried to cut through the wire faster than the enemy artillery and machine guns could kill them. It was a 1914-style attack with 1914-style results: a massacre.

Wild Bill Donovan moved along the line, trying to urge on his men, until his luck ran out. At about 10:00 A.M., he felt a smash, "as if somebody had hit me on the back of the leg with a spiked club," and "fell like a log" with a bullet through his thighbone. He crawled into a shell hole and refused evacuation until the attack ended. For the rest of the morning, company after company hurled itself against the enemy wire, which the American artillery had not damaged in the least. The German artillery fired box barrages, obliterating Doughboys by the score and deluging the area with gas. The tanks finally came up, but within a few minutes all of them had either broken down or been reduced to scrap. Corpses and body parts lay scattered along the ground and hanging in the wire. Corporal Martin Hogan's left hand had been smashed by an enemy bullet, but he had to remain on the field until late in the day before he could crawl to a dressing station. Leaving the battlefield, he saw "men being carried with legs shattered, with blood-drenched clothes from the flow of ghastly body wounds, and I passed one man sitting against a tree with half his head torn away. . . . He must have seated himself here after the first shock to rest and have died moments later."[10]

Finally, even Wild Bill Donovan, the ever-forward leader who had always attacked regardless of losses, decided the killing had to stop. In the late morning, the New York regiment's commander, Colonel Harry Mitchell, forwarded a message from Major General Summerall ordering the attacks to resume. Donovan, risking court-martial, refused. The regiment's losses, he told Mitchell, had been too heavy. The Ohioans stopped attacking at about the same time. Both regiments were utterly shattered; during the afternoon, headquarters and support personnel, including cooks, were called to reinforce the front.[11]

To Father Duffy, the lessons of the day's attacks were obvious. "Success," he observed, "is not always the reward of courage":

> Since 1915, no commanders in the [British and French] armies would dream of opposing to strongly wired and entrenched positions the naked breasts of their infantry. They take care that the wire, or part of it at least, is knocked down by artillery or laid flat by tanks before they ask unprotected riflemen to try conclusions with its defenders. When the wire is deep, and still intact, and strongly defended, the infantry can do little but hang their heroic bodies on it.

But he was only a chaplain. "The opinion of our Corps Commander, General Summerall," he admitted, "was the one that counted most."[12]

Summerall, unwilling to consider the possibility that the Americans might have something to learn from their war-wizened European allies, drew different conclusions from the day's events. With Pershing and other American generals, he had gone into the war with the assumption that spirit and drive won battles, and he was not about to change course now. He would not listen to any discouraging talk, and even tried to sweep it away by general decree. "There has been," he admonished his troops in V Corps, "a tendency to exaggerate losses and casualties" with expressions like "All shot to pieces," "Held up by machine guns or machine gun fire," "Suffered enormous losses," and "Men all exhausted." From now on, he declared, "officers and soldiers are forbidden to use such expressions in official messages, reports, conversations or discussions. They are generally misleading and always do harm. An exact statement of the facts will convey the necessary information."[13]

To Summerall's frustration, the decree did not expunge every iota of negativity. On one occasion, he visited a 32d Division command post and told the regimental surgeon a story about the cheerful, smiling soldiers he had encountered near the front. The doctor, knowing that the men Summerall had seen were only replacements new to the battle, countered angrily that the frontline troops were tired, filthy, and sick, with trench foot and "full of vermin." Their morale, he declared, was "absolutely gone." "Well," Summerall responded drily before turning away in disgust, "you had better capitulate to the Germans."[14] Nothing was fit to enter the general's ears except talk of attack and victory.

On the evening of the fifteenth, Summerall swept into divisional headquarters and demanded to know why the 83d Brigade had not advanced. Finding the response not to his liking—"he wanted results, no matter how many men were killed," said Father Duffy—he relieved Lenihan, Harry Mitchell, and some junior officers on the spot. Then he snatched up the phone and called MacArthur. The 84th Brigade had not done much better than the 83d, he said; it must take the Côte de Châtillon by the evening of the next day. MacArthur, knowing what Summerall wanted to hear, replied that the 84th would take the hill on time, "or report a casualty list of 6,000 dead. That will include me."[15] Summerall shed no tears this time, but he left MacArthur in command.

MacArthur's response had not been all bluff. He really did mean to launch an all-out attack on the following day, and to lead it in person. Journalists, already attracted by the brigadier's flamboyance, found his apparent indifference to enemy fire irresistible. At the end of one attack, two reporters met MacArthur at his command post in an old stone farmhouse and pointed excitedly to his sleeve, where a bullet had apparently passed through his trademark turtleneck sweater. "When did brigadier generals get to be expendable?" one of the newsmen gushed. "Well," MacArthur modestly replied, "there are times when even general officers have to be expendable."[16]

★

ONE week of fighting had practically wrecked the once-proud 82d Division. Each of its four regiments had been reduced by approximately two-thirds. The men were miserable and demoralized, with many sick from exhaustion, insufficient and poor food, and exposure. They had also run low on ammunition. General Duncan nevertheless ordered his men to attack, at 8:00 A.M. on October 15.

Lieutenant Herman Ulmer, commanding a company of the 325th Regiment in place of a captain who had just been killed, formed up his troops just before dawn. His regiment occupied the center of the divisional line, with the 326th on its left around St. Juvin and the 328th on its right midway between Sommerance and St. Georges. At 6:45 A.M., a barrage of high explosives and shrapnel fell on the American lines with a resounding crash. It was some of the heaviest shellfire Ulmer had ever seen, and it landed with a sinister purpose. Explosions cut off the three frontline companies on all sides, announcing a box barrage that prevented reinforcement or withdrawal. Then the German infantry attacked, two divisions aiming to retake St. Juvin and drive the Americans back across the Aire. Short of ammunition, the frontline companies held for as long as they could. Many Doughboys fought to the death, but eventually the companies dissolved. Some Doughboys surrendered; others scattered and ran.

With its front broken, the 325th fell back one hundred yards and occupied shell holes along the St. Juvin–St. Georges road. As they did so, the Germans took over the original American front line along the crest of a ridge and began setting up machine guns. Ulmer's men watched, helpless to respond. They had received no new supplies since using up almost all of their ammunition the previous day. When the Germans resumed their attack, there would be no way to repulse them. The 82d Division would be driven out of St. Juvin, and back across the Aire.

With nothing to lose, Ulmer decided to order a bayonet charge before the Germans could install their machine guns along the ridge.

> The signal for a charge was given and the line rose to a man—the men yelling like Indians and running toward the German line with the dash of sprinters. As expected, the Germans did not wait to meet us. Seeing a determination to carry out the charge, they turned and fled, leaving behind them besides their dead and wounded, seven machine guns well supplied with ammunition. These our men turned to good account, holding our line with this enemy material until more of our own ammunition came up. To me this was beyond all question the most thrilling incident of the entire war.[17]

The 326th Regiment and the 77th Division, fighting in and around St. Juvin, likewise repulsed the German attack, and the original front lines were restored. But the 82d Division had reached the end of its tether. Its frontline strength had fallen to 150 officers and 4,138 soldiers, one-third of its original numbers.[18]

★

THE German counterattack hit the Statue of Liberty Division's 306th Regiment with staggering force. Fortunately, the fields in the Aire Valley were extremely wet and the enemy artillery shells sank deep in the mud before exploding in geysers of mud, stones, and water.[19] The German infantry was bravely persistent, however, pushing some of the Americans all the way back into St. Juvin, and driving a wedge down the tiny Agron River west of town, almost all the way to the Aire. The Americans in St. Juvin, supported by heavy machine guns, eventually knocked the Germans back out of the town, and with elements of the 82d Division retook Hill 182. The incursion west of St. Juvin was more dangerous and had to be dealt with by a reserve battalion that attacked along the north bank of the Aire and broke up the German formations before they could dig in.

The German counterattack put an end to any attack plans on the right, but on the left the 307th Regiment continued with its own plans to cross the Aire and take Grandpré. Getting across the river here was only half the trouble. The town was a major strongpoint in its own right, far different from most other French villages. Built into the face of the Aire Valley's steep northern ridge, it had one east-west main street bisected by two other streets coming over the ridge from the north. Into the center of the town jutted a rocky promontory surrounded by thirty-foot cliffs and surmounted by a sixteenth-century château. The Germans had fortified the château and dug emplacements along the cliff, turning the promontory into a nearly impregnable citadel.[20] Even if the town along the river fell, the Germans could withdraw into the citadel and wreak havoc on the occupying Americans.

The first two assaults on Grandpré did not go well. At 7:30 A.M., after a one-hour artillery bombardment, the 307th Regiment's First Battalion moved toward the river through a thin mist. Machine guns and artillery pinned down the assault companies as soon as they reached the railroad cut on the south bank. The Doughboys dashed forward from the railroad in small parties and took cover in trees and bushes along the river, but try as they might they could find no crossing place. Twice, groups of brave or foolhardy Americans attempted to swim across the fifty-foot-wide and six-to-eight-foot-deep river, but each time the Germans shot them dead in the water. Another attempt by the Third Battalion at 3:00 P.M. also ended in failure. Enraged at the lack of progress, the regiment's colonel left his command post and stalked up to the railroad cut. There he called out the First Battalion's commander, Major Philip Gardiner, and relieved him for "lack of initiative." Gardiner's replacement, Captain Erwin B. Newcomb, had only joined the regiment a few days before.[21]

Scouts meanwhile roved along the river, and at 5:00 P.M. one of them discovered a fording place. Captain Newcomb immediately ordered several companies of his battalion to wade across the river at dusk and occupy a small island just below Grandpré. While they did so, the Doughboys along the railroad cut would fire to suppress the enemy emplacements in the town, including those in the church steeple and in a building with a large red cross on its roof. Engineers would move up after dark with lumber and build a double-plank footbridge. The Doughboys accomplished both missions successfully, but they were not yet done.

After the engineers finished the plank footbridge, Captain Newcomb sent more troops across it to reinforce the detachment on the island. The engineers then constructed another footbridge across the canal on the island's other side, thus establishing a link with the town proper. Lieutenant Frederick A. Tillman commanded the canal crossing and the night attack on Grandpré that followed. "It was so dark you could see nothing," he later testified. "It had began to rain. This did not make us any more uncomfortable as practically all of us had either waded the river or fallen off the bridge in the darkness. I personally had fallen in three times." The Americans nevertheless completed the crossing without opposition, climbed a steep clay bank, cut through a belt of barbed wire, and crawled cautiously toward the town's southern outskirts. The rain fell more heavily as the Americans penetrated the wire, muffling the sounds of the wire clippers. Amazingly, the German outposts still suspected nothing. Then a Doughboy lost his footing on the slippery bridge and fell into the canal with a resounding splash. A German sentry fired a flare, and the Americans froze. Tillman was sure the game was up: "I thought for a minute that all was over but our last stand and I aimed my pistol at the spot and waited. Every man froze in his tracks, the light fell almost directly over the ford, burned, and went out. We were safe and I passed a whispered order down the line and we moved on."[22]

It was 3:30 A.M., October 16. The battle for Grandpré, and a new, very different phase of the Meuse-Argonne offensive, was about to begin.

CHAPTER 25

*"Large Bodies Move Slowly, Though with Great
Momentum When They Start"*

Pershing relinquished command of First Army to Hunter Liggett—now a lieutenant general—on October 16, but did not leave without regrets. He had conceived the army, created it, nurtured it, and led it through three of the bloodiest weeks in American history. No wonder, then, that he had trouble letting go. For the first few days after Liggett took over, Pershing could not bring himself to leave headquarters at Souilly. Instead, he kept "hovering around" and "worrying everybody with endless talk." Finally Liggett lost patience and told Black Jack to "go away and forget it."[1]

Pershing's departure, however reluctant, allowed him to return to his strengths as an administrator, politician, and a diplomat. Many powerful men still wanted to divvy up the AEF, and only Pershing could fend them off. At the same time, he knew how to represent the army's interests to the War Department and the politicians in Washington, and ensure that it continued to receive the training, equipment, and supplies that it needed. Moreover, as commander in chief and a national military icon, Pershing would head the United States armed forces during the upcoming armistice talks and whatever might follow. If he could be tough with the British and French, people could expect him to be much harder on the Germans.

First Army also benefited from the change of leadership. As a battlefield general, Pershing had been mediocre. His management of the Meuse-Argonne offensive had been uncreative, and his understanding of tactics remained rooted in the nineteenth century. His obsession with the cult of the offensive had shattered several American divisions and sacrificed thousands of men for victories that a little creativity and forethought might have won more cheaply. True, the French had pushed Pershing relentlessly and demonstrated a wasteful disregard for American casualties; yet they would push Liggett too, without the same bloody results. Pershing and Foch agreed that First Army must drive forward without regard to losses, but Liggett, as events would prove, did not.

"Large bodies move slowly, though with great momentum when they start," the war correspondent Frederick Palmer said of Liggett, whose generous girth was legendary. "The sceptic's question about Liggett was whether or not he had energy in keeping with his mentality."[2] Everyone knew he was smart. He had the capacity for seeing all sides of a problem, grasping the essentials, and arriving at well-reasoned solutions. The problem was that he only solved problems after careful study and deliberation. His card playing in the first hours of an attack was symbolic of this. In the go-get-'em culture of the AEF in 1918, Liggett seemed out of place, an archaic behemoth in a youthful, fast-moving world. I Corps had done well under his command. But could he make First Army fight?

Liggett's first acts were typical of the man. Upon learning on October 12 that he would take command of First Army in four days, he had departed I Corps for an extensive tour of the front lines to inform himself of the "temper of the troops and their commanders."[3] He asked questions and gathered information, but came to no snap decisions. He threw no Summerall-style tantrums, and relieved no officers on the spot. Instead, Liggett listened quietly, even modestly, and then returned to Souilly to ponder and devise a plan.

First Army, he learned, was in sorry shape. On paper, it totaled over a million soldiers in seventeen divisions at the front and in reserve. Nearly one hundred thousand of those soldiers, however, were stragglers. Walking along roads, loitering at field kitchens and aid stations, stealing from supply dumps, and hiding out in woods, the stragglers reflected the army's abysmal morale. Clearly, firm countermeasures were necessary. General Bullard's solution had been to place "an unbroken line" of military policemen behind every one of his sanguinary attacks. Other commanders authorized policemen to bomb skulkers out of dugouts when they refused to leave, or sent stragglers to the front wearing humiliating placards. Liggett reinforced the police, established stragglers' posts on every road, and ordered patrols to scour the back areas for "strays and hideaways." But he also understood straggling as a symptom of a wider problem. After three weeks of terrible weather and some of the worst fighting that any American had ever seen, the

Doughboys had taken almost all they could bear. "Such endless hammering in bad weather was a terrific strain on young troops," Liggett concluded. "There was serious need for rest and reorganization."[4]

Pershing didn't agree with Liggett's conclusion. The *Kriemhilde Stellung* had been breached, he argued; now was the time to press the attack. But with what? Three divisions, the 3d, 5th, and 82d, had been reduced to about a quarter of their authorized combat strength, between four and five thousand men. The 32d Division, captor of Côte Dame Marie, had been reduced to a scant two thousand effectives. Three more—the 4th, 33d, and 77th—had been in the front lines since September 26 and were long overdue for a rest. The 29th and 42d, fresh a few days before, had been nearly crippled. Reserve divisions were moving up, but they could not take over the entire front at once. "It was essential," Liggett insisted, "to gather up the army as a team," resting, repairing, reorganizing, and refitting so that, in time, "our full weight might be felt in one concerted blow." He estimated it would take another two weeks before First Army could resume the offensive. Pershing fumed, but eventually relented.[5]

The two weeks would not be spent in inactivity. Local attacks would continue in order to secure good jumping-off points for the final offensive, which Liggett tentatively scheduled for the end of the month. The most important of those attacks would take place on the left, where the 78th Division, supported by the French Fourth Army to the west, would take over from the exhausted 77th and try to secure Grandpré and the heights to its north. This would have the double benefit of breaking the western branch of the *Kriemhilde Stellung,* and diverting German reserves away from the center, where Liggett intended to launch his large-scale attack. At the same time, V and III Corps in the center would clear out places like the Bois des Rappes, the Bois de Clairs Chênes, the northern edge of Bois de Bantheville, and especially the Côte de Châtillon, placing First Army in position to rip open the middle of the *Kriemhilde Stellung* at the appropriate moment. Finally, the French XVII Corps would continue attacking east of the Meuse, hoping to draw German reserves toward that flank and away from the center.

Liggett could take one consolation: on October 16, First Army finally reached all of the objectives that Pershing had expected it to take on September 26.

★

THE troops of the 26th "Yankee" Division, a National Guard formation recruited from the northeastern United States, were a little reminiscent of the

New England Minutemen that George Washington had encountered when he first took command of the Continental army at Cambridge, Massachusetts, in 1775. Like their colonial progenitors, the Yankees fought hard, but in their own way—under their own, pseudodemocratic form of discipline, and according to their own schedule. Outsiders who presumed to tell them what to do were unwelcome; only their own, New England–bred officers would do. Their commander, Major General Clarence Edwards, came from Cleveland, but the troops accepted him because his father had been born in Massachusetts. And his personality suited them. At West Point and in the army commands that followed, old soldiers said, he used to maintain discipline in his company by calling out the toughest man and beating him up in front of the others. The Yankee Doughboys called him "Daddy" and would do anything for him.[6]

The 26th Division's 104th Regiment moved into the lines east of the Meuse on October 16 as a temporary part of the French 18th Division, which was assaulting—although that may be too strong a word—the Heights of the Meuse to the right of the 29th Division. Thrown into battle with the same thoughtlessness that the French had shown toward the 29th Division, the Yankees attacked at dawn into the northeastern Bois d'Haumont. Sixteen French tanks supported the infantry assault, but within minutes all of them had broken down or been destroyed. Slaughtered by Maxims, the Yankee Doughboys could make no headway against the German defenses.

As Lieutenant Ralph Robard advanced at the head of his platoon, which had taken 75 percent casualties, shrapnel from a German hand grenade opened up a thirteen-inch gash across his spine. He crawled into a shell hole more than half filled with icy water while enemy fire scattered the remainder of his platoon. The cold water slowed the bleeding and kept Robard barely conscious. Then two Germans crawled into the hole. Thinking Robard dead, "for by this time only the ugly wound was showing above the water and I was lying head down with just my nose exposed for breathing purposes," the Germans opened fire on his men. The lieutenant waited for an opportunity and then turned, ignoring the pain in his back, and killed one of them. The other leapt on top of him, and the two grappled until Robard received a pistol shot in the shoulder and fainted. He never remembered whether or not he had killed the German before losing consciousness.[7]

Over the next few days the 26th Division's other regiments entered the lines, replacing the French 18th Division and relieving some elements of the 29th Division. In the midst of their preparations to renew the attack, however, Pershing relieved General Edwards, who had offended the commander in chief and many others with his independence and borderline insubordina-tion. This ill-timed move outraged almost all of the division's officers and men and threw its command structure into confusion on the eve of an im-portant attack. On October 23 and 24, the Yankees attacked toward Belleu Bois, Hill 360, and the Bois d'Ormont, making significant gains on the first day but bogging down on the second. Further attacks on the twenty-sixth and twenty-seventh likewise made little progress, although on the latter date Private Michael J. Perkins of Boston blasted open a German pillbox with grenades and rushed inside with his trench knife, killing several Germans and capturing twenty-five more, and earning for himself a Medal of Honor. By the time it left the front at the end of the month, the Yankee Division's official casualty count was 3,818.

First Army's straggling epidemic hit the 26th Division particularly hard, partly because of the heavy fighting and bad weather, and partly because of the departure of the popular General Edwards and much of his staff. Private F. C. Wilder of the Yankee Division's 101st Regiment tried to rest in an old, deep German dugout during one frosty late October night, but the lice, or "cooties," that swarmed over him and his three companions made sleep im-possible. Hoping to escape the vermin, Wilder went downstairs into the unlit bowels of the dugout. Hearing someone breathing in the darkness, he asked, "Who's here?"

"Are you after me?" the voice asked fearfully.

"No," Wilder responded. "Why do you ask?"

"Because I am hiding here. I have been here almost two days."

"What are you hiding for?"

"To be honest with you, I am afraid," the voice confessed. "I am from Company ----- and I know that this war is nearly over. I have been through the whole thing and have never been a coward before. But I'll admit that I am one now. I want to go back to the States and I know that if I go over the top again, I will be killed."

"Don't be afraid of me squealing," Wilder reassured the frightened sol-dier. "The best of luck to you."[8]

☆

THE 29th Division maintained a tenuous hold on Molleville Farm on the morning of October 16. A strong counterattack could have shattered the thin line of Doughboys clinging to the woods on the clearing's northern edge, but the exhausted Germans remained inactive. Instead, the weary Doughboys of the 115th and 116th Regiments, weak from lack of food and with swollen and bleeding feet, stumbled up the wooded ridge north of Molleville Farm for a few hundred yards into the Bois de la Grande Montagne. The woods' thickness rendered mortars and one-pounders useless, so the troops simply sprayed Chauchats and fired rifles randomly as they advanced.[9] At the end of the day, they scratched shallow holes in the mud and collapsed. Since October 8, the division had taken 3,936 casualties.

They stayed on that muddy, wooded hillside for another week. The Germans bombarded them endlessly, and the smell of gas that "made one yearn to vomit" mingled with the stench of corpses in various stages of ripeness. Food—when it arrived, which wasn't often—sometimes became contaminated with gas, causing dysentery. Desertion and shell shock were rife, and morale poor. Yet on October 23 the attack order came again, this time with the objective of taking the massive Etrayes Ridge just to the north. The 116th and 113th Regiments from left to right would advance in a northeasterly direction, in conjunction with the Yankee Division to the east and behind a massive artillery barrage.[10]

The Germans, as happened so often, seemed to know the Americans were coming. At 4:30 A.M., an hour before the attack, they dropped four to five hundred shells, half of them gas, on the area around Molleville Farm. Caught unprepared without their masks, dozens of Doughboys coughed their lungs out. And when the American artillery barrage began at 5:30 A.M., the Germans responded with one twice as strong, massacring the infantry as they waited in their jump-off positions. To make matters worse, the rolling barrage that preceded the infantry moved forward fitfully and sometimes fell on the Doughboys, forcing them to halt under fire. Fortunately the machine gunners made up for the artillery's ineptitude, firing three hundred thousand rounds and pummeling the enemy defenses. The Germans resisted stoutly at first with Maxims concealed in underbrush and on platforms in trees, but surrendered in progressively larger groups as the Americans advanced. Etrayes Ridge fell by midnight. The Blue and Gray Division remained there until the end of the month, when the 79th Division relieved it.[11]

✸

MAJOR General Hines, III Corps' commander, went to get a tooth pulled on October 20, while his 3d and 5th Divisions suffered terrible losses in desperate attacks against well-defended German positions. That evening, nursing his sore jaw at headquarters, the general looked over field reports and summarized the day's events in his diary. "Resistance is slight," he wrote. The attacks continued the next morning, and the Americans captured a few hills and ridges after further bloody fighting. "The men are now undoubtedly beginning to feel their own power," Hines wrote. On the twenty-third, the 3d and 90th Divisions—the latter having replaced the shattered Red Diamond Division—attacked again. They seized some positions that the Germans had abandoned and were stopped elsewhere by devastating enemy fire. "The Bosche is well sick of it," Hines wrote, "and has the peace idea so firmly fixed in his head that fighting seems to him useless."[12]

The Ivy Division took no part in these attacks. Devastated by constant fighting, it had departed the lines on the eighteenth. Old Fritz Wise, the tough-love colonel who had led Marines in Belleau Wood, assessed what remained of his command: "Smeared with mud from tin hats to shoes. Bushy, bristling beards on every face; full of mud, too. The same red-rimmed, burnt-out eyes I had seen come out of the Bois de Belleau. The only thing clean about them was their rifles."[13] Sergeant Major James Block imagined how civilians would react if the Doughboys could march down New York's Fifth Avenue looking as they did just after leaving the front lines. "I wonder," he mused, "if the plaudits of the multitude would be mightier than when they bade those men farewell, or if with mingled feelings of pride, of sorrow, of sympathy, of a fuller realization of the meaning of war, of a deeper sense of patriotism, that multitude would not look upon the scene in solemn reverence, too deeply stirred to give expression to their feelings."[14]

★

THE remnants of the 3d Division's 30th Regiment withdrew from the Bois de la Pultière on October 16, to be reorganized into a provisional company. Of its officers, only two lieutenants remained. But the division—according to the generals, anyway—still had something left to give. Two days later, it shifted eastward into the zone formerly occupied by the 4th Division. On the nineteenth, the 7th Regiment's First and Third Battalions merged into a provisional company totaling 301 men, and joined the remnants of Second Battalion to form a weak provisional battalion. General Preston Brown, the 3d Division's scrappy new commander, ordered the provisional battalion to launch an "at all costs" attack the next day. Its objectives, Hill 299 and the Bois de Clairs Chênes, had been designated essential jump-off points for First Army's full-scale attack at the end of the month.[15]

The attack jumped off at 7:00 A.M. Among the soldiers in the leading wave was Private Bill Houghton of Ansonia, Connecticut, whose company fought under the command of Captain Charles Harris. The baby-faced Harris was about twenty-one years old, reputedly the youngest captain in the AEF and also a good officer. At 7:00 he looked at his watch and motioned the troops to get moving. "O.K., men," he said, "we've got a job to do—let's go." The Americans spread out as the Maxims opened fire, and penetrated the woods in groups of two to three soldiers. At 9:00 A.M., they outflanked the Germans to the right and reached the woods' northern edge. The line was shaky, however, and when German infantry filtered in from the Bois des Rappes to the west, all formation disappeared in a free-for-all melee.

Private Houghton lost track of Captain Harris as men ran, jumped, and fought among the trees. Screams and gunfire drowned out words of command, and an officer had to grab Houghton and a buddy as they crouched behind some trees in order to make them know he was there. "Look, you two," he shouted into their ears. "There's a wounded man over at the other side of that clearing. Here are two Red Cross bands. If you put them on, take off your cartridge belts, and lay your rifles down, the Germans might not shoot at you. And you could possibly save the guy's life." "What the hell," Houghton and his buddy said. "Why not?" And they went. The Germans didn't fire, and they brought the wounded man safely back. Deciding they were good at this sort of thing, the officer sent them off again.

"Boys," he said, "I've got some very bad news. Captain Harris has been seriously wounded. He's in a trench by that road over there. The Germans have the route completely covered by machine-gun fire." Figuring that the Germans would be reluctant to fire on their own men, the officer gave Houghton and three other Doughboys some prisoners to use as stretcher-bearers. He was right, the Germans didn't fire; but after picking up the captain the party became lost in the woods and blundered on a large column of enemy infantry. Houghton's buddy tried a bluff that had succeeded before, with demoralized soldiers, and walked right up to the Germans, yelling "Hands up!" This time it didn't work. The Germans fired, and the Americans dropped Captain Harris and ran. After a while Houghton felt guilty and convinced another Doughboy to go back for the captain. The Germans captured them and forced them to carry the wounded officer back to their headquarters. Harris, dying with a bullet through the lung, looked up and said, "Houghton, I guess it's just not our day."

The Germans assigned a boy soldier about fifteen years old "with a grin a mile long" to escort them back. After a while, Houghton realized that he still had a large knife in his pocket and that the teenager was the only German in sight. He could easily have killed the boy and dashed for the American lines. A storybook soldier hero would have done it. Houghton didn't.

The real reason was I just didn't have it in my heart to kill a young boy in cold blood like that. I'd fired my rifle any number of times in combat, but that was different. All in all, I'm glad I didn't do it. There was only about three weeks of the war left; maybe the young fellow survived.[16]

✧

THE German infiltration from the Bois des Rappes eventually unnerved the Americans, who withdrew from the Bois de Clairs Chênes to their original positions. Furious at the retreat—they had been told to take the woods "at all costs"—the 7th Regiment's colonel, W. J. Morrow, gathered 150 engineers and infantry and led them straight back into the Bois de Clairs Chênes. Maxims and minenwerfers exacted a heavy toll, but the Americans recovered their line on the woods' northern edge by sundown. There they dug little strongpoints, beat off a German counterattack, and huddled down to spend the night. Hill 299, a pivotal height that commanded the surrounding area, still lay ahead.[17]

Major General Preston Brown threw everything into the attack the next morning, ordering the remains of the 7th Regiment, a company from the 4th Regiment, a provisional battalion from the 38th Regiment, three companies of the 6th Engineers, and the Seventh Machine Gun Battalion to take Hill 299. Colonel Morrow led the attack. "It was a job for no weaklings," a participant later stated; "no man who thought he was too tired, no officer who wanted to get to the rear."[18] Incredibly, the attack succeeded in capturing Hill 299, but then the Germans poured out from the Bois des Rappes, and the Americans in the Bois de Clairs Chênes began to retreat. Without quick action, the troops occupying Hill 299 would be cut off. There were no reserves.

Colonel Morrow gathered up the few remaining scraps of 3rd Division and took control of the situation. Shouting, "Come on, now, we're going back to the front. We're going to get the old line back again," he and some officers took sixteen runners and signalmen and started through the woods, picking up stragglers along the way. Like a magnet, he pulled the scattered Doughboys together and got them to repulse the Germans and reestablish their lines.[19] The Bois de Clairs Chênes and Hill 299 had indeed been taken "at all costs." The cost was the Rock of the Marne Division, which as a fighting formation had ceased to exist. The remnants hung on until they were relieved on the night of October 26–27. Since September 30, the division had taken 7,712 casualties—not counting stragglers.

Jack Barkley was one of the thousands of Doughboys who did not make the official casualty lists. Shortly after the capture of Hill 299, he collapsed in utter exhaustion. "Jesse and I had been sitting down for a few minutes, and when we were ready to go on I couldn't get up. My legs just wouldn't work."[20] His buddies carried him back to the strongpoint they had established in the quarry, and down the road past Montfaucon. Passing in and out of consciousness, he didn't know until much later that his part in the war had ended.

★

THE 5th Division had lost the Bois des Rappes, and General Hanson Ely, who took command of the division on October 18, wanted it back. A "blue-eyed man of massive physique, who met all situations smilingly and with a firm jaw," Ely was a fighter; he had commanded a regiment of the 1st Division at Cantigny, and a brigade of the 2d Division at Blanc Mont. His division was at only about one-fourth of its normal strength, and extremely tired, but the Germans were not much better off. Not relishing the probable results of a head-on assault against the woods, on October 18 and 19 Ely tried to take it with small groups of infantry. Each effort failed, however, and he finally decided that "only a direct attack could be successful in wresting the woods from the Hun."

The direct attack took place on the morning of October 20, when, after a fifteen-minute artillery barrage, a battalion of the 11th Regiment charged headlong into brutal enemy fire. The Americans managed to capture and hold a few yards of shell-shattered trees on the woods' southern edge, but suffered extremely heavy casualties. Ely now decided "that only a surprise attack could force the enemy to give up the place," and this time it worked. On the twenty-first, refreshed by their first hot food in a week, the troops of the 11th Regiment assaulted the Bois des Rappes after only a five-minute barrage. As luck would have it, the Germans had just inserted two new divisions into the line. The Americans caught them unprepared, capturing the entire woods along with 175 prisoners.[21] The 90th Division began taking over the lines that evening.

The Red Diamonds rested for nine days, returning to the front on October 29 with the mission of attacking Aincreville, by that time one of the last remaining strongholds of the *Kriemhilde Stellung*. In theory, the division should have recovered enough to carry out the attack without much trouble. But nine days had not been enough. Ely ordered the 61st Regiment's Second Battalion to take Aincreville in a standard frontal assault after a preparatory barrage, but the battalion's commander came up with a new plan of attack that took into account the shakiness of the men under his command. He told the lieutenant and sergeants of the attacking company to keep it secret from their men.

At 2:30 A.M. on October 30, one hundred men from Company F under the command of Lieutenant R. W. Young moved forward silently in two waves, without any barrage. The sergeants advanced with the second wave, making sure that the men went forward and not back. Lieutenant Young led the first wave until the enemy machine guns discovered it and opened fire. Yelling for his men to lie down and take cover, Young surreptitiously took a captured German flare pistol out of his pack and fired a green star-rocket. This, all his men knew, was the signal that the Germans used to call down an artillery barrage. Young waited, watching his men until their wild eyes and panicky movements revealed that they knew what the rocket meant. Then he yelled, "Beat it for the town, it's your only chance!" and frantically waved them forward. The ruse worked. Reasoning in an instant that the town's buildings offered their only hope of safety, the soldiers jumped up and ran pell-mell for Aincreville, taking out some machine-gun nests along the way. Young assembled them in the outskirts and made them take cover. At daybreak, they came out of their shelters and successfully mopped up the town, taking few casualties aside from Young. A German sniper killed him.[22]

✷

THE 90th Division entered the lines on October 22. Made up of draftees from Texas and Oklahoma—thus the initials on its badge, T.O., and its nickname, "Tough Ombres"—it consisted of the 357th, 358th, 359th, and 360th Regiments. It arrived in England and France in the early summer of 1918 and took almost two thousand casualties during the St. Mihiel offensive. On September 26 it had suffered another eighteen hundred casualties while making bloody and useless diversionary attacks in the direction of Metz. Transferred to the Meuse-Argonne, the Tough Ombres launched multiple attacks on October 23, 24, and 25, capturing the town of Bantheville and some surrounding woods, but the Germans drove them back from Le Grand Carré Farm after inflicting one thousand casualties.

Most of the German resistance that Private Vincent Reed and his comrades in the 358th Regiment encountered was from snipers. Private Jack Ward, a hulking Indian friend of Reed's, was on outpost duty when a German sniper bullet went through his helmet, grazing his head. Shouting furiously that "there ain't no Dutchman going to get away with that and live," Ward went out and killed the sniper.[23] Yet vignettes such as Reed's don't tell the whole story. Even a few days at the front in the Argonne could reduce men to living wrecks. Supply Sergeant Norvel Clotfelder of Mazie, Oklahoma, hadn't seen much combat by October 27, but that evening he wrote in his diary: "They (Germans) shell roads, bridges, and river every time. Germans have it over us on observation. One shell wounded three this evening. Have dysentery and fever. Am so weak I can hardly get around. Irregular meals, dead horses, bad water, insufficient covering, and constant nerve tension are enough to kill anyone. Have seen men so badly shell shocked that they could not be held still when they heard a shell."[24] Compared to most of the other First Army divisions, however, the Tough Ombres would be considered as fresh as daisies when the offensive resumed on November 1.

✱

THE weakened and demoralized 32d Division, which had taken an official total of 5,211 casualties since the beginning of the month, waited for relief until October 19 and 20, when the 89th "Middle West" Division replaced it at the front. The 89th consisted of regular army soldiers and draftees from Arizona, Colorado, Kansas, Missouri, Nebraska, New Mexico, and South Dakota, and was arranged into the 353d, 354th, 355th, and 356th Regiments. It had arrived in England in the early summer of 1918, and participated in the St. Mihiel offensive. With the 90th Division it had launched diversionary attacks in that sector on September 26 and suffered fourteen hundred casualties. Its commander, Major General William Wright, took command of the division just before St. Mihiel. He had attended West Point without graduating, and was a good officer with an affinity for leading from the front. Some considered his division, along with the 1st, 2d, and 42d, to be among the best divisions in the AEF.[25]

The Middle West's assignment, to clear the Bois de Bantheville, was extremely difficult. The Germans had it filled with machine-gun nests, and although Wright's men handled them carefully, taking them out one at a time rather than in costly frontal assaults, the enemy was a past master at this sort of game. Every night, German soldiers infiltrated into woods that the Americans thought they had captured, and fired with rifles and Maxims into the 89th's flanks and rear. Wright often thought the woods had been cleared of the enemy, only to discover the Germans stronger than ever before. The woods did not fall firmly under the Middle West's control until October 23, by which time about fifteen hundred Americans had become casualties and "some of the bloodiest and most tragic pages in the history of the 89th Division" had been written.[26] The 89th's toughest battles, however, would not take place until after November 1.

✱

SHORTLY after midnight on October 16, General MacArthur personally led a reconnaissance to the German wire on the Côte de Châtillon. An airplane had detected a gap in the wire, and he wanted to know if his 84th Brigade could exploit the weak point in the morning. The men moved forward slowly, running at a crouch or sliding through the mud on their bellies, until they reached the wire. As the Americans scanned the enemy defenses, a German artillery barrage crashed down and forced them to scramble into shell holes for cover. MacArthur waited until the barrage had finished, and then crawled from soldier to soldier, hissing that they should follow him back to the American lines. When they did not respond right away, he assumed that they had fallen asleep from fatigue. Then he discovered that they were dead—all of them. Stunned but still determined, he made his way back to headquarters alone. "It was God," he later said. "He led me by the hand, the way he led Joshua."[27]

Major Ravee Norris, the Alabama officer who had condemned MacArthur's earlier plan for a nighttime bayonet attack as "nothing short of murder," came up with an idea for exploiting the gap in the wire. Hearing his commander, Lieutenant Colonel Walter E. Bare, discussing plans for attacking the Côte de Châtillon, Norris butted in. "I have been up there forty-eight hours! I am to make the attack! Am I to have nothing to say about it?" Bare asked him what he meant. "We will never take that hill by just attacking it from the front," Norris replied. Instead, while the artillery and machine-gun barrage kept the Germans' heads down, he and a hundred picked men would infiltrate along a hedge leading to the gap, and pass through it to another hedge running along the southeast face of the Côte de Châtillon. Then, when the barrage lifted and infantry launched the main assault up the hill, Norris's men would pop up and fire into the German defenders' left flank. Bare agreed with the plan, and after further discussion with Colonel Matthew Tinley, who commanded the Iowans of the 168th on the right, he modified it to involve simultaneous attacks on both sides of the Côte de Châtillon. The plan was complex, but it made maximum use of suppressing fire by Norris's men, machine guns, and artillery.

The artillery began shelling the Côte de Châtillon at about 10:00 A.M., and as the first shells exploded Norris's detachment, under the command of Captain Tom Fallow, ran along the hedge and through the wire. By the time the barrage lifted they had reached positions along the hedge's other side. Norris, following from a distance, fell with a bullet through the heel just as he passed through the gap in the wire. At the same instant, he heard three shrill blasts from Fallow's whistle. Looking up, Norris saw his men firing from the hedge and moving toward the Germans' flank. In a short time the enemy broke and fled, allowing the rest of the American infantry to cut through the wire and charge toward the crest.

The Iowans had meanwhile seized La Tuilerie Farm, pierced the German wire, and pushed up the hill, only to be driven back again. The Alabamans' success on the west allowed the Iowans to resume their attack on the right, and the two regiments, after fighting bitterly and beating off repeated enemy counterattacks during the afternoon, seized the hill. After it was over, a sergeant came down and found Norris still lying on the ground amid the German wire. "Captain we've got the hill," he yelled, "and a lot of these God damned Heines as well." Norris, who had spent several hours straining his eyes and ears to figure out what was happening, laughed with relief, his eyes full of tears.[28]

Among the heroes of the day was Private Thomas Neibaur, a diminutive young man from Sharon, Idaho. An automatic rifleman with the 167th Regiment, Neibaur reached the crest of the Côte de Châtillon and was setting up his position when a Maxim hit him through both legs. He nevertheless stuck to his post, helping to break up repeated enemy counterattacks, killing four Germans who fought him hand to hand, and capturing eleven prisoners. Most men just fought to keep themselves and their buddies alive. Sergeant Harold Denny of the Iowa regiment was with his men that morning, "expecting confidently to be relieved," when his company captain called all the sergeants to his command post and told them of the impending attack on the Côte de Châtillon. "I know it's tough that we've got to hit it again," the captain said, for he cared about his men, "but the brigade has been ordered to take the hill, even if it is wiped out in doing it.

"Now, men," the captain continued, "it's serious. We're going to have losses. We've only 85 left. We must keep casualties as low as possible. We'll advance one man from each squad at a time. I think that way we can hold losses to a minimum.

"Go back to your men and get them busy at something. Get them to polishing up their rifles, so they know that they'll shoot. Get them to digging to warm up and to take their minds off things. Get their morale as high as you can; we'll need it."

"It won't be very bad," Sergeant Denny and his comrades told one another, but they knew it would be awful. And it was. "After I had got back to the hospital the next day," Denny recalled, "I still heard the crack-crack-crack of the machine guns we faced all day, and could not sleep."[29] They had earned their rest. The Rainbow Division would not enter combat again until a few days before the end of the war.

★

AFTER the war ended, Colonel Walter Whitman of the 325th Regiment asked his officers and men to send him notes for a regimental history that he intended to write. Some of the material he deemed unsuitable for publication and scratched out. Among the unacceptable material was an account by Captain Bozier Castle of B Company, who complained of the "useless sacrifice of the lives of many of America's patriotic sons" during attacks from October 16 to 20. "The military government of the United States has nothing to be proud of because of victories won on the Meuse-Argonne Front," Bozier declared, "but because of the courageous and unskilled heroic efforts displayed by her soldiers, and that her numerical strength was greater than the effective bullets of the enemy."[30]

The generals had opinions of their own that they also kept to themselves. On October 20, the commander of I Corps, Major General Dickman, reported:

> The 82nd Division, as is known personally to the Army Commander, was not a well trained or well disciplined division when it was put into line. The dwindling away of the 164th Brigade to, roughly, 1300 men after one day of light fighting is also known to the Army Commander and is a further indication of the condition of this unit when it was attached to the 1st Corps. The fact that the division indicated strongly that it expected to be relieved due to hardships, losses and continual fighting, after it had been in action two, five, six and ten days, respectively, is a further indication of the condition of this unit when it was attached to the 1st Corps.

A division inspector reported on the same day that, although the fighting strength of the division had been reduced to three thousand rifles with lieutenants commanding some battalions, "the morale and spirits of the remaining infantry in ranks [is] excellent and unbroken and . . . they are still ready for a fight. The spirit, however, of his brigadiers and colonels was not so good."[31]

Not much remained of the All-American Division on October 16, but it stayed in the line, butting repeatedly against the German defenses around Champigneulle. Each time the Doughboys advanced with heavy casualties, only to be blasted back to their starting points by German artillery and counterattacks. Corporal Fred Takes was trying to sleep at 5:00 A.M. on the eighteenth when he received orders to attack at dawn. He couldn't believe it;

only thirty-five men remained in his company. And neither could his comrades: "We were all disgusted thinking they wanted to kill us all off. We were wet and cold as it had rained all night. The captain said he knew none of us was hardly able for any more scrapping. He said to go as far as we could and then get in a shell hole." Takes took the captain at his word. At H hour, feeling tired and weak, he and several other Doughboys plodded forward several yards and jumped into a shell hole, where they stayed until an officer rousted them out later in the afternoon. Thankfully, the attacks ended on October 19, and after another eleven days in the lines the division was relieved on the thirtieth. "Talk about a happy bunch," Takes wrote in his diary, "but we had to keep it to our selves, it wouldn't do to scream."[32]

☆

THE relief signal for the 77th Division came on the morning of October 16. The Statue of Liberty Doughboys, who had been fighting since September 26, gratefully marched away from the front lines—all except the 307th Regiment's First Battalion, which was too busy storming the fortified town of Grandpré.

Lieutenant Frederick A. Tillman's Doughboys had crossed the Aire overnight on two hastily built bridges, and after a brief scare caused by a soldier falling into the river they had cut through the enemy wire without being detected. They lay on the ground for an hour or two and tried not to fall asleep. As the first streaks of dawn lit the horizon, Tillman and the other officers roused their men and moved them into the town—the sentries and machine-gun nests along the river having already been quietly eliminated. As the Doughboys walked cautiously down a street, a German sentry bolted around a corner and ran straight into the muzzle of an American officer's pistol. Trading information for his life, the sentry pointed out his company's positions. Following his directions, an American platoon captured twenty-seven Germans before they left their barracks. Another American detachment was quietly establishing an outpost when a German machine gunner walked casually by. Yelling *"Mein Gott,"* the German whipped out his pistol and fired it at a lieutenant's head. Fortunately he was a poor shot, and the American ran for his life as the German emptied his pistol after him. The shots spread the alarm, and machine guns opened fire on Tillman and his men from three directions. By that time the Americans had entered the town at several points, and a directionless, chaotic street fight ensued, replete with grenades, snipers, machine guns, and close-quarters combat from house to house.[33]

The Doughboys reached the main square at 9:00 A.M. Two hours later, they secured the streets leading east and south from the main square and the railway station. More savage fighting followed, as patrols pushed from street to street only to be sent tumbling back by showers of grenades. By early afternoon, however, the Germans had begun to crack. Some fled, and forty were captured; others, cowering in cellars and dugouts, were killed by American grenades. The citadel remained firmly in German hands, but that was no longer the 77th Division's problem. That afternoon, First Battalion crossed the little plank footbridges back to the south bank of the Aire. The 78th Division was taking over.

✳

At dawn on October 16, while Lieutenant Tillman led his men of the 307th Regiment into Grandpré, a courier stepped into a battalion dugout of the 78th Division's 311th Regiment and handed a message to its major. A few minutes later a captain came out of the dugout and passed the word for the men to prepare light combat packs, rolling the blankets seperately so that they could be ditched if necessary. "I think that's the order we've been waiting for," a Doughboy said.

"I agree," Private Earl Searcy replied. "I think we're in for it."

A lieutenant walked by. "We go over at 6:30," he barked. "Every man on his toes!"

"What's the plan?" the men asked him.

"Column of twos through the village, wade the [Aire] river, then form a skirmish line," he replied. "Those are captain's orders."

"How far away did you say the Germans were?" a Doughboy called out to the lieutenant.

"About a kilo," he replied. "See that hill? That's where they are. After we cross the river, we skirmish, then go for 'em."[34]

Searcy's outfit, the 78th "Lightning" Division, had been organized at Camp Dix, New Jersey, in September 1917. Commanded by a decorated Spanish-American War and Philippine Insurrection veteran, Major General James H. McRae, it consisted of draftees from Delaware, New Jersey, New York, New England, and Illinois—Searcy's home state. Arranged into the 309th, 310th, 311th, and 312th Regiments, the division sailed from America to England in June 1918. Trained by the British over a period of two months, it had been kept in reserve during the St. Mihiel offensive. The 78th sparred a bit with the Germans after that battle ended, but it remained green and untested when it entered the lines in place of the 77th Division on the night of October 15–16.

The Lightning Division had no opportunity to adjust to the front before entering combat. H hour, General Dickman decreed, would be 6:00 A.M. on the sixteenth. Guides from the 77th Division were supposed to lead the new troops into line and point out the German defenses and the routes of attack. In the rain and fog of the night preceding the attack, however, almost all of the guides got lost. The 78th Division's officers could not correct them, because they didn't have any maps. General Duncan, commanding the 82d Division, called up I Corps headquarters at midnight and suggested that Dickman cancel the 78th's attack. The infantry remained well behind the front, he warned, and the gas shells intended to play a large role in the preparatory barrage would not arrive until the seventeenth. But Dickman didn't listen. The Doughboys would just have to attack as they arrived.[35]

Both the 78th's objectives lay on the ridge above Grandpré: on the left, just above the town proper, the deep and dense Bois de Bourgogne; on the right, the smaller but very rugged Bois des Loges. The latter wood, according to a later observer, "might have been designed by the devil and handed to the Germans as a gift. It was a series of ravines, like a giant corrugated iron roof, thick enough to conceal machine guns and to protect the defenders from detection by artillery, yet thin enough to give them murderous fields of fire." Dickman considered it one of the most imposing enemy strongpoints on the entire battlefield—but he still sent his troops against it unprepared.[36]

The 78th attacked with the 312th, 311th, 310th, and 309th Regiments in line from left to right. On the right, the 309th and 310th arrived at their jump-off positions with only minutes to spare. Crossing the Aire on footbridges near St. Juvin, they advanced across the open ground below the Bois des Loges and Champigneulle. They moved forward in short rushes, and as men fell to long-range machine-gun and artillery fire, their neighbors moved over to fill the gaps. The enemy fire increased as the infantry approached their objectives, obscuring the lines with the smoke and debris of exploding shells for minutes at a time as the troops retreated downslope out of the clouds, then, rallied by their officers, turned and rushed back in. This went on for much of the day until the attack stalled, on a line parallel with Hill 182, north of St. Juvin.[37]

On the left, the 312th did not get in position until 2:00 P.M., leaving Searcy's 311th to go forward alone. The regiment departed Chevières, crossed the railroad embankment, and approached the Aire. As the troops looked for crossing places, they could see German dugouts and huts on the hillside opposite. American machine guns opened fire on these, hoping to keep the enemy under cover, but it didn't work. In an instant, Maxims opened fire from the

Aire's north bank. Private Searcy and his inexperienced comrades looked up in confusion; maybe, they thought, their own guns were firing on them by accident. It took them a moment to realize the truth, and for the officers to call their men back to the railroad embankment. By then, dozens of Americans had fallen dead or wounded. "Oh God, I'm shot," cried Searcy's pal Ervin, doubling over and clutching his stomach. He lost consciousness, but seemed to recover after a few minutes. "I'm sleepy," he called. Then, "I'm cold; cover—"and he was dead.

The Americans sheltered behind the embankment while officers debated what to do. The decision came in the same mold that it had for so many other green formations in the Meuse-Argonne: go over, attack, and win, whatever the cost. Searcy looked at the river where they would cross. A bridge had once been there, but the Germans had blown it up; all that remained were its shattered supports. The Doughboys would have to use these to steady themselves as they crossed, for the current was swift. The whole area was under German observation. "We've got to go, boys, that's all I know," the captain told Searcy and a friend, then admitted: "There won't be ten of us get across that river." Then, just before H hour at 3:00 P.M., a courier came with word from the battalion major to stay put until further orders. Relieved, Searcy and his comrades settled down "behind that friendly—a very, very friendly—railroad embankment in a comparatively satisfied and relieved sense of security."[38]

The 312th meanwhile moved into Grandpré. The 77th Division troops told their replacements that the town had been taken. They were wrong. Lieutenant Tillman and his men had captured only the east-west main street and the lower town, near the banks of the Aire. The upper town, extending along either side of the citadel, remained in enemy hands. Private Leonard Kurtz's regimental intelligence section had its hands full trying to determine a way to penetrate the upper town, and especially to get around the citadel. Every day he joined patrols, navigating by way of corpses—such as a dead German, staring glassily at the sky, that they dubbed the "Astronomer"—into the fields and woods to the east and west. But it seemed the Germans had every route covered. For now the Americans remained trapped in Grandpré, fighting house to house against enemy soldiers who crept down from the heights above.[39]

The attacks resumed the next morning, October 17. On the right, the 309th did not get going until late afternoon, so the 310th attacked without support on either flank. Fortunately, the recent heavy rains had made the fields so muddy that the German artillery shells buried themselves several feet deep before exploding. This helped minimize casualties among the assault waves, which penetrated the Bois des Loges about a hundred yards to an east-west road. Its success helped to distract the Germans from the Aire, where Searcy's 311th crossed one company at a time. Searcy's captain was sure they would all be slaughtered, but nevertheless led from the front as the Doughboys crossed, holding rifles above their heads with water up to their necks. Pleasantly shocked that the Germans had not resisted the crossing, the Americans let up a cheer on the far bank and then "drew up into one of the prettiest skirmish formations" that Searcy had ever seen. The regiment moved forward a little farther and then dug in along the St. Juvin–Grandpré road. Unfortunately, many of the troops had ruined their gas masks in the crossing, and died when the inevitable German gas barrage began.[40]

On October 18, the American artillery backed up the infantry by dumping thousands of canisters of phosgene gas onto the German positions, but to no appreciable effect, and the Germans replied in kind. Meanwhile, the 310th, supported by some companies of the 309th, continued its attacks into the Bois des Loges. The Doughboys started out about 1:00 A.M., moving carefully through the woods under brilliant moonlight and eventually reaching positions near its northern edge with light casualties. At daybreak, however, the Germans got wise to what had happened and laid an artillery barrage on the woods before launching a counterattack. Vicious fighting continued all day as some American companies clung to the woods' northern edge, while parties of German infantry and machine gunners moved down gullies on both flanks. After terrible losses, particularly in officers, the regiment withdrew to its original positions in the southern Bois des Loges.[41] Private Searcy had been pulled into reserve with the rest of his battalion, and did not participate in the 311th's attack on the eighteenth, which was just as well, for the assault went nowhere.

The 312th in Grandpré, meanwhile, tried to outflank the citadel to the left, where a narrow valley ascended to Talma Farm in the Bois de Bourgogne. French troops had taken the farm on the seventeenth, only to be driven out by a counterattack, so the Americans took a crack at it on their own. Two companies crept cautiously up the valley just after dawn, until they were three hundred yards from their objective. Then the fog lifted, and the Americans found themselves in a death trap. Maxims opened fire from above on three sides and cut the companies to pieces, killing or wounding all the officers and most of the men. The survivors had no choice but to play dead until nightfall, when they crawled back down the valley to Grandpré.[42]

The Lightning Division spent the nineteenth engaged in further bitter fighting in the Bois des Loges, with the 309th and 310th Regiments attacking repeatedly with heavy losses and little gain. The 311th drove a wedge up the open slopes between Grandpré and the Bois des Loges, capturing a strongly defended farm after a grenade attack and repulsing a counterattack. The problem now was the continued German possession of the citadel. From there, they dominated the lower town of Grandpré. They also could see everything that happened to the east, and their artillery and machine guns took the 309th, 310th, and 311th in constant enfilading fire from the left flank, making additional advance impossible. Major General McRae ordered a heavy artillery bombardment on the strongpoint, saturating it and the surrounding area with mustard and phosgene gas, which the Americans finally had in quantity. A predawn infantry attack into the upper town of Grandpré to the citadel, and around either flank, followed the bombardment. In Grandpré, infantry seized some houses in the upper town and audaciously tried to scale the citadel walls, but the Germans came out of their hillside dugouts and dropped an avalanche of potato-masher grenades on the Americans, hurling them back. On the left, however, the Doughboys successfully took and held Talma Farm. It would prove useful later on.[43]

Three days of rest and preparation followed, and on October 23 the Americans came again. McRae had given up on the Bois des Loges, withdrawing the 309th and 310th from there while some weary 82d Division infantry moved in to hold the line. He concentrated all of his artillery on the citadel, which the 312th attacked with every soldier it could muster. The attack, so brutal that it "could have been led by Richard the Lion-Hearted with a battle-ax," went forward directly against the citadel, and up the valley leading to Talma Farm.[44] Concealed machine guns in the Bois de Bourgogne caused terrible casualties, and the Americans became desperate to pinpoint their locations.

Private Kurtz, with bullets buzzing past him "like bees," had established an intelligence station in the farmyard, and some Doughboys brought him twenty terrified German prisoners. One of the prisoners panicked and ran, and the Americans shot him dead. Kurtz had the rest of them brought to him one at a time. Several burly Doughboys gathered menacingly about each prisoner as he approached, "to produce an atmosphere conducive to eliciting information." The method was crude, but it worked. Each of the Germans cried that while he, himself, was not a machine gunner—"they seemed to divine by intuition, or perhaps it was obvious, that machine gunners were not popular"—he did happen to know where the Maxims were located.[45]

Effective intelligence gathering such as this helped the Americans to extinguish the German nests one at a time. Slowly, methodically, the enemy defenses were picked apart, and finally an American platoon drove east from Talma Farm and reached the citadel. More Lightning Division Doughboys poured through the gap that the platoon had opened and cleared the Germans from the rocky promontory. The conquest marked the first major penetration of the ridgeline above the Aire Valley. Several more days of fighting followed, during which the 312th—which had taken 50 percent casualties—slowly worked north through the Bois de Bourgogne, but the western branch of the *Kriemhilde Stellung* had finally been broken.

With that, the final piece of Liggett's plan fell into place. First Army was in position for the attack that would end the war.

"The Americans Are Here. We Can Kill Them but
We Can't Stop Them."

—LETTER FROM A GERMAN OFFICER, NOVEMBER 1918[1]

The Central powers were crumbling. Allied military success in the Middle East, the Balkans, and Italy led to the surrender of Turkey on October 31 and Austria-Hungary on November 4; Bulgaria had left the war a month earlier. Germany fought on, but the kaiser's government was falling to pieces. Ludendorff resigned his post on October 26, and as the kaiser left Berlin for the Belgian resort town of Spa on the thirtieth, German politicians began discussing his abdication. The sailors of the German High Seas Fleet refused orders to put to sea on October 30 and prepared for mutiny. Civil unrest, inspired partly by the Bolshevik takeover in Russia, became widespread, and there was talk of revolution.

The German army too was in a dismal state. Its officers no longer believed in victory, and its soldiers were losing the will to fight even in defense of the homeland. On the western front, Foch's concentric offensive had enjoyed terrific success almost everywhere along the lines. In northern France and Flanders, British and Belgian forces—augmented by two U.S. divisions—had recaptured Lille and the Channel ports of Ostend and Zeebrugge, reaching the Scheldt River on October 31. Farther south, French forces liberated the city of Laon and drove steadily toward the German frontier.

Marshal Foch called a conference of the Allied military leaders at Senlis on October 25 to assess the state of the German army and discuss possible armistice terms. Field Marshal Haig, his usual skeptical, acid-tongued self, declared that although a "very great part of the German forces had been beaten," they could still pull back to a shorter front and make "a very effective stand." The British and French, he pointed out, were "pretty well exhausted," badly short of men and without replacements. With a cut at Pershing, who sat stony and impassive as usual, Haig added that "the American army was not yet organized, not yet formed, and had suffered a great deal on account of its ignorance of modern warfare . . . it requires time to get in shape." He proposed mild armistice terms, amounting primarily to a German evacuation of the conquered territories and Alsace-Lorraine.

Foch spoke in more upbeat terms. The German army had not disintegrated, he agreed, but it was nonetheless "thoroughly beaten." Over the past three months it had shed 250,000 prisoners and four thousand guns. As for the Allies, he lectured, "Victorious armies are never fresh. . . . Certainly the British and French armies are tired; certainly the American army is a young army, but it is full of idealism and strength and ardor. It has already won victories and is now on the eve of a victory; and nothing gives wings to an army like victory." His conclusion: "We must push it." Pétain agreed, and insisted that any armistice terms must include an occupation of Germany up to the Rhine.

Pershing spoke last. "There should be no tendency toward leniency with Germany and her Allies in fixing the terms of an armistice," he opined. The German army was "constantly in retreat" and showed no signs of recovering. The supposedly exhausted British and French troops were "now attacking with as much vigor as ever." Refusing to respond directly to Haig's remark about American ignorance of modern warfare, he added that the AEF "is constantly increasing in strength and training, its staff, [and] its services and its higher commanders have improved by experience." He agreed with Foch that Germany should be occupied up to the Rhine.[2]

Five days later, Pershing wrote to the Allied Supreme War Council and more vigorously expressed his views on how the war should end:

> It is the experience of history that victorious armies are prone to overestimate the enemy's strength and too eagerly seek an opportunity for peace. The mistake is likely to be made now on account of the reputation Germany has gained through her victories of the last four years. . . . I believe the complete victory can only be obtained by continuing the war until we force unconditional surrender from Germany, but if the Allied Governments decide to grant an armistice, the terms should be so rigid that under no circumstances could Germany again take up arms.[3]

The Allied premiers, who felt confident of imposing their will on Germany without calling for unconditional surrender, resented Pershing's intrusion

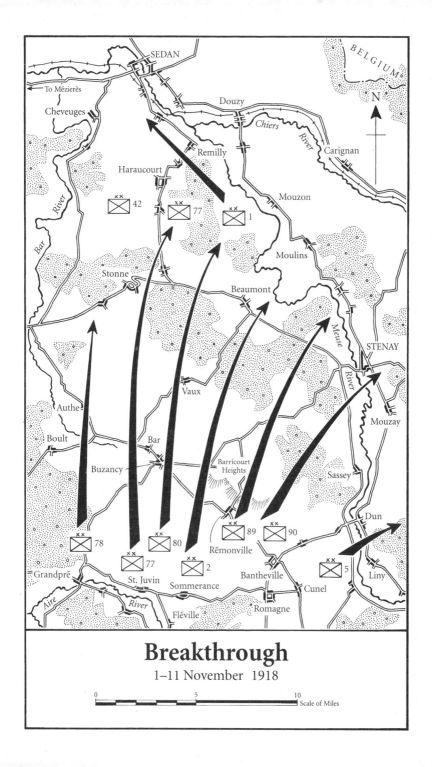

Breakthrough
1–11 November 1918

into political affairs. "Political, not military," Lloyd George grumbled. "Someone put him up to it." "Theatrical," snarled Clemenceau, "and not in accordance with what he has said to Marshal Foch." Advised gently by Woodrow Wilson's foreign policy adviser, Edward House, that he had indeed overstepped his bounds, Pershing did not press his political opinions further. Yet he also did not change his mind. "If unconditional surrender had been demanded," he stated in his memoirs published in 1931, "the Germans would, without doubt, have been compelled to yield, and their troops would have returned to Germany without arms, virtually as paroled prisoners of war." Then there would have been no German soldiers "marching back to their homeland with colors flying and bands playing, posing as the victims of political conditions."[4]

Booted out of the halls of state, Pershing nevertheless hoped to ensure that the Germans were beaten rapidly and thoroughly. To that end, he pressed Liggett to send First Army into the attack as quickly and as vigorously as possible. But Liggett, while agreeing with Pershing on the need to whip the Boche, was a much more methodical man. The jump-off for the final offensive had originally been set for October 28, but when the commander of the French Fourth Army begged for a postponement to the beginning of November, Liggett was "secretly delighted."[5] He had been working night and day, but there remained much to do before First Army was ready to attack.

Liggett's approach to preparing First Army began with the individual Doughboy. The confidence and aggressiveness that characterized the American soldiers in the days leading up to September 26 had all but disappeared by mid-October, as the swarms of stragglers attested. Hard fighting, poor supply, and bad weather contributed to this, as did a widening gulf between staff officers and common soldiers. Although the Doughboys had not by any means lost faith in their cause, many suspected that the staff neither knew nor cared what happened to them. Such beliefs were already widespread in the British and French armies. Liggett had no intention of allowing them to become so in the AEF.

Addressing his corps commanders on October 23, Liggett explained that "in the present operation our success is not so apparent to the lower ranks as they do not visualize the strategy of the whole front. Our immediate front does not appear to them a glorious success, especially in comparison with the advances of the other Allied Armies." The only way to make the soldiers see the big picture, he believed, was "by our higher commanders . . . gaining personal contact with the lower ranks and explaining to them the situation."

With this in mind, Liggett proposed a plan designed "to produce the desired psychological results for our next attack."

> I believe it would be well to insist that division, brigade and regimental commanders visit daily all of their lower units and gain more personal contact with the men. There is no question in my mind that the spirit exists to soundly thrash the German in our next attack. This spirit can be made use of if our officers will only appear more frequently among the men with the firm conviction of thrashing the German in the next attack.

Of course, just being there to hector the men with brave talk was not enough. Staff officers also needed to revise their tactics. There must be no more crowding men in the lines, no more mindless frontal assaults without regard to losses. America's manpower resources were not inexhaustible. Casualties must be kept to a minimum.[6]

Liggett's tactical plan for the offensive's final phase emphasized the concepts of fire and maneuver, and combined arms. In fire and maneuver, one group of infantry fired to suppress an enemy emplacement while a second group maneuvered to destroy it. Combined arms dictated that riflemen attack in coordination with supporting arms, including machine guns, mortars, one-pounders, tanks, artillery, and even planes. These concepts were not new. The U.S. Army had introduced and promoted them well before the war began. In the rush to create the AEF, however, young officers had received only cursory training in battlefield tactics. Moreover, the almost fanatical manner in which officers were indoctrinated into the cult of the attack subsumed older lessons that counseled forethought and patience. In the Meuse-Argonne, many Doughboys died unnecessarily because of foolishly brave officers who led their men head-on against enemy machine guns.[7]

In the two weeks' preparation allotted to him, Liggett could only remind his officers to employ better tactics. Many of them had already learned the lesson the hard way. By mid-October, veteran troops already employed fire and maneuver, combined arms, infiltration, and other tactics essential to the modern battlefield. Unfortunately, by the time the offensive resumed on November 1 even the battle-seasoned divisions had been heavily diluted with raw replacements, many only weeks removed from farms or row houses in the United States. Some of Second Lieutenant John G. Baker's worst memories of the war would be of "draftee replacements in the front lines . . . who said they had never fired a rifle and who didn't understand many simple commands and terms. I can remember lying in an exposed fox hole showing a fresh replacement how to put a clip in his rifle. Another replacement was confused by the order to 'fix bayonets.' A corporal saw him examining his bayonet, figuring there was something wrong with it." Officer replacements— "90-day wonders"—could be even worse than enlisted men, because they scorned advice and got other men killed.[8]

Providing the men with equipment proved difficult. Supplies of rifles, machine guns, and support weapons were only barely adequate. By November 1, the tank corps' complement of Renaults had been reduced to eighteen, and only 475 American and French planes remained combat ready. Ammunition, however, existed in ample supply, including—for the first time—gas. During the opening bombardment on September 26, there had been one American or French artillery piece per 14.7 yards of front; on November 1, there would be one gun per 20.3 yards. Each gun had fired an average of 188 shells on September 26, however, while 235 shells left each muzzle on November 1. William L. Langer's 1st Gas and Flame had only fired smoke on September 26, but on November 1 it received plenty of chlorine gas shells and fired as many as it could.[9]

The November 1 attack would also benefit from Billy Mitchell's changed approach to air tactics. Hitherto, he had concentrated his bombers against roads, bridges, railways, and supply dumps behind the enemy lines. For the new attack, he directed them to focus on enemy frontline infantry and artillery, in direct coordination with the attacking Doughboys. Liggett also demanded that division commanders make more frequent and effective use of the pursuit squadrons allotted to them, and ordered field officers to communicate and coordinate with the fliers. The Americans would not achieve aerial supremacy—the Germans still had plenty of planes, though not enough pilots—but at least the Doughboys would see as many Spads as Fokkers overhead.[10]

★

Foch and Pershing advised Liggett to make his main thrust on the left, in the I Corps sector from Grandpré to Landres–et–St. Georges, but he rejected the idea as "certain to entail frightful losses." The Germans had shifted most of their reserves to that sector in expectation of just such an attack. If the Americans *did* break through, converging enemy artillery fire could hit them from both flanks. Instead, Liggett decided that Summerall's V Corps should make the main thrust in the center, supported on the right by Hines's III Corps.

The capture of the main strongpoints of the Heights of Cunel and Romagne, including the Côte de Châtillon, Hill 288, Côte Dame Marie, the Bois de Bantheville, and the Bois des Rappes, had provided V Corps with excellent jumping-off positions. If Summerall captured one more major obstacle, Barricourt Ridge, he would rupture the central *Kriemhilde Stellung* and force the Germans to withdraw from before I Corps to the left and the Heights of the Meuse to the right. The plan looked doable, particularly since the recent strong attacks made by the 26th Division on the right and the 78th Division on the left had drawn German reserves away from the center and toward the flanks, as indeed Liggett had intended they would.[11]

From right to left, the attacking units would be the 26th and 79th Divisions (French XVII Corps); the 5th and 90th Divisions (III Corps); the 89th and 2d Divisions (V Corps); and the 80th, 77th, and 78th Divisions (I Corps). The main thrusts would be made in the center by the 90th, 89th, and 2d Divisions, particularly the latter two, which faced Barricourt Ridge. The 1st and 42d Divisions would follow in close reserve, prepared to support the expected breakthrough. Summerall, with his motto "We will go through," appeared everywhere in the days preceding the attack, racing from headquarters to headquarters and spouting slogans like "There is no excuse for failure," "No man is ever so tired that he cannot take one step forward," and "The best way to take machine guns is to go and take 'em. Press forward."[12] His methods may have been old-fashioned, even a little silly. But he got results.

★

DAWN broke "like thunder" on November 1, as artillery lieutenant Bob Casey's men dragged their 75mm field guns forward behind the advancing 89th Division. His gunners did not enjoy the advance. The Germans had shelled them even before they limbered up their guns that morning, and the fire intensified with every step forward. Half of Casey's men were already dead or wounded, along with many of his horses. Every little while a piece of shrapnel hit a horse, and the men stopped to unhitch the animal before moving on. The surviving horses had to pull twice as hard. Casey saw that one of the horses in the lead team was bleeding from six wounds. "He had lost an eye, the remnants of which hung in an oystery mass over his nose. I felt like shooting him but he was still pulling and we needed his help."

Topping a hill, Casey came upon the remains of enemy trenches that the American artillery—which included huge howitzers and railway guns—had demolished. They "were filled with a hash of blood and entrails that looked like the offal of a packing plant. There were no wounded men—few corpses that one could identify as such." The view ahead was more bearable, if not exactly attractive:

> The light had struggled briefly to penetrate the pall of battle and then had given up the effort. A cold white mist, choking with mustard, rolled northward with the wind. New shell craters added wisps of smoke to the noisome vapors. The sun hung like a red lantern over the woods. Ahead the entire panorama of battle was spread in the dim light—a line of infantry, slowly advancing in extended order. The line of the barrage was just ahead of them—plainly marked by churning earth, smoke puffs whiter than the morning mists, and the drums of melanite rolling and echoing.[13]

After a while Casey encountered a stream of prisoners filing toward the rear. As always, the German enlisted men looked haggard and happy; the officers, proud, clean, and professional. One young lieutenant stopped as the guns passed and rubbed his eyes in amazement. Seeing that Casey was an officer, he walked over and saluted. "Artillery here!" he said. "It is so hard to believe. I congratulate you on your men."

The two officers, American and German, stood together for a while, watching the panorama of war roll by. The German looked toward the horizon beyond the spire of Remonville, where the American artillery was butchering a column of his soldiers. "Excellent shooting," the German said with a specialist's admiration for his craft. "Your guns are marvelously accurate."

"Your artillery is pretty good," Casey responded. "We have just come through your barrage."

"You could never have come through your own," said the German. "I, too, am an artilleryman. . . . The war will soon be over, *Gott sei dank!*" With that, the officer saluted and rejoined the column of prisoners marching down the hill.[14]

✯

THE Doughboys jumped off at 5:30 A.M. under cover of the same kind of heavy fog that had screened the advance on September 26. Following a massive—and, for once, extremely accurate—artillery barrage, including plenty of gas, the infantry made rapid progress. The 2d and 89th Divisions made the deepest penetration in the center as they drove toward Barricourt Ridge. The 5th and 6th Marines led the 2d Division's attack, which passed through lines held by the 42d Division. Major Thomas Reilly of the Rainbow's New York regiment watched the Marines go:

> As the light came up and the mist cleared, it looked as if a volcano was riding right up the hill to the front. The Marine units just marched behind it in a line of skirmishers and the usual attack formation. I suppose, though, that coming through the woods and trenches must have broken it up as it didn't look any too regular at that stage.[15]

Reilly didn't get to see how the Marines could fight—and die.

Months of combat had hardened Private William Francis, a Marine scout from Dallas, Texas. When German artillery shells landed near him that morning, he only chuckled at his good luck, "for now, in a way, I did not care whether I was killed or not." He was equally casual with a German sniper who shot at him as he delivered a report, for "a man didn't pay any attention to being shot at these days." As he advanced across an open field with a company of the 5th Marines later that morning, however, a Maxim opened fire from woods five hundred yards away. There was no cover, and the machine gun "mowed the boys down as if they had been wheat before a scythe." The Marines dove to the ground and returned fire, but it was a long while before Francis could make out the German position. He pointed out the position to a buddy and told him to fire on it with his Browning Automatic Rifle, but the man was dead. Another Marine crawled forward to take the Browning, and was instantly killed. Francis kept firing with his rifle as Marines died one by one all around him.

Francis felt a bullet tear off the heel of his boot and turned around; the shot had come from another Marine. He also saw his captain with the second wave, paralyzed with indecision. What had become of all those lessons on tactics?

> We had a new Captain, it was the first time he was ever under shell fire, and he was nearly wild with nervousness, not because he was afraid but because he didn't know how to take a machine gun, or if he did he had forgotten how in the excitement.

Battle-seasoned Marines took control of the situation by instinct.

> After firing for quite a bit I crawled to my left into the woods and got a rifle grenade with the intention of slipping along the edge of the woods and firing at the Germans from their flank. In the meantime the company on our left had flanked the enemy while we were drawing their fire.

The German position was destroyed, and the surviving Marines, who had to be restrained from executing the captured machine gunners, continued. The company had been almost entirely wiped out.[16]

The Marines took heavy casualties in the first hours—almost fourteen hundred of them fell dead or wounded in the offensive's first two days—but after the first line of enemy machine guns had been breached enemy resistance crumbled practically to nothing. Advancing past Landres–et–St. Georges to Landreville and Bayonville, the 2d Division covered six miles and took the western slopes of Barricourt Ridge in one exhilirating afternoon. To the right, meanwhile, the Middle Westerners of the 89th Division broke through quickly, thanks in part to the bravery of Doughboys like Sergeant Arthur Forrest and Lieutenant Harold Furlong, who earned Medals of Honor by wiping out enemy machine guns. The 89th seized the crest of Barricourt Ridge by 4:00 in the afternoon. Several hundred German prisoners marched past Major General Wright's headquarters, including, he noted matter-of-factly, a woman in uniform.[17] The Tough Ombres of the 90th Division did well too, advancing about two miles to the eastern slopes of Barricourt Ridge at the foot of Hill 343.

✶

EARLIER in the war, attacking armies had trouble exploiting breakthroughs such as this. Lacking wireless communication, generals could not keep pace with the attack, direct troop movements, and employ reserves effectively. George C. Marshall, whom Liggett had appointed his chief of operations, adopted a novel solution to this problem. At First Army headquarters, groups of junior officers sat around and "bitterly bemoaned the fact that they were being denied the opportunity of taking part in the active fighting." Marshall decided to "give them a stomachful of battle" while at the same time attempting a little "experiment in communications." He selected several officers and provided each one with cages full of carrier pigeons. After a brief course of instruction in how to handle the birds, he sent the officers to the front with instructions to accompany the commanders of the assault battalions. Four times a day, the officers were to release pigeons to First Army headquarters with exact reports on the location of the assault troops and the resistance they faced. The officers took to their mission enthusiastically and released the messages as scheduled. Marshall relayed their reports to the corps and division commanders, thus helping them to keep in touch with the front lines.[18]

On the left, I Corps advanced only a short distance against strongly defended positions—as Liggett had predicted. Why the Germans fought so hard to defend the region was more than anybody could figure. Pounded by artillery and drenched with gas, it reeked with corruption and decay. Soldiers of the Blue Ridge Division, who had grown up in the beautiful rolling hills of western Virginia and Pennsylvania, were shocked by what they saw. "What a battlefield!" Major Jennings Wise exclaimed.

> The Kriemhilde Stellung had been torn to shreds by the American guns. Upon the fields, along every approach, and in trenches, still lay the dead. The whole country had been drenched with gas. Although the fields were sodden and every road-ditch was a running stream of water, the odor of charred things was everywhere as if the earth were still smoldering. One felt that all about him the hot breath of an unseen, evil power was fuming; and was glad for once that the rain was falling to destroy the hot poison in the air. . . . Amid the universal desolation one felt as if he were treading haunted ground.[19]

The Germans paid a heavy price to hold on to this little corner of Hell. Private Rush Young observed the toll as his reserve regiment moved up:

> As we advanced, the roads and fields were strewn with dead Germans, horses, masses of Artillery, transports, ammunition limbers, helmets, guns, and bayonets. The whole earth had been gassed by shells from our artillery. The small streams were flowing red with blood from the dead bodies of German soldiers and horses. They had been trying to take cover along the banks of the roads and streams. All along the road were bodies that had been half buried, some with their feet sticking out of the ground.[20]

Liggett, who had just been promoted to lieutenant general, didn't mind the lack of progress on his left flank. He had asked I Corps to "threaten furiously," nothing more. When Pershing complained, and Dickman seemed downcast that his troops had not advanced farther, Liggett consoled them. There would, he said, "be no enemy in front of that corps the next day, as the advance in the center would force the German to go north, and to go fast." He was right. That evening, General Gallwitz and the other German commander in the sector agreed to abandon the remnants of the *Kriemhilde Stellung,* and withdraw to the half-finished, last-ditch defensive line, the *Freya Stellung.* "Undoubtedly," Gallwitz admitted, "we had suffered a defeat!"[21] More than that; for the German army, November 1 had been a disaster.

November 2 ushered in the period of open warfare that the AEF had planned for since the beginning of the war. Now, theoretically, the individual Doughboy would come into his own and fight like Americans knew how to fight. But in most places the Germans ran too fast to be picked off by rifles or skewered with bayonets. Where the enemy did resist, he usually fired a few bursts from his Maxim and then packed off, leaving the Americans with empty dugouts—or nasty surprises. Nobody, the Doughboys learned, knew how to set a booby trap like the Germans. Such traps could be anything from rows of buried six-inch shells connected by trip wires, to spiked ceremonial helmets attached to single grenades. The Doughboys' passion for souvenirs was well known, and the Germans took advantage of it by booby-trapping Lugers, trench knives, backpacks, and other items.[22] They also poisoned food, or so the Doughboys believed. "On one occasion," recalled Captain William Reddan of the 29th Division, whose regiment had suffered badly under French command, "somebody found several tins of beef, Austrian rations."

> Having in mind the "booby-traps" it was thought risky to eat it; after considerable debate the suggestion was made that a can of beef be opened, placed on a mess tin and given to one of the French soldiers. If he ate it and lived all would be well. If he died? The only thing we could do for him then would be to see that he was given a military funeral. For the next few hours a close watch was kept on the "Frog." When there seemed to be no ill effects we started a small fire and for the first time in four days enjoyed a warm feed.[23]

The biggest advances now took place on the left, where I Corps pushed forward six miles as the enemy fled. Progress was slower in the center, where the 2d, 89th, and 90th Divisions struggled with supply-line traffic jams, disorganization, and somewhat stiffer enemy resistance. The most frustrating action took place on the right, where the 5th Division attempted to cross to the east bank of the Meuse in time to cut off the German forces withdrawing from the Heights. General Hines, commanding III Corps, had "forbidden the talking about peace in this Corps, impressing on the command that now is the time above all others to hit the Bosch hard, and that there can be no talk of peace or after war problems until the Hun is crushed." Tempted by the sight of slow-moving columns of trucks, wagons, and artillery withdrawing north along the road from Sivry-sur-Meuse to Dun, the Red Diamonds did their best. Scouts tried desperately to find crossing places out of sight of the German machine-gun emplacements that dotted the slopes above the river's east bank, but to no avail. Each time Doughboys swam the river the Germans fired flares and machine-gunned them in the water.[24]

Rain reduced vision and muffled sounds on the night of November 2–3, allowing engineers to complete a footbridge over the Meuse near Brieulles, opposite Liny. They finished just at dawn; then Red Diamond infantry dashed across the bridge to low, open ground between the river and a canal on the other side. The Germans detected the crossing as it began and directed machine-gun and rifle fire on the infantry. Trapped—the canal had not yet been bridged, and there was no way to get back across the Meuse without getting killed—the Doughboys and some of the engineers sprinted to the high canal bank, where they took cover. The Germans on the hills above could not see them there, but the Americans also could not leave the embankment without facing certain death. There was no way forward, either, for the canal was too wide and deep. Instead, the Doughboys worked north along the embankment for about six hundred yards, where they found the remains of an old iron bridge that the Germans had destroyed. On the other side, the Americans could see a three-hundred-yard-deep cove or indentation in the opposite slope. The cove was packed with enemy machine-gun nests; but once they had been gotten rid of, it would provide excellent shelter from the German emplacements farther up the slope to the north and south. The commanding American officer decided to bring up the engineers and build two parallel bridges there overnight.[25]

Engineers built the bridges during the night of November 3–4, while more infantry crossed the Meuse and crowded along the canal embankment. The engineers declared their work finished at 2:00 A.M., and an eight-man infantry patrol started across the canal. They had just reached the opposite side when the Germans woke up, firing from the top and both sides of the cove onto the footbridges and along the canal bank. The patrol clattered back across the canal, followed by a swarm of bullets. The infantry behind the embankment tried to silence the enemy in and around the cove, firing Stokes mortars and rifle grenades until their ammunition was completely exhausted, but the German guns kept firing. Finally the American commander, Lieutenant Colonel Courtney H. Hodges, ran along the embankment, ordering the Doughboys to stand up at a prearranged signal and open fire on the cove with every weapon they could find. All the commotion had fully aroused the Germans, however, and when the Americans opened their small-arms barrage, it seemed that every machine gun in Germany fired right back.[26]

The Americans hugged the canal embankment all day on the fourth, listening as their artillery shelled the enemy positions on the other side. The barrage lifted at 5:00 P.M. and the infantry, now reinforced to two companies, leapt up and opened fire on the cove while assault squads rushed the bridges. The upper bridge remained intact, but the lower bridge had been wrecked, forcing some of the men to wade waist-deep through the water over its remains. Shooting as they ran forward, the assault squads deployed on the other side of the canal and sprinted toward the cove. They stormed the bullet-riddled enemy machine-gun nests and butchered their crews. There was no opportunity to celebrate the establishment of the bridgehead. Shortly after the Americans entered the cove, a French barrage landed among them and caused severe casualties. Another four hundred yards upstream, meanwhile, another infantry battalion had crossed the Meuse and canal on a makeshift bridge of telegraph poles lashed together with rafts and duckboards. By dawn on November 5, the Red Diamond Division pushed an entire infantry brigade across the river at these two crossing points. The crossings near Liny continued over the next few days—Captain Edward Allworth won his Medal of Honor here by swimming the river under enemy fire—but the Germans held the Americans off for long enough to withdraw most of their men and equipment safely to the north.

✶

TWENTY-FIVE miles northwest of the 5th Division's crossing near Brieulles, the 89th Division reached the Meuse during the night of November 4–5 at the town of Pouilly. Corporal Rudolph A. Forderhase of the 356th Regiment followed a steep path that night to a hill overlooking the riverbank. He found his battalion assembled there under the command of Captain Arthur Wear, who was visibly upset. Divisional headquarters had been hounding the captain and other officers with angry questions and peremptory demands. Why weren't the troops advancing faster? Why hadn't more prisoners and supplies been taken? Why hadn't the river been crossed? The facts—that the men were exhausted; that they had been fighting tough rear guards without artillery support; that the Germans had destroyed the bridges over the Meuse and burned all boats and boat-building materials—meant nothing to General Wright and his staff. The river must be crossed, and immediately.

Captain Wear called for volunteers. The river had swollen beyond its normal banks, thanks to recent rains and obstructions that the Germans had placed downstream, and the water was cold and deep. But he needed someone to swim across the river and gather information on the strength and disposition of the enemy. Many men volunteered; Wear selected half, and watched them file down to the river. Then he and the rest of the battalion staff moved to the hill's summit to await the dawn. Several hours later, just as the sun appeared above the horizon, a few wet and exhausted men walked up the hill. They were all that remained of the patrol. The rest had either been killed by the enemy or drowned in the river. The survivors had been unable to gather any information of value. Wear listened to them silently and then walked away down the hill. A few minutes later, Corporal Forderhase heard a shot. Wear had killed himself. All he left behind was a note asking someone to write his brother and say that he was "weary and tired." The armistice was six days away.[27]

Wear's suicide did not dissuade other officers from ordering more cross-river reconnaissances over the succeeding days. On November 8, Sergeant Waldo Hatler of the 356th Regiment swam the river near Pouilly and returned with information that earned him a Medal of Honor. On the next day Private Harold Johnston, also of the 356th, earned a Medal of Honor for a similar exploit at the same place. These acts of bravery set the stage for the Middle West Division's full-scale river crossing on November 10. Several miles farther north, meanwhile, Sergeant Ludovicus Van Iersel, a native of Holland serving with the 2d Division's 9th Regiment, earned yet another Medal of Honor on November 9 by crossing the river at a damaged bridge near Mouzon and gathering important information.

Twelve miles northwest of Pouilly, the 77th Division reached the Meuse at the town of Villers before dawn on November 6, and attempted to establish a bridgehead on the other side. Second Lieutenant Floyd Smith of Detroit, a member of the 305th Regiment, arrived in Villers to find the engineers saying they could not build a bridge because of German machine guns on the opposite bank. Smith called for some American machine gunners to cover the engineers, and while they were setting up he decided to take a closer look at the German positions. He selected a crossing place near the remnants of a destroyed bridge, where the debris-choked water flowed below the Germans' line of sight. Smith and a sergeant hopped from piece to piece of the wreckage, carrying a two-by-four to cover the gaps.

Halfway across, Smith jumped onto some planking that started floating downstream away from the old bridge. With no way back, he slipped into the water and swam to the opposite bank. He found a ditch there and crawled in it for some distance before sticking his head up to look around. He found himself staring face-to-face with two German machine gunners sitting in their nest about ten feet away. Startled, the men surrendered. Smith then saw several dozen German soldiers in shallow foxholes behind some willow trees along the riverbank. Placing his prisoners between himself and the enemy soldiers, Smith stood up, yelled to the American machine gunners on the opposite bank, and pointed to the willows. The Americans opened fire and the Germans behind the willows fled, leaving the engineers to build their bridge in peace.[28]

✫

ELSEWHERE, the pursuit continued. By November 4, First Army had advanced thirteen miles against fast-weakening resistance. On the same day the Germans began a full-scale general withdrawal aimed at breaking contact with the American advance and establishing new lines along the northeast bank of the Meuse River below Sedan. On the fifth, Pershing threw Bullard's Second Army into the pursuit on the right, while Liggett's First Army continued to push the Germans back toward the northern Meuse. By the sixth, the spires of Sedan were in sight.

One of the most embarrassing and potentially disastrous episodes in U.S. military history followed. It began with a conference on the third between Pershing and General Paul Maistre, who commanded the French Group of Armies of the Center. Maistre's command, which included the French Fourth Army, immediately to the left of First Army, had been pursuing the Germans too; but it had not progressed as quickly as the Americans. It remained, consequently, farther away from the city of Sedan than I Corps, which looked set to get there within a few days. Technically, Sedan fell within the prescribed zone of advance of the French Fourth Army. But what if I Corps got there first? Pershing suggested to Maistre that in such a case the army boundaries should be ignored and I Corps should take Sedan. Maistre, according to Pershing, not only "offered no objection, but on the contrary warmly approved."[29]

The agreement seems innocuous enough at first glance. But Sedan was no ordinary city. In 1870, during the Franco-Prussian War, the Prussians had won a critical victory there, capturing the French emperor Napoleon III and destroying his army. They had followed up their victory by declaring the unification of Germany under the kaiser in the palace of Versailles, and by annexing Alsace-Lorraine. Another humiliation had come in 1914, when the German army seized the city a second time. For the French, a people always keen on symbolism, recapturing the city was an important matter of national pride. "To suggest that someone else take Sedan," a historian has remarked, was "very much as if Rochambeau had tried to shoulder George Washington aside at Yorktown in order to accept Cornwallis's surrender."[30]

For Pershing, however, capturing Sedan was also a matter of pride. In his memoirs, he stated that "it was the ambition of the First Army and mine that our troops should capture Sedan." But who did he mean by "First Army"? He couldn't have meant Liggett, who was not consulted in the matter, and who described the subsequent attempt to grab the city as a "tactical atrocity." He could not have meant Dickman, Summerall, or the other corps and division commanders, who were too busy with genuinely important tactical considerations to worry about symbolic victories. And he could not have meant the Doughboys, to whom Sedan was just another French city; all they wanted was to stay alive until the war ended. For Pershing, however, the capture of Sedan would come as the crowning vindication—the proof that all his labors to create First Army, keep it whole and independent, and guide it through the bloody battlefields of the Meuse-Argonne had not been in vain. It would also, from his point of view, mark the glorious, symbolic victory that America needed to put her stamp on the peace settlement and the postwar world—an "I was here" message carved into French soil.[31]

On the afternoon of November 5, General Fox Conner, AEF chief of operations, arrived at First Army headquarters at Souilly. His friend and counterpart, the First Army chief of operations, Colonel George C. Marshall, was there; but Liggett and his chief of staff, Brigadier General Hugh Drum, were away. Conner chatted with Marshall for about half an hour before declaring that Pershing wanted First Army to capture Sedan, and that orders to that effect should be issued immediately. Marshall, remarking that "this was a rather important order," called for a stenographer and dictated the following message from Pershing to the commanding generals of I and V Corps:

> 1. General Pershing desires that the honor of entering Sedan should fall to the First American Army. He has every confidence that the troops of the 1st Corps, assisted on their right by the 5th Corps, will enable him to realize this desire.
>
> 2. In transmitting the foregoing message, your attention is invited to the favorable opportunity now existing for pressing our advantage throughout the night. Boundaries will not be considered binding.

Conner read the message and ordered it to be issued immediately, but Marshall had second thoughts and suggested that he run it by either Drum or Liggett. Conner grudgingly agreed to give him half an hour. Drum finally arrived at his office just before the time expired, and Marshall showed him the message. Drum approved, and Marshall dispatched it. Liggett was neither consulted nor informed until long after it had gone out.[32]

First Army's divisions, meanwhile, had been shuffled somewhat since November 1. By the morning of the sixth they were arrayed, from left to right, as follows: 42d, 77th (I Corps); 1st, 2d, 89th (V Corps); 90th, 5th (III Corps); and 79th, 26th (French XVII Corps). The division nearest to Sedan, then, was the 42d; the French 40th Division straggled along to its left rear, across the army boundary line. Dickman naturally assumed that the Rainbow, as the closest formation to the city, should have the honor of capturing it. He issued orders to that effect, and by 4:30 P.M. on the sixth, troops of the 42d were marching past Chéhéry, just southwest of Sedan and two miles inside the French Fourth Army's zone of operations. The seriousness with which Dickman interpreted his mission came through in a message that the Rainbow's commander, General Menoher, issued at 11:00 P.M. to his officers and men:

> Orders from the 1st Corps are most positive and explicit that the pursuit be kept up night and day without halting, and that Sedan must be reached and taken tonight, even if the last man and officer drop in his tracks. If the troops have stopped for tonight, they will be aroused at once and sent forward.[33]

Officers accordingly woke up their tired men and goaded them on through the darkness: Sedan must be taken immediately!

Dickman, Menoher, and their officers and men did not realize how V Corps' commander, the hard-driving Summerall, had interpreted the message that Marshall had sent out on November 5. In his mind, the concluding statement that "boundaries will not be considered binding" could mean only one thing: Pershing had declared a free-for-all march on Sedan. To the division that got there first would fall the glory. Summerall's beloved Big Red One had been first in everything else, and he was determined that it should also be first at Sedan. At 2:00 P.M. on November 6, he appeared at the headquarters of 1st Division, now under the command of Brigadier General Frank Parker, and ordered it to march immediately on Sedan. It would, of course, have to pass through the I Corps zone to get there, but Summerall knew nothing of Dickman's dispositions, or even where the enemy was. Nor did he bother to inform Dickman of what he was doing. Parker, with slightly more courtesy, sent a messenger to I Corps, but he told nothing to Menoher or the 77th Division's commander, General Alexander.

The Doughboys of the 1st Division, far from sharing Summerall's craving for glory, were furious at being forced to march several miles overnight. The marches of the preceding days had already left them exhausted. They "plowed," said Lieutenant Colonel Theodore Roosevelt Jr., "like mud-caked specters through the dark, some staggering as they walked." Informed of Summerall's orders, they cursed heartily as they moved out.[34] The gap that their departure left between the 2d and 77th Divisions remained open. Summerall, with other things on his mind, did not take the trouble to call up reserves to fill it.

The officers and men of the 42d and 77th Divisions had no idea that the Big Red One was coming. Hearing troops moving in the dark where they had no right to be, sentries opened fire. The bone-tired 1st Division soldiers, who had not been told whether to expect friends or enemies, returned fire; and some substantial skirmishes resulted. Columns of infantry, artillery, ammunition, and supplies crashed into one another at crossroads in the dark, causing tremendous confusion. Everyone had his orders and was determined to get through. Wagon drivers cursed and lashed whips at one another. Men got into fistfights. It was as if I and V Corps had turned on each other and declared war.

General Douglas MacArthur, sporting yet another hole in the sleeve of his sweater from a sniper's bullet, and fresh from a feast consisting of "potato soup, potato fricassee, potatoes creamed, potato salad . . . finished with potato pie," was woken up in the early morning of November 7 by an aide. A regiment of the 1st Division, the aide said, was at that moment marching directly across the 84th Brigade's line of advance, between it and the enemy. Sensing that he would have to act quickly to prevent a debacle, MacArthur rushed forward to warn his men not to open fire. He then walked over to the 1st Division officers to exchange information. As they stood next to the marching column, MacArthur noticed a bedraggled Doughboy staring at him "in a rather wishful way." The general assumed that the soldier envied the Camel cigarette he was smoking and offered him one from a crumpled pack. Thanking MacArthur as he lit the cigarette, the soldier said: "I was thinking, if you had just a'bin a Boche general 'stead of an American one we would all of us got the D.S.C." MacArthur laughed. "If you don't get a medal," he said as he handed the soldier the pack, "in any event you do get a package of cigarettes." The Doughboy understood the relative value of things at the front. "To tell the truth, sir," he said with a grin, "I would rather have the cigarettes than the medal."[35] A little later, a 1st Division detachment, confused by MacArthur's unorthodox attire, decided that he *was* a German general and arrested him. It took him some time to explain his real identity.

Other officers and generals came close to getting into fistfights alongside their men. Told by a Rainbow colonel that the 1st Division was preventing him from carrying out his orders, Parker sniffed that "he intended to advance on Sedan no matter what the plans of the Forty-second were." Menoher and Alexander furiously demanded to know what the hell Summerall thought he was doing, and Dickman became nearly apoplectic, screaming over the telephone to anyone who would listen. For Liggett, the episode became "the only occasion in the war when I lost my temper completely." Around noon on November 7, someone called Liggett to complain about the 1st Division's antics. Flabbergasted, the general sped to I Corps headquarters as fast as his staff car could drive. He found Dickman and his staff in such a welter of anger and confusion that "had the enemy chosen to counter attack in force at the moment a catastrophe might have resulted." Recovering his temper, Liggett issued an order for Summerall to withdraw the 1st Division.

The order came just in time. Lieutenant Colonel Roosevelt, commanding the 26th Regiment, had followed Summerall's orders so enthusiastically that he nearly provoked an international incident. Declaring "that his mission was to enter SEDAN and unless orders were changed such was his intention," Roosevelt had plunged right into the midst of the rapidly advancing French 40th Division. The French naturally issued a "loud wail," singling out Roosevelt and declaring that if he did not get out of their way, they would open fire on his regiment. The colonel remained implacable, however, and had not Liggett ordered the withdrawal a serious fight might have developed. As it was, it took the 1st Division many hours to extricate itself from I Corps, during which time it and the 42d and 77th Divisions remained paralyzed and powerless to advance. The French, meanwhile, occupied Sedan.

Summerall, the author of 1st Division's boneheaded maneuver, discreetly absented himself from V Corps headquarters before Liggett could confront him. Later, with the big man safely out of arm's reach, Summerall claimed that he had only been following orders; after all, the November 5 order had said that boundaries would not be considered binding. To this disingenuous explanation, Liggett responded that "no reasonable interpretation" of the order "would permit of the atrocity of marching one division across the front of another in pursuit of an enemy." But although Dickman and others raged, calling for Summerall and Parker to be court-martialed, there was little that Liggett could do. Pershing, perhaps understanding that his fixation on capturing Sedan had helped to instigate the fiasco, shrugged the whole thing off. The officers and men in the line summed up the episode succinctly. "Someone was glory hunting," said Lieutenant Colonel Clarence Huebner, who participated in the 1st Division's march. "An army officer is dangerous when he begins to be a glory hunter."[36]

✦

On the evening of November 9, Foch wired a message to Pershing and the other Allied army commanders:

> The enemy disorganized by our repeated attacks is withdrawing along the whole front. It is important to maintain and hasten our action. I appeal to the energy and initiative of Commanders-in-Chief and their armies to secure decisive results.[37]

Early the following morning, Pershing forwarded the message to Liggett and ordered him to continue First Army's attacks all along the line. There must be no letup. Everyone knew that armistice terms were under discussion, but the results of those discussions could not be guaranteed. If First Army slowed down and gave the Germans time to recuperate and reorganize, they might decide to stall for time, prolonging the war for weeks or even months. Attacking now, so the thinking went, would save casualties in the long run. "Fighting," said Liggett, "was our concern and our only concern until we were ordered to stop."[38]

Abandoned by its allies and facing collapse on the western front along with revolution at home—sailors had raised the red flag in Kiel on November 3, to be followed over the following days by sailors, soldiers, and civilians in other ports and cities—the German government had decided to seek an armistice as quickly as possible. On the seventh, a German armistice delegation left Spa and crossed the battle lines into France. Two days later the dejected delegates stepped into Foch's railway carriage in the Forest of Compiègne and began negotiations for an armistice. "When I saw them in front of me, aligned on the other side of the table," Foch gloated, "I said to myself: 'There's the German Empire!' "[39] On the tenth the kaiser, told that his army and navy would no longer follow his orders, abdicated and fled to Holland. That evening the German government gave its delegates permission to sign the armistice, which they did at 5:10 the following morning. At 11:00 A.M., they agreed, all hostilities would cease.

The Doughboys' feelings veered between exaltation and heartbreak as the war's end approached. For the first time, they thrilled at the sight of clouds of friendly aircraft overhead, compared to only a few German planes; "at last, the supremacy of the air seemed to have been gained by the

Allies." They also learned what it meant to feel like liberators. During the first six weeks of the offensive, they had captured only blasted fields and forests, or crumbled and deserted villages. In November they marched through pristine towns and hamlets filled with people. After four years under German occupation, however, the villagers seemed stunned, uncertain whether to treat the Americans as liberators or enemies. As the 77th Division entered La Besace:

> Any large piece of white rag that could be found was floating above the house tops to mark the location of the village so that it would not be shelled. . . . As the shells crashed around the outer rim of the village the villagers retreated into the houses almost in a panic. The small population consisted of women, old men and very small children and it is quite possible that the fathers of some of those children may have been German. . . . These poor French people were uncertain whether or not to be afraid of us.[40]

With news of the kaiser's abdication on November 10, men dared to tell one another that the fighting would end soon. But the tragedies continued right up to the last moment. Many Doughboys would never forget those last-second assaults and bombardments that killed or maimed men before they could enjoy the fruits of a world at peace.

Private Connell Albertine of the Yankee Division, which on November 10 and 11 launched repeated and universally futile attacks in the woods east of the Meuse, watched some German artillery shells fall at the foot of a hill on the war's final day. Someone yelled, "Medical Corps men—litter bearers—hurry—hurry!" and Albertine ran over to see what had happened. A soldier had been badly wounded, and he died after they put him on a stretcher. Albertine and his buddies dug a shallow grave with their bayonets as a chaplain administered the last rites. They had almost covered the dead soldier when the Germans resumed shelling the area, showering the men with rocks, dirt, and shrapnel. The chaplain told them to clear out, and they left the dead soldier partially exposed, his toes sticking four inches out of the dirt.[41]

Private Henry Gunther, a twenty-three-year-old Baltimorean serving with the 79th Division's 313th Regiment, had "gotten in bad" with the officers and men of his company. For days, he had been looking for opportunities to "make good," but the Germans just kept running. They wouldn't fight and give Gunther a chance to prove that he was not a coward. More and more, he felt "a smoldering hatred of himself and the world," a conviction that others despised him, and that he could never redeem himself. And so, five minutes before 11:00 A.M. on the morning of November 11, he crawled ahead of his platoon toward a German machine-gun nest near Damvillers, east of the Meuse. The Germans shouted and waved for him to go back, but he kept coming, so they killed him. "There was," reported a *Baltimore Sun* correspondent, "a little more ceremony than usual to the burial they gave Gunther, because he had died making good. There could not be much ceremony to most of the burials that took place all the rest of that day and most of the next, because there were so many of them."[42]

Private Casper Swartz of the 314th Regiment spent the bitterly cold night of November 9–10 lying on the ground under two tattered blankets that he shared with two other soldiers.

> Well we almost froze, as the edges of the blanket that was not on our bodies were froze stiff, as our blankets were damp from the rain we were in yesterday, there were a few fellows so cold they could not walk at all, their legs seemed to be paralyzed—Us fellows that could walk, would take the guys by each arm and move them around until they could walk themselves—a few were hauled back to the first aid station.

The next morning he watched in horror as a German airplane swooped over his regiment, killing a wounded lieutenant lying on a stretcher.

> The Pilot had made several very low passes over us and trying to shoot us, he was so low, once he flew over, and when he passed where I was he leaned on the left side of the aeroplane, and he had a dirty smile on his face, he had a long slender face and dark skin like a good sun tan, he was only about sixty five feet above the ground flying just about fast enough to keep the aeroplane in the air. Our orders were never to shoot at an aeroplane [but after the wounded lieutenant's death] we took it upon ourselves and opened fire on him . . . do not know if we hit the pilot in any part of his body or not, he opened up his throttle and started to climb to higher altitude, the aeroplane left and did not come back any more.[43]

★

CAPTAIN Louis Gottschalk led a battalion of the 32d Division's 128th Regiment across a fog-draped field near Peuvillers, east of the Meuse, on the morning of November 10. Unable to see more than a few feet ahead, the captain and his men did not notice the woods encroaching on both sides as they advanced. When the fog lifted, it was too late. Maxims opened fire at close range from right and left, and as the Americans hit the dirt Germans attacked out of the woods. Gottschalk formed his men in a defensive perimeter, and for several minutes the troops fought point-blank and hand to hand, blazing away with rifles and Chauchats and hurling hand grenades. The enemy infantry eventually retired, but the machine guns in the woods kept plugging away, pinning the Americans down in the field.

Captain Gregory Dempsey, running forward with a message for Gottschalk's isolated battalion, was brought down by a German machine gun that raked him above the knees. Two of Dempsey's friends, Lieutenant Richard Mulcahy and Sergeant John Rasmussen, grabbed a blanket and dashed across the field to rescue him. Maxims cut both of them down. Rasmussen fell near Dempsey with a bullet through the leg. Dempsey warned him to keep quiet and still, but the panic-stricken sergeant tried to crawl and the machine gun finished him off. Mulcahy, lying farther away, called out in agony until midnight, when he died. Dempsey and most of the other wounded men remained behind when the rest of Gottschalk's battalion pulled out after dark; they were not recovered until after the armistice. Stretcher-bearers found Major Daniel Martin, who had been shot through the spine, and carried him off the field. "Think there's any hope for me or any use of carting a man around who is paralyzed from the waist down?" he asked them, and died a few minutes later.[44]

☆

THE 5th Division's 11th Regiment, which had crossed the Meuse and advanced rapidly northwest, attacked on the morning of November 10 toward the town of Louppy. Wading across a small stream, the Americans entered the town and found the Germans determined to defend it house by house. The Doughboys cleared them out and then stormed a château where the Germans had barricaded themselves in, armed with machine guns. Finally, after hand-to-hand fighting and serious casualties, the Americans captured the town and established a line on its north side. As they did so the German artillery bombarded Louppy and its château, setting several houses afire. The flames burned through the night.[45]

The next morning, November 11, Lieutenant E. P. Lukert joined the 11th Regiment's commander, Colonel Robert Peck, in the church steeple at Louppy. Peck, who had joined the regiment on October 30, had not participated in the terrible fighting before the Heights of Cunel and Romagne. He knew that the armistice would go into effect at 11:00, but had no intention of allowing the war to end without launching one last attack. To Lukert's horror, the colonel ordered the regiment to attack the ridge above Louppy at 10:30 A.M. With peace imminent, the ridge no longer had any tactical value. It amounted to nothing more than another battle honor for the colonel to boast about when he returned home. He would be able to tell his friends that he ended the war fighting instead of sitting on his hands.

A few minutes before 10:30, a German officer walked toward the American lines, waving a white flag. Speaking perfect English, he asked the sentries to lead him to their colonel. They did so, no doubt congratulating themselves that the enemy intended to surrender, but the German officer's message was different. "We wish to cease firing and avoid further bloodshed," he told Peck as Lukert stood nearby. "My division is four miles away—but I am ordered to cover that retreat and permit the removal of our material. This I must do, and will. I know you will attack in a few minutes—one grand finish so to speak, and I am prepared to meet you—on that crest." Pointing, the German declared that he had approximately sixty-five machine guns, all trained on the open ground that the Americans would have to cover. "They are laid and waiting to stop your advance up that hill," he said. "Will you come and cause more casualties, or will you give us a respite until eleven o'clock, when we can withdraw without further fighting?"

"No; is that so!" the official 5th Division history quoted Peck as replying. "Then that spoils all my schemes!" Lukert, who was there, only remembered him gruffly telling the German that he would "act as he deemed fit," and sending him away. In any event, the attack was canceled—due, in Peck's official report, to "heavy fog." Lukert "was darn glad of it. Instead we collected the dead—the last heroic dead—and buried them near the Church."[46]

✷

THE 89th Division spent the afternoon and evening of November 10 crossing the Meuse near Pouilly. As night fell, engineers dragged pontoons from their hiding places in the woods and tried to build bridges at the town, but without success; the Germans heard them working and drove them off. The colonel of the 356th Regiment decided on a different approach. Ordering some of the engineers to remain near Pouilly and hammer on boards as if they were still at work, he had more pontoons—"borrowed without leave" from the neighboring 2d Division—and catamaran rafts floated another two thousand yards downstream. There the engineers lashed the pontoons together and used them to ferry two battalions of the 356th across the river. For silence, the metal pontoons were covered with hay and wooden boards, and the troops made it across without being detected. By midnight they reached the heights north of Pouilly with almost no casualties. Elsewhere, a combined group of Marines and soldiers of the 356th crossed on a bridge without taking the same precautions, and took 30 percent casualties in the process.[47]

Corporal Rudolph Forderhase had crossed the Meuse on the makeshift ferry, and as dawn broke on November 11 he felt relieved that his officers seemed determined to avoid unnecessary casualties during the war's last hours. Wading across a shallow lake covered by a thin crust of ice, Forderhase followed his captain through dense fog that limited visibility to a few feet. Suddenly the captain stumbled into a pit, almost on top of two young German soldiers. They had anticipated his arrival by raising their arms in surrender. The captain ordered Forderhase, who spoke German, to ask them why they had not fired their Maxim. They could have killed dozens of men, and then withdrawn easily under cover of the fog. The Germans told Forderhase that they knew the war was about to end and saw no point in sacrificing lives needlessly. Other Germans were not so scrupulous, and the corporal saw several of his comrades and many enemy soldiers fall dead before the cease-fire order came.[48]

★

Iowa farmer Joe Romedahl of the 33d Division, now with Second Army, "lost all faith in the rumors about peace" after lunch on November 10, when the men of his platoon lined up and marched toward the front. They stopped briefly for supper at dark and then started out again, wading through knee-deep mud as they neared their destination. Soldiers of another division passed them going back and offered their pity. General Bullard, they said, drove Second Army as relentlessly as he had driven his old corps in First Army. He had ordered another major attack for the eleventh. Romedahl's unit arrived at the front at 3:00 A.M., many of the men crying with exhaustion after their twelve-hour hike. He had just fallen asleep when a sergeant shouted for him and another soldier—a Minnesotan named Torgerson—to occupy a shell-hole outpost in no-man's-land. They stayed there until dawn, wet, muddy, and shivering uncontrollably.

Returning to the main American lines on the foggy morning of November 11, Romedahl gobbled a can of corned beef and prepared to attack.

> Suddenly we were all ordered to jump out of our trench and start over the top. For some distance everything seemed to be quiet, but all at once the German soldiers turned their machine guns at us so we could run only a short distance at a time, then drop flat on the ground so the bullets would pass over

us (at least we hoped so), but I saw some hit the ground close to me and some just over my head.

The Americans sloshed across an ice-cold creek, where some became stuck in the mud with their heavy packs and had to be hauled up the opposite bank. As they continued they passed several wounded Doughboys who had lain there since a failed attack on the previous day. One soldier begged Romedahl to stop and help him back. He refused; the officers had told their men to stop for nothing.

The Maxims fired faster as the Americans pressed their attack. Every few feet Romedahl and his comrades dropped, took cover, and waited for the enemy fire to slacken before dashing forward again. Each time there were fewer soldiers than before. Romedahl had just dropped flat after one dash when he heard Torgerson groan several feet away. Turning, he asked the Minnesotan if he had been hit. Torgerson did not reply, but crawled slowly toward his friend. He died before reaching him.

Romedahl jumped up again at an officer's command and started forward. Hearing a cry for help, he saw another friend named Garrett stuck up to his waist in a mud- and water-filled crater. Romedahl took his hand and pulled him out. As he finished a Doughboy ran up, shouting that everyone had been ordered to fall back. Romedahl needed no urging, but turned and ran as fast as he could, Garrett gasping and staggering just behind. The German machine gunners could have cut most of them down, but they stopped firing as the Americans recrossed the creek and dove into their trenches. As they did so a big German shell landed nearby, shaking the ground and sending dirt and shrapnel flying in all directions. Garrett, soaking wet and covered with mud, went to pieces and started to cry. As Romedahl tried to calm him down he noticed some movement behind him. Out in no-man's-land, German soldiers were walking around and laughing, some of them hopping up and down and throwing their helmets in the air.[49]

✦

ARTILLERY officer Bob Casey, just promoted from lieutenant to captain, sat somberly with his battery on the morning of November 11, brooding over the men who had died and his own survival. At 9:00 A.M., a messenger reported that all firing would cease in two hours. Casey heard only sporadic firing in the distance and was happy to keep it that way. His own battery shut down at 9:45, and the men stood about, looking at their watches as the minutes ticked away. Fifteen minutes later, a whiz-bang burst at a bridge over a nearby creek, leaving seven bodies by the side of the road. Then the American heavy artillery decided to get rid of all of their accumulated ammunition by firing it at the enemy. The Germans retaliated, and soon the shelling reached an intensity that Casey had rarely seen before. He recorded the final minutes in his diary.

10:37 A.M.: "A shell just lit in the old sawmill. Men are out in the road running madly about. Other men are staggering out of the wreck and dropping as they emerge. Ambulances have stopped and litter bearers are on their way across the clearing. Twenty men killed—thirty-five wounded. The war has twenty-three minutes still to go."

10:38 A.M.: "An 11th F.A. kitchen is near the road to the south of us. The battery alongside our shack has dropped into silence when this new bombardment started. Most of the men had gone down to the kitchen for breakfast. A shell—short of the road—smashed into the soup cannon. Fourteen dead. Four wounded. In twenty-two minutes we shall have peace."

10:40 A.M.: "A crash almost at our elbows has shaken the whole hillside. At first we credited the disturbance to the Germans but the facts are otherwise. The heavies of the 11th have opened up again with maximum charge. They are seeking to pay for fourteen lives. There is quite a jamboree about the 155 gun pits. Adjutants, majors, and volunteer workers of all ranks are howling 'cease firing.' Nobody pays any attention to them."

10:59 A.M.: "The guns are so hot that the paint is rising from them in blisters. The crews are sweating despite the autumn chill of the air. To them the peace approaches as a regrettable interruption."

11:00 A.M.: "The silence is oppressive. It weighs in on one's eardrums."[50]

★

BUGLER Wayne DeSilvey of the 28th Division, fighting in Bullard's Second Army near St. Mihiel, experienced "absolutely the worst shell fire I have ever been under" from midnight until eleven o'clock. During the last twenty minutes, it seemed like more men died than during any other day in the entire war. Wounded by shrapnel just before the end, he lay untended on the battlefield for two hours before receiving aid.[51] The shelling made Corporal Harold Pierce, also with the 28th Division, sick at heart. "It seems so foolish," he wrote, "to keep up the killing till the last minute. But the killing the artillery does is so impersonal and miles away. He cannot see the tortured, horrible looks of the slaughtered or feel the remorse the doughboy feels when he sees a man he has shot. I stay close to a hole, filled with horror at the thought of being killed at the last minute." As the shelling continued to intensify,

Pierce lost faith in all the talk about peace. Using a German watch, he counted down the minutes to 11:00, but as the hour passed the firing continued. Disheartened, he decided that the war would go on forever. As his watch marked 11:20, however, the firing diminished, "like machinery in a large factory suddenly being shut off, gradually, a few last scattering shots, a last shot, then a strange hushed stillness, a peculiar feeling too sudden to be real." His watch was twenty minutes fast.

The troops did not welcome the arrival of peace with any cheering or demonstrations of joy. Instead they walked about silently, as if stunned:

> Men at the guns leave the pieces hot from the final barrage and sit down. Doughboys in dugouts and shell holes emerge cautiously, unbelievingly. . . . Outside of saying we hope it is really true we talk little of the Armistice. It may only be for a few days anyhow and the war will be on again in all its cruelty. It is too unreal, a battery is likely [to] start at any time and wake us from this dream.[52]

Will Schellberg, who had nearly been killed by an exploding shell at 10:30 A.M., thought that he "was in heaven or dreaming."[53] "We hardly knew what to do with ourselves for a while," recalled Private Robert Dwight; "it seemed rather queer to not hear the screech of a shell or the sharp reports of rifles and machine guns."[54] It took time, sometimes hours or days, for the Doughboys to get over the feeling of paralysis and disbelief. "What's an armistice?" asked Jack Barkley.

> It sounded like some kind of a machine to me. The other boys around didn't know what it meant either. That was one thing we hadn't heard any rumors about. We figured out after a while that it had something to do with fighting, but we thought it was a kind of temporary pause, like a truce. When the official word came through that it meant peace, we couldn't believe it. Finally Jesse said, "Well, kid, I guess it really does mean the war is over." I said, "I just can't believe it's true." But it was.[55]

Then curiosity took hold. Orders against fraternization had gone out, but the sight of Germans shouting and dancing in no-man's-land was too much for many Doughboys to resist, and they went out to meet their erstwhile enemies. Joe Romedahl's outfit helped the Germans to collect wounded from both sides and then joined them in building a bonfire: "We stood around it together to try and dry our clothes and keep warm, while our rifles and bayonets lay on the ground. Just a little while before, we had been trying to kill one another; but now everyone was so glad that the war was over that we forgot all about it."[56] Knowing the Americans' passion for souvenirs, the Germans gladly offered helmets, Lugers, and various trinkets in exchange for cigarettes and food. Suspicions died slowly for some. One German soldier offered a watch to Private Casper Swartz and his friends:

> The first guy he offered it to would not accept it, he was afraid of it, as he thought it was a booby-trap—then he offered the watch to another guy and he didn't want to take it, he too thought it was a booby-trap, the fellow asked the German why he wanted to give the watch away, he said "I am so glad the war is over and that he wanted to go back home, and this is the only thing that I can give in appreciation of what has happened, the war is over." Then they asked him to open the watch front and back, so if it was intended to explode when opened, it could explode in the Dutchman's hands, the watch did not explode, so one of our fellows accepted the watch.[57]

Other Americans had lost their taste for souvenirs. On leaving the front some weeks before, Sergeant William Triplet of the 35th Division had absentmindedly picked up a bullet-pierced German helmet. A pudgy Red Cross man—not a doctor, but a concessionaire of the type who sold nickel packs of chewing gum for a dime—saw the helmet and offered to buy it. Triplet handed it to him. "See here," the man said to his friend, "that's the coat of arms of the Fifth Prussian Guards. And look at this, that's one Kraut they can write off the roster." The two oohed and aahed at the blood and brains in the lining, and then asked Triplet how much he wanted for the helmet.

> I'd intended keeping it as a souvenir, the ancient head-hunting, scalp-taking, skulls-on-poles instinct that is so close under the epidermis of the most civilized men. But it had a hole in it, it was getting heavier, and was a damned nuisance swinging and bumping my leg every step. Also it would start smelling bad tomorrow.

"It's all yours, sir," Triplet said, and started to move on, feeling disgusted with the Red Cross man for wanting the trophy and himself for picking it up in the first place. Then the man held out his hand, and the sergeant instinctively took it. Finding a half-dollar coin in his palm, Triplet silently tilted his hand and dropped it in the mud. "Well," the man huffed as Triplet walked away, fuming inwardly at "that sanctimonious, philanthropic, bloodthirsty son of a slut thinking he could buy a helmet full of Hun brains with his profit from ten packs of Spearmint. Even in the American Revolution we were paying the

Tuscaroras five continental dollars for a British scalp. They bought ours for one pound sterling."[58]

✳

AFTER dark the Germans really began to celebrate, making use of the thousands of flares in their supply dumps. Private Swartz described the scene in his diary:

> We could see how we were surrounded by the Germans, when they set off the different signal rockets, it was a very beautiful sight, as they had a lot of different kinds. After the Germans were through celebrating we tucked ourselves in for the night, as we were not allowed to celebrate in any way, except dig in to hold our line, in case anything would start up.[59]

French civilians celebrated too, shouting, singing, and getting drunk. Sometimes American soldiers joined them. In one town, "civilians and soldiers joined hands and made an endless chain circling through town and I don't think there was a bottle of wine left in the town."[60] Others, like Corporal Alvin C. York, stayed away from the party:

> I don't know that I can jes exactly tell my feelings at that time. It was awful noisy, all the French were drunk, whooping and hollering. The Americans were drinking with them, all of them. I never done anything much. Jes went to church and wrote home and read a little. I did not go out that night. I had jes gotten back there and were all tired. I was glad the armistice was signed, glad it were all over. There had been enough fighting and killing. And my feelings were like most all of the American boys. It was all over. And we were ready to go home. I felt that they had done the thing they should have done, signing the armistice.[61]

Many thought sadly of lost comrades, the dead and incurably maimed. Minds moved back to shared laughter, hardship, fatigue, and terror that would both enrich and scar the rest of their lives.

Thoughts of the future, and how they would readjust to civilian life, kept other men silent. For George S. Patton, whose bullet wound on September 26 had kept him out of combat for the remainder of the war, news of the Armistice plunged him into a deep depression. In some doggerel poetry that he broodingly scribbled on Armistice Day, he contemplated the "festering sewer / full of the fecal Pacafists / Which peace makes us endure." In place of the martial heroes born in war, he predicted that "little lives / Will blossom as before, / Pale bloom of creatures all too weak / To bear the light of war." He could only look forward to the time when "The tuneless horns of mighty Mars / Once more shall rouse the Race. / When such times come, Oh! God of War / Grant that we pass midst strife, / Knowing once more the white-hot joy / Of taking human life." "War," he told Pershing, "is the only place where a man really lives."[62]

"When I Get Back, You Can Wager I Will Be a Home Loving Man"

In the 1970s, Henry Berry interviewed dozens of aged veterans about their role in the First World War. He asked one "very dignified gentleman" of eighty-two years for his feelings about the Meuse-Argonne.

"Now," the veteran said, "do you want my frank opinion?"

"Absolutely," Berry replied.

"Well, I think it was a fucked-up mess."

That, recorded Berry, "was the general opinion of all the men I saw."

☆

THE relief that the Doughboys felt on the signing of the Armistice and the conclusion of the Meuse-Argonne campaign did not last long. Almost immediately, their thoughts turned to one thing: home, and how soon they would get there. The fighting had ended. America's job was done. What were they waiting for? Surely the time had come to pack up, board ships, and sail back across the Atlantic. "From the moment the firing ceased," remembered Corporal Carl Noble of the 5th Division, "the boys' talk changed. Before this one might hear them say, 'If I ever get back to the States,' but now everyone was saying, 'When I get back.' . . . They began to wonder how soon. Some thought we would start at once and be back early in December. Others thought it would be Christmas time or New Year's Day before we saw the States again. I thought we wouldn't make it before February."[1]

Many Doughboys did not realize that the Armistice had not ended the war, but only suspended hostilities. In Foch's railway carriage on November 11, the German delegates had agreed to withdraw from all of the occupied territories, including Alsace-Lorraine. Their signatures also committed the German government to surrender most of its military arsenal, including artillery, machine guns, and airplanes along with thousands of trucks and railway carriages and—most humiliating—the bulk of the German navy. To enforce these terms, Allied forces would occupy western Germany up to the Rhine River. The final peace agreement would not be signed, however, until the conclusion of the Versailles Conference in the summer of 1919.

In the interim, the Doughboys had to wait. Some marched to join the Army of Occupation in Germany, where they spent the next several months coming to more or less uneasy terms with the German civilians. Others lingered at camps in France and Belgium, returning to the old routine of drilling and marching that they had endured months earlier. Crammed into unsanitary, overcrowded camps, where some soldiers died in training accidents and others fell ill with influenza, many wondered if they would ever make it home at all. With the worldwide epidemic nearing its height and over ten thousand Doughboys contracting the disease every week, men blamed the army for packing them together in unhealthy camps and thought ever more desperately of home.

British troops waiting for demobilization mutinied at Calais in January 1919. The Yanks might have done so too had they been forced to wait much longer. Sooner or later, however, the order came. Eight hundred thousand Doughboys were demobilized by the end of 1918, and another 2.7 million by the end of June 1919. Corporal Noble left France in July and arrived home in August, but there were horror stories of soldiers who were not permitted to leave until much later. Private Connell Albertine of the Yankee Division heard rumors of one soldier who had shouted "To hell with France!" as he boarded his transport, and whose unit had been sent back to camp. Terrified that the same thing would happen to them, Albertine's outfit crept aboard meek as lambs, even allowing supply officers to divest them of their prized souvenirs.[2] Even after their transports left dock, soldiers worried that they would turn back, sink, or—worst of all—sail to Russia or the Middle East.

Even as these fears dissipated, anything but a party atmosphere prevailed on the homeward-bound ships. Many Doughboys began to sense how far apart they had grown from civilization after days and weeks at the front. One Doughboy in Corporal Donald Kyler's company of the 1st Division had liberated a miniature dachshund from a German trench and brought it on board against regulations. An officer caught the soldier taking his dog for a surreptitious walk on deck after dark and placed him under arrest. He ordered the dog, a quiet, gentle animal that the Doughboys had adopted as a mascot, to be thrown overboard. The sight of the dachshund's pleading eyes as it swam desperately behind the ship led Kyler to question the savage discipline that he had once embraced as an enthusiastic young soldier. "In time," he mused, "I became what I thought was a good soldier. At least I became a fanatical one. But now . . . I know that I was not a good soldier. Not in a democratic sense. In fact, I had become as militaristic, or more so, than the enemy against whom we had gone to war. It has been said that we fought the war to make the world safe for democracy. But in producing men like myself, democracy was not safe. My way was the way that authoritarianism has followed throughout history."[3]

Lieutenant Maury Maverick, also of the battle-tested 1st Division, sat one night on ship in the officers' dining room as some chaplains discussed the war. One, who reminded Maverick of a baboon, spoke of the Germans as cowards, and another railed against enemy war atrocities.

> I got pretty well bored with this kind of guff and nonsense. I suggested that if our opponents were mere cowards, then we weren't such brave men for having whipped them. Then the parson, both brave and bold, stood up and pointed his accusing finger at me: "Do you mean to tell me that you admire the German fiends, the despoilers of women, the destroyers of churches, the Huns, the vandals—?" and so on, and so on. By that time I was sore. With barrack-room language, I repeated that the Germans were just as good soldiers as we were. I said something else about Christian preachers urging men to kill each other.

On arrival in New York, Maverick and some others were hauled before a colonel from the Inspector General's Department and charged with speaking "derogatory to the morale of the American troops." Fortunately, Maverick recalled, "the colonel had some brains. In about fifteen minutes he dismissed us all and told us to go to town and enjoy ourselves."[4]

Officers worried that repeated episodes of disobedience might lead to outright mutiny. Some placated the enlisted men with ceremonial acts such as the "death of Sam Browne," in which they shed the belts that had set them apart as officers. Secretary of War Newton Baker witnessed one such ceremony upon the SS *George Washington* as it returned from France:

> The ship's band one night paraded around the deck, led by some junior officers, bearing signs of a jesting and jocular character pertaining to the death of Sam Browne. As the band went by the officers joined the procession, taking

off their belts and carrying them in their hands. The several thousand soldiers on the ship saw the procession and cheered far into the night.[5]

For the most part, however, the soldiers had no gripe with lieutenants, captains, and even majors and colonels. It was the generals they resented, the men who had sent them into the Meuse-Argonne meat grinder, driving them forward in senseless attacks without thought for the consequences. Generals Bullard, Alexander, and Summerall were especially despised. Liggett, for all his evident concern for the Doughboys' welfare, rarely appeared in their diaries, letters, and memoirs. To the soldiers, he and his fellow generals were simply the men who had sent them to fight and die.

★

"GENERAL Pershing seemed to me to be the nicest, cleanest man I had met in France," Sarah Sand wrote after witnessing a review of soldiers and nurses in April 1919. "He fairly captured my heart with his careworn face and husky, much abused voice; he looked that day like a man who had almost reached the limit of his strength, although in passing down the line after line of men he walked so fast that the rest of the officers could scarcely keep up with him." To most of the Doughboys, he appeared as a stiff, distant figure—"that sonuvabitch," said one, who "roared past our column in his big staff car, spattering every one of us with mud and water from head to foot." He inspired no sense of loyalty, no enthusiasm for victory; he lacked, said the British officer and theorist B. H. Liddell Hart, the "personal magnetism which can make men lay down their lives gladly." The gulf between the general and his soldiers remained wide despite the efforts that he had made to visit the front during the fighting. His attempts to "appease" the Doughboys after the Armistice by relaxing army regulations were accepted without gratitude.[6]

Historians have been even harder on Pershing than the men who fought under him, deriding his leadership as "too narrow, too self-centered, too authoritarian, somewhat vain, lacking in flexibility and innovativeness, and bound by tradition and experience to the extent that he was unable to master the requirements of the modern battlefield."[7] His emphasis on training the Doughboys to use rifles and bayonets instead of grenades, machine guns, and other weapons of the modern battlefield has come in for particular criticism. "He thought he was spreading a new gospel of faith when actually it was an old faith exploded," said Liddell Hart. "That was the one flaw in the great structure he had built. It may even be said that he omitted but one factor from his calculations—German machine guns—and was right in all his calculations but one—their effect."[8]

Yet the criticism can be overstated. True, the lack of training in weapons, tactics, and combined arms had bloody results. Machine gunners didn't understand indirect fire; artillerymen didn't know when and how to use high explosives, shrapnel, smoke, and gas; and the infantry failed to coordinate effectively with support weapons, including grenades, mortars, machine guns, artillery, tanks, and aircraft. But it was not all Pershing's fault. Many of the AEF's problems in the Meuse-Argonne resulted from years of unpreparedness, and America's late entry into the war. In the desperate days of the spring and summer of 1918, there had been no time for training of almost any sort. The Doughboys not only had learned nothing about tactical concepts like combined arms and fire and maneuver; they also, in many cases, had not even been taught how to fire their rifles. For all the talk of rifles and bayonets, American rifle marksmanship was often quite poor. And even if Pershing had emphasized different concepts in training, it is unlikely that he would have been able to implement them systematically before the war ended. It is questionable whether the AEF in 1918 was capable of anything more than the clumsy tactics it employed in the Meuse-Argonne.

Nor, for those soldiers who did receive intensive training in rifles and bayonets rather than heavier weapons, was the effort always wasted. In places like the Argonne Forest, the Bois de Montrebeau, and the Bois des Rappes, combat had frequently degenerated into the kind of individualistic, soldier versus soldier fighting in which Americans had historically excelled. Critics of this style of fighting, moreover, were often visionaries who promised more of other weapons than they were yet able to deliver. Liddell Hart, like Patton, viewed the tank as a potentially decisive weapon, and lambasted Pershing for ignoring it; yet in the Meuse-Argonne the Americans had used every tank they could get their hands on. The Renaults were slow and mechanically unreliable, however, and with few exceptions they had little impact on the course of the battle.

Much the same could be said of the U.S. Army Air Service. Billy Mitchell's comments on the Meuse-Argonne dripped contempt for the infantry:

> The infantry on the ground just knocked its head against a stone wall. It was terrible for us to look down from the air and see the uncoordinated, not to say disorganized, nature of the combat which resulted from not using the airplanes sufficiently for reconnaissance. . . . If the Germans had had the power

of offense they had possessed earlier in the year, they would have cut our ground troops to pieces, but now they had not "got the punch" and were maintaining a passive defense, which was lucky for our army.[9]

Yet he too had failed to prove the value of his service on the battlefield. Mitchell always spoke of what his aircraft could do, but the troops never believed it. To them, the U.S. Army Air Service was a joke: afraid to confront the enemy head-on, and absent when it mattered. Mitchell countered—accurately, for the most part—that the infantry had not trained in signals and liaison, and knew nothing of aircraft. Yet the fliers also lacked training in air-ground cooperation, and Mitchell's own tactics, which concentrated his planes in mass formations behind the enemy lines, made such cooperation a tricky proposition at best. For their part, the Germans hardly noticed the American air service's presence until the last ten days of the war.

The Doughboys were quick learners, and despite the deficiencies in their training they adapted to the conditions of modern warfare in an astonishingly short period of time. During six weeks in 1918, they learned lessons on tactics and weaponry that had taken the British and French years to absorb. The sad thing is that it didn't need to take even that long. Pershing and his generals had bristled at British and French arrogance in presuming to teach them how to fight, but they might have done as well to ponder their own arrogance in refusing to learn. Allied lectures on tactics and weaponry were often delivered in insufferably hectoring tones, but they were well intentioned for all that. By 1918, the British and French had learned many painful lessons about fighting the Germans. But Pershing and his generals stopped up their ears. They charged into the Meuse-Argonne with all the élan of the French in 1914, and twice the stupidity. Thousands of Doughboys died fighting for objectives that could have been won at half the cost.

When Pershing spoke of a lack of initiative and drive in the European armies, however, he was correct in one important respect. The French army, shattered by years of horrendous fighting, had by 1918 lost most of its capacity to attack. Fearing a repeat of the 1917 mutinies, French officers did not push their men hard. Instead, as the Americans in the Meuse-Argonne witnessed on the right and left flanks, the French withdrew before determined enemy resistance. The Americans, young and naive, seemed by contrast only too willing to fight and die. French officers commanding American troops in XVII Corps east of the Meuse responded by treating the Doughboys as cannon fodder and throwing them into attacks without reconnaissance or support. This and other episodes of apparent French callousness—preserving their own lives while wasting others—convinced the Americans that their allies could teach them nothing, and vindicated their arguments against amalgamation. In a secret study, the AEF operations chief, Brigadier General Fox Conner, compared casualty figures and advances made by U.S. divisions under French and American command. "Under American Command," he concluded, "identical divisions advanced farther against greater resistance in less time, and suffered less casualties."[10] The lesson seemed obvious, and would be applied again in later wars: Americans were better off doing things in their own way.

✯

THE central question for Pershing and his generals was whether the Meuse-Argonne offensive had ended in victory. None of them doubted that it had. "The success" in the Meuse-Argonne, Pershing asserted, "stands out as one of the great achievements in the history of American arms." At the cost of about 122,000 casualties, including 26,277 dead, First Army had killed or wounded 100,000 Germans, taken 26,000 enemy prisoners, and captured 874 artillery pieces and more than 3,000 machine guns. It had defeated the German army so badly that Liggett, for one, was convinced that another day or two of fighting would have "reduced it to a mob." In forty-seven days, First Army had advanced all the way to Sedan, Mézières, and the upper Meuse. Had the war continued for another day, the Americans most likely would have occupied Longuyon, a critical junction of the railroad that supplied all of the German armies in Belgium and France. In sum, all of First Army's stated objectives had been met.[11]

The British and French were less impressed by First Army's achievement. True, it had met all of its objectives—but very late, and at terrible cost. The German forces facing it were wasted and demoralized—anything but the kaiser's best. Gallwitz, they asserted, had been fighting nothing more than a rearguard action in the Meuse-Argonne; and he had succeeded, preventing an American breakthrough until ten days before the end of the war. In Flanders, the British had faced even stronger enemy forces and advanced over twice the distance at half the cost. Foch, Haig, Clemenceau, and Lloyd George would offer the Americans flattery and praise, but nothing would convince them that Pershing's First Army had played anything more than an auxiliary role in winning the war.

Pershing was closer to the truth. First Army *had* won a great victory. Gallwitz's defense of the Meuse-Argonne, though brilliantly conducted, amounted to much more than a rearguard action. His orders were to defend the region at all costs. And unlike in Picardy and Flanders, where the Germans could afford to trade space for time, Gallwitz had little room for maneuver. As the last viable defensive position between Verdun and the north-south railway that supplied most of the kaiser's western armies, the *Kriemhilde Stellung* had to be held. Gallwitz's tools for doing so were worn, but far from blunt. Well trained, supplied, and equipped, the German artillery in 1918 was still the best in the world. The German air service, though crippled by a shortage of trained pilots, remained formidable as well. And the German army was no pushover. Even in October, with the war's outcome no longer in doubt, a sizable number of Gallwitz's soldiers remained willing to fight to the death. Masters of defense, the Germans used the difficult terrain and their plentiful machine guns and artillery to maximum effect. True, the Americans had taken far greater casualties than necessary, and learned many bloody lessons about twentieth-century warfare. But they had also occupied dozens of enemy divisions—the Americans said forty-four—that might have been used against the Allies in Picardy and Flanders.[12]

In the final analysis, First Army had not won the war, but it had appreciably helped to hasten its end, and it had accomplished the limits of which it, or practically any other army, was capable under the circumstances. That was much more than the French could have done in its place, and about equal to what the British could have achieved—albeit with a smaller casualty list. A more difficult question is whether the Meuse-Argonne was worth the cost. Did all those Doughboys need to die? The dictates of national pride, politics, and diplomacy said yes. America, Pershing and his countrymen believed, had to prove that she could stand alone and powerful on the world stage. Morality—according to some constructions, at least—also dictated that American soldiers must fight and die in the cause of right and justice. The Doughboys themselves never came up with one definitive answer. Some veterans believed they had fought the good fight. Others said it had all been a terrible waste. For most, it was a little of both.

★

"Our biggest conflict or engagement took place in the Argonne Forest, where a man's life wasent worth a nickle," Corporal Frank Schmitt of the 28th Division wrote to his father in December 1918. "Father dear I have seen Death in every shape and form during my seven months over here, imaginable, and have seen and been places, I shudder everytime I think of them, And have learned what a home and Life really means, and when I get back, you can wager I will be a home loving man."[13] For most of the Doughboys returning home, the old tales of patriotism, sacrifice, and eternal glory had lost their savor. Ernest Wrentmore, the boy soldier of the 5th Division, returned to America on a stretcher, a physical and emotional wreck with shrapnel in his legs and gas-scorched lungs:

> There was no glory. Instead, it brought to him a wounded body, and memories of sights that will always cause heartaches and tears. It brought him hardship and exposure almost beyond man's conception—hunger, cold, and sleepless nights, the sight of mangled bodies of friends and buddies; the knowledge of desolation; and the sorrow and agony that is the aftermath of war. It left him with memories that can never be erased—memories that bring, again and again, visions of an eternity spent in a hell on earth.[14]

Nurses like Sarah Sand also lost some faith in the ideals on which they had been raised. Shortly after arriving in New York, she and hundreds of her fellow nurses attended a play called *The Follies of 1919*. The play lightheartedly traced the experiences of a Red Cross nurse behind the front lines, and ended with her marrying and settling down to a life of happiness and tranquillity. Such tales might once have impressed the young women, but not anymore. The war, they knew, could never entirely be left behind them:

> Of course it was only a play. In true life the World War nurses could never entirely escape from the thoughts of their wounded and dying comrades who had started out so bravely to "Save Democracy for the Future" and who had taken part in this "War to End All War." We had stood by their bedsides in their misery and suffering and in spite of our best efforts, we had seen the light fade from their eyes and their bodies stiffen in death.[15]

The women who had served in France had all changed, but each in a different way. Nurse Mary Elizabeth Downs said that the war had made her "stronger physically, and broad-minded and in every way a success," but "in an unsettled state of mind." Edna Sue Gamage appreciated the need for "more efficient people in the world," and felt disgusted with the "smaller things of life." Pearl May Harris felt resentment at corruption, mismanagement, and sexism in the army. Sara Mildred Tucker simply learned to "appreciate our boys as never before."[16]

Men's politics had not necessarily changed. Some emerged from the war more conservative, and others more liberal. In the early 1920s there was a brief explosion of radical politics of both the right and left, with many veterans participating in both. There is no conclusive evidence, however, that the radicalism resulted from anything more than the unstable world politics of the time, or the temperament of youth. Most of the ex-Doughboys probably felt about as Republican, Democratic, or Socialist as they had before the war began. And their devotion to country remained the same. In Europe, disillusion—fed as much if not more by civilian discontent with the old order than by anything the veterans said or did—caused in many places a reassessment of the meaning and importance of patriotism and national glory. In America, no fundamental changes took place. Instead, there was a subtle perception shift, particularly of the meaning of the "social contract" between the soldier and his country.[17]

The Grand Old Flag remained worth fighting for; but the Doughboys' perceptions of how and why men should defend the country—and what they should receive in return—had changed. "Would you go again if necessary?" people asked Joe Romedahl. "The only answer to that question," he answered them, "is that one does not have a choice when our country is at war. We must go when we are called to help defend our country; however I would add that I would not go through the same experience again for all the money in the world."[18] In serving, most Doughboys believed that they had done the right thing, so that their children would not have to fight again. A crowd of civilians gathered around Corporal C. Earl Baker's train as it pulled into the station at Huntington, Pennsylvania, desperately seeking sons and brothers, husbands and lovers. Among the crowd was a family with a baby girl named Argonne in honor of where her father had fought, and a young wife looking for her husband. The woman went from soldier to soldier, clutching sleeves and asking, "Where's Tom?" "Has anyone seen Tom?" She did not know that he had been killed, and no one had the nerve to tell her. "We'd faced the worst the Hun could throw against us," Baker remembered, "but no one wanted to be the one to tell Mabel and her baby daughter that Tom was not with us."

> In the midst of our joy at being home, there was not a one of us who didn't silently mourn the comrades who'd gone west ahead of us. None of us had escaped without small wounds, gas inhalation or the emotional trauma they called shell-shock then. Most of us would suffer for the rest of our days with recurrent dysentery and nightmares. But the carefree boys of Company F had come home men. We'd fought the war that would end all wars. Little [baby] Argonne would never have to lie in a bloody trench.[19]

Nor, for all the horrors the soldiers had experienced, were all their memories bad. War, as veterans have always attested, is not without its redeeming elements. A one-armed veteran told Colonel Arthur Woods "what a terrible thing the war was, yet said that in some ways he had hated to have it end and to give up his friends and the spirit there was in his company. He missed the comradeship of it and the lift of it."[20] Alvin York, who loathed the war, nevertheless sensed that in some respects it had made him a better man:

> The war brings out the worst in you. It turns you into a mad fightin' animal, but it also brings out something else, something I jes don't know how to describe, a sort of tenderness and love for the fellows fightin' with you. I had kinder got to know and sorter understand the boys around me. I knowed their weakness as well as their strength. I guess they knowed mine. If you live together for several months sharing and sharing alike, you learn a heap about each other. It was as though we could look right through each other and knowed everything without being hid. I'm a telling you I loved them-there boys in my squad. They were my buddies.[21]

Over time, however, the Doughboys' pride in a job well done and fond memories of wartime comradeship became tinged with feelings of neglect. Thoughts that the government might owe them something did not at first enter their minds. Military service, Woodrow Wilson and his successors in the 1920s believed, amounted to nothing more or less than a civic duty. An unwounded Doughboy did not, by this view, require any pension to give his service meaning. On returning home, healthy soldiers received a discharge allowance of sixty dollars and the option to convert their temporary wartime risk insurance into permanent life insurance—with regular premium payments, of course—and nothing more. This policy was not at first unpopular. Raised in a culture that told men to stand up for themselves, the men of the First World War generation took pride in their willingness to do without government aid. It took the hardships of disability, unemployment, and finally economic depression to build a sense of entitlement.[22]

✶

RETURNING home to her native Nebraska in 1919, Sarah Sand thought of how "thousands of soldiers were coming home wounded, with broken, handicapped bodies. Some were diseased, others injured with slow and deadly gasses that would destroy their lungs and still others with shell-shocked minds. Will these comrades ever again know real happiness? Or must they spend the remaining days of their lives on some hospital cot, suffering for their devotion to their country?" It took years for such questions to enter the realm of popular discussion. In 1925, the silent movie blockbuster *The Big*

Parade exposed the trauma of wounded veterans to public view for the first time, showing matinee idol John Gilbert returning home minus a leg and depicting his struggles to readjust to civilian life. All over the United States, many people realized for the first time, hundreds of thousands of wounded Doughboys still struggled to pull together their lives.[23]

In theory, every wounded soldier received a disability pension—or "compensation," in the parlance of the 1920s. In addition, the Soldier's Rehabilitation Act of 1918 established the Federal Board for Vocational Education, which aimed to treat the disabled veteran "as a civilian needing advice and assistance . . . to train him to meet the needs of the occupation he has elected, to urge him to make the most of his opportunity to overcome his handicap by taking thorough-going instruction, to help him to secure desirable permanent employment, and to keep in close touch with him after he goes to work."[24] Veterans unable to work in any capacity received small subsistence allowances in addition to their regular government "compensation." Another law passed in 1919 assigned military hospitals caring for wounded veterans to the Public Health Service. It also created a few new veterans' hospitals and worked with private institutions by contract. The Veterans' Bureau managed these programs after its creation in 1921, and with two other federal agencies—the Bureau of Pensions of the Interior Department and the National Home for Disabled Volunteer Soldiers—distributed aid to the more than two hundred thousand veterans officially recognized as wounded.

"There was a statement made in Washington by one of the most prominent leaders," veteran Harry Zander wrote in 1933, "that our battle casualties had been most *wonderfully* taken care of, and all that remained were a few *doubtful* cases that could not get compensation because they did not have a disability incurred in service." Yet Zander knew from personal experience that thousands of veterans, particularly victims of gas, disease, and battle trauma or shell shock, had struggled for years to gain official recognition as war casualties, often without success. While one doctor might diagnose a veteran with a gas-related illness, for example, all it took was one dissenting opinion for a soldier's case to be questioned and his compensation cut in half, if not eliminated altogether. To further complicate matters, medical men knew little about the long-term effects of gas, service-related disease, or battle trauma. "Medical Opinion," Zander wrote, "claims that men gassed, or who have had the Flu, either died or got well and after one year would not allow compensation."[25]

Joseph Attura, who had been born in Italy in 1897 and immigrated to the United States in 1916, enlisted in the 1st Division a year later and served with distinction. He was gassed in May 1918, but after a few months in the hospital he went AWOL, rejoined his unit, and served with it in the Meuse-Argonne until the end of the war. After returning home in 1919 the gas damage to his lungs resurfaced, causing chronic pain and debilitation as he tried to build a life with three children in New York City. After frequent hospital stays interrupted his attempts to land a steady job, he made the mistake in 1929 of reporting to the Brooklyn Naval Hospital. After a few days the hospital decided that he suffered not from gas-related illness but from syphilis. Orderlies called him a "faker" and mockingly gave him glasses of water to "help" him out of coughing fits. The doctors kicked Attura out of the hospital after ten days and reported his supposed condition to the Veterans' Bureau, which cut his pension to practically nothing. He spent the following two years trying to get the diagnosis overturned; he became depressed, outraged, and increasingly sick. In 1931 the Veterans' Bureau found that he did not have syphilis and reinstated his pension. It was too late; he died a few months later.[26]

Walking down an Atlanta street after the war, Zander happened upon one of his old comrades from the Meuse-Argonne. "Miller," he stammered, taking the old friend by the hand with tears in his eyes.

> Miller was shabby and worn looking. He had not even had a shave in days—his scraggly beard attested to that, and his red hair too, had lost its lustre and was dull and mixed with a lighter shade. Only his eyes were the same . . . the same haunted fearful look I remembered so well out there on the battlefield. I knew that for Miller the hell of war was not ended . . . that he still lived those days over again . . . the result of which faced him continually.

"Harry," Miller said over coffee in a nearby café, "you know since I came back what it has been. I can't establish my claim and the government doctors insist they can't find anything—and yet I cannot hold out on any kind of work." Zander knew how he felt; his own disability claim had been cut from eighty dollars a month to fifty, and then to eight; now the government was trying to eliminate it entirely.[27]

Episodes of soldiers who had been mentally incapacitated by their experiences in the Meuse-Argonne but received no recognition, compensation, or vocational assistance were too numerous to count. Families of mentally ill soldiers who became violent or committed suicide received no government assistance. Zander, a veterans' activist, recorded three sample cases. In one, "a young boy leaves home. Goes through the entire campaign overseas and when he returns he is so out of tune with the world that he cannot adjust himself. Try as hard as he will to get work—he meets with no success. He disappears in a few weeks never to be heard of." His family lived on county poor funds. In the second case, a veteran got a job with an electrical company but committed suicide by jumping off a pole. His mother, a widow with a handicapped daughter, received no aid. In the third case, a veteran returned home so traumatized that he shrieked in his sleep and refused to go to bed without his rifle. He became an alcoholic and was killed in a car accident—and his mother received nothing.[28]

Soldiers who did not have to cope with physical or psychological wounds faced another major problem in their readjustment to civilian life: unemployment. The U.S. Employment Service urged veterans to resume their previous lines of work: "You have probably been broadened by your Army experience," a pamphlet informed the returning Doughboys, but "this does not mean that you will better yourself by taking up a new kind of work . . . advancement will come more rapidly if you go back to the job where you are known." Employers did not always welcome them back, however. Many jobs had disappeared, and sometimes the veterans seemed no longer physically or mentally suited for their old lines of work. The war, Donald Kyler said, "warped my personality away from what is generally considered as good in America . . . molded and stiffened my character [and] lessened my sensitivity to the value of human life. That rigidity was detrimental to my career in industry and to my personal life."[29]

Local municipalities and industries such as the Ford Motor Company offered employment to veterans, and institutions like the American Legion launched job drives, but thousands of ex-Doughboys nevertheless drifted from job to job, unable to hold any of them down. Even former generals had trouble getting by. Bullard, the ever-forward ex-commander of III Corps and Second Army, "gagged" at any suggestion of government aid to veterans and raged at the bolshevism he saw creeping everywhere into American society. Yet he also struggled to maintain his accustomed social rank after retiring from the army, despite the support of some wealthy friends. In 1928, seeking to "recapture his past glory," he posed in uniform for a Lucky Strike cigarette advertisement. The Luckies, he said, had "helped get the AEF through the strain of battle and allowed weight-conscious soldiers to handle their tension without snacking."[30]

Continued unemployment and financial difficulties finally energized the veterans to ask for something more from the state than sixty dollars, and in 1924 the American Legion and other organizations convinced Congress to pass the Adjusted Service Certificate Law. This law provided the veterans with additional aid—but not right away. Instead the veterans were given bonus certificates redeemable in 1945. No one minded the delay very much in the economic boom of the mid- to late 1920s, when many veterans finally found stable work that allowed them to get back on their feet. In the economic depression that followed the stock market crash of 1929, however, the Doughboys found themselves in desperate need of those bonus certificates.

The American Legion stepped forward again, convincing Congress in 1931—over President Herbert Hoover's veto—to permit the Doughboys to borrow up to 50 percent of the certificates' value. More than half of the 4.3 million veterans borrowed money, but it was often not enough to tide them over the hard times.[31] Congress refused to allow full redemption of the certificates, and the veterans became increasingly outraged, their demands more radical. Calling on the government to fulfill its portion of the social contract—they had done their part by enlisting or being drafted into the army and serving overseas—the veterans and their families formed a "Bonus Army" that marched on Washington, D.C., in June 1931. A month later, Hoover sent U.S. Army troops under the command of General Douglas MacArthur and Major George S. Patton to destroy the Bonus Army's shantytown and send the veterans home. MacArthur, who like many others feared that the Bonus Army had been infiltrated by Communists, did his job with gusto, driving the Doughboys out with bayonets and tear gas. For veterans across the country, including those who had not participated in the bonus movement, MacArthur's attack marked the final betrayal by a country ungrateful for their sacrifices.

✫

ANOTHER group of veterans had even greater cause for feeling that their sacrifices had been unappreciated. So far as most whites were concerned, blacks had proven themselves poor soldiers. Tales of the 92d Division's failure at Binarville evolved into incredible stories of cowardice that white soldiers readily believed. White officers who had commanded black troops deliberately concocted some of the stories. Captain John Stringfellow of the 80th "Blue Ridge" Division recalled meeting a white major from the 92d Division behind the front in early October. The major told him:

> One night we were in the trenches. We were waiting for Zero hour. Finally, about dawn it came. They were ordered over the top and wouldn't budge. At last the Colonel came up in the trenches and going along the lines kept saying, *"Men, you are making history for your Race!"* (here his voice dropped almost

to a whisper as he paused, then continued) *And they kept on making history!* Tell you, Stringfellow, the thing I was most afraid of was that some of those Germans across no man's land would hop up with white sheets on, and start for us. I'd have been trampled to death.

Stringfellow believed the major, and laughed heartily.[32]

Captain W. A. Sirmon of the 82d Division passed some 92d Division soldiers who had been relegated to labor battalions after their unit's collapse at Binarville and asked them why they had fled at the noise of their own barrage, as he had heard. He quoted one of the black soldiers, "a plain old Georgia negro," as replying:

> White folks, you knows no nigger aint gwine t' do nothin' fo' no other nigger. Dey had nigger officers over us an' dar wunt no white folks at all around. We was jes' natchully scared. Ef we'd a had some white officers, we wouldn't run, no suh. But jus' lak I said, no nigger aint gwin' t' do nothin' with no other nigger bossin' 'im.

Sirmon, "knowing negoes" as he thought, "got his point."[33]

Such fantasies, which exculpated white officers from responsibility for the division's failures, received wide credence at the highest levels. Bullard, who never outgrew the racism inherent in his rural Alabama upbringing, insisted that black troops did not belong at the front. He ascribed their presence there to the machinations of political idealists seeking "racial uplift" and trying to create artificial conditions of equality where none were justified. "All of this constructive equality," said Bullard, "I regarded as an injustice: it is not real." Sending blacks to the front not only endangered the American army and French civilians—the Negro, said Bullard, was "a more sensual man than the white man," and thus more prone to commit rape—it was unfair to the blacks themselves:

> I fear that it will always be so with Negroes wherever they are in contact with whites. This thought and my experience led me to this conclusion: If you need combat soldiers, and especially if you need them in a hurry, don't put your time upon Negroes. The task of making soldiers of them and fighting with them, if there are any white people near, will be swamped in the race question.

On the other hand, Bullard sneered, "if racial uplift or racial equality is your purpose, that is another matter."[34]

For all the contempt with which white soldiers treated them, most blacks viewed their military service with pride. The 368th Regiment had, they admitted, not succeeded—but neither had many white units like the 35th Division. The 93d Division, fighting with the French in the Champagne, had acquitted itself extremely well. So far as African Americans were concerned, they had more than proven themselves. They had served selflessly, and in many cases died for a government that denied them their basic rights. To the question of whether they would receive recognition or recompense, however, white America delivered a resounding no. From 1919 to 1921, race riots spread through towns and cities in the South and Midwest, killing hundreds of people—almost all of them African Americans—and destroying millions of dollars' worth of property. The riots fostered a vicious circle of racial hatred, with many blacks becoming increasingly radical and violent in their demands for equal rights, and whites, fearful of Bolshevik infiltration and race war, demanding brutally harsh measures to put them down.[35]

☆

ANOTHER postwar movement took place out of the public view. Deep down, the Meuse-Argonne opened a lasting perception gap in American society. On one side stood the combat veterans; on the other, everyone else. Civilians "shunned" Donald Kyler, and he didn't blame them. He knew that he had changed, and not, in his view, for the better. "Soon after I left the army," he confessed, "I realized that my philosophy was of the past. It was not in conformity with modern trends, and that I would have to be very careful not to become involved in some unlawful act. So I became a citizen—but not a good one. For many years I have worked diligently, paid my taxes, and stayed outside the main channel of American life." "War does something to a person," said Corporal Clarence Mahan. "We were scared, but we had to develop a numbness and an unfeeling attitude toward it all. Otherwise, we would have lost our minds. . . . To see blood and carnage everywhere as men, horses, and mules are blown to bits developed in us a certain savagery and hate that pushed us on toward a terrible enemy with a willingness to see him destroyed." Fearful of how the war had changed him and what it would mean to his civilian friends and relations, Mahan, a native of Sullivan, Indiana, tried to lock his feelings deep inside:

> Before I reached home, I decided that I must clear my mind of all the terrible experiences of the past two years, as much as possible. It would not be right to make my family and friends sad and uncomfortable by inflicting upon

them the horrors in which they had no part. Now I was home with the expectations of building a new and better life.

After wandering around for years, he landed a job as an automobile mechanic and met his future wife. "Her love and the home we established," said Mahan, "helped me forget the horrors of war. Soon I began to collect the bits and pieces of the two years of war and hide them away in a hidden corner of my mind."[36]

Friends and loved ones knew the veterans were hiding something, but could not figure out why. Ex-Doughboys struggled to explain. Sergeant H. T. Williams of the 29th Division admonished civilians not to ask "why soldiers don't talk about the war":

> <u>Do Not</u> censure the soldier for his reticence. Do not ask him to tell you about the war. He would prefer to go alone into the silent places;—alone, save for the memories of friendships formed in action and ending only with death, of comrades who were true until the end.[37]

According to Lieutenant Louis Ranlett of the 2d Division:

> It is true that the boys do not talk about the war. The reason is not because the war is something not to be thought of. The boys would talk if the questioners would listen. But the questioners do not. They at once interrupt with "It's all too dreadful," or, "Doesn't it seem like a terrible dream?" or, "How can you think of it?" or, "I can't imagine such things." That is as bad as telling a humorist you've heard that one before. It shuts the boys up.[38]

The Doughboys' reticence extended long after the war ended—not, as Ranlett argued, because they didn't want to talk, but because nobody seemed willing to listen. In Europe, particularly Britain, France, and Germany, and in Australia, soldiers' memoirs became big business in the publishing industry in the late 1920s and 1930s, particularly after the English-language publication of Erich Maria Remarque's *All Quiet on the Western Front* in 1929. Some veterans endorsed Remarque's vision of naïveté and disillusionment, and others rejected it. Either way, European readers bought memoirs by the hundreds of thousands and encouraged their veterans to write more. In America, the memoir publishing craze never took hold. Hundreds of American veterans published memoirs; some of them, such as Hervey Allen's *Toward the Flame* (1926), were of as high a literary quality as anything appearing in Europe. Aside from adventurous, romantic tales written by pilots like Eddie

Rickenbacker or ambulance drivers like Ernest Hemingway, however, American readers weren't interested. Books written by infantrymen just didn't sell. Nor, with the flash-in-the-pan exception of *The Big Parade,* did movies about American soldiers. The biggest-grossing war movies, like *Wings* (1927) and *The Dawn Patrol* (1930), were about fliers; or, like *All Quiet on the Western Front* (1930), about Germans.[39]

The Doughboy, then, never became as fixed in the American public imagination as the Tommy in Britain, the Digger in Australia, or the Poilu in France. Who was he? At the war's beginning, he was like any other American soldier in any other era—young, confident, naive, eager for adventure, and mostly believing in the cause and country for which he fought. Perhaps the only thing that set him apart in 1917 was his immigrant roots. By the end of 1918, however, he had become something very different and unique. Of all the soldiers in American history, the Doughboy is the first to have experienced modern industrialized warfare. He did so without preparation of any kind—military or psychological—and suffered terribly as a result. Yet no other soldier in American history or perhaps the history of the world learned how to fight in such a short period of time. Over a period of just a few months, four million volunteers and draftees endured, adapted, and finally overcame all obstacles to become first-rate soldiers. In the process they lost some of their youth, confidence, and naïveté. But they had shown, far more than any number of generals, diplomats, or politicians could ever have done, that America had an important role to play on the world stage.

✦

ONE of the last instances of public recognition of America's World War I veterans came on November 11, 1921, when the remains of the Unknown Soldier were entombed at Arlington National Cemetery. President Warren G. Harding led the ceremony, along with Pershing, Foch, Wilson, and numerous other generals, officers, and politicians. Their grandiloquent speeches—from Harding, a "series of platitudes . . . terrifically repeated"—threatened to overshadow the presence of dozens of men who had actually fought.[40] Among them were several Medal of Honor winners, including three members of the Lost Battalion—Nelson Holderman, George McMurtry, and Charles Whittlesey—along with Samuel Woodfill and Alvin C. York.

York, to his dismay, received celebrity treatment in the months immediately following the end of the war. Paraded around New York City, he was offered advertising, book, and movie deals worth more money than he had ever thought existed in the world. Disgustedly, he turned them all down, yearning only to return to his old cabin, his family, and his hound dogs in Fentress County, Tennessee.

> I would have been interested in helping to make the pictures if I didn't have to be in it myself and if they would do it, not to make a heap of money for themselves or for me but jes to show what the boys done done over there, and also to show what faith will do for you if you believe in it right. But I knowed they weren't interested in that. They jes wanted me to show how I done killed the Germans in the Argonne.

Far from glorying in his exploit, York was haunted by thoughts of the men he had killed.

> I didn't want to kill a whole heap of Germans nohow. I didn't hate them. But I done it jes the same. I had to. I was cornered. It was either them or me, and I'm a-telling you I didn't and don't want to die nohow if I can live. If they done surrendered as I wanted them to when I hollered to them first, and kept on hollering to them, I would have given them the protection that I give them later when I tuk them back. But they wouldn't surrender, and there was no way out for me but to tech them off. Jes the same I have tried to forget. I have never talked about it much. I have never told the story even to my own mother.

After the ceremony ended, York returned to Tennessee. The Rotary Club of Nashville had donated money to buy him a new farm in Pall Mall, but all he got was an unfinished home under a heavy mortgage. To pay for this and other expenses, and to further the cause of rural education, York embarked on numerous speaking tours throughout the United States. He died in 1964.[41]

Woodfill, a longtime regular, experienced such difficulty in readjusting to civilian life after the war's conclusion that he decided to rejoin the army with his old rank of sergeant, even though he had ended the war as a captain. After "a brief step into the glaring limelight," at the entombment of the Unknown Soldier, Woodfill returned to his unit.[42] His Indiana farm meanwhile fell into debt, and he received three months' leave from the army to work as a day laborer on a dam in order to pay the mortgage. Hearing of his troubles, Cincinnati newspapers collected $10,000 to pay off the debt, and in 1923, after thirty years' military service, Woodfill retired with a small pension. He stayed on his farm until his death in 1951, struggling with debt all his life.

The mobs of newspapermen, advertising agents, and movie agents who pounced on York shortly after the end of the war also besieged Charles Whittlesey. The former Lost Battalion commander enjoyed the attention no more than York did; but unlike the reclusive Tennessean, Whittlesey compromised. In the 1919 movie *The Lost Battalion,* he played himself. Stiff and uncomfortable with the manufactured sets and ridiculous script, Whittlesey went through the motions, his mind elsewhere. After the filming ended, he fled celebrity like a plague. Good causes—Red Cross drives, veterans' disability campaigns—brought him out for public appearances. But all the while he was withering inside. First his ideals slipped away. In college, Whittlesey had been a Socialist; and in the immediate aftermath of the war he nurtured the hope that something good would come of the fighting—social progress, international amity, lasting peace. He had tried to foster these ideals in 1919 by speaking out in favor of an equitable, nonvindictive peace treaty with Germany, and in support of various charities. But no one seemed willing to listen. The Treaty of Versailles imposed the punitive peace terms that he had decried; the United States shunned the League of Nations; and society seemed determined to return to the prewar status quo, or "business as usual." By the time of the Unknown Soldier ceremony in 1921, Whittlesey had lost faith in causes.

Next to go, after his ideals, was his self-respect. People called him a hero. He knew he was anything but. Instead of pointing fingers at Generals Alexander and Johnson for the men who died in Charlevaux Valley, Whittlesey blamed himself. He had been too impetuous in the advance, and too slow to withdraw. His stubbornness had kept the Germans at bay; but would it, after all, have been better to surrender? What purpose did they serve by holding on, except to leave more men dead? Every day, ex–Lost Battalion soldiers appeared at his law office, speaking of disabilities, unemployment, and sleepless nights, and whether or not they blamed him, he felt responsible for their plight.

Whittlesey did everything he could for the veterans and the families of those who had died. And the appeals kept coming. By the autumn of 1921, he was "besieged by wounded soldiers and widows of soldiers seeking aid." He visited hospitals, attended funerals of gas victims and suicides, and comforted grieving relatives. Each case wore him down a little more and increased his sense of guilt. "Raking over the ashes like this," he told a friend, "revives all the horrible memories. I'll hear the wounded screaming again. I have nightmares about them; I can't remember when I last had a good night's sleep." In one nightmare, he awoke in the middle of the night feeling the face of a young American soldier touching his cheek, "cold in death."

Whittlesey hardly said a word at the entombment of the Unknown Soldier. He sat rigid, his eyes staring fixedly ahead, as if he saw something that the others could not. At one point he turned to McMurtry and said, "I keep wondering if the Unknown Soldier is one of my men. . . . I should not have come here." Nine days later, at a Red Cross fund-raiser in New York City, he shared the stage with Foch and dozens of wounded men, many of them multiple amputees. On the twenty-sixth he put his ill younger brother Elisha, who had volunteered as an ambulance driver during the war and contracted an illness that ruined his lungs, on a train to visit their parents in Pittsfield. A few hours later he boarded the United Fruit liner *Taloa*, bound for Havana.

Whittlesey had no business in Havana. That evening on board the ship, he discussed the Army-Navy football game with a fellow veteran and talked briefly in the smoking room with a Cuban businessman who had served in the Spanish-American War. At 11:15, he got up, said "good night," and walked out onto the fog-covered deck. The next morning a steward entered Whittlesey's cabin and found it vacant, with eight sealed envelopes lying on his desk. One was addressed to the captain, and said simply that he had gone overboard. Another, written to a friend, read: "Just a note to say good bye. I'm a misfit by nature and by training, and there's an end of it." His body never was found.[43]

✳

In April 1919, Secretary of War Newton D. Baker came to France to visit Pershing and oversee the process of demobilization and the occupation of western Germany. With him came nine-year-old Warren Pershing, the general's son. They had not seen each other for over two years. Wearing a miniature sergeant's uniform, the boy accompanied his father on his official visits and tours of inspection. Together they visited a small American military cemetery at Beaumont, where twelve hundred American soldiers who had died during the Meuse-Argonne lay buried. Amid the crosses stood the French mayor and some children, laying wildflowers on the graves. The mayor promised Pershing that his people would always remember the Doughboys "sleeping so far away from their homes." With tears in his eyes, the general responded that he would trust no one else to care for the graves so well as "the dear people of France." On Memorial Day, he delivered a formal address at Romagne, where nearly ten thousand soldiers had already been buried in what would become the largest U.S. military cemetery on the Continent. He had spent the whole morning working on his speech:

> It is not for us to proclaim what they did, their silence speaks more eloquently than words, but it is for us to uphold the conception of duty, honor, and country for which they fought and for which they died. It is for us the living to carry forward their purpose and make fruitful their sacrifice.

And now, Dear Comrades, Farewell. Here, under the clear skies, on the green hillsides and amid the flowering fields of France, in the quiet hush of peace, we leave you forever in God's keeping.

On September 1, 1919, Pershing and his son boarded the *Leviathan,* which entered New York harbor a week later. Signal guns, official delegations, and noisy crowds welcomed his arrival. Two days later, Congress appointed him to the highest military position in the nation, "General of the Armies of the United States"; and on the tenth, resplendent on horseback, he led a victory parade of the 1st Division from 110th Street to Washington Square. Manhattan's streets and parks spilled over with hundreds of thousands of men, women, and children waving American flags. A week later a similar parade took place in Washington, D.C. "They have returned in the full vigor of manhood, strong and clean," he told the crowd. "In the community of effort, men from all walks of life have learned to know and to appreciate each other. . . . They will bring into the life of our country a deeper love for our institutions and a more intelligent devotion to the duties of citizenship."

Pershing's words delighted the crowds, who interrupted him more than twenty-five times with their applause. In time, however, the old-fashioned patriotic lexicon lost its luster, even for him. "Let's not talk high-sounding phrases," he said shortly after his retirement in 1924. "Let's not use old words, shop-worn words, like 'glory' and 'peace' without thinking exactly what they mean. There's no 'glory' in killing. There's no 'glory' in maiming men. There are the glorious dead, but they would be more glorious living. The most glorious thing is life. And we who are alive must cling to it, each of us helping." He clung to life for another quarter century, entering Walter Reed Hospital in Washington, D.C., in 1941 and fading slowly until his death in 1948. Warren Pershing gave his father a simple soldier's headstone at Arlington National Cemetery, distinguishable only by the relatively large area of grass surrounding it.[44]

NOTES

———•◦•———

Quotations from soldiers' diaries, letters, and other manuscripts retain the original grammar, spelling, and punctuation.

The American Battle Monuments Commission's *Summaries of Operations* for individual divisions, with their accompanying maps, have been used heavily throughout the preparation of this book. Except where otherwise noted, casualty figures are taken from the official army figures provided in these summaries.

ABBREVIATIONS

DLC	Library of Congress
MHI	Military History Institute
NARC	National Archives, College Park, Maryland.
USAWW	*United States Army in the World War*
VHP	Veterans History Project
WWIS	World War I Survey

PREFACE

1. Reese Russell Collection, Veterans History Project (VHP), AFC/2001/001/18879, Library of Congress (DLC).
2. Dennis Nolan papers, box 2, MHI.
3. Paul F. Braim, *The Test of Battle,* 144–45.
4. See Robert F. Braim and Robert H. Ferrell, *America's Deadliest Battle.*

CHAPTER 1: *"All the Promotion in the World Would Make No Difference Now": John J. Pershing*
1. Quoted in Frank E. Vandiver, *Black Jack,* 1:593.
2. Donald Smythe, *Guerrilla Warrior,* 211.
3. Gene Smith, *Until the Last Trumpet Sounds,* 129.
4. Smythe, *Guerrilla Warrior,* 212–13.
5. Quoted in Donald Smythe, *Pershing,* 2.
6. Vandiver, 1:590.
7. John J. Pershing, *My Experiences,* 1:1–2.
8. *Washington Post,* May 10, 1917.
9. Quoted in Smythe, *Pershing,* 5.
10. Smythe, *Pershing,* 6; Smith, 139.
11. Pershing, 1:18.

12. Ibid.

13. Edward M. Coffman, *The War to End All Wars,* 24–27.

14. Pershing, 1:37.

15. As a former professor and lifelong student of history, Wilson believed that Abraham Lincoln had erred during the U.S. Civil War by meddling in his generals' deliberations. Both he and Baker thought they should concentrate instead on civilian affairs and leave their generals to run the armed forces. "Our field of operations was necessarily removed a great distance from Washington," Baker later explained, and "it was quite impossible for us to form accurate judgments of the varying incidents in the field of operations. [Therefore] we could not do less than to give [Pershing] full authority and leave him untrammeled by attempts to formulate plans of action which, made at a great distance, would not be informed with knowledge of the situation which the commander at the front had when the plans reached him" (quoted in David F. Trask, *The AEF and Coalition Warmaking,* 11–12). Ironically, American soldiers found Wilson *too* detached from military operations and accused him—unfairly—of not caring about whether they lived or died.

16. George C. Marshall, *Memoirs of My Services,* 3.

17. Smythe, *Pershing,* 13; Pershing, 1:42.

CHAPTER 2: *The Cult of the Attack*

1. Hugh A. Drum papers, box 15, MHI.

2. Pershing, 1:38.

3. Smythe, *Pershing,* 45.

4. Trask, 16–17.

5. *United States Army in the World War, 1917–1919* (USAWW), 14:316; James W. Rainey, "Ambivalent Warfare," 34.

6. Mark E. Grotelueschen, *The AEF Way of War,* 14–16; Rainey, "Ambivalent Warfare," 38.

7. Ibid.

CHAPTER 3: *"Right or Wrong, My Country"*

1. Joseph N. Rizzi, *Joe's War,* 1–3.

2. Michael E. Hanlon, "The Origins of Doughboy," online.

3. William L. Langer, *Gas and Flame in World War I,* xvii–xix.

4. James H. Hallas, *Doughboy War,* 9, 12; Martin Marix Evans, *American Voices of World War I,* 7.

5. Hallas, 12.

6. Edward G. Lengel, "The University of Virginia Ambulance Drivers of the First World War," 22–23; Evans, 11.

7. Charles M. DuPuy, *A Machine Gunner's Notes,* 25.

8. Quoted in Byron Farwell, *Over There,* 66.

9. Russell L. Stultz, *History of the Eightieth Division,* 72.

10. Arthur H. Joel, *Under the Lorraine Cross,* 8; William S. Triplet, *A Youth in the Meuse-Argonne,* 161.

11. Farwell, 60–61; DuPuy, 23; quoted in Alan D. Gaff, *Blood in the Argonne,* 18; Conrad Lanza to Hugh Drum, September 8, 1926, Drum papers, 82d Division files, box 16, MHI.

12. Coffman, 69–73.

13. Farwell, 102.

14. Evans, 19.

15. Hallas, 38–41.

CHAPTER 4: *"Retreat, Hell. We Just Got Here"*

1. Quoted in John Terraine, *Douglas Haig*, 433.
2. George Aston, *The Biography of the Late Marshal Foch*, 154–55; A. Hilliard Atteridge, *Marshal Ferdinand Foch*, 71.
3. Quoted in Trask, 63, 74.
4. George C. Marshall, 11; John S. Stringfellow, *Hell! No!*, 77.
5. Joel, 20.
6. Joe Romedahl, *An Iowa Soldier in World War I*, 62; DuPuy, 57.
7. Corporal Robert Harbison, 80th Division, 320th Infantry Regiment, WWI Survey (henceforth WWIS), MHI.
8. Walter D. Corning, *The Yanks Crusade*, 30–31.
9. Coffman, 217.
10. It would remain the worst single-day casualty toll for the Marines until the Battle of Tarawa in 1943.
11. Quoted in Trask, 71–72.

CHAPTER 5: *"An Independent American Army"*

1. Hallas, 108.
2. Ibid., 129–30, 132.
3. Rod Paschall, *The Defeat of Imperial Germany*, 169.
4. DuPuy, 50; Joel, 16–17.
5. Paschall, 164–67.
6. Braim, 79.
7. Smythe, *Pershing*, 175–76; Vandiver, 2:937–39.
8. Smythe, *Pershing*, 177; quoted in Trask, 105.
9. MacArthur need not have fretted. Metz was a strong fortress and strategically insignificant; see Trask, 22.
10. Pershing and his generals had hoped that such huge divisions would be able to absorb heavy punishment and keep on fighting.
11. Quoted in Smythe, *Pershing*, 186–87.

CHAPTER 6: *"Here Is the Golden Dream": The Meuse-Argonne*

1. Braim, 89.
2. Report of commanding officer, First Army, Drum papers, box 12, MHI.
3. Braim, 97, 109; George S. Viereck, *As They Saw Us*, 234–35.
4. Ferdinand Foch, *The Memoirs of Marshal Foch*, 404–5, 411.
5. Foch, 404–5; Paschall, 181–82; report of commanding officer, First Army, Drum papers, box 12, MHI.
6. Conrad H. Lanza, "The Start of the Meuse-Argonne Campaign," 67.
7. U.S. Army, *Staff Ride*, Field Orders No. 20, Chapter 1, Part 3, 19–20.
8. Quoted in Carlo D'Este, *A Genius for War*, 226.
9. Quoted in ibid., 201, 205.
10. Quoted in ibid., 207. Patton also met with Colonel J. F. C. Fuller, the visionary second in command of the British tank force, who taught him about armored theory and tactics.
11. Quoted in ibid., 226.
12. During the battle, Patton devised a system of marking each tank with symbols of card suits—spades, hearts, diamonds, and clubs—to correspond with the four platoons in a tank company. The five tanks per platoon were thus labeled, for example, the one, two, three, four, and five of spades, hearts, diamonds, and clubs.

CHAPTER 7: *"The Only Way to Begin Is to Commence"*

1. James M. Cain, "The Taking of Montfaucon," 114–15.
2. Private James E. Collins, 33d Division, 124th Machine Gun Battalion, October 23, 1997, letter from grandson, Steven D. Collins, WWIS, MHI.
3. Hallas, 197.
4. Ibid., 195–96.
5. Sergeant Russell E. Stultz, 80th Division, 318th Infantry Regiment, WWIS, MHI.
6. Hallas, 195.
7. George C. Marshall, 137–39.
8. Ibid., 151.
9. Quoted in Farwell, 221.
10. George C. Marshall, 149; Braim, 91.
11. George C. Marshall, 154.
12. James J. Cooke, *Billy Mitchell,* 51.
13. Ibid., 61–64.
14. Ibid., 63.
15. Ibid., 62.
16. William Mitchell, "The Air Service in the Argonne-Meuse," 552.
17. Cooke, 56.
18. William Schellberg, *Your Brother Will,* 42, 49–50.
19. Ashby Williams, *Experiences of the Great War,* 75.
20. Roy Hoopes, *Cain,* 65.
21. Ashby Williams, 79.
22. Robert J. Casey, *The Cannoneers Have Hairy Ears,* 198–99.
23. Ibid., 197.
24. Coppard, *With a Machine Gun to Cambrai,* 39; Stultz, WWIS, MHI.
25. Joel, 32.
26. Vera Brittain, *Testament of Youth,* 395.
27. Langer, x–xi.
28. T. Ben Meldrum, *A History of the 362nd Infantry,* 23.
29. E. Lester Muller, *The 313th of the 79th in the World War,* 99.
30. Ray N. Johnson, *Heaven, Hell, or Hoboken,* 89–90.
31. Casey, 175–76.
32. Ray N. Johnson, 89–91; Quoted in D'Este, 253.
33. Henry W. Smith, *A Story of the 305th Machine Gun Battalion,* 62; Corning, 66.
34. L. Wardlaw Miles, *History of the 308th Infantry,* 119.
35. Gaff, 119–22.
36. Ashby Williams, 77.
37. Joel, 33.
38. Muller, 130; Raymond S. Tompkins, *Maryland Fighters in the Great War,* 79.

CHAPTER 8: *"You Boys Are My Kind. Now Let's Go In!": September 26*

1. Joel, 33; Casey, 178.
2. Ferrell, *America's Deadliest Battle,* 41–42; *The Official History of the 315th Infantry, U.S.A.,* 52; Edward V. Rickenbacker, *Rickenbacker,* 128.
3. Quoted in Richard L. Miller, *Truman,* 132–33; Harry S. Truman, *Memoirs,* 129–30; Monte M. Poen, *Letters Home by Harry Truman,* 57.
4. Casey, 178–79.

5. Edward C. Lukens, *A Blue Ridge Memoir,* 59; Meldrum, 26; Joseph B. Sanborn, *The 131st U.S. Infantry,* 203; Robert L. Dwight, "R. L. Dwight's WWI Diary," online.

6. *Official History of the 315th Infantry,* 52; DuPuy, 77; Muller, 105; Braim, 97.

7. Ray N. Johnson, 92.

8. Maximilian Boll, "My First Journey," 81; Edgar B. Jackson, *Fall Out to the Right of the Road,* 307; Joel, 35.

9. Casey, 179; H. G. Proctor, *The Iron Division,* 254; Lukens, 63.

10. Rizzi, 80.

11. Ray N. Johnson, 93–94.

12. Ibid., 94.

13. Robert L. Bullard, *Personalities and Reminiscences of the War,* 270.

14. Ibid., 268.

15. Abel Davis, *The Story of the 132d Infantry,* 10–12; Frederick L. Huidekoper, *The History of the 33rd Division,* 1:68–69, 2:502–6.

16. Charles D. Dermody, "A Yank in the First World War," online; Sergeant Willie Sandlin of the 132d Regiment—a muscular, stern-eyed mountaineer from Perry County, Kentucky—extinguished three machine-gun nests, killing twenty-four Germans and earning a Medal of Honor.

17. Huidekoper, 3:79; Captain George Mallon and Sergeant Sydney Gumpertz of the 132d Regiment won Medals of Honor here by racing from gun to gun, shooting some crews and beating down others with their fists. They captured four howitzers, eleven machine guns, one antiaircraft gun, and more than one hundred prisoners.

18. Sanborn, 203.

19. Cronkhite's remarks about blacks, though outraging many southerners, were merely patronizing: "I met some junior officers who said they were not keen on saluting Negro officers," he said. "They would not feel that way if they understood the spirit of the salute. If one of them came from a town where there was an old Negro character, one of those old fellows who do odd jobs and is known to everybody, he'd at least nod his head and say, 'Howdy, uncle.' Now suppose through some freak of nature this old Negro should be transplanted into an officer's uniform; the salute would be merely saying to him 'Howdy, uncle,' in a military way" (Arthur E. Barbeau and Florette Henry, *The Unknown Soldiers,* 56).

20. Frank T. Floyd, *Company "F" Overseas,* 52.

21. Stultz, WWIS, MHI.

22. Lukens, 62.

23. Ibid., 56, 64–65.

24. *Company F History,* 29–33; Josiah C. Peck, *The 319th Infantry A.E.F.,* 25.

25. Bullard, 268; Frederick Palmer, *Our Greatest Battle,* 371–72.

26. Christian A. Bach and Henry Noble Hall, *The Fourth Division,* 163.

27. Drum papers, 4th Division files, box 16, MHI.

28. *History of Company F, 316th Infantry,* 52.

29. Muller, 48; Cain, 110.

30. Tompkins, 82.

31. The 79th Division actually faced two regiments of the German 117th Division, both of them badly mauled after fighting all summer on the Somme and amounting in total to perhaps 3,300 men.

32. Elbridge Colby, "The Taking of Montfaucon," 134; Schellberg, 43.

33. Joel, 35–36.

34. Boll, 84.
35. Ibid., 84–86.
36. Joel, 36–37; Colby, 134.
37. DuPuy, 78–83.
38. Private Casper W. Swartz, 79th Division, 314th Regiment, WWIS, MHI; Muller, 139–41.
39. Rexmond C. Cochrane, *The 79th Division at Montfaucon,* 19.
40. Colby, 134–36.
41. DuPuy, 88, 93–94; Muller, 58–62; William B. Clark, *War History of the 79th Division,* 10.
42. Tompkins, 84.
43. Drum papers, 4th Division files, box 16, MHI.
44. Gerald F. Gilbert Jr., 79th Division, 316th Ambulance Company, WWIS, MHI.
45. Hal Thurman Kearns, "A Chaplain Overseas," in *St. Lawrence University in the World War,* 336–40.
46. USAWW, 9:140.
47. Lieutenant Robert Weise, 37th Division, 147th Regiment, WWIS, MHI.
48. Ray N. Johnson, 94–96.
49. Morris Martin Collection, VHP, AFC/2001/001/1034, DLC.
50. Harold H. Burton, *600 Days' Service,* 64.
51. Martin, VHP, DLC.
52. Ibid.
53. Captain Farley E. Granger collection, 91st Division, 361st Regiment, WWIS, MHI; Meldrum, 28.
54. Granger, WWIS, MHI; Captain Granger's son and namesake is the Hollywood movie actor Farley Granger Jr.
55. Casey, 190. Four soldiers—Sergeants Phillip Katz and Chester West of the 363d Regiment, and Sergeant Lloyd Seibert and Lieutenant Deming Bronson of the 364th Regiment—performed deeds on this day that earned them Medals of Honor.
56. Hunter Liggett, *A.E.F.,* 174.
57. Bullard, 144.
58. Ibid., 143; quoted in Coffman, 250.
59. Quoted in Ferrell, *Collapse at Meuse-Argonne,* 1.
60. Private Milton B. Sweningson, 35th Division, 138th Regiment, WWIS, MHI.
61. Clair Kenamore, *From Vauquois Hill to Exermont,* 104–5; Wold Medal of Honor citation.
62. Kenamore, 112–15, 125–26; Skinker Medal of Honor citation.
63. Kenamore, 117–18.
64. Ibid.
65. Quoted in D'Este, 256.
66. Edward P. Rankin Jr., *The Santa Fe Trail Leads to France,* 12.
67. Quoted in D'Este, 257.
68. D'Este, 257–59.
69. Kenamore, 123.
70. Triplet, 171–73.
71. Ferrell, *Collapse at Meuse-Argonne,* 42.
72. Interview with James E. Ruffin by James R. Fuchs, Springfield, Missouri, April 19, 1966, Truman Presidential Museum and Library, online at http://www.trumanlibrary.org/oralhist/ruffin.htm; Evan A. Edwards, *From Doniphan to Verdun,* 59; Kenamore, 127.
73. Ferrell, *Collapse at Meuse-Argonne,* 42–45; Kenamore, 129–30.
74. Corporal Donald Call of the 344th Tank Battalion, a New York City native, won a Medal of Honor during this attack.

75. Ferrell, *Collapse at Meuse-Argonne,* 44.
76. Nolan papers, box 2, MHI; Palmer, 57.
77. Private Duncan M. Kemerer, 28th Division, 111th Regiment, WWIS, MHI.
78. Jackson, 309.
79. Ibid., 314.
80. Proctor, 267–68.
81. Ibid., 246, 257.
82. Private Alfred R. Hoyles, 77th Division, 307th Regiment, WWIS, MHI.
83. Grotelueschen, 300, 314; Robert H. Ferrell, *Five Days in October,* 7–8.
84. W. Kerr Rainsford, *From Upton to the Meuse,* 158–59.
85. Miles, 120–21.
86. Ibid., 122.
87. Rainsford, 167.
88. Miles, 123.
89. Ibid., 124.
90. Henry W. Smith, 64; Miles, 127.
91. Sarah Sand Stevenson, *Lamp for a Soldier,* 23–24.
92. United States Army War College, Historical Section, "The Ninety-Second Division," 2–15.
93. Charles H. Williams, *Sidelights on Negro Soldiers,* 70–71.
94. United States Army War College, "The Ninety-Second Division," 26.
95. Ibid., 27.
96. Edwin J. Tippett Jr., *Who Won the War?,* 137–38.
97. William Mitchell, *Memoirs,* 258–59.
98. Quoted in Stultz, 384.

CHAPTER 9: *"We Began to Realize What Artillery Really Meant": September 27*
1. Herman R. Furr, *314 Machine Gun Battalion History,* 34.
2. Bach and Hall, 174–75.
3. Cain, 107–16.
4. Schellberg, 44.
5. Tompkins, 87.
6. Private Andrew J. Kachik, 79th Division, 314th Regiment, WWIS, MHI.
7. Joel, 38.
8. Boll, 87.
9. Tompkins, 87.
10. *History of Company F,* 55; Tompkins, 87–88.
11. DuPuy, 95.
12. Sergeant Edward A. Davies, 79th Division, 315th Regiment, WWIS, MHI.
13. Hoopes, 67; Cain, 118–19; Muller, 55–58.
14. Lieutenant Clair Groover, 79th Division, 313th Regiment, WWIS, MHI.
15. Ray N. Johnson, 98.
16. Martin, VHP, DLC.
17. Burton, 67.
18. Meldrum, 30–31.
19. Granger, WWIS, MHI.
20. Martin, VHP, MHI.
21. *The Story of the 91st Division,* 29; Lieutenant Frank L. Thompson, 91st Division, 348th Machine Gun Battalion, WWIS, MHI.

22. Bronson Medal of Honor citation.

23. Triplet, 187.

24. Rizzi, 102–3.

25. Triplet, 187–90.

26. Rizzi, 92–93.

27. Triplet, 193.

28. Sergeant Triplet later got a chance to look at one of these rifles firsthand thanks to an American tank commander. "Look at what they sniped me with," the tanker complained in a hurt voice, lugging "a long, evidently heavy something off the tank track. Even in the dusk I could see that it looked like an M-98 Mauser expanded to six feet long with a bi-pod support under the monstrous barrel. 'This thing throws an armor-piercing bullet the size of your thumb, went through my front plate, the driver, the rear bulkhead, and smashed hell outa the engine' . . . the monster must have weighed fifty pounds and my little finger fitted the muzzle at the second joint. Bolt action, single-shot, and a broken collar bone per shot. Quite a gun" (Triplet, 216).

29. Quoted in Kenamore, 154; Edwards, 61; Ferrell, *Collapse at Meuse-Argonne,* ix.

30. Miller, 137–38; Poen, 58.

31. Triplet, 195.

32. Ibid., 197–99.

33. Rizzi, 93.

34. Private Alexander H. Case, 35th Division, 137th Regiment, WWIS, MHI.

35. Edwards, 65.

36. Rizzi, 93.

37. Corporal Harold W. Pierce, 28th Division, 112th Regiment, WWIS, MHI.

38. Arthur McKeogh, *The Victorious 77th Division,* 2.

39. Henry W. Smith, 65; quoted in Gaff, 126.

40. United States Army War College, "The Ninety-Second Division," 28–29.

41. Quoted in James J. Cooke, *Pershing and His Generals,* 132.

42. Palmer, 141–42.

43. Tompkins, 80.

44. Groover, WWIS, MHI.

45. Casey, 182–83.

46. Mitchell, "The Air Service in the Argonne-Meuse," 558.

47. Mitchell, *Memoirs,* 258–59.

48. Rush S. Young, *Over the Top with the 80th,* n.p. Mitchell's measures may have prevented large-scale attacks, or the Germans—perhaps reasoning that their planes would be more useful over the front lines—may simply have chosen not to carry them out.

49. Quoted in Smythe, *Pershing,* 197.

CHAPTER 10: *"Words Can Never Describe It, Nor Is the Mind Imaginative Enough to Conceive It": September 28*

1. USAWW, 9:144.

2. Casey, 188.

3. John L. Hines papers, diary, MHI.

4. Young, n.p.

5. Boll, 89; DuPuy, 99; *Official History of the 315th Infantry,* 67.

6. William Bell Clark, *War History of the 79th Division,* 17.

7. Davies, WWIS, MHI.

8. DuPuy, 98; *Official History of the 315th Infantry,* 71, 157.

9. Davies, WWIS, MHI.

10. *History of Company F,* 58.

11. Atwood, Distinguished Service Cross citation; *History of Company C, 304th Field Signal Battalion,* 38. Kuhn relieved Colonel Charles after hearing of this incident.

12. *History of Company F,* 59–61.

13. Anonymous typescript, December 1, 1918, in Granger, WWIS, MHI.

14. Ray N. Johnson, 101–2.

15. Burton, 74.

16. Miller, Medal of Honor citation.

17. Ferrell, *Collapse at Meuse-Argonne,* 62–63.

18. Edwards, 65.

19. Wayne DeSilvey, "The Diary of Bugler Wayne DeSilvey," online.

20. Proctor, 278, 282.

21. Pierce, WWIS, MHI.

22. Ibid.

23. Ibid.

24. Miles, 129.

25. *History of the 306th Infantry,* 67; Schaffner, Medal of Honor citation.

26. Miles, 132; Gaff, 126; Rainsford, 176.

27. Henry W. Smith, 66; Charles H. Williams, 164; United States Army War College, "The Ninety-Second Division," 30–31. Elser blamed everything on his men, calling their conduct "utterly and absolutely disgraceful." He added that "the colored soldiers have no confidence in their officers." He meant their *black* officers, but he might as well have included himself (Evans, 142). Five black officers were later tried for cowardice on September 28. Four of them were ordered to be executed, and the fifth received a sentence of life imprisonment.

28. Pershing, 2:294; Smythe, *Pershing,* 197–98.

CHAPTER 11: *"There Were Very Few Heroes That Morning": September 29*

1. Lukens, 73–75.

2. Henry Berry, *Make the Kaiser Dance,* 71, 76.

3. Frederick M. Wise and Meigs O. Frost, *A Marine Tells It to You,* 268–69.

4. Young, n.p. His battalion of the 80th Division had temporarily been assigned to the 4th Division.

5. Sergeant Major James Block, 4th Division, 59th Regiment, WWIS, MHI.

6. George L. Morrow, *The Fifty-Eighth Infantry in the World War,* 100–101; Wise and Frost, 184.

7. Mitchell, *Memoirs,* 259.

8. Conrad H. Lanza, "The End of the Battle of Montfaucon," 355; Boll, 90.

9. Davies, WWIS, MHI; *Official History of the 315th Infantry,* 73, 157.

10. Boll, 93–94; Irwin J. Rentz, "World War I Diary," 31.

11. *History of Company F,* 64.

12. Harry Frieman Collection, VHP, AFC 2001/001/23600, DLC.

13. Hallas, 250.

14. Master Engineer Leroy Y. Haile, 79th Division, 304th Engineer Regiment, WWIS, MHI.

15. Casey, 197.

16. Dwight, online.

17. Ray N. Johnson, 102–4.

18. Granger, WWIS, MHI.

19. *Story of the 91st Division,* 32.

20. Accounts by Granger, Hutchinson, and Parker are in Granger, WWIS, MHI.

21. Meldrum, 36.

22. Granger, WWIS, MHI.

23. Ferrell, *Collapse at Meuse-Argonne,* 83.

24. Kenamore, 191.

25. Triplet, 220.

26. Lanza, "Supporting an Infantry Division," 411.

27. Charles B. Hoyt, *Heroes of the Argonne,* 104.

28. Triplet, 222–23.

29. Kenamore, 209.

30. Edwards, 79.

31. Ferrell, *Collapse at Meuse-Argonne,* 91; Kenamore, 11–12.

32. Ferrell, *Collapse at Meuse-Argonne,* 91.

33. Triplet, 233.

34. Kenamore, 13–14.

35. Lanza, "Supporting an Infantry Division," 419.

36. Quoted in Miller, 143. Traub later bragged to Congress that on this day he had bravely withstood a barrage of three hundred shells meant just for him while a German plane strafed him specifically—one dud shell falling a few feet from him while the plane's bullets slopped harmlessly into muddy ground. He evaded any hint of censure for his conduct (Ferrell, *Collapse at Meuse-Argonne,* 124).

37. Rankin, 25–26.

38. Miller, 143.

39. Rizzi, 103.

40. Private Maurice M. De Frehn, 28th Division, 112th Regiment, WWIS, MHI.

41. "Buck Private" O'Neil, *History & Rhymes,* 51.

42. "War Diary Company A 112th Infantry 28th Division June 12, 1918 to Nov. 13, 1918, Inclusive," in WWIS, 28th Division, 112th Regiment, MHI.

43. *History of the 110th Infantry,* 99–100.

44. George W. Cooper, *Our Second Battalion,* 152–53; "War Diary Company A 112th Infantry," MHI.

45. Charles F. Minder, *This Man's War,* 325–27.

46. Rainsford, 178.

47. Miles, 133.

48. Smith, Medal of Honor citation.

49. Gaff, 127–31; Berry, 354–55.

50. Pershing, 2:304.

51. Vandiver, 2:961–62; Pershing, 2:303–4; Smythe, *Pershing,* 200–201.

52. Quoted in Smythe, *Pershing,* 200.

53. Timothy K. Nenninger has rightly pointed out that Pershing visited the front more often than many other generals would have done, and that during the Meuse-Argonne inspectors general were assigned to every division with the mission of submitting reports on things like supplies, casualties, morale, and fatigue. Pershing read all of those reports. All the more remarkable, in my opinion, that he made such little allowance for these factors in his planning—keeping many divisions in the line and ordering them to attack repeatedly until they were on the verge of dissolution (Timothy K. Nenninger, " 'Unsystematic as a Mode of Command,' " 745–46).

54. Vandiver, 2:964–65.

55. Ibid., 2:964.

CHAPTER 12: *Relief: September 30*

1. Many of Pershing's troops were sick with influenza. Twenty-five hundred of them died of the disease in September, and forty thousand were admitted to hospitals (Paschall, 183).
2. DuPuy, 99.
3. Drum papers, 79th Division file, box 16, MHI.
4. Meldrum, 38.
5. Quoted in Laurence Stallings, *The Doughboys,* 239–40.
6. Kenamore, 240.
7. Rizzi, 116.
8. Rankin, ix.
9. Minder, 328–29.
10. Rainsford, 188–91.
11. Gaff, 133.
12. Evans, 142.
13. The 368th Regiment took 318 casualties during the Meuse-Argonne offensive, 58 of them dead. None of those casualties were noted in the rush to affix blame after the war. Popular accounts of the "Lost Battalion" acidly noted the failure of the regiment to protect Major Whittlesey's left flank, and all but accused them of responsibility for the force's encirclement. For his part, Colonel Brown reported that his company and battalion commanders had all "utterly failed" to carry out his orders. He especially blamed "the inefficiency and cowardice of the company officers who repeatedly withdrew their companies and platoons, without orders and without suffering losses which could possibly justify such action." Of his own responsibility nothing was said. Shortly after the battle ended, the 92d Division's commander removed thirty company officers from the 368th, all for incompetence and overall "worthlessness" (United States Army War College, "The Ninety-Second Division," 34).
14. The official tally is taken from figures provided in the American Battle Monuments Commission's divisional summaries; see also Paschall, 188–89.
15. Martin, VHP, DLC.
16. Harvey Cushing, *From a Surgeon's Journal,* 463, 473.
17. Pershing, 2:327.
18. Lettie Gavin, *American Women in World War 1,* 44.
19. Stevenson, 46–48.
20. James J. Cooke, *The All-Americans at War,* 92.

CHAPTER 13: *"God Damn It, Don't You Know We're Going Over the Top": October 4*

1. Stowers, Medal of Honor citation.
2. The history of the 93d Division is much better documented than that of the 92d Division. See especially Frank E. Roberts, *The American Foreign Legion: Black Soldiers of the 93d in World War I* (Annapolis, Md.: Naval Institute Press, 2004); Stephen L. Harris, *Harlem's Hell Fighters: The African-American 369th Infantry in World War I* (Washington, D.C.: Brassey's, 2003); and Arthur W. Little, *From Harlem to the Rhine.* An extensive study of the 369th Regiment also appears in Richard Slotkin, *Lost Battalions.*
3. Pershing, 2:307.
4. USAWW, 8:82.
5. USAWW, 2:619, 8:83; Smythe, *Pershing,* 204.
6. Pershing, 2:323.
7. Lanza, "The First Battle of Romagne," 495–96; Viereck, 250.
8. USAWW, 9:189; Ferrell, *America's Deadliest Battle,* 55.

9. USAWW, 9:191–92.

10. Pershing, 2:321; Viereck, 248–49.

11. Morrow, 107.

12. Ibid., 109–10; Bach and Hall, 183.

13. Morrow, 111.

14. Block, WWIS, MHI.

15. Young, n.p.

16. Jennings C. Wise, *The Great Crusade,* 195; Edley Craighill, *History of the 317th Infantry,* 63.

17. *History of the 318th Infantry Regiment,* 67; Stultz, 432–33.

18. Ibid., 433.

19. Jennings Wise, 199–202.

20. Young, n.p. In about six months of on-and-off fighting during World War I, the United States suffered 72,807 casualties from poison gas, with 1,462 dying outright and many more crippled or with drastically shortened lives. By contrast, in the three and a half years of the war during which gas was in use, the Germans suffered 200,000 gas casualties against about 190,000 each for the British and French. The proportionately much higher rate of gas casualties suffered by the Americans is a measure of their inexperience and lack of proper training.

21. *Company F History,* 42–44.

22. Stultz, 436.

23. Clarence Lovejoy, *The Story of the Thirty-Eighth,* 148–49.

24. John Lewis Barkley, *No Hard Feelings!,* 3–4, 162–63.

25. Frederic V. Hemenway, *History of the Third Division,* 103.

26. Barkley, 164–70.

27. William G. Haan diary, in Private Edward T. Lauer papers, 32d Division, 121st Field Artillery Regiment, WWIS, MHI.

28. Paul W. Schmidt, *Co. C, 127th Infantry, in the World War,* 98–106.

29. Haan diary, WWIS, MHI; Hartger Jonker Jr., *The "Old Command,"* 37–38; Lieutenant Harold C. Woehl, 32d Division, 126th Regiment, WWIS, MHI.

30. Bullard, 110–11.

31. Grotelueschen, 36–38; Harbord, *The American Army in France,* 101.

32. Stallings, 59.

33. Corporal Donald Kyler, 1st Division, 16th Regiment, WWIS, MHI.

34. The Germans saturated the 1st Division lines with gas during the three days preceding the attack, causing almost one thousand casualties (Cochrane, *The 1st Division in the Meuse-Argonne,* 19).

35. Grotelueschen, 134; Private Herbert L. McHenry, 1st Division, 16th Regiment, WWIS, MHI.

36. *History of the First Division during the World War,* 194; Roberts Medal of Honor citation.

37. Kyler, WWIS, MHI.

38. Maury Maverick, *A Maverick American,* 127–33.

39. Ibid.

40. Charles B. Fullerton, *The Twenty-Sixth Infantry in France,* 65–66.

41. Lanza, "The First Battle of Romagne," 501.

42. Charles M. Clement, *Pennsylvania in the World War,* 2:410. The headstones in Apremont's cemetery still bear the scars of this battle today.

43. Nolan papers, box 2, MHI; Kovach, *The Life and Times of MG Dennis E. Nolan,* 35.

44. Pierce, WWIS, MHI.

45. In Private William S. Mertz, 28th Division, 111th Regiment, WWIS, MHI.

CHAPTER 14: *The Lost Battalion: "Our Mission Is to Hold This Position at All Costs"*
1. USAWW, 9:148.
2. Robert Alexander, *Memories of the World War,* 203.
3. Captain A. T. Rich, "Report of Inspection of the 77th Division," October 8, 1918, Drum papers, 77th Division files, box 16, MHI.
4. Quoted in Gaff, 134.
5. Ibid., 135.
6. John W. Nell, *The Lost Battalion,* 85.
7. Gaff, 137–38.
8. *History of the 306th Infantry,* 70.
9. Report of Brigadier General Evan Johnson, Drum papers, 77th Division files, box 16, MHI; Alexander, 206–7.
10. 307th Regiment report, Drum papers, 77th Division files, box 16, MHI.
11. Gaff, 143–44.
12. Miles, 150.
13. Ibid., 151. These pits are still easily visible.
14. Major Charles Whittlesey, supplementary report on 308th Regiment, and Revnes trial record, Drum papers, 77th Division files, box 16, MHI.
15. Gaff, 146–47.
16. Newspaper articles and reports, Drum papers, 77th Division files, box 16, MHI.
17. Alexander, 214.
18. Gaff, 148–50.
19. Quoted in ibid., 164.
20. Reports in Drum papers, 77th Division files, box 16, MHI.
21. Miles, 154–58, 241.
22. Quoted in Gaff, 215; inspector's report, 154th Brigade report in Drum papers, 77th Division files, box 16, MHI; Alexander, 219. Colonel Stacey reported to the 77th Division's chief surgeon on October 5 and was evacuated to a hospital the same day. His condition initially was entered as "Medical—Not Determined." The hospital inspector reported that the colonel was extremely nervous, and panicky from loss of memory. He decided that Stacey suffered from neurasthenia, or nervous collapse, and concluded "that he does not possess the necessary qualifications to command a combat unit in action" (Drum papers).
23. Miles, 160; Thomas M. Johnson and Fletcher Pratt, *The Lost Battalion,* 135–37; Ferrell, *Five Days in October,* 36.
24. Quoted in Gaff, 174; McMurtry testimony, Drum papers, 77th Division files, box 16, MHI.
25. Richard Slotkin, *Lost Battalions,* 337–40.
26. Quoted in ibid., 338.
27. Ibid., 342.
28. USAWW, 9:212.
29. Viereck, 250.

CHAPTER 15: *"Just Plain Murder": October 5*
1. Block, WWIS, MHI.
2. Frederick Wise and Meigs Frost, *A Marine Tells It to You,* 281.
3. Bach and Hall, 187–88; Morrow, 113–14.
4. Jennings Wise, 210–11; Bullard, 276.
5. Young, n.p.

6. Jennings Wise, 213–14.

7. Young, n.p.

8. Hemenway, 69.

9. Barkley, 170–72.

10. Woehl, WWIS, MHI.

11. Schmidt, 107–9.

12. Charles E. Butler, *The Yanks Are Coming,* 83–85.

13. *History of the First Division,* 189; Butler, 86.

14. *History of the First Division,* 199–201.

15. Quoted in Gaff, 189–90; Nell, 96.

16. Gaff, 191–92.

17. Miles, 163–64.

18. Drum papers, 77th Division files, box 16, MHI.

19. Ferrell, *Five Days in October,* 62.

CHAPTER 16: *"It Is Not a Dishonorable Deed to Give Up": October 6*

1. Barkley, 176–77.

2. Ibid., 181.

3. Hemenway, 70.

4. Barkley, 183–89.

5. Quoted in Ferrell, *Five Days in October,* 55.

6. Liggett, 186–88; Ferrell, *Five Days in October,* 54–55; Coffman, 323–24.

7. Alvin C. York, *Sergeant York,* 198–215; letter to the author from Dr. Michael Birdwell.

8. *Infantry in Battle,* 190–92.

9. Gaff, 202–5.

10. Revnes trial papers, February 18, 1919, in Drum papers, 77th Division files, box 16, MHI; Gaff, 204–5. After the war, Revnes was court-martialed on the grounds that he did "misbehave himself before the enemy in that he sought to induce Major Charles W. Whittlesey . . . shamefully to surrender himself and the force of which he was in command." The tribunal at first found him not guilty; but on reconsideration they decided that he was guilty, though not "shamefully," and sentenced him to be dismissed. The judge advocate, considering the circumstances, overturned Revnes's sentence and ordered him released from arrest.

11. 308th Regiment report and Revnes trial papers, Drum papers, 77th Division files, box 16, MHI.

12. Alexander, 219–20.

13. Ibid., 223; Drum papers, 77th Division files, box 16, MHI. First Lieutenant Harold Ernest Goettler, a pilot in the 50th Aero Squadron, and his observer, Second Lieutenant Erwin R. Bleckley of the 130th Field Artillery, were killed by enemy ground fire while attempting to drop supplies to the Lost Battalion on October 6. They received posthumous Medals of Honor.

CHAPTER 17: *"Their Faces Told the Whole Story of Their Fight": October 7*

1. Berry, 81–82. George Clark, *Devil Dogs: Fighting Marines of World War I* (Novato, Calif.: Presidio, 1990), has a chapter on the battle of Blanc Mont.

2. Barkley, 192–219. He was awarded a Medal of Honor for his exploit.

3. G. W. Garlock, *Tales of the Thirty-Second,* 244–54; Edmund P. Arpin Jr., "A Wisconsinite in World War I," 127–30.

4. James J. Cooke, *The All-Americans at War,* viii.

5. Quoted in ibid., 87.

6. Ibid., 89.

7. Pierce, WWIS, MHI.

8. York, 215–16.

9. *History of the 110th Infantry,* 102.

10. Pierce, WWIS, MHI.

11. World War I Organization Records, 28th Division, boxes 10 and 14, files 228-11.4, 228-33.1, RG 120, NARC.

12. Pierce, WWIS, MHI.

13. Clement, 2:591; report of 55th Bde commander, in Joe Ansel folder, 28th Division, 109th Regiment, WWIS, MHI; World War I Organization Records, 28th Division, boxes 10 and 14, RG 120, NARC; Ferrell, *America's Deadliest Battle,* 85.

14. Cooper, 158.

15. Gaff, 231–34.

16. Gaff, 239–40; Drum papers, 77th Division files, box 16, MHI.

17. Drum papers, 77th Division files, box 16, MHI.

18. Ibid.; Gaff, 240.

19. *Washington Sunday Star,* May 1, 1927.

20. Ferrell, *Five Days in October,* 65–66; Gaff, 246.

21. Drum papers, 77th Division files, box 16, MHI; Langer, 66.

22. Miles, 169; Drum papers, 77th Division files, box 16, MHI. Although 554 is the number usually given for the size of the force trapped in the Charlevaux pocket, the exact tally has never been finally determined. Many ex-soldiers and descendants would falsely claim to have participated in Whittlesey's noble defense. "The list of walk-ins, walk-outs, carried-outs, and dead or missing," says historian Robert Ferrell, "came to resemble the inflated passenger list for the *Mayflower*" (*Five Days in October,* 80). Also unknown is the number of German troops surrounding them. Some accounts claim that the Americans far outnumbered the Germans—an assertion that, if true, sets the affair of the Lost Battalion in an entirely new light.

23. Gaff, 259–60; Slotkin, 372.

CHAPTER 18: *"York, I Hear You Have Captured the Whole Damned German Army": October 8*

1. Huidekoper, 1:101–2.

2. Henry F. Seal, *"Ever Forward,"* 105.

3. Ibid., 107.

4. Seal, 108; Gregory Medal of Honor citation.

5. F. C. Reynolds, *115th Infantry U.S.A. in the World War,* 129; Regan and Costin Medal of Honor citations.

6. Huidekoper, 1:105.

7. Davis, 24; *History of the 124th Machine Gun Battalion,* 21.

8. Miles, 175; George M. Sparks, *The 327th Under Fire,* 56–57.

9. Other members of York's detachment later testified that there were about a hundred Germans in the group around the shack. If so, the number of men that he captured personally probably amounted to about two dozen (York, 237–59).

10. Douglas Mastriano, "Alvin York and the Meuse-Argonne Offensive," 23–29.

11. York gave two accounts of how he replied to the major. This was his official account. In his memoir, dictated to Tom Skeyhill ten years after the war, York said he pointed his .45 at the German and told him he had better (York, 229, 266).

12. York, 217–66.

13. Pershing, 2:332

CHAPTER 19: *"We Are Going to Have a Very Hard Day": October 9*

1. Private Berger Loman, a Norwegian native fighting in the 132d, earned a Medal of Honor on this date by taking out German machine guns in the Bois de Chaume.
2. Dermody, online; Huidekoper, 3:177.
3. *History of the 124th Machine Gun Battalion,* 23.
4. USAWW, 9:547.
5. Bullard, 274.
6. Hines papers, diary, MHI.
7. Bach and Hall, 190.
8. Ibid., 191–92.
9. Ashby Williams, 114.
10. Clarence E. Lovejoy, *The Story of the Thirty-Eighth,* 149–55.
11. Haan diary, Lauer, WWIS, MHI.
12. Garlock, 244–45.
13. Michigan and Wisconsin War History Commissions, *The 32nd Division in the World War,* 102.
14. Woehl, WWIS, MHI; Jonker, *The "Old Command,"* 37–39.
15. Joseph M. Donnelly, *A History of Company "G,"* n.p.; Haan diary, Lauer, WWIS, MHI.
16. Kyler, WWIS, MHI.
17. *Infantry in Battle,* 146–49; *History of the First Division,* 208. The only exception to the day's success came on the right, where the 91st Division's 181st Brigade, inserted into the lines between the 1st and 32d Divisions, failed to take Hill 255 northwest of Gesnes. But it hardly mattered. With the 32d Division at Côte Dame Marie, and the 1st Division in possession of Hills 272 and 263, that hill would eventually fall as a matter of course.
18. Kyler, WWIS, MHI.
19. Sparks, *The 327th under Fire,* 64.
20. Viereck, 256; Sparks, 60–64.
21. York, 272.
22. Minder, 354.
23. Viereck, 258–59.
24. USAWW, 9:546, 549.

CHAPTER 20: *Beyond the Argonne: October 10*

1. Joseph D. Lawrence, *Fighting Soldier,* 88.
2. Cutchins, *History of the Twenty-Ninth Division,* 162.
3. Lawrence, 86–100; Cutchins, 164; U.S. Army, 29th Division, *Source Book,* 50.
4. U.S. Army, 29th Division, *Source Book,* 118–19, 200.
5. Huidekoper, 3:99.
6. Bullard, 274; Bach and Hall, 192.
7. Stultz, 488.
8. Ashby Williams, 124.
9. *Infantry in Battle,* 37, 232–35, 376–77.
10. Woehl, WWIS, MHI; Haan diary, Lauer, WWIS, MHI.
11. McHenry, *As a Private Saw It,* 65–67.

CHAPTER 21: *Last Gasp: October 11*

1. USAWW, 9:552.
2. Seal, 24, 38, 114. Although Molleville Farm has been rebuilt, the woods surrounding it still contain nearly intact gun pits, trenches, and bunkers.

3. Edward Loudenbeck collection, VHP, AFC/2001/001/1937, DLC.

4. Bach and Hall, 193–96.

5. Stultz, *History of the Eightieth Division,* 496–97; Stultz, WWIS, folder 74, MHI; Ashby Williams, *Experiences of the Great War,* 127; Lukens, 87.

6. Lukens, 91–92; Ashby Williams, 132–33.

7. Bullard, 280.

8. Ferrell, *America's Deadliest Battle,* 114.

9. Woehl, WWIS, MHI.

10. Emil B. Gansser, *On the Battle Fields of France in 1918,* 142.

11. Colonel Walter M. Whitman collection, 82d Division, 325th Regiment, WWIS, MHI; Corporal Fred H. Takes, 82d Division, 325th Regiment, WWIS, MHI.

12. S. L. A. Marshall, *The American Heritage History of World War I,* 445; Smythe, *Pershing,* 208.

13. Smythe, *Pershing,* 207.

14. Trask, 142–45.

15. Smythe, *Pershing,* 88–94, 208.

16. Quoted in ibid., 216.

17. Georges Clemenceau, *Grandeur and Misery of Victory,* 81–87.

18. Braim, 130; Smythe, *Pershing,* 206, 217; Trask, 144–45.

19. Braim, 122–23.

20. James J. Cooke, *The U.S. Air Service in the Great War,* 181.

21. Mitchell, "The Air Service in the Argonne-Meuse," 559; Cooke, *The U.S. Air Service in the Great War,* 192.

CHAPTER 22: *"Like the Heat from a Blast-Furnace Door": October 12–13*

1. U.S. Army, 29th Division, *Source Book,* 60.

2. William J. Reddan, *Other Men's Lives,* 175–207; U.S. Army, 29th Division, *Source Book,* 61.

3. Ibid.

4. Frederick Wise and Meigs O. Frost, 277; Barkley, 223.

5. Block, WWIS, MHI.

6. Lawrence, 120–21.

7. Young, n.p.

8. Lowell Thomas, *Woodfill of the Regulars,* 9–11, 65.

9. Ferrell, *America's Deadliest Battle,* 109.

10. Thomas, 276–90.

11. Ernest L. Wrentmore, *In Spite of Hell,* 152–53.

12. Kyler, WWIS, MHI.

13. Douglas MacArthur, *Reminiscences,* 15.

14. Geoffrey Perret, *Old Soldiers Never Die,* 87.

15. James J. Cooke, *The Rainbow Division in the Great War,* 10–11; another famous member of the regiment, the poet Joyce Kilmer, had been killed in July.

16. MacArthur, 66.

17. Perret, 105; MacArthur, 66; D. Clayton James, *The Years of MacArthur,* 217.

18. Francis P. Duffy, *Father Duffy's Story,* 263.

19. York, 280.

20. Colonel Walter M. Whitman papers, 82d Division, 325th Regiment, WWIS, MHI.

CHAPTER 23: *"The Best Day's Work": October 14*

1. Barkley, 225–26.

2. Wrentmore, 163.

3. *Official History of the Fifth Division,* 145; Lieutenant James A. Leach Jr., 5th Division, 11th Regiment, WWIS, MHI.

4. *Official History of the Fifth Division,* 145; Wrentmore, 165.

5. Wrentmore, 167–75.

6. Gansser, 148–49.

7. *Official History of the Fifth Division,* 145–54.

8. Haan diary, Lauer, WWIS, MHI.

9. Schmidt, 118.

10. Woehl, WWIS, MHI.

11. Horace L. Baker, *Argonne Days,* 54–57; Michigan and Wisconsin War History Commissions, 107.

12. Woehl, WWIS, MHI; World War I Organization Records, 32d Division, boxes 20–21, RG 120, NARC; Garlock, 248–49. Strom and his men received DSCs.

13. Schmidt, 119–21; Michigan and Wisconsin War History Commissions, 107.

14. Haan diary, Lauer, WWIS, MHI.

15. Quoted in Cooke, *Rainbow Division,* 171.

16. Perret, 105.

17. Quoted in Cooke, *Rainbow Division,* 172.

18. Henry J. Reilly, *Americans All,* 681; Cooke, *Rainbow Division,* 173–74.

19. Duffy, 270.

20. Reilly, 692; Cooke, *Rainbow Division,* 171–72; Hallas, 279; Duffy, 271.

21. Cooke, *Rainbow Division,* 174.

22. Colonel Walter Whitman papers, 82d Division, 325th Regiment, WWIS, MHI.

23. Takes, WWIS, MHI.

24. Alexander, 244.

25. *History of the 306th Infantry,* 76–77.

26. Ibid., 80–81.

27. Alexander, 246–47; Henry W. Smith, 67; *History of the 306th Infantry,* 84–85.

28. Alexander, 247–52.

CHAPTER 24: *"There Are Times When Even General Officers Have to Be Expendable": October 15*

1. U.S. Army, 29th Division, *Source Book,* 256; Seal, 115–19.

2. John S. D. Eisenhower, *Yanks,* 259; Hines Papers, MHI; Smythe, *Pershing,* 215; Captain Robert H. St. James, 3d Division, 7th Regiment, WWIS, MHI; Hemenway, 71.

3. Wrentmore, 178–86.

4. *Infantry in Battle,* 401–2; *Official History of the Fifth Division,* 156.

5. Gansser, 150.

6. Woehl, WWIS, MHI; Schmidt, 123–25; Haan diary, Lauer, WWIS, MHI.

7. Viereck, 263.

8. Elmer W. Sherwood, *Diary of a Rainbow Veteran,* 180.

9. Cooke, *Rainbow Division,* 177; Lawrence Stewart, *Rainbow Bright,* 124–25.

10. Hallas, 280; Martin J. Hogan, *The Shamrock Battalion of the Rainbow,* 248–49.

11. Cooke, *Rainbow Division,* 176–77.

12. Duffy, 276–77.

13. Hallas, 285.

14. Lauer, WWIS, MHI.

15. Duffy, 277; James, *The Years of MacArthur,* 222.

16. Perret, 106; Henry D. Stansbury, *Maryland's 117th Trench Mortar Battery in the World War,* 99.

17. Letter, April 11, 1924, in Whitman, WWIS, MHI.

18. Cooke, *Rainbow Division,* 106.

19. *History of the 306th Infantry,* 90.

20. Thomas Fleming, "Two Argonnes," 44–48.

21. Report, October 18, 1918, in Raymond Sheldon papers, MHI; Rainsford, 230.

22. Reports by Lt. F. A. Tillman and Capt. Newcomb, Raymond Sheldon Papers, MHI.

CHAPTER 25: *"Large Bodies Move Slowly, Though with Great Momentum When They Start":*
October 16–31

1. Quoted in Smythe, *Pershing,* 218.

2. Frederick Palmer, 359.

3. Liggett, 205.

4. Bullard, 267; Liggett, 207–8.

5. Smythe, *Pershing,* 217; Braim, 135; Liggett, 207.

6. Frank P. Sibley, *With the Yankee Division in France,* 17–18; Smythe, *Pershing,* 215.

7. Hallas, 281.

8. Ibid., 286.

9. Seal, 140; U.S. Army, 29th Division, *Source Book,* 119.

10. Casey, 238; U.S. Army, 29th Division, *Source Book,* 151.

11. Ibid., 15, 43; Seal, 77; Millard E. Tydings, *The Machine Gunners of the Blue and Gray*
Division, 34–37; *Infantry in Battle,* 74–75.

12. Hines papers, diary, MHI.

13. Frederick Wise and Meigs O. Frost, 283.

14. Block, WWIS, MHI.

15. Hemenway, 144–45; St. James, WWIS, MHI.

16. Berry, 147–49.

17. *Infantry in Battle,* 404.

18. Lovejoy, 161.

19. St. James, WWIS, MHI; *Infantry in Battle,* 404–5.

20. Barkley, 255.

21. *Official History of the Fifth Division,* 161–64.

22. *Infantry in Battle,* 12–14.

23. Vincent Reed collection, VHP, AFC/2001/001/2431, DLC.

24. Ibid.; Norvel Clotfelder collection, VHP, AFC/2001/001/2386, DLC.

25. William L. Wright, *Meuse-Argonne Diary,* 1–2.

26. Cochrane, *The 89th Division in the Bois de Bantheville,* 26.

27. Perret, 106–7; MacArthur, 67.

28. Reilly, 678–86.

29. Hallas, 282.

30. Whitman, WWIS, MHI.

31. Drum papers, 82d Division files, box 16, MHI.

32. Takes, WWIS, MHI.

33. Tillman report in Sheldon papers, MHI.

34. Earl B. Searcy, *Looking Back,* 82–83.

35. Cochrane, *The 78th Division at the Kriemhilde Stellung,* 12.

36. Fleming, 44–48; Cochrane, *The 78th Division,* 13; Joseph T. Dickman, *The Great*
Crusade, 167–68.

37. *A History of the Three Hundred Tenth Infantry,* 129–31.

38. Searcy, 84–86.

39. Leonard P. Kurtz, *Beyond No Man's Land,* 45; *History of the Three Hundred Tenth Infantry,* 138.
40. Ibid., 134; Searcy, 87; Cochrane, *The 78th Division,* 22–23.
41. Cochrone, *The 78th Division,* 16; *History of the Three Hundred Tenth Infantry,* 135–36.
42. Kurtz, 55–56.
43. Cochrane, *The 78th Division,* 18–19; Kurtz, 56–57.
44. Stallings, 331.
45. Kurtz, 58–60.

Victory: November 1–11

1. Hallas, 302.
2. USAWW, 10:19–23.
3. Ibid., 10:29–30.
4. Smythe, *Pershing,* 221; Pershing, 2:369.
5. Liggett, 218.
6. Drum papers, 82d Division files, box 16, MHI.
7. Nenninger, "Tactical Dysfunction in the AEF," 178.
8. Lieutenant John G. Baker, 32d Division, 127th Regiment, WWIS, MHI.
9. USAWW, 8:362; "Artillery and Ammunition Expended in the A.E.F.," memo dated April 22, 1920, Drum papers, box 14, MHI; Langer, 76–78.
10. USAWW, 8:367.
11. Liggett, 216.
12. Palmer, 587–88; quoted in Coffman, 344–45.
13. Casey, 299–301.
14. Ibid.
15. Quoted in Hallas, 299.
16. Evans, 156–57.
17. Wright, 138.
18. George C. Marshall, 182–84.
19. Jennings Wise, 232–33.
20. Young, n.p.
21. Liggett, 222; Viereck, 275.
22. Floyd, 77.
23. Reddan, 227.
24. Hines papers, diary, MHI; *Official History of the Fifth Division,* 199.
25. Leach, WWIS, MHI; *Official History of the Fifth Division,* 201–5.
26. Ibid., 207.
27. Evans, 158; Hallas, 303.
28. Henry W. Smith, 79.
29. Pershing, 2:381; for a discussion of why Maistre agreed to the proposal, see Donald Smythe, "A.E.F. Snafu at Sedan," 136.
30. Smythe, "A.E.F. Snafu at Sedan," 136.
31. Pershing, 2:381; Smythe, "A.E.F. Snafu at Sedan," 135.
32. George C. Marshall, 189; Smythe, "A.E.F. Snafu at Sedan," 138. Drum added the order's last sentence as an afterthought.
33. Quoted in Reilly, 795.
34. Smythe, "A. E. F. Snafu at Sedan," 140.
35. MacArthur, 69.
36. Smythe, "A.E.F. Snafu at Sedan," 143–45; Coffman, 353.

37. USAWW, 8:113.
38. Liggett, 234.
39. Quoted in Martin Gilbert, *First World War,* 497.
40. Henry W. Smith, 76–77.
41. Connell Albertine, *The Yankee Doughboy,* 228–29.
42. Tompkins, 105; Gunther was officially recognized as the last American soldier killed in the war.
43. Swartz, WWIS, MHI.
44. Garlock, 262–64.
45. Leach, WWIS, MHI.
46. Lieutenant E. P. Lukert Jr., 5th Division, 11th Regiment, WWIS, MHI; *Official History of the Fifth Division,* 251.
47. *Infantry in Battle,* 108–12.
48. Evans, 159–60.
49. Romedahl, 87–92.
50. Casey, 328–29.
51. DeSilvey, online.
52. Pierce, WWIS, MHI.
53. Schellberg, 66.
54. Dwight, online.
55. Barkley, 271.
56. Romedahl, 87–92.
57. Swartz, WWIS, MHI.
58. Triplet, 234.
59. Swartz, WWIS, MHI.
60. Sergeant Andrew Madsen, 32d Division, 123d Field Artillery Regiment, WWIS, MHI.
61. York, 284.
62. Quoted in D'Este, 271–72.

CONCLUSION: *"When I Get Back, You Can Wager I Will Be a Home Loving Man"*

1. Hallas, 311–12.
2. Albertine, 268–71.
3. Kyler, WWIS, MHI.
4. Maverick, 138–39.
5. Quoted in Jennifer D. Keene, *Doughboys, the Great War, and the Remaking of America,* 137.
6. Stevenson, 95–96; Smythe, *Pershing,* 238; Basil Henry Liddell Hart, *Reputations,* 314–15; Keene, 133.
7. Braim, 163.
8. Liddell Hart, 314–15.
9. Mitchell, *Memoirs of World War I,* 261.
10. Drum papers, April 2, 1919, letter from Conner to Drum, box 14, MHI.
11. Pershing, 2:391; Braim, 145; Liggett, 238.
12. Braim, 145.
13. Corporal Frank Schmitt, 28th Division, 109th Regiment, WWIS, MHI.
14. Wrentmore, 193.
15. Stevenson, 112.
16. Lengel, "University of Virginia Base Hospital 41 in the World War," 29.
17. Keene, 161–78.
18. Romedahl, 11–12.

19. C. Earl Baker, *Doughboy's Diary,* 124–25.

20. Hallas, 329.

21. York, 212–13.

22. Keene, 171; decades later, as MHI questionnaires attest, the Doughboys still felt proud of their independence from government aid, believing that it set them apart from "softer" generations, like those of World War II and Vietnam.

23. Stevenson, 112; the shock of presenting such a subject to the American public may be compared to *The Best Years of Our Lives* in 1946, or *The Deer Hunter* in 1978. Laurence Stallings, a World War I veteran who also lost a leg, wrote the script for *The Big Parade.*

24. Charles A. Prosser, "A Federal Program for the Vocational Rehabilitation of Disabled Soldiers and Sailors," 117.

25. Harry W. Zander, *Thirteen Years in Hell,* 288.

26. Private Joseph J. Attura, 1st Division, 18th Regiment, WWIS, MHI.

27. Zander, 282.

28. Ibid., 301–2.

29. Quoted in Keene, 164; Kyler, WWIS, MHI.

30. Keene, 163–65; Allan R. Millett, *The General,* 448, 461.

31. Keene, 180.

32. Stringfellow, 244–45.

33. Sirmon, *That's War,* 248–49.

34. Bullard, 292, 297–98.

35. Slotkin, 436–43.

36. Kyler, WWIS, MHI; Corporal Clarence Mahan, 1st Division, 1st Supply Train, WWIS, MHI.

37. Sergeant Robley W. Glaus, 29th Division, 116th Regiment, WWIS, MHI.

38. Hallas, 328.

39. By using American actors to play German roles, speaking in American accents, some of the Doughboys' feelings and concerns about the war were advanced—but only surreptitiously.

40. Slotkin, 477.

41. York, 236, 300; Michael E. Birdwell, "Gobble Like a Turkey," 164–68.

42. Thomas, 319.

43. Slotkin, 475–80; Gaff, 281–85.

44. Smythe, *Pershing,* 254–61, 309.

When writing a book of this scope on limited resources of time and money, there is no point in reinventing the wheel. I have therefore relied heavily on the American Battle Monuments Commission's *Summary of Operations* series for First Army's operational activities in the Meuse-Argonne. These highly detailed booklets, written during the Second World War by teams of officers working in official reports and memoranda, provide reliable accounts of the day-to-day activities of individual companies, battalions, regiments, brigades, and divisions. Any scholar bold enough to write a full-scale operational history of the Meuse-Argonne—which this book does not pretend to be—must move beyond the ABMC booklets and conduct the bulk of his or her research in the official AEF records in RG 120 at the National Archives in College Park, Maryland. "A few days" in these records, as historian Robert Ferrell has aptly written, "will not suffice for anything beyond random impressions" (*Collapse at Meuse-Argonne,* 155). It is, rather, a task requiring months if not years of work if the researcher is to do the records justice.

Utilizing the ABMC booklets has allowed me to concentrate my research on memoirs, diaries, letters, and other published and unpublished material pertinent to the focus of my book: the experiences of common soldiers. Even with the official records set aside, the task has been vast enough. The largest collection of primary source material relating to the experiences of American soldiers during the First World War resides at the U.S. Army Military History Institute in Carlisle, Pennsylvania. This huge collection—a national treasure—of questionnaires, diaries, memoirs, letters, and other papers is supplemented by a library of published unit histories and personal accounts that is second to none in the United States. Another important collection of unpublished primary source material—now partially digitized—resides at the Veterans History Project at the Library of Congress's American Folklife

Center in Washington, D.C. In addition, several hundred published and un-published memoirs, diaries, and letters, many of them extremely rare, are available through interlibrary loan and, increasingly, on the Internet. Other unpublished materials are available in libraries and museums all over the country, and in private hands. As an avid collector who has spent twenty years researching the experiences of common soldiers in the First World War, I can attest that I have only scratched the surface of what is out there.

UNPUBLISHED SOURCES

U.S. ARMY MILITARY HISTORY INSTITUTE, CARLISLE, PENNSYLVANIA

World War I Survey Collection for the 1st, 2d, 3d, 4th, 5th, 26th, 28th, 29th, 32d, 33d, 35th, 36th, 42d, 77th, 78th, 79th, 80th, 82d, 89th, 90th, 91st, 92d, and 93d Divisions, including questionnaires, diaries, memoirs, and other unpublished materials.

Lucien Grant Berry papers.
Karl Bretzfelder papers.
Hugh A. Drum papers.
Glenn W. Garlock papers.
John L. Hines papers.
Dennis Edward Nolan papers.
Paul Ransom papers.
Raymond Sheldon papers.
Orlando W. Ward papers.

VETERANS HISTORY PROJECT, AMERICAN FOLKLIFE CENTER, LIBRARY OF CONGRESS

James Frederick Campbell Collection (AFC/2001/001/24108)
Tenus Christensen Collection (AFC/2001/001/3401)
Norvel Clotfelter Collection (AFC/2001/001/2386)
George Duwel Collection (AFC/2001/001/622)
Harry Frieman Collection (AFC/2001/001/23600)
Charles Gerwitz Collection (AFC/2001/001/286)
Joseph Gleeson Collection (AFC/2001/001/10911)
Theodore Kohls Collection (AFC/2001/001/723)
Edward Loudenbeck Collection (AFC/2001/001/1937)
Mark McCave Collection (AFC/2001/001/1376)
Michael McCoog Collection (AFC/2001/001/24386)
William McKnight Collection (AFC/2001/001/10877)
Morris Martin Collection (AFC/2001/001/1034)
Thomas Millea Collection (AFC/2001/001/1681)
Michael Moran Collection (AFC/2001/001/10867)
James Platt Collection (AFC/2001/001/1125)
Vincent Reed Collection (AFC/2001/001/2431)
Alva Reid Collection (AFC/2001/001/5008)
Guy Rowe Collection (AFC/2001/001/3498)
Reese Russell Collection (AFC/2001/001/18879)
Lloyd Staley Collection (AFC/2001/001/2435)
Charles Taylor Collection (AFC/2001/001/1770)
Coy Vance Collection (AFC/2001/001/8201)

NATIONAL ARCHIVES, COLLEGE PARK, MARYLAND

Record Group 111.11, Records of the Office of the Chief Signal Officer, Still Pictures (General), 1860–1982.

Record Group 120.9.3, Records of the American Expeditionary Forces. Historical Files: Operations Reports, Unit Histories, Messages. 28th and 32d Divisions.

INTERNET RESOURCES

Chopin, Mathew. "Through the Valley of Death." Online at http://www.geocities.com/louisiana_doughboy/index.htm.

Dermody, Charles D., Sr. "A Yank in the First World War." Online at http://www.htc.net/~dermody/yankww1.htm.

DeSilvey, Wayne. "The Diary of Bugler Wayne DeSilvey." Edited by Phil Reese. Online at http://www.worldwar1.com/dbc/desilvey.htm.

Dwight, Robert L. "R. L. Dwight's WWI Diary." Transcribed by the author's grandson, Bill McPherson. Online at http://home.stny.rr.com/wmcpherson/rlddiary.html.

Gustafson, Robert R. "Diary & Photos: Battle in the Argonne and Playing with Pershing's Band." Online at http://www.worldwar1.com/dbc/rgustafson.htm.

Hanlon, Michael E. "The Origins of Doughboy." Online at http://www.worldwar1.com/dbc/origindb.htm.

Huber, Allen D. "The Diary of a Doughboy." Edited by Robert Huskey. Online at http://www.usgennet.org/usa/mo/county/stlouis/missourians/john-huskey.htm.

Livergood, William A. "Diary of William A. Livergood: A Tale of a Soldier Who Served in the World War in France." Online at http://www.laroke.com/larryk4674/2001/poppop.htm.

Scherr, Arthur. "Diary of Corporal Arthur W. Scherr, 107th Field Signal Bn., 32nd Division (Red Arrow Division), Wisconsin National Guard." Online at http://www.100megsfree2.com/jjscherr/scherr/Diary.htm.

Tudury, Henry Jetton. "The Diary of Henry Jetton Tudury: Mississippi's Most Decorated Doughboy of World War I." Edited by Charles Sullivan. Online at http://www.geocities.com/henry_tudury/diary.htm.

OTHER MANUSCRIPT SOURCES

Balthaser, Walter R. "Memoirs . . . from the Pen of Walter R. Balthaser." Property of Merritt Balthaser.

Boll, Maximilian A. W. "My First Journey, 1917–1919." Stanford, Calif.: Hoover Institution Archives.

Rentz, Irwin J. "World War I Diary." Property of John D. Rentz, Reading, Pennsylvania.

PUBLISHED SOURCES

Albertine, Connell. *The Yankee Doughboy*. Boston: Branden Press, 1968.

Alexander, Robert. *Memories of the World War, 1917–1918*. New York: Macmillan, 1931.

American Battle Monuments Commission. *American Armies and Battlefields in Europe*. Originally published 1938. Reprint. Washington, D.C.: United States Army Center of Military History, 1992.

———. *1st Division Summary of Operations in the World War*. Washington, D.C.: United States Government Printing Office, 1944.

———. *2d Division Summary of Operations in the World War*. Washington, D.C.: United States Government Printing Office, 1944.

———. *3d Division Summary of Operations in the World War*. Washington, D.C.: United States Government Printing Office, 1944.

———. *4th Division Summary of Operations in the World War*. Washington, D.C.: United States Government Printing Office, 1944.

———. *5th Division Summary of Operations in the World War*. Washington, D.C.: United States Government Printing Office, 1944.

———. *26th Division Summary of Operations in the World War*. Washington, D.C.: United States Government Printing Office, 1944.

———. *28th Division Summary of Operations in the World War*. Washington, D.C.: United States Government Printing Office, 1944.

———. *29th Division Summary of Operations in the World War*. Washington, D.C.: United States Government Printing Office, 1944.

———. *32d Division Summary of Operations in the World War*. Washington, D.C.: United States Government Printing Office, 1944.

———. *33d Division Summary of Operations in the World War*. Washington, D.C.: United States Government Printing Office, 1944.

———. *35th Division Summary of Operations in the World War*. Washington, D.C.: United States Government Printing Office, 1944.

———. *36th Division Summary of Operations in the World War*. Washington, D.C.: United States Government Printing Office, 1944.

———. *37th Division Summary of Operations in the World War*. Washington, D.C.: United States Government Printing Office, 1944.

———. *42d Division Summary of Operations in the World War*. Washington, D.C.: United States Government Printing Office, 1944.

———. *77th Division Summary of Operations in the World War*. Washington, D.C.: United States Government Printing Office, 1944.

———. *78th Division Summary of Operations in the World War*. Washington, D.C.: United States Government Printing Office, 1944.

———. *79th Division Summary of Operations in the World War*. Washington, D.C.: United States Government Printing Office, 1944.

———. *80th Division Summary of Operations in the World War*. Washington, D.C.: United States Government Printing Office, 1944.

———. *81st Division Summary of Operations in the World War*. Washington, D.C.: United States Government Printing Office, 1944.

———. *82d Division Summary of Operations in the World War*. Washington, D.C.: United States Government Printing Office, 1944.

———. *89th Division Summary of Operations in the World War*. Washington, D.C.: United States Government Printing Office, 1944.

———. *90th Division Summary of Operations in the World War*. Washington, D.C.: United States Government Printing Office, 1944.

———. *91st Division Summary of Operations in the World War*. Washington, D.C.: United States Government Printing Office, 1944.

———. *92d Division Summary of Operations in the World War*. Washington, D.C.: United States Government Printing Office, 1944.

———. *93d Division Summary of Operations in the World War*. Washington, D.C.: United States Government Printing Office, 1944.

American Troops at the Argonne. Hearings before the Committee on Military Affairs, U.S. Senate, 65th Congress, 3rd session. Washington, D.C.: Government Printing Office, 1919.

Army War College, Historical Section. *The Ninety-Second Division, 1917–1918: An Analytical Study*. Washington Barracks, D.C.: Army War College, 1923.

Arpin, Edmund P., Jr. "A Wisconsinite in World War I: Reminiscences of Edmund P. Arpin, Jr." Edited by Ira Berlin. *Wisconsin Magazine of History* 51, 1 (Autumn 1967), 3–25; 51, 2 (Winter 1967–68), 124–38; 51, 3 (Spring 1968), 218–37.

Aston, George. *The Biography of the Late Marshal Foch*. New York: Macmillan, 1929.

Atteridge, A. Hilliard. *Marshal Ferdinand Foch: His Life and His Theory of Modern War*. New York: Dodd, Mead, 1919.

Bach, Christian A., and Henry Noble Hall. *The Fourth Division: Its Services and Achievements in the World War Gathered from the Records of the Division*. Garden City, N.Y.: Christian A. Bach, 1920.

Baker, C. Earl. *Doughboy's Diary*. Shippensburg, Pa.: Burd Street Press, 1998.

Baker, Horace L. *Argonne Days: Experiences of a World War Private on the Meuse-Argonne Front, Compiled from His Diary*. Aberdeen, Miss.: The Aberdeen Weekly, 1927.

Barbeau, Arthur E., and Florette Henry. *The Unknown Soldiers: African-American Troops in World War I*. Originally published 1974. Reprint. New York: Da Capo Press, 1996.

Bareither, Terry M., ed. *An Engineer's Diary of the Great War*. West Lafayette, Ind.: Purdue University Press, 2002.

Barkley, John Lewis. *No Hard Feelings!* New York: Cosmopolitan Book Corporation, 1930.

Berry, Henry. *Make the Kaiser Dance*. New York: Doubleday, 1978.

Birdwell, Michael E. "Gobble Like a Turkey: Alvin C. York and American Popular Culture," in Michael E. Birdwell and W. Calvin Dickinson, eds., *Rural Life and Culture of the Upper Cumberland*. Lexington: University Press of Kentucky, 2004, 159–77.

Braim, Paul F. *The Test of Battle: The American Expeditionary Forces in the Meuse-Argonne Campaign*. Newark, Del.: University of Delaware Press, 1987.

Brittain, Vera. *Testament of Youth: An Autobiographical Study of the Years 1900–1925*. New York: Macmillan, 1933.

Britten, Thomas A. *American Indians in World War I: At Home and at War*. Albuquerque: University of New Mexico Press, 1997.

Bruce, Robert B. *A Fraternity of Arms: America and France in the Great War*. Lawrence: University Press of Kansas, 2003.

Buck, Beaumont. *Memories of Peace and War*. San Antonio, Tex.: Naylor, 1935.

Bullard, Robert Lee. *Personalities and Reminiscences of the War*. Garden City, N.Y.: Doubleday, Page, 1925.

Burton, Harold H. *600 Days' Service: A History of the 361st Infantry Regiment of the United States Army*. Cleveland: privately printed, 1919.

Butler, Charles E. *The Yanks Are Coming*. New York: Vantage Press, 1963.

Cain, James M. "The Taking of Montfaucon," in Roy Hoopes, ed., *The Baby in the Icebox and Other Short Fiction by James M. Cain*. New York: Holt, Rinehart and Winston, 1981, 104–19.

Carter, Robert L. *Pictorial History of the 35th Division*. St. Louis: Robert L. Carter, 1933.

Casey, Robert J. *The Cannoneers Have Hairy Ears: A Diary of the Front Lines*. New York: J. H. Sears, 1927.

Cheseldine, R. M. *Ohio in the Rainbow: Official Story of the 166th Infantry, 42nd Division in the World War*. Columbus, Ohio: F. J. Heer, 1924.

Clark, William Bell. *War History of the 79th Division, National Army*. Williamsport, Pa.: privately printed, 1918.

Clemenceau, Georges. *Grandeur and Misery of Victory*. New York: Harcourt, Brace, 1930.

Clement, Charles M., ed. *Pennsylvania in the World War: An Illustrated History of the Twenty-Eighth Division*. 2 volumes. Pittsburgh: State Publications Society, 1921.

Cochrane, Rexmond C. *The 1st Division in the Meuse-Argonne, 1–12 October 1918*. Army Chemical Center, Md.: U.S. Army Chemical Corps Historical Office, 1959.

———. *The 26th Division East of the Meuse: October 1918*. Army Chemical Center, Md.: U.S. Army Chemical Corps Historical Office, 1960.

———. *The 29th Division in the Côtes de Meuse: October 1918*. Army Chemical Center, Md.: U.S. Army Chemical Corps Historical Office, 1959.

———. *The 33rd Division along the Meuse: October 1918*. Army Chemical Center, Md.: U.S. Army Chemical Corps Historical Office, 1958.

———. *The 42nd Division before Landres–et–St. Georges: October 1918*. Army Chemical Center, Md.: U.S. Army Chemical Corps Historical Office, 1960.

———. *The 78th Division at the Kriemhilde Stellung, October 1918*. Army Chemical Center, Md.: U.S. Army Chemical Corps Historical Office, 1957.

———. *The 79th Division at Montfaucon, October 1918*. Army Chemical Center, Md.: U.S. Army Chemical Corps Historical Office, 1960.

———. *The 89th Division in the Bois de Bantheville, October 1918*. Army Chemical Center, Md.: U.S. Army Chemical Corps Historical Office, 1960.

———. *The Use of Gas in the Meuse-Argonne Campaign: September–November 1918*. Army Chemical Center, Md.: U.S. Army Chemical Corps Historical Office, 1958.

Coffman, Edward M. *The War to End All Wars: The American Military Experience in World War I*. New York: Oxford University Press, 1968.

Colby, Elbridge. "The Taking of Montfaucon." *Infantry Journal* 47, 2 (March–April 1940), 128–40.

Company F History, 319th Infantry. Flemington, N.J.: Ryman Herr, 1920.

Cooke, James J. *The All-Americans at War: The 82nd Division in the Great War, 1917–1918*. Westport, Conn.: Praeger, 1999.

———. *Billy Mitchell*. Boulder, Colo.: Lynne Riener, 2002.

———. *Pershing and His Generals: Command and Staff in the AEF*. Westport, Conn.: Praeger, 1997.

———. *The Rainbow Division in the Great War*. Westport, Conn.: Praeger, 1994.

———. *The U.S. Air Service in the Great War, 1917–1919*. Westport, Conn.: Praeger, 1996.

Cooper, George W. *Our Second Battalion: The Accurate and Authentic History of the Second Battalion 111th Infantry*. Pittsburgh: Second Battalion Book Company, 1920.

Coppard, George. *With a Machine Gun to Cambrai: The Tale of a Young Tommy in Kitchener's Army, 1914–1918*. London: H.M.S.O., 1969.

Corning, Walter D. *The Yanks Crusade: A Book of Reminiscences*. Chicago: privately published, 1927.

Craighill, Edley. *History of the 317th Infantry*. Tours, France: Deslis Frères, 1919.

Crawford, Gilbert. *The 302nd Engineers: A History*. New York, privately printed, 1920.

Cushing, Harvey. *From a Surgeon's Journal: 1915–1918*. Boston: Little, Brown, 1936.

Cutchins, John A. *History of the Twenty-Ninth Division, "Blue and Gray," 1917–1919*. Philadelphia: MacCalla & Co., 1921.

Davis, Abel. *The Story of the 132d Infantry A.E.F.* Privately printed, 1919.

D'Este, Carlo. *A Genius for War: A Life of General George S. Patton*. London: HarperCollins, 1995.

Dickman, Joseph T. *The Great Crusade: A Narrative of the World War*. New York: D. Appleton, 1927.

Donnelly, Joseph M. *A History of Company "G": 125th Infantry, 32nd Division, World War I*. Houghton, Mich.: Privately printed, 1973.

Doughty, Robert A. *Pyrrhic Victory: French Strategy and Operations in the Great War*. Cambridge, Mass.: Harvard University Press, 2005.

Duffy, Francis P. *Father Duffy's Story: A Tale of Humor and Heroism, of Life and Death with the Fighting Sixty-Ninth*. New York: George H. Doran, 1919.

DuPuy, Charles M. *A Machine Gunner's Notes: France 1918*. Pittsburgh: Reed & Witting, 1920.

Edwards, Evan Alexander. *From Doniphan to Verdun: The Official History of the 140th Infantry*. Lawrence, Kans.: The World Company, 1920.

Eisenhower, John S. D., with Joanne Thompson Eisenhower. *Yanks: The Epic Story of the American Army in World War I*. New York: The Free Press, 2001.

Ettinger, Albert M., and A. Churchill Ettinger. *A Doughboy with the Fighting Sixty-Ninth: A Remembrance of World War I*. Shippensburg, Pa.: White Mane Press, 1992.

Evans, Martin Marix, ed. *American Voices of World War I: Primary Source Documents, 1917–1920*. London: Fitzroy Dearborn, 2001.

Farwell, Byron. *Over There: The United States in the Great War, 1917–1918*. New York: W. W. Norton, 1999.

Faulkner, Richard S. " 'Up in the Argonne': The Tragedy of Lieutenant Justus Owens and the 82nd Division in the First World War." *The Georgia Historical Quarterly* 80, 2 (Summer 1996), 276–98.

Ferrell, Robert H. *America's Deadliest Battle: Meuse-Argonne, 1918*. Lawrence: University Press of Kansas, 2007.

———. *Collapse at Meuse-Argonne: The Failure of the Missouri-Kansas Division*. Columbia: University of Missouri Press, 2004.

———. *Five Days in October: The Lost Battalion of World War I*. Columbia: University of Missouri Press, 2005.

———, ed. *Dear Bess: The Letters from Harry to Bess Truman, 1910–1959*. New York: W. W. Norton, 1983.

Fleming, Thomas. "Two Argonnes." *American Heritage* 19, 6 (October 1968), 44–48, 88–94.

Floyd, Frank T. *Company "F" Overseas*. Pittsburgh, Pa.: Pittsburgh Printing Company, 1921.

Foch, Ferdinand. *The Memoirs of Marshal Foch*. Translated by T. Bentley Mott. Garden City, N.Y.: Doubleday, Doran, 1931.

Fullerton, Charles B. *The Twenty-Sixth Infantry in France*. Montabaur-Frankfurt, Germany: Martin Flock, 1919.

Furr, Herman R. *314 Machine Gun Battalion History, Blue Ridge (80th) Division*. Officers and Men of the Battalion, 1919.

Gaff, Alan D. *Blood in the Argonne: The "Lost Battalion" of World War I*. Norman: University of Oklahoma Press, 2005.

Gansser, Emil B. *On the Battle Fields of France in 1918*. Grand Rapids, Mich.: privately printed, 1958.

Garlock, G. W. *Tales of the Thirty-Second*. West Salem, Wis.: Badger Publishing Company, 1927.

Gavin, Lettie. *American Women in World War 1: They Also Served*. Boulder: University Press of Colorado, 1997.

Gilbert, Martin. *First World War*. London: Weidenfeld and Nicolson, 1994.

Grotelueschen, Mark Ethan. *The AEF Way of War: The American Army and Combat in World War I*. Cambridge, Eng.: Cambridge University Press, 2007.

Hallas, James H. *Doughboy War: The American Expeditionary Force in World War I*. Boulder, Colo.: Lynne Rienner, 2000.

Harbord, James G. *The American Army in France, 1917–1919*. Boston: Little, Brown, 1936.

Harlowe, Jerry. *Your Brother Will: The Great War Letters and Diary of William Schellberg.* Ellicott City, Md.: Patapsco Falls Press, 1992.

Haterius, Carl E. *Reminiscences of the 137th U.S. Infantry.* Topeka, Kans.: Crane & Company, 1919.

Hemenway, Frederic Vinton. *History of the Third Division, United States Army, in the World War, for the Period, December 1, 1917, to January 1, 1919.* Cologne, Germany: M. Dumont Schauberg, 1919.

The History of Company C, 304th Field Signal Battalion, U.S. Army, American Expeditionary Forces; A Brief History and Roster of the Outpost Company of the Signal Battalion of the 79th Division from Organization to Demobilization, 1917–1919, John P. Flood, Captain Sig. C., U.S.A., Commanding. Philadelphia: Shade Printing Company, 1920.

History of Company F, 316th Infantry 79th Division, A.E.F. in the World War, 1917–18–19. Philadelphia: Company F Association of the 316th Infantry, 1930.

History of the First Division during the World War, 1917–1919. Philadelphia: John C. Winston, 1931.

History of the 110th Infantry (10th Pa.) of the 28th Division, U.S.A., 1917–1919: A Compilation of Orders, Citations, Maps, Records and Illustrations Relating to the 3rd Pa. Inf., 10th Pa. Inf., and 110th U.S. Inf. Pittsburgh: Association of the 110th Infantry, 1920.

History of the 124th Machine Gun Battalion, 66th Brigade, 33rd Division A.E.F. Privately printed, 1919.

History of the 306th Infantry. New York: 306th Infantry Association, 1935.

A History of the Three Hundred Tenth Infantry, Seventy-Eighth Division U.S.A., 1917–1919. New York: Schilling Press, 1919.

History of the 318th Infantry Regiment of the 80th Division 1917–1919. Richmond, Va.: William Byrd Press, 1919.

Hogan, Martin J. *The Shamrock Battalion of the Rainbow: A Story of the "Fighting Sixty-Ninth."* New York: D. Appleton, 1919.

Hoopes, Roy. *Cain.* New York: Holt, Rinehart and Winston, 1982.

Hoyt, Charles B. *Heroes of the Argonne: An Authentic History of the Thirty-Fifth Division.* Kansas City, Mo.: Franklin Hudson, 1919.

Huidekoper, Frederic Louis. *The History of the 33rd Division A.E.F.* Vols. 1–4 of *Illinois in the World War,* ed. T. C. Pease. Springfield: Illinois State Historical Library, 1921.

Infantry in Battle. Washington, D.C.: The Infantry Journal, 1939.

Jackson, Edgar B. *Fall Out to the Right of the Road!* Verona, Va.: McClure Press, 1973.

James, D. Clayton. *The Years of MacArthur.* Volume 1, *1880–1941.* Boston: Houghton Mifflin, 1970.

Joel, Arthur H. *Under the Lorraine Cross: An Account of the Experiences of Infantrymen Who Fought with the Lorraine Cross Division in France during the World War.* Privately printed, 1921.

Johnson, Ray Neil. *Heaven, Hell, or Hoboken.* Cleveland, Ohio: O. S. Hubbell Printing Co., 1919.

Johnson, Thomas M., and Fletcher Pratt. *The Lost Battalion.* Indianapolis: Bobbs-Merrill, 1938.

Jonker, Hartger, Jr. *The "Old Command": Service History of Company "L," 126th Infantry.* Privately printed, 1919.

Keene, Jennifer D. *Doughboys, the Great War, and the Remaking of America.* Baltimore: Johns Hopkins University Press, 2001.

Kenamore, Clair. *From Vauquois Hill to Exermont: A History of the Thirty-Fifth Division of the United States Army.* St. Louis, Mo.: Guard Publishing, 1919.

Kimball, Guy E. *One Soldier's Experience with the American Expeditionary Force in World War I, 2 October 1917 through 1 October 1918.* Privately printed, 1982.

Kovach, Karen. *The Life and Times of MG Dennis E. Nolan, 1872–1956: The Army's First G2.* Fort Belvoir, Va.: History Office, Office of the Chief of Staff, U.S. Army Intelligence and Security Command, 1998.

Kurtz, Leonard P. *Beyond No Man's Land.* Buffalo, N.Y.: Foster & Stewart, 1937.

Langer, William L. *Gas and Flame in World War I.* New York: Alfred A. Knopf, 1965.

Lanza, Conrad H. "The Battle of Montfaucon, 26 September 1918—An Artilleryman's View." *Field Artillery Journal* 23, 3 (May–June 1933), 226–48.

———. "The End of the Battle of Montfaucon." *Field Artillery Journal* 23, 4 (July–August 1933), 347–67.

———. "The First Battle of Romagne." *Field Artillery Journal* 23, 6 (November–December 1933), 493–507.

———. "The Start of the Meuse-Argonne Campaign." *Field Artillery Journal* 23, 1 (January–February 1933), 57–71.

———. "Supporting an Infantry Division." *Field Artillery Journal* 23, 5 (September–October 1933), 405–25.

Lawrence, Joseph Douglas. *Fighting Soldier: The AEF in 1918.* Edited by Robert H. Ferrell. Boulder: Colorado Associated University Press, 1985.

Lengel, Edward G. "The University of Virginia Ambulance Drivers of the First World War." *Magazine of Albemarle County History* 57 (1999), 1–33.

———. "University of Virginia Base Hospital 41." *Magazine of Albemarle County History* 59 (2001), 1–30.

———. *World War I Memories: An Annotated Bibliography of Personal Accounts Published in English since 1919.* Lanham, Md.: Scarecrow Press, 2004.

Liddell Hart, Basil Henry. *Reputations, Ten Years After.* Boston: Little, Brown, 1928.

Liggett, Hunter. *A.E.F.: Ten Years Ago in France.* New York: Dodd, Mead, 1928.

———. *Commanding an American Army: Recollections of the World War.* Boston: Houghton Mifflin, 1925.

Little, Arthur W. *From Harlem to the Rhine: The Story of New York's Colored Volunteers.* New York: Covici, Friede, 1936.

Lovejoy, Clarence E. *The Story of the Thirty-Eighth.* Coblenz, Germany: Görres-Druckerei, 1919.

Lukens, Edward C. *A Blue Ridge Memoir.* Baltimore: Sun Print, 1922.

MacArthur, Douglas. *Reminiscences.* New York: McGraw-Hill, 1964.

McHenry, Herbert L. *As a Private Saw It: My Memories of the First Division, World War I.* Indiana, Pa.: A. G. Halldin, 1988.

McKeogh, Arthur. *The Victorious 77th Division (New York's Own) in the Argonne Fight.* New York: John H. Eggers, 1919.

Malcolm, Gilbert, and James M. Cain. *79th Division Headquarters Troop: A Record.* Privately printed, 1919.

Marshall, George C. *Memoirs of My Services in the World War, 1917–1918.* Boston: Houghton Mifflin, 1976.

Marshall, S. L. A. *The American Heritage History of World War I.* New York: American Heritage, 1964.

Mastriano, Douglas. "Alvin York and the Meuse-Argonne Offensive." *Military History* 23, 6 (September 2006), 23–29.

Maverick, Maury. *A Maverick American.* New York: Covici Friede, 1937.

Meldrum, T. Ben. *A History of the 362nd Infantry.* Ogden, Utah: A. L. Scoville Press, 1920.

Michigan and Wisconsin War History Commissions. *The 32nd Division in the World War, 1917–1919*. Milwaukee, Wis.: Wisconsin Printing Company, 1920.

Miles, L. Wardlaw. *History of the 308th Infantry, 1917–1919*. New York: G. P. Putnam's Sons, 1927.

Miller, Richard Lawrence. *Truman: The Rise to Power*. New York: McGraw-Hill, 1986.

Millett, Allan R. *The General: Robert L. Bullard and Officership in the United States Army, 1881–1925*. Westport, Conn.: Greenwood Press, 1975.

Minder, Charles F. *This Man's War: The Day-by-Day Record of an American Private on the Western Front*. New York: Pevensey Press, 1931.

Mitchell, William. "The Air Service in the Argonne-Meuse: The Action in the Air over the Argonne Forest." *World's Work* 38, 5 (September 1919), 552–60.

———. *Memoirs of World War I: "From Start to Finish of Our Greatest War."* Reprint. Westport, Conn.: Greenwood Press, 1975.

Morrow, George L. *The Fifty-Eighth Infantry in the World War, 1917–1918–1919*. Privately printed, 1919.

Muller, E. Lester. *The 313th of the 79th in the World War*. Baltimore: Meyer and Thalheimer, 1919.

Nell, John W. *The Lost Battalion: A Private's Story*. Edited by Ron Lammert. San Antonio, Tex.: The Historical Publishing Network, 2001.

Nenninger, Timothy K. "Tactical Dysfunction in the AEF, 1917–1918." *Military Affairs* 51, 4 (October 1987), 177–81.

———. " 'Unsystematic as a Mode of Command': Commanders and the Process of Command in the American Expeditionary Forces, 1917–1918." *Journal of Military History* 64 (July 2000), 739–68.

Official History of the 82nd Division, American Expeditionary Forces, "All American" Division. Indianapolis: Bobbs-Merrill, 1919.

The Official History of the Fifth Division, U.S.A. Washington, D.C.: The Society of the Fifth Division, 1919.

The Official History of the Three Hundred and Fourth Engineer Regiment, Seventy-Ninth Division, U.S.A. during the World War. Philadelphia: 304th Engineer Regiment, 1920.

The Official History of the 315th Infantry U.S.A.: Being a True Record of Its Organization and Training, of Its Operations in the World War, and of Its Activities Following the Signing of the Armistice. Philadelphia: Historical Board of the 315th Infantry, 1920.

Olsmith, Vernon G. *Recollections of an Old Soldier*. San Antonio, Tex.: privately printed, 1963.

O'Neil, "Buck Private." *History & Rhymes of Our Boys in the Great War*. Privately printed, 1926.

Palmer, Don, and Jack Koons. *Billets and Bullets of 37 Division: Cartoons and Ragtime*. Jack Koons, 1919.

Palmer, Frederick. *Our Greatest Battle: The Meuse-Argonne*. New York: Dodd, Mead, 1919.

Paschall, Rod. *The Defeat of Imperial Germany, 1917–1918*. Chapel Hill, N.C.: Algonquin Books, 1989.

Peck, Josiah C. *The 319th Infantry A.E.F.* Paris: Herbert Clarke, 1919.

Perret, Geoffrey. *Old Soldiers Never Die: The Life of Douglas MacArthur*. New York: Random House, 1996.

Pershing, John J. *My Experiences in the World War*. 2 vols. New York: Frederick A. Stokes, 1931.

Poen, Monte M., ed. *Letters Home by Harry Truman*. New York: G. P. Putnam's Sons, 1984.

Proctor, H. G. *The Iron Division National Guard of Pennsylvania in the World War*. Philadelphia: John C. Winston, 1919.

Prosser, Charles A. "A Federal Program for the Vocational Rehabilitation of Disabled Soldiers and Sailors." *Annals of the American Academy of Political and Social Science* 80, Rehabilitation of the Wounded (November 1918), 117–122.

Rainey, James W. "Ambivalent Warfare: The Tactical Doctrine of the AEF in World War I." *Parameters* 13, 3 (September 1983), 34–46.

———. "The Questionable Training of the AEF in World War I." *Parameters* 22, 4 (Winter 1992–92), 89–103.

Rainsford, W. Kerr. *From Upton to the Meuse with the Three Hundred and Seventh Infantry.* New York: D. Appleton, 1920.

Rankin, Edward P., Jr. *The Santa Fe Trail Leads to France: A Narrative of Battle Service of the 110th Engineers (35th Division) in the Meuse-Argonne Offensive.* Kansas City, Mo.: Dick Richardson, 1933.

Rarey, George H. "American Tank Units in the Foret d'Argonne Attack." *Infantry Journal* 32, 2 (March–April 1928), 389–95.

Reddan, William J. *Other Men's Lives (Experiences of a "Doughboy") 1917–1919.* Bloomfield, N.J.: privately published, 1936.

Reilly, Henry J. *Americans All: The Rainbow at War. Official History of the 42nd Rainbow Division in the World War.* Columbus, Ohio: F. J. Heer, 1936.

Reynolds, F. C., ed. *115th Infantry U.S.A. in the World War.* Baltimore: Read-Taylor, 1920.

Richards, J. Stuart. *Pennsylvanian Voices of the Great War: Letters, Stories and Oral Histories of World War I.* Jefferson, N.C.: McFarland, 2002.

Rickenbacker, Edward V. *Rickenbacker.* Englewood Cliffs, N.J.: Prentice-Hall, 1967.

Rizzi, Joseph N. *Joe's War: Memoirs of a Doughboy.* Edited by Richard A. Baumgartner. Huntington, W.Va.: Der Angriff, 1983.

Romedahl, Joe. *An Iowa Soldier in World War I.* Edited by Mildred Romedahl Steele. Boone, Iowa: JRS/MRS Enterprises, 1993.

St. Lawrence University in the World War 1917–1918: A Memorial. Canton, N.Y.: St. Lawrence University, 1931.

Sanborn, Joseph B. *The 131st U.S. Infantry (First Infantry Illinois National Guard) in the World War.* Chicago: privately printed, 1919.

Schellberg, William. *Your Brother Will: The Great War Letters and Diary of William Schellberg, Machine Gun Company, 313th Infantry, "Baltimore's Own," 157th Brigade, 79th Division.* Edited by Jerry Harlowe. Ellicott City, Md.: Patapsco Falls Press, 1992.

Schmidt, Paul W. *Co. C, 127th Infantry, in the World War: A Story of the 32nd Division and a Complete History of the Part Taken by Co. C.* Sheboygan, Wis.: Press Publishing Company, 1919.

Scott, Emmett J. *Scott's Official History of the American Negro in the World War.* N.p.: Emmett J. Scott, 1919.

Seal, Henry F. *"Ever Forward": World War I 1917–1919, History of the 116th U.S. Infantry Regiment 29th Infantry Division Organized from the 1st, 2nd, and 4th Infantry Regiments, Virginia National Guard, at Camp McClellan, Anniston, Alabama 4 October 1917.* Richmond: Virginia Department of Military Affairs, 1953.

Searcy, Earl B. *Looking Back.* Springfield, Ill.: The Journal Press, 1921.

Sherwood, Elmer W. *Diary of a Rainbow Veteran.* Terre Haute, Ind.: Moore-Langen, 1929.

Sibley, Frank Palmer. *With the Yankee Division in France.* Boston: Little, Brown, 1919.

Sirmon, W. A. *That's War: An Authentic Diary.* Atlanta, Ga.: The Linmon Company, 1929.

Slotkin, Richard. *Lost Battalions: The Great War and the Crisis of American Nationality.* New York: Henry Holt, 2005.

Smith, Eugene R. "The American Dreyfus (Robert Rosenbluth)." *American Heritage* 45, 7 (November 1994), 93–94.

Smith, Gene. *Until the Last Trumpet Sounds: The Life of General of the Armies John J. Pershing*. New York: John Wiley & Sons, 1998.

Smith, Henry W. *A Story of the 305th Machine Gun Battalion, 77th Division A.E.F.* New York: Modern Composing Room, 1941.

Smythe, Donald. "A.E.F. Snafu at Sedan." *Prologue* 5, 3 (1973), 135–49.

———. *Guerrilla Warrior: The Early Life of John J. Pershing*. New York: Charles Scribner's Sons, 1973.

———. *Pershing: General of the Armies*. Bloomington: Indiana University Press, 1986.

Sparks, George McIntosh, ed. *The 327th under Fire: History of the 327th Infantry, 82nd Division in the Great World War*. Privately printed, 1920.

Stallings, Laurence. *The Doughboys: The Story of the AEF, 1917–1918*. New York: Harper & Row, 1963.

Stansbury, Henry D. *Maryland's 117th Trench Mortar Battery in the World War, 1917–1919*. Baltimore: John D. Lucas Printing Co., 1942.

Stevenson, Sarah Sand. *Lamp for a Soldier: The Caring Story of a Nurse in World War I*. Bismarck, N.D.: North Dakota State Nurses' Association, 1976.

Stewart, Lawrence. *Rainbow Bright*. Philadelphia: Dorrance, 1923.

The Story of the 91st Division. San Francisco: 91st Division Publication Committee, 1919.

Stringfellow, John S. *Hell! No! This and That, a Narrative of the Great War*. Boston: Meador, 1936.

Stultz, Russell L. *History of the Eightieth Division, A.E.F. in World War I*. Edited by Lee S. Anthony. Roanoke, Va.: The Descendants of the 80th Division Veterans, 2004.

Sweeney, William Allison. *History of the American Negro in the Great World War*. N.p.: G. G. Sapp, 1919.

Terraine, John. *Douglas Haig: The Educated Soldier*. London: Hutchinson, 1963.

Thomas, Lowell. *Woodfill of the Regulars: A True Story of Adventure from the Arctic to the Argonne*. Garden City, N.Y.: Doubleday, Doran, 1929.

Thompson, Hugh S. *Trench Knives and Mustard Gas: With the 42nd Rainbow Division in France*. Edited by Robert H. Ferrell. College Station: Texas A&M University Press, 2004.

Tippett, Edwin James, Jr. *Who Won the War? Letters and Notes of an M.P. in Dixie, England, France and Flanders*. Toledo, Ohio: Toledo Type-Setting & Printing Co., 1920.

Tompkins, Raymond S. *Maryland Fighters in the Great War*. Baltimore: Thomas & Evans, 1919.

Trask, David F. *The AEF and Coalition Warmaking, 1917–1918*. Lawrence: University Press of Kansas, 1993.

Triplet, William S. *A Youth in the Meuse-Argonne: A Memoir, 1917–1918*. Edited by Robert H. Ferrell. Columbia: University of Missouri Press, 2000.

Truman, Harry S. *Memoirs*. Volume 1, *Year of Decisions*. Garden City, N.Y.: Doubleday, 1955.

Tydings, Millard E. *The Machine Gunners of the Blue and Gray Division (Twenty-Ninth)*. Aberdeen, Md.: Harford Printing and Publishing Co., 1920.

United States Army in the World War, 1917–1919. 17 vols. Washington, D.C.: Center for Military History, 1988–92.

U.S. Army. American Expeditionary Force. General Staff College. *Staff Ride: Meuse-Argonne Operations*. France, 1919.

U.S. Army. 29th Division. *Source Book: Operations of the 29th Division East of the Meuse River October 8th to 30th, 1918*. Fort Monroe, Va.: Coast Artillery School, 1922.

United States Army War College, Historical Section. "The Ninety-Second Division, 1917–1918: An Analytical Study." Washington Barracks, D.C.: Army War College, 1923.

Vandiver, Frank E. *Black Jack: The Life and Times of John J. Pershing*. 2 vols. College Station: Texas A & M University Press, 1977.

Viereck, George S., ed. *As They Saw Us: Foch, Ludendorff and Other Leaders Write Our War History*. Garden City, N.Y.: Doubleday, Doran, 1929.

Westlake, Thomas H. *History of the 320th Infantry Abroad*. New York: McGraw-Phillips, 1923.

Williams, Ashby. *Experiences of the Great War: Artois, St. Mihiel, Meuse-Argonne*. Roanoke, Va.: Stone Printing and Manufacturing, 1919.

Williams, Charles H. *Sidelights on Negro Soldiers*. Boston: B. J. Brimmer, 1923.

Wilson, Bryant, and Lamar Tooze. *With the 364th Infantry in America, France, and Belgium*. New York: Knickerbocker Press, 1919.

Wise, Frederic May, and Meigs O. Frost. *A Marine Tells It to You*. New York: J. H. Sears, 1929.

Wise, Jennings C. *The Great Crusade: A Chronicle of the Late War*. New York: The Dial Press, 1930.

Wrentmore, Ernest L. *In Spite of Hell*. New York: Greenwich Publishers, 1958.

Wright, William L. *Meuse-Argonne Diary: A Division Commander in World War I*. Edited by Robert H. Ferrell. Columbia: University of Missouri Press, 2004.

York, Alvin C. *Sergeant York: His Own Life Story and War Diary*. Edited by Tom Skeyhill. Garden City, N.Y.: Doubleday, Doran, 1928.

Young, Rush Stephenson. *Over the Top with the 80th*. Washington, D.C.: privately printed, 1933.

Zander, Harry W. *Thirteen Years in Hell*. Boston: Meador Publishing Company, 1933.

A C K N O W L E D G M E N T S

———•·•———

My thanks must go first of all to the professional and always cour-
teous staff of the U.S. Army Military History Institute in
Carlisle, Pennsylvania, where I conducted most of my research,
particularly to Richard J. Sommers and Richard Baker. I am also grateful to
Eileen Simon of the Veterans History Project at the Library of Congress;
Sharon Culley and Holly Reed of the still photos room at the National
Archives in College Park, Maryland; Eric Vettel, Heidi Hackford, and
Arthur Link of the Woodrow Wilson Library in Staunton, Virginia; Jen-
nifer Keene of Chapman University; Michael Birdwell of Tennessee Tech-
nological University; Joseph P. Rivers, superintendent of the Meuse-Argonne
American Cemetery at Romagne; and Ted Crackel, editor in chief of the
Papers of George Washington. Also providing advice or research assis-
tance at various stages were Jonathan Casey and Eli Paul of the National
World War One Museum at Liberty Memorial in Kansas City; David L.
Snead of Liberty University; Michael E. Hanlon; John W. Chambers III;
David Homsher; Randal Gaulke; Roger Cirillo; and Steve McGeorge. The
Descendants and Friends of the 314th Infantry Regiment A.E.F., particu-
larly John H. Shelter; John, Roy, and Steve Rentz; and Merritt Balthaser
provided manuscripts and other assistance in the history of the 79th
Division.

I cannot adequately thank my friend and guide to the Meuse-Argonne
battlefields, Frédéric Castier of the Arthur S. Tozar Museum and the 1st Infantry Division Veterans' Association. Fred's expert knowledge of the terrain
and local connections were critically important in helping me to make sense
of this complicated battle; we also had a lot of fun rambling through woods
and fields to discover bunkers, trenches, gun pits, and artifacts! I would also

like to thank Rick Britton, who once again outdid himself in preparing the maps; John Sterling, David Patterson, and Patrick Clark at Henry Holt; and my agent, Peter Matson. Thanks are due especially to all the members of my family: my wife, Laima; my children, Mike, Laura, and Tom; my brother, Eric; and my parents, Alan and Shelbia.

INDEX

Adjusted Service Certificate Law (1924), 426–27

Adler, Julius Ochs, 344

African Americans, 13, 36–37, 92, 120–22, 143, 159–60, 190, 194–95, 427–29. *See also* American Expeditionary Forces, 92d Division, 93d Division

Aincreville, 368–69

Aire River, 3, 57, 58, 61, 62, 109, 113, 116, 141, 220–21, 246, 250, 303, 309–11, 342–45, 356–58, 377

Aisne-Marne offensive (summer 1918), 48, 60, 95, 115, 117

Aisne River, 41, 45, 57, 61, 209

Albertine, Connell, 402, 414

Alexander, Robert, 117–18, 221–22, 224, 228, 230–31, 245, 253–54, 272–73, 342–43, 398, 400, 416, 433

Allen, Hervey, 430

All Quiet on the Western Front (Remarque), 430

   movie, 431

Allworth, Edward, 326, 332–34, 349–50, 394

Alsace-Lorraine, 22, 92, 382, 396

American Battle Monuments Commission, 2, 3

American Expeditionary Force (AEF). *See also* Doughboys; *and specific battles*

   First Army, 26, 49–53, 59–62, 72–73, 115, 118, 124, 144, 191–92, 198–99, 311–13, 315–16, 361, 397–401, 419–20

   Second Army, 308, 313, 396, 406–9, 426

   Tenth Army (fictional), 60

I Corps, 62, 107–8, 115, 122, 144, 154, 160, 178, 187–88, 199, 221–22, 230–31, 245–46, 250, 256, 303–4, 305, 309, 313, 316, 360, 376, 386–87, 391–92, 396–401

III Corps, 62, 90, 95, 122, 125–26, 144, 148, 186, 195, 199–200, 202, 233, 235, 256, 286, 306–8, 313–14, 316, 345, 347–48, 361, 364–65, 386–87, 392, 398, 426

V Corps, 26, 62, 96, 103–5, 122, 124, 144–45, 160, 167, 186, 195, 199, 205, 209, 221, 233, 256, 286, 288–89, 305, 308, 313, 329, 345, 354, 361, 386–87, 397–400

1st Division (Big Red One), 19, 34, 42–45, 47–48, 62, 69, 90, 95, 160, 183, 199, 205, 212–18, 221, 230, 233, 242–44, 245, 246, 250–52, 263, 264–65, 265, 288, 292–94, 303–4, 305, 315, 322, 327, 340, 368, 370, 387, 398–401, 414–16, 424–25, 435

2d Division, 42, 45–48, 70, 255–56, 368, 370, 387–90, 392, 395, 398–99, 405, 430

3d Division ("Rock of the Marne"), 45, 48, 62, 160, 199, 205–9, 239–41, 247–48, 256–58, 287, 288–89, 289, 302–3, 316, 321, 331–32, 334, 347–48, 361, 364, 365–68

4th Division ("Ivy"), 3, 26, 48, 62, 90, 94–96, 100–102, 122, 125–26, 144, 148–49, 162–64, 186, 199–202, 235–36, 256, 286–87, 301, 306–8, 313, 316, 321–22, 331, 347, 361, 365

American Expeditionary Force (*continued*)

5th Division ("Red Diamond"), 3, 34, 307, 315–16, 322–27, 331–36, 345, 347–48, 361, 364–65, 368–69, 387, 392–94, 398, 404–5, 413, 421

26th Division ("Yankee"), 35, 42, 48, 106, 361–64, 387, 398, 402, 414

27th Division, 35, 195

28th Division ("Keystone"), 35, 48, 62, 108, 113–18, 123, 138, 141–42, 144, 155–58, 177–80, 195–97, 199, 218, 220–21, 224, 230, 244–46, 250, 265–69, 272–73, 278, 294, 408–9, 420–21

29th Division ("Blue and Gray"), 3, 62, 256, 275–78, 285, 298–301, 305–6, 316–22, 345–47, 361–64, 392, 430

30th Division, 195

32d Division ("Red Arrow"), 35, 42, 48, 62, 160–61, 199, 205, 209–11, 218, 241–43, 263–65, 288, 290–92, 303, 308, 316, 333, 335–39, 345, 351–52, 355, 361, 370, 403–4

33d Division ("Prairie"), 35, 38, 62, 90–94, 122, 125, 144, 199, 256, 275–76, 278, 283–85, 301, 305, 316, 345, 347, 361, 406–7

35th Division ("Santa Fe"), 35–36, 62, 106, 108–15, 117, 122–23, 135–41, 144, 154, 160, 172–78, 183, 187–88, 198, 214, 410, 429

37th Division ("Buckeye"), 62, 79, 88–90, 100–104, 106, 122–24, 127, 131–35, 144, 152–54, 160, 165–66, 170, 172, 187, 205, 209

40th Division ("Sunshine"), 117

42d Division ("Rainbow"), 6, 42, 48, 52, 66, 315–16, 322, 327–29, 333, 335, 339–41, 345, 352–55, 361, 370–73, 387, 389, 398–400

77th Division ("Statue of Liberty"), 35–36, 60, 62, 80–81, 108, 117–20, 122–23, 142–45, 158–59, 180–83, 189–90, 195–97, 199, 218, 252–53, 278, 296–97, 303, 309, 311, 316, 341–45, 356–58, 361, 374–77, 387, 395–96, 398–400, 402

78th Division ("Lightning"), 36, 375–81, 387

79th Division ("Kuhn's Singing Army"), 33, 35, 44, 49, 62, 73, 82, 88, 96–102, 104, 122–24, 126–30, 144, 148–51, 160, 164–65, 186–87, 202, 205, 364, 387, 398, 402

80th Division ("Blue Ridge Boys"), 3, 62, 68, 74, 81–82, 88, 90, 92–95, 122–23, 125, 144, 146, 148, 161, 186, 199–205, 236–39, 256, 286–89, 301–2, 307–8, 315, 322–23, 355–56, 387, 391, 427

82d Division ("All-American"), 62, 178, 193, 230, 250–51, 265–67, 267, 273, 278–82, 292, 294–96, 303, 309–11, 316, 329–30, 341–42, 344–45, 357, 361, 373–74, 376, 379, 428

89th Division ("Middle West"), 351, 370, 387–88, 390, 392, 394–96, 398, 405–6

90th Division ("Tough Ombres"), 365, 368–70, 387, 390, 392, 398

91st Division ("Wild West"), 6, 62, 88, 104–7, 122, 132–35, 144, 152–54, 166–72, 177, 187, 191, 209, 211, 242, 288, 308, 338

92d Division, 36, 62, 120–22, 143–44, 159–60, 427

93d Division, 36, 121, 194–95, 429

1st Infantry Brigade, 265

1st Tank Brigade, 64, 80

6th Marine Brigade, 47, 388–90

7th Brigade, 286

8th Brigade, 11, 14

55th Brigade, 179, 218, 267

56th Brigade, 267

83d Brigade, 327–28, 339, 353–55

84th Brigade, 52, 327–28, 339, 352–53, 355, 371–73, 399

153d Brigade, 224, 231, 343

154th Brigade, 223–25, 245

157th Brigade, 126

181st Brigade, 288–89, 308

1st Gas and Flame Regiment, 77, 208, 272, 386

4th Infantry Regiment, 205–9, 240–41, 247–50, 256–63, 288–89, 331–32, 348, 367

5th Marine Regiment, 162, 255–56, 388–90

6th Cavalry Regiment, 13

6th Engineer Regiment, 367

6th Infantry Regiment, 323, 333, 335

7th Cavalry Regiment, 16

7th Infantry Regiment, 205, 208–9, 240–41, 258–59, 263, 288, 331, 348, 365–67

9th Infantry Regiment, 395

10th Cavalry Regiment ("buffalo soldiers"), 13

11th Infantry Regiment, 323, 333, 335, 368, 404–5

16th Infantry Regiment, 213–16, 292–94

18th Infantry Regiment, 213–16, 242–43, 293–94

20th Engineer Regiment, 38

26th Infantry Regiment, 213, 217–18, 243, 251–52, 265, 293–94, 400

28th Infantry Regiment, 213, 216–18, 242–44, 293–94

30th Engineer Regiment ("Gas and Flame"), 77

30th Infantry Regiment, 205, 288–89, 302–3, 308, 321, 331, 332, 365

37th Engineer Regiment, 33

38th Infantry Regiment, 205–6, 288–90, 308, 331, 367

39th Infantry Regiment, 95, 286–87, 301, 306–7

47th Infantry Regiment, 95–96, 286–87, 306–7

58th Infantry Regiment, 95, 162–63, 200–201

59th Infantry Regiment, 95, 162–63, 235–36

60th Infantry Regiment, 323–27, 332–35, 348–51

61st Infantry Regiment, 323, 333, 348–51, 368–69

101st Infantry Regiment, 363

104th Infantry Regiment, 362

109th Field Artillery Regiment, 180

109th Infantry Regiment, 115–17, 141, 157–58, 178, 218, 220, 244, 267

110th Engineer Regiment, 30, 177

110th Infantry Regiment, 115–17, 141, 155–56, 178, 187, 218, 220, 267–68

111th Infantry Regiment, 115, 141, 158, 180, 220, 267, 369

112th Infantry Regiment, 115–17, 141, 155–58, 178–80, 220, 267–69

113th Infantry Regiment, 276, 298–300, 305, 317–18, 364

114th Infantry Regiment, 276, 305, 317–21

115th Infantry Regiment, 276–77, 300–301, 305, 363–64

116th Infantry Regiment, 276–77, 298, 305–6, 346–47, 363–64

117th Engineer Regiment, 353

125th Infantry Regiment, 209, 291–92, 303, 338–39

126th Infantry Regiment, 209–10, 241, 291, 303, 336, 351

127th Infantry Regiment, 209–10, 241–42, 336, 338–39, 351–52

128th Infantry Regiment, 209, 211, 263–65, 336–38, 351, 403–4

129th Field Artillery Regiment, 86

129th Infantry Regiment, 90

130th Infantry Regiment, 90

131st Infantry Regiment, 90, 278, 301

132d Infantry Regiment, 90, 278, 283–85, 301

137th Infantry Regiment, 109, 113–15, 135, 140, 154–55, 173, 175

138th Infantry Regiment, 109–13, 115, 135, 154–55, 173, 175

139th Infantry Regiment, 109, 113–15, 135–37, 140, 154–55, 173–76

140th Infantry Regiment, 113, 115, 135–41, 154–55, 173–74, 177

145th Infantry Regiment, 103–4

147th Infantry Regiment, 103–4

148th Infantry Regiment, 132

165th Infantry Regiment, 327, 328, 339–41, 353–54, 389

166th Infantry Regiment, 327, 339, 341, 353–54

167th Infantry Regiment, 327, 339–41, 352–53, 371–73

168th Infantry Regiment, 327, 339, 352–53, 371–73

305th Infantry Regiment, 119, 181, 223, 227, 245, 343, 395

306th Infantry Regiment, 119, 158–59, 181, 223, 227, 273, 343–45, 357

American Expeditionary Force (*continued*)

307th Infantry Regiment, 119, 181, 189, 223–25, 227, 231, 245, 273, 343, 357–58, 374–75

308th Infantry Regiment, 119–20, 143, 159, 181–83, 189–90, 223–34, 245, 369–74, 343

309th Infantry Regiment, 375–80

310th Infantry Regiment, 375–80

311th Infantry Regiment, 375–80

312th Infantry Regiment, 375–80

313th Infantry Regiment, 82, 97–102, 129–30, 150, 165, 402–3

314th Infantry Regiment, 97–100, 102, 128–30, 164, 403

315th Infantry Regiment, 98–99, 130, 148–50, 164–65

316th Infantry Regiment, 36, 96–97, 99, 150–52, 165, 187

317th Infantry Regiment, 1, 202–3

318th Infantry Regiment, 201–2, 202–5, 236–39, 287

319th Infantry Regiment, 93, 204–5, 287–88, 302, 307

320th Infantry Regiment, 93, 148, 287, 302, 307

325th Infantry Regiment, 265, 294–95, 309–10, 330, 341–42, 355–56, 373

326th Infantry Regiment, 265, 294–95, 309–11, 341–42, 356

327th Infantry Regiment, 265–66, 279, 294–95, 309–11

328th Infantry Regiment, 265–68, 279, 294–95, 309, 341–42, 356

353d Infantry Regiment, 370

354th Infantry Regiment, 370

355th Infantry Regiment, 370

356th Infantry Regiment, 370, 394–96, 405–6

357th Infantry Regiment, 369

358th Infantry Regiment, 369–70

359th Infantry Regiment, 369

360th Infantry Regiment, 369

361st Infantry Regiment, 104–7, 132–34, 153–54

362d Infantry Regiment, 104–7, 132–34, 153, 166–72

363d Infantry Regiment, 104–7, 132, 134, 154, 167, 172

364th Infantry Regiment, 104–5, 132–34, 154, 167, 172

368th Infantry Regiment,, 120–22, 143–44, 159–60, 190, 222–23, 227, 429

369th Infantry Regiment ("Harlem Hellfighters"), 194–95

371st Infantry Regiment, 194

Lost Battalion, 6, 81, 120, 189, 221–34, 244–46, 250–54, 265–74, 369–74, 431–34

1st Light Tank Battalion, 64

7th Machine Gun Battalion, 367

12th Machine Gun Battalion, 285

128th Machine Gun Battalion, 177

306th Machine Gun Battalion, 180, 225, 252–53, 296

344th Tank Battalion, 64, 109, 110–12, 214, 218–20

345th Tank Battalion, 64, 214

348th Machine Gun Battalion, 172

amalgamation controversy, 24–26, 39, 183, 197, 418–19

ambulance service, 33–34, 102, 107, 144, 171, 186, 192

ammunition, 78, 79, 88, 92, 110, 123, 128, 134, 137, 144–45, 155, 159, 165, 181, 182, 186, 188, 198, 199, 200, 205, 225, 230, 248, 249, 253, 259–62, 270, 277, 281, 284, 292, 300, 313, 324–25, 332, 336, 347, 355–56, 386, 391, 393, 399, 408,

arrival in France, 42–45

artillery, 4, 6, 27–28, 33–34, 43, 45, 52, 58–59, 62–64, 71, 73, 75–76, 78–80, 85–88, 92–93, 97, 100–1, 104, 106, 113–14, 116, 118, 122–23, 126, 128, 131, 133, 135–36, 138, 140, 142, 145, 147, 149, 151–52, 154–55, 157, 162–65, 173–74, 177–80, 183, 189, 191, 198–99, 202–3, 210, 212, 219, 232, 252, 263, 272, 287–88, 293, 300, 302, 306–7, 313, 340, 352–53, 364, 371, 378–79, 386–88, 407–8, 417

casualty figures, 4, 47–48, 52, 95, 100, 115, 186–88, 190–93, 195, 205, 209, 213, 218, 220, 256, 265, 287, 305, 327, 363, 367, 369–70, 419 communications and signals, 34, 52, 78–79, 102, 114–15, 126–27, 298, 311, 390

criticism of, 184–85, 195–97

demobilization, 414

deserters, 35, 298, 333, 364

engineers, 33–34, 79, 91–92, 95, 127

equipment, 33–34, 43, 73–79, 119–21, 198, 386

final offensive of, 359–61, 380, 384–86, 396–97, 401

food and water shortages, 73, 123, 125, 144–45, 164, 166, 173, 181, 192, 222, 230, 231

gas warfare, 77, 80, 97, 208, 272, 341, 376, 378–79, 386, 388, 391, 417

logistics and supplies, 26, 34, 52–53, 69–72, 123–24, 144–46, 183–85, 197, 311–12, 386, 392

machine-gun training, 27–28, 33–34, 45, 78–79, 93, 123–24, 197–98, 313

manpower replacement, 222, 311–12

medical care, 10, 102–3, 107, 123, 126, 135, 144–45, 171, 186, 190–93, 197, 222, 230–31, 237, 311, 353

morale, 147, 202, 355, 360–61, 363–64

Nurse Corps, 192–93

officers and command, 36, 37, 46, 52, 82, 108, 115, 121, 123–24, 143, 160, 184–85, 192, 231, 347–348, 384–86, 427–28

organization of, 26–29

racial tensions in, 36–37, 120–22, 190, 194–95, 427–28

regional and ethnic diversity of, 34–37

Signal Corps, 193

tactics, 27–29, 33–34, 45, 52–53, 78, 123–24, 144, 185, 311–13, 354, 359–60, 385–86, 416–19

Tank Corps, 6, 23, 27–28, 34, 63–65, 80, 101, 110–12, 116, 149, 157–58, 164, 169, 178–79, 198, 218–20, 313, 417

training, 18–19, 26, 31–39, 43–45, 77–79, 108, 115, 117–19, 121, 198, 308–9, 417–18

trench warfare and, 23, 27–28, 58–59, 74

U.S. Army Air Service, 6, 23, 34, 60, 62–63, 72–73, 86, 124, 145–46, 149, 163, 198, 200, 214, 309–10, 314–15, 386, 417–18

weapons, 27–28, 33–34, 44, 45, 78, 93–94, 108, 119, 123–24, 313

American Legion, 426, 427

American Revolutionary War, 18, 36, 100

Anderson, Johannes, 278

Andrews, Avery D., 26

Angelo, Private, 112

Animals

dogs, 206, 278, 414–15

horses and mules, 69–71, 75, 86, 93, 107, 123, 126–27, 129–30, 138, 160, 170, 183, 187, 206, 237, 242, 251, 309, 370, 387, 391, 429,

pigeons, 102, 181, 230, 232, 390

Apremont, 114, 155–56, 158, 178–80, 187, 218–19, 221, 267

Arabian Peninsula, 23

Ardeuil, 194–95

Argonne Forest, 2–3, 6, 57–62, 115–20, 141–44, 189, 195–99, 221–34, 245–46, 250, 252–54, 256, 265–67, 275, 282, 294–97, 303–5, 420–21. *See also* American Expeditionary Forces, 28th Division, 77th Division, 82d Division; Lost Battalion; *specific military objectives and towns*

Ariétal Farm, 243, 251–52

Arlington National Cemetery

Pershing's grave at, 435

Unknown Soldier's tomb at, 431–34

Armistice

celebrations of, on battlefields, 409–13

final skirmishes before, 401–9

signed, 401

terms discussed, 315, 359, 382, 401

Army Boys on the Firing Line, The, 348

Arpin, Edmund P., 263–64

Askew, Henry, 38

Attura, Joseph, 424–25

Atwood, John Baird, 151

Australia, 24

armed forces of, 43, 48, 430

Austria-Hungary, 21–23, 35–36, 39, 381

armed forces of, 198, 285

Avocourt, 82, 145, 147

Baesel, Albert, 132

Bagans, Lt., 150

Baker, C. Earl, 422

Baker, Horace, 336–38
Baker, John G., 385–86
Baker, Newton D., 16–19, 26, 312, 415–16, 434
Balkans, 23
Baltic, SS, 19–20
Baltic states, 23
Baltimore Sun, 403
Bantheville, 131, 333, 369
Bare, Walter E., 371
Barkley, John Lewis "Jack," 6, 206–9, 240–41, 247–51, 258–63, 288–90, 321, 331–32, 367–68, 409
Baronvaux Creek, 132, 135
Barricourt Ridge, 387, 390
Bart, Frank J., 255
Baulny, 140, 154, 177
Bayonville, 390
Beaumont American Military cemetery, 434
Belgium, 21, 22, 39, 414
  armed forces of, 381
Bell, George, Jr., 91
Belleau Wood, Battle of, 46–47, 162, 255, 365
Belleu Bois, 363
Bellevue Signal Ridge, 195
Bergmaier, Private, 98
Berry, Henry, 413
Bertog, Private, 283–84
Béthincourt, 1, 93, 146
Bethlehem Steel Works, 112
Big Parade, The (movie), 423–24, 431
Binarville, 144, 159–60, 181, 190, 222–24, 227, 427–28
Blackford, Staige Davis, 33
Blanc Mont Ridge, 3, 255–56, 272, 368
Block, James, 201, 235, 322, 365
Bois 268, 151, 152
Bois de Bantheville, 291, 316, 333, 361, 370, 387
Bois de Beuge, 151, 207
Bois de Bourgogne, 343, 376, 378–80
Bois de Boyon, 173
Bois de Brieulles, 148–49, 162, 163
Bois de Chaume, 275–76, 278, 283–85, 301
Bois de Chauvignon, 351
Bois de Chênes, 298, 300
Bois de Chêne Sec, 241

Bois de Cheppy, 105
Bois de Cierges, 153, 167, 171
Bois de Clairs Chênes, 348, 361, 365–67
Bois de Consenvoye, 275–78, 300
Bois de Cuisy, 100–102
Bois de Cunel, 208, 256–58, 287–90, 302
Bois de Dannevoux, 125
Bois de Fays, 3, 148, 198–201, 235–36, 286, 301
Bois de Forêt, 199–200, 306–7, 321, 331, 348
Bois de Forges, 92
Bois de Gesnes, 339
Bois de la Côte Lémont, 148
Bois de la Grand Montagne, 275–76, 364
Bois de la Morine, 241
Bois de la Naza, 223, 231, 273
Bois de la Pultière, 288–89, 324–25, 331–33, 347–51, 365
Bois de la Reine, 298, 300
Bois de la Tuilerie, 129
Bois de Malancourt, 99
Bois de Malaumont, 199, 200, 287, 302
Bois de Moncy, 243, 294
Bois de Montfaucon, 103
Bois de Pommes, 82
Bois de Romagne, 291, 304, 339–40, 352, 353
Bois de Septsarges, 96, 125–26
Bois des Loges, 343, 376–79
Bois des Ogons, 3, 126, 148–49, 162–65, 198–99, 202–5, 208, 236–39, 286–87, 302
Bois des Rappes, 3, 316, 333, 348–51, 361, 366–68, 387
Bois d'Etraye, 275
Bois de Valoup, 241–42, 291–92
Bois d'Haumont, 362
Bois d'Ormont, 317–21, 363
Bois Plat Chêne, 301
Boll, Maximilian, 88, 98, 129, 148, 164
Bolsheviks, 39, 381
Bonus Army march (1931), 427
Boone, Daniel, 206
Borne de Cornouiller, 301
Boureuilles, 109, 115, 116
Boxer Rebellion, 115, 207, 212
Brabant, 276
Brabant-sur-Meuse, 278

Breckenridge, Lucien, 231
Brett, Serano, 111
Brezy-le-Sec, 205
Brieulles, 201, 393–94
Brittain, Vera, 76–77
Bronson, Deming, 134
Brooklyn Naval Hospital, 425
Brown, Fred, 122, 143, 159–60
Brown, Preston, 365, 367
Buanthe Creek, 109–10, 136, 137
Buck, Beaumont Bonaparte, 205, 239–40, 289, 347
Budd, Kenneth, 181
Bulgaria, 22, 381
Bullard, Robert Lee, 45, 62, 90, 92, 102, 107–8, 125, 199, 201–2, 212, 235, 286–87, 301–2, 306–8, 313, 360, 396, 406, 408, 416, 426, 428
Bureau of Military Operations, French, 22
Butler, Charles, 242–43

Cain, James M., 6, 66, 74, 97, 126–27, 130–31
Calais; 414
Cameron, George Hamilton, 62, 96, 124, 205, 209, 288, 308, 313
Camp Allen (Pa.), 33
Camp Dix (N.J.), 375
Camp Doniphan (Okla.), 140
Camp Funston (Kans.), 32
Camp Green (N.C.), 95
Camp Lee (Va.), 32
Camp Lewis (Wash.), 32
Camp Meade (Md.), 96
Camp Mills (N.J.), 32, 327
Camp Sill (Okla.), 32
Canada, 24
Cantigny, Battle of, 45, 69, 90, 95, 213, 368
Caporetto offensive, 39
Casey, Bob, 75, 79, 85–86, 107, 145, 147, 165–66, 387–88, 407–8
Castle, Bozier, 373
Champagne (France), 47, 50, 61, 194–95, 221, 255–56, 429
Champigneulle, 343, 373–74, 376
Champ Mahaut, 117, 141–42, 230
Champrocher Ridge, 279

Charles, Oscar J., 151, 187
Charlevaux Mill, 223–27, 233, 245
Charlevaux Valley, 223, 226–27, 229, 244–45, 252–54, 271–71, 273, 433
Charpentry Ridge, 154
Charpentry, 114, 136, 138, 140, 143–44
Château-Thierry, Battle of, 45, 47
Châtel Chéhéry, 198, 250, 267–69, 398
Chaudron Farm, 155
Cheppy, 3, 109–13, 138
Chevières, 343
Chin, Henry, 270
China, 115
    Chinese Americans, 270
CIA, 328
Cierges, 96, 152, 198, 208
Civil War, 3, 4, 35, 36, 323, 328
Clay, Alexander, 38
Clemenceau, Georges, 183–84, 195, 197, 312, 384, 419
Clotfelder, Norvel, 369–70
Cockey, Joshua, 129–30
Collins, James L., 11–12
Compton, Paul, 220
Condon, Ed, 86
Conger, Arthur, 160
Conner, Fox, 26, 397–98, 419
Conscientious objectors, 32, 35
Consenvoye, 276, 278, 285
Continental Army, 362
Cornay, 198, 266, 279, 294–95, 303
Corning, Walter, 44
Corrado, Corporal, 98
Costin, Henry, 277
Côte Dame Marie, 290–92, 303, 308, 316, 335–39, 345, 351, 361, 387
Côte de Châtillon, 329, 339–41, 351–53, 361, 371–73, 387
Côte des Perrières, 117
Craig, Malin, 250
Cronkhite, Adelbert, 81–82, 92–93, 202–5, 236, 239, 286, 288, 307
Cuba, 18, 36, 197, 265
Cuisy, 95, 96
Cunel, Heights of, 58–59, 61, 96, 144–45, 149, 198–200, 202, 233, 256, 282, 288, 301–2, 307–8, 316, 387
Cunel (town), 324, 331–33, 335
Cushing, Dr. Harvey, 192

Damvillers, 275
Dannevoux, 1, 94
Darragh, Thomas, 179
Davies, Edward, 130, 149–50, 164
Davis, William D., 134
Dawes, Charles G., 26
Dawn Patrol, The (movie), 431
De Angelo, Mike, 207, 248–49
"Death of Sam Browne" ceremonial acts, 415–16
De Frehn, Maurice, 178–79
Delaplane, Channing "Dogface," 7, 135, 137–40, 154–55, 173–77
Democratic Party, 17
Dempsey, Gregory, 404
Denny, Harold, 372–73
Depôt de Machines (supply dump), 181, 189
Dermody, Charles D., 283–85
DeSilvey, Wayne, 155, 408–9
Diamond, Jack "Legs," 35
Dickman, Joseph, 313, 373, 376, 391, 397–98, 400
Dixon, Roy, 283–84
Dodd, Robert, 270
Donaldson, Michael A., 341
Donovan, William "Wild Bill," 328, 340–41, 353–54
Dorey, Halstead, 348
Dos Passos, John, 15
Doughboys. *See also* African Americans, American Expeditionary Force, *and specific battles and military units*
    aftermath of war for, 1–2, 420–31
    attitudes toward air service, 6, 73, 198, 205–6, 314–15, 417–18
    attitudes toward generals, 416–17
    attitudes toward tanks, 63, 238
    await demobilization, 413–20
    battle fatigue and shell shock of, 30, 184–88, 191–92, 197, 202, 237, 322–23, 364, 424–26
    Bonus Army march, 427
    character and morality of, 66–69
    diversity of, 35–37
    illnesses of, 68, 186, 192–93, 312, 364, 414
    inexperience of, 62, 69
    medical care for, 102–3, 107, 123, 126, 135, 144–45, 171, 186, 190–93, 197, 222, 230–31, 237, 311, 353
    memoirs and movies of, 430–31
    pensions and aid for, postwar, 423–34
    poison gas and, 1, 23, 76–77, 80, 126–28, 174, 191–92, 197, 200, 203–4, 235, 272, 324, 421, 425, 434
    public recognition of, 431–33
    racism of, 36–37, 71, 427–28
    reason for name, 31
    relations with British, 27, 44
    relations with French, 25, 27, 42–45, 48–49, 101, 110, 149, 178, 210, 238, 299, 317, 321, 362, 392
    training of, 29, 31–39, 69, 78–79, 417–20
Downs, Mary Elizabeth, 421
Drum, Hugh Aloysius "Drummie," 26, 69–72, 250, 315, 397–98
Drum, John, 70
Duffy, Father Francis, 328–29, 340, 354–55
Duncan, George B., 230, 250, 265–66, 279, 309, 341, 355, 376
DuPuy, Charles, 33, 36, 44, 130, 186–87
Dwight, Robert L., 88, 409

Early, Bernard, 279–80, 282
Eastman, "Monk," 35
East Prussia, 22
Eclisfontaine, 133–35, 144, 154
Edwards, Clarence "Daddy," 362–63
Elser, Max, 143, 159
Eltinge, LeRoy, 63
Ely, Frank, 279, 294
Ely, Hanson, 368
Epinonville, 106–7, 132–35, 144, 153–54, 198
Etrayes Ridge, 364
Etraye, 275
Etzel-Giselher Stellungen, 58
Exermont, 109, 114, 173–76, 199, 214–18, 242

Fallow, Tom, 371
Federal Board for Vocational Education, 424
Field Service Regulations (U.S. Army), 27–28
"Fighting 69th" New York Regiment (Civil War), 328
Fiske, Harold B., 26
Fismes, 48

Fismette, 48

Flabas, 275

Flanders, 24, 40–41, 195, 381, 419, 420

Fléville, 135, 199, 214–16, 246, 250, 292–93, 309

Floyd, "Nigger," 207, 247–49, 331–32

Flynn, Sergeant, 338

Foch, Ferdinand, 41, 42, 47, 49–52, 61, 195–97, 221, 297, 312–13, 360, 381–82, 384, 386, 401, 414, 419, 431, 434

Follies of 1919, The (play), 421

Forderhase, Rudolph A., 394–95, 406

Ford Motor Company, 426

Forges, 92

Forges Creek, 91–93

Forrest, Arthur, 390

Fourteen Points, 253, 315

France, 1, 39, 414, 418
  arrival of American troops in, 42–45
  attitudes toward Americans, 25, 27, 43–45, 48–49, 101, 110, 149, 178, 210, 238, 299, 317, 321, 362, 392, 419
  economic disarray of, 39
  German offensives in, 24–25
  military conduct and policies of, 22–24, 41, 47–52, 60–61
  origins of war and, 21–22
  proposals for amalgamation, 24–25, 28
  relations with First Army, 183–84, 195, 197, 312–13, 360, 419–20
  supplies equipment to A.E.F., 73, 77–78

Francis, William, 389

Franco-Prussian war (1870), 22, 396

Franz Ferdinand, Archduke, assassination of, 21

Frasier, Lyman S., 251–52

French armed forces, 22, 39–40, 47–50, 62, 70, 195, 276, 381, 396
  Second Army, 69, 195–97
  Fourth Army, 122, 190, 195, 255, 361, 384, 396, 398
  1st Cavalry Division, 122, 245
  XVII Corps, 62, 195–97, 256, 275–76, 286, 305, 316, 361, 387, 398, 418
  XXI Corps, 45
  1st Cavalry Division, 122, 245
  5th Cavalry Division, 62

18th Division, 275–76, 298, 317, 362
  26th Division, 275
  40th Division, 398, 400
  Groupement Durand, 122
  air service, 72, 101, 244, 314, 386
  artillery, 45, 49, 62, 168, 177–78, 200, 276, 386
  colonial Senegalese soldiers, 275
  failures of, 418–19
  gas warfare, 76
  Lost Battalion and, 224, 227
  mutinies in, and resistance to attack, 23–24, 41
  Pershing and Mitchell's view of, 72
  tanks, 97, 101, 238, 259
  tensions with Americans, 250
  train American soldiers, 44–45, 108, 121

Freya Stellung, 58, 391

Frieman, Harry, 165

Furlong, Harold, 390

Gallipoli (1915) Battle of, 23

Gallwitz, Max von, 60, 123, 146, 164, 198–99, 233–34, 285, 296–97, 305, 314, 352, 391, 419–20

Gamage, Edna Sue, 421

Gansser, Emil, 308–9, 335, 351

Gardiner, Philip, 357

Garlock, Glen, 265

Garrett, Private, 407

George Washington, SS, 415–16

German Americans, 35–36, 180

German armed forces, 24, 39, 59
  Fifth Army, 59–60, 234, 285, 296–97
  I Reserve Corps, 245
  1st Guards Division, 175
  5th Guards Division, 175, 214
  37th Division, 214
  41st Division, 294–95, 352
  52d Division, 154, 175, 214
  air service, 72, 93–94, 124, 136–38, 145–46, 163, 198–200, 204–6, 214, 314–15, 420
  artillery, 22, 41, 47, 52, 57–59, 61, 70, 75–76, 78, 91–92, 94, 96–97, 106–7, 113, 124, 126, 129–31, 133–36, 138–39, 143–44, 147–49, 151–53, 155–59, 161, 163, 166–70, 174–75,

German armed forces (*continued*)
177–78, 181, 186, 195, 198–200,
202–5, 208, 211, 214–16, 218–19, 221,
233, 235, 237, 239, 242, 246–47, 256,
261–63, 267, 269, 277–78, 282, 287,
299, 306, 318, 322, 329–30, 335, 341,
343, 345, 353, 364, 369, 371, 407–8,
419–20
assessment of American forces by, 45–46,
198–99
command of, 315
defeat of, 381–82, 391, 396, 419–20
defenses of, 57–60, 109–10
fleet and submarines, 15, 20, 24, 31,
38–39, 381
gas warfare, 41, 76–77, 79–80, 146, 151,
166, 168, 174, 191–92, 200, 203–4,
278–79, 286, 300–301, 303, 306, 333,
341, 349–53, 364, 378
intelligence service, 60, 199
machine guns, 211
offensive of 1918, 39–41, 45, 47–49
propaganda to black troops, 121
reserves, 59–60, 161, 198
Stosstruppen, 23, 40, 48, 245
strength of, 198–99
Germany
Allied Army of Occupation in, 414
armistice terms and, 382–84, 414
Nazi Party and, 315
origins of war and, 21–23
peace initiatives of, 253–54, 315
unrest in, 381, 401
Geronimo, 13
Gesnes, 153–54, 167–72, 209–11, 241–42,
290
Gettysburg, Battle of, 4, 113
Gilbert, Gerald, Jr., 102
Gilbert, John, 424
Gilligan, Patrick, 189
Golfe de Malancourt, 99–100
Göring, Hermann, 199
Gottschalk, Louis, 403–4
Grandmaison, Louzeau de, 22, 286
Grandpré, 58, 61, 309, 342–43, 357–58,
361, 374–80, 386
Granger, Farley, 6, 107, 133, 166, 167–68,
169, 171–72
Grassey, Captain, 322

Great Britain, 21–22, 39, 418
amalgamation proposals, 24–25, 28
assessment of First Army by, 419
British Expeditionary Force, 22–24, 31,
33–34, 39–41, 44–45, 49–50, 62, 72,
195, 381
Fifth Army, 40
mutiny at Calais, 414
Great Depression, 2, 427
Greek Americans, 36
Gregory, Earl, 277
Gunther, Henry, 402–3

Haan, William, 209, 211, 243, 263–65,
290–92, 303, 335–36, 338–39,
351–52
Haig, Sir Douglas, 40, 41, 49, 312, 381–82,
419
Haile, LeRoy, 165
Hamilton, Clad, 113–14, 173
Hannay, J. R. R., 228
Harbord, James G., 45, 118, 212
Harding, Warren G., 431
Harris, Charles, 365–66
Harris, Pearl May, 421
Hatler, Waldo, 395
Hawke, Frederick, 330
Hemingway, Ernest, 15, 431
Herschowitz, Jack, 182, 183
Hewit, "Big Ben," 96, 150–52, 164–65
Higgins, Robert, 238
Hill 180, 220, 265–66, 279
Hill 182, 150, 344–45, 357, 376
Hill 188, 194
Hill 202, 114
Hill 212, 243
Hill 218, 112–13, 135–39
Hill 223, 265–68, 279
Hill 231, 177–78, 187
Hill 240. *See* Montrefagne
Hill 242, 352–53
Hill 244, 267–69, 272
Hill 250, 198, 207, 240, 247–49, 256,
258–59, 289
Hill 253, 208, 240, 258–63, 288–90
Hill 254, 351
Hill 255, 241–42
Hill 258, 290–92, 303, 338–39
Hill 260, 335

Hill 263, 294
Hill 268, 207–8
Hill 269, 243–44, 263–65, 293
Hill 272, 214, 243, 251–52, 289, 292–94
Hill 274 (Suicide Hill), 149–50, 164, 203–5
Hill 275, 287
Hill 282, 100
Hill 286, 290–91
Hill 287, 290–91
Hill 288, 339–41, 387
Hill 295, 126
Hill 299, 331–32, 348, 365, 367–68
Hill 343, 390
Hill 360, 363
Hindenburg, Paul von, 315
Hindenburg Stellung, 195, 309
Hines, John Leonard, 26, 95, 102, 125–26, 148, 200, 286, 308, 313, 347, 364–65, 386, 392
Hitler, Adolf, 315
Hodges, Courtney H., 393
Hogan, Martin, 353–54
Holderman, Nelson, 227–29, 232–33, 431
Hollingshead, Lowell R., 369–71
Hoover, Herbert, 427
Hospitals, 27, 130, 187, 191–93, 237, 372, 423–25
Hott, John, 227
Houghton, Bill, 365–67
House, Edward, 384
Howland, Henry, 110, 112–14
Hoyles, Aldred, 117
Huebner, Clarence, 400–401
Hutchinson, William, 168–72

Illinois National Guard, 38
Industrial Workers of the World "Wobblies," 91
Infantry Drill Regulations (U.S. Army), 27
Influenza, 192–93, 312, 414
Intelligence, 26, 59–60, 198, 207
Iraq, 23
Isonzo, Battles of the, 23
Italian Americans, 36, 117, 207
Italy, 22–23, 39
Ivoiry, 104, 106, 131, 133, 144, 198

Jacks, L. V., 165
James, Jesse, 207, 247–49, 331–32, 368

Janis, Elsie, 193
Jankoska, Captain, 303
Japan, 14, 22
Jewish soldiers, 117, 165, 182, 207
John, Ralph, 143
Johnson, Evan, 223–24, 228, 231, 245, 273, 433
Johnson, Ray, 79, 89–90, 103–4, 131, 152–53, 166
Johnson, Thomas, 273–74
Johnston, Ewart, 277
Johnston, Harold, 395
Johnston, William, 105, 167
Judah, Noble, 341

Kachik, Andrew, 128–29
Kearns, Rev. Hal, 102
Kelley, Reginald, 346–47
Kelly, John J., 255–56
Kemerer, Duncan, 116
Kerensky, Alexander, 23, 39
Kriemhilde Stellung belt, 58, 61–62, 145, 149, 153–54, 161, 198–99, 202, 205, 209, 230, 252, 256, 282, 288–91, 304–5, 308–9, 311, 321, 339, 345, 351, 361
   central, broken, 387–91, 420
   western, broken, 380
Kuhn, Joseph, 97–98, 101, 127, 130–31, 149–50, 164
Kurtz, Leonard, 377, 379
Kyler, Donald D., 213–15, 292–94, 327, 414–15, 426, 429

La Besace, 402
La Besogne, 279, 294, 296
labor battalions, 35, 36, 428
Lafayette, 26, 38
Lafayette Escadrille pilots, 73
La Forge, 220, 244, 250, 266
La Grange aux Bois Farm, 153, 167
Landres-et-St. Georges, 340–41, 353, 386, 390
Landreville, 390
Langer, Wiliam L., 31–32, 77, 386
Langley, Jesse R., 100
Langres, 63
Laon, 381
La Palette Pavilion, 227, 245, 272

La Tuilerie Farm, 351–52, 372
Laughton, Rev. James R., 68–69
La Viergette, 369
Lawrence, Joseph, 298–300, 322
League of Nations, 433
Leavenworth Staff College, 70
Le Chêne Tondu Ridge, 156–58, 179–80, 220, 224, 246, 267, 369, 273
Le Chesne, 61
La Fère, 195
Le Grand Carré Farm, 333, 369
Lejeune, John A., 255
Lenihan, Michael, 353, 355
Lenin, V.I., 39
Lewis, Michael, 243
Liddell Hart, B. H., 416–17
Liggett, Hunter, 7, 62, 107–8, 114, 118, 160, 214, 220–21, 228, 230, 243, 245–46, 250–51, 265–67, 369, 279, 294, 303, 309, 314
    commands First Army, 313, 359–61, 380, 384–87, 390–91, 396–401, 416, 419
Lille, 381
Lindsey, Julian, 282
Liny, 393–94
Lithuanian Americans, 36
Little Big Horn, Battle of, 16
Lloyd George, David, 41–43, 312, 384, 419
Longuyon, 419
Lost Battalion. *See* American Expeditionary Force: Lost Battalion
Lost Battalion, The (movie), 433
Loudenbeck, Edward, 306
Louis XVI, King of France, 113
Louppy, 404–5
Lovett, "Wild Bill," 35
Lucknow, battle of (India), 232, 253
Ludendorff, Erich von, 40–41, 47–48, 296–97, 315
Lukens, Edward, 88, 94, 161, 307–8
Lukert, E. P., 404–5
Lusitania, sinking of, 15, 89

MacArthur, Douglas, 5–7, 52, 60, 268, 327–29, 339–40, 352, 355, 371, 399, 427
Madeleine Farm, 149, 164, 198, 208, 249, 287, 289

"Mademoiselle from Armentieres" (song), 66–68
Mahan, Clarence, 429–30
Maistre, Paul, 396
Malancourt, 99, 100, 102, 127
Malbrouck Hill, 276–77
Mamelle Trench, 208, 289–90, 302
March, Peyton C., 312
Marcq, 309, 343
Marne River, 45, 117, 205
    First Battle of, 22
Marshall, Elizabeth, 19
Marshall, George C., 6, 19, 43, 69–72, 390, 397–98
Martin, Daniel, 404
Martin, Morris "Speedy," 104–6, 132–34, 191
Maverick, Maury, 216–18, 415
Max of Baden, Prince, 315
McAndrew, James, 250
McKeogh, Arthur, 182–83, 189
McKinley, William, 70
McMahon, John E., 323, 348, 351
McManigal, John, 174–76
McMurtry, George, 222–23, 227, 230, 232–33, 271, 273, 431, 433–34
McRae, James H., 375, 379
Menoher, Charles T., 327, 339–40, 353, 398, 400
Metz, 50, 52, 59–60, 369
Meuse, Heights of the, 57, 59, 61, 91–92, 148, 195, 233, 235, 256, 275–78, 282, 305, 362, 392
Meuse-Argonne, Battle of. *See also specific geographical areas and military units*
    command and tactics in, 385, 416–20
    cost of, 420
    eve of offensive, 73–82
    final offensive and victory in, 384–412
    German defense installations in, 57–60
    phase 1, 85–193
    phase 2, 194–254
    phase 3, 255–315
    phase 4, 317–58
    phase 5, 359–80
    preparation for, 60–65, 69–72
    planning for, 50–52, 195–97
    size and importance of, 4–7

Meuse-Argonne American Cemetery and Memorial at Romagne, 2–3, 434–35
Meuse River, 57–59, 61–62, 91–92, 94, 276, 278, 285, 305–6, 345, 361
  crossings, 393–96, 405–6
Mexican expedition of 1916–17, 18–19, 31, 70, 118, 197, 323
Mexico, 14–15
Mézières, 61, 62, 419
Miller, Oscar F., 153–54, 167
Miller, Walter E., 32
Minder, Charles, 180–81, 189, 296
Mitchell, Harry, 354, 355
Mitchell, William "Billy," 6, 63, 72–73, 124, 145–46, 198, 200, 206, 314–15, 328, 386, 417–18
Mitchell, Willie P., 237–38
Molleville Farm, 3, 275–76, 300, 305–6, 346–47, 363–64
Monaco, Tony, 32
Monroe, Henry. *See* Wrentmore, Ernest L.
Monson, John J., 182–83
Montblainville, 141, 144, 156
Montfaucon, 57–59, 61–62, 96–104, 123, 125–31, 143–44, 148–49, 183–84, 195–97
  Memorial at, 3
Montrebeau Wood, 154–55, 172–78, 214–16
Montrefagne (Hill 240), 214, 216, 242–43, 246, 292–93
Moore, Samuel E., 33
Morel, Sergeant, 110
Morrow, W. J., 367
Morton, Charles G., 276, 305–6
Moseley, George Van Horn, 26
Moselle River, 59
Moulin de l'Homme Mort, 159, 222
Muir, Charles H. "Uncle Charley," 115–17, 218, 220, 230
Mulcahy, Richard, 404

Nantillois, 96, 126, 130, 148, 163, 204–5, 236–38
Napoleonic wars, 31
Napoleon III, emperor of France, 396
National Defense Act (1916), 18
National Guard, 18, 35, 37, 70, 108, 195
National Home for Disabled Volunteer Soldiers, 424

Native Americans, 13, 207, 247–48, 270, 331, 369
Nayhone, Sergeant, 207, 258–59
Neibaur, Thomas, 372
Nell, John, 223, 244
Newcom, George, 227
Newcomb, Erwin B., 357–58
New Deal, 2
New York American, 273
Nicholson, "Slicker Bill," 126–27, 130–31, 165
Nivelle offensive, 41
Noble, Carl, 413–14
Nolan, Dennis, 4, 26, 52, 72, 115, 160, 179–80, 187, 218–20, 267
Norosoff, Private, 207
Norris, Ravee, 340, 371–72

Office of Strategic Services (OSS), 328
Officers' Reserve Corps, 18
Omaha Beach cemetery, 2
Operation Michael, 40
Ostend, 381
Ottoman Empire, 22–23
Ourcq River, 117, 205
Our Greatest Battle (Palmer), 5

Palestine, 23
Palmer, Frederick, 5, 95, 144, 360
Paris, 22, 45
Parker, James S., 175
Parker, Frank, 398, 400
Parker, H. W., 112
Parker, John Henry "Gatling Gun," 106, 167–68, 170–72
Passchendaele, Battle of, 41
Patton, Beatrice, 63–64, 80, 111
Patton, George S., 6, 7, 26–27, 63–64, 80, 109–12, 178, 192, 218, 328, 411–12, 417, 427
Peck, Robert, 404–5
Peixotto, Ernest, 69
Pensions, Bureau of, 424
Pepper, Benjamin, 100
Perkins, Michael J., 363
Péronne, 195
Pershing, Anne (daughter), 12
Pershing, Helen (daughter), 12, 14
Pershing, Helen Warren "Frankie" (wife), 11–14, 311

Pershing, John J. "Blackjack," 4, 7, 108, 218, 325, 412, 431
  air services and, 72–73
  Allies criticize, 184, 195, 197, 312–13, 382, 384
  appointed commander in chief, 15–19
  armistice talks and, 359, 382–84
  arrives in Paris and plans tactics, 19–20, 26–29
  assessment of leadership and tactics of, 416–20
  background and early career of, 13–15, 31, 118
  black divisions and, 122
  Clemenceau and, 183–85, 195–97
  creates American First Army, 49–50
  death of wife and children, 11–14
  demands independent U.S. army, 26, 39, 49
  doctrine of rifle and bayonet and, 27–29, 34, 46, 118
  drive to attack and willpower belief of, 41, 52–53, 60–65, 114, 124, 143–44, 160, 199, 243, 354
  final drive to victory and, 386, 391, 396, 401
  Foch and, 50–52, 195–99, 312–13
  Lost Battalion and, 221, 233, 246, 250–51
  Marshall and, 69, 71
  Memorial Day address at Romagne, of 1919, 434–35
  Meuse-Argonne phase 1 and, 85, 96, 101–3, 105, 137, 143–44, 147, 160, 172
  Meuse-Argonne phase 2 and, 199, 256
  Meuse-Argonne phase 3 and, 256, 275, 282, 285–86, 301–2, 308, 311–13
  Meuse-Argonne phase 4 and, 315–16, 345, 347–48, 351
  Meuse-Argonne plan for three stages of advance, 59–65
  Montfaucon and, 101–2, 123–24
  nicknamed "Black Jack," 13
  officers and, 37, 70, 90, 108, 160, 179–80, 212, 265, 308, 313, 347–48, 362–63
  origins of war and, 15
  relinquishes First Army command to Liggett, 311–15, 359–61, 361
  return home of, in 1919 and honors for, 435

  Sedan confusion and, 396–97, 400
  spring offensives of 1918 and, 41–43, 45
  St. Mihiel offensive and, 50–53
  supply and manpower shortages and, 311–13
  understanding of troops' hardships, 201, 220
  War Department and, 312
  Wilson and, 18–19
Pershing, Mary Margaret (daughter), 12
Pershing, Warren (son), 12, 13, 434–35
Pétain, Henri-Philippe, 23, 41, 45, 49, 52, 197, 382
Philippine Insurrection, 13, 18, 36, 70, 95, 107, 115, 118, 197, 205, 209, 212, 265, 323, 375
Picardy, 195, 420
Pierce, Harold, 141–42, 156–58, 220, 266, 268–69, 408–9
Poland, 23
Polish Americans, 36, 117
Portugal, 22
Portuguese Army Corps, 40
Pouilly, 394–96, 405–6
Prescott, A. F., 143, 182
Presidio fire of 1915, 12
Princip, Bavrilo, 21
Prinz, Heinrich, 270
Prisoners of war
  American, 176, 199
  German, 98–99, 110, 112, 130, 134, 189, 330, 388
Pruitt, John H., 256
Prussians, 396
Public Health Service, 424
Pulveritis, Private, 322
Putnam, Israel, 100

"Questions a Platoon Leader Should Ask Himself" (memorandum), 118–19
"Questions for a Battalion Commander to Ask Himself" (memorandum), 118

race riots, 37, 429
Rainsford, Walter, 189
Ranlett, Louis, 430
Rasmussen, John, 404
Ravin de Boulasson, 266
Red Cross, 192–93, 421

Reddan, William J., 6, 317–21, 392
Reed, Vincent, 369
Regan, Patrick, 277
Reilly, Thomas, 389
Remarque, Erich Maria, 430
Rendinell, Joseph E., 47
Rentz, Irwin, 164
Reserve Officers' Training Corps, 18
Revnes, Maurice S., 252–53
Richêne Hill, 300, 301
Richthofen, Baron Manfred von, 199, 205
Rickenbacker, Eddie, 73, 86, 430–31
Ridge 198, 226, 228–29, 244, 273
Ristine, Carl L., 113–14, 135–36, 154–55, 173
Rizzi, Joe, 6, 30–31, 89, 136–37, 140, 178, 188
Robard, Ralph, 362
Robb, George S., 194–95
Roberts, Harold, 214
Rockenback, Samuel D., 64
Romagne, 291, 316, 333, 335–39
Romagne, Heights of, 58–59, 61, 96, 109, 136, 144–45, 149, 198–99, 205, 207–9, 214, 221, 233, 240, 256, 282, 288–92, 302–3, 308, 316, 335, 345, 387
Romania, 22, 23
Romedahl, Joe, 43, 406–7, 409–10, 422
Roosevelt, Franklin D., 2, 216
Roosevelt, Theodore, 13–16
Roosevelt, Theodore, Jr., 7, 399–400
Ross, Lloyd, 339
Runyon, Damon, 6, 273
Russell, Reese, 1–4
Russia, 21–24, 112
  revolution in, 39, 381
Russian Americans, 36, 165
Russo-Japanese War, 14

St. Georges, 339, 341–42, 353, 356
St. Hubert's Pavilion, 158–59
St. Juvin, 309–11, 341–45, 356–57, 376
St. Mihiel offensive, 50, 52–53, 64, 69–73, 77, 108, 213, 255, 265, 323, 327, 369, 370, 375, 408
St. Mihiel (town), 408
Samogneux, 275–76
Sand, Sarah, 120–21, 193, 416, 421, 423–24
San Juan Hill, Battle of, 13, 70, 95, 133

Sauerwein, Major, 110
Savage, Murray, 280, 295
Schaffner, Dwite H., 158–59
Schellberg, Will, 73, 98, 100, 127–28, 409
Schmidt, Paul, 210–11, 241–42, 338, 351–52
Schmitt, Frank, 420–21
Scott, Hugh Lenox, 16, 18
Searcy, Earl, 375, 377, 378
Séchaut, 194, 195
Sedan, 57, 61, 396–401, 419
Septsarges, 96
Serbia, 21–23
Shaffer, Paul, 187
Shannon, James, 268–69
Sheldon, Raymond, 250
Shepherd, Lemuel, 162, 255–56
Simpich, Ernest, 174–75, 176
Sioux Ghost Dance rebellion, 13
Sirmon, W. A., 428
Sivry-sur-Meuse, 284, 301
Skinker, Alexander, 110
Slack, Clayton, 278
Smith, Floyd, 395–96
Smith, Frederick, 181–82
Smith, Henry, 142–43
Soissons counteroffensive, 47–48, 212
Soldier's Rehabilitation Act (1918), 424
Somme, Battle of, 15, 23, 31, 41
Sommepy, 255
Sommerance, 304, 309–11, 329–30, 339, 341, 356
Sophie, Arch Duchess, 21
Souilly First Army headquarters, 89, 147, 163, 183, 184, 397
South Africa, 24
Spanish-American War, 13, 18, 33, 107, 115, 118, 205, 209, 212, 375
Stacey, Cromwell, 182–83, 223, 225, 231
Stayton, Edward, 177
Stenay–Le Chesne line, 61
Stevens, J. A., 96
Stewart, Lawrence, 353
Stowers, Freddie, 194
Stringfellow, John, 427–28
Strom, Edward B., 338
Summerall, Charles P., 212, 214, 230, 243–44, 263, 265, 293, 303, 313, 329, 354–55, 386–87, 397–99, 400, 416
Supreme War Council, 382, 384

Swartz, Casper, 100, 403, 410–11
Sweeny, Mary, 193
Sweeny, Sunshine, 193
Sweezey, Claude B., 101, 102
Sweningson, Milton B., 109
Syrian Americans, 207

Takes, Fred, 310, 342, 373–74
Talma Farm, 378–80
Tannenberg (1914), Battle of, 23
Taylor, John, 309–10
Thacher, Archibald, 343–44
Thomas, John, 151
Thompson, Frank L., 134
Tillman, Frederick A., 358, 374, 377
Tinley, Matthew, 371
Tom Swift and His War Tank, 348
Torgerson, Private, 406, 407
Toward the Flame (Allen), 430
Traub, Peter, 108, 114–15, 135, 137,
    154–55, 172–73, 176–77
Triplet, William S., 35, 113, 135–39,
    173–74, 410–11
Tronsol Farm, 167, 172
Truman, Harry, 6, 86, 110, 138, 177–78,
    187–88
Truman, Ralph E., 177
Tucker, Sara Mildred, 421
Turkey, 22, 381
Turkish Americans, 36
Tuscania, sinking of, 38–39

Ulmer, Herman, 342, 355–56
United Press, 233
U.S. Army. *See also* American
    Expeditionary Force *and specific
    military units*
  Army Reserve, 18
  Army War College, 97, 107
  attack on Bonus Army, 427
  draft and recruiting, 1, 18, 32
  Enlisted Reserve Corps, 18
  General Staff College (Langres), 27
U.S. Congress, 18, 426, 427, 435
  Senate Military Affairs Committee, 13
U.S. Employment Service, 426

Van Iersel, Ludovicus, 395
Varennes, 3, 113–14, 116

Vauquois Hill, 108–10, 113–14
Vera Cruz intelligence mission, 328
Verdun, Battle of, 15, 23, 31, 50, 57–58,
    73–74, 97, 183
Versailles Conference, 414
  Treaty of, 433
Very, 106, 136
Vesle River, 48, 117, 205
Veterans' Bureau, 424, 425
Vidmer, George, 344
Villa, Pancho, 12, 14
Villers, 395
Vollmer, Lieutenat, 280–82

Wagner, Richard, 58
Walker, Norman, 12
Ward, Jack, 369
War Department, 16, 28, 212, 312, 328,
    359
  black soldiers and, 36–37
  conscientious objectors and, 251
Warren, Francis Emroy, 13, 15–16
Washington, George, 362, 396
Wear, Arthur, 394–95
Weise, Robert, 103
Wellmann, Richard, 245, 272
West Point, 13, 97, 107, 212
Weygand, Maxime, 195–97
Whitman, Walter, 309, 373
Whittlesey, Charles "Galloping Charlie,"
    6, 80–81, 118–20, 159, 182–83,
    189–90, 222–33, 244–46, 252–54,
    296, 369–74, 431–34
Whittlesey, Elisha, 434
Wilder, F. C., 363
Wildish, Allen, 215, 292
Wilhelm, Karl, 229
Wilhelm II, Kaiser of Germany, 15, 315,
    381
  abdication of, 401–2
Williams, Ashby, 74–75, 82, 287, 302, 307–8
Williams, H. T., 430
Wilson, Woodrow, 15, 17–19, 25–26, 42,
    253, 315, 384, 423, 431
Wings (movie), 431
Wise, Frederic "Old Fritz," 162, 235–36,
    321, 365
Wise, Jennings, 203–5, 236–37, 391
Wittenmyer, Edward, 343

Woehl, Harold, 241, 291, 303, 308, 336
Wold, Nels, 109–10
women, 14, 192–93, 421
Wood, Raiford, 310
Woodfill, Samuel, 6, 323–27, 431, 432
Woods, Arthur, 423
World War I
  aftermath of, 1–4, 413–35
  beginning of, 14–15, 21–23
  casualties, 23
  cemeteries and battlefields, 2–4
  end of, 401–12
  U.S. entry into, 1, 15–20, 24
World War II, 2–4, 344
Worsham, Elijah, 133

Wrentmore, Ernest ("Henry Monroe"), 6,
  326–27, 332–35, 348–51, 421
Wright, William, 370, 390

YMCA volunteers, 193, 273
York, Alvin C., 3, 6, 251, 266–67, 279–82,
  293–96, 329–30, 411, 423, 431–32
Young, R. W., 369
Young, Rush, 146, 148, 162–63, 201–2, 204,
  236–39, 322–23, 391
Young China Association, 270

Zander, Harry, 424, 425–26
Zeebrugge, 381
Zimmerman telegram, 15

ABOUT THE AUTHOR

EDWARD G. LENGEL is an associate professor of history at the University of Virginia. He is the author of several books on military history, including *General George Washington: A Military Life*. A recipient, with the Papers of George Washington documentary editing project, of the National Humanities Medal, he has made frequent appearances on television documentaries and was a finalist for the George Washington Book Prize. A lifelong student of the First World War and an avid collector, he lives in Charlottesville, Virginia, with his wife and three children.